THE
A B C and X Y Z
OF
BEE CULTURE

A Cyclopedia of Everything Pertaining to
the Care of the Honey-bee; Bees, Hives,
Honey, Implements, Honey-plants,
etc. Facts Gleaned from the
Experience of Thousands
of Bee-keepers, and
Afterward Veri-
fied in Our
Apiary.

By A. I. Root and E. R. Root
131st Thousand

MEDINA, OHIO
THE A. I. ROOT COMPANY
1910

To the throng of eager questioning
brothers and sisters in the art of bee
culture, in our own and other countries, this work is especially dedicated
by   The Authors

1877 Preface

In preparing this work I have been much in 'ebted to the books of Langstroth, Moses Quinby, Prof. A. J. Cook, King, and some others, as well as to all the bee-journals; but, more than to all these, have I been indebted to the thousands of friends scattered far and wide who have so kindly furnished the fullest particulars in regard to all the new improvements as they have come up in our beloved branch of rural industry. Those who questioned me so much a few years ago are now repaying by giving me such long kind letters in answer to any inquiry I may happen to make that I often feel ashamed to think what meager answers I have been obliged to give them un.ler similar circumstances. A great part of this A B C book is really the work of the people; and the task that devolves on me is to collect, condense, verify, and utilize what has been scattered through thousands of letters for years past. My own apiary has been grea ly devoted to testing carefully each new device, invention, or process as it came up. The task has been a very pleasant one; and if the perusal of the following pages affords you as much pleasure I shall feel amply repaid.

November, 1877.   A. I. ROOT.

Preface to Later Editions

Many years have passed since the original preface by A. I. Root was written. Since that time there have been fourteen distinct editions, of anywhere from 2000 to 15,000 copies, making a total of 131,000. While the original work contained only about 200 pages it will be seen that this one has over 600. So rapid have been the advances in apiculture that it has been necessary to make frequent revisions, and so extensive have been the changes that some editions seem almost like new works. As these pages are kept in standing type changes can easily be made.

After the revision of 1883, ill health and interest in other matters compelled A. I. Root to drop the subject of bee culture to a great extent. Since that time the work of revision has devolved almost entirely upon his eldest son, the writer. About the time that we took up this work we began to assume editorial charge of Gleanings in Bee Culture, a semi-monthly magazine, and since 1887 we have had almost entire charge of both except that we have been very ably assisted in the last year or two by a younger brother, H. H. Root. In order that we might keep in close touch with the best practices in vogue, we made a num-l er of extended trips, visiting some of the most successful bee-keepers in the country. taking along with us camera and note-book. One year we traveled thus equipped over seven thousand miles, covering a large portion of the West and at other times the entire eastern p irt of the country. Many of the photographs taken at the time are scattered throughout the work. This extended travel among bee-beepers, together with a large acquaintance and general correspondence, has enabled us to incorporate, as we believe, new and valuable matter in these pages; and the work, so far from being an A B C only, is also an X Y Z of bee culture. Originally, A. I. Root intended it to be a work purely for beginners; and while it still is primarily for that class, yet we have sought in the later editions to incorporate general matter of interest and of value to the advanced bee-keeper.

So great have been the general changes in the practices and general systems of management that it has been found necessary during the last fifteen or twenty years to re-write almost whole articles. So much of new matter and new subjects has been added that practically three-fourths of the present volume is the work of the reviser. In this connection we are desirous of acknowledging our indebtedness to specialists who have written certain articles of a technical nature, which articles will be found scattered here and there throughout the work. Inasmuch as some of these are the work of two or three people, the discriminating reader will notice here and there a change of style. Although this is unavoidable we believe that the general teachings harmonize throughout

We offer no apologies for lack of literary style. Much of the work of revision and the re-writing of new articles has been done under pressure of other work; but we have endeavored to use the simplest and pl inest language possible to describe each process, device, or method.   ERNEST R. ROOT.

Preface to 1910 Edition

In the 1910 edition a number of what might be called moving pictures are scattered throughout the work, showing the successive steps of various manipulations described. A large amount of new matter has been added, especially to the following subjects: Absconding Swarms, Apiary, Bees as a Nuisance, Comb Foundation, Comb Honey, Diseases of Bees, Entrances, Extracted Honey, Extractor, Exhibits of Honey, Feeding and Feeders; Frames, to Manipulate; Fruit Blossoms, Introducing, Laws Relating to Bees; Pollen, Queen-Rearing, Robbing, Swarming, Wax, Wintering. The following subjects have been entirely re-written: Bees and Fruit, Glucose, Honey, Honey Adulteration, Sugar, Migratory Bee-keeping, Nectar, Cane Sugar, Spring Management of Bees. The general subject of Bees as Pollenators, under the head Fruit Blossoms and Pollen, has received special attention in the present edition.

As far as possible the reviser has sought to have all technical articles written by specialists in their particular lines. For example, everything relating to the chemistry of honey has been written by Prof. Hugh Bryan, of the Bureau of Chemistry of the United States Department of Agriculture. Dr. E. F. Phillips, of the same Department, has prepared a number of articles on technical subjects; and R. E. Snodgrass, who has probably made the most extended study of the anatomy of the bee of any scientist in the world, has prepared the article in the appendix on The Anatomy of the Bee.

Particular attention has been paid to the matter of general proof-reading in the 1910 edition. While W. P. Root, general proof-reader of the publishing house of the A. I. Root Company, has done the major part of the work, he has been very ably assisted by F. A. Allen, Phillipsburg East, Quebec, Canada, and Miss Wilhelmina C. Duecker, of Medina, a former school-teacher.

The article on The Anatomy of the Bee did not reach the publisher's hands until after the regular article in its alphabetical order had been printed. As Snodgrass' work is so much in advance over the work of previous scientists, it was decided to place his article at the end of this work as an appendix.

In order that the reader may trace out the authorships of the various articles, a list is appended of those originally written by A. I. Root, those by E. R. Root, those jointly by A. I. Root and E. R. Root, and those by W. K. Morrison and other writers.

July 15, 1910.   ERNEST R. ROOT.

ARTICLES BY A. I. ROOT:

Age of Bees; Catnip; Milkweed; Mustard; Rocky Mountain Bee-plant; Ventilation; Water for Bees; Whitewood.

ARTICLES BY E. R. ROOT:

Alfalfa; Anatomy of the Bee; Apiary; Artificial Fertilization; Banat Bees; Barrels; Basswood; Bee-bread; Beginning with Bees; Bee-space; Bees and Grapes; Bees as a Nuisance; Bee paralysis; Bees on Shares; Bleaching Honey-comb; Box Hives; Buckwheat; Canada Thistle; Candied Honey; Catclaw; Comb Foundation; Comb Honey; Contraction; Diseases of Bees; Entrances; Exhibits of Honey; Extractor; Feeding and Feeders; Foul Brood, American and European; Frames, Self-spacing; Frames, to Manipulate; Fruit-blossoms; Goldenrod; Heartsease. Hives; Hive-making; Hoarhound; Honey-dew; Honey-peddling; Huajilla; Increase; Introducing; Italianizing; Locality; Marigold; Migratory Bee-keeping; Moving Bees; Nucleus; Orange-blossom Honey; Organization of Bee-keepers; Overstocking; Poisonous Honey; Pollen; Pollination of Plants; Priority Rights; Profits in Bees; Propolis; Queen-rearing; Rats; Record-keeping of Hives; Reversing; Skep; Spacing Frames; Spanish Needle; Spreading Brood; Spring Management; Veils; Vinegar; Weight of Bees; Willow; Willow-herb.

ARTICLES JOINTLY BY A. I. AND E. R. ROOT:

Absconding Swarms; After-swarming; Anger of Bees; Ants; Artificial Pasturage; Asters; Bee-hunting; Bee-moth; Bees; Candy for Bees; Clover; Drones; Dysentery; Enemies of Bees; Extracted Honey; Horsemint; Hybrids; Italian Bees; Laying Workers; Queens; Raspberry; Robbing; Sage; Stings; Swarming; Uniting Bees.

ARTICLES BY W. K. MORRISON.

Ants in South America; Bees, Stingless; Carpet Grass; Catalpa; Century Plant; Cotton; Dandelion; Egyptian Bees; Eucalyptus; Gallberry; Hives, Evolution of; Honey Adulteration; Honey and its Colors; Honey-plants; Locust, Honey; Logwood; Mesquite; Nectar; Palmetto; Pepper-tree; Sunflower; Tupelo; Dictionary of Bee-keepers' Terms.
Campanilla.—Leslie Burr.
Eye, Compound; Parthenogenesis; Scent of Bees.—Dr. E. F. Phillips, Bureau of Ent., Wash., D. C.
Bee-keeping for Women.—Mrs. Anna B. Comstock.
Honey as a Food.—W. K. Morrison and Dr. C. C. Miller.
Honey-comb.—Prof. Edward F. Bigelow and A. I. and E. R. Root.
Out-apiaries.—Dr. C. C. Miller and E. R. Root.
Laws Relating to Bees.—W. K. Morrison and Dr. E. F. Phillips.
Phacelia.—Dr. C. C. Miller.
Smoke and Smokers; Wax; Wintering.—E. R. and H. H. Root.
Mangrove.—W. S. Hart.
Anatomy of the Bee in the appendix.—R. E. Snodgrass, Bureau of Entomology, Washington, D. C.
Glucose, Honey, Honey Adulteration, Sugar, Cane sugar.—Prof. A. Hugh Bryan, Bureau of Chemistry, Washington, D. C.
Picture Gallery Notes.—W. P. Root.

Introduction to the First Edition

About the year 1865, during the month of August, a swarm of bees passed overhead where we were at work, and my fellow-workman, in answer to some of my inquiries respecting their habits, asked what I would give for them. I, not dreaming he could by any means call them down, offered him a dollar, and he started after them. To my astonishment, he, in a short time, returned with them hived in a rough box he had hastily picked up, and, at that moment, I commenced learning my A B C in bee culture. Before night I had questioned not only the bees but every one I knew, who could tell me any thing about these strange new acquaintances of mine. Our books and papers were overhauled that evening; but the little that I found only puzzled me the more, and kindled anew the desire to explore and follow out this new hobby of mine; for, dear reader, I have been all my life *much* given to hobbies and new projects.

Farmers who had kept bees assured me that they once paid, when the country was new, but of late years they were of no profit, and everybody was abandoning the business. I had some headstrong views in the matter, and in a few days I visited Cleveland, ostensibly on other business, but I had really little interest in any thing until I could visit the bookstores and look over the books on bees. I found but two, and I very quickly chose Langstroth. May God reward and for ever bless Mr. Langstroth for the kind and pleasant way in which he unfolds to his readers the truths and wonders of creation to be found inside the bee-hive.

What a gold-mine that book seemed to me as I looked it over on my journey home! Never was romance so enticing—no, not even Robinson Crusoe; and, best of all, right at my own home I could live out and verify all the wonderful things told therein. Late as it was, I yet made an observatory hive and raised queens from worker eggs before winter, and wound up by purchasing a queen of Mr. Langstroth for $20.00. I should, in fact, have wound up the whole business, queen and all, most effectually, had it not been for some timely advice toward Christmas, from a plain practical farmer near by. With his assistance, and by the purchase of some more bees, I brought all safely through the winter. Through Mr. Langstroth I learned of Mr. Wagner, who, shortly afterward, was induced to recommence the publication of the *American Bee Journal*, and through this I gave accounts monthly of my blunders and occasional successes.

In 1867, news came across the ocean from Germany, of the honey-extractor; and by the aid of a simple home-made machine I took 1000 lbs. of honey from 20 stocks, and increased them to 35. This made quite a sensation, and numbers embarked in the new business; but when I lost all but 11 of the 35 the next winter, many said, "There! I told you how it would turn out."

I said nothing, but went to work quietly and increased the 11 to 48 during the one season, not using the extractor at all. The 48 were wintered entirely without loss, and I think it was mainly because I took care and pains with each individual colony. From the 48 I secured 6162 lbs. of extracted honey, and sold almost the entire crop for 25 cents per lb. This capped the climax, and inquiries in regard to the new industry began to come in from all sides. Beginners were eager to know what hives to adopt, and where to get honey-extractors. As the hives in use seemed very poorly adapted to the use of the extractor, and as the machines offered for sale were heavy and poorly adapted to the purpose, besides being "patented," there really seemed to be no other way before me then to manufacture these implements. Unless I did this I should be compelled to undertake a correspondence that would occupy a great part of my time without affording any compensation of any account. The fullest directions I knew how to give for making plain simple hives, etc., were from time to time published in the *American Bee Journal;* but the demand for further particulars was such that a circular was printed, and, shortly after, a second edition; then another, and another. These were intended to answer the greater part of the queries; and from the cheering words received in regard to them it seemed that the idea was a happy one.

Until 1873 all these circulars were sent out gratuitously; but at that time it was deemed best to issue a quarterly at 25 cents per year, for the purpose of answering these inquiries. The very first number was received with such favor that it was immediately changed to a monthly at 75 cents. The name given it was *Gleanings in Bee Culture*, and it was gradually enlarged until, in 1876, the price was changed to $1.00. During all this time it has served the purpose excellently of answering questions as they came up, both old and new; and even if some new subscriber should ask in regard to something that had been discussed at length but a short time before, it is an easy matter to refer him to it or send him the number containing the subject in question.

When *Gleanings* was about commencing its fifth year, inquirers began to dislike being referred to something that was published half a dozen years before. Besides, the decisions that were then arrived at perhaps needed to be considerably modified to meet present wants. Now you can see whence the necessity for this A B C book, its office, and the place we propose to have it fill.

December, 1878.   A. I. ROOT.

Introduction to the 1908 Edition

The Development of Bee Culture in the United States.

Before the reader plunges into the subject-matter of this work he may be interested in knowing something of the early beginnings and the phenomenal growth of bee culture to its present stage of development. It will not be necessary to trace the early history of apiculture in foreign lands any more than to state that it was not until the invention of movable combs, handled in a very crude way, that the science of bee culture began to take any step forward; and it was not until a little later that the perfected frame of our own Father Langstroth was brought out that bee culture may be said to have assumed any commercial importance in this country.

In the early '50's bees were kept only in box hives, and in a very small and primitive way. A yield of ten or fifteen pounds of dirty chunk honey per skep was considered a good yield; but after the Langstroth invention, by which the brood-nest of the colony could be investigated and manipulated, yields of anywhere from thirty-five to seventy-five pounds per colony of beautiful honey were common averages, and one hundred or two hundred pounds of extracted nothing extraordinary; indeed, a single colony in a good locality has been known to furnish anywhere from four hundred to seven hundred pounds. While such an output per hive is extraordinary, it goes to show what was made possible through the Langstroth invention. So important was it that it may be truthfully said that the art of keeping bees was almost entirely revolutionized, not only in this country but in many parts of Europe as well.

In the early '60's the honey-extractor and comb foundation were brought out. These, together with the invention of the movable frame, lifted bee culture up to a plane where there was "money in it." Very soon a large number were keeping anywhere from fifty to one hundred colonies. Others began to have a series of out-apiaries running anywhere from five hundred to three thousands colonies. In the meantime bee-supply factories sprang up all over the United States. Thousands and thousands of queen-bees were reared and sent through the mails, to improve stock. Periodicals on bees came into existence; the old *American Bee Journal*, edited by the lamented Samuel Wagner, a contemporary of Langstroth, did much to expound the new principles in the early days of modern bee culture. Shortly after, *Gleanings in Bee Culture*, edited by A. I. Root, came into existence. A devoted follower of Langstroth, he threw his whole soul into the keeping of bees. So ardent was his enthusiasm that his little quarterly, and shortly after a monthly, grew amazingly; and, even after the editorial management was transferred from father to sons, as noted in the preface, it continued to grow until it now has a circulation of over thirty-three thousand copies. It has passed from the stage of a small monthly to a dignified illustrated magazine issued twice a month.

The honey business continued to develop from small beginnings so that there was a total aggaegate of from one hundred and fifty to one hundred and seventy-five million pounds of honey produced and marketed annually in the United States. These figures can scarcely be comprehended; but if this amount were all loaded into freight-cars it would make a solid trainload, without a break, something like fifty miles long. Some States, in good years, notably California, have been known to produce as much as five and even six hundred cars in a season. Other States will produce anywhere from one hundred to two

INTRODUCTION.

hundred; but in most of the Eastern States the amount produced is sold locally, so that it does not show up in carloads as it does in some of the Western States, particularly those in the alfalfa and mountain-sage districts; and it may be said that the amount of honey that is annually produced at the present time in the arid and mountainous districts is very small in comparison with what probably will be produced in years to come. The new irrigation projects, both State and national, will make room for immense acreages of alfalfa, and this will doubtless mean in the near future a trebling of the amount of this beautiful honey.

In addition to the large amount of literature on bees that is being distributed, there are numerous local and State bee-keepers' societies that hold bee conventions in various parts of the country. and some of these are affiliated with the National Bee-keepers' Association with a membership of nearly twenty-five hundred.

Besides these different organizations there have been held various field-day exhibitions in different parts of the country. At a recent one held in Jenkintown, near Philadelphia, at the apiary belonging to the authors of this work, over a thousand people interested in bee culture were present to witness the various operations in the handling of bees.

But this is not all. So great has been the growth of the bee-keeping industry that even our national government is giving substantial recognition to the business. The Bureau of Entomology of the United States Department of Agriculture sets aside something like nine thousand five hundred dollars per annum for the study of apiculture. Some five or six trained experts are devoting their whole time to the study of bees, including one bacteriologist, who is giving his entire attention to the investigation of bee diseases. In addition to all this, many State agricultural colleges and experiment stations are giving more or less attention to the subject—so much so that bee culture has come to be recognized as one of the great national industries.

Honey is now found on the tables of nearly all of our best families. A large percentage of the cakes and cookies now manufactured by some of the extensive baking companies contain honey, for it has been found that honey is not only a sweetener but a preservative as well. As an indication of the large amount of honey used for the purpose, it may be interesting to note in this connection that the National Biscuit Company is said to have placed an order for one hundred cars of honey. We have also been informed that the independent bakers have formed an association to buy honey and other supplies. This organization buys for its members anywhere from ten to twenty-five carloads of honey at a time. Honey is also used in a large way by the makers of soft drinks. They require a sweet that has plenty of flavor, and honey fills the bill.

Beeswax, of which there are now annually hundreds of tons produced, is now used in the arts and sciences as it never was before; and while paraffine and ceresine have to a limited extent taken its place, yet there is a peculiar quality about the product from the hives that makes it far superior to these mineral waxes. The very fact that it can command two or three times the price of its inferior competitors gives some idea of its value.

But there is an ethical as well as a commercial side to bee culture that should be mentioned. Thousands of people all over the world have found health and happiness in the keeping of bees; for, be it noted, they may be kept in any back yard in any climate, and yield not only a large amount of pleasure but profit as well. Many thousands more make bee-keeping a side issue in connection with some other business or profession, and who, by such work as this, are enabled to increase their already modest income, thus making a comfortable living.

In addition to all this, the study of bees opens up a new world and a new science. The professional and business man finds that he can give his fagged brain a rest and a respite from the cares of the day. It is no small wonder, then, that the A B C of 1877, of 200 pages in the early days, should find so extensive a demand for it that it should not only be increased in size, but reach the enormous sale of 131,000 copies.

If there was ever a rural pursuit that made greater progress in half a century in this country than bee culture the writer does not know it; and yet many are so optimistic that they believe the industry is only in its infancy.

Jan. 1, 1908.   ERNEST R. ROOT,

A. I. ROOT AT HOME AMONG HIS FLOWERS.

A.

ABSCONDING SWARMS.—Per- haps nothing is more aggravating in bee culture than to have our bees all on a sud- den abscond for parts unknown, without so much as stopping to give us a parting word of farewell, or a single token of recog- nition of the debt they owe us, in the shape of gratitude for our past kindnesses in pro- viding them with a home, shelter, etc. Per- haps no part of animated creation exhibits a greater love of home than does the honey- bee. No matter how humble or uninviting the surroundings, bees seem much attached to their home; and as they parade in front of their doorway after a hard day's work, plainly indicate that they have a keen idea of the rights of ownership, and exhibit a willingness to give their lives freely, if need be, in defense of their hard-earned stores. It is difficult to understand how they can ever be willing to abandon it altogether, and with such sudden impulse and common consent. No matter if they have never seen or heard of such a thing as a hollow tree, but have for innumerable bee generations been domesticated in hives made by human hands, none the less have they that instinc- tive longing that prompts them to seek the forest as soon as they get loose from the chains of domestication. It is possible that the bees, as they go out foraging, keep an eye out for desirable places for starting new homes, and it may be that they have the hollow trees picked out some time before they decide to leave. Many incidents have been reported that pretty clearly show this to be the case. We once found our bees working strongly on a particular locality about a mile and a half from the apiary, where the white clover was blooming with most unusual luxuriance. Very soon after, a colony swarmed, and the bees, after pour-

ing out of the hive, took a direct line for a tree in this clover-field, without so much as making any attempt to cluster at all. Did they not figure out the advantage of having only a few rods instead of over a mile to carry their honey, after having patiently gathered it from the blossoms, little by little? Perhaps it will be well to remark here, that it is very unusual for a swarm to go to the woods without clustering; the bees usually hang from 15 minutes to an hour, and many times several hours; in fact, we have known them to hang over night; but perhaps it would be well to take care of them inside of 15 or 20 minutes if we would make sure of them. Long before swarming- time, hives should all be in readiness, and they should also be located near where the new colony is to stand. If one is going to have a model apiary, he should not think of waiting until the bees swarm before he lays it out, but take time by the forelock, and with careful deliberation decide where every hive shall be before it is peopled with bees, if he would keep ahead and prevent his bees from taking "French leave."

But they sometimes leave, even after they have been carefully hived in modern hives on frames of foundation. If the swarming mania gets well under way in a bee-yard, a swarm is more apt to come out the second time, even when hived in a new location in a different hive, than where there is only a very little swarming. It was once thought that giving a frame of unsealed brood to these second-time absconders would hold them. While this, no doubt, acts as a re- strainer, yet when a swarm leaves its new quarters we would recapture it, hive it back into the hive, and then carry hive, bees, and all down cellar and keep them there several days until they get over their mania. They may then be set out on their permanent summer stands.

The plan of holding the bees with un- sealed brood does very well if one can get them into the hive; but it is necessarily somewhat like the one of catching birds with a handful of salt; how are we to obvi- ate losing the occasional swarm that goes off without clustering at all? or the quite frequent cases of coming out unobserved, or

1

when no one is at home? We are happy to say there is a very certain and safe remedy for all cases of first swarming, in having the wings of the queen clipped so she can not fly; this plan is in very general use, and answers excellently for all first swarms; but, alas! the after-swarms are the very ones that are most apt to abscond, and we can not clip the wings of *their* queens, because they have not yet taken their wedding-flight. What shall we do? In the first place, second or after swarms should *not be allowed*. If the parent hive, after it has cast its first swarm, is treated as recommended under the head of AFTER SWARMS, there will be no further swarming from that colony for that season. We recommend the Heddon method. See page 4.

Clipping the wings of the queen or putting on drone-traps (see DRONES) will prevent losing first swarms by absconding, it is true; but it does not always prevent losing the queen. She goes out with the bees as usual, and, after hopping about in front of the hive, sometimes gets ready to go back at about the same time that the bees do, after having discovered she is not in the crowd. Even if she gets some little distance from the hive, the loud hum they make as they return will guide her home many times; but unless the apiarist is at hand at such times to look after affairs, many queens will be lost, and the bees will rear a lot of young queens, and go into after-swarming in good earnest, making even the first swarm an "after-swarm." A German friend, who knows little of bee-culture, once told us our bees were swarming, and if we did not ring the bells, etc., they would certainly go to the woods. As we quietly picked up the queen in passing the hive, we told him if they started to go away, we would call them back. Sure enough, they did start for the woods, and had gone so far that we really began to be frightened ourselves, when, away in the distance, we saw them suddenly wheel about, and then return to the hive at our very feet. While he gave us the credit of having some supernatural power over bees, we felt extremely glad we had taken precautions to clip all our queens' wings but a few days before. After this we felt a little proud of our control over these wayward insects, until a fine swarm of Italians started off under similar circumstances, and, despite our very complacent, positive remarks, to the effect that they would soon come home, they went off and stayed "off." In a humbler, and, we dare say, wiser frame of mind, we investi-

gated, and found they had joined with a very small third swarm of black bees, and had just come from one of the neighbor's hives. We tried to "explain," but it required a five-dollar bill to make matters so clear that we could carry back our rousing swarm of yellow bees, and sort out the black unfertile queen, that they might be made to accept their own. Thus you see how many a slip there is, in bee culture, between cup and lip, and how very important it is that you keep posted, and also "post" yourself in some conspicuous place near or in the apiary if you allow natural swarming, and do not want your golden visions—and bees—to take to themselves wings and fly away.

ABSCONDING FOR WANT OF FOOD.

Perhaps bees oftener desert their hives because they are short of stores than from any other cause; and many times, in the spring, they seem to desert because they are nearly out. They issue from the hive, and alight in a tree very much like a normal swarm during the swarming season. The remedy, or, rather, preventive, for this state of affairs, is so plain we hardly need discuss it. After they have swarmed out, and are put back into the hive, give a heavy comb of sealed stores; if that can not be obtained, feed them a little at a time, until they have plenty, and be sure that they have brood in the combs. If necessary, give them a comb of unsealed larvæ from some other hive, and then feed them until they have a great abundance of food. One should be ashamed of having bees abscond for want of food.

ABSCONDING IN EARLY SPRING.

This seems to occur just at a time when we can ill afford to lose a single bee; and, worse still, only when our stocks are, generally, rather weak, so that we dislike the idea of losing any of them. In this case they do not, as a general thing, seem to care particularly for going to the woods, but rather take a fancy to pushing their way into some of the adjoining hives, and, at times, a whole apiary will seem so crazy with the idea as to become utterly demoralized.

A neighbor, who made a hobby of small hives—less than half the usual size—one fine April day had as many as 40 colonies leave their hives and cluster together in all sorts of promiscuous combinations. To say that their owner was perplexed, would be stating the matter very mildly.

Similar cases, though perhaps not as bad, have been reported from time to time, ever since novices commenced to learn the sciences of bee culture; and although cases of swarming out in the spring were known once in a great while before the recent improvements, they are nothing like the mania that has seemed to possess entire apiaries— small ones — since the time of artificial swarming, honey-extractors, etc. We would by no means discourage these improvements, but only warn beginners against making too much haste to be rich. We would not commence dividing our bees until they are abundantly strong. They should go into winter quarters with an abundance of sealed honey in tough old combs as far as may be ; and should have hives with walls thick and warm, of some porous material, such as chaff or straw, with a good thickness of the same above, and we shall have little cause to fear any trouble from bees absconding in the spring.

ABSCONDING NUCLEUS SWARMS.

A very small nucleus—if it contains no more than a couple of hundred bees—is liable to swarm out. Queen-breeders, in attempting to mate queens in baby nuclei containing only one or two section-boxes, had considerable trouble in keeping the bees in the hive, especially when the young queen went out to mate. Accordingly it was found necessary to make the baby hives much larger, with frames 5⅜x8 inches, and two nuclei to a hive. See QUEEN-REARING. With these there is not much trouble from swarming out, providing that they are well supplied with bees, some brood, and honey.

ABSCONDING FOR MORE SATISFACTORY QUARTERS.

There is still another kind of absconding that seems to be for no other reason than that the bees are displeased with their hive, or its surroundings, and, at times, it seems rather difficult to assign any good reason for their having suddenly deserted. We have known a colony to swarm out and desert their hive because it was too cold and open, and we have known them to desert because the combs were soiled and filthy from dysentery in the spring. They very *often* swarm out because they are out of stores, and this generally happens about the first day in spring that is sufficiently warm and sunny. We have known them to swarm out because their entrance was too large, and, if we are not mistaken, because it was too small.

We have also known them to swarm out because they were so "pestered" with a neighboring ant-hill—see ANTS—that they evidently thought patience ceased to be a virtue.

ABSCONDING IN THE SPRING.

They often swarm out in spring where no other cause can be assigned than that they are weak and discouraged, and in such cases they usually try to make their way into other colonies. While it may not always be possible to assign a reason for such behavior with medium or fair colonies, we may rest assured that good strong colonies, with ample supplies of sealed stores, seldom, if ever, go into any such foolishness.

By way of summing up, it may be well to say: If you would not lose your bees by natural swarming, clip the wings of all queens as soon as they commence laying; then look to them often, and know what is going on in the apiary every day during the swarming season; if you would not have runaway swarms in the spring, and while queens are being fertilized, confine your experiments to pecks of bees instead of pints.

ADULTERATION OF HONEY. See HONEY ADULTERATION.

AFTER-SWARMING.—We might define this by saying that all swarms that come out, or are led out by a VIRGIN QUEEN, are termed after-swarms; and all swarms that come out within eight or fifteen days after the first swarm are accompanied by such queens. There may be from one all the way up to a half-dozen or even more, depending on the yield of honey, amount of brood or larvæ, and the weather; but whatever the number, they are all led off by queens reared from one lot of queen-cells, and the number of bees accompanying them is, of necessity, less each time. The last one frequently contains no more than a pint of bees, and, if hived in the old way, would be of little use under almost any circumstances; yet when supplied with combs already built and filled with honey, such as every enlightened apiarist should always keep in store, they may be made the very best of colonies, for they have young and vigorous queens, and often are equal to any in the apiary the next season.

There is one very amusing feature in regard to these after-swarms. When they have decided to send out no more swarms, all the young queens in the hive are sent out, or, it may be, allowed to go out with the last one ; and every few days during the swarming season, some "new hand" writes us about the wonderful fact of his having found three or four, or it may be a half-dozen queens in one swarm. On one occasion, a friend, who weighed something over 200, ascended to the top of an apple-tree during a hot July day to hive a very small third swarm. He soon came down, in breathless haste, to inform us that the swarm was *all queens;* and, in proof of it, brought two or three in his closed-up hands.

Years ago after-swarming was considered a sort of necessary evil that had to be tolerated because it could not be obviated; but in no well-regulated apiary should it be allowed. Many consider it good practice to permit one swarm—the first one. After that all others are restrained. Cutting out all the queen-cells but one may have the effect of preventing a second swarm; but the practice is objectionable—chiefly because one *can not be sure* that he destroys all but one. If there are two cells the occupant of one of them, when she hatches, is likely to bring out an after-swarm; indeed, we may say that, as long as there are young queens to hatch, there are likely to be after-swarms up to the number of three or four.

But the practical honey-producers of to-day consider cell-cutting for the prevention of these little swarms as waste of time, although they may and do cut out cells to prevent prime or first swarms. There are some who deem it advisable to prevent swarming altogether. The plan usually adopted to prevent second swarms is about as follows:

The wings of all queens in the apiary should be clipped, or else there should be entrance-guards over the colonies. As soon as the first swarm comes forth, and while the bees are in the air, the queen, if clipped, is found in front of the entrance of the old hive. She is caged, and the old hive is lifted off the old stand, and an empty one containing frames of foundation or empty combs is put in its place. A perforated zinc honey-board is next put on top, after which, the supers, now on the old stand. The queen in her cage is placed in front of the entrance, and the old hive is next carried to an entirely new location. In the mean time the swarm returns to find the queen at the old stand; and when the bees are well started to running into the entrance she is released, and allowed to go in with them. Most of the old or flying bees that happen to be left in the old colony, now on the new location, will go back to the old stand to strengthen further the swarm. This will so depopulate the parent colony that there will hardly be bees enough left to cause any after-swarming, and the surplus of young queens will have to fight it out among themselves—the

"survival of the fittest" being, of course, the only one left. She will be mated in the regular way, and the few bees with her will not, of course, follow her, as there will not be enough of them to make a respectable after-swarm.

HEDDON'S METHOD.

The first swarm is allowed to come forth; and while it is in the air the parent colony is removed from its stand and placed a few inches to one side, with its entrance pointing at right angles to its former position. For instance, if the old hive faced the east, it will now look toward the north. Another hive is placed on the old stand, filled with frames of wired foundation. The swarm is put in this hive, and at the end of two days the parent hive is turned around so that its entrance points in the same direction as the hive that now has the swarm. Just as soon as young queens of the parent colony are likely to hatch it is carried to a new location during the middle of the day or when the bees are flying the thickest. The result is, these flying bees will go back to the hive having the swarm. This, like the other method described, so depletes the parent hive that any attempt at after-swarming is effectually forestalled.

A variation from this plan makes it easier and just as good. Hive the swarm on the old stand and set the old hive close beside it, both facing the same way. A week later, when most bees are out, remove the old hive to a new stand That leaves the old colony just as much depleted as the longer way; and the depletion coming more suddenly will more thoroughly discourage all thought of further swarming.

AGE OF BEES.—It may be rather difficult to decide how long a worker bee would live if kept from wearing itself out by the active labors of the field; six months certainly, and perhaps a year; but the average life during the summer time is not over three months, and perhaps during the height of the clover-bloom not over six or eight weeks. The matter is easily determined by introducing an Italian queen to a hive of black bees at different periods of the year. If done in May or June, we shall have all Italians in the fall: and if we note when the last black bees hatch out, and the time when no black bees are to be found in the colony, we shall have a pretty accurate idea of the age of the blacks The Italians will perhaps hold out under the same circumstances a half longer. If we introduce the Italian queen in September, we shall find black bees in the hive until the month of May following—they may disappear a little earlier, or may be found even later, depending upon the time they commence to rear brood largely. The bees will live considerably longer if no brood is reared, as has been several times demonstrated in the case of strong queenless colonies. It is also pretty well established that black bees will live longer in the spring than Italians—probably because the latter

ALFALFA BLOSSOM.

are more inclined to push out into the fields when the weather is too cool for them to do so with safety; they seldom do this, however, unless a large amount of brood is on hand, and they are suffering for pollen or water.

During the summer months, the life of the worker-bee is probably cut short by the wearing-out of its wings, and we may, at the close of a warm day, find hundreds of

these heavily laden, ragged-winged veterans making their way into the hives slowly and painfully, compared with the nimble and perfect-winged young bees. If we examine the ground around the apiary at nightfall, we may see numbers of these hopping about on the ground, evidently recognizing their own inability to be of any further use to the community. We have repeatedly picked them up, and placed them in the entrance, but they usually seem only bent on crawling and hopping off out of the way where they can die without hindering the teeming rising generation.

AGE OF DRONES.

It is somewhat difficult to decide upon the age of drones, because the poor fellows are so often hustled out of the way, for the simple reason that they are no longer wanted; but we may be safe in assuming it is something less than the age of a worker. If kept constantly in a queenless hive they might live for three or four months.

AGE OF THE QUEEN.

As the queen does little or no outdoor work, and is seldom killed by violence as are the drones, we might expect her to live to a good old age, and this she does, despite her arduous egg-laying duties. Some queens die, seemingly, of old age, the second reason, but generally they live through the second or third, and we have had them lay very well even during the fourth year. They are seldom profitable after the third year, and the Italians will sometimes have a young queen "helping her mother" in her egg-laying duties, before she becomes unprofitable.

If a very large amount of brood is found in a hive, two queens will often be found, busily employed, and this point should be remembered while seeking to introduce valuable queens.

ALFALFA, OR LUCERNE. (Medicago sativa). This one of the clovers is very closely related to, and indeed greatly resembles, sweet clover, which latter is described under the head of CLOVER. Alfalfa has, now come to be one of the most important honey-plants of the great West—especially those arid regions that have to be irrigated. It is grown most extensively in Colorado, Wyoming, Arizona, Nevada, Utah, Kansas, Nebraska, New Mexico, Washington, Oregon, Idaho, and is now making rapid strides in California, Texas, and other States.

It has been grown, in an experimental way, in many of the Eastern States; but outside of irrigated regions, and some parts of the West not irrigated, it is not known to yield honey to any considerable extent. While it makes an excellent forage-plant in a few localities in the East, permitting from two to four cuttings, it is grown as a hay, particularly in the Western States mentioned; for there is no other forage-plant that will yield the same value per acre of fodder or hay in the regions that have to be irrigat-

METHOD OF STACKING ALFALFA HAY.

ed. It yields anywhere from 3 to 5 tons per acre, and gives from 3 to 5 cuttings to the season, and, under favorable circumstances, it is even claimed that 6 and 7 have been made. For the best hay it should be cut when the blooming commences; but, unfortunately for the bee-keeper, this alsocuts off the supply of nectar when it is flowing at its very best; for alfalfa, when in bloom in the irrigated regions, is perhaps the greatest

honey-plant in the world. But notwithstanding the interests of the bee-keeper, the ranchers cut their alfalfa just as soon as it begins to bloom, irrespective of the fact that it is "killing the goose that lays the golden egg" for the bee-keeper. After cutting, it is stacked in the open field* in a stack that will run anywhere from 10 to 100 tons in capacity.

As one goes through the irrigated regions of Arizona, California, Idaho, Utah, and Colorado, in a Pullman car going at the rate of 50 or 60 miles an hour, he sees hundreds and hundreds of such stacks; and where one stack has been cut into, or opened up, he sees not the dull grayish-brown hay of the East, but a beautiful grass-green clover hay; and it seems to keep green, no matter how old it is, provided it is not faded out by the intense sunlight that pours down with such relentless fury on the Great American Desert. But it is only the top layers that are faded. A few inches below, the hay is of the beautiful green color.

The irrigation needed to grow it for forage makes the crop almost certain; and those bee-keepers located in the vicinity of alfalfa-growing can rely almost as certainly on a crop of honey, the very finest, richest, thickest in the world. Of all the honey we have ever tasted we know of nothing, not even clover (which has formerly held the first rank), that can equal it. It runs from 12 to 13 lbs. to the gallon, while most eastern honeys run from 11 to 12 lbs. This heaviness of body is due to the dryness of the atmosphere in which it grows; for where alfalfa flourishes at its best, hives made of the best seasoned white pine will shrink and twist and check in a manner that is truly astonishing to a "tenderfoot." A light dry atmosphere a mile above the level of the sea, in the regions of Denver, almost entirely devoid of dews and frosts, a cloudless sky, occasional hot winds, a bright sun that pours down, unobstructed by cloud or mist, causes every thing to dry up, and even honey to thicken—so much so that it is difficult to throw it out of combs with the best extractors. Indeed, we found that some bee-keep-

*In the irrigated regions it scarcely ever rains, and therefore great barns for the storage of the hay are not necessary.

THE WAY ALFALFA HAY IS STACKED ON 1000 AND 5000 ACRE FARMS IN THE WEST.

ers were obliged to place their extractors in warm rooms, and even warm the combs sometimes before extracting, so thick is the honey. And then to do any thing like a good job of extracting one must give the extractor-baskets a h gh rotative speed, and this necessarily puts a great strain on the wire cloth and the bracing of the extractor.

We have already spoken of the superb quality of alfalfa honey. If any one takes a liking to it, as we have done, he will be almost spoiled for eating any other honey. Some of it is so thick and fine that it can be almost chewed like so much delicious wax candy. The flavor is a little like that of white clover, with a slight trace of mint that is very pleasant. In color it is quite equal to it, and in every other way it has no superior, although in some parts of the West the color is a light amber. In the very hot portions of the United States it is disposed to be darker than in the colder localities. The Colorado alfalfa is as a rule the lightest in color.

The nectar from alfalfa is secreted so abundantly during the time it is in bloom that anywhere from 100 to 500 colonies can be supported in a given location. In Colorado, however, it is found more profitable to have apiaries containing no more than from 100 to 150 colonies, owing to the very great overstocking in many of the best localities. Bee-keepers have rushed to this land of gold and golden honey in such numbers that in the great alfalfa-growing regions apiaries are stuck in very closely, from half a mile to a mile apart, so it is not now profitable to have more than 100 colonies to the yard. In other localities not so much overstocked, from 200 to 300 colonies can be kept in a single apiary.

For a given acreage there is no plant or tree, unless it is basswood, that will support as many colonies. In several localities in Colorado and Arizona, within a radius of five miles there will be anywhere from two to seven thousand colonies, the like of which can not be found anywhere else in the world, probably.

In Kansas and Nebraska, in the unirrigated regions, it is being grown more and more; where, too, it is so dry, and the soil so alkaline, it was supposed nothing would grow. It has been found that the roots of the alfalfa will pierce the hardpan, reach down into the moist subsoil, and leach out the alkali. Some of these lands have thus been transformed into productive ranches. With the onward march of the alfalfa has come the busy bee to take its share of the wealth.

There is scarcely a prettier sight than alfalfa when in bloom. The beautiful bluish or violet tinted flowers present a mass of color that is truly striking to one who has never seen the like of it before; and the fields are measured, not by the acre, but by the square mile. Indeed, we rode through one ranch in a Pullman car, going probably 50 miles an hour, that seemed all of 40 min-

Plate I.

THE CELEBRATED ALFALFA PLANT AND ROOT.

The plant represented in this plate grew in a rich, loose soil, with a heavy clay subsoil and an abundant supply of water, the water-level ranging from 4 to 8 feet from the surface at different seasons of the year. The diameter of the top was 18 inches, and the number of stems 360. The plate shows how these crowns gather soil around them, for the length of the underground stems is seen to be several inches, and this represents the accumulation of nearly this much material about it.

This is one of the largest plants that I have yet found. The specimen, as photographed, was dug April 30, 1898.—*Dr. Headden, in Bulletin No. 35, "Alfalfa."*

utes in going through it—not acres, but miles and miles of it as far as the eye could reach on each side of the track; and stacks and stacks of it, aggregating 100 tons to the pile, more than one could count if he were to try. Imagine, if you please, the effect of seeing such a field all in bloom, and mowing-machines going through it cutting it down. Imagine, too, the happy hum of the bees going to and from these immense fields. Then, truly, is the harvest of both rancher and bee-keeper.

No time is lost. The rancher is eager to get the whole cut as *soon as possible*. The bee-keeper, on the other hand, hopes that his rancher co-laborer may make as *slow* work as possible; for as the mowing-machines go through the field. the bee-keeper sees a gradual decrease in the flow of nectar. At the rate the mowers are progressing he can tell to a day when the hay will all be cut, and when the honey or the nectar will cease to flow. In producing con b honey he supplies his colony with just enough sections so the bees may fill every one of them at the close of the honey-flow which he knows in advance to a day. When the hay is all cut, then he awaits the new growth, the new bloom, and then, again, there is a scramble for honey on the part of the bee-keeper and the bees, and another scramble to get the hay down before it grows to be too old or out of bloom.

There is a growing tendency of late for the ranchman in some localities to cut the hay *before* it comes into bloom. It is claimed that the early cutting makes a better quality of hay. However that may be, if the practice should become universal one of the greatest honey-plants of the world will be cut off from the bees. In any case, fortunate is that bee keeper who is located in the vicinity of those alfalfa-fields devoted to the growing of alfalfa *seed;* for all such have the benefit of the entire blooming until the flower fades and the seed-pod takes its place. It is in these regions especially that a large number of colonies per yard can be supported.

Most of the best alfalfa-fields in the West have been taken by bee-keepers; and unless one can take a range vacated by another by death or otherwise, or get it by purchase, it is a matter of common honor that the new comer, should keep out; still, there are some who will squeeze in just a few colonies and gradually encroach upon the territory until there is not much in it for any one.

APPEARANCE OF THE ALFALFA.

To one who is unacquainted with the plant, alfalfa looks a good deal like sweet clover; and when the two plants are young it takes even an expert to detect the difference; but as they grow older the alfalfa assumes more of a heavy bushy character; and the other. sweet clover, takes on more the appearance of a treelike weed.

CULTIVATION OF ALFALFA.

While it seems to grow best in the raid regions watered by irrigation ditches, it also grows in localities where there is not too much rainfall or the soil is not too wet. It seems to do best on a light sandy soil with a loose or porous subsoil, and the roots run for 4 to 12 feet down—on the average perhaps 5 or 6 feet. The seed may be sown broadcast or in drills about 12 inches apart. The amount per acre varies greatly. Some think that 10 lbs. is sufficient, while others argue in favor of 30 lbs. The average amount seems to be from 15 to 20 lbs. If too small an amount of seed is sown, the plants grow large and coarse; whereas if a larger amount is used, a larger number of plants result in smaller stems and better hay.

Alfalfa is what is called a perennial—that is, it lives on from year to year, and the great difficulty of growing it in the East is to get it to make a stand. If it can be once started it will grow on from year to year with very little trouble.

The average life of the plants under ordinary conditions seems to be about twelve years, although some claim they will live as long as fifty years; but good authorities seem to doubt the statement.

Of late years the culture of alfalfa has been taken up in the Central, Southern, and Eastern States to a considerable extent, and with some success. It ought to be understood, however, it is most useful where "soiling" is practiced. European farmers who live in a similar climate prefer sainfoin to alfalfa, claiming it produces a finer hay, and is otherwise more suitable. For Southern Europe soola is preferred. All three are similar in habit and culture, but alfalfa is the rankest grower. See SAINFOIN.

For some of the data just given, and for the half-tone illustration shown on page 8, we are indebted to Bulletin No. 35, entitled "Alfalfa," from the State Agricultural College, Fort Collins, Col., by Dr. W. P. Headden, Chemist.

ANATOMY OF THE BEE. For the main facts of this article we are indebted to "The Honey-Bee," a scientific work by Thos. Wm. Cowan, editor of the *British Bee Journal*. Material gathered from other sources is duly acknowledged.

We will first call attention to the alimentary canal—that is, the organs of digestion and assimilation. What is digestion? Cowan says, "It is the separation of the nutrient part of food from the non-nutrient, and the conversion of the nutrient into a liquid fit to mingle with the blood, and thus nourish the body of the insect." We all know how the bee gathers up its food through its wonderful and delicate little tongue. It then passes into a little tube just below the point a, in the engraving, called the "œsophagus," or

know what the bees were working on. Suspecting that they were gathering juices from over-ripened raspberries on the vines, we grasped a bee by its waist and abdomen, and pulled until the parts were separated, when there was revealed the little honey-sac, which had di-engaged itself from the abdomen. This contained a light purple or wine-colored liquid. The size of this honey-sac, as nearly as we recollect now, was a good big eighth of an inch; and we should judge that the bee had all it could contain in its little pocket. Cheshire says that, when the honey-sac is full, it is ⅙ of an inch in diameter. This would agree with our observations.

HONEY-BEE DISSECTED: AFTER WITZGALL.

STOMACH-MOUTH.

The wonderful stomach-mouth, h, solves a very difficult problem. Honey or nectar swallowed by the bee goes directly into the honey-sac, where it may remain for days unchanged, just as if in a glass can. When the bee desires, it takes honey or pollen from the honey-sac into the chyle stomach, where it is changed into chyme. This chyme the nurse bees feed to the brood, as also to the queen and the drones. But how can chyme be passed from the chyle-stomach out through the honey-sac without having a lot of raw nectar mixed with it? The stomach-mouth solves the problem by moving up and joining itself to the œsophagus, leaving the honey-sac shut out entirely. This will be better understood by referring to the drawings by Dr. Breunnich.

"gullet." We find a similar organ in our own bodies, leading from the mouth and communicating directly with the stomach. This œsophagus passes through the waist of the bee, or thorax, as it is called, and to the honey-stomach g in the abdomen. It is in this little sac, although it can hold but a tiny drop at a time, that millions and millions of pounds of nectar are carried annually and stored in our combs. This sac g is located in the fore part of the abdomen.

Several years ago we had a curiosity to

TRUE STOMACH.

This corresponds to the stomach in our own bodies, and performs the same function in the way of digestion in converting the nutrient particles of the food into blood. The inside walls of the stomach have cer-

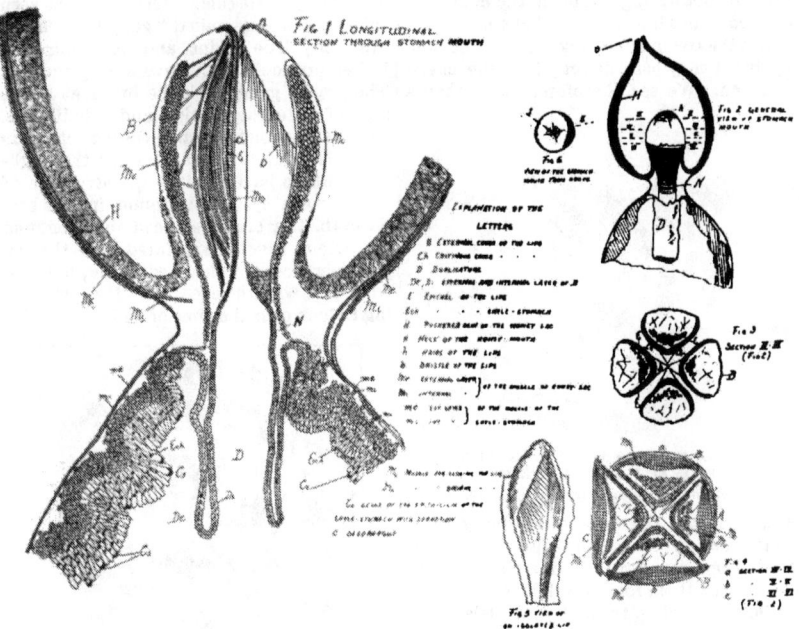

ENLARGED DRAWING SHOWING STOMACH-MOUTH, BY DR. BRUENNICH.

tain cells which perform certain offices; but without more definite engravings it will be impossible to describe them in detail.

The next organ is the small intestine, or, as it is sometimes called, the "ileum." In the human body the small intestines are much more elaborate. It is into this that the food, after its digestion, passes, and where, by absorption, the nutrient particles not already absorbed pass into the blood, and so on throughout the system.

It will be noted, also, at l, some small radiating filaments. These are called the malpighian tubes. It is not certain what their office is, but it is thought that these are the urinary organs.

At the end of the small intestine, k (page 10), will be seen an enlargement, m. This is called the colon. Although the appearance of the colon in the bee is different from that in the human body, yet its functions are very much the same; and if allowed to become dammed up by excreta (that is, by retention during winter) it is liable to cause disease in the bee, just the same as in the human body. See DYSENTERY. Mr. Cowan, the author of the book mentioned at the outset, says:

From the colon, what remains of the undigested food is expelled by the anal opening. For this purpose strong muscles exist, by which the colon is compressed and the excreta ejected.

The quantity of the excreta voided, usually of a dark-brown color, is regulated by the nature of the food; bad honey, an improper substitute for honey (such as glucose) producing a larger amount, while good honey and good syrup produce less, a larger proportion of it being digested and absorbed. It is, therefore, important that bees should have good food, as, in a healthy condition, workers never void their fæces in the hive, but on the wing. In the winter it is retained until voided on their first flight.

So you see, then, that bad food makes mischief, just the same as it does in the human body, and it is in this colon that the overplus of fæces is stored during winter.

HOW THE BEE "MAKES" HONEY.

After the nectar is gathered it is then transferred from the tongue to the œsophagus and thence to the honey-stomach, g (page 10). It has been shown by experiment that there are many more pollen grains in the nectar than in honey; hence the little stomach-mouth, h, comes into play in separating the grains from the honey. On arrival at the hive, the bee regurgitates—that is, expels the contents of the honey-sac into the cell; but during its stay in the honey-sac the nectar has undergone a change.

But the bee may not regurgitate the honey, for it may pass directly into the chyle-stomach. We see, therefore, that when a

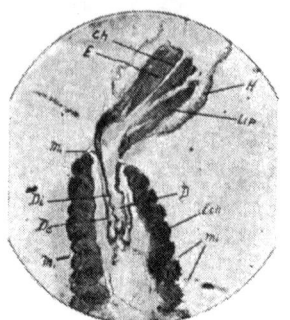

FIG. 7.—LONGITUDINAL SECTION THROUGH THE STOMACH-MOUTH.—*Bruennich*.
This is further explained in Fig. 1—6.

swarm issues, the bees, after filling their honey-sacs to their full capacity (a very small drop), can carry with them a supply of food to last them for several days; and even while on the wing, through that little stom-

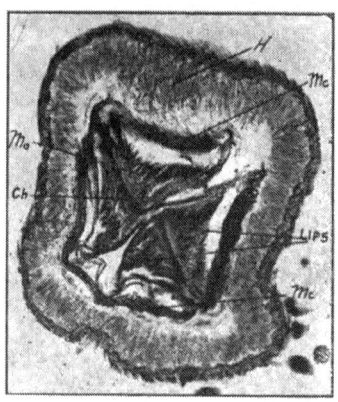

FIG. 8.—TRANSVERSE SECTION THROUGH THE STOMACH-MOUTH IN THE MIDST OF OF THE LIPS, THE HONEY-SAC BEING EMPTY.—*Bruennich*.

ach-mouth, they may take nourishment. So much for the alimentary canal, its office in digestion, and the honey-stomach.

THE NERVOUS SYSTEM.

By referring to the general engraving there will be seen parallel and medial lines passing almost the entire length of the bee, and finally communicating with the brain,

a. Along at irregular intervals will be seen thickened masses called "ganglia." These are really little brains, and, as in our own bodies, preside over the involuntary muscles. The largest ganglion is the brain, at *a*—the seat of voluntary action and intelligence. One is surprised in reading through chapters 10 and 11 of Mr. Cowan's work how thoroughly scientists have studied the structure of the nervous system as found in the bee. Even the tiny brain has been dissected, and its various functions pointed out—that is, what parts communicate with the antennæ, what part with the eyes, etc. It is interesting to look over the sizes of different brains

FIG. 9.—SAME AS FIG. 8, BUT THE HONEY-SAC NOT QUITE EMPTY.—*Bruennich*.

found in different insects. We quote here a paragraph found on page 70 of Mr. Cowan's book:

It is generally admitted, that the size of the brain is in proportion to the development of intelligence; and Dujardin, who made careful measurements, gives the following sizes: In the worker bee the brain is the $\frac{1}{174}$ of the body; in the ant, $\frac{1}{290}$; the ichneumon, $\frac{1}{400}$; the cockchafer, $\frac{1}{3920}$; the dytiscus, or water-beetle, $\frac{1}{4200}$.

In man the proportion is 1 to 40, but we all know that he is of the very highest order of intelligence. However, it is not surprising to learn that the bee has the largest brain of any of the insects, exceeding by far even that of the ant, whose intelligence has been admired over and over again.

THE RESPIRATORY SYSTEM.

It is also interesting to inquire how the bee breathes. By referring to the engraving (page 10) we observe a couple of large air-sacs, called the "trachea," corresponding somewhat to the lungs These are located on either side of the abdomen, as at *t*. They are then divided and subdivided into small, er trachea, and these in turn ramify all through the entire body. Instead of fresh air being received in at the mouth, as with us, fresh supplies are admitted through little mouths called "spiracles." Ten of these are located in the abdomen—five on each side—and are situated just about on the margin of the scales, between the dorsal and ventral segments. Four others are situated on the thorax, or waist, two on each side. You may, therefore, decapitate a bee and it will continue breathing as before. If you place a pencil dipped in ammonia near its body, the headless insect will struggle to get away; and if the pencil touches its feet, the ganglia already spoken of communicate the sensation to the other ganglia, and at once all the feet come to the rescue to push off the offending object, or,

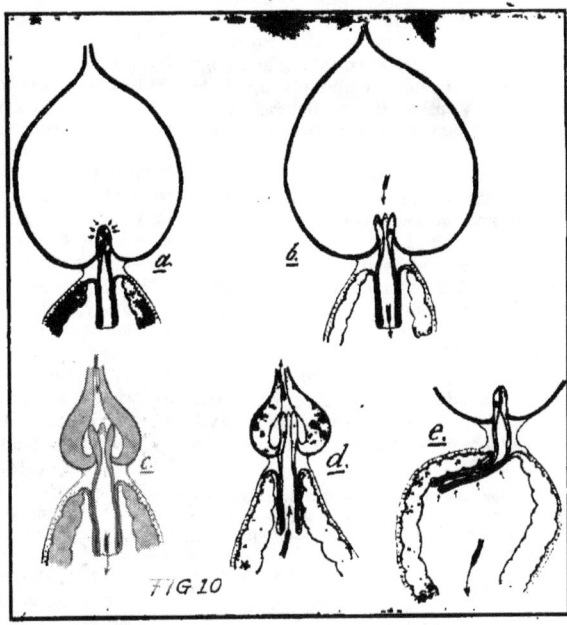

THE GENERAL SCHEME OF THE STOMACH-MOUTH OF THE HONEY-BEE IN DIFFERENT SITUATIONS.—*Bruennich.*

a, a field or swarm bee fasting,
b, the same eating honey.
c, a brood-bee eating pollen.
d, a brood-bee feeding the brood.
e, Valvular close from the chyle-stomach against the honey-sac, when the first is contracting itself for removing its contents into the small intestine.

it may be, to take closer hold so the sting may do its work: for, if bees are daubed with honey they will die very soon from strangulation, because these little mouths or spiracles are closed. A bee may swim around in a trough of water, and, though its head be entirely out, it will drown just the same, because these spiracles or breathing-mouths are submerged under water. On a hot day, if the entrance of a hive be closed the bees will soon begin to sweat: and, thus becoming daubed, the delicate spiracles are closed, causing suffocation and death. Such bees look as if they had been boiled.

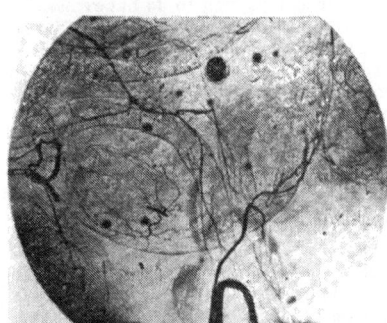

FIG. 1.—Delicate ends of the finely divided tracheas carrying air into all parts of bee's body.—*Bruennich.*

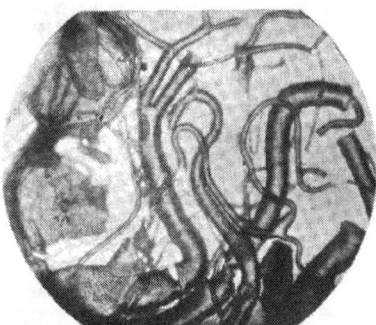

FIG. 2.—Larger tracheas showing chitinous spires which prevent tubes from collapsing.—*Bruennich.*

It was formerly supposed that royal jelly was a secretion from certain glands: but that idea has been completely upset by Schiemenz, Von Planta, and Schönfeld who have proved that it is chyme from the chyle-stomach.

This chyme is produced in what is called the chyle-stomach, shown at *l*, in the cut on page 10; and worker larvæ are fed on this concentrated food for three days, after which they are weaned. "On the fourth day this food is changed and the larva is weaned; for the first pap has a large quantity of honey added, but no undigested pollen, as Prof. Leuckhart had stated. The drone larvæ are also weaned, but in a different way; for, in addition to honey, a large quantity of *pollen* is added after the fourth day." And right here we can not do better than quote from Mr. Cowan:

Microscopic examination showed that, in the queen and worker larvæ, there was no undigested pollen; whereas in the drone larvæ, after the fourth day, large numbers of pollen grains were found. In one milligram, no less than 15,000 pollen grains were counted, and these were from a number of different plants. . . . This work of Dr. Planta's, we think conclusively proves that the food is not a secretion, and that the nurses have the power of altering its constituents as they may require for the different bees. . . . Royal jelly is, therefore, chyle food, and this is also most likely the food given to the queen-bee. Schoenfeld has also recently shown that drones are likewise dependent upon this food, given to them by workers, and that, if it is withheld, they die after three days, in the presence of abundance of honey. This, he thinks, accounts for the quiet way in which drones perish at the end of the season. It will now be easily understood, that if weaning of the worker larvæ does not take place at the proper time, and if the first nourishing food is continued too long, it may be the cause of developing the ovaries, and so produce fertile workers, just as the more nourishing food continued during the whole of the larval existence in the case of a queen develops her ovaries, or even in the absence of a queen the feeding of workers on this rich food may tend to have the same effect. This, then, is the solution of royal jelly and brood food.

For a more exhaustive treatment of the whole subject, see Cowan's work, The Honey-bee, Cook's Manual of the Apiary, or Cheshire's Bees and Bee-keeping, Vol. I.

ANGER OF BEES. We confess we do not like the term "anger," when applied to bees, and it almost makes us angry when we hear people speak of their being "mad," as if they were always in a towering rage, and delight to inflict severe pain on every-thing and everybody coming near them. Bees are, on the contrary, the pleasantest, most sociable, genial, and good-natured lit-tle fellows one meets in all animated crea-tion, when one understands them. Why, we can tear their beautiful comb all to bits right before their very eyes, and without a particle of resentment; but with all the patience in the world they will at once set to work to repair it, and that, too, without a word of remonstrance. If you pinch them they will sting; and anybody who has ener-gy enough to take care of himself would do as much had he the weapon.

We as yet know very little of bees com-paratively; and the more we learn, the easier we find it to be to get along without any clashing in regard to who shall be master. In fact, we take all their honey now, almost as fast as they gather it; and even if we are so thoughtless as to starve them to death, no word of complaint is made.

There are a few circumstances under which bees seem "cross;" and although we may not be able to account exactly for it, we can take precautions to avoid these un-pleasant features, by a little care. A few years ago a very intelligent friend procured some Italians, an extractor, etc., and com-menced bee culture. He soon learned to handle them, and succeeded finely; when it came time to extract, the whole business went on so easily that he was surprised at what had been said about experienced hands being needed to do the work. He had been in the habit of doing this work as directed, toward the middle of the day, while the great mass of the bees were in the fields; but in the midst of a heavy yield of clover honey, when the hives were full to overflow-ing, they were one day stopped by a heavy thunder-shower. This, of course, drove the bees home, and at the same time washed the honey out of the blossoms so completely that they had nothing to do but remain in the hives until more was secreted. Not so with their energetic and enthusiastic owner. As soon as the rain had ceased, the hives were again opened and an attempt made to take out the frames, as but a few hours be-fore; but the bees that were all gentleness then, seemed now possessed of the very spirit of mischief and malice: and when all hands had been severely stung, they con-cluded that prudence was the better part of valor and stopped operations for the day. While loads of honey were coming in all the while, and every bee rejoicing, none were disposed to be cross; but after the shower, all hands were standing around idle; and when a hive was opened, each was ready to take a grab from its neighbor, and the result was a free fight in a very short time.

There is nothing in the world that will induce bees to sting with such wicked recklessness as to have them get to quarreling over combs or honey left exposed when they have nothing to do. From a little carelessness in this respect, and nothing else, whole apiaries have been so demoralized that people were stung when passing along the street several rods distant. During the middle of the day, when bees were busily engaged on the flowers, during a good yield, we have frequently left filled combs standing on the top of a hive from noon until supper time without a bee touching them; but to do this after a hard rain, or at a time when little or no honey is to be gathered in the fields, might result in the ruin of several colonies, and you and your bees being voted a nuisance by the whole neighborhood.

Almost every season we get more or less letters complaining that the bees have suddenly become so cross as to be almost unmanageable, and these letters come along in July, after the clover and linden have begun to slack up. The bees are not so very unlike mankind after all, and all you have to do is to avoid opening the hives for a few days, until they get used to the sudden disappointment of having the avenues through which they were getting wealth so rapidly, cut off. After a week or ten days they will be almost as gentle as in the times when they gathered half a gallon of honey daily, if you are only careful about leaving hives open too long, or leaving any bits of honey or comb about.

It is not easy to explain why bees sting so remorselessly and vindictively after having had a taste of stolen sweets, yet nearly all the experience we have had of trouble with stinging has been from this very cause. Bees from colonies that have a habit of robbing will buzz about one's ears and eyes for hours, seeming to delight in making one nervous and fidgety if they succeed in so doing, and they not only threaten, but oftentimes inflict, the most painful stings, and then buzz about in an infuriated way, as if frantic because unable to sting one a dozen times more after their sting is lost. The colonies that furnish this class of bees are generally hybrid, or perhaps black bees having just a trace of Italian blood. These bees seem to have a perfect passion for following one about, and buzzing before the nose from one side to the other (until one gets cross-eyed in trying to follow their er-

ratic oscillations), in a way that is most especially provoking. One such colony annoyed us so much while extracting that we killed the queen, although she was very prolific, and substituted a full-blood Italian. Although it is seldom a pure Italian follows one about in the manner mentioned, yet an occasional colony may contain bees that do it; at least we have found such, where the workers were all three-banded. That it is possible to have an apiary without any such disagreeable bees, we have several times demonstrated; but oftentimes you will have to discard some of your very best honey-gatherers, to be entirely rid of them.

On occasions like this it is advisable to use robber-traps. See ROBBERS.

With a little practice the apiarist will tell as soon as he comes near the apiary whether any angry bees are about, by the high keynote they utter when on the wing. It is well known that with meal feeding we have perfect tranquillity although bees from every hive in the apiary may be working on a square yard of meal. Now, should we substitute honey for the meal, we should have a perfect uproar, for a taste of honey found in the open air during a dearth of pasturage, or at a time when our bees have learned to get it by stealing instead of honest industry, seems to have the effect of setting every bee crazy. In some experiments to determine how and why this result came about, we had considerable experience with angry bees. After they had been robbing, and had become tranquil, we tried them with dry sugar; the quarrelsome bees fought about it for a short time, but soon resumed their regular business of hanging about the well-filled hives, trying to creep into every crack and crevice, and making themselves generally disagreeable all around. If a hive was to be opened, they were into it almost before the cover was raised, and then resulted a pitched battle between them and the inmates; the operator was sure to be stung by one or both parties, and, pretty soon, some of the good people indoors would be asking what in the world made the bees so awfully cross, saying that they even came indoors and tried to sting. Now, why could they not work peaceably on the sugar as they do on the meal, or the clover-blossoms in June? We dampened the sugar with a sprinkler, and the bees that were at work on it soon started for home with a load; then began the high key-note of robbing, faint at first, then louder and louder, until we began to be almost frightened at the mischief that might ensue. When the dampness was all licked up, they soon subsided into their usual condition. The effect of feeding honey in the open air is very much worse than that of feeding any kind of syrup, and syrup from white sugar incites robbing in a much greater degree than that from brown sugar; the latter is so little relished by them that they use it only when little else is to be found. It is by the use of damp brown sugar that we get rid of the greater part of what are usually termed angry bees, or bees that prefer to prowl around, robbing and stinging, rather than gather honey " all the day," as the greater part of the population of the apiary does. The sugar should be located *several rods away*, and should be well protected from the rain, but in such a way as to allow the bees to have free access. When no flowers are in bloom, they will work on it in great numbers; but when honey is to be found, you will see none but the prowling robbers round it. These, you will very soon notice, are mostly common bees and these having a very little Italian blood. We have seen Italians storing honey in boxes while the common bees did nothing but work in the sugar-barrels. Where you work without a veil, it is very convenient to have these annoying bees out of the way, and, even if they belong to our neighbors, we prefer to furnish them with all the cheap sugar they can lick up.

HOW THE SOURCE FROM WHICH BEES ARE GATHERING AFFECTS THEIR TEMPER.

It has been found that bees are crosser when working on some blossoms than on others. For example they seem to be more inclined to sting when working on buckwheat than on clover. This is probably due to the fact that the latter yield nectar all day while the former will in most localities yield an hour or two in the morning and again toward night. The stoppage of the flow seems to affect the bees adversely.

In the same way they are cross when working on honey-dew from hickory and oaks. This yields heavily in the morning and lets up and stops during the middle hours of the day. The morning dews soften the saccharine matter secreted on the leaves of these trees, and when it dries up again the nectar supply is cut off and the bees are cross. During 1909, when there was so much honey-dew from oaks and hickories from all over the country, bees that year were reported to be exceptionally cross.

To make bees good-natured, a honey-plant must be a continuous yielder *all day*. So long as it keeps up its supply, there is quiet.

In discussing this general subject we have attempted to show some of the causes that make bees cross, in order that beginners may be forewarned and on their guard. Now, it may seem a little strange if, under the head of OUTDOOR FEEDING, under the head of FEEDING and HOW TO STOP ROBBING, under the head of ROBBING, we should recommend the very thing that we have warned the beginner not to do—that is, to expose sweets in the open air to which they may help themselves. When the reader has read over some of the chapters in this work he will be able to stop robbing by *doing the very thing* that starts it in the first place, on the principle that " like cures like." After one has had some experience he can actually stop robbing by putting out a counter-attraction in the shape of feed outdoors; and when the bees are busy with this feed one may open up the hives and do any thing he pleases. The different cases of this kind will be discussed under the sub-title of FEEDING OUTDOORS under the general head of FEEDING AND FEEDERS; of EXTRACTORS, and again under the sub-title HOW TO STOP ROBBING, under the head of ROBBING.

Where one has only a single hive and no neighbors who keep bees, the case is something like Robinson Crusoe on the island; no chance for stealing, and consequently nothing to be cross about. Bees are seldom cross, unless through some fault or carelessness of their owners. See ROBBING; also STINGS.

ANTS. Although we have given the matter considerable attention, we can not find that ants are guilty of any thing that should warrant, here in the North, the apiarist in waging any great warfare against them. Some years ago a visitor frightened us by saying that the ants about our apiary would steal every drop of honey as fast as the bees could gather it. Accordingly we prepared ourselves with a tea-kettle of boiling water, and not only killed the ants but some grapevines growing near. Afterward there came a spring when the bees, all but about eleven colonies, dwindled away and died, and the hives filled with honey, scattered about the apiary unprotected, seemed to be as fair a chance for the ants that had not " dwindled " a particle, as they could well ask for. We watched to see how fast they would carry away the honey, but, to our astonishment, they seemed to care more for the hives that contained bees than for those containing only honey. We soon determined that it was the warmth from the cluster that especially attracted them; and as the hives were directly on the ground, the ants soon moved into several that contained only a small cluster and for a while both used one common entrance. As the bees increased, they began to show a decided aversion to having two families in the same house, although the ants were evidently inclined to be peaceable enough until the bees tried to "push" matters, when they turned about and showed themselves fully able to hold possession. The bees seemed to be studying over the matter for a while, and finally we found them one day taking the ants, one by one, and carrying them high up in the air, and letting them drop at such a distance from their home that they would surely never be able to walk back again. The bees, as fast as they became strong colonies, drove the ants out; and our experience ever since has been, that a *good* colony of bees is never in any danger of being troubled in the least by ants. One weak colony, after battling awhile with a strong nest of the ants, swarmed out; but they might have done this any way, so we do not lay much blame to the ants.

But ants do prove to be very annoying in those apiaries where there is any attempt to keep the grass down with a lawn-mower. The little hillocks that they make all over the yard disfigure it to some extent, as well as forming more or less obstruction to the scythe and lawn-mower. While, as we have already said, ants do little if any damage to hives in the North, yet as it is so easy to eradicate them it may be well to consider methods for their extermination.

HOW TO DESTROY ANTS' NESTS.

With a crowbar or a sharp stick and a mallet make a hole an inch or so in diameter, and about a foot deep, down through the center of the nest. Around this hole make two or three other similar ones, or more if the nest is a large one. Go to the drugstore and get about a dime's worth of bisulphide of carbon. Be careful with the stuff, for it is very explosive, and the fumes of it should not be allowed to collect in the room where there is a gasoline flame or any stove or lamp burning. From this bottle pour about a tablespoonful of the liquid in each hole; then immediately stop each up with a plug of earth, for it is desired to have the fumes of the bisulphide penetrate all the

galleries of the nest, thus destroying ants, larvæ, and eggs. In a day or so it will be found that every thing formerly animate in and about that nest is dead—*very* dead.

But if the nests are not very large, one can secure almost as good results by using coal oil or gasoline in place of the bisulphide. But in using these, about twice or three times the quantity should be poured in each hole. We have tried both gasoline and kerosene, and have found each effective in destroying the nest. Of the two, the kerosene (or coal oil as some call it) seems to be preferable. In using bisulphide of carbon, gasoline, or kerosene, be careful about spilling or pouring any of it on the top of the nest, as that will kill the grass, leaving a brown spot right where it should be green. The bisulphide is more apt to kill the grass than the gasoline or coal oil, as it is much more powerful. All things considered we would recommend the use of kerosene.

The best time to destroy ants' nests is to go early in the spring, before the ants have had an opportunity to make much of a hillock; then there will be less liability of killing the grass: or, rather, a better opportunity for the grass to recover from its "dose" during the early spring rains.

ANTS IN THE SOUTH.

These insects are much more troublesome in the Southern States, and all warm climates, in fact, than in the North. Sometimes they are so large and powerful that they even set about to destroy the colony. We would first find the nest, and proceed to destroy by the use of kerosene or gasoline. If these do not prove to be powerful enough, use bisulphide of carbon, making three or four holes to the square foot of nest; but in the case of the bisulphide, one must be careful to have each hole stopped up tight with plugs of earth, otherwise the gas will escape, and the effect of the liquid will be largely lost.

But there is a species of ants in warm climates that have nests in trees that are inaccessible. Other ants are so small, and come such long distances, that it is almost impossible to find their nest. In such cases it has been recommended to place within their reach some syrup or honey mixed with arsenic, Paris green, London purple, or strychnine. It is unnecessary to say that all vessels containing such poisonous mixtures should be placed in a box covered with screen just fine enough to keep out bees, and coarse enough to admit the ants. They will work on these poison- ous mixtures, and carry them home to their young, with the result that both mature insects as well as larvæ will be destroy- ed, no matter where the nest may be.

E. H. Schæffle, of Murphys, Cal- ifornia, who rec- ommends this method of feed- ing ants with poisoned sweets, says the plan is very effective, for their visita- tions will soon cease. But he stipulates that the box contain- ing the poison- ous sweet should be placed in the trail of the ants. When it does not seem prac- ticable to de- stroy the pests they may be kept away from the hive temporarily by pouring a lit- tle narrow trail of kerosene clear around the hive or hives. The ants will □ come

THE AUTHORS' APIARY IN CUBA.

Some eight or ten years ago we owned and operated an apiary in Cuba, the same run for honey as well as bees and queens; but the poor seasons finally com- pelled us to abandon it. . . The hives here shown are in straight rows and close together. Experience showed that this was a mistake, for there were no distinguishing objects by which the bees could mark their homes, and as a result there .was more or less confusion and robbing.

THE ROOF APIARY OF C. H. W. WEBER, CINCINNATI, OHIO.

In cities bees are often put on the roofs of the buildings. In all such cases it is advisable to provide shade, for the heat of the summer will be intense in hot weather. If the roof becomes too hot for comfort it is advised to paint it white.

up to the oily line, and there stop.

Mr. Poppleton, of Florida, has graphically described in *Gleanings* the

CARNIVOROUS ANTS.

With one exception these ants are the worst ene- mies bees have here in Florida, and only constant vigilance from September to December inclusive will prevent the loss of many colonies every season. These ants are usually found in our hummock lands, and only occasionally in clean pine woods; are red in color; of very large size, frequently mea- suring nearly or quite half an inch in length; are strictly nocturnal in their habits, being seldom seen in daytime except when disturbed or waging battle with a colony of bees; are usually found in decayed wood, through which they cut out galleries for use as living-apartments. A favorite place is in a partly decayed saw-palmetto root in the ground. Nearly every cabbage-palmetto tree contains a colony of them among the boots near its top, and for this rea- son a thick palmetto grove is one of the worst places an apiary can be located. They are also found in piles of old boards, and on the ground under old boards or logs. They also like to enter our houses and locate in trunks, boxes, drawers, and in almost any place where they can find a few inches of space to occupy. They are frequently found in the tops of our hives if there is sufficient space above the bees under the cover.

At sundown they start on their nightly quest for food; and if near an apiary a few of them will usually be seen running on some of the hives. As long as only two or three can be seen on any one hive, no special attention need be given them; but if a dozen or more are seen it means that they have probably selected that hive for their own use, and it needs close watching. They will continue their regular attentions to that one hive, gradually increasing in numbers until they decide they are strong enough, when nearly the entire colony of ants will boldly attack the bees by biting off wings and legs, and crippling them so they are of no more use. Bees fight back courageously, the battle continuing for hours, and sometimes a day or two, according to the relative strength of the two belligerents. The inside of the hive and the ground near by will be strewn with dead ants and dead and crippled bees; but it always ends with the destruction of all the bees, and the moving in and occupation of the hive by the ant colony. When ants have once chosen a certain colony of bees to work on, the beemaster has got to destroy the ants, root and branch, or they will in time destroy the bees. If a part only of the ants are destroyed they will simply bide their time until they have built up strong enough, and then do the work. I know of few or no living creatures more presistent in evil works than are these bee-killing ants. They also, in certain localities, do great damage to queen-rearing nuclei.

During the fall months I make it a practice almost every evening after dark in my home apiary, and as often as possible in the out-apiaries, to see by the light of a lantern the front of every hive; and any one on which I see three or four or more ants running over has a marker placed on it. If the number of ants on any one of these marked hives increases each night I give that hive especial attention until the ants get numerous enough to begin to worry the bees. When this occurs, bees commence to whine, as I call it—that is, utter a fine sharp note with their wings. As the ants get bolder the cry of the bees becomes louder and more frequent—so much so that I have frequently heard it fully fifty feet away. The ants usually worry the bees continually for several nights, when suddenly the whole colony of ants starts in on a battle royal, which continues for hours or even a day or two, until every bee is disabled or driven out. A great many of the ants will also be killed; but how the bees do this is a mystery to me.

When the battle has once been joined, the beekeeper has a difficult task to save the bees: but this can usually be prevented. When the ants become plentiful enough at the hive to begin worrying the bees, there is usually a trail of going and returning ants from their nest to the hive, and this can usually be located and traced to their nest, which, when found, should be left undisturbed until the following day, when all the ants will be at home. If the nest can not be found the first time trying, I search again and until it is found. As soon as the nest is found, or search for it is given up for that night, I sprinkle some insect powder on their trail near the hive; also wherever on or around the hive I can do so to worry the ants and not injure the bees. This will usually keep the ants from doing any more harm that night.

The next day when all the ants are at home, I take a kettle of boiling water, tear open the nest, and, if possible, kill every ant and egg. If a few of them are left they are likely to gather together, increase in time to their former strength, and again attack

that same colony of bees. Whenever the nest is found in a box or piece of wood that can be easily moved with all the ants, the easiest and best plan is to carry them into the chicken-yard, break open the nest, and the hens will gladly do the rest of the business. They are very fond of both ants and eggs; and they not only find them good to eat, but give their owner lots of fun watching the old rooster especially, kick and scold every time an ant bites one of his feet. I have had many a hearty laugh watching this performance.

These ants are a great pest here in Florida. They destroy in the aggregate a great many colonies every fall. I know of one apiary which was entirely lost, largely, I judge, from what I hear, by these ants. At the best they are a great nuisance because they compel the bee-keeper to remain at home watching them at a season of the year when nothing is doing in the apiary, and the apiarist could, but for them, be away on a holiday, or have some outside business. O. O. POPPLETON.
Stuart, Fla., Dec. 9, 1905.

Ants are a serious pest to bees in many tropical countries, notably in South America, where they are omnipresent and almost omnipotent. A species similar to that described by Mr. Poppleton in Florida exists all over tropical America, and particularly in the southern continent. He has so graphically described it, there is no necessity to enlarge on it further. The worst feature of these ants is their readiness to travel, so that, when one does destroy their nests, there is

MORRISON'S ANT-PROOF BEE-HIVE SHED.

no assurance the apiary is safe from their attacks. Another bad feature is their habit of traveling by night; in fact, nearly all their depredations are made in the dark.

To circumvent them, it is necessary to destroy all their nests within a radius of 100 yards of the apiary by the application of bisulphide of carbon to their nests. But this precaution alone will not suffice, and it will be necessary to adopt further measures. Luckily it is not difficult to do this, as tropical bee-keepers are obliged to keep their beehives under a shed, for excellent reasons.

In erecting a shed, therefore, we can take measures to prevent effectually the ants having access to the hives at all. All we have to do is to add cups to all the posts used to support the structure. The illustration preceding, shows very clearly how this is accomplished with but little expense or trouble. The cups are filled with coal-tar, creosote, or crude petroleum, all of which the ants positively dislike for two reasons—they stick to their feet and the smell is vile. No ant will attempt to cross such a mess as this, hence the bees are secure. The warm climate keeps the tar, etc., always soft; and if some rain falls into the cups it does no harm, as the water also tastes of the tar.

In working with the bees care should be taken to see nothing is left which will form a " bridge " whereby the ants will manage to reach the bee-hives while the apiarist is absent. One of the worst things that can happen is to allow the ants to get a taste of the bees, for once they do they are sure to linger around waiting for an opportunity to get into the hive.

APIARIST. One who keeps bees, or a bee-keeper; and the plot of ground, including hives, bees, etc., is called an

APIARY. As you can not well aspire to be the former until you are possessed of the latter, we will proceed to start an apiary.

LOCATION.

There is scarcely a spot on the surface of the earth where mankind finds sustenance that will not, to some extent, support bees, although they may do much better in some localities than in others. A few years ago it was thought that only localities especially favored would give large honey crops; but since the introduction of the Italians, and the new methods of management, we are each year astonished to hear of great yields here and there, and from almost every quarter of the globe. It will certainly pay to try a colony or two of bees, no matter where you may be located.

Bees are kept with much profit, even in the heart of some of our large cities. In this case the apiary is usually located on the roof of the building, that the bees may be less likely to frighten nervous people and those unacquainted with their habits. Such an apiary should be established like those on the ground in all essential points.

It is not always possible to select just the location for an apiary that we might like, and we are therefore compelled to take what we can get ; but where conditions permit it is advisable to select the rear of a village lot ; or, if located on a farm, back of the house in an orchard. The ground should be rolled and smoothed down so that a lawn-mower can run over every portion of it, as the grass should be kept down around the hives. And then, a smooth plot of ground renders the use of a wheelbarrow or hand-cart for handling loads much more pleasant and convenient. An ideal spot would be an orchard of young trees seventy-five or a hundred feet from the road or highway. Usually the rear end of a village lot just back of the house will answer very nicely. If the apiary *must* be located close to the highway, then a high board fence should be placed between the bees and the street. A hedge of osage orange, or evergreens ; a trellis of some sort of vine : trees, shrubbery, or any thing that will cause the bees to raise their flight to a height of ten or twelve feet above the traffic of the street may be used. In any case, the bees should never be allowed to go direct from their hives on a line that would encounter vehicles or pedestrians: otherwise their owner may have a lawsuit on his hands for alleged damages from bee-stings. See BEES AS A NUISANCE.

TOO MUCH SHADE DETRIMENTAL.

If the orchard where the bees are to be located is made up of *old* trees, then there can be from four to five hives grouped under each tree. If, on the other hand, it consists of young ones, then not more than one or two hives should be placed at a tree, and in that case always on the north side, to be in the shade. The hives should be so located that they will get the morning sun up to eight or nine o'clock, and the afternoon sun from three or four o'clock on. Too much shade is detrimental, and too much hot sun pouring directly on the hives is equally bad. Experience has shown conclusively that a very dense shade over bees in the morning hours is detrimental. Colonies located on the *west* side of a building or barn, or under densely foliaged trees, so that they do not get the morning sun, will not, as a rule, be as far along by the time the honey-flow comes on as those that have only moderate shade. On the other hand, an *afternoon* shade does not do as much harm as one in the forenoon.

Well, suppose one does not have trees of any sort in his yard—what shall he do? One of four courses lies open: First, to use double-walled hives ; second, single-walled hives with shade-boards ; third, single-walled hives having on the south side of them some sort of vine that can be reared up within a year or two. A grapevine trellis,

APIARY OF M. H. MENDLESON.

This apiary occupies a very unique position down in the bottom of the canyon, where it is well protected. The ground has been leveled off and terraced, and the rows of hives are straight and parallel. This is one of the most picturesque spots for an apiary in the world. From it some of the finest sage honey of California is obtained, and no wonder; for the mountain sage is always in sight and in reach of the bees. The patches of white, black, and button sage on the mountain-sides can be plainly seen.

When the author visited this yard in 1901, he considered it one of the best-located yards in all California—well protected, and the bee-pasturage at close range. But for the fact that there is only about one good yield of sage honey in five years, this would be a veritable bee-paradise indeed.

THE AUTHORS' APIARY AT JENKINTOWN, PA.

This is an exhibition apiary in the suburbs of Philadelphia, used to demonstrate the various processes and methods of handling bees. Here are also shown to the visitors the various races, their characteristics and markings.

This yard is intended to be a model one in every respect, and has been so pronounced. The ground is nicely terraced, and here and there are flower-gardens so arranged as to give a pleasing effect.

In June, 1905, and again in 1906, a general field-day of bee-keepers was held at this apiary. Experts were present to describe and illustrate their various methods of handling bees to the crowds that assembled from all over the country. At the field meet of 1906 there were something over 1000 bee-keepers present, making by all odds the largest gathering of bee-keepers that this country has ever seen. This affair was a success in every way, and it is possible that other meets will be held at this yard in the future.

APIARY OF J. WEBSTER JOHNSON, TEMPE, ARIZONA.
This method of shading an apiary in Arizona, where the temperature during the hottest weather often goes above 100 degrees, is almost universal. The roof consists of dried grass or leaves laid on top, and secured by wires laid over the whole.

say 8 feet high and 10 or 12 feet long, running from east to west, well covered with a vine, can be made to protect anywhere from five to ten hives. On this trellis, grapevines or any other quick-growing vine may be reared to provide shade during the heat of the day. The fourth and last plan is to use overhead trellis, making use of straw, dried grass, or brush for a covering such as is used in Arizona and Cuba. See cuts pages 22 and 23. These trellises are about 7 feet high, and run from east to west,* so that the sun, nearly overhead as it is in Arizona, never strikes the hives from morning till night. These trellised shades, if there are no trees, are indispensable in hot localities. They thoroughly protect the bees, prevent combs melting down, and render the work of the apiarist pleasant.

But some bee-keepers prefer to use shade-boards. These consist of large covers cleated at the ends, and made of two or three boards of the cheapest lumber that can be had. They should be large enough to project a foot over the front and rear, and an equal distance on each side. They are then held securely in place by a stone weighing 15 or 20 pounds.

But whenever one manipulates these hives he is required to lift a heavy stone and remove an awkward shade-board before he can do any work with the bees.

When bee-hives are placed in long rows close together, as under a shed or on a roof, it is very essential that the hives differ from each other in appearance so that the bees may distinguish their own hive from all the rest. This differentiation may be accomplished in various ways; first, by painting the hives different colors; second, by using a different entrance or alighting-board; third, by laying a stone or brick on some boards and not on others; fourth, by placing a piece of brush on the front of some hives, etc. The idea is to place some distinctive mark by which each hive may be quickly recognized by its tenants. The best place to make such mark is at the entrance so that all the bees can see it, both on leaving and returning.

WINDBREAKS.

The most perfect windbreak is an inclosure of woods on three sides, with an opening to the south. This, however, is not

* In Cuba or other humid countries the sheds should run north and south, for the hives need the sun in the morning and late afternoon to dry them. Protection is required only during the heat of the day when the sun is overhead.

SIDE AND END VIEW OF THE SAME APIARY.

The side-braces shown are necessary to prevent a heavy wind from blowing the structure over. It should be noted that these sheds are almost indispensable in hot countries. In dry atmospheres they should be arranged east and west; in the humid they should be placed north and south, to dry out the hives after a tropical rain.

available to all. An apiary so situated that there is a clump of woods on one side and buildings on the other two sides, leaving only a southern aspect, is well sheltered from the prevailing winds. But, as already stated, if there are woods or buildings around the east side of the bee-yard, enough so as to shade the hives until about noon, the bees will not build up as fast in the spring as those that can get the morning sun up to ten or eleven o'clock. In the absence of any natural or accidental protection whatever, it is quite essential that some sort of windbreak be provided. If it is desirable to put up something permanent, and something which would not rot out or require repairs, outskirt the apiary with rows of hardy-growing evergreens, such as are seen in our own apiary in the following pages. These, for the first few years, would afford but a scanty protection; but in 10 years' time they answer their purpose admirally. In 1879, we enclosed our apiary with evergreens. They have proved to be very thrifty, and now (1910) are quite good-sized trees.

HIVE-STANDS.

It will be next in order to consider whether we shall put the hives directly on the ground or on some sort of stand. Many bee-keepers use four half-bricks, so arranging them that they will come directly under the four corners of the bottom-board. To secure a proper level, it will be necessary to use a spade or pickax to cut down the soil in spots sufficiently to let one or more bricks come down to the grade of the others. It is desirable, however, to have the forward bricks a little lower than the rear in order that the water may run out of the entrances. Other bee-keepers use short strips of old boards or pieces of scantling, cut off in lengths equal to the width of the hive, and leveled in the same manner as the bricks. But the bricks and old boards allow the hives to come too near the ground—enough so to cause dampness, and, sometimes, when the bricks settle, the rotting of the under side of the bottom-board.

Mr. R. C. Hollins, of Sladenville, Ky., drives four notched stakes into the ground, made of stuff three inches wide, one inch thick, and one or two feet long. The part driven into the ground should be dipped in creosote, linseed oil, or, better still, carbolineum, a kind of wood preservative used by railway companies to preserve ties. The

APIARY OF ERNEST W. FOX, HILLSBORO, WISCONSIN.

This apiary is ideal in that it has a solid windbreak of woods on two sides; of ground gradually sloping toward the bee-cellar, making it easy to get the hives to it. In the spring the colonies will naturally be lighter to carry up hill. This same sloping feature makes it easy to transport the heavy supers to the wagon or honey-house on the lower grounds.

illustration here given will show the idea. The stakes should project up above the ground from one to six inches. Four inches will ordinarily be high enough. In that case the stakes need not be more than 18 inches long. The length of them, however, will depend a good deal on the character of the soil and the preference of operator—whether the hive shall be high or low.

The stakes should be driven by line, and accurately measured off and afterward leveled with a bottom-board and spirit-level. If the stakes stick up six inches above the

ground it will add greater convenience to the handling of the bees; but in cool spring weather there should be some sort of board reaching from the ground up to the alighting-board, so that bees coming in somewhat chilled may crawl from the ground up into the hive.

Another arrangement that has been used to a considerable extent is what is known as the Heddon hive-stand. It is made of four rough boards of cheap lumber from four to six inches wide, and one inch thick.

HEDDON HIVE STAND.

The dimensions should, of course, be of the size of the bottom-board. The manner of putting together will be plain from the cut. This stand is preferred by a large number of bee-keepers.

A modified form, and a much better one, is shown at the top of next column. It has

the obvious advantage of a slanting front from the ground to the bottom-board.

Another arrangement that is favored by a good many is a double hive-stand made as shown in the accompanying illustration. The legs should not be less than two inches square, and the ends to come in contact with the ground should be dipped in tar, or some sort of wood-preservative. The side-boards, if the legs are a foot long, may be anywhere from three to six inches wide—four inches will be a nice compromise. The whole should be securely nailed and made to conform to a level floor. When a sufficient number have been made they can be spaced off and leveled up in the yard ready to receive pairs of hives, or even three if thought necessary.

This arrangement has much to recommend it. It permits keeping the hives in groups of two or three, so that they may be operated at a convenient distance from the ground. It also allows carrying out the general plan of shaking swarms, as explained further on under the head of SWARMING; of forming nuclei, or doubling up in the fall. Say there are two hives on the same stand, and both of them weak, and neither of them strong enough to go through the winter. Place all the combs and bees in one hive, and put it in the space exactly between where the two stood. Now move the other hive away entirely. The flying bees of both hives will go back to the one now at a point midway between where the other two stood.

SNAPSHOTS OF THE AUTHOS' HOME APIARY IN WINTER.

The colonies are either in double-walled hives or single walled with an outside winter-case slipped over. Upper right-hand view shows a case made of building-paper

But an important feature of this hive-stand is that it permits of being moved from one out-apiary to another without "pulling up stakes;" and a stand that will hold two or three hives is cheaper than two or three separate stands.

If the entrances of the hives are less than a foot above ground it is desirable to have some sort of board leading from the ground up to the entrance, unless the alighting-board itself is of good size, as shown in the illustration, in which case the incoming bees will be able to land without difficulty.

ARRANGEMENT OF HIVES.

Having decided upon the location, kind of shade, windbreaks, and hive-stands, how shall we arrange the hives in the apiary? This question can best be answered by studying the plans adopted by some of the prominent apiarists. Where there is no natural shade the one shown on page 22 is a very good one.

PLANS FOR APIARIES.

A PART OF AN APIARY ARRANGED ON THE STRAIGHT-ROW PLAN.

C. A. Hatch, of Ithaca, Wis., a prominent and extensive bee-keeper, arranges his hives on the plan shown above, which, as will be seen, will work nicely in connection with the double hive-stand shown on page 25.

The stars in the preceding diagram indicate the entrances. There are two lanes, or alleyways, one six feet wide, for the bees, and one ten feet wide, for the apiarist, and his horse and wagon, etc. It will be noticed that the hives are arranged in pairs, in such a way that they face each other with entrances six feet apart. In the next alley their *backs* are toward each other.

S. E. MILLER'S PLAN OF AN APIARY.

This plan is similar to the one used by Mr. Hatch, but is arranged with a view of still greater economy of space, not losing sight of the scheme of a highway for bees, and an alley for the apiarist. Instead of being in pairs they are arranged in groups of five each. Little circles in front of the hives indicate the entrances. The hives should be 18 inches apart to give room for a lawn-mower. It would hardly do to put them closer than 12 inches, for long timothy grass will grow up between, and then it is difficult to clean it out; and if not cut out it is in the way of putting on the supers. The groups can be from 10 to 20 feet apart; but if put exactly 16 feet apart, and the hives in the group 18 inches apart, an apiary of 80 colonies can be accommodated on a plot 75 feet square, or in the back yard of an ordi-

nary town lot. One advantage of this grouping plan is, that the apiarist can sit on one hive while he is working on another; and his tools, such as smoker, honey-knives, bee brushes, etc., are right at hand for the whole five hives. Where there is only one hive on a stand, the tools have to be carried to each hive.

The general scheme is as pretty in practice as it is in theory; and it is an actual fact that one can crowd more colonies on a given area (and yet leave room to run wagons or carts among the hives), than with any other plan with which we are acquainted.

The Miller plan is specially well adapted to a location in a grove; but as trees often vary in size the foliage is sometimes lopsided or scant on some of the trees, and hence it is not always practicable to put five hives at each tree. It is our practice to place in front of the smallest trees only one hive; in front of those a trifle larger, two hives; those still larger, three hives, and when they are of fair size, five, as in the Miller plan. Arranging the hives thus, gives each group of one, two, three, or five, as the case may be, an individuality of its own, thus affording the bees a better chance to distinguish their own group; but in every case the precaution must be observed of placing the hives on the *north* side of the tree. Where

HOME APIARY OF THE AUTHORS IN SUMMER.

This photo shows the windbreak of evergreens surrounding the yard. The house-apiary is shown in the background, the upper story of which is used as a workshop. A trellis of grapevines is placed in front of each hive. In summer there is ample shade, and in the full and early spring the leaves are shed, leaving plenty of sun to strike the hives when it is most needed.

there are two and three in a group, one can have the entrances pointing toward the south; or if there are only two in a group he can have one hive with its entrance pointing toward the west, and the other hive toward the east. In any case I would avoid having hives face the north.

The following diagram shows how the hives on the three and two plan may be arranged, considering, of course, that the tree is just south of the hive, and one, two, three, or four feet from it.

We have tested the plan for apiaries arranged with one alleyway for bee-flight and one for the apiarist; and so have a good many competent bee-men. The bees seem to recognize this narrow alleyway as their own allotted highway; and when they are working heavily, said highways are literally full of bees, while the broad ones are more free. In some apiaries in California we found double rows of hives, with a double alleyway between them, instead of being parallel, diverge from a common center, like the spokes of a wheel. Of course, in this case the honey-house or work-shop should be at the hub, or center of the system.

KEEPING GRASS DOWN AROUND THE HIVES.

Having decided on the location and plan of the apiary, the next question that would natural y arise is, Shall the grass be allowed to grow and be kept down to an even height with a lawn-mower? or shall the sod be cut off entirely, and the hives be placed on a smooth plot of clay leveled off like a brick-yard? In favor of this last arrangement it may be said that queens can be easily found, and that, when the sod is once removed, all that is necessary is to go around the hives with a hoe or scraping-knife to shave off the weeds as fast as they come. If they are kept down thus, and the plot is sprinkled with a thin layer of sawdust raked over evenly, we have an almost ideal spot for bees. While ground floors of this kind are nice and pretty to look at, it means a great deal of labor and expense, because there is almost constant warfare against weeds. They will crowd their heads up through the sawdust; and at the present low prices at which honey sells, it may be doubted whether one is warranted in going to such expense and trouble. The great majority of bee-keepers, however, after having leveled the plot, leaving the sod, consider it sufficient to keep the grass

down with a lawn-mower. If it is mown once or twice a week, the yard not only looks pretty but practically there is no inconvenience resulting from the short grass. A lawn apiary is much prettier, and about as convenient in every way as one with a brick-yard bottom.

KEEPING DOWN THE GRASS AT THE ENTRANCES OF THE HIVES.

It is not practicable to run a lawn-mower any closer than about two inches to a hive; and it is, therefore, our practice to sprinkle salt in front of the entrances and around the hives. This kills all vegetation up to a point where the lawn-mower can reach it.

But a good many apiarists do not even have the time to use a lawn-mower. As it would be a great task to keep the grass down in front of the hives where it would obstruct bees returning heavily laden from the fields, it is a very common practice to use a board little longer than the entrance, and a foot or 18 inches wide. This board should be cleated on the back, and attached to the hive so that the bees may have an easy runway clear up to the entrance. These boards may be planed and painted; but ordinarily we would recommend rough unplaned stuff—the cheaper the better. This gives the bees a good foothold, and at the same time saves some expense. See ENTRANCES.

SHEEP FOR KEEPING DOWN GRASS IN THE APIARY.

One of our neighbors lets loose a few sheep in his apiary occasionally. It is well known that our woolly friends can gnaw the grass closer than any other stock. If a few of them be turned into an apiary for a day or two they will cut down all the vegetation close to the hives, not leaving even a sprig of any sort. One would naturally suppose that the bees would sting the animals, with the possible result that a hive or two would be overturned; but in actual practice no trouble results. Once in a great while a sheep is stung; but instead of running and bellowing like a calf, or kicking and rearing like a horse, these animals quietly walk off to a bush and plunge their heads into it, and keep them there until all is quiet. A bee can not possibly hurt them except around the eyes and nose. But it is so seldom that they are attacked that one can not consider it cruelty to animals to use them as lawn-mowers. If one does not care to have them stung at all he can turn them into the apiary just at night, and before daylight drive them out again. But we have been in a yard where two or three sheep were allowed to graze all the season through, and in all that time they were not stung more than once or twice, and yet the grass was kept down *automatically over every square foot of the apiary.*

One would suppose the droppings might be somewhat offensive; but our neighbor assures us that this is not the case, as the manure very soon sun-dries, and it is of such a nature that it makes no trouble in the first place.

THE HOUSE-APIARY.

This is a term that is used to designate a structure enclosing a whole apiary. The hives are usually arranged on shelves next to the outside walls and having direct communication with the outside.

As a general thing, an outdoor apiary is cheaper and more satisfactory than one in a building. For the house-apiary, the capital to put up the building must be furnished at the outset; and one that will take 50 colonies will cost much more than the same number of hives intended for outdoor use. But there are conditions under which the house-apiary may be and is used to advantage—in fact, affords the only method of keeping bees at all. Where land is valuable, such as in or near the city, or in localities occasionally visited by thieves, where bees, honey, and every thing, so far as possible, must be kept under lock and key, it is a necessity. A small building, also, to accommodate 35 or 40 colonies, even when these conditions do not exist, may often be used very advantageously in connection with the regular apiary outdoors. When robbers are bad, or when the day is rainy, the work can continue right on, because the apiarist can leave the outdoor bees and resume operations inside, free from robbers in the one case, or protected from inclement weather in the other. Until very recently, house-apiaries have not been regarded with very much favor among practical bee-keepers, principally on account of faulty construction, and because bee escapes, when house-apiaries began to come into use in certain quarters, were not known; but since the advent of these labor-saving devices, the troubles arising from bees leaving the hives, and crawling over the floor to die, or to be trampled on if not already dead, at the first visit of the apiarist, are done away with. These and other inconveniences have been almost wholly removed; and perhaps the only reason why the house-apiary is not more generally used is because of the expense, or first cost.

HOW TO CONSTRUCT A HOUSE-APIARY.

The building may be oblong, square, octagonal, or round. The round or octagonal form will, perhaps, save steps during the operation of extracting; because, if the building is only 12 or 14 feet in diameter, the extractor may be put in the center of the room, and every hive will be equally distant, or practically so, and the combs may be transferred from hive to extractor, and *vice versa*, without taking more than one step; whereas, if the building is oblong some hives will be further from the seat of operations. The house-apiary building we are using is octagonal; but we found it a very expensive thing to make, and we were greatly annoyed by a leaky roof; and the only way to make it tight, with its many angles, was to cover it with tin. We would, therefore, construct a plain square building, say 12 feet across. For a roof we would adopt the plain gable, covering it with shingles. Where the winters are cold the building should *by all means be double-walled* with sawdust, or some sort of packing material should be poured in between the two walls. Unless it is warmly packed there will be bad wintering. Our own building is lined on the inside with tarred paper, and re-covered with manilla paper; but we are not sure that we would recommend it for any one else, because holes are constantly being punched through it. A better way would be to line it with wood—some cheap flooring would be good enough. If the joints are made tight, so that the packing-material will not leak, plain No. 2 barn-boards would answer. Through the roof, and extending through the center of the ceiling, we would have a ventilator-shaft, made of wood, about a foot square, and so arranged that it can be closed at will. During summer weather the smoker should be set directly beneath the shaft, and the ventilator opened for the escape of smoke. It should always be closed before leaving the building, because it is desirable to have the room perfectly dark, except at the small openings, where bee-escapes are to be placed, as we shall soon explain.

As to a door and windows there should be only one window, and that opposite the door, so as to allow a draft to pass directly through, because the building at best becomes very sultry in hot summer weather. An ordinary tight-fitting door should be used, hinged in the usual way. To the outside of the door-frame there should be a wire-cloth screen-door. At the top of the door the wire cloth should extend up as seen in the cut below; that is to say, it should be nailed on the outside, and should extend four or five inches beyond the bottom inside edge of the frame, leaving a bee-space between the frame and cloth. This is to allow the bees that collect in the room during the time of working, as for instance

during extracting, to escape in accordance with the natural instinct that prompts them to crawl upward. The window should have wire cloth nailed on the outside in like manner, the same extending above the window-casing as in the figure.

A better method is that shown in the larger cut where the edges of the wire cloth are formed into bee-escapes.

A better arrangement still, and the expense is but slight, is ordinary screen windows. At two of the upper corners attach Porter honey-house bee-escapes as shown in the engraving in the next column. This will be more reliable, as the robbers can not by any possibility return through

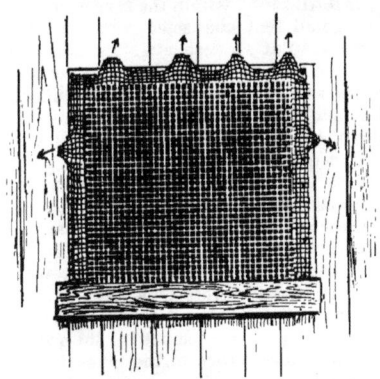

the Porter, while they may learn the way back through the projecting screen.

At several points, close on a line with the floor, should be one-inch holes, on the outside of which should be more Porter honey-house bee-escapes. The purpose of the opening in these escapes is, to let the bees that happen to be inside after working crawl out toward the light; and, once outside, they will enter their own hives, with the possible exception of a few young ones, and they will be accepted at any of the entrances.

A few years ago it was not deemed necessary to have anything but end-boards to hold up the frames. These boards resting on the floor or shelf were secured against the side of the building. It remained then to close up the open side with a tight-fitting division-board, and the top with a quilt. But in practice this was found to be very

PORTER HONEY-HOUSE BEE-ESCAPE.

objectionable; and those who manage house-apiaries now prefer to use ordinary outdoor hives instead, primarily because the bees can be more easily confined to the hives; and, secondarily, because the indoor and outdoor hives are one and the same, and interchangeable.

The entrances of the hives are so arranged that they communicate with openings through the side of the building; and then ordinary covers should be used to confine the bees strictly within the hives. In lieu of a cover a thin ⅜ board, or something of that sort, may answer just as well; but so far as possible we would so construct the house-apiary so that every thing outdoors may be moved inside, and *vice versa*, whenever requirements make it necessary. The dimensions of the house-apiary inside should be just large enough to take a row of your hives without wasting space.

For entrances to the hives from the outside there should be a two-inch round hole, lined with a tin tube that has first been painted, and then dusted on the inside with some fine sand while the paint is fresh, so as to make it rough enough for the bees to cling to the inside surface. These tin tubes should be inserted at the time of the construction of the building, and before the packing-material has been poured in, and should be high enough for the bottom of the tube to come flush with the top of the bottom-board. To connect this tin tube to the hive entrance is not difficult.

As the entrance through the house-apiary is 2 inches in diameter, it will be necessary to have a raised rim about 2 inches deep, the same width and length as the regular hive you are using. The side of the rim next to the building should be cut away for the 2-inch entrance, or else the whole side be left off entirely. This rim should be nailed down in position.

This rim will, of course, take the place of the regular bottom-board. It is not absolutely necessary to make it two inches deep; it can be only one inch deep if preferred. The entrance then, instead of being at the ends of the frames, will be at the sides, or make a side entrance.

On account of convenience in handling frames, it is necessary to have the hive's side against the building.

To economize still further the space of the building, there should be another tier of hives about four feet above the floor; and these should be supported by shelving that reaches clear around the room. The same arrangement with regard to entrances may be employed as described for the bottom tier.

Now let me insist again. Do not delude yourself with the idea that you can build hives cheaper, and have them a part of the building. You are making a great mistake if you do. The ordinary outdoor hives are in every way much more handy. And another thing, do not be satisfied to put just a mere quilt on top of the frames. It is absolutely necessary that the bees be confined strictly to their own hives, otherwise they will be crawling from one hive to another, killing queens occasionally, getting on the floor, getting mashed, to say nothing of the inconvenience to the apiarist when he desires to do any work inside.

PUTTING CROSS COLONIES IN HOUSE-APIARY.

We have always observed that the crossest bees are but little inclined to sting *inside* of a building. When they fly from the combs that you are handling, they find themselves inclosed; and this so disconcerts them that they immediately fly to the screen windows and escape. James Heddon says, "If you have a cross colony, put it in the house-apiary and see how tame it will become."

HOUSE-APIARIES FOR WINTERING.

As the building is double-walled, and is (or ought to be) packed, colonies will require less protection than outdoors. Indeed, about all that is necessary to put them into winter quarters will be to put on an extra comb-honey super, tuck in a chaff cushion, replace the cover, and then the bees are prepared. In very severe cold weather, a small fire, or heat from a large lamp in the room, may, perhaps, be used to advantage; but artificial heat in wintering should be used sparingly and with care, for oftentimes it does more harm than good.

APIS DORSATA. See BEES.

APIARY, OUT. See OUT-APIARIES.

ARTIFICIAL FERTILIZATION. After the reader has read the subjects of DRONES, QUEENS, and QUEEN-REARING, he will fully understand that the mating of the drone and queen in a state of nature takes place on the wing in the air, but it never occurs inside the hive. Nature has seemed to design, for the purpose of avoiding in-breeding, that the queen shall find her mate in the open air, where, according to the law of chance, she will in all probability meet some drone not directly related to her. Attempts have been made at various times to bring about fertilization within the hive or within some small tent connected with the hive-entrance. But all such attempts have resulted in failure, because the drones and queens, as soon as they find they are confined in a small inclosure, will bump against the sides of the mosquito-netting or wire cloth, vainly seeking to escape.

There have been some few reports of where success has been accomplished; but they seem to come from obscure persons who were probably not familiar with the fact that queens will often take several flights in the air before they meet a drone. One might therefore, put a wire-cloth cage over a hive, and then remove it; the queens and the drones return to the hive; but as both again seek the air on some future occasion, and meet, our friend the experimenter concludes that the act of copulation took place in his cage, when in fact it did not occur until at a subsequent time in the air.

So far it has not been feasible to control more than one parentage in the rearing of queens, and that the mother. No matter how choice the queen may be, nor how excellent her stock, yet she may mate in the open air with a drone from very inferior stock. In the breeding of domestic animals it is possible to mate together a choice male and a choice female. Much could be accomplished in the way of improved stock if we could also control the male parentage of bees; and we do not know but that in-breeding, according to modern methods now known in stock-raising, might secure for us a race of bees greatly superior to any thing we now know.

Just at present it seems very desirable that bees with longer tongues be bred, so that the nectar in the deep corolla-tubes of red clover, in the horsemint of Texas, and the mountain sages of California, as well as of hundreds of other flowers, could be reached. Tons and tons of honey might thus be secured that otherwise goes to waste. See TONGUE OF WORKERBEE.

ARTIFICIAL HEAT. As strong colonies early in the season are the ones that get the honey and furnish the early swarms as well, and are in fact the real source of profit to the bee-keeper, it is not to be wondered at that much time and money have been spent in devising ways and means whereby all might be brought up to the desired strength in time for the first yield of clover honey. As market-gardeners and others hasten early vegetables by artificial heat, or by taking advantage of the sun's rays by means of greenhouses, etc., it would seem that something of the kind might be done with bees; in fact, we have, by the aid of glass and the heat of a stove, succeeded in rearing young bees every month in the year, even while the weather was at zero, or lower, outside; but so far as we can learn, all artificial work of this kind has resulted in failure, so far as profit is concerned. The bees, it is true, learned to fly under the glass and come back to their hives; but for every bee that was raised in confinement, two or three were sure to die, from one cause or another, and we at length decided it was best to wait for summer weather, and then take full advantage of it.

Later, we made experiments with artificial heat while the bees were allowed to fly out at pleasure; and although it seemed at first to have just the desired effect, so far as hastening brood-rearing was concerned, the result was, in the end, just about as before; more bees were hatched, but the unseasonable activity, or something else, killed off twice as many as were reared, and the stocks that were let alone in the good old way came out ahead. Since then we have rather endeavored to check very early brood-rearing, and with better results.

A few experiments with artificial heat have apparently succeeded, and it may be that it will eventually be made a success; but my impression is, that we had much better turn our energies to something else, until we have warm settled weather. Packing the hives with chaff, sawdust, or any other warm, dry, porous material, so as to economize the natural heat of the cluster, seems to answer the purpose much better, and such treatment seems to have none of the objectionable features of working with artificial heat. The chaff needs to be as close to the bees as possible; and to this end we would have all the combs removed except such as are needed to hold their stores. Bees thus prepared seem to escape the ill effects of frosty nights in the early part of the season, and we accomplish for brood-rearing exactly what was hoped for by the use of artificial heat.

For the benefit of those who may be inclined to experiment, we would state that we covered almost our entire apiary with manure, on the plan of a hot-bed, one spring, and had the mortification of seeing almost all die of spring dwindling. Another time we kept the house-apiary warmed up to a summer temperature with a large oil-lamp, for several weeks, just to have them beat those out of doors. The investment resulted in losing nearly all in the house-apiary with spring dwindling, while those outside stayed in their hives as honest bees should, until settled warm weather, and then did finely, just because we were "too busy to take care of them" (?), as we used to express it. After you have had experience enough to count your profitable colonies by the hundred, and your crops of honey by the ton, it will do very well to experiment with greenhouses and cold-frames; but beginners had better let such appliances alone unless they have plenty of money to spare for more bees.

ARTIFICIAL PASTURAGE. Although there used to be quite a trade in seeds and plants to be cultivated for their honey alone, we can give little encouragement to those who expect to realize money by such investments. There is certainly a much greater need of taking care of the honey that is almost constantly wasting just for lack of bees to gather it. A field of buckwheat will perhaps occasionally yield enough honey to pay the expense of sowing, as it comes in at a time when the bees in many places would get little else; and if it does not pay in honey, it certainly will in grain. If one has the money, and can afford to run the risk of a failure, it is a fine thing to make some accurate experiments, and it may be that a farm of one or two hundred acres, judiciously stocked with honey-bearing plants, trees, and grains, would be a success financially. It has been much talked about, but none, so far as we know, have ever put the idea in practice. To beginners we would say: Plant and sow all you can that will be sure to pay aside from the honey crop, and then, if the latter is a success, you will be so much ahead; but beware of investing much in seeds that are for plants producing nothing of value except honey. Alsike and white Dutch clover, buckwheat, rape, alfalfa, and the like, it will do to invest in; but catnip, mignonnette, Rocky-Mountain bee-plant, etc., etc., we would at present handle rather sparingly.

The question, "How many acres of a good honey-bearing plant would be needed to keep 100 colonies busy?" has often been asked. If ten acres of buckwheat would answer while in full bloom, we should need perhaps ten other similar fields sown with rape, mustard, catnip, etc., blossoming at as many different periods, to keep them going the entire warm season. It would seem 500 acres should do nicely, even if nothing were obtained from other sources, but at present we can only conjecture. A colony of bees will frequently pay for themselves in ten days during a good yield from natural pasturage; and if we could keep up this state of affairs during the whole of the summer months, it would be quite an item indeed. Alfalfa, sainfoin, sweet clover, buckwheat, rape, alsike clover, crimson and red clover, cow peas of the South, and some others, are the only cultivated plants that have given paying crops of honey, without question, so far as we have been informed. See HONEY-PLANTS in Index.

ARTIFICIAL SWARMING See SWARMING, ARTIFICIAL, and NUCLEUS.

ASTERS. Under this head we have a large class of autumn flowers, very often called daisies in some localities, most of which are honey-bearing; they may be distinguished from the helianthus, or artichoke and sunflower family, by the color of the ray-flowers. The ray-flowers are the outer colored leaves of the flower, which stand out like rays; in fact, the word aster means star, because these ray-flowers stand out like the rays of a star. Many of the yellow autumn

flowers are called asters, but this is an error; for the asters are never yellow, except in the center. The outside rays are blue, purple, or white. You may frequently find half a dozen different varieties growing almost side by side. Where there are many acres of them, they sometimes yield considerable

ASTER.

honey, but other seasons they seem to be unnoticed by the bees. Better move your bees to where they grow naturally, when you have determined by moving a single hive first, as a test, whether they are yielding honey in paying quantities.

Where asters and goldenrod abound largely, it may be best to defer feeding until these plants have ceased to yield honey, say the last of September.

In some localities, notably along the bottom lands and during some years, the asters may yield considerable honey, on the amber order, of good heavy body, but of a flavor that would not ordinarily be considered suitable for table use. It must go to the confectioner or to the baker. Commercially it is scarcely known on the market.

As we stated at the outset, asters are very numerous. It has been estimated that there are about 120 different species in the United States alone, and about 60 in the northeastern part of North America. Of this entire number all but a dozen are purple or blue. So numerous is the family, and so slight the variations between the different species, that botanists are often puzzled to distinguish them.

A very common variety is the *A. patens*, with bright bluish-purple flowers. These are low-growing, with wide-spreading branches, and branchlets terminating in a solitary flower-head. They grow along the dry riversides in early August.

The New England aster, *Novæ Angliæ*, has stout hairy stems some eight feet high, with some large violet-purple or sometimes pinkish flower-heads. These are conspicuous in late summer.

Another species is a tall swamp variety with long showy pale-lavender ray-flowers. One of the most common asters is *A. cordifolius*. As its name indicates, the leaves are heart-shaped; but it is not the only species of this numerous family with leaves of that shape. It has many pale-blue or almost white flowers.

A beautiful specimen is the "seaside," a purple aster—*A. spectabilis*. This is a low-growing plant with large bright heads having the usual purple ray-flowers. It grows on sandy soil near the coast.

In general we may say that the aster, like the goldenrod, is conspicuous during the fall of the year throughout almost all the United States; and, like the goldenrod, it might almost be called our national flower.

B.

BANAT BEES. See BEES.

BARRELS. The regular size used for the storage and shipping of honey is anywhere from 31 to 32 gallons. Barrels of 45 to 50 gallons capacity, however, are a little too heavy; being very unwieldy they are liable to be broken or jammed by freight-handlers in shipping. As to the kind of barrel, second-hand alcohol or whisky barrels that can be obtained at the drugstores may be used, providing they are not charred on the inside. The ordinary alcohol-barrel is gummed or glazed on the inside with a preparation of glue that does not dissolve. As a general rule, whisky-barrels are charred, and therefore unsuitable. Before taking barrels of any kind it is very necessary to determine what the character of the lining is on the inside. Molasses or syrup barrels may be used, if they be thoroughly cleansed; but barrels that have a sour or musty smell should not be considered for a moment; for, even if cleaned, they might taint and ruin the honey.

After the barrel has been cleaned it should be put in a dry place, so that it will dry thoroughly, inside and out; and this reminds me that you should never use barrels, the wood of which has become soaked with water; for honey has the quality of absorbing moisture from the wood; that is to say, a wet barrel filled with honey will actually become dry. The staves shrink, and then, of course, the honey leaks out. If one does a large business in shipping honey in barrels he should buy new ones. The staves should be made of sound kiln-dried stuff; and nothing but iron hoops, not wooden ones, should be used. The barrels should be kept in a dry place, and then, before using, they should be well coopered and tested, as will be explained.

KEGS.

Wooden packages holding from 100 to 150 lbs. are used quite extensively in some parts of the East. They are usually made of cypress, and, when well made, make a very good package. The general directions that apply to barrels will equally apply to kegs.

BARRELS THE FREQUENT CAUSE OF COMPLAINT.

It may be said that no slovenly, careless, or slipshod bee-keeper should use barrels. He will be too careless to see that they are tight. He will put his honey into them, ship them, and in all probability the barrels will begin to leak *en route;* and he will receive a complaint from the consignee that "the honey arrived in bad condition," "half of it gone." There have been more ill feelings and hard words because of inexcusable carelessness or lack of proper knowledge concerning this matter of shipping honey in barrels than, perhaps, any other one thing connected with the marketing of honey. If the directions we have given are carefully followed, and good barrels are selected, there will be little or no trouble.

Another frequent source of complaint arises from the fact that the barrels are filled too full. Honey, during the process of candying, will expand. If it is put into the barrel long before it is candied, the barrel should not be filled quite full. Just before shipping put in a little more and then ship. We have received several consignments of honey that had candied, in barrels. The barrels had been filled full, the honey had candied, and burst the barrel.

HOW TO TEST BARRELS FOR LEAKS.

Barrels that are intended for the storage of honey should not be kept in a cellar but in a *dry place.* Before filling, the hoops should be driven down tight all around. To test for leakage, Mr. N. E. France, Platteville, Wis., a bee keeper of large experience, recommends the following plan :

Drive one of the bungs in, and then with the mouth placed tightly over the other bunghole blow in until there is quite a pressure in the barrel. To do this, place the mouth over the hole, exhaust the lungs, draw in a fresh supply through the nose, exhaust the lungs again, and so on until you have forced in all the air possible. Place the side of the palm next to the mouth, then with a quick sliding motion move the mouth simultaneously with the palm, and close the opening. Now listen for air-leaks. If there are any, there will be a hissing in one or more places. Dip the free hand into some water, and push it along to where the air seems to be hissing out. This will prove beyond a doubt whether there is a leak at that point. If there is one, there will be a sputtering or bubbling. Note the place, and then hunt for other leaks. But all this time, of course, the palm of one hand should be held over the bung through which the air was forced. Wherever the air is found leaking through, drive the hoops down still further until the openings are closed. Then, again, force air into the barrel and try for leaks as before.

Do not, under any circumstances, test a barrel for leakage with water, as it soaks up the wood, and the latter would swell up and close the leak. After the honey is put into the barrel it would absorb the water, and the barrel would leak just at the time it could be least afforded—when it would be half way on its journey.

THE NEED OF PARAFFINING OR WAXING BARRELS.

We are well aware that some of our best honey-producers say it is not necessary to wax or paraffine barrels inside ; but our experience shows that it is very important, not so much so for the purpose of closing up any possible leaks as to prevent the honey from soaking into the wood of the barrel, or the wood itself from giving a taint to the honey. The average person has little idea of the amount of honey that can be soaked up inside of an unwaxed barrel, and be charged up to the shipper. After having tested the barrel for leaks by the air-pressure plan recommended, and made it tight, wax or paraffine the inside of the barrel ; but don't depend on the waxing to close up the leaks—the barrel should be tight before.

Paraffine, being a good deal cheaper than beeswax, and melting at a lower temperature, is, therefore, to be recommended. Melt up about 10 or 12 lbs.; and when quite hot pour it through a large funnel into one bunghole of the barrel. Quickly drive in the bung, roll it around, twirl it on each head ; then give it another spin so as to cover perfectly all around the chime. This operation will warm the air inside to such an extent that the liquid will be forced into every crevice. As soon as the inside is covered, loosen the bung with a hammer ; and if the work is well done the bung will be thrown into the air with a loud report. Pour out the remaining liquid, warm it up again, and treat the other barrels in a like manner.

The operation as a whole takes but very little time ; and if one has taken pains to make the barrel tight by the air-pressure plan, the coating of paraffine on the inside will make it doubly secure. Second-hand barrels especially should be paraffined ; and even new barrels should be so treated to prevent a great loss of honey that would · necessarily soak into the wood. Steel barrels are not recommended.

BARRELS OR SQUARE CANS.

In California, Colorado, and other hot dry States, barrels and kegs should never be used. The ordinary 60-pound tin cans, described under EXTRACTED HONEY, are the only suitable shipping-packages. Indeed, they are the only package that nine-tenths of the bee-keepers of this land can use safely. While they cost considerably more per pound, yet the honey is nearly always reported as going through in good order. Even if one has a hole punched in it, only 60 pounds of honey is lost ; while in the case of a leak or break in a barrel, anywhere from five to eight times that amount is wasted. Through the entire West—and that is where the great bulk of the extracted honey in the United States is produced—the square tin can, two in a case, is used exclusively ; and we would strongly urge the average bee-keeper to use them in preference to barrels. While the tin package costs a little more per pound, it also brings a little more on the market ; for the buyer can take as large or small a quantity as he needs. Where the purchaser hesitates to buy a whole barrel of honey for his own local trade, he will readily take one or more cans of 60 lbs. each.

REMOVING CANDIED HONEY FROM BARRELS.

Good thick honey will usually become solid at the approach of frosty weather, and perhaps the readiest means of getting it out of the barrel in such cases is to remove one of the heads, and take it out with a scoop. When it is quite hard, you may at first think it difficult to force a scoop down into it ; but if you press steadily, and keep moving the scoop slightly, you will soon get down its whole depth. If the barrel is kept for some time near the stove, or in a very warm room, the honey will become liquid enough to be drawn out through a large-sized honey-gate.

A more wholesale way of removing candied honey is to set the barrel or keg in a tub or wooden tank of water, the latter being kept hot by a small steam-pipe. In 24 or 36 hours the honey in the barrel will be melted, and can then be drawn out in the usual way.

BASSWOOD (or Linden) (*Tilia Americana*, *Tilia heterophylla*, *argentea*, and other *Tiliæ*). Excepting, perhaps, alfalfa, sage, and white clover, basswood (often known as "linden") furnishes more honey than any other one plant or tree known in this country. It is true that it does not yield honey every season ; but what plant or tree does? It occasionally gives us such an immense flood of honey that we can afford to wait a season or two, if need be, rather than depend on sources that yield more regularly, yet in much smaller amounts. If a bee-keeper is content to wait, say ten or fifteen years, for the realization of his hopes, or if he has an interest in providing for the bee-keepers of a future generation, it will pay him to plant basswoods. A tree that was set out about ten years ago in one of our streets now furnishes a profusion of blossoms, almost every year ; and from the way the bees work on them we should judge it furnishes considerable honey. A hundred such trees in the vicinity of an apiary would be, without doubt, of great value. See AR-TIFICIAL PASTURAGE. Our 4000 trees were planted in the spring of 1872, and in 1877 many of them were bearing fair loads of blossoms. We made some experiments with basswood seeds, but they proved mostly fail-

ures, as have nearly all similar ones we have heard from. By far the better and cheaper way is to get small trees from the forest. They can be bought for about one cent each. These can be obtained in almost any quantity, from any piece of woodland from which stock has been excluded. Cattle feed upon the young basswoods with great avidity, and pasturing our woodlands is eventually going to cut short the young growth of these trees from our forests, as well as of many others that are valuable. We planted trees all the way from one to ten feet in height. The larger ones have, as a general rule, done best.

The cut will enable any one to distinguish at once the basswood when seen. Clusters of little balls with their peculiar leaf attached to the "seed-stems" are to be seen hanging from the branches the greater part of the summer ; and the appearance, both before and after blossoming, is pretty much the same. The blossoms are small, of a light-yellow color, and rather pretty ; the nectar is deposited on the inner side of the thick fleshy petals. When profuse it will sparkle like dewdrops if a cluster of blossoms is held up to the sunlight.

Climatic influences have their effect upon basswood. Among the hills of York State the leaves assume mammoth proportions. We measured one that was 14 inches long. While this leaf was among the largest, yet the leaves were, on the average, about twice the size of those in our own locality. In Illinois we noticed that the basswoods seemed to be less thrifty than in Ohio. The leaves seemed to be smaller, and the bark of the trees of a little different appearance. The next engraving represents quite accurately the typical forms, however.

The European basswood, or linden (fully as good a honey-producer as the American species) is famous as an avenue tree, as it furnishes a fine shade and is unaffected by the grime and dirt of the cities. The famous street of Berlin, Unter-den-Linden, is shaded by this species. It is known in England as the "lime" tree, and is there a great favorite for street planting. The famous "lime-tree walk" of Cambridge University is well known. This tree takes precedence over all others for street planting in the northern United States. It blooms earlier than its American sister.

It is rather to be regretted that basswood is not more plentiful, being one of the main stays, where it grows, of the honey-producer, and one of the most valuable woods in man-

AMERICAN BASSWOOD, OR LINDEN.

ufacture. It will hardly do for outside exposure to the weather; but it is admirably adapted for packing-boxes, and is used in *immense* quantities for the manufacture of furniture, forming the bottoms and sides of drawers, the backs of bureaus, dressing-cases, etc., and it is also employed extensively in the manufacture of paper.

It has often been charged that we are cutting off our own noses by using it for one-piece sections—that we are "killing the goose that lays the golden egg." Well, it is true that apiarian-supply makers use quite a little; but still, the amount *they* use is very insignificant in comparison with that employed by furniture-manufacturers, various packing-box concerns, and wood-pulp and paper-makers.

After all, there is one redeeming feature, the basswood is a very rapid grower. We thought at one time that we had used nearly all the basswood in this section, to say nothing of the enormous quantities shipped in from Michigan and other States; yet somehow the farmers still bring in beautiful nice white basswood lumber; but where they get it in our vicinity is a puzzle. At least some of this lumber is from a second growth of trees that sprouted from the stumps of old trees—said trees having been cut for us ten years ago. If basswood will replace itself in ten or even twenty years, so that it can be used again for lumber, there is yet hope that it will continue to bless the beekeeper.

Over against this is the stubborn fact that our basswoods are disappearing, and rapidly, too, over all the country. During 1899, when there was such a great advance in pine lumber, basswood was used very largely for house-building, with the consequence that millions of feet were used up.

Basswood, and perhaps most other foresttrees, require shade, especially when young. Much to our surprise, some that were planted directly under large white-oak trees have done better than any of the rest. Who has not noticed exceedingly thrifty basswoods growing in the midst of a clump of briers and bushes of all sorts? We would plant the trees not more than 12 feet apart.

The best yield of honey we ever had from a single hive, in one day, was from basswood bloom, the amount being 43 lbs. in three days. The best we ever recorded from clover was 10 lbs. in one day. Honey from the basswood has a strong aromatic or mint flavor, and we can tell when the blossoms are out by the perfume about the hives. The taste of the honey also indicates to the apiarist the very day the bees commence work on it. The honey, if extracted before it is sealed over, when it is coming in rapidly, has the distinctive flavor so strong as to be very disagreeable to some persons. A lady likens it to the smell and taste of turpentine or camphor, and very much dislikes it when just gathered; but when sealed over and fully ripened in the hive, she thinks it delicious, as does almost every person.

BEE-BREAD. A term in common use, applied to pollen when stored in the combs. In olden times, when bees were killed with sulphur to get at the honey, more or less pollen was usually found mixed with the honey; it has something of a "bready" taste, and hence, probably, came its name. Since the advent of the extractor and section boxes, it is very rare to find pollen in the honey designed for table use. See POLLEN.

BEE-DRESS. See VEILS.

BEE-ESCAPES. See COMB HONEY, also EXTRACTING.

BEE-HUNTING. We have given the warning so often, against leaving sweets of any kind about the apiary, and about being careful not to let the bees get to robbing each other, that it may seem a little queer to be directed how best to encourage and develop this very robbing propensity in these little friends of ours.

The only season in which we can trap bees is when they will rob briskly at home; for while honey is to be found in the flowers in plenty, they will hardly deign to notice our bait of even honey in the comb. Before starting out, it will be policy to inform yourself of all bees kept in the vicinity, for you might otherwise waste much time in following lines that lead into the hives of your neighbors. You should be at least a mile from any one who has a hive of bees when you commence operations, and it were safer to be two miles. We do not mean by this to say that there are no bee-trees near large apiaries, for a number have been found within half a mile of our own, and an experienced hand would have but little trouble in finding more, in all probability; but those who are just learning would, very likely, be much perplexed and bothered by domesticated bees mixing with the wild ones.

Perhaps the readiest means of getting a line started is to catch bees that will be found on the flowers, especially in the early part of the day. Get them to take a sip of the honey you have brought for the purpose, and they will, true to their instinctive love of gain, speed homeward with their load, soon to return for another. To find the tree, you have only to watch and see where they go. Very simple, is it not? It certainly is on paper, but usually involves much hard work when carried out in practice. You can get along with very simple implements; but if your time is valuable, it may pay to go out fully equipped. For instance, a small glass tumbler will answer to catch bees with; and after you have caught one, you can set the glass over a piece of honey-comb. Now cover it with your handkerchief to stop its buzzing against the glass, and it will soon discover the honey and load up. Keep your eye on it; and as soon as it is really at work on the honey gently raise the glass and creep away, where you may get a good view of the proceedings. As soon as it takes wing it will circle about the honey, as a young bee does in front of the hive, that it may know where to return; for a whole "chunk" of honey, during the dry autumn days, is quite a little gold-mine in its estimation. There may be a thousand or more hungry mouths to feed, away in the forest at its leafy home, for aught we know.

If you are quick enough to keep track of the bee's eccentric circles and oscillations, you will see that these circles become larger and larger, and that each time the bee comes round it sways to one side; that is, instead of making the honey the center of its circles, it makes it almost on one edge, so that the last few times the bee comes round it simply comes back after it has started home, and throws a loop, as it were, about the honey to make sure of it for the last time. Now you can be pretty sure which way its home lies almost the very first circuit it makes, for it has its home in mind all the time, and bears more and more toward it.

If you can keep your eye on it until it finally takes the "bee-line" for home, you do pretty well, for a new hand can seldom do this. After the bee is out of sight, you have only to wait until it comes back, which it surely will do, if honey is scarce. Of course, if its home is near by, it will get back soon; and to determine how far it is, by the length of time the bee is gone, brings in another very important point. The honey that bees get from flowers is very thin; in fact, it is nearer sweetened water than honey, and if you wish a bee to load up and fly at about a natural "gait," you should give it honey diluted with water to about this consistency. Unless you do, it will not only take a great deal more time in loading up, but the thick honey is so much heavier the bee will very likely stagger under the load, and make a very *crooked* bee-line of its homeward path. Besides, it will take much more time to unload. Sometimes, after circling about quite a time, the bee will stop to take breath before going home, which is apt to mislead the hunter unless he is experienced; all this is avoided by filling your honey-comb with honey and water, instead of the honey alone.

Now, it takes quite a little time to get a bee caught and started at work; and that we may get busy, we will have several bees

started at the same time. To do this expeditiously, we will use a bee-hunting box made as in the following cut.

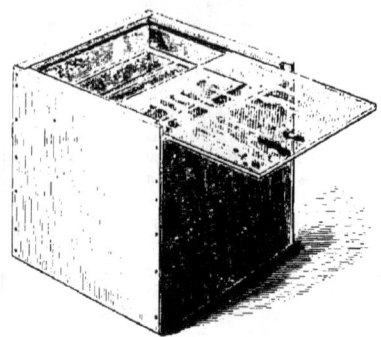

BOX FOR BEE-HUNTING.

This is simply a light box about 4¼ inches square; the bottom is left open, and the top closed with a sheet of glass that slides easily in saw-cuts made near the upper edge. About a half-inch below the glass is a small feeder quite similar to the one figured in FEEDING AND FEEDERS.

HOW TO USE THE HUNTING-BOX.

Take with your box about a pint of diluted honey in a bottle. If you fill the bottle half full of thick honey, and then fill it up with warm water, you will have it about right. In the fall of the year you will be more likely to find bees on the flowers in the early part of the day. When you get on the ground, near some forest, where you suspect the presence of wild bees, pour a little of your honey into the feeder, and cautiously set the box over the first bee you find upon the flowers. As soon as the box is well over the flower, close the bottom with your hand, and the bee will buzz up against the glass. Catch as many as you wish, in the same way, and they will soon be sipping the honey. Before any have filled themselves, ready to fly, place your box on some elevated point, such as the top of a stump in an open space in the field, and draw back the glass side. Stoop down now, and be ready to keep your eye on one bee whichever way it may turn. If you keep your head low, you will be more likely to have the sky as a background. If you fail in following one, you must try the next; and as soon as you get a sure line on a bee as it bears finally for home, be sure to mark it by some object that you can remember. If you are curious to know how long they are gone, you can, with some white paint in a little vial. and a pencil-brush, mark one of them on the back.* This is quite a help where you have two or more lines working from the same bait. When a bee comes back, you will recognize it by the peculiar inquiring hum, like robbers in front of a hive where they have once had a taste of spoils. If the tree is near by, each one will bring others along in its wake, and soon your box will be humming with a throng so eager that a further filling of the feeder from the bottle will be needed. As soon as you are pretty well satisfied in which direction they are located, you can close the glass slide and move along on the line, nearer the woods. Open the box, and you will soon have them just as busy again; mark the line and move again, and you will very soon follow them to their home. To aid you in deciding just where they are, you can move off to one side and start a cross-line.† Of course the tree will be found just where these lines meet; when you get where you think they should be, examine the trees carefully, especially all the knot-holes, or any place that might allow bees to enter and find a cavity. If you place yourself so that the bees will be between you and the sun, you can see them plainly, even if they are among the highest branches. Remember you are to make a careful and minute examination of every tree, little and big, body and limbs, even if it does make your neck ache. If you do not find them by carefully looking the trees over, go back and get your hunting-box, bring it up to the spot, and give them feed until you get a quart or more at work. You can then see pretty clearly where they enter. If you do not find them the first day, you can readily start them again almost any

time, for they are very quick to start, when they have once been at work, even though it is several days afterward. Bees are some times started by burning what is called a "smudge." Get some old bits of comb containing bee-bread as well as honey, and burn them on a small tin plate, by setting it over a little fire. The bees will be attracted by the odor of the burning honey and comb, and, if near, will sometimes come in great numbers.

A spy-glass is very convenient in finding where the bees go in, especially if the tree is very tall; even the toy spy-glasses sold for 50 cents or a dollar are sometimes quite a help. The most serviceable, however, are the achromatic opera-glasses that cost from $3.00 to $5.00. With these we can use both eyes, and the field is so broad that no time is lost in getting the glass instantly on the spot. We can, in fact, see bees with them in the tops of the tallest trees almost as clearly as we can see them going into hives placed on the ground.

After you have found the tree, probably you will be in a hurry to get the bees that you know are there, and the honey that *may* be there. Do not fix your expectations too high, for you may not get a single pound of the latter. Of two trees that we took a few years ago, one contained just about as much honey as we had fed them, and the other contained not one visible cell full! The former were fair hybrids, and the latter well-marked Italians. If the tree is not a valuable one, and stands where timber is cheap and plentiful, perhaps the easiest way is to cut it down. This may result in a smashed heap of ruins, with combs, honey, and bees all mixed up with dirt and rubbish, or it may fall so as to strike on the limbs or small trees, and thus ease its fall in such a way as to do very little injury to the tree or forest. The chances are rather in favor of the former, and on many accounts it is safer to climb the tree and let the bees' part down with a rope. If the hollow is in the body of the tree, or so situated that it can not be cut off above and below, the combs may be taken out and let down in a pail or basket; for the brood-combs, and such as contain but little honey, the basket will be rather preferable. The first thing, however, will be to climb the tree; and as we should be very sorry to give any advice in this book that might in any way lead to loss of life, we will, at the outset, ask you not to attempt climbing unless you are, or can be, a very careful person. An old gentleman who has been out with

*Since this was written, an A B C scholar says: "Bees vary in their flight. But I have found that on an average they will fly a mile in five minutes, and spend about two minutes in the hive or tree. Of course, they will spend more time in a tree when they have to crawl a long distance to get to the brood-nest, hence we may deduce the rule : Subtract two from the number of minutes absent, and divide by ten. The quotient is the number of miles from the stand to the tree. (See GLEANINGS, 1887, page 431.) This applies to a partially wooded country. Perhaps in a clearing they could make better time, On a very windy day it takes them longer to make trips."

† The same writer says further : "It is a waste of time to look for the bee-tree, or to make cross-lines, until you get beyond the tree. When the bees fly back on the line, you may rest assured that you are beyond the tree. Move your last two stands closer together (lining the bees carefully), so that they are only ten or fifteen rods apart. Now, as you have bees flying from two directions into the tree you will probably discover where they are immediately. But if you fail to find them easily, take a stand at one side, eight or ten rods, and cross-line. This is the only place that I find a cross-line of any advantage." —See *Gleanings in Bee Culture, Vol. XV.,* page 771.

us remarked that he once knew a very expert climber who took all the bees out of the trees for miles around, but was finally killed instantly by letting his hands slip, as he was getting above a large knot in the tree. We do not wish to run any risks where human life is at stake.

CLIMBERS FOR BEE-HUNTERS.

For climbing trees 12 or 18 inches in diameter, a pair of climbers should be used, such as can be obtained at any telephone office.

If the tree is large, the climber provides himself with a withe or whip, of some tough green bough, and bends this so it will go around the trunk, while an end is held in each hand. As he climbs upward, this is hitched up the tree. If he keeps a sure and firm hold on this whip, and strikes his feet into the trunk firmly, he can go up the most forbidding trees rapidly and safely. Some light cord, a clothes-line for instance, should be tied around his waist, so he can draw up such tools as he may need. Those needed are a sharp ax, hatchet, saw, and an auger to bore in to see just how far the hollow extends. If the bees are to be saved, the limb or tree should be cut off above the hollow, and allowed to fall. A stout rope can be then tied about the log hive, passed over some limb above, the end brought down and wrapped about a tree until the hive is cut off ready to lower. After it is down, let it stand an hour or two, or until sundown, when all the bees will have found and entered the hive; then cover the entrance with wire cloth, and take it home.

There are some trees, indeed, so large that it would be impossible to climb them with the implements already given. A very ingenious plan, however, has been put into execution by Mr. Green Derrington, of Poplar Bluff, Mo. We give his description, together with an engraving made from a photograph which he sent.

I send you a photograph of a very large tree, which I climbed by means of spikes and staples. To prevent the possibility of falling I put a belt under my arms. To this I attached two chains. At the end of each chain is a snap. My method of climbing is as follows: After ascending the ladder as far as I can go I drive into the side of the tree a large bridge spike, far enough into the wood to hold my weight. A little further up I drive another spike. In between the spikes I drive the first staple, and to this I attach the first chain by means of the snap, and ascend by the nails as far as the chain will allow me; I then drive another staple, and attach the other chain, and next loosen the lower snap. After driving in more spikes, I again ascend as high as the chain will allow me, and attach the other chain to

A BEE-TREE, ELEVEN FEET IN DIAMETER, CLIMBED BY GREEN DERRINGTON.

another staple. In this manner I can make my ascent with perfect security.

The tree stands close to the Black River, in a graveyard, and from it I obtained 50 lbs of honey. Regular climbers are excellent for small trees, say from two to three feet in diameter; but the tree illustrated has such a rough and uneven bark, and is so large that it would be difficult to climb it without the aid of spikes and the staples I have men-

tioned. On account of the large knots it would be impossible to use a rope, or something similar, to hitch up by climbers, as described in the A B C book. Knots are not in my way when I use spikes and staples. GREEN DERRINGTON.
Poplar Bluff, Butler Co., Mo.

HOW TO GET BEES OUT OF BEE-TREES OR FROM BETWEEN THE SIDINGS OF A HOUSE WITHOUT MUTILATING EITHER THE TREE OR THE HOUSE.

It sometimes happens that a colony of bees will take their abode in some fine shade tree in a park, which the authorities will not allow to be cut; or they will domicile in the woods of some farmer, who, while he will allow the bee-hunter to get the bees, will not let him cut the tree; or, as it often happens, a colony will make its home between the plaster and the clapboarding of the house. How, then, can such bees and their honey be secured without doing any damage to the tree or the building that gives them a home and protection? The matter is made very easy by the use of the modern bee-escape. For particulars regarding this device, see COMB HONEY and EXTRACTED HONEY.

Having the bees located in the bee-tree the hunter prepares a small colony of bees or a nucleus, putting it into a light hive or box which can be carried to the scene of operations. He takes along with him a hammer, a saw, some nails, and lumber, with which he can make a temporary platform. On arriving on the spot he lights his smoker and then prepares to set up this platform directly opposite or in front of the flight-hole of the bee-tree, or the knot-hole, we will say, of the dwelling. This he constructs out of the lumber which he has brought. Before doing so it will be necessary for him to blow smoke into the flight-hole, in order to prevent bees from interfering with the building of the temporary hive-stand. He next puts a Porter bee-escape over the flight-hole of the tree, in such a way that the bees can come out but not go back in. Last of all he places his hive with the bees which he has brought, with its entrance as near the bee-escape (now placed over the old entrance) as he can.

His work is now complete, and he leaves the bees to work out their own salvation.

The bees from the tree, as fast as they come out, are, of course, unable to return. These, one by one, find their way into the hive on the temporary platform. At the end of four or five weeks the queen in the tree or dwelling will have very few bees left, and there will also be but very little brood for that matter, through lack of bees to take

care of it, for her subjects are nearly all in the hive on the outside.

At this time Mr. Beehunter appears on the scene. He loads his smoker with fuel (brimstone), removes the bee-escape and brimstones the old colony, or what is left, which by this time is probably not more than a handful of bees with the queen.

Again he leaves the scene of operation; but the bee-escape is not replaced. What happens now? The bees in the hive, including those that were captured, rob all the honey out of the old nest in the tree or house in the course of three or four days, carrying it into the hive on the extemporized platform.

The bee-hunter now takes away the hive, removes the temporary hive-stand, and carries the bees home. If they be taken a mile or a mile and a half they will stay where placed.

In the meantime, no damage has been done either to tree or building, as the case may be. All that will be left in the tree will be some old dry combs which, in the form of wax, probably would not amount to fifty cents, if the time of rendering be taken into account.

This method of taking bees could not very well be practiced where the bees are located in inaccessible positions, as in high trees; but it will be found very useful where a colony is located in some building or shade-tree in a park.

We are indebted for the general principles here set forth to Mr. Ralph Fisher, of Great Meadows, N. J., who has practiced this plan with great success.

DOES BEE-HUNTING PAY?

If you can earn a dollar per day at some steady employment, I do not think it would, as a rule; yet there are doubtless localities where an expert would make it pay well in the fall of the year. With the facilities we now have for rearing bees, a bee-keeper could stock an apiary much quicker by rearing the bees than he would by bringing them home from the woods, and transferring. In the former case he would have nice straight combs, especially if he used foundation; but the combs from the woods would require a great deal of fussing, and yet would never be nearly as nice as those built on foundation, even then. So much by way of discouragement. On the other hand, a ramble in the woods, such as bee-hunting furnishes, is one of the most healthful forms of recreation one can find, because it gives one a chance to study, not only the habits of the bees, but the flowers as well;

A DISSECTED BEE-TREE.
This shows the general arrangement of combs in the cavity. Fortunately in this case the swarm was accommodating enough to make the nest close to the ground, where it could be easily captured.

for in hunting for a bee to start with we find many plants that are curious and many that we would not otherwise know bees frequent.

BEE-KEEPING AS A SPECIALTY. See BEGINNING WITH BEES.

BEE-KEEPING FOR WOMEN.

[It is presumed, of course, that no ordinary *man* would be *entirely* competent to write on a subject of this kind. In looking about for some lady to do this, the authors could think of no one more able than Mrs. Anna B. Comstock, author of a charming work for beginners on "How to Keep Bees." Mrs. Comstock is the wife of Prof. J. Henry Comstock, of Cornell University, and both of them entomologists. We engaged her to write the article, and here it is:]

Two questions invariably "pop-up" at us when this matter of feminine bee-keeping is discussed: One is, "Why shouldn't a woman keep bees?" and the other is, "Why should a woman keep bees?" Like most other questions these may be answered more or less rationally with proper consideration.

Taking the "why shouldn't" question first, we are bound to confess that nowadays there is no effective reason why a woman should not do almost any thing that she takes into her enterprising little head to do. But quite aside from the consideration of woman's prowess, there are one or two reasons that might deter some of the faint-hearted fair from undertaking bee keeping. There is no use of trying to gloss over the fact that there is a great deal of hard work and heavy lifting in the care of a profitable apiary. The hard work is really no objection, as most women of whatever class are at it any way. But lifting heavy hives is certainly not particularly good exercise for any woman, although I must confess that I have never lifted half so strenuously when caring for bees as I used to on the farm when we moved the cook-stove into the summer kitchen, accomplishing this feat by our feminine selves, rather than bring to the surface any of the latent profanity which seems to be engendered in the masculine bosom when taking part in this seasonal hegira.

There are at least two ways of obviating this feminine disability in bee-keeping. One, practiced successfully by several women, is through the use of a Boardman hive-cart, which almost solves the problem if the bees are wintered out of doors, and do not have to be carried up and down cellar stairs; the other method is to get some man to do the lifting and carrying. It may be the husband, the father, the brother, the son, or the hired man; but as this work can be done at a time which can be planned for, it is not so difficult for the men of the establishment to give the help needed. I am sure my husband would say that I am quite enthusiastically in favor of the man solution of this problem; but his opinion does not count for much, because he loves the bees so enthusiastically that I have to beg for a chance to work with them at all, although he virtuously points out the hives to people as "Mrs. Comstock's bees."

Another "shouldn't" reason might be that women are afraid of bee-stings. This falls flat, from the fact that women are not a bit more nervous than men in this respect. This year when I was struggling to hive a swarm from a most difficult position, an interested man stood off at a safe distance in a most pained state of mind. He was a courteous gentleman, and he felt that it was outrageous for me to have to do the work alone, but he did not dare to come to my aid, and I think he considered my temerity in dealing with the swarm as almost scandalous.

Thus having disposed of all the reasons I can think of why women shouldn't keep bees, I turn gladly to the more interesting reasons why she should look upon the apiary as one of her legitimate fields of labor. There are so many reasons for this that I could not enumerate them even if a complete number of a bee journal were given me for the purpose. So I shall speak of just a few of the most cogent reasons. I should put first of all, and as embracing all other reasons, that bee-keeping may be made an interesting avocation which can be carried on coincidentally with other employments; it is an interesting study in natural history; it cultivates calmness of spirit, self-control and patience; it is a "heap" of fun; incidentally it may supply the home table with a real luxury; and it may add a very considerable amount to any woman's spending-money. It can also be carried on as a regular business, to support a family.

But it is as an avocation that I am especially interested in the apiary. Any woman who keeps house needs an avocation to take the mind and attention completely off her household cares at times. There is something about the daily routine of housekeeping that wears mind and body full of ruts, even in the case of those who love to do housework better than any thing else. Talk about the servant question! It is not the servant question, but the housework question. If some means could be devised by which housework could be performed with inspiration, zeal, and enthusiasm, the servant problem would solve itself; but this ideal way of doing housework can be carried on only when the spirit is freed from the sense of eternal drudgery. I am not a wizard to bring about this change; but I know one step toward it, and that is the establishment of some permanent interest for woman that will pull her out of the ruts and give her body and mind a complete change and rest. Embroidery, lacemaking, weaving, painting, and several other like occupations, may serve this purpose in a measure; and, perhaps, if carried on in the right way, may achieve more in this line than they do at present. But these are all indoor occupations; and what a woman needs is something to take her out of doors where she can have fiea air. Excess of perspiration induced by the cook-stove is weakening; but honest sweat called forth in the open air by an application of generous sunshine is a source of health and strength.

Bee-keeping is one of the best of these life-saving, nerve-healing avocations; it takes the mind from household cares as completely as would a trip to Europe, for one can not work with bees and think of any thing else. Some of the attributes which make bee-keeping an interesting avocation I will mention: First of all, bees are such wonderful creatures, and so far beyond our comprehension, that they have for us always the fascination of an unsolved problem. I never pass our hive without mentally asking, "Well, you dear little rascals, what will you do next?" Bees are of particular interest to woman for several reasons: if she likes good housekeeping, then the bee is a model: if she likes a woman of business, again is the bee a shining light; if she is interested in the care of the young, then is the bee-nurse an example of perfection; if she believes in the political rights of woman, she will find the highest feminine political wisdom in the constitution of the bee commune. In fact, it is only as a wife that the bee is a little too casual to pose as ideal, although as a widow she is certainly remarkable and perhaps even notorious.

Another phase which makes bee-keeping a pleasing avocation for women is that much of the work is interesting and attractive. I never sit down to the "job" of folding sections and putting in starters without experiencing joy at the prettiness of the work. And if there is any higher artistic happiness than comes from cleaning up a section holding a pound of well-capped amber honey

and putting the same in a dainty carton for market, then I have never experienced it; and the making of pictures has been one of my regular avocations. By the way, woman has never used her artistic talent rightly in this matter of cartons. Each woman beekeeper ought to make her own colored design for the carton, thus securing something so individual and attractive as to catch at once the eye of the consumer.

As a means of cultivating calmness, patience, and self-control the bee is a well-recognized factor. Bees can be, and often are, profoundly exasperating; and yet how worse than futile it is to evince that exasperation by word or movement! No creature reacts more quickly against irritation than the bee. She can not be kicked nor spanked; and if we smoke her too much, we ourselves are the losers. There is only one way to manage exasperation with bees—that is, to control it; and this makes the apiary a means of grace.

The money-making side of bee-keeping is a very important phase in arousing and continuing the woman's interest in her work. I think woman is by birth and training a natural gambler, and the uncertainties of the nectar supply and of the honey market add to rather than detract from her interest in her apiary. I know of several women who have made comfortable incomes and supported their families by bee-keeping; but, as yet, I think such instances are few. However, I believe there are a large number of women who have added a goodly sum yearly to their amount of spending money, and have found the work a joy instead of drudgery. Personally, I have had very little experience with the commercial side of bee-keeping. Once when our maddeningly successful apiary grew to forty hives when we did not want more than a dozen at most, and the neighborhood was surfeited with our bounty, we were "just naturally" obliged to sell honey. We enjoyed greatly getting the product ready for market, and were somehow surprised that so much fun could be turned into ready cash. As a matter of fact, both my husband and myself have absorbing vocations and avocations in plenty, so that our sole reason for keeping bees is because we love the little creatures, and find them so interesting that we would not feel that home was really home without them; the sight of our busy little co-workers adds daily to our psychic income. We are so very busy that we have very little time to spend with them, and have finally formulated our ideal for our own bee-keeping, and that is to keep bees for honey and for "fun." We shall have plenty of honey for our own table, and just enough to bestow on the neighbors so they will not get tired of it; and fun enough to season life with an out-of-door interest and the feeling that no summer day is likely to pass without a surprise.

BEE-KEEPERS' SOCIETIES. See ORGANIZATION OF BEE-KEEPERS.

BEE LEGISLATION. See LEGISLATION ON BEES.

BEE-MOTH. When you hear a person complain that the wax-worm killed his bees, you can set him down at once as knowing very little about bees; and if a hive is offered you that has an attachment or trap to

square box is, in fact, all we want for a hive; but as we must have the combs removable, we require frames to hold them; and if these frames are made so that bees can get all around and about them, we have done all we can to make a moth-proof hive.

Of course, colonies will at times get weakened; and under the best of care, with common bees especially, worms will sometimes be found in the combs. Now if you have the simple hives shown in these pages you can very quickly take out the combs, and with the point of your knife remove every web and worm, scrape off the debris, and assist the bees very much. Where there is an accumulation of filth on the bottom-board, lift out all the combs, and brush it off, and be sure you crush all the worms

A sample of how the eggs and cocoons of the bee-moth are deposited on wood. Sometimes the wood is grooved or eaten out. The illustration fails to convey the real filthiness of the mass.

catch or kill moths, you may set the vender down as a vagabond and swindler. You can scarcely plead ignorance for *him;* for a man who will take upon himself the responsibility of introducing hives, without knowing something of our modern books and bee-journals, should receive treatment sufficiently rough to send him home, or into some business he understands.

When a colony gets weakened so much that it can not cover and protect its combs, robbers and wax-worms help themselves as a natural consequence; but neither rarely do any harm if there are plenty of bees, and a clean tight hive. If a hive is so made that crevices will admit a worm, and not allow a bee to go after it, it may make some trouble in almost any colony; and we can not remember that we ever saw a patented moth-proof hive that was not much worse in this respect than a plain simple box hive. A plain

therein, for they will crawl right back into the hive if carelessly thrown on the ground.

If you keep only Italians, or even all hybrids, you may go over a hundred colonies and not find a single trace of wax-worms. At the very low price at which Italian queens can now be purchased, it would seem that we are very soon to forget that a bee-moth ever existed; and the readiest way we know to get combs that are badly infested free from worms is to hang them, one at a time, in the center of a full hive of Italians. You will find all the webs and worms strewn around the entrance of the hive in a couple of hours, and the comb cleaned up nicer than you could do it if you were to sit down all day at the task.

Occasionally you will find that webs and cocoons are deposited back of the division-board or in some crack or crevice of the hive. Sometimes they will be located between the tops of the sections and the super-cover. The illustration on page 47 gives a fair sample of how they may be built up against the wood. In such cases you will find how the moth has burrowed or gnawed into the wood.

HOW TO KEEP EMPTY COMBS SECURE FROM THE WAX-WORMS.

With Italians only, you may have no trouble at all, without using any precaution; but where black bees are around you, kept in the old-fashioned way, or in patent hives, you will be very apt to have trouble unless you are careful. Suppose, for instance, you take a comb away from the bees during the summer months, and leave it in your honey-house several days. If the weather is warm you may find it literally infested with small worms, and in a few days more the comb will be entirely destroyed. Combs partly filled with pollen seem to be the especial preference of these greedy, filthy-looking pests, and we have sometimes thought they would do but little harm were it not for the pollen they find to feed on. A few years ago we used to have the same trouble with comb honey when taken from the hive during the early part of the season; but of late we have had less and less of it; and during late years we have hardly seen a wax-worm in our comb honey at all, and we have not once fumigated our honey-house. We ascribe this to the increase of Italians in our own apiary, and those all about us, for the most of the bees in the woods are now partly Italianized. These have driven the moth before them to such an extent that they bid fair soon to become extinct. Perhaps much has been also done by keeping all bits of comb out of their way; no rubbish that would harbor them has been allowed to accumulate; and as soon as any has been found containing them, it has been promptly burned. Those who take comb honey from hives of common bees are almost sure to find live worms sooner or later.

How do worms get into a box of honey that is pasted up tightly, just as soon as the bees are driven out? Possibly just as they get into a comb taken from the hive during warm weather. The moth has doubtless been all through the hive, for it can go where a bee can, and has laid the eggs in every comb, trusting to the young worms to evade the bees by some means after they are hatched. This explanation, we are well aware, seems rather unreasonable, but it is the only one we can give. In looking over hives of common bees, we have often seen

moths flit like lightning from crevices, and have sometimes seen them dart among the bees and out again; but whether they can deposit an egg so quickly as this, we are unable to say. In taking combs from a hive containing queen-cells to be used in the lamp nursery we have always had more or less trouble with these wax-worms. The high temperature and absence of bees are very favorable to their hatching and growth, and after about three days worms are invariably found spinning their webs. If they are promptly picked out for about a week no more make their appearance, showing clearly that the eggs were deposited on the combs while in the hive.

When queen-cells are nearly ready to hatch, we often hear the queens gnawing out, by holding the comb close to the ear. In the same way we hear wax-worms eating their galleries along the comb; and more than once we have mistaken them for queens. They are voracious eaters, and the "chanking" they make, when at full work, reminds one of a lot of hogs. As they are easily frightened you must lift the combs with great care either to see or hear them at their work.

Their silken galleries are often constructed right through a comb of sealed brood, and they then make murderous work upon the unhatched bees. Perhaps a single worm will mutilate a score of larvæ before it is dislodged. These are generally found at the entrance of the hive in the morning; and numerous letters have been received from beginners, asking why their bees tear the unhatched brood out of the combs and carry it out of the hives. Possibly the moth is at the bottom of all or nearly all these complaints.[*] If you examine the capped brood carefully you will see light streaks across the combs where these silken galleries are; and a pin or a knife-point will soon pry his wormship out of this retreat. As the young worms travel very rapidly it is quite likely that the eggs may have been deposited on the frame or edges of the comb. It is a little more difficult to understand how they get into a honey-box with only a small opening, but we think it is done by the moth while on the hive.

You may, perhaps, have noticed that the moth-webs are usually seen between one comb and another, and they seldom do very much mischief unless there are two or more combs side by side. Well, if in putting away

---

[*] Brood that has been chilled in early spring or overheated from any cause will be carried out in the same way.

BEESWAX-MOTHS.

your surplus combs for winter you place them two inches or more apart, you will seldom have any trouble, even should you leave them undisturbed until the next July. There is no danger from worms, in any case, in the fall, winter, or spring, for the worms can not develop unless they have a summer temperature, although they will live a long time in a dormant state if not killed by severe freezing weather. We have kept combs in our barn two years or more; but they were not removed from the hives until fall and were kept during the summer months in a close box where no moth could possibly get at them. We have several times had worms get among them when we were so careless as to leave them exposed during warm weather; and one season we found nearly a thousand combs so badly infested that they would have become almost worthless in less than a week. The combs were all hung up in the honey-house, and about a pound of brimstone was thrown on a shovel of coals in an old kettle. This was placed in the room, and all doors and windows carefully closed. Next morning we found most of the worms dead; but a few encased in heavy webs still lived. After another and more severe fumigation, not a live one was to be found, and our combs were saved. We have several times since fumigated honey in boxes in the same way. The following extract from Burt's *Materia Medica* contains some hints valuable to apiarists as well as to doctors:

In the form of *sulphurous-acid fumes*, or gas, sulphur is the most powerful of all known agents as a disinfectant and deodorizer. To disinfect a room and clothing from infectious diseases, as smallpox, etc., first close up the chimney and paste up all crevices of the windows and doors to prevent the escape of gas. Now raise all carpets, and hang up the cloths so that the fumes of gas may have complete access to them. When this is done, set a tub in the center of the room with six inches of water in it. In the center of this water place a stone that comes just above the water. On this stone set an iron vessel with two pounds of sulphur broken up into quite fine pieces or lumps; on this pour a few ounces of alcohol, to make the sulphur burn readily; set the alcohol on fire, and leave the room, closing the door behind you. It is well to repeat this fumigation three or four times.

After the bees have died in a hive, it should never be left exposed to robbers and moths, but should be carried indoors at once, or carefully closed up. If you have not sufficient bees either by artificial or natural swarming to use the combs before warm weather, keep careful watch over them, for a great amount of mischief may be done in a very few days. We once removed some combs, heavy with honey, in August, and,

thinking no worms would get into them so late, we delayed looking at them. A month later honey began to run out on the floor; and upon attempting to lift out a comb it was found impossible to do so. When all were lifted up at once, a mass of webs nearly as large as one's head was found, in place of honey and combs. So much for not keeping a careful watch over such property.

The practice in late years is to use bisulphide of carbon—the same drug that is spoken of under the head of ANTS. The combs to be treated are placed in a tool-box or small room. A pint or a quart of the liquid, depending on the size of the inclosure, is then placed in an open vessel *above* the combs. The stuff is very volatile and evaporates quite rapidly; and the fumes, being heavier than air, settle down, passing around and through the combs.

One should be very careful in handling this drug lest he inhale the fumes of it, although a few breaths would probably cause no harm except a little dizziness. Every thing being in readiness, pour out the liquid in the right place, and shut up the inclosure. On account of the fearfully explosive nature of bisulphide of carbon, it is advisable to use a large box or cupboard outdoors. One can, of course, use it in a building or room; but first be sure there is no lighted fire, a lamp, nor any thing that might ignite explosive gas.

HOW TO KEEP EMPTY COMBS.

When combs are left in spring, after the death of the bees in a hive, there is no safer place to put them than in the care of a good strong colony. Brush off the dead bees and put the combs in a clean hive on the stand of a strong colony, and then place the colony *over* this hive of empty combs, so that they will be obliged to pass through the hive of combs to go in or out. In other words, give the bees no entrance except that of the lower hive, allowing free communication between the two. The combs will then be kept free from worms and mold, with no care whatever on your part, except to keep the entrance so small for two or three days at first that robbers will not trouble.

After the weather has become warm, three or four stories of empty combs may be piled over a queen-excluder on top of a hive containing a colony; then a frame of brood in the upper story will make sure that the bees traverse all the combs.

BEE-MOTH IN HIGH ALTITUDES.

In Colorado, at least in the region of Denver, where the elevation is fully a

COMBS INFESTED BY THE LESSER WAX-MOTH.

This photograph was sent us by George W. Tebbs, Hespeler, Ontario, Canada, who wrote that the frame
was taken from a hive which had originally contained an Italian colony, but
which had been empty during the winter.

mile above the level of the sea, the ordinary wax-moths are unknown. The great elevation seems to be more than they can stand. There is, however, a very small wax-worm, but it is not the same that ordinarily troubles bee-keepers.

The Government Entomologist for New South Wales, Australia, Mr. Sidney Olliff, wrote an article on the subject of bee-moths for the New South Wales *Agricultural Gazette.* There is so much of value in it, especially as it describes the same pest we have here, that we have decided to reproduce it in these columns. The illustration accompanying it is especially accurate.

The bee-moths, or beeswax-moths, of which there are two distinct kinds commonly found in Australia, are so well known, and have been so frequently figured and described, that it will not be necessary to give very detailed or technical descriptions of them here. A considerable number of inquiries have been received during the past few years regarding these destructive moths, chiefly from amateur bee-keepers; and it may, therefore, be useful to publish a few notes concerning the habits and seasonal appearance of these insects in Australia, more especially as I am able to add some information regarding remedial and preventive measures for the suppression of the pests, which have been found satisfactory by experienced bee-keepers. The larger of the beeswax-moths—properly known as *Galleria mellonella*, Linn., but sometimes called by the name *Galleria cereana*, Fabr.—appears to be by far the more destructive of the two insects. It is a very widely distributed species, being found throughout Europe and North America, in India, and even in the cold regions of Northern Siberia; indeed, it appears to have a range that is co-extensive with that of the hive-bee itself. In warm countries it is much more abundant, and therefore destructive, than in temperate or cold

climates, a fact which is probably accounted for by the varying number of broods or generations which occur in a season under different climatic conditions. With us in New South Wales the first brood of moth appears in the early spring from caterpillars which have passed the winter in a semi-dormant condition, within the walls of their silken coverings, and turn into pupæ or chrysalids only upon the approach of warm weather. These winter (or hibernating) caterpillars feed very little, and usually confine their wanderings to the silken channels which they have made for themselves before the cool weather set in. Upon the return of desired warmth these caterpillars spin a complete cocoon for themselves and then turn into the chrysalis stage, whence, from ten days to a fortnight, perfect moths appear. These then lay eggs in any convenient spot, such as the sides and bottoms of the frames, on the walls of the hive itself, or on the comb. In each case I have had an opportunity of observing the process, the moth chose the sides of the frames, as near to the brood-comb as possible, the young larvæ having a very decided preference for this comb. The larvæ having once made their appearance (usually in from eight to ten days after the laying of the larval eggs) their growth is exceedingly rapid, the average time before they are ready to assume the chrysalis stage being only some thirty days. The average duration of the chrysalis period is about a fortnight, so it can easily be seen with what great capabilities for rapid reproduction we have to deal. As we have said, the number of generations, or broods, which develop in a season, *i. e.*, between early spring and late autumn, varies with locality and climate; but it may be worth while to record that, in my opinion, we have sufficient evidence to prove the existence of four broods in the Sydney district under ordinary circumstances. I have myself bred three generations, or broods, from a comb received in early spring from the Richmond River; and I am convinced that a fourth might have been bred from the same stock but for an unfortunate accident to the eggs obtained from my third brood. Upon first hatching, the larva is pale yellow in color, with a slightly darkened head; and, when full grown, it is of a dull grayish flesh color, with a dark reddish-brown head. Its average length is about an inch, and, like the majority of the caterpillars of moths, it has sixteen legs. The chrysalis of the larger beeswax-moth is of the ordinary type, and is inclosed in a very compact cocoon of tough white silk, usually spun up in one of the silken channels or galleries made by the larva to which we have previously referred. The perfect insect, or moth, has reddish brown-gray forewings, which are distinctly lighter in color toward the outer or hinder margins. The sexes can readily be distinguished by the outline of the wings, as will readily be seen by a glance at the plate accompanying this article.

The second species of beeswax-moth is known a² *Achræa grissella*, Fabr., the lesser beeswax-moth, or honey-moth, etc. Although not nearly so destructive as the larger kind, it does considerable damage in old and neglected hives. The moth is much smaller than *Galleria mellonella*, with which, by the way, I have found it associated in the same hive on more than one occasion. It is of a dead gray color, and has a yellow head. This species is not nearly so particular in choosing its food as the former kind (*G. mellonella*), and may frequently be found feeding on the *debris* which commonly collects on the bottom of a neglected hive.

It is a well-known fact, that beeswax-moths do not attack the Italian (Ligurian) bee to any serious extent, which, indeed, are rarely attacked at all. It is the ordinary black or hive bee that suffers so greatly.

In conclusion I would express my thanks, among other kind correspondents, to Dr. Dagnell Clark, the Rev. John Ayling, and Messrs. Abram & Riddle, who have been kind enough to forward to the Department specimens or information.

So far as I am aware, very few recognizable figures of the bee-moths have been published ; hence the plate attached, from the pencil of Mr. E. M. Grosse, will doubtless prove very acceptable. With the exception of an excellent wood-cut in Dr. Taschenberg's "Die Insecten" (Brehm's Thierleben, Vol. IX., page 432) of the larger species, I have not been able to find a figure showing the stages or habits of these moths.

EXPLANATION OF PLATE.

BEESWAX-MOTHS.

Fig. 1.—Larva or caterpillar of Larger Beeswax-moth (*Galleria mellonella*, Linn.), side view (much enlarged).

Fig. 2.—The same viewed from above (much enlarged).

Fig. 3.—Cocoon of same, extracted from bee-comb (enlarged).

Fig. 4.—Larger Beeswax - moth (*Galleria mellonella*, Linn.), male (much enlarged).

Fig. 5.—Forewing of same, female.

Fig. 6.—Larva or caterpillar of Lesser Beeswax-moth (*Achræa grissella*, Fabr.), side view (much enlarged).

Fig. 7.—Pupa or Chrysalis of same (much enlarged).

Fig. 8.—Lesser Beeswax - moth (*Achræa grissella*, Fabr.), (much enlarged).

In the background above, a comb from a frame hive is represented, showing brood-comb tunneled by the larvæ of the larger beeswax-moth (*Galleria mellonella*, Linn.).

⁂ The natural sizes of the insects are indicated by hair-line.

BEE PARALYSIS. See DISEASES OF BEES.

BEE-SPACES. This term is applied to spaces left by the bees both between combs they build and between the parts of the hive and the combs. It varies all the way from ¼₆ to ¼; but ¼₆ is considered the correct average. But in hive-construction it has been found that a space of ¼ inch will be more free from the building of bits of comb and the depositing of propolis than a little wider spacing. Any less space than ¼₆ will be plugged up with propolis and wax.

Father Langstroth, in the great invention which he gave to the world—the first *practical* movable frame — made the discovery that bees recognize and protect passageways which we now call bee-spaces. Taking advantage of this fact he made a frame for holding comb bee-spaced all around. All who preceded him had failed to grasp the fact that bees would leave such spaces unfilled with wax or propolis. Before Langstroth's time it was necessary to pull out frames stuck fast to the hives with propolis, or tear or cut loose the combs with a thin-bladed knife, before they could be removed for the purpose of inspection.

By bringing out his bee-spaced frame the "father of modern apiculture" solved, with one great master-stroke, a problem that had been puzzling the minds of bee-keepers for centuries.

In later years, manufacturers of hives have been compelled to recognize this great principle, that there are certain parts inside hives that must be bee-spaced from every other part or else be stuck or glued together in a way that will make them practically inseparable. For example, the bottoms of supers containing the sections must be ¼ inch above the tops of the brood-frames in the lower part of the hive. The sections themselves must be held a bee-space away from the separators or fences. It has come to be a general practice to put the bee-space in the bottom-board, leaving the bottoms of the frames in the brood-nest nearly flush with the bottom of the hive. This makes it necessary to have the sides and ends of the hive project above the general level of the frames about ¼ inch. In the same way the supers have a bee-space on top but not on the bottom. If a super be removed, and a hive-cover be put in its place, there will still be a space between the cover and the brood-frames.

BEES. Throughout this work we deal particularly with Italians, the common black bees of this country, and the crosses between the two, because they are used almost exclusively by bee-keepers. The crosses are often incorrectly denominated "hybrids;" but as that name has been generally adopted, we retain it. For particulars regarding these bees the reader is referred to HYBRIDS, which see. The Italians are spoken of specifically, also, under the heading of ITALIANS, elsewhere in this work.

BLACK OR GERMAN BEES.

Black bees are so common in nearly every vicinity that very little description is necessary. As the name indicates, they are black. One variety in the South is of a brownish black; another distinctly black, and, if any thing, a trifle smaller.

Comparing the Germans with the Italians, they are more inclined to rob, are not as good workers, but are equal when nectar is abundant, or when there is dark honey like that from buckwheat to be gathered. They are much more nervous; and when a hive of them is opened they run like a flock of sheep from one corner of the hive to another, boiling over in confusion, hanging in clusters from one corner of the frame as it is held up, and finally falling off in bunches to the ground, where they continue a wild scramble in every direction, probably crawling up one's trousers-leg, if the opportunity offers. Their queens are much harder to find, the bees are not so gentle, and, worse than all, they have a disagreeable fashion of following the apiarist about from hive to hive in a most tantalizing way. This habit of poising on the wing in a threatening manner before one's eyes is extremely annoying, and some bees will keep it up for a day at a time unless killed. We generally make very short work by smashing them between the palms of our hands, or batting them to death with little paddles we keep near. It is useless to strike at individual bees while they are in the air, for one is much more liable to miss than to hit them. Our practice is to take two sticks, one in each hand, and work them back and forth in front of our face very rapidly, just about as one would operate a fan on a hot day. This rapid movement excites anger in the bees, with the result that they make a dive for the whirling sticks; and in less time than it takes to tell it, one by one they get their heads rapped, and go down into the grass.

Comb honey from the blacks is a little whiter, if any thing, than that made by pure Italians, because the capping is raised up, leaving a slight air-gap between it and the surface of the honey in the cell. But this difference in the whiteness of capping is so very slight as compared with that on comb honey made by the Italians that it really cuts

no figure in the market. The blacks are also much easier to shake off the combs than pure Italians, which can hardly be shaken off, that some prefer blacks or hybrids, when extracting, for that reason alone.

CARNIOLANS.

The Carniolans, evidently a variety of black bees, which they very much resemble, were introduced into this country in 1884, or thereabout. They are said to be very gentle; but the few colonies we have tried are no more so than average Italians, and in one case they were more vindictive than the Cyprians. As stated, they resemble blacks, and might easily be mistaken for them; but there is a difference. They are larger, and their abdomens are of a more bluish cast, the fuzzy rings being very distinct. They are gentler, as a rule, and do not, like the blacks, boil over in confusion when the hive is opened, although one of our Carniolan colonies did this very thing. They have not the fixity of character of the Italians—colonies of the same race differing quite widely. The general verdict is, that they are excessive swarmers, and this trait alone makes them very undesirable. Their close resemblance to black bees makes it difficult to detect the crosses of the two races. This fact, coupled with their great swarming propensity, will largely prevent their meeting with general favor.

But Carniolans have one good trait in their favor, and that is, they deposit as little propolis as any bees ever known. Some colonies that we had, actually deposited almost none. In the production of comb honey this is quite an important item.

CAUCASIANS.

This is a race that looks very much like Carniolans and the common black bee of this country, but it resembles the latter more than the former. So close is the general resemblance that even experts in some cases have been unable to distinguish them. But there is a vast difference in their general habits and temperament.

The claim has been made that Caucasians are the gentlest bees known; and this claim, in part at least, has been established, although they are no more so than some good strains of pure Italians. Bee-men are not agreed, however, as to their honey-gathering qualities. Some consider them very inferior, while others believe they are equal to any race in this respect. All admit that they are bad propolizers, sticking large chunks of gum in all parts of the hive—a trait that be comes more manifest as cold weather comes on. In this one respect they differ materially from Carniolans.

About the most serious objection that can be urged against them (and the same may be said of Carniolans) is very strong resemblance to the common blacks. It will be simply impossible to detect their crosses; and unscrupulous dealers might send out such crosses, or even black bees, and palm them off as Caucasians. But the deception could not continue long, as Carniolans behave very differently on the combs. There is also a strain of yellow Caucasians; but these we have never tested, and therefore are unable to give any opinion as to their merits.

BANAT BEES.

The black strain of these bees looks very much like the black Caucasians; and their general characteristics, so far as we have been able to observe, are about the same also. A yellow variety of the same bees is also reported.

TUNISIANS.

This black race, natives of North Africa, are sometimes called "Punics." They have been tested to some extent in this country, but so far have not been able to establish any claim in their favor that would entitle them to consideration on the part of American bee-keepers. They are cross, and so inclined to smear everything with a red bee-glue that they are entirely unsuited for the production of comb honey. They are no better honey-gatherers than gentler races; and the fact that they do not excel in any way, and are so far surpassed by other bees in desirable qualities, should bar them from introduction into this country.

EGYPTIANS.

The Egyptian bee is reputed the most beautiful species of *Apis*. It has been nam-ed *Apis fasiata* by entomologists; has been cultivated for thousands of years by the Egyptians, and was probably the first species reduced by mankind to domestic purposes.

In the time of the ancient historian Herodotus, apiaries were transported up and down the Nile so as to keep pace with the seasons in Upper and Lower Egypt. This practice is continued at the present day to a limited extent. Inscriptions on tombs show the practice in use 4000 years ago, at least, and the honey-bee highly reverenced by the people of that age.

The Egyptian bee is so much smaller than the Italian that the two do not hybridize very well; on the contrary, the queen, if compelled to mate with a European drone, frequently dies soon after fertilization. It is probably, however, the mother-species of the Cyprian, Holy-Land, and Grecian bees.

 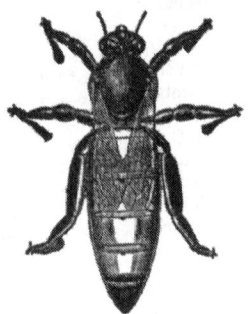 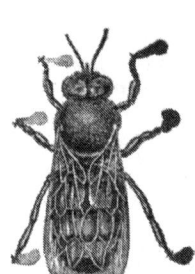

WORKER.   QUEEN.   DRONE.

It is a fast, excellent worker, but reputed to possess an irritable temper though kept domesticated for thousands of years. Possibly in a climate similar to that of Egypt it would exhibit a better temper than in Northern Europe. It could hardly be otherwise.

In color Egyptians are almost identical with Italians, but in addition have a coat of white hairs, which adds to their appearance. There are varieties, or races, of the same species in countries next to Lower Egypt. One feature of these bees would please Americans, namely, their ability to keep themselves pure and uncontaminated with other races. There is a similar species in Senegal known as *Apis Adansonii*, of which we know but little.

ALBINOS.

Albinos are either "sports" from Italians, or, what is more generally the case, a cross between Holy-Lands and Italians. After testing them in our own apiary we find them little different from common Italians. The fringe, or down, that appears on the rings of the abdomen of young bees is a trifle whiter than usual, yet no one would observe it unless attention were called to it. The queens are very yellow, while the workers, as honey-gatherers, are decidedly inferior, even in the second generation; and when we select light-colored bees or queens for several successive generations, unless careful we develop only a worker progeny lacking ability as honey-gatherers and endurance. By selection we can get almost any thing we want, and that quite speedily with bees; for we can produce several generations in a single season if need be.

EASTERN RACES OF BEES.

Cyprians, Holy-Lands, or Syrians, are mentioned later under the head of ITALIANS. Of other Eastern races I can do no better than to quote what Mr. Frank Benton, formerly Apicultural Expert of the U. S. Department of Agriculture, has said of them in a special bulletin issued by the Department, entitled " Honey-bee," containing 118 pages. Mr. Benton spent some months in the jungles of India, in search of new bees. For this reason, if for no other, he is able to give us authoritative information. From the bulletin above mentioned we make the following extracts:

THE COMMON EAST-INDIAN HONEY-BEE.
(*Apis Indica*, Fab.)

The common bee of Southern Asia is kept in very limited numbers and with a small degree of profit in earthen jars and sections of hollow trees in portions of the British and Dutch East Indies. They are also found wild, and build when in this state in hollow trees and in rock-clefts. Their combs are composed of hexagonal wax cells, and are arranged parallel to

 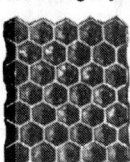

FIG. 1.— WORKER-CELLS OF COMMON EAST-INDIAN HONEY-BEE (APIS INDICA), NATURAL SIZE.

each other like those of *A. mellifica*, but the worker brood-cells are smaller than those of our ordinary bees, showing 36 to the square inch of surface instead of 29; while the comb where worker-brood is reared, instead of having, like that of *A. mellifica*, a thickness of seven-eighths inch, is but five-eighths inch thick. (Fig 1.)

The workers. — The bodies of these, three-eighths inch long when empty, measure about one-half inch when dilated with honey. The thorax is covered with brownish hair, and the shield or crescent between the wings is large and yellow. The abdomen is yellow underneath. Above it presents a ringed appearance

the anterior part of each segment being orange yellow, while the posterior part shows bands of brown of greater or less width, and covered with whitish-brown hairs; tip black. They are nimble on foot and on the wing, and active gatherers.

The queens.—The queens are large in proportion to their workers, and are quite prolific; color, leather or dark copper. *The drones.*—These are only slightly larger than the workers; color, a jet-like blue-black, without yellow, their strong wings showing changing hues like those of wasps.

Manipulations with colonies of these bees are easy to perform if smoke be used ; and, though they are more excitable than our common hive-bees, this peculiarity does not induce excessive stinging, but seems rather to proceed from fear. The sting is also less severe.

Under the rude methods thus far employed in the management of this bee no great yields of honey are obtained, some 10 or 12 pounds having been the most reported from a single hive. It is quite probable these little bees would yield more if imported into this country, since they could no doubt visit many small flowers not frequented by the hive-bees we now have, and whose nectar is, therefore, wasted; but very likely they might not withstand the severe winters of the North unless furnished with such extra protection as would be afforded by quite warm cellars or special repositories.

Here is something exceedingly interesting regarding the smallest honey-bees in the world. Just take a look at the size of the cells as shown in the figure, natural size, and then compare them in your mind's eye with comb in your own apiary. Well, here is what Mr. Benton has to say :

THE TINY EAST-INDIAN HONEY-BEE.
(*Apis florea*, Fab.)

This bee, also a native of East India, is the smallest known species of the genus. It builds in the open air, attaching a single comb to a twig of a shrub, or small tree. This comb is only about the size of a man's hand, and is exceedingly delicate, there being on each

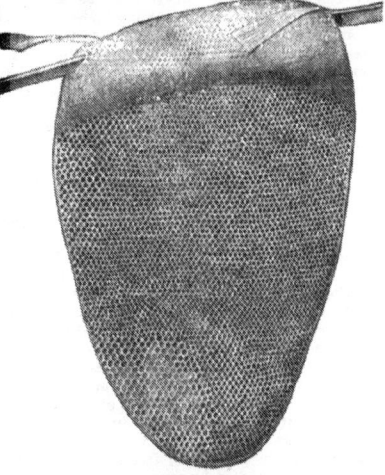

FIG. 3.—COMB OF TINY EAST-INDIAN HONEY-BEE (API FLOREA), ONE-THIRD NATURAL SIZE.

side 100 worker-cells to the square inch of surface (Figs. 2 and 3). The workers more slender than house-flies, though longer-bodied, are blue-black in color, with the anterior third of the abdomen bright

FIG. 2.—WORKER-CELLS OF TINY EAST-INDIAN HONEY-BEE (APIS FLOREA); NATURAL SIZE.

orange. Colonies of these bees accumulate so little surplus honey as to give no hope that their cultivation would be profitable.

GIANT BEES OF INDIA.
(*Apis dorsata*, Fab.)

A few years ago a great deal used to be said regarding the East Indian "giant" honey-bees, *Apis dorsata*, and the possibilities of having them imported and domesticated in this country. Much truth and nonsense have evidently been circulated in regard to them. Mr. Benton, having been in their native land, gives us something here that can be relied on.

This large bee, which might not inappropriately be styled the Giant East-Indian bee, has its home in the far East—both on the continent of Asia and the adjacent islands. There are probably several varieties of this species, more or less marked, and very likely *Apis zonata*, Guer., of the Philippine Islands, reported to be even larger than *Apis dorsata*, will prove on further investigation to be only a variety of the latter. All the varieties of these bees build huge combs of very pure wax—often 5 to 6 feet in length and 3 to 4 feet in width, which they attach to overhanging ledges of rocks or to large limbs of lofty trees in the primitive forest jungles. When attached to the limbs of trees they are built singly, and present much the same appearance as those of the tiny East-Indian bee, shown in the accompanying figure (Fig. 3). The Giant bee, however, quite in contradistinction to the other species of apis mentioned here, does not construct larger cells in which to rear drones, these and the workers being produced in cells of the same size. Of these bees—long regarded as a myth by bee-keepers of America and Europe—strange stories have been told. It has been stated that they build their combs horizontally, after the manner of paper-making wasps; that they are so given to wandering as to make it impossible to keep them in hives, and that their ferocity renders them objects greatly to be dreaded. The first real information regarding these points was given by the author. He visited India in 1880-81 for the purpose of obtaining colonies of *Apis dorsata*. These were procured in the jungles by cutting the combs from their original attachments, and it was thus ascertained (as might have been expected in the case of any species of apis), that their combs are always built perpendicularly; also that colonies placed in frame hives and permitted to fly freely did not desert their habitations, and that, far from being ferocious, these colonies were easily handled by proper precautions, without even the use of smoke. It was also proved by the

quantity of honey and wax present that they are good gatherers. The execution at that time of the plan to bring these bees to the United States was prevented only by severe illness contracted in India.

These large bees would doubtless be able to get honey from flowers whose nectaries are located out of reach of ordinary bees, notably those of the red clover, now visited chiefly by bumble-bees, and which it is thought the East-Indian bees might pollinate and cause to produce seed more abundantly. Even if not further utilizable, they might prove an important factor in the production, throughout the Southern States, of large quantities of excellent beeswax, now such an expensive article.

There are a few in this country who believe the introduction of the giant bees here would result disastrously to the business; that, as the English sparrow has driven out some of our American song birds, so *Apis dorsata* might drive out the Italians and black bees by taking the nectar that would otherwise go to *Apis mellifica*, and thus indirectly rob the bee-keeper. It is also stated that *Apis dorsata* could not be domesticated, but would run wild all over the country; but from all the information we can gather we have no fear of any of these things. The facts prove that they have not run out *Apis Indica, Apis florea*, and other Eastern bees in their own habitats; furthermore, it is doubtful whether they would be able to stand our changing climate, even in the South; for it must be understood that India and the Philippines have a much warmer climate than our Southern States.

HOW BEES GROW.

Having devoted so much space to the different races of bees, it is now in order to discuss *how* they grow.

During warm weather, while bees are gathering honey, open your hive about noon, and put in the center a frame containing a sheet of foundation; examine it every morning, noon, and evening, until you can see eggs in the cells. By inserting it between two combs already containing brood you will very likely find eggs in the cells the next day.

If you have never seen an egg that is to produce a bee, you may have to look very sharp the first time, for they are white like polished ivory, and scarcely larger than one of the periods in this print. They will be seen in the center of the cells attached to the comb by one end. The egg under the microscope much resembles the cut. It is covered, as you notice, with a sort of lace-like penciling, or net-work it might properly be called. Immediately on discovering eggs, mark down the date. If the weather is favorable, these eggs will hatch out in about three days or a little more, when, in place of the egg, you will, if you look sharp enough, see a tiny white worm or grub floating in a minute drop of milky fluid. If you

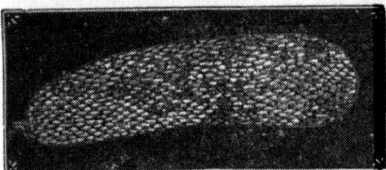

A QUEEN'S EGG UNDER THE MICROSCOPE.

watch you will find bees incessantly poking their heads into these cells; and very likely the milky fluid is placed on and about the egg a little before the inmate breaks its way out of the shell. We infer this, because we have never been able to get the eggs to hatch when taken away from the bees,[*] al-

3 4 5 6 9 12 15
THE DAILY GROWTH OF LARVÆ.

though we have carefully kept the temperature at the same point as in the hive. The net-work, as shown in the cut above, allows the milky fluid to penetrate the shell of the egg to furnish nourishment for the young bee at just the time required. These worms are really young bees in their larval state, and we shall in future call them larvæ. They thrive and grow very rapidly on their bread-and-milk diet, as you can see if you look at them very often. They will more than double in size in a single half-day, and in the short space of 12 days will expand from a mere speck (the larva just hatched) to the size of a full-grown bee, filling the cell completely. This seems almost incredible, but there they are, right before your eyes. We presume it is owing to the highly concentrated nature of this "bread-and-milk" food that the workers are so constantly giving them that they grow so rapidly. If you take the comb away from the bees for a little while you will see the larvæ opening their

[*] Since this was written it has been proven that eggs, removed from the hive, when subjected to proper temperature will hatch if supplied artificially with the milky food; otherwise, not.

mouths to be fed, like a nest of young birds, for all the world.

Figures under the cut represent the age in days from the laying of an egg. First the larva just having broken the egg-shell on the third day; next, a larva on the fourth day. During the fifth and sixth days they grow very rapidly, but it is difficult to fix any precise mark in regard to size. On the ninth day, the larva, having straightened itself out, the worker-bees cap it over. We have made a pretty accurate experiment on this point, and it was just six days and seven hours after the first egg hatched, that the bees completely capped it over. Just when larvæ begin to have legs and eyes, we have not discovered; but we found that the wings develop toward the last of the growth.

Regarding this point, Frank Cheshire, in his work on "Bees and Bee-keeping," says:

The chorion of the egg breaks, usually after three days (the time varies according to temperature), and a footless larva, with thirteen segments, exclusive of the head, alternately straightens and bends its body to free itself of the envelope. It is extremely curious that, before hatching, the larva presents rudimentary legs, which disappear—a fact which some have supposed to indicate "atavism," a reference to an ancestral type in which the larva bore feet; but this does not seem to be valid, for reasons which would encroach too much on our space. Toward the end of the larval period, the three segments following the head have little scales beneath the skin on the ventral side, which are the beginnings of the legs, and which can not be seen until the creature has been immersed in alcohol: the budding wings outside these, on second and third segments, are, by the same treatment, brought under view, as are also the rudiments of the sting in queen or worker larvæ, the male organs appearing in that of the drone. After sealing, the fourth segment begins to contract, and the fifth becomes partly atrophied, so that, soon, the former constitutes only a partial cover for the base of the developing thorax, and the petiole between it and the abdomen, while the latter becomes the narrow, first abdominal segment. It has been explained that the last three segments disappear in forming the sting; and now we find the fourth forming the petiole, leaving nine of the thirteen original segments, of which three go to the thorax and six to the abdomen.

After the larvæ are 6 days old, or between 9 and 10 days from the time the egg was laid, you will find the bees sealing up some of the largest. This sealing is done with a sort of paper-like substance; and while it shuts the young bee up, it still allows it a chance to breathe through the pores of the capping. It is given its last food, and the nurses seem to say, "There! you have been fed enough; spin your cocoon, and take care of yourself."

After this, as a general thing, the young bee is left covered up until it gnaws off the capping and comes out a perfect bee. This will be in about 21 days from the time the egg was laid, or it may be 20 if the weather is very favorable; therefore it is shut up 11 or 12 days. Now, there is an exception to this last statement, and it has caused not a little trouble and solicitude to beginners. During very warm summer weather, the bees, for one reason or another, decide to let a part of their children go "bareheaded," and therefore we find, on opening a hive, whole patches of immature bees looking like silent corpses with their white heads in tiers just about on a level with the surface of the comb. At this stage of growth they are motionless, of course, and so the young bee-keeper sends a postal card, telling us the brood in his hives is all dead. Some have imagined that the extractor killed them, others that it was *foul brood;* and we often think, when reading these letters, of the family which moved from the city into the country. When their beans began to come up, they thought the poor things had made a mistake by coming up wrong end first; so they pulled them all up, and replanted them with the bean part in the ground, leaving the proper roots sprawling up in the air. We can rest assured that the bees almost always know when it is safe to let the children's heads go uncovered.

It is very important, many times, to discover just when a queen was lost or a colony swarmed; hence you should learn these data thoroughly : The development of a bee occupies 3 days in the egg, 6 in the larval state, and 12 days sealed up.

The capping of worker-brood is nearly flat; that of the drones so much raised or convexed that we can at a glance tell when drones are reared in worker-cells, as is sometimes the case.

The young bee, when it gnaws its way out of the cell, commences to rub its own nose, straighten out its feathers, and then push its way among the busy throng, doubtless rejoicing to become one of that vast commonwealth. Nobody says a word, nor, apparently, takes any notice of the youngster; but for all that, they, as a whole, we are well convinced, feel encouraged, and rejoice in their own way at a house full of young folks. Keep a colony without young bees for a time, and you will see a new energy infused into all hands just as soon as young bees begin to gnaw out.

If you vary your experiment by putting a frame of Italian eggs into a colony of common bees, you will be better able to follow the newly emerged young bee as it matures.

The first day it does little but crawl around; but about the next day it will be found dipping greedily into the cells of unsealed honey, and so on for a week or more. After about the first day it will also begin to look after the wants of the unsealed larvæ, and very soon assists in furnishing the milky food for them. While so doing, a large amount of pollen is used, and it is supposed that this larval food is pollen and honey, partially digested by these young nurses. Bees of this age, or a little older, supply royal jelly for the queen-cells, which is the same, probably, as the food given very small larvæ. Just before they are sealed up, larvæ to produce worker-bees and drones are fed on a coarser, less perfectly digested mixture of honey and pollen. Young bees have a white downy look until they are a full week old, and continue a peculiar young aspect until they are quite two weeks old. At about this latter age they are generally active comb-builders of the hive. When a week or ten days old they take their first flight out of doors; we know no prettier sight in the apiary than a host of young Italians taking a playspell in the open air, in front of their hive. Their antics and gambols remind one of a lot of young lambs at play.

It is also very interesting to see these little chaps bringing their first load of pollen from the fields. If there are plenty of other bees in the hive of the proper age, they will not usually take up this work until about two weeks old. The first load of pollen is to a young bee just about what the first pair of pants is to a boy-baby. Instead of going straight into the hive with its load, as the veterans do, a vast amount of circling round the entrance must be done; and even after the young bee has once alighted it takes wing again before rushing all through the hive, to jostle nurses, drones, and perhaps the queen too; saying as plainly as could words, "Look! Here am I. I gathered this, all myself. Is it not nice?"

We might imagine some old veteran, who had brought thousands of such loads, answering gruffly, "Well, suppose you did; what of it? You had better put it in a cell and start off after more, instead of making all this row and wasting time, when there are so many mouths to feed." We said we might imagine this, for we have never been able to find any indication of unkindness inside a bee-hive. No one scolds or finds fault, and the children are never forced to work, unless they wish. If they are improvident, and starvation comes, they all suffer alike, and, we do believe, without a single bit of hard feeling or censure toward any one. They all work together, just as your right hand assists your left; and if we would understand the economy of the bee-hive, it were well to bear this point in mind.

Shortly following the impulse for pollen-collecting, comes that for honey-gathering; and the bee is probably in its prime as a worker when a month old. At this age it can, like a man of 40, "turn its hand" to almost any domestic duties; but if the hive is well supplied with workers of all ages, it now probably does most effective service in the fields. See AGE OF BEES.

When a colony is formed of young bees entirely, they will sometimes go out into the fields for pollen when but five or six days old. Also when a colony is formed wholly of adult bees they can build comb, feed the larvæ, construct queen-cells, and perform work generally that is usually done by younger bees; yet it is probably better economy to have bees of all ages in the hive.

BEES AND FRUIT. Every now and then we hear complaints of how bees will attack and eat up fruit; and to a casual observer, at least, they apparently do bite through the skin, extract the juices, until the specimen is shriveled up to a mere semblance of its former shape and size. Careful investigation has shown repeatedly that bees never attack sound fruit no matter how soft the skin nor how juicy and pulpy the contents within the skin.

Some years ago, Prof. N. W. McLain, then in the employ of the Department of Agriculture, Washington, D. C., conducted an elaborate series of experiments in which

GRAPES FIRST PUNCTURED BY BIRDS AND DESPOILED BY BEES.

he placed sound fruit, consisting of grapes, peaches, apricots, and the like, in hives containing bees that were brought to the verge of starvation. This fruit was left in the hives day after day, but it was never once molested. Then he tried breaking some of the fruit, and in every case all such specimens were attacked by the bees sucking up the juices until nothing but a dried skin and the stones or seeds were left.

Years later, Prof. H. A. Surface, economic zoologist at Harrisburg, Pa., tried a similar experiment, but in no case did the bees attack the sound fruit, although they partook freely of that which he had broken.

At the Wilmington State Fair, held Sept., 1908, in Delaware, Mr. Joel Gilfillan, of Newark, Del., had on exhibition a three-story observation hive containing two combs of bees. In the third story was hung a peach, a pear, and a bunch of grapes. This was kept on exhibition during the entire fair where the general public could see it. As is shown, this fruit was never once visited by the bees. The general verdict of those who saw it, fruit-men and farmers alike, was that bees would and could not injure *sound* fruit.

The authors have had, during the past thirty years, between three and four hundred colonies located in a vineyard at their home apiary. Notwithstanding hundreds and hundreds of pounds of grapes are raised every year, the bunches hanging within three or four feet of the entrance of the hives, the sound fruit is never attacked; but progressive fruit-growers and horticulturists there is a general acknowledgment that bees do not attack sound fruit; that the little damage they do to damaged fruit is compensated for a hundred times over by the indispensable service they perform in pollinating fruit-blossoms early in the season when no other insects or means of mingling the pollen exists. Indeed, some of our best fruit-growers are now keeping a few hives of bees in each of their orchards. Often they invite bee-keepers to locate yards of bees either in the orchards or as near as it is practicable to put them.

ONE OF THE EXHIBITS OF BEES AT THE GRANGE FAIR IN WILMINGTON, DELAWARE, HELD IN SEPTEMBER, 1908.
A card in the hive read, "Bees do not injure sound fruit."

But a casual observer might easily get the impression that bees not only suck damaged fruit dry, but actually puncture and eat up sound fruit. Some years ago a neighbor sent word to us that he would like to have us come up to his vineyard and he would give us undisputable proof that our bees were actually puncturing his grapes and sucking out the fruit. We looked at the luscious bunches as they were hanging down, and, sure enough, there were small needle like holes in almost every berry that the bees were working on. It looked like a clear case of "caught in the act" evidence against them. For the time being we were unable to offer a satisfactory explanation. We brought the matter to the attention of an old farmer who had been a bee-keeper for many years. Finally one morning he sent word to us that he had found the guilty culprit, and that if we would come down to his place *early* some morning he would point him out. This we did. He showed us a little bird, quick of flight, and almost never

during a dearth of honey, a broken or otherwise bruised bunch of grapes will occasionally be visited by a few bees.

The writer of this article has attended various horticultural and pomological conventions, both State and national. Among the

APRICOTS DAMAGED BY BIRDS; FRUITS THUS INJURED ARE SUCKED DRY BY BEES, WHICH STORE THE JUICE AS HONEY.

to be seen around the vines when any human being was present. This bird, about the size of a sparrow, striped, and called the Cape May warbler (*Dendroica tigrina*), has a long sharp needlelike beak. It will alight on a bunch, and, about as fast as one can count the grapes, will puncture berry after berry. After his birdship has done his mischief he leaves, and then come the innocent bees during the later hours of the day and finish up the work of destruction by sucking the juices and the pulp of the berry until it becomes a withered skin over a few seeds. While the birds during the early hours of the day are never seen, the bees, coming on later, receive all the credit for the mischief.

The Cape May warbler is not the only bird guilty of puncturing grapes. There are many other species of small birds that learn this habit, and among them we may name the ever present sparrow and the beautiful Baltimore oriole, the sweet singer that is sometimes called the swinging bird, from its habit of building its nest on some overhanging limb.

For further information regarding grape-puncturing birds, write to Dr. Merriam, of the United States Department of Agriculture, Washington, D. C.

WHEN BEES MAY DAMAGE FRUIT.

But there are times when bees do a real damage; and it is then that their owner should compromise, or, better yet, seek means to avoid trouble in the first place. In the fruit-drying ranches of California, apricots and peaches are cut up into small pieces and laid upon trays exposed to the sun's says. If there is a dearth of honey at this time, and a large number of bees in the locality, this fruit is quite liable to be attacked. The bees may visit it in such large numbers that they suck out the juices, leaving nothing but the shriveled form of the fruit. The property is no doubt damaged and its sale ruined. Before such a catastrophe can happen, the bee-keeper should move his whole yard to a point three or four miles distant from any fruit-drying operations. Failing to do so the fruit-grower, if the bees caused trouble, might enter suit for damages, and possibly recover the value of his crop. The bee-keeper, therefore, when the drying season is on, should take the precaution to move his bees away at once or make arrangements with his neighbor whereby he is to give immediate notice if the bees begin work on the fruit.

Years ago we had trouble with a cidermaker. He claimed that our bees would lick up the cider from the press as fast as he could make it. We easily adjusted this difficulty by screening his building with mosquito-netting.]

In every case of this sort the bee-keeper should avoid trouble. If he is a member of the National Bee-keepers' Association he might put up a stiff defense, it is true.; but in the case of the fruit-drying ranches and the cider-mills, the bee-keeper had better err on the safe side by avoiding suit for damages, because no bee-keepers' union or any other organization, or lawyers either, for that matter, would be able to give much assistance where it was clearly proven that the bees were doing an actual damage.

BEES EXONERATED BY A JURY.

In 1900, trouble arose between two brothers named Utter, at Amity, N. Y. One was a bee-keeper and the other a fruit-grower. The latter averred that the former's bees punctured his peaches, and that, in consequence of their alleged damage, he was unable to raise any fruit. There had not been very good feeling between the brothers for years. The fruit-grower brought suit against the bee-keeper, and the case was tried on December 17, 18, and 19, 1899, at Goshen. There was no lack of legal talent on either side. The case was a very hard-fought one from beginning to end. Among some thirty odd witnesses examined, the Government expert, Mr. Frank Benton, of the United States Department of Agriculture, Washington, D. C., gave in his testimony to the effect that bees never puncture sound fruit; that it is practically impossible for them to do so, owing to the fact that they have no cutting jaws like those found in the wasp and other insects of that character. He also showed how wasps and birds will, under some conditions, puncture fruit; that these minute holes they make will, during a dearth of honey, be visited by bees. Other expert testimony was offered, nearly all of which exonerated the bees. After all the evidence was in and the pleas were made, the jury retired, and in a short time returned a verdict for the defendant. The fruit-grower had failed to make out a case against the bees.

For further particulars regarding this the reader is referred to the General Manager of the National Bee-keepers' Association.

In case trouble arises, the owner of the bees will do well to read the next subject, "Bees as a Nuisance," and also the other subject found in its alphabetical order, "Laws Relating to Bees."

BEES AS A NUISANCE. It would seem almost out of place to discuss this question in a work intended for perusal and study by those who believe (and rightly, too) that bees are not a nuisance; but, as we shall show, there are very good reasons why we should calmly discuss this question in order to avoid trouble that may arise in the future. Certain difficulties have arisen between the keepers of bees and their neighbors. Perhaps the bees, after a long winter confinement, have taken a flight and soiled the washing hung on a line in a neighbor's yard. Possibly some of his children have been stung, or there have been times when he has been annoyed while in the peaceable possession of his own property by bees coming on his premises, and smelling around, as they sometimes do during the fruit-canning season when the aroma of sugar and juicy fruits is flowing out through the doors and windows of the kitchen. Possibly the offended neighbor keeps chickens, and members of his feathered tribe have trespassed on the grounds of the bee-keeper. The result of all this is that bad feelings arise. Complaint is made to the village fathers ; an ordinance is passed declaring bees within the limits of the corporation to be a nuisance, and requiring the keeper to remove them at once or suffer the penalty of fine or imprisonment, or both.

In some instances, live stock has been stung ; a cow or a calf or a horse may get near the entrances of the hives, which, we will say, are within a foot of a dividing line between the two properties. Perhaps the stock is stung nearly to death. Damage is claimed and a lawsuit follows, with the result that a feeling of resentment is stirred up against the bee-keeper. But this is not all. Possibly the bee-keeper has an apiary in his front yard, bordering on the general highway. A nucleus may be robbed out, with the result that the bees go on the warpath, and begin to sting passersby. Perhaps a span of horses is attacked ; a runaway follows ; damages are claimed, and another lawsuit is begun.

In the foregoing we have supposed *possible* instances. It is proper to state that they are only types of what has occurred and may occur again, so it behooves us to be careful.

In the case first mentioned (the aggrieved neighbor's washing soiled by the stains from bees affected with dysentery), it is well for the bee-keeper to send over several nice sections of honey, or offer to pay for the damage done to the washing. Nothing makes a woman more angry than to have her nice clean white linen, after she has scrubbed, rinsed, and hung it out to dry, daubed with nasty, ill-smelling brown stains. But if our bee-keeping friend will take pains to offer an apology *before* the woman makes complaint, and show a disposition to make the matter good, trouble may be averted. And right here it should be said, if the bees are in the cellar do not set them out on a wash-day ; or if they are outdoors, and the sun comes out bright so they begin to fly strongly from the hives, send word to your neighbors and ask them not to hang out their washing, if it is wash-day, for a few hours. Send along a few boxes of honey, and keep the folks across the way "sweetened up." Ninety-nine neighbors out of a hundred will put up with a great deal of inconvenience, and say, "Oh! that is all right. It won't take long to rinse out the clothes again."

Take, for example, more serious cases—where horses or cattle have been stung. If you have been foolish enough to place hives near the highway or your neighbor's line fence where he has loose stock, you may have to pay pretty dearly for it before you get through. The remedy is prevention. Always put bees in a back yard, and not too close to your neighbor's line fence. Be careful, also, to prevent robbing. See that there are no weak nuclei with entrances too large. As soon as the honey-flow stops, contract

occasions. We supplied our neighbor with clover seed for this field; and when he came to cut the crop the horses would occasionally be stung while drawing the mower. In one case there came very near being a serious mixup, as the team came very near running away with the mowing-machine.

Two years later, corn was planted in this same field. When the horses were cultivating up and down the rows they were attacked again by the bees, for they were going in great droves across this field to a patch of clover beyond. Notwithstanding we had a high board fence to raise the flight of the bees above the team when near our yard, there was more or less trouble. On one occasion the driver was stung pretty severely

SCHEME FOR PROTECTING HORSES WHILE CULTIVATING A FIELD NEXT TO A BEE-YARD

the entrances of all the weaker colonies. If extracting is done after the honey flow, great caution needs to be exercised. The extracting-room should be screened off, and bee-escapes provided. Wherever possible, take off all surplus by the use of bee-escapes rather than by shaking. See ROBBING and EXTRACTING.

WHAT TO DO WHEN BEES ATTACK NEIGHBORS' HORSES.

But it sometimes happens that something must be done at once to avert an attack upon teams of horses working in fields adjoining a bee-yard. We have one outyard located near a field where our neighbor's horses have been attacked by the bees on several

and the animals became unmanageable. Fortunately the driver got them under control without any serious consequences.

Now, our neighbor is a kindly man; and when he telephoned what had happened we saw that something would have to be done. We told him to go to the harness-shop and secure some large horse-blankets that would cover the necks and backs of the horses, and we would pay the bill. We then directed him to secure some large squares of mosquito-netting and fold this around the horses' heads. In the meantime we supplied him with veils for himself and man.

When the next day came for cultivating, the blankets were put on and we went down to watch developments. We found that the blankets helped very materially, as they protected the animals from the onslaught of bees around their backs and necks where they could not brush or switch them off. Our neighbor did not think it was necessary to put the mosquito-netting over the heads, as he said his horses did not mind bees on the face, as they could be brushed off on the fore-legs. With these large blankets the horses went up and down the rows with very little trouble.

We found upon investigation that the bees were not disposed to be cross, but in going to and from the fields in search of honey they were interrupted in their flight. The switching of the tails of the horses angered them with the result as stated.

But suppose your neighbor is unreasonable and ugly, and he brings suit for damages; or suppose that your bees are located in a city or village, and that the town council has declared your bees a nuisance.

Do not move the bees if you have used reasonable precaution, but write at once to the Manager of the National Bee-keepers' Association, whose address will be found by writing to any bee-journal or the publishers of this work. If you are a member of the Association you will be entitled to protection, and possibly all or a part of the court expenses will be paid by the organization. The Association does not undertake to defend its members against criminal carelessness of such a kind as we have already described; but when the bee-keeper has exercised every precaution, then it endeavors to protect his rights. This means that you should become a member *before* you get into trouble. The annual fee for membership and protection is $1.00.

Well, we will say the attorneys have been retained, and the Association is back of you. Any number of decisions have been handed down to prove that bees are not a nuisance *per se;* that, when they are properly kept, and due precautions are used, they can not be driven out of the corporation. There are several precedents from various courts, even from the Supreme Court of Arkansas, to show that bees have the right to be kept within a corporation like any other live stock, so that any ordinance not in conformity with these decisions can be declared unconstitutional. Several ordinances declaring bees to be a nuisance have been repealed. See DECISIONS, under head of LAWS RELATING TO BEES, found elsewhere in its alphabetical order.

BEES, CROSS. See ANGER OF BEES.

BEES, HANDLING. See FRAMES, MANIPULATING; also EXHIBITS.

BEES ON SHARES. In some localities, notably in California, Colorado, and the great West, bees are often kept on shares. While this method of doing business has usually been conducted quite successfully and satisfactorily to both parties, yet nevertheless many disputes and troubles have arisen, perhaps because there was a lack of contract; or if there was one there was nothing in it to cover the point in dispute.

The following form of contract was very carefully drawn by an attorney, and it is hoped will meet every condition.

ARTICLES OF AGREEMENT.

This Agreement, made and entered into at ——, this —— day of ——, 190—, by and between —— of ——, party of the first part, and hereinafter called the owner, and ——, of ——, party of the second part, and hereinafter called the employee.

Witnesseth: First, that said owner has agreed, and in consideration of the covenants and agreements herein contained and to be performed by said employee, does hereby agree to provide a good location for keeping bees, at or near ——, and furnish and put thereon, on or before the —— day of ——, 190—, not less than —— colonies of healthy bees, and then and thereafter at such times as needed during the continuance of this contract, to provide and furnish at his own cost and expense, all hives, tools, implements, machinery, and buildings necessary to enable said employee to carry on successfully the business of producing and securing honey and wax from said bees; and further to pay one-half of the cost and expense of all sections, cans, bottles, shipping-cases, and packages that may be required to put the honey and wax into marketable shape; and in case it shall be necessary to feed said bees, to provide and furnish feeders and the sugar for making the syrup; and said owner further agrees to give and deliver on the said premises, to said employee, as and for his compensation for labor done and provided by him in caring for said bees and securing honey and wax, the full one-half of all marketable honey and wax produced by and secured from said bees.

Second: In consideration of the above covenants and agreements, the said ——, employee, hereby agrees to enter the employ of said owner on said —— day of ——, 19—, and at once care for said bees in a proper manner; do, perform, and provide all labor necessary to carry on successfully the business of producing and securing honey and wax ready for market; pay one-half the cost and expense of all sections, cans, bottles, shipping-cases, and packages that may be required to put the honey and wax into marketable shape; feed the bees, when necessary that they shall be fed, and deliver on the premises to the said owner the full one-half of all the marketable honey and wax produced and secured from said bees, and to accept the remaining half as and for his full compensation for labor done and provided by him in the care of said bees and the production and securing of honey and wax.

Provided, and it is mutually agreed and understood by and between the parties hereto, that said employee shall double up all of sa'd hives at the close of the season or leave them reasonably strong and well supplied with stores and prepared for winter; and if any of said colonies of bees are lost through the carelessness or negligence of said employee, said owner may recover from said employee as damages an amount not greater than one-half what it would cost to replace said bees and queens; all increase of swarms (artificial or natural) to belong to said owner. It is further mutually agreed and understood that in case no honey is secured, or the amount runs below ten (10) pounds per colony, said owner shall pay to said employee, as and for his compensation for all labor done and provided by him on and about said bees, an amount not exceeding —— cents per hour for each and every hour of labor so done, and provided by said employee on and about said bees, and in such case all honey to belong to said owner.

Signed in duplicate by said parties, the day and year first above written.

Signed in presence of   —— ——

—— ——   —— ——

The foregoing comprises the essential features of a contract; but local conditions may render it necessary to make some modifications.

The last clause in the above contract is inserted as a matter of fairness to the employee. If no honey should be secured, the employee has performed his part of the contract in good faith, and, moreover, has improved the apiary—perhaps increased it —so that it will be in better condition the following year for a honey crop. For this betterment it is no more than right that the owner should pay the employee a reasonable sum, whatever amount may be agreed on; or, if preferred, a certain number of colonies. One can readily see that, in case the honey season was an absolute failure, the employee would suffer a total loss except for a provision of this kind, and that the owner would still have his bees, his implements, and every thing necessary to carry on the business for another season.

By the above contract it is to the interest of both parties to keep down increase. The employee must know, if he is a practical bee-keeper, that, the greater the increase, the less the honey; and he will, therefore, bend all his efforts and skill to keep the colonies in the best possible condition to obtain a crop of honey.

Keeping bees on shares is practiced quite extensively in Colorado and California. It very often happens that a bee-keeper lately arrived from the East desires to try a locality to see whether it will be suited to his health, and whether or not he can make the

keeping of bees a success. He accordingly finds a bee-keeper whose other business leads him to desire some one competent to manage them for him. But where one is well settled in a locality, and has the means whereby he can purchase the bees, he had better do so—better even go in debt; but in this case, to secure the owner I would agree that, in case the honey crop is insufficient to pay for at least half the bees, he will then agree to content himself with half the honey crop on the terms here proposed.

BEES, STINGLESS. The bees of the Western Hemisphere are stingless—at least a very large proportion of them. Their habitat extends from the boundary between the United States and Mexico down to Buenos Aires, in Argentina, embracing an area of 8,000,000 square miles. One comparatively unimportant species inhabits most of the West India islands. There are a few species in Asia and Africa.

By entomologists these bees are usually classed under two great genera—*Melipona* and *Trigona;* but some naturalists are disposed to add another, *Tetrasoma*. There is an extraordinary variety of these bees, which is supposed to embrace at least 100 species, whereas there are not more than 8 species of *Apis*. The variation in size is also great, for some are no larger than a mosquito, while others are considerably larger than the hive bee. A number of naturalists are at work studying them with a view to their proper classification and arrangement by species.

There is an equal variation in the number of bees per colony, for some consist of only a few (100) individuals while others are supposed to contain not less than 100,000 bees.

Some build only small nests, not much larger than an orange; others, again, construct a home as large as an ordinary flour-barrel. Some build in a hole in the ground; others in the open air, as wasps and hornets do, while quite a number build their nests in the hollows of forest-trees.

An intermediate species occupies the position midway between bees and wasps, and is generally spoken of as the honey-gathering wasp. Wasps are carnivorous, hence it is hardly fair to class this one with these hawks of the insect tribe.

Early travelers in South and Central America did not fail to notice the stingless bees, and they are quite frequently referred to by them. Capt. Basil Hall, in the 18th century, noticed apiaries of them in Peru; and Koster, in his Travels in Brazil, carefully mentions them. Spanish writers on Cen-

3

tral America casually noted them in the 16th century; but no European seems to have been interested enough in them to make a comprehensive study of their life-history and habits. That work was left for the twentieth-century naturalists. Geoffrey St. Hillaire, a naturalist-explorer, did something to awaken interest by his now classical observations on honey-gathering wasps of Paraguay, of which he furnished a com-

from their chief enemy, the lizard. The logs are robbed at stated intervals, the keeper being well satisfied if he can secure a gallon of honey per hive at a robbing, depending somewhat on the species used for domestication.

Apparently no effort has ever been made to invent a hive suitable to their wants. It is noticeable that the natives use only those species whose homes are made in hollow

STINGLESS WORKER.   ITALIAN WORKER.   ITALIAN QUEEN.
(Magnified two times.)

plete account in 1825 (Paris). Azara, a similar explorer, also called attention to them in his travel through Paraguay. He describes a species twice as large as *Apis mellifica*.

Other explorers have mentioned them from time to time, but nothing of real value was elicited until lately. Their study has now been taken up in earnest. White men have been inclined to dismiss them as worthless for practical purposes; but the natives of South America are certainly not of that opinion. On the contrary, they regard them as superior to the "stinging fly" of the white man. In Southern Mexico, Central America, and South America, they are quite frequently kept in a domesticated state by the native inhabitants — that is to say, they have them in hollow logs which have been brought from the forests. These "hives" are generally hung up by ropes around their dwellings to protect the bees

trees, no effort being made to utilize the many other species whose nests are made in holes in the ground or on tree-branches.

The quality of the honey and wax varies very much, some of it being quite good and some quite the opposite. The wax is apt to be mixed with propolis to a great extent; but at least one species inhabiting the upper tributaries of the Orinoco, in Columbia, furnishes a desirable wax which has been frequently sold in this country.

While the stinging bees cannot sting they *bite* and worry in a way to surpass bees possessed of a sting. At the Philadelphia field-day meeting at which a thousand bee-keepers were present, in June, 1906, two colonies of a large species of stingless bees were exhibited. A hive of them was torn apart and opened for inspection. Did those stingless bees take such intrusion without making any objections? Not at all.

ITALIAN QUEEN.   (Mag. two times.)   STINGLESS QUEEN.

PROF. H. A. SURFACE, ZOOLOGIST, AT HARRISBURG, PENNSYLVANIA, WITH HIS BEGIN-
NER CLASS IN BEE-KEEPING.

They attacked their despoilers in a way they will not soon forget. They would bite, grasp the hair, eye-lashes, twist and pull, and even crawl into the ears and nose of their tormentors. So vicious was their on-slaught that they drove one man, who had a hand in breaking up their home, from the scene of action. While the pain of their bite is infinitessimal, yet the high-note hissing sound, getting into the hair, pulling at the eyes and eye-lashes, and, crawling into the nostrils and ears, almost makes one crazy.

It is fair to state that stingless bees do not offer such attack unless provoked to fury: ordinarily they can be handled without any protection whatever.

BEE-ESCAPES. See COMB HONEY, also EXTRACTING.

BEGINNING WITH BEES. The beginner will find he will be able to understand the articles in this work much more readily if he can in some way manage to visit a bee-keeper in his vicinity. If he can afford it, it would be well for him even to go some distance to see some progressive bee-keeper, and spend a whole day where he will be able to pick up tricks of the trade, and a fund of information that might take him weeks or months to dig out of text-books.

Even if he knows of no one but an old-fashioned box-hive bee-keeper, he should see him; but, far better, visit some practical man who will be able to point out the queen, and illustrate the *modus operandi* of opening a hive and handling the frames—in short, make a practical demonstration of many of the manipulations here explained. If there is no bee-keeper he can visit he should send to his nearest dealer and get a one or two frame nucleus with a queen. Let him follow carefully the directions on the outside of the shipping-box; then, with the bees before him, read and study his A B C's. Without an actual demonstration of some sort, much that is written here will otherwise be like pure Greek to the average beginner in bees. Having seen the bees, and learned how to open a hive, what next?

We would strongly urge the importance of a small beginning with as little expense as possible; for nothing is more discouraging after having plunged into the business extensively (blindfolded as it were) than to lose a large portion of the bees, either through bad wintering or from some other cause—all for the want of a little practical experience, or even a theoretical knowledge. Many a person has met with disaster from starting out with bees on altogether too large a scale. Sometimes one is offered a bargain of 25 or 30 colonies including hives, bees, implements, smokers, etc., at a ridiculously low price, and the temptation becomes strong to buy. He'd better not, unless having read the several articles indicated in the fine print on the first page of this work.

After investing $25.00, put no more into the business until the bees bring in some returns. In other words, *make the bees pay their way*. It is a very easy matter to throw away some good money into the venture and get no returns; because bee-keeping as a business is something that depends more upon the weather than perhaps any other. For this reason we do not advise any one to rely on bees as a sole means of livelihood. True it is that there are many bee-keeping specialists; but they are men who have gradually grown into the business, and as a general rule have a specially favorable location, keeping somewhere from 500 to 1000 colonies.

The keeping of bees is generally more successfully carried on in connection with some other business. Many a professional man desires some sort of light recreation, and a few bees will afford him just the diversion he needs. Farmers, fruit-growers, or horticulturists, may keep from 50 to 100 colonies without greatly interfering with any other work; and nearly every one, as explained under APIARY, can keep a few colonies in his back yard. Ten or twenty colonies will yield almost a certain return of a much larger revenue, per colony, than ten times that number. See PROFITS IN BEES, elsewhere.

Having considered some of the difficulties and uncertainties of bee-keeping, one may now inquire whether he desires to go into the business at all. With the knowledge that from 10 to 20 colonies can usually be handled successfully, and at a good profit, the beginner will naturally desire to try his hand at it. How shall he make his start? Whenever possible, buy bees in your own vicinity. Regarding the price, a strong colony of Italian bees, with tested queen, in a new Dovetailed hive, or in any modern hive, in fact, might be worth $10.00. This should be considered the outside price. Usually bees that are hybrids or blacks, in movable-frame hives, second hand, sell from $3.00 to $5.00 per stock, including hive. If there are no modern bee-keepers in the vicinity one may have to purchase a box hive or two with the combs all built solidly into the hive—see BOX HIVES. The price of these, if they

are blacks or hybrids, is generally from $1.00 to $3.00 per hive.

To move colonies in box hives, turn the hive upside down, and tie over the end a piece of cheese-cloth. The moving should be done at night, or at least on a cool day, carrying them a distance of at least a mile and a half, otherwise many of the bees will return to their old location. See MOVING BEES.

In some localities it may not be possible to buy bees of any one. In such case send to the nearest dealer for a one or two frame nucleus. If one doesn't mind expense, let him purchase four or five nuclei and then proceed to build them up as described under NUCLEUS and FEEDING.

Before purchasing any bees he should get of his dealer or manufacturer five or ten modern hives in the flat. As there are several such hives on the market, all of them fairly good, the beginner may be at a loss to know which of them to choose. For comb honey we would recommend the Danzen-

THREE-FRAME NUCLEUS FOR SHIPPING.

baker or Dovetailed hive. For particulars see HIVES. They are sold by all the dealers; and as these hives are used largely by expert bee-keepers who carry on the business quite extensively with good results, the novice will not go far astray by adopting them.

As soon as the hives are received in the flat, nail them up and paint them. With every lot of hives there will be sufficient nails of the right kind to put them together. If one can not afford to take the time himself, let him employ some carpenter, who, with the printed directions, will be able to put them together in a workmanlike manner. (A carpenter is not needed, however.)

Having the hives all in readiness, five or ten, as the case may be, one can, with his two or three nuclei, build them up by feeding, and then divide as recommended under NUCLEUS and FEEDING.

If the beginner is successful thus far, he may then, with some assurance, purchase of his dealer one or two Italian queens, which he can easily introduce to the nuclei. See INTRODUCING. In dividing or forming nuclei, one should, of course, give the new queen he just purchased to the bees that are made queenless. After he has had a little more experience in watching and studying bees he may then be able to do something at queen-rearing. See QUEENS and QUEEN-REARING. To avoid trouble with robbers he should then read very carefully the subject of STINGS and ROBBING. Toward the close of the season he should next take up WINTERING, as found in its alphabetical order, reading this carefully; for more disasters in apiculture result from failure to winter bees properly than from any other cause.

Nuclei, or, better, pounds of bees, can be purchased of some of the dealers. These will be placed in light shipping-boxes, and usually contain 500 to 1000 bees, one or two frames of brood, and a little honey. As the express charges on nuclei will be double first-class, it is always cheaper and better to buy in pound packages, or common bees in one's own vicinity where possible, and, after transferring, introduce Italian queens.

BELLFLOWER. See CAMPANILLA.

BLACK BROOD. See DISEASES OF BEES.

BLACK LOCUST. See LOCUST.

BLEACHING COMB HONEY. See COMB HONEY.

BOX HIVES. It seems as if any description in a work designed to teach modern apiculture would be entirely out of place; but since many have never seen any thing but a movable-frame hive, and the old box hive is occasionally referred to in various portions of this work, perhaps a brief description should be given.

These hives, as the name indicates, are merely boxes containing neither brood-frames nor any movable fixtures. They usually consist of a rude rough box about a foot square, and from 18 to 24 inches high. Through the center there would be two cross-sticks, the purpose of which was to help sustain the weight of the combs built in irregular sheets within the hive.

At the close of the season it was the custom for the apiarist to go around and "heft" his hives. Those that were heavy were marked to be brimstoned; and those that were light were left to winter over for next season if they could. The bees of the first named were destroyed with sulphur fumes, and then the bee-bread, honey, and every thing were cut out.

In the more modern box hives there were glass boxes that could be drawn out from an upper part, leaving the lower intact. In this case the bees were not destroyed. In any case there was no opportunity to inspect combs, hunt queens, divide, or perform any of the hundred and one operations of modern apiculture.

When one compares the crudity of these methods with those that are described in this book, he sees what wonderful progress has been made in apiculture.

BRASSICA. See MUSTARD; also RAPE; also SEVEN-TOP TURNIP.

BROOD. See BEES; also DISEASES OF BEES.

BROOD, SPREADING. See SPREADING BROOD.

BOTTLING HONEY. See EXTRACTED HONEY; also PEDDLING HONEY and CANDIED HONEY.

BUCKWHEAT. (*Polygonum.*) This, in certain sections, is one of the most important honey-plants. It is grown principally on the hillsides of Eastern New York and Pennsylvania, and in these localities, where are thousands of acres within a radius of a few miles, immense quantities of buckwheat honey are annually produced. On one hilltop in Schoharie Co., N. Y., near Gallupville, where we stood, we were told that within a radius of three miles the bees had access to 5000 acres of buckwheat, all of which was within the range of our eyes. So great is the acreage of it in New York that anywhere from 2000 to 3000 colonies can be kept in some counties; and this means hundreds of bee-keepers who are specialist honey-growers and farmers, almost all of whom keep at least a few colonies. The latter class reason this way: That the growing of buckwheat as a grain is one of the most profitable branches of farming; that the nectar in the blossoms properly belongs to them, and if they keep a few colonies they will virtually get two crops from one field—honey and the buckwheat grain.

We have ridden a bicycle through the buckwheat region of New York, traveling all day, without losing sight of buckwheat-fields that seemed to cover every available piece of ground on both sides of the road. So immense are the fields that the atmosphere seems to be heavily charged with the aroma of the bloom, and if one is not a lover of buckwheat honey the odor is somewhat sickening.

One bee-keeper in the heart of the buckwheat country (W. L. Coggshall, of West Groton), who lives near Cayuga Lake, har-

lina and Texas. But it is in Eastern New York, on the hillsides, that it seems to thrive best. Stalks of the celebrated Japanese variety that would measure two feet high in Ohio will reach five or six feet in length in the more favored locations in New York. There is something in the climate and soil of those great hills that makes the growing of this plant much more profitable

NATURAL SIZE

JAPANESE BUCKWHEAT.

vested one year with his 1000 colonies 78,000 lbs. of honey; another year 50,000 lbs.; and for a good many years his crops have ranged along into the carloads. While this is not all buckwheat honey by considerable, yet a good big portion of it is.

But the growing of buckwheat is by no means confined to the East. It is grown in small acreages, of, say, one to five acres, in most of the North Central States. It also is a paying crop for seed and honey in the South, being grown largely in South Caro-

in the East than in the West, although it is always a paying crop for the grain in nearly every locality where ordinary grain crops can be grown.

THE QUALITY OF BUCKWHEAT HONEY.

Buckwheat honey itself is of a deep dark purplish tint, and looks very much like New Orleans or sorghum molasses. It is usually of heavy body; and the flavor, to one who is a lover of clover and basswood, and who has never been accustomed to buckwheat honey,

JAPANESSE BUCKWHEAT THIRTY-FOUR INCHES HIGH IN A LITTLE OVER THREE WEEKS FROM THE TIME THE SEED WAS PLANTED.

is more or less rank; and yet those who have always been used to buckwheat honey, or at least a good many of them, prefer it even to clover or basswood.

A lady from the East once called at our store and looked over our honey. We showed her several samples of choice clover and basswood comb honey.

"I do not like this," she said. "It looks like manufactured sugar honey. Haven't you any buckwheat?"

"Yes, but we did not suppose you would like that, because such honey rarely sells in our locality."

We then placed before her some sections of buckwheat honey, and these suited her exactly.

"*That* is real bee honey," said she, with a look of satisfaction, and she carried home several sections.

It seems that her father had been a bee-keeper, and about all the honey she ever saw was buckwheat: and unless it had the strong flavor and dark color of the honey she was familiar with in her childhood days it was not honey to her, and there are thousands and thousands like her in the East.

Yes, there is a fancy trade that prefers buckwheat; and this trade is so large that buckwheat honey in the New York market brings almost as high a price as the fancy grades of white; but in the Western markets, principally in Chicago, "the stuff" goes begging a purchaser, and sells as an off grade of poor honey.

Notwithstanding the color of buckwheat honey itself is purplish, the cappings of the combs, especially if made by black bees, are almost pearly white. Buckwheat comb honey—some of it at least—is very pretty, and especially when it is put up by practical bee-keepers who know how to produce a first-class grade of any honey.

IS BUCKWHEAT A RELIABLE SOURCE FOR HONEY, AND WHEN?

In York State, buckwheat can be depended upon almost every year for a crop of honey but in the West it is rather uncertain—some years yielding no honey, and others doing fairly well. But when it does yield, the bees work on it almost entirely in the morning, the nectar supply lasting until about ten or eleven o'clock. There are, however, exceptions.

In the East, if we are not mistaken, on account of the immense acreage, the bees are kept busy gathering honey from morning till night; and owing to the fact that it can be depended on almost absolutely for a yield of honey—when even basswood or clover fails, as it does sometimes in any locality—the bee-keeper is able to make at least expenses and something besides. Indeed, some years when there is almost a total failure of white honey, the York State honey-producers are enabled to make a fair living from buckwheat alone.

DIFFERENT VARIETIES OF BUCKWHEAT.

The first buckwheats of which very much became known were designated as the black and the gray. Later on, the silverhull came into prominence. Both of these varieties were finally displaced almost entirely by the celebrated Japanese. This variety is not only very much more prolific, but the kernels, or seeds, are very much larger—so much larger, indeed, that it necessitates the use of larger screens on the part of the millers who make a business of grinding it. At the present time the Japanese is grown almost exclusively. The illustration shown on page 70 is a very excellent one of the buckwheat plant in general; and while the kernels shown are a little larger than the natural size (engravings usually exaggerate), yet they are much larger than the old varieties of silverhull and gray.

The Japanese is an enormous yielder, having been known to produce at the rate of 80 bushels per acre, and the crop has become so profitable in localities favoring its growth that it is not an uncommon thing for a single farmer to raise anywhere from 500 to 1000 bushels.

BUCKWHEAT A PAYING FARM CROP.

We have set it down as a rule in this work that it is not profitable to grow any honey-plant unless the seed will pay the expense of the crop. In this case buckwheat, as we have shown it, is one of the most profitable grains that can be grown, and outside of any honey it may yield, there is " good money in it." In our own locality the yield of nectar from buckwheat is so irregular and so scant from season to season that we do not get very much honey; and yet when it does yield it affords an excellent diversion for the bees, keeping them out of mischief when there would be an absolute dearth of honey from every other source; hence even in Ohio it pays to grow it.

HOW TO PREPARE THE SOIL FOR GROWING BUCKWHEAT, AND WHEN TO SOW.

Two crops of buckwheat can be grown in a season, but usually they do not pay. In such case the first must be sown very early—so early that it is liable to be killed by frosts after it comes up. Very hot weather coming on while it is in bloom proves unfavorable to the maturing of the seed. Buckwheat ordinarily should be sown after some other crop, anywhere from July 1 to the middle of August, depending on the locality. Almost any soil can be used for growing it; but the better the soil, the larger the crop, of course. Some recommend loose mellow ground, or clover sod turned under. Others say plow immediately after sowing oats or planting corn, as by thus working the soil *early* it becomes settled and holds the moisture which buckwheat demands; and the result is, the seed fills better. After plowing, the ground should be thoroughly harrowed, and then the seed sown with a drill. If a fertilizer is used, it should be put in at the same time with the seed and run through the drill. One experienced grower says the sowing should be done while the ground is dry and dusty, and never immediately after a rain. After sowing, the surface should be immediately rolled to compact the soil, as the grain sprouts more quickly, sometimes showing above ground in less than four days.

Mr. J. H. Kennedy, of Quenamo, Kan., tells us of a crop of 116 bushels of Japanese buckwheat that cost him next to nothing. After turning under his oat stubble in July, as it was too early to put in wheat he sowed the ground to buckwheat with a drill. This came off so soon that the ground was in almost as good condition, apparently, for sowing wheat as it was when first prepared. He then put the drill right on to the buckwheat stubble, and next season reported that the wheat sown on this stubble looked exactly as well as the rest sown on other ground. It is probable that a plant so different in its habits from wheat will take little if any of the necessary plant food for wheat from the soil; and it is a common remark that nothing fits the ground so nicely for a succeeding crop as buckwheat.

The amount of seed to the acre varies according to the locality. On good land, two pecks per acre is recommended as enough; on thin soil, three pecks. One can increase the yield on thin soils by the use of 50 lbs. of phosphate and 50 lbs. of plaster mixed and drilled in, according to W. L. Coggshall, of West Groton, N. Y., to whom we have already referred. The same authority estimates that buckwheat is one of the best crops to subdue rough land, and that it always leaves the ground in good condition for potatoes and oats, and almost any crop, except corn.

Buckwheat as a fertilizer of soil is one of the best. Sometimes after late sowing, early frosts nip the stalks. In such cases we would always recommend plowing it under before the plants wilt. It will more than pay for its cost as a fertilizer, and some buckwheat-growers, we understand, enrich their soil every so often in this way, even when the frost does not come in to spoil the crop. In this case they wait till after the blooming to get the honey and then plow under. Indeed, several prominent men recommend plowing in two or even three crops of buckwheat, one after another, if short of manure, when it is desired to get the ground into a high state of cultivation.

The best crop of buckwheat we ever had was after plowing under a crop of red clover. The influence of clover and abundant rains matured the grain in just 65 days after the sowing; and as the seed was not sown in the first place till after the 15th of August, our experiments showed that, under favorable circumstances, buckwheat is a very speedy crop. There was no killing frost that season until the last of October, but this, of course, is unusual.

SOWING BUCKWHEAT AND CRIMSON CLOVER AT THE SAME TIME.

During the last two or three years we have had excellent success in sowing crimson clover with buckwheat, especially where both were put in along the last of July or first of August. They come up together; but the buckwheat, being stronger, takes the ground, and the crimson clover makes but little showing until after the buckwheat is harvested. Then the crimson clover, during the cool moist fall weather, rapidly covers the ground. If frost should kill the buckwheat, the crimson clover will rise up above it and hide its black unsightliness in a very brief period; and the dead buckwheat seems to be just the sort of mulching that the clover needs. The finest crop of crimson clover we ever grew or saw was sown this way, and turned under the following June, for planting potatoes.

Caution.—It is a fact that buckwheat honey occasionally contains 33 per cent of water, and is, therefore, too thin, according to the formula of the national pure-food law passed July 31, 1906, which limits the amount of water in honey to 25 per cent. It will be necessary, therefore, to evaporate thin honey to make it conform to the law.

This may be done by means of a honey-evaporator, or by storing it for a while in a hot dry room. Bee-keepers need not hesitate to go to the extra trouble involved by the law, since the honey is really so much improved, and ought to command higher price.

C.

CAGES FOR QUEENS. See INTRODUCING.

CAMPANILLA. A plant that stands first in importance to the bee-keepers of Cuba is the campanilla, or bellflower, a species of the morning-glory. There are several varieties, but only two of them seem to yield honey—the campanilla blanca and the campanilla marada.

Campanilla blanca, or white bellflower, is of most importance. It is a perennial, the vines sometimes obtaining the size of from two to three inches in diameter, and is generally found growing among trees and shrubs or along fences and stone walks. The height of bloom is about Christmas, for which reason it is also called the "aguinaldo blanca de la pasque," and at this season of the year it is a common sight to see almost every tree, shrub, and fence along the road one solid mass of white-aguinaldo bloom. The odd feature about this plant is its irregular blooming. It will bloom only every other day, and then, again, several days in succession. The days of blooming are always universal. One day every vine is in full bloom; the next day not a single vine is to be seen in bloom in miles of travel.

Campanilla marada, or pink bellflower, is an annual. It blooms during the months of October and November. It is found principally in western Cuba, in the region known as the "vuelta abajo," the great tobacco region; and it is the growing of tobacco that makes possible the great amount of this particular variety of the bellflower, for tobacco seed is, as a rule, always sown on virgin soil. Large tracts of land, on both mountain and coast, are cleared every year, just to grow one crop of tobacco-plants. When the plants are big enough to be transplanted they are pulled and shipped by railroad, ox-cart, or mule-train, to where the tobacco is to be grown. These tobacco-seed beds are, by the next year, and for years to come, covered by the vines of the campanilla marada, which, in western Cuba, springs up wherever the land has been cultivated.

The honey from the bellflowers, in color and flavor, is equal to alfalfa or sage. The comb built during the bellflower flow is pearly white, and when melted it produces wax as white as tallow.

CAMPECHE. See Logwood.

CANADA THISTLE (*Cardus arvensis*), though condemned by agriculturists and experiment stations, and outlawed everywhere, is a very important honey-plant in some parts of Canada. While bee-keepers, of course, will do nothing to spread it, and should do everything id their power to kill it out, yet if it *must* exist there is no wrong in getting a little something out of it, and that something is a great deal to the bee-keeper. This thistle is much like the common thistle of the central-northern States, but a little smaller, with a bluish-purple head of flowers.

The honey is of very fine quality, good color, and will rank with the best clover or

standards for pure honey allow 8 per cent to be present. New honey generally contains more sucrose than old honey. There are present in honey before heating some enzymes (unorganized ferments) which have the power to invert the sucrose. Hence on ageing, if heat has not been applied to kill this action the per cent of sucrose decreases. Sucrose on hydrolysis or inversion forms equal parts of dextrose and levulose, these latter being the predominant sugars of honey. See Sugar.

CANDIED HONEY. All liquid honey, and some comb honey, is liable to cloud and partially solidify at the approach of cold weather; that is, it assumes a granular mealy condition, somthing like moist Indian meal, and again like moist fine white granulated sugar. The granules of candied

CAMPANILLA, OR BELLFLOWER.

basswood in almost any market. It is a commercial asset to the bee-keeper only in those localities where it has come to be a pest among the farmers, who would exterminate it root and branch if they could. Our laws are now so rigid that the weed will probably never get very far in the States; and any farmer who has any regard for his own interests will stamp it out on sight.

CANE SUGAR. This is the common name applied to the sugar-sucrose. Sucrose is made from the sugar-cane and also from the sugar-beet. When derived from the beet it should go under the name of beet sugar. Sucrose is found in pure honey in amounts varying from nothing up to 8 per cent. Only in a very few cases has pure honey been found which showed the higher figures. The

honey are about the size of grains of ordinary table salt, but may be much finer with some grades of honey. Comb honey granulates to a very limited extent, and only after a much longer period, than extracted. While cold weather is much more conducive to granulation, yet in some localities, and with some honeys especially, it takes on the semi-solid form even in *warm* weather. Some honeys will candy in a month after being taken from the comb, and others will remain liquid for two years. The honey most likely to granulate is extracted alfalfa, which does so in from three to five months. Mountain sage from California remains liquid for a year or longer. Ordinary comb honey in sections, if well ripened in the hives before it is taken off, will usually remain liquid for a year. After that time, especially if it has been subjected to cold during the previous winter, there are likely to be a few scattering granules in each cell. These gradually increase in number until the comb, honey, and wax become almost one solid mass. In such condition it is fit neither for the market, the table, nor for feeding back, and should be treated by the plan we will describe presently.

IS GRANULATION A TEST OF PURITY?

In the eyes of the general public, granulated honey is not pure, many thinking it has been "sugared," either with brown or white sugar. But the very fact that it granulates solid is one of the best proofs of its purity. If honey granulates only partially, in streaks, it *may be* evidence of the fact that it has been adulterated with glucose. But even pure honey will assume this condition, while honey that is nearly two-thirds or three-quarters glucose granulates very little. Here, again, it must not be taken as positive evidence that, because honey refuses to granulate, or does so only slightly, therefore it is adulterated. The purity of any honey can usually be determined through the taste by an expert bee-keeper who has tested various grades of honey, and knows their general flavor. But here, again, even taste must not be considered an infallible test. Doubts can be removed only by referring a sample or samples to an expert chemist. See HONEY ADULTERATION.

TO PREVENT CANDYING OF HONEY.

There is no plan that will act as an absolute preventive; but by a method which we will describe, granulation can be deferred for one and possibly two years. Even after treatment, if the honey is subjected to a freezing and thawing temperature for a series of days it will be almost sure to start candying again. Continuous cold weather with the mercury slightly above zero is not as favorable as alternate cold and warm weather.

After the first few days the honey will appear slightly cloudy. This murky appearance grows more pronounced, and granulation proceeds more rapidly, until the point of solidification is reached. But there is no excuse for having honey at any time, either comb or extracted, kept in a zero or freezing temperature; for all practical purposes we can prevent honey candying for a year on the average.

There are two methods commonly in vogue to prevent honey from candying again. One is, to put it in a double boiler or vat, and gradually raise the temperature to 150 or 160 degrees Fahr., holding it at that point till all the honey is melted. It should then be put into bottles or tin cans, and sealed while hot. While this plan is very good, a much better one, in our opinion, is to melt the candied honey very slightly and keep it at a temperature of 140° Fahr., for three days. Do not let it go above 145°. The process of melting will be very slow, and a continuous slow heat so acts on the honey that it will remain liquid much longer than when the heat is applied more rapidly and raised to a higher point. It is then sealed hot, as in the other case.

For full particulars on bottling honey to keep it in a liquid condition, see EXTRACTED HONEY.

To liquefy honey in the candied state, or heat it to prevent its getting into that condition, the honey should be placed in a double boiler—that is to say, a tank with double walls, having the space between the walls filled with water. This may be placed on the stove and filled with honey. The double boiler used by the Rauchfuss brothers, of Denver, Col., is shown in the engraving on page 76, and its manner of construction will be apparent.

Where one doesn't have such a boiler, and can not afford one, he could make a very good substitute by taking a common wash-boiler. Into this put some blocks about an inch square. On these blocks place three or four tin pails, or as many as will go into the boiler. Should he have something larger than a wash-boiler it would be all the better. The honey is then filled into the tin pails. If candied solid it may be handled with a spade. Water is poured into the wash-boiler until it comes within two inches of the top of the pails. The whole is then placed on the stove, and subjected to a slow heat. When the water reaches a temperature of 160, or nearly that, let the fire be checked; the honey should not become any hotter, because it may otherwise injure the flavor as well as the color. Honey should never be brought to a boiling temperature except to kill the germs of foul brood, when all such honey should be fed back provided it has boiled at least two hours.

Mr. C. W. Dayton, of Chatsworth, Cal., has another and very simple outfit to liquefy honey. As it can be made out of materials found in any bee-keeper's yard, at very small cost, many will, perhaps, prefer it to the Rauchfuss double boiler above described.

As will be seen from the illustration, Mr. Dayton makes use of second-hand kerosene-cans, which may be purchased for five cents apiece. He cuts off the top at a convenient height, then washes out the cans thoroughly. For the purposes of liquefying he uses eight on top of an ordinary cook-stove. To keep the honey from burning he gets some band iron, $\frac{1}{4} \times \frac{1}{16}$, at some hardware store, and makes a series of hoops on which the cans are to stand while heating. Eight of them

DOUBLE BOILER FOR LIQUEFYING HONEY.

are placed together as shown; when, to conserve the heat further, a tin cover large enough to slip down over the whole is provided.

With the help of this outfit Mr. Dayton says he can melt up 200 lbs. of honey in a very short time. We should like to suggest that these cans would be more convenient to handle were he to take heavy wire, make some bails and hook them into holes punched

DAYTON'S OUTFIT FOR LIQUEFYING CAN-
DIED HONEY.

on two opposite sides He would then have a very serviceable pail at a small cost; and, when the honey was melted, he could lift it off the stove and pour it into some other receptacle from the corner of the cans. This

corner makes the finest kind of pitcher mouth, avoiding any spilling of the honey.

MELTING UP HONEY IN A CAPPING-MELTER.

Under the head of "Extractors," pages 186 and 187, we describe the use of capping-melters with a set of illustrations. This outfit is also well adapted for melting up candied honey, especially candied *comb* honey. Ordinary candied extracted will run through it very readily without any danger at all of impairing the flavor, and, what is more, it will be strained in the process. In the case of candied comb honey, the wax and honey will be very nicely separated by the device shown on page 187; in fact, when comb honey candies, we do not know what else to do with it except to run it through a capping-melter, selling the honey for what it will bring as extracted and the wax at its market price. If the capping-machine is properly handled the quality of neither the wax nor the honey will be in any wise affected, and the combined price of the two will probably exceed what one could obtain if he attempted to sell, if he could at all without melting up.

Under EXTRACTED HONEY, sub-head BOTTLING HONEY, will be found several other devices for melting up honey that might likewise be used to advantage.

CAUSE OF GRANULATION.

As already stated, the primal cause is alternating cold and warm weather. At any very cold temperature, prolonged for days, honey probably would not candy at all, but chill into a hard waxy mass, readily softening again in a warm atmosphere. As some honeys differ chemically, it may be assumed that some other cause operates to bring about the solid condition than warm and cold changes. Just what that is, we do not know; only we do know that stirring or violent agitation hastens granulation; and we also know that, if some granulated honey is mixed with ordinary liquid extracted, the latter will candy much more rapidly; for when honey *once starts* to granulate, the process goes on very rapidly, although it may take from ten days to six months for the honey to pass entirely from the liquid condition into the solid.

AIKIN'S PAPER-BAG HONEY-PACKAGE FOR CANDIED HONEY.

FREAKS OF HONEY-CANDYING.

This problem of honey-candying is very interesting. It sometimes happens that of two lots taken from the same barrel or can, and placed in two self-sealing packages, the honey in one will soon candy while in the other it will remain liquid, notwithstanding that both packages have been subjected to the same temperature and general conditions. If this happened in the case of sealed packages only we might suppose that the sealing of one package was less perfect than the other; but that the candying does not depend on the sealing altogether is shown by the fact that the two lots of honey may not be sealed at all, and yet one of them turns to a solid while the other remains liquid. It should be stated that these instances are by no means frequent; indeed, they are rare; yet they occur just often enough to excite our curiosity.

Another interesting fact is that, while honey may candy solid within six months from the time it is taken from the comb, when kept in the same cans under the same conditions for a period of two or three years a gradual change takes place, or at least has been known to do so. We have seen alfalfa honey after it had been in glass jars seven years, and were told that it had candied solid within a few months after being taken from the extracting-cans. At the time we saw it (seven years after), it was going back to the liquid condition. Some cans were almost entirely liquid, and others had streaks of candied honey reaching out like the branches of an evergreen-tree all through the package. These same jars are being watched with the expectation that the honey will ultimately turn back to the liquid state. But there is no probability that it will taste the same as before it candied. Indeed, there is every evidence to show that so far it has ungone a slight chemical change. Whether that change is due to the continued effect of light upon the granules is not known.

THE SCIENCE OF GRANULATION.

While we do not know very much as yet about the theory of honey-candying, yet we do know that, while the nectar of flowers may be, chemically, cane sugar, yet after it has been stored in the hive by the bees, and partially digested or worked over as explained under HONEY elsewhere, it is known to science as invert sugar. Ordinary honey is a combination of dextrose, levulose, and water, in approximately equal proportions. "Honey candies upon standing," says Dr. Headden. of the Colorado Experiment Station at Fort Collins, "because of the ability of its dextrose to assume a crystalline form much more readily than the levulose." At the Colorado State bee-keepers' convention, he showed samples of free dextrose and levulose. The former looked like very nice light-colored brown sugar; the latter appeared like a cheap grade of dark-colored molasses. The doctor went on to explain that, if candied honey were subjected to a sufficient pressure, the greater portion of the levulose could be obtained, leaving the solid mass largely dextrose. The levulose of honey candies slightly, but is very different in appearance from its dextrose constituent.

HOW TO GET CANDIED HONEY OUT OF BROOD-COMBS AND YET SAVE BOTH THE COMB AND THE HONEY.

Where honey candies at all in brood-combs, it will usually be only partially. After uncapping, M. M. Baldridge, of St. Charles, Ill., recommends placing all such combs in the extractor, and throwing out any portion of the honey remaining liquid. He next lays the combs in the bottom of a clean wash-boiler, and, from an elevated dipper pours water slowly into the cells. He then turns the comb over and treats the other side the same way. As fast as the combs are splashed with water he places them

in a hive or super. After they have all been doused he takes them out and sets them over strong colonies. He says the bees, by aid of the water liquefy the whole mass, clean the combs, and save both the combs and honey.

Candied comb honey in sections can scarcely be treated in this way, as it would be impracticable to uncap the cells. These should be treated in a capping-melter, as directed a couple of pages back.

HOW TO MARKET CANDIED HONEY.

Some years ago attempts were made to put up candied honey in small packages for retail purposes; but it was not until the year 1901 that any real progress was made. At that time R. C. Aikin, of Loveland, Colo., began to put up his honey in cheap lard-pails. He allowed it to candy, and then sold it direct to consumers. The packages being cheap he could afford to put

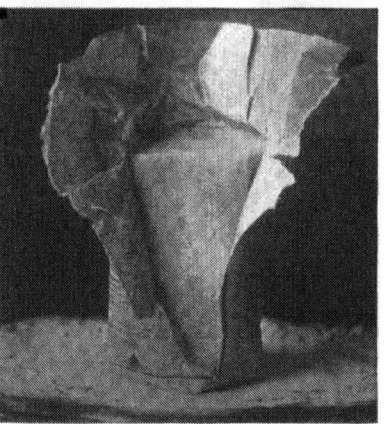

AIKIN'S PAPER-BAG PACKAGE DISSECTED FOR THE TABLE.

the honey on the market at a price that would compete with ordinary sugar. A little later on he conceived the idea of using stout paraffine-paper bags instead of pails, and has made a complete success of it.

Alfalfa honey in Colorado is well known to granulate very rapidly. As soon as the graining begins to show he draws the honey off into the bags, and allows them to stand in a cool place, when it soon candies. Illustrations on the previous page show the style of the bag after it has been filled and the top edges folded down. The honey readily candies into solid bricks, and will stand all kinds of rough treatment. The only expense is for bags, which can be bought of supply-dealers, in 2-lb. size, for $7.00 per 1000, and other sizes in proportion. It was thought for a time that the Eastern clover and basswood honeys would not candy solid enough when put up in this shape; but experience shows that they can be handled in that package as well as alfalfa, providing they are already graining when the bags are being filled, or if a little old candied honey is mixed in to expedite the process. *This is*

CANDIED HONEY IN OYSTER-PAILS.

Another package, somewhat similar to the Aikin bag, is the ordinary oyster-pail. When honey begins to granulate it can be drawn

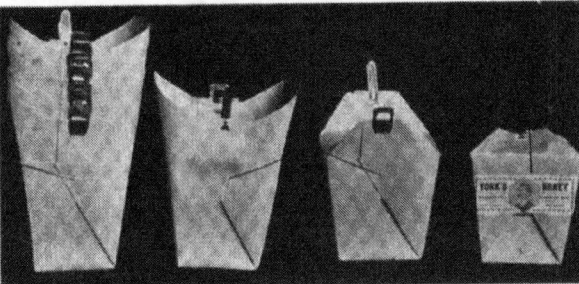

SQUARE OYSTER-PAILS FOR CANDIED HONEY.

off into pails of proper sizes, the covers put on, and the honey allowed to stand. In the course of two or three weeks in cool weather it should become quite solid; but it should be remembered that at an extremely cold temperature honey will not candy; but does so readily during alternately warm and cool weather. Oyster-pails have the advantage that bee-keepers can buy them at any grocery, and they are almost as cheap as the Aikin paper bags. They have the merit, also, that honey can be sold in them in a practically liquid condition without fear of leaking. They can also be handled quite roughly. If the honey should candy, all the better.

CUTTING CANDIED HONEY INTO BRICKS.

But honey in 60-lb. square cans that is candied solid requires a good deal of treatment before it can be gotten out, put into bags, and candied again. The cans must be first immersed in a boiler of water

ROUND OYSTER - PAILS FILLED WITH CANDIED HONEY.

very important in the case of honey intended to candy in bags or pails.

The smaller illustration in the preceeding page shows how the paper can be peeled off, leaving a nice solid brick of honey. On each paper package are printed directions for liquefying, reading like this:

The candied condition of this honey is proof of its purity. If preferred liquid. put it into a pail, and the pail into warm water, but not hotter than you can hold your hand in. NEVER LET IT BOIL, for boiling spoils the honey flavor. To remove the bag, cut from top to bottom, then peel it AROUND.

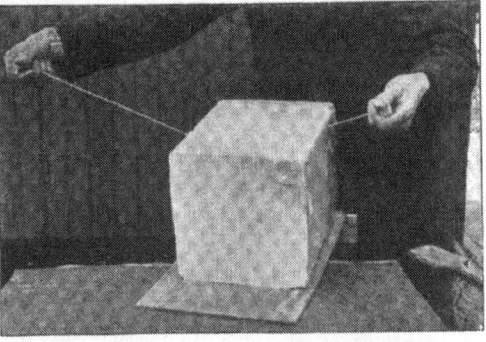

SLAB OF HONEY NEARLY CUT THROUGH BY WIRE.

about 160°, and kept there for hours at a time, before it melts enough to be poured out. Our honey-man, Mr. Jesse A. Warren, conceived the plan of stripping the tin away from the honey within, leaving it in the form of a solid cake. With a pair of snips he cuts off the top and bottom of the can, then slits it down at one corner. He next takes a strand of steel wire, attaching a

SLAB OF HONEY CUT OFF.

handle to each end and slips it under the cake of honey about two inches. The wire is then folded around the cake, the two ends crossed, and with a handle in each hand the operator draws slowly, sinking the wire gradually into the cake from all four sides, until continuous pulling causes it to pass clear through. A thin-bladed knife is now inserted in the slit where the wire entered, and slabs off a chunk like that shown in the next plate. Other pieces are slabbed off in like manner. These are then cut up into bricks, using the same general plan — bricks all the way from 5 oz. up to 2 lbs. They are wrapped in paraffine paper, on which are general directions explaining how to liquefy.

CUTTING CANDIED HONEY WITH A MACHINE.

The plan just described answers a very good purpose where only a very small quantity of candied honey is to be cut up. A far better apparatus is the ordinary butter-cutter shown in the accompanying illustration, and sold by the Cleveland Galvanizing Works, Cleveland. The same thing, or something like it, could be obtained of any dealer in dairy supplies.

This butter-cutter, as will be seen by the illustration, employs the same principle — a wire drawn taut for cutting butter. Since butter has about the same consistency as hard-candied honey, the same machine will slice up a cake of candied honey in uniform bricks, and do it more quickly and neatly than can possibly be done with a single strand by hand in the manner explained.

In using the machine, care should be taken not to crowd the frame holding the strands of wire too fast as it is a job, that can not be rushed without danger of breaking the wires. A gentle continuous pressure is what is required.

For the perpendicular cuts a couple of heavy weights are applied in such a way that, after the cake of honey is put in place, the horizontal frame and its wires gradually work their way through the mass. When the cake is cut the other way on the horizontal line, the operator takes hold of the gate, as it were, pulling gently.

All that then remains is to take a thin-bladed knife, pick up each brick and lay it on a piece of paraffine paper. The brick is then neatly wrapped, when it is slipped inside of a special carton made just large enough to receive it. The carton is then covered with another wrapper, neatly let-

BUTTER-CUTTER FOR CUTTING CANDIED HONEY INTO BRICKS.

tered in gold, and containing directions how to liquefy the honey when desired. As a rule, the consumer is advised to use the honey in the candied form by explaining that it can be spread on bread like so much butter.

Our people have found it advantageous to adopt the 1¼-lb. brick or 48 to the 60-lb. cake from the square can. It sells in our market from 25 to 30 cents retail, thus making a good margin on 10-cent honey.

CAUTION.

Do not attempt to cut the tin off from the can of candied honey unless the honey is very solid. If it is slightly mushy there will

MACHINE FOR CUTTING CANDIED HONEY INTO BRICKS.

be trouble. The mass of candied honey will squash out of shape, and run all over every thing. There is no use in trying to cut up honey like this into bricks. It should either be melted or put into oyster-pails, where the process of solidifying can be completed. It may be questioned whether it pays to cut off square cans and take the honey in a solid chunk; but it enables one to fill rush orders for candied honey on short notice. Second-hand cans are worth only a few cents; whereas to melt the honey out and re-candy costs fuel and time.

GENERAL REMARKS ON HOW TO MAKE HONEY CANDY QUICKLY.

As we have already explained, continuous zero weather is not nearly so favorable as weather somewhere near the freezing-point, now moderating up to the thawing-point, then freezing, then thawing, etc. When the weather remains continuously cold, set the honey out in pails or bags in a room where the temperature goes a little below freezing, leaving it for a day or two, then bringing it into a warm room. After it is thoroughly

warmed up, put it into the cold room again, and so continue with changes of temperature. Stir the honey occasionally, and always make it a rule to have some candied honey mixed with that which you desire to bring to a solid condition, which greatly hastens the process.

EDUCATING THE PUBLIC TO CANDIED HONEY.

The question may arise whether it would be everywhere practicable to sell candied honey in any one of the forms described. It could hardly be deemed advisable to furnish buyers or commission houses knowing neither the shipper nor the real character of such honey. The packer or producer must first introduce it to his own customers — people who know him. The nature of the honey must be explained; how put up; that only the purest and best can be solidified in this manner; that it can be liquefied by putting the pail in water about as hot as the hand can bear, etc. In short the trade must be educated to it. The fact that no unripe or glucosed honey can be put up in bags or bricks will be a strong "talking-point" on the purity of the honey. When the facts *once become known*, old prejudices give way.

We have been putting up honey, both in bags and in brick form, sliced by wire, and the trade keeps so strong that we are scarcely able to supply the demand. The grocers

CANDIED BRICK HONEY, WRAPPED AND READY FOR MARKET.

have actually come after it. One of our neighbors buys the honey, slices it up with a wire, and wraps it in paper. By so doing he says he more than doubles his money. His customers buy the honey cheaper: he is pleased and they are pleased.

A short time ago we cut up some brick honey with a wire into packages weighing 5 ounces. These sold for a nickel. They went off so fast we could not supply the demand. For the sake of experiment we cut up one 60-lb. can of candied honey into 160 cubes. The honey cost 6¼ cents per pound. We re-tailed these cubes at 5 cents each, or 13½ cents a pound—doubling on our money.

After the trade gets educated to buying honey in this form no effort at all is neces-sary to sell it. The cost of the package is practically nothing, and all trouble from the honey candying again is overcome, because the trade has been educated to know that such honey is the pure article.

The time may come when candied honey will be known on the market as a common article of commerce; because when the pub-lic gener lly understands that such honey *must be of the best quality, and absolutely pure,* it will sell without any hesitation.

CANDY FOR BEES. There is just one kind of candy that is used universally by bee-keepers for queen-cages. While excel. lent for this purpose it should not be used as winter food unless in pans, where, if it be-comes soft, it will not run down and kill the bees.

It is none other than what is popularly termed the "Good" candy, after I. R. Good. of Nappanee, Indiana, who introduced it into this country. It was, however, first made by a German named Scholz, many years before. See "Langstroth on the Honey-bee," p. 274, 1875 edition. By Europeans it is, therefore, called the Scholz candy.

HOW TO MAKE IT.

Make a stiff dough with first quality of extracted honey and powdered cane sugar. Do not use beet sugar. These were all the directions given at first; but it would seem that, from the difference in results, more specific instructions are nec-essary. Mr. J. D. Fooshe (or, rather, his wife, who does it for him) has been very successful in making the candy. Their method is as follows: 'Take good thick hon-ey and heat (not boil) until it becomes very thin; then stir in pulverized white sugar.* After stirring in all the honey will absorb, take out the mixture and thoroughly

* Confectioners' sugar — a grade of pulverized sugar—will not answer, as it generally contains starch. While such sugar is all right for frosting for cakes it is death to bees. Be sure the sugar is pure cane—not beet.

knead it with the hands. The kneading makes it more pliable and soft, so it will absorb, or. rather, take up, more sugar. For summer use it should be worked, mixing in more sugar until the dough is too stiff to work readily, when it should be allowed to stand a day or two; if then so soft as to run, a little more sugar should be kneaded in. Much will depend upon the season of the year. More sugar is required in proportion to the honey in warm or hot weather than for cool or cold weather. It should not be too hard in winter, nor so soft in summer as to run and daub the bees. For this rea-son the honey, before mixing, should be heated so as to be reduced to a thin liquid. In shipping bees, the main thing to look out for is to see that the candy does not run nor yet get hard. It is one of the nice points in making this candy to have it just right. Don't delude yourself with the idea that a second quality of honey will do. Al-ways use the nicest you have. We get the best results with first quality of clover ex-tracted. Sage honey, for some reason or other, has the property of rendering the candy in time as hard as a brick. and, there-fore, should not be used.

There is not very much trouble in mailing queens to Australia, if the candy can be made just right so as not to become too hard nor too soft on the journey. If it retains a mealy, moist condition, the bees will be pretty sure to go through all right. See Benton cage, under INTRODUCING.

HARD CANDY FOR WINTER AND SPRING FEEDING—HOW TO MAKE.

Into a porcelain, granite, or copper kettle (do not use iron) pour a quantity of granu-lated sugar; add a very little water, and place it on the stove. Stir just enough to make a very thick syrup, and keep stirring until the sugar is all dissolved; then cease. Heat gradually, and keep a good fire until it boils. Care will have to be taken that the mixture does not overcook. To de-termine when it has boiled enough, dip the finger into cold water, then into the boil-ing syrup, and *immediately* back into the water. When cooked enough, the film of syrup will crack on the finger as the joint is bent. If one hesitates to thrust his wet finger into boiling syrup, let him dip out a little with a spoon and drop the contents into cold water. If the residue hardens so that it is brittle, and breaks between the fingers, the kettle should be lifted off; but the finger test is the more accurate. This is what is called "cooking to a hard crack."

CARPET GRASS AND BLOSSOMS—LIFE SIZE.

At this stage, remove the syrup from the stove. It can now be poured into greased shallow tin pans, and when cooled hard it will have a crystalline rock-candy appearance if the work has been done right.

These cakes may be placed crosswise on the brood-frames and covered with old carpeting if in cool or cold weather.

Where a larger quantity of candy is to be given at a time, it is advisable to take a common brood-frame of the old Langstroth type, without any spacers on it, and lay it on a greased sheet of tin which can be obtained at any tin-shop. As the hot syrup begins to cool pour it into the frame until level full, and allow the candy to set. This may then be hung in the brood-nest like a comb of sealed stores. For winter feeding, nothing is better except sealed stores.

If preferred, stir the syrup while cooking, causing it to grain. When poured into pans, as before directed, it will be hard and white. Some prefer to have their candy made this way as it is less sticky, and therefore pleasanter to handle. But the one objection to the granulated candy is that it forms into granules; and as the bees take it up, these granules drop down on the hive-bottom to a greater or less extent, and are carried out and wasted. All things considered, we prefer hard crystalline candy.

If you don't care to make the candy yourself, place these directions before your candy-man and instruct him to heat the candy to 310° F. by his candy-thermometer.

Caution: — Whoever makes the candy should clearly understand that if the mixture is scorched, even the slightest, it will make unfit food for spring or winter feeding. When the syrup is cooked nearly enough, there is great danger of burning, and it is *then* that the greatest care should be exercised.

CANS FOR HONEY. See EXTRACTED HONEY.

CARNIOLANS.—See BEES.

CARPET GRASS. Carpet grass (*Lippia nodiflora*) is one of the best honey-plants known, but has not come to the front yet, in bee-keeping circles. In Central California it produces abundantly, and has been reported in the Bermudas, where it is the leading honey-plant, and also in the West Indies and Texas. It is known as a "sand-binder," so that, in Florida, it would be a boon for this purpose alone, but it is a splendid yielder of good honey besides. Stock will eat it, and it holds up its head when every thing else is burned up by sun heat. The term carpet grass, or, better, carpet weed, suits it admirably, for it covers the ground like a carpet. It grows only a few inches high, as might be supposed from its creeping habit. It is one of those plants which it will pay bee-keepers to study.

CATALPA (*Catalpa speciosa*), or hardy catalpa, is one of the few trees profitable to grow for lumber alone in the central portions of the United States. It is a bee-keeper's tree, and for that reason is mentioned here. While not quite equal to the black locust, either for honey or for its economic value as a timber tree, it has the merit of not being attacked by borers, as the black locust usually is, and it is now being grown to some extent as an investment by farmers in the Central States. It does not rank very high as a honey-bearer, but where extensively planted we shall doubtless hear of favorable reports later on.

There are other catalpas, but so far as known none are valuable for timber-planting; and some farmers, neglecting the difference, have lost money by investing in the other species.

The experts of the United States Department of Agriculture are of opinion after examining a number of catalpa plantations in Ohio, Indiana, Illinois, and Missouri that it will yield as large profit as any ordinary farm crop. The *net* profit is stated to be from $5.00 to $7.00 per year when properly cared for. The greatest value of the timber is for use as fence-posts, cross-ties, and telegraph-poles, the branches being used as firewood. It is not thought advisable to wait till it reaches saw-log dimensions. It requires good soil and is best grown from seed. Where a bee-keeper wishes to improve the honey-bearing flora of his locality the better course would be to grow the young trees for others to plant, selling them at a nominal figure when planted within reach of the bees in his own apiary.

Prof. W. J. Green, of the Ohio Experiment Station, who has devoted considerable study to the question of commercial culture of the hardy catalpa, has this to say:

Most seedsmen have been careless regarding the kind of seed which they sold, hence the majority of the trees which have been grown from these seeds are of the wrong kind, because the hardy catalpa does not produce as much seed, and is more difficult to procure. It is impossible, when the trees are small, to tell what they are. After they have attained some age it is possible to distinguish the different kinds. They are easily distinguished by the blossoms and seed. The station is now making considerable effort to introduce the true hardy catalpa, and we have quite a number of trees which we expect to send out to different parts of the State for the sake of experiment. We do not expect to sell the trees nor give them away, but we shall require the party to conduct an experiment to pay for the trees.

The catalpa frequently, on good soil, makes an increase in diameter of an inch a year. I saw trees in Creston a few days ago that were planted only ten years ago, and one of them was more than a foot in diameter. On ordinary soil they would not grow as fast. There are some near Wooster that are about twenty years old, not very much larger than the one mentioned at Creston. We have some on the station ground that are ten to twelve feet high, three years from planting. I know of a grove where the trees are planted eight feet apart each way, and at twenty years of age are worth on an average $1.00 per tree for posts and poles. I hope that you will plant a grove of this tree, for it is surely very valuable, and I do not know of any species of tree that will be likely to yield greater profit.—*Gleanings in Bee Culture*, March 15, 1904.

Those who intend to plant catalpa in the North should take pains to get the true seed of the *hardy* catalpa (*Catalpa speciosa*). The Southern catalpa (*Catalpa catalpa*) will not answer, neither will the Japanese (*Catalpa bignonoides*).

CATCLAW (*Acacia greggii*) or mimosa. This is quite an important honey plant or tree, rather, in Texas. It yields immense quantities of excellent honey that ranks with the best white honey of the North. While possibly it would not sell alongside of our clovers, yet in localities where it is produced it is praised very highly for table use, no honey being classed higher except that from the "guajilla," which see.

The catclaw is a bushy tree with low-spreading branches, attaining a height of anywhere from 15 to 20 feet. It derives its name from the bushy and fuzzy blossoms suggestive of the furry coat of a cat, and the peculiar kind of claws or hooks, shaped very much like the claw of a common house cat. If one tries to push through the bushes or among the branches he will conclude that, unless he "backs up," he may "remain hooked." Perhaps he will anyhow.

The illustration on the following page shows a small twig, life size. The leaves are small and in clusters while the blossoms have a cottony or downy look. One of the seed-pods, after the blossoms have been cast off, is shown at the upper left-hand corner of the plate.

The tree comes into bloom about the first of May, and yields honey for a considerable length of time before going out of bloom. In July there is a second crop.

Like the guajilla and mesquite it grows in the semi-desert regions of Texas and Arizona where it would be impossible to carry on farming without irrigation. There are vast areas in both States mentioned that will probably never be used for any thing more useful to man than catclaw, guajilla, and mesquite; so that the onward march of civilization will not displace these honey-trees with more profitable farm crops. We may reasonably conclude that catclaw will remain one of the permanent sources of honey supply, whatever we think may be the possible or probable future of the basswood of the Northern States.

I am not sure but it would pay to introduce these valuable honey-bearing trees in other semi-arid regions. It has been introduced into Southern Europe, whence large

CATCLAW LEAF, TWIG, AND BLOSSOM.—LIFE SIZE.

quantities of its flowers are exported to France and England. It is there known as mimosa.

CATNIP. (*Nepeta Cataria*). This is a near relative of GILL-OVER-THE-GROUND, which see. Quinby has said that, if he were to grow any plant exclusively for the honey it produces, that plant would be cat-

nip; and very likely he was not far from right. But as we have never yet had any definite report from a sufficient field of it to test it alone, either as to quality or quantity of the honey, we remain almost as much in the dark in regard to it as we were at the time he made the statement, many years ago. Several have cultivated it in small patches, and have reported that in a state of cultivation it apparently yielded more honey than in its wild state, for bees were found on it almost constantly, during several months in the year; yet no one, we believe, is prepared to say positively that it would pay to cultivate it for this purpose.

CAUCASIANS. See BEES.

CENTURY-PLANT (*Agave Americana*), American aloe, or maguey, is undoubtedly the most liberal yielder of nectar among the long list of American honey-plants. Unluckily for us it is limited in this country to the extreme South and Southwest, but is very common in old Mexico, where it is one of the most common and most sought-after plants in the country, being the source from which Mexicans derive their beer (pulque), and also their brandy (mescal). The sweet juice is tapped from the plant, and this is converted into liquors of varying degrees of intoxicating power. When in flower this juice ascends to the immense flower panicles, where it exudes through the nectaries, setting the bees wild with delight. It exudes so liberally it may be collected without the aid of bees at all. In addition, the agaves are liberal yielders of fine fibers, all of the sisal of commerce being collected from them; but the one here mentioned is seldom used for this purpose. The species commonly cultivated for sisal in Mexico (*Agave ixtli*) does not produce nectar at all, so far as the writer has seen. This plant is doubly interesting to a bee-keeper, because it is probably the only plant which can be cultivated in this country exclusively for the honey it will yield. It thrives on semi-arid land which can be had free, and the culture required is merely nominal, hence it promises better returns than any plant yet tried exclusively for the honey it will produce. In spite of its name it blooms as often as most other cacti, and it does not take long to grow. The long flower-stem seen in the illustration shoots up with marvelous rapidity; and when the golden-yellow flowers appear, hundreds of bees cluster on them as if they were taking syrup from a feeder. The nectar can be gathered by hand. There is a common impression that this plant takes something like a century to reach maturity; but where the climate is suitable it does not exceed ten years in any case; and once the plantation begins to flower, it keeps up its annual procession of blooms, though not from the same plant.

The most suitable localities for century plants in this country are in the vicinity of Yuma, Arizona; Needles, California; Southwestern Texas and Southern Florida.

CLIPPING QUEENS. See QUEENS.

CLOVER. Perhaps no class of honey-plants yields more or better honey than the clover family. In the northern portions of the United States we find white clover common in our pastures. It is honey from this plant which gives the name of "clover" to most of the honey bearing that name. Closely related to it is the white Dutch, which is often found on lawns in cities; in fact, it is the only white clover from which the seed can be gathered and used, large quantities being mixed with lawn-grass seed. Alsike and red clovers are coming to be more and more cultivated as fodder. Where the clovers of our pastures give way to intensive agriculture, the alsike and red clovers, and, in the western country especially, alfalfa, are taking their place.

The failing of white clover from the pasture lands has been met by rapid counter-spreading of sweet clover along the roadsides and railway tracks, and over the country generally. A few years ago this plant was scarcely known; but now it extends over the entire country.

The alfalfa, referred to under this heading elsewhere, is being introduced all over the western country. Indeed, at the present time it may be said to be the most important crop ever raised on irrigated land. In quantity and quality of its honey it comes near surpassing the white clover, which has for years carried off the honors; for any honey said to be equal to white clover receives the highest encomium.

There are other clovers, such as the crimson, which are being introduced to some extent. Sainfoin is largely grown, has somewhat the characteristics of alfalfa, and is now being introduced to some extent in this country from Europe, where it is a very important fodder-plant.

Having discussed in a general way the clovers that have any connection with bee-keeping, we will now consider the different varieties.

WHITE CLOVER (Trifolium repens).

This at one time was considered the most important source of honey in the world;

CENTURY PLANT.

and in the central and eastern States it still holds first honors in spite of the fact that intensive agriculture has crowded it out of

WHITE CLOVER.

the pasture lands in some sections, leaving it to find a foothold only in vacant lots, fence-corners, and roadsides. Unfortunately the seed of this plant can not be saved.

RED CLOVER (*Trifolium pratense*).

COMMON RED CLOVER.

The common red clover yields honey largely some seasons, but not so generally as does the white, nor do the bees work on it for as long a period. While working on red clover bees bring in small loads of a peculiar dark-green pollen. By observing this we can usually tell when they are gathering red-clover honey. Italians often do finely on red clover, while the common black bees will not even so much as notice it. The cultivation is much like that of alsike, mentioned further on: but the safest way for a beginner is to consult some good farmer in his own neighborhood, because different localities require slightly different treatment. The same will apply to saving the seed, which can hardly be done profitably without the use of a clover-huller made especially for the purpose.

PEAVINE, OR MAMMOTH CLOVER.

This is the largest kind of red clover known, as its name indicates; and it does, many seasons, furnish a very large amount of honey. As a rule, however, like the red clover mentioned above, it is seldom visited by the common bees; but nearly every season it is visited more or less by Italians; which some seasons (where very large fields are near by) store remarkably large amounts of very fine honey from this one source alone. In bloom principally throughout the months of August and September, it is a very important honey-plant. Although the hay is hardly equal to that from common red clover, it is, perhaps, the best forage-plant known to plow under. Once well started it will grow on almost any soil; and let a good stand be secured and plowed under, the ground gets in condition to furnish a fair crop of almost any thing.

ALSIKE CLOVER.

This was formerly supposed to be a hybrid, since in appearance it is so nearly intermediate between the white and red clovers; hence its name, *Trifolium hybridum*, Linn. It is now known to be a distinct species. While it yields fully as much honey as the red, the petals are so short that bees find no difficulty in reaching it. If you imagine a large head of white clover, with extremities of the petals tipped a beautiful pink—equal in beauty to a dahlia if they were not so common—you will have a very good idea of the alsike. The leaf is much like that of other clovers, except that, in color, it is a soft clean bright green, without the spots of down that are seen on the white and red clovers.

If alsike clover came into bloom at a season when bees could get little else, as buckwheat does, we would place it, instead of buckwheat, first on the list of plants for artificial pasturage.* Where white clover does not grow spontaneously, alsike is undoubtedly, ahead of every thing else now known. It not only produces honey in large quantities, but the quality is not excelled by any thing known in the world. It is true, many people prefer basswood, mountain sage, and other aromatic flavors, at first taste; but we

*If alsike is cut, or even pastured off, just before coming into bloom, it will blossom again, just after white clover is gone, and give a crop of clover honey just when we most need it. One of our leading honey-men says this fact alone, learned at a convention, has been worth more than $50.00 to him.

PEAVINE, OR MAMMOTH RED CLOVER.—LIFE SIZE.

believe every one tires of these after a time, while clover stands almost alone, as the great staple for every-day use, with our "bread and butter."

CULTIVATION, AND SOWING THE SEED.

The cultivation is so much like that of red clover that what applies to one will do for the other. The seed of alsike is much smaller and less quantity is required; the general rule being four pounds to the acre. As it blossoms only the second year, or very sparingly the first, with ordinary cultivation it can be sown almost any time, and, in fact, it is often sown on wheat on the snow in March. In this way we can see just how evenly we are getting it on the ground. The farmers near us who furnish the finest seed say they have the best success with that sown with oats in the spring. Although alsike will produce some honey with almost any cultivation, it is important to have the ground nicely prepared, if we wish to get large yields of either hay or honey. On good mellow ground, finely pulverized, we may get a growth of 3 ft. in height, and a profusion of highly colored blossoms that will astonish one who has never seen such a sight; especially when the field is roaring with the hum of busy Italians. Such heavy growth being liable to lodge badly during wet weather, it may be well to sow a sprinkling of timothy seed with it. When put in early, good soil sometimes produces considerable bloom the first season, but not much is to be expected until the second year, when it is at its height. It will continue to yield years afterward to a greater or less extent, for it seems to cling to the soil. It may be sown in the spring on fall wheat; but where timothy has been sown with the wheat in the fall previous, it is apt, on some soils, to choke out the alsike. Apparently, even one sowing will go a long way.

SAVING THE HAY.

Raised for hay and honey, without any reference to saving the seed, it gives at least two good crops every season; in this case it is cut when in full bloom. In our locality it usually blooms the last of June, and sometimes furnishes considerable honey before the white clover is out. The hay is admitted by all to be equal to any of the grasses or clovers in use, while pasturage, after the clover is cut, is most excellent for all kinds of stock.

Its value for milch cows is shown by the following, taken from *Gleanings in Bee Culture*, Vol. XIII., page 161:

AS A FORAGE-PLANT

it has no superior, producing a large flow of very rich milk. June 15th, when I shut the stock out of the alsike, I allowed them to run in a field of red clover that was just coming into blossom, and at the end of the third day the five cows had shrunk their milk to the amount of 9 quarts to the milking. Then, in October, to test it further for feed, as there was quite a growth of leaves on the ground I again allowed the cows in the field. You may imagine my surprise when I found, at the end of a week, they had made a gain of 10 quarts to the milking.

  Millington, Mich.   M. D. YORK.

SAVING THE SEED.

The seed is always saved from the first crop of blossoms, and it should be allowed to stand about two weeks longer than when cut for hay. If you wish to get a good price for your seed, it must be very nicely cleaned. It is thrashed out with a clover-huller, made expressly for clover seed, and then cleaned with a fanning-mill with appropriate sieves. Timothy seed is very nearly the same size, making it difficult to remove it all, unless by a fanning-mill having the proper blast arrangement. As the alsike weighs 60 lbs. to the bushel, and timothy only 45, there is no great difficulty in doing it effectually.

We need scarcely add, that whoever raises seed for sale should exercise the most scrupulous care to avoid sending out foul seeds of any kind; and where Canada thistles or weeds of that class prevail, we would, under no circumstances, think of raising seed to be sent all over the land. If they are in your neighborhood, raise hay and honey, and let seed be furnished by some one who is differently situated.

PROFIT OF THE CROP.

The seed has for a number of years sold for from $5.50 to $8.00 per bushel, and the average yield of seed is about four bushels per acre, 60 lbs. being reckoned as a bushel. It retails for 15 to 18 cents per pound. See CLOVER.

The following, taken from *The Farmer*, of St. Paul, Minn., not only shows what profit may be realized in raising alsike, but is another proof of its value as a hay crop. The reader will observe that the writer is in no way interested in bees.

WILL IT PAY FARMERS TO RAISE ALSIKE WITHOUT ANY REFERENCE TO BEE-KEEPING AT ALL?

About 20 years ago I bought my first alsike-clover seed, and sowed it alone on the south side of a hill. The season was dry, and it grew only about a foot high; and as it was said the first crop produced the seed, I cut it for seed and felt disappointed at getting so little that I was ready to pronounce it a humbug, and plowed it up the same fall. Some years afterward I saw a bushel of seed at the Dane

County Fair, at Madison. I inquired of the owner, Mr. Woodward, how he liked it, and if it was a profitable crop. He said he got four bushels of seed per acre, and sold it at $10. per bushel; that the hay, after being hulled, was better than the best red-clover hay, and that his cattle ate it in preference to any other hay. I bought two bushels of the seed and sowed about one bushel to twelve acres, mixing one-third timothy, by measure, where I wanted it for pasture or hay, and about the same quantity of pure alsike where I wanted it for seed. It does not raise seed the same year it is sown, but, like red clover, the next year. I have sown it with wheat, barley, and oats. It does best with spring wheat or barley.

I hulled 110 bushels this year from 20 acres. I expect to get $7.00 per bushel, and I have at least 25 tons of good hay, after hulling, worth enough to pay all expenses of cutting and hulling. Some years ago I sold my whole crop on the Board of Trade in Chicago for $11.00 per bushel.

Mr. George Harding, of Waukesha, a breeder of Cotswold sheep and short-horn cattle, and one of Wisconsin's most wide-awake farmers, showed me a small field of one of his neighbors that he said produced seven bushels of alsike seed per acre, and that he sold it in Milwaukee for $12.00 per bushel. I have 80 acres in alsike; and so long as it pays me as well as it has done, I will sow it.

The first crop the next year after sowing is the seed crop. It can be cut for seed for several years. It is not a biennial plant like red clover, but a perennial. It has one tap root with many branches, and does not heave up by frost, like red clover, which has but one tap root.

I prefer it to red clover for several reasons. When sown with timothy it matures with it (Medium red clover matures before timothy is fit to cut.) I cut about the 10th to 15th of July; red clover should be cut (here) about the 20th of June. Alsike is not easily injured by dew or light rains after being cut. It has none of the "fuzz" that red-clover has, making it so unpleasant to handle as hay or seed. The stem is not so coarse nor so hollow, and has more branches, leaves, and blossoms. The blossom is of a pink color. Red clover must be cut when we are in the busiest time working our corn. Alsike is cut after corn work is over. This is of great advantage in a corn region.

Alsike makes a good fall pasture after the seed is cut. My stock will eat it in preference to red clover, timothy, or blue grass. Blue grass, or, as it is often called in this country, June grass, is a good early and late grass, but in midsummer it dries up; and had it not been for clover we should have been badly off for pasturage this dry year.

Dane Co., Wis.   (HON.) MATT. ANDERSON.

The next, from *Gleanings in Bee Culture*, Vol. XIV., page 327, is of so much importance in regard to raising alsike, or other honey-yielding plants, that we give it here entire:

A SUGGESTION TO BEE-KEEPERS IN REGARD TO HAVING ALSIKE RAISED BY THE FARMERS OF THEIR OWN NEIGHBORHOOD.

I have managed to supplement the natural supplies for my bees during the last five or six years as follows: I first tried sweet clover with but poor success, so I took up alsike clover, and this is the way I work:

About this time of the year I buy from 200 to 400 lbs. of best alsike clover seed in Montreal at wholesale price. This year I can get it for 12 cts., perhaps less. I expect to buy my supply next week. It will cost me ½ ct. freight, and I shall probably sell it to the farmers who are *within two miles of my apiary*, for 10 cts. per lb. At this price it is readily taken up by all who are "seeding down" land suitable for alsike, as the price in the stores here is from 16 to 18 cts. Three pounds mixed with timothy will seed an acre very well, so you see I get pasturage which will last from two to five years, of the very best quality of honey, at the small cost of $7.50 for one hundred acres. I can not conceive of any plan which, with me, would be cheaper, less trouble, or that would give as quick and reliable returns. I could get a good deal of seed used by selling it at cost; but I find that taking off two or three cents per pound makes a great difference in the amount sown. As white and alsike clover are the most reliable honey-plants we have here—very rarely failing entirely—the results have been very marked and satisfactory.

To those who wish to try this plan I would say, Work up the matter personally; canvass every farmer within two miles and more in every direction from your apiary (those living more than two miles should pay cost of seed), showing them a sample of your seed, pointing out its advantages, etc. Although alsike-clover hay will not weigh so heavy as red clover, it is far sweeter and better, and all stock much prefer it to eat. One pound of seed, also, will go as far as two pounds of red clover, as the seeds are so much smaller.

Canvassing the farmers should be done at *once*, as every good farmer plans his work and buys his seed early. After you have finished canvassing, add up your orders, send to a reliable seedsman, distribute, and get pay for your seed, and your work for the season is done; but it should be repeated every season, to enlarge your "base of supply" as much as possible. Of course, you will have to wait one season before the alsike will bloom.

In localities where different apiaries are near together, if the seed is furnished under cost the parties should make up the amount of the difference *pro rata*, according to the number of colonies they have.

A WORD OF CAUTION ABOUT SOWING ALSIKE.

First, get the *very best* seed you can find. Poor seed is an abomination. Don't sow it on dry, sandy land, for alsike delights in a moist soil.

This simple plan of increasing pasturage may not be new, but I never heard it mentioned, though doubtless some have tried it.

Danville, Quebec, Can.   GEO. O. GOODHUE.

We need hardly add, that the above plan can be carried out with buckwheat, rape, and any other honey-yielding plants that are of value to farmers.

Some bee-keepers are beginning to find that it pays to furnish alsike-clover seed free of charge to their neighbors within a mile or a mile and a half of their bee-yards, because, they aver, when the seed is once in the soil the plant continues to reseed itself so it will spread all through the farming country, both to enrich the farmer, giving him a better quality of hay when mixed with other clovers and timothy, and at the same time increase the annual honey crop of the bee-keeper. One or two years after the free giving of seed, the farmers will begin to find out its value, and will then want it and be willing to pay for it. Some bee-keepers then furnish it at half price.

So excellent is the quality of the hay that many farmers grow alsike year after year, notwithstanding that red clover or peavine yields a larger tonnage, but not necessarily more milk or cheese per acre. It is in such localities that an increase of the annual honey crops is noted.

Mr. Wm. McEvoy, one of the most extensive bee-keepers of Ontario, also foul-brood inspector there, finds it profitable to furnish seed to his neighbors. He writes in *Gleanings in Bee Culture* for March 1st, Vol. XXXIV :

HOW CAN WE SECURE MORE HONEY OF THE BEST QUALITY? ALSIKE CLOVER VS. ALFALFA.

This is the all-important question, and I am well aware that nearly every one, if he answered, would say, "By increasing and moving the bees to where they can gather honey from clover." This can be done; but will the increase of bees not lead to encroaching on other bee-keepers' rights? It certainly will if the parties moving bees from place to place do not provide for their share of the pasture. Almost any locality can be made a good one by seeding down 20 acres each year for three years with alsike clover. I am going in for increasing, and starting out-apiaries in places where no bees are kept, and will supply enough alsike-clover seed to seed down 20 acres each year for three years. It will cost me only about the price of 300 lbs, of extracted honey each year; and for this little outlay I shall be immensely paid with a fine quality of the best honey. Woodburn, Ont., Can., Feb. 12, 1906.

Following the practice of Mr. McEvoy, we have for several years been furnishing alsike clover seed to farmers at half price providing that the fields where it was to be sown were within half a mile of some one of our yards. We have also furnished it free to those who would sow it in fields within a few rods of the yards.

By continuing this policy we have enormously increased the alsike-clover acreage within half a mile of our yards. Our men observed that the amount of clover honey gathered has noticeably increased, and that less feeding of sugar syrup in the fall has been found necessary. After the alsike is once introduced it will keep on self-sowing, and, what is more, the farmers will discover that it will take root where the ordinary red clovers fail to make any satisfactory showing. Whenever the ground becomes "clover-sick," or whenever there is any ground on which the ordinary red clovers do not seem

to make a satisfactory growth, the alsike will usually do nicely. Farmers all over the country are beginning to learn the value of this forage-plant, particularly when sown with timothy.

After a few years it will not be necessary to furnish seed free and at half price, for the farmer will find the crop so valuable that he will pay full price for it; but he must be educated at first by giving him a bonus.

WINTER-KILLING AND ITS EFFECT ON THE CLOVERS.

There are two kinds of winter-killing. One is known as the " heaving-out" process, by which the alternate freezing and thawing of a water-soaked soil breaks the roots of the clovers, dismembering them until there seems to be but little of them left. The other kind of winter-killing is from what might be called the dry process. In this the ground is frozen to a great depth, freezing the roots and plants solid. While it may thaw and freeze somewhat, it is claimed "that the severe cold wind blowing over the surface when the ground is not protected, if it continues for any length of time, will kill almost any clover." But on the other hand it is claimed that white clover suffers less from winter-killing than any of the clovers. Unlike the common red, peavine, and alsike, it has no great tap-root. It is essentially a vine like the strawberry, having shallow roots at frequent intervals shooting down into the ground for short distances. During the heaving process of winter-killing, the white clovers are lifted up and down, and apparently are but little harmed by the process except in cases where there is very severe cold without snow that attacks root and branch alike.

THE EFFECT OF DROUTH AND WINTER SNOWS ON THE CLOVERS.

One authority says the drier it is in the fall, up to a certain limit, and the more prolonged, the more the root system is strengthened and the more it grows. If this drouth is followed by winter or spring rains, plants will grow amazingly.

Nearly all the writers agree that clover has freaks of yielding enormously some years and failing almost entirely in others. Some of them assert that a drouth in the fall is not hurtful, but beneficial, providing *other conditions that follow* are favorable. Others assert that a severe drouth in the fall is invariably followed by a failure of clover honey the following year, and there is considerable proof to support the statement. All acknowledge that a drouth may be so severe that the clover may be killed and is killed.

Some years ago a prominent writer made the positive prediction that we could depend on a crop of honey from clover if we only have deep snows in winter. Referring to this, one bee-keeper says, in the winter of 1907 there was comparatively little snow, and yet there was a bumper crop in the summer of 1908; and then he adds, " As an actual fact, the amount of clover honey is not measured by the quantity of bloom; for I have seen the fields white with an abundance of it, but only a fair crop. I can remember one year when we had a great scarcity of bloom, and yet we had a good crop of clover honey. I have also seen fields white with clover, but no honey." He then goes on to say that he has seen the clover parched by drouth in June—not a blossom in sight, and, at the very time of year when there should be bloom if ever. Then a series of soaking rains came on, and, presto! bloom and a crop of honey. He winds up by saying, " In the fall and latter part of the summer of 1897 or '8 we had a very dry time—not so dry as last fall, but dry enough—so dry that it was spoken of as being remarkably so. . . I had a bumper crop the following summer."

Another writer, Mr. John McLauchlan, of London, Canada, confirming the quotation just made, says :

The fall of 1899 or 1900, I forget which, was exceptionally dry in this district right through from August 15 until winter set in. This was followed by a very dry spring with very little grass of any kind until the later part of May, when a series of warm rains commenced which continued almost daily until about the 20th of June. The effect was marvelous. By the end of June the fields and roadsides were one beautiful mass of white clover and alsike, and the honey crop was the best my memory can recall.

JOHN MCLAUCHLAN.
London, Canada, Feb. 22.

Mr. E. Lamont, of New Dover, Ohio, says: " Late summer and fall drouths, as a rule, harm clovers but little. . . . I doubt if, in the long run, the conditions brought about by last year's dry spell are a damage to the bee-keepers of the white-clover districts;" and then, implying that a wet fall is too much of a good thing, he adds : " I am satisfied that a rank growth of clover at any time, except white clover, does not yield the nectar that it otherwise would. This is proven conclusively in the case of red and alsike clovers that are cut for seed, as there is never so much seed on the low ground, where the growth is rankest." And then he concludes by saying that he believes it is an advantage, in point of nectar secretion, that clovers should have an occasional setback by drouth.

SWEET CLOVER (*Melilotus alba* and *officinalis*).

Within the last few years this plant, commonly denominated a weed by town councils and by ignorant farmers, is finding its way over the entire United States. We can remember a few years ago when a plant of sweet clover was unknown around here. The first few plants that we ever saw created quite a sensation, both on the part of the bee-keeper and of the general public, because, during the time they were in bloom, they were fairly covered with bees. So far from being a noxious weed it is really a valuable forage-plant in some localities ; and while white clover, for some unaccountable reason, is not yielding as it did some years ago, *sweet* clover, a wonderful honey-plant, seems determined to make up for the loss by spreading itself from one end of the country to the other. It takes special delight in growing on waste places, even on the hardest and roughest clay, along common wagon-roads and railroads. It is scattered over the former by being carried on the wheels of wagons when the roads are muddy, and, as a consequence, the plants may be found along most of the highways of the country. Over the steam roads the rapidly moving trains, by reason of the great suction generated, gather up the seeds and drop them along their journey, with the result that the seed is scattered by the cars from one end of the country to the other : but it never occupies any good arable fields of the farmer, for it is very easily exterminated. From the very fact that it will grow in waste places where nothing else could eke out a living, we can say that it is really adding to the wealth of the country. In some localities it affords the only forage-plant that will grow, and as such is very valuable. In other localities where it grows by the roadsides and along railway tracks, it furnishes a little honey to the bees during that time of the year when no nectar can be obtained from any other source ; and if it were grown in great patches instead of in streaks a mile or a hundred miles long it would be much more important as a honey-plant; because bees do not ordinarily fly much more than one or two miles, the amount of acreage of the plant within range of their flight is very limited.

There are two kinds of sweet clover, the white and the yellow. The white is almost universal, while the yellow is seen only in occasional patches. The former is larger, stronger, and more thrifty than the yellow. The latter seems to be almost exactly the same thing, only that it is smaller, and the flowers yellow; but it has this distinct advantage, that it blooms two or three weeks earlier than the white variety.

QUALITY OF SWEET-CLOVER HONEY.

We have tasted a number of samples that came from localities where nothing but sweet clover is grown. While the color is of a slightly greenish cast, and the body good, the flavor is only fair. We should hardly consider it equal to ordinary white clover or alfalfa, yet a little of it in any honey improves the flavor. This flavor is due to an attribute known as *cumarin*, extracted from the sweet-clover plant, and used as a substitute for vanilla. Hence, when a small quantity of pure sweet-clover honey is put into other honey it gives a vanilla taste so highly prized by many.

Sweet clover is quite an important honey-plant in Utah. One of our subscribers, Mr. J. C. Swaner, has had considerable experience with this plant. In *Gleanings in Bee Culture* for Jan. 1, Vol. XVII., he writes:

Sweet clover grows here along the water-courses, moist waste places, the roadsides, and in neglected fields. It grows from six inches to as many feet in height, according to the location, and is covered with an abundance of bloom from top to bottom, yielding in most seasons an abundance of nectar, which, after being gathered and stored, produces honey of the very best quality and color. It does not generally bloom the first year; but in the second it commences about the first of July, and keeps up a continual bloom until killed by frost furnishing bees with pasturage, generally from the middle of July until the latter part of August.

Sweet clover is sometimes used for pasturage, and also for making hay, if cut when young, but it is a long way behind alfalfa for that purpose. Though it is sometimes relished by stock, very few would sow it for feeding. When eaten while green it is in a measure a cause of hoven, or bloat, in cows. If you wish good milk or butter you had better not feed it to milch cows, as it imparts a very disagreeable taste. Eaten off by stock it soon recovers, producing an abundance of bloom for the bees.

As sweet clover is a biennial it is not a very hard weed to eradicate, and seldom troubles cultivated fields, though it does sometimes seed a field; and if such field is planted to grain the following season, it will come up, and is cut off only with the reaper. Next season, if the same field be neglected, it will quite likely be covered with sweet clover, and that, too, sometimes as high as your head. But where a field is cultivated as it should be for two seasons, the clover entirely disappears. The plant requires a little moisture in the soil the first year; but after that it will grow without. I consider it, for my part, a great deal better to see a roadside lined with it than with sunflowers, etc.

Now, to sum up, sweet clover yields our main honey crop in this locality. It is our best honey; and I may say without boasting, it compares favorably with the finest grades known.

Salt Lake City, Utah.   J. C. SWANER.

SWEET CLOVER IN COLORADO.

It is remarkable that sweet clover can be made to grow where nothing else will take root. We have seen it on the alkali lands of Colorado and California—lands where nothing could exist, except, perhaps, a kind of alkali weed that is absolutely useless to either man or beast; and yet we hear how sweet clover is regarded as a noxious weed by State legislatures and township trustees. Even in Ohio, mayors are ordered to cut down along municipal roadsides all weeds, including sweet clover, and yet there is nothing so good as a soil-binder for loose lands as sweet clover. We should not be surprised if it were worth millions of dollars to railroad companies to prevent the washing away of embankments, for that is where it does best, on hard yellow clay or other soil where nothing else can grow and take root.

There are big dumps near Cleveland where refuse, cinders, and slag of every sort are thrown; but we have noticed how sweet clover seems to find its way along the edges of these dumps, and it seems to be creeping all over, making the waste land productive of at least some good.

SWEET CLOVER FOR INOCULATING SOIL.

It has been clearly demonstrated by experiments conducted in several States that sweet clover is excellent for preparing soil which requires inoculating with bacteria before it will grow satisfactorily some of the well-known clovers, notably alfalfa, which frequently refuses to grow unless this is done.

The following letter by a practical farmer in the *Rural New-Yorker* explains just how this is accomplished:

INOCULATION FOR ALFALFA.

At present I have about 15 acres of alfalfa, all of it seeded the first time, part inoculated when seeded. I have used soil from an old alfalfa-field, and that where sweet clover grows along the roadside, as it does everywhere in this locality when permitted, and I have thought I obtained the best results from the use of sweet-clover soil. I have seen sweet clover five or six feet in height growing along the road on the hardest kind of subsoil two or three feet below the surface soil. I believe the bacteria on such sweet clover to be more vigorous as a nitrogen-gatherer than that obtained from alfalfa as it is usually grown. The proper time to apply the soil to the intended alfalfa-field is after the ground is plowed and leveled, before the seed is sown. I understand a bright sunshine will kill the bacteria. It should be sown on a cloudy day, and immediately cultivated in the ground. I have always sown the soil broadcast by hand, using a pail to carry dirt in. If I had to purchase the soil, 1 think 100 pounds might do. Use more if it can be readily obtained. If taken from an alfalfa-field I should want to know that the bacteria were well developed. The bacteria will not be present to any extent in alfalfa that is manured heavily enough to supply the nitrogen requirements of the plant. In one field of alfalfa I inoculated a strip about two rods wide in the middle to find out the benefits of inoculation. The narrow strip has been a great contrast to the adjoining ground, and I am convinced that the yield was twice as great, of a better grade of hay than that which was not inoculated. There was a perfect stand on that inoculated. It was inoculated with sweet-clover soil. The field has been sown three years, and last year the yield was four tons per acre; and I believe that, if it had all been inoculated when seeded, it would have been at least six tons. There was not quite the difference this last year between that which was inoculated and that which was not, which proves it will inoculate itself in time. I have a 96 acre farm, 70 acres under plow, and sell on an average 150 hogs per year, besides lots of other stuff. —Fremont, Ind.

Land which, for some reason not easily explained, has become "clover sick," can be redeemed by the use of sweet clover by the same method. There may be exceptions to this, but, as a general statement, it is true, for there have been too many experiments to admit of doubt.

H. R. Boardman, in *Gleanings*, Vol. XXII., writes of it as follows:

AS A FORAGE-PLANT.

I once supposed, as most people do now, that sweet clover was entirely worthless as a forage-plant for stock—that nothing would eat it; but I have demonstrated to my entire satisfaction that horses, cattle, and sheep, will not only learn to eat it, but will thrive upon it, both in pasture and dried as hay, and that hogs are fond of it in the green state. I say, they *learn* to eat it, because most stock have to acquire a taste for it, not taking readily to it at first. I gave it a fair trial for pasture last summer. My horses and family cow fed upon it almost entirely during the dry part of the season. They became fat and sleek, without the help of grain or other feed. The milk and butter from the cow showed no objectionable flavor. The amount of feed furnished was something surprising. It has a habit of continually throwing out or renewing its foliage and its bloom; also, when cut or fed back, it keeps constantly fresh.

East Townsend, O. H. R. BOARDMAN.

It is now well established that cattle do *sometimes* eat sweet clover green, although some consider it objectionable as pasturage. Prof. Tracy, of the Mississippi Agricultural College, and Prof. Charles E. Thorne, of the Ohio Agricultural Experiment Station, Wooster, speak highly of it as a hay plant, but say, as do others, that stock must *learn* to eat it. Livingston's catalogue calls it "quite valuable for soiling." Its general character as a good honey-plant is

well established, and it may be well worth while to give it a thorough test. On some alkali lands of the West it is the only plant that will live and thrive.

The following, by Alva Agee, editor of the *National Stockman and Farmer*, is striking testimony to the value of sweet clover as a soil-renovator. No two men are held in higher esteem by scientific farmers in this country than Alva Agee and F. E. Dawley, both very successful farmers on their own account.

TEST SWEET CLOVER.

How many of our readers are going to test sweet clover as a soil-improver for thin land? This is a legume, making free use of the air's nitrogen and growing rank on land that is poor. Its value as a soil renovator certainly has not been appreciated. We should have more definite data on this subject. When the clover is cut early for hay, as is done in the case of alfalfa, the hay is nutritious and Hon. F. E. Dawley, of the New York Institutes, who has grown it for many years as a cover crop in an orchard, says that his cattle like the hay after it has been sweated in the mow. The ability of sweet clover to furnish a big amount of humus-making material to poor land is probably its most attractive point. There is prejudice against this plant because live stock does not graze it, as a rule, and it is a weed where not wanted, but I believe it will furnish more nitrogen and good humus to a very poor soil than any other plant we have, provided the sweet clover bacteria are present in the ground. In that respect it is like alfalfa and all other legumes.

Farmers' Bulletin No. 18, of the general government, in speaking of the value of sweet clover on poor soils, says: "As a restorative crop for yellow loam and white lime lands this plant has no superior, and for black prairie soils it has no equal."

CRIMSON CLOVER.
(*Trifolium incarnatum*).

This species, if grown largely, would certainly have one special advantage over any of the other clovers, in that it comes into bloom before any other, and very soon after apple-blossoms; in fact, it fills the gap between apple-bloom and white clover. The color of the bloom is quite distinct from that of the common red clover; in fact, it looks more like a great long tapering strawberry than any thing else. Almost every season, while ours is in bloom, people stop their teams to look at it and inquire about it; and on Decoration day sometimes they come for miles just to get huge bouquets of these great crimson blossoms that almost startle one by their beauty and brightness. In visiting other bee-keepers where they have succeeded in growing it. we found a similar report; and one who has never seen an acre of crimson clover in bloom can scarcely comprehend the beauty, not only of its gorgeous blossoms, but by the beautiful clean bright-green foliage that distinguishes it, as well as the colors of the blossoms, from any other plant.

While this variety is not exactly new, the idea that it can be sown during July or August, and yet winter over as far north as the State of Ohio, is a comparatively new discovery. In States south of the Ohio River it may be sown in September, October, and even November. In our locality we obtain excellent results by sowing it the same time we do buckwheat (for particulars see BUCKWHEAT); or it may be sown with all sorts of garden crops, especially those that are to come off soon, all through the months of July and August. With very favorable fall weather it may succeed, or partially succeed, through the month of September. Some of our best crops have been secured by broadcasting it among early corn, just before it is cultivated the last time. If you want to raise some nice turnips, without any additional expense, mix thoroughly an ounce of turnip seed with 5 pounds of crimson clover before the clover is sown. In sowing it among corn, as mentioned above, we use a broad-cast seed-sower, the operator sitting on the back of a horse so as to get him above the tops of the corn.

SOWING CRIMSON CLOVER IN THE SPRING.

As the clover is a hardy cold-weather plant, sowing it in the spring is not, so far as we can learn, a success. The trouble is, when put in in the spring, even if put in quite early, the blooming time is quite apt to come just when the weather is hot and dry; and a drouth is almost sure to cause

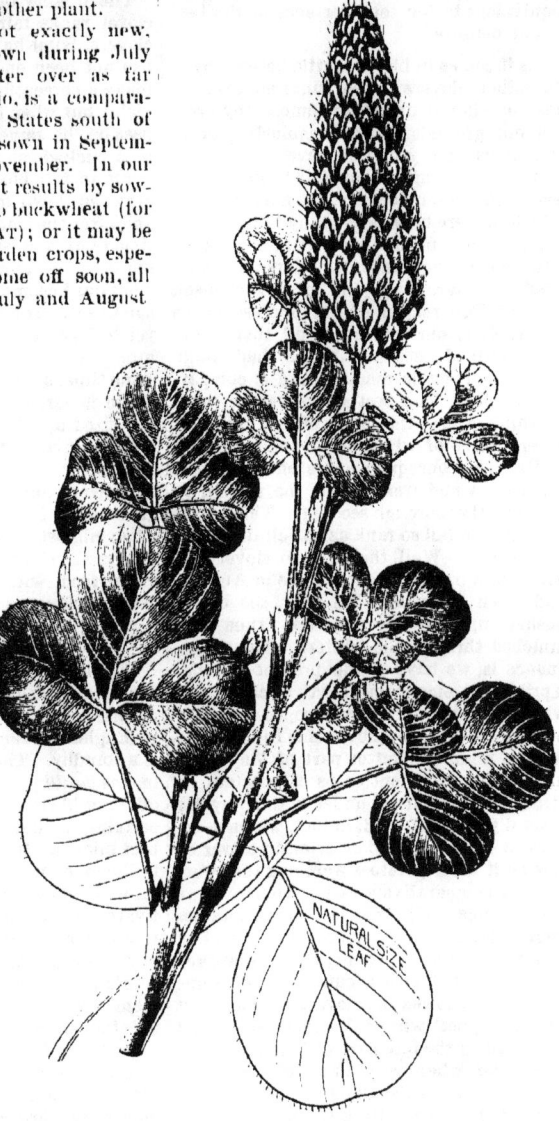

CRIMSON CLOVER.

failure. If, however, the seed is put in quite early, and the spring months happen to be cool, with plenty of rain clear into July and even August, it sometimes makes an excellent crop. When sown as above, it naturally makes a large amount of feed, equal to any of the clovers; and some of our experiment stations have estimated that a good stand plowed under while in bloom is equivalent to ten tons per acre of the best stable manure.

As it comes in bloom a little before any of the other clovers (when wintered over), it may be plowed under for almost any crop. On our grounds we sow regularly four or five acres each year, and have had no failure. It is no more than fair to state, however, that in our locality, the northern part of Ohio, there have been many failures. In fact, one of our standard writers on agriculture says thousands of dollars have been wasted by farmers trying to grow crimson clover. The reason of our success is, we think, first, our ground is all thoroughly underdrained; second, it has had large amounts of stable manure, and is comparatively rich. The best stand we ever had, we think, was in the spring of 1899. We had several acres of wheat last year that lodged badly. The consequence was, enough wheat rattled out and was left on the ground to make pretty thorough seeding. This wheat grew up the fall so rank as to fall down before winter. Well, the crimson clover was sown right on the wheat stubble in August; and when the wheat fell over, the clover pushed up through and was thus well mulched through the winter. The consequence is, we have at the present writing, April 25, a tremendous growth of clover and wheat together. This we propose to turn under as soon as the clover is in full bloom— say the middle or latter part of May. We have grown excellent crops of potatoes on crimson clover turned under in this way, for several years past; and, in fact, we have secured a splendid stand of crimson clover by sowing it after potatoes were dug that were planted comparatively early. One year we sowed crimson clover as fast as the potatoes were got out of the ground; that is, as fast as we dug fifteen or twenty rows we worked up the ground with a cutaway and Acme harrow, and sowed the clover. The first put in (in August) wintered splendidly. That put in along the fore part of September did fairly; but where we did not get the seed in until the last of September or fore part of October, it was mostly a failure. Perhaps one other reason why we succeeded is that our seed of late years has been of our own growing. It is an easy matter to grow seed; and where it is worth only $2.50 a bushel, the present price, we think the seed can be

grown profitably in our locality—that is, on good ground with the conditions mentioned.

QUALITY OF CRIMSON-CLOVER HONEY.

The quality of the honey from crimson clover ranks fairly with that of any of the clovers. Some have called it superior. There has not been enough of it in our locality to make a perceptible difference in the honey-yield; but when in bloom there are as many bees on the same area as we ever saw, even in a buckwheat-field. As we plow it under while in full bloom, the bees are gradually crowded down to the last heads standing; and after the last head goes under, for some time there will be quite a lot of bees swarming over the ground, apparently wondering what has become of their abundant pasturage in so short a space of time. We have as yet had no reports, to our knowledge, from hundreds of acres or more in blossom at the same time, as is often the case with alfalfa, white clover, and sometimes red clover. A fair-sized apiary needs many acres of any plant to give a good yield of honey.

Another great advantage it has over almost everything else for poultry is that it is green and luxuriant through the winter when almost every other plant is killed by the frost. If you want to give your poultry green feed, with but little trouble, get in crimson clover as soon as a crop is harvested.

SAINFOIN CLOVER (Onobrychis sativa).

This excellent farm crop, has been grown for ages in Europe, and at the present day is raised very extensively, more particularly in England, France, and Belgium, where it is a standby. The name "sanfoin" literally means *healthy hay*, presumably because it does not bloat animals to which it is fed. It certainly makes fine hay—possibly the very best known. It also produces choice honey in liberal quantity—the honey almost identical with white-clover honey. Grown and cultivated very much as alfalfa is with us it has this difference—it is not suited to a semiarid country. It has been grown quite successfully at the Ottawa, Ontario, experiment station, and throughout all Ontario. Sainfoin does not yield as much hay as alfalfa, being finer in the vine, and not so tall. It commences to bloom shortly after fruit-blossoms fall, and stays in bloom long enough to allow bees ample time to gather a crop. The blossoms do not come all together, but in succession, hence it is not practical to cut it just before blooming time, as is now done with alfalfa. It would seem to be a grand crop for those who raise

fruit-blossoms fall, and stays in bloom long enough to allow the bees ample time to gather a crop. The blossoms do not come all together, but in a succession, hence it would not be practical to cut it just before blooming, as is now done with alfalfa. It would seem to be a grand crop for those who raise fine horses and cattle, also poultrymen who feed cut clover. It is not likely it will ever yield so large a crop as alfalfa, but in every other respect it is probably superior.

PIN CLOVER, OR ALFILARILA.

Pin clover, or alfilarila (*Erodium cicutarium*), is one of the leading honey and pollen yielders of California and Arizona. It is regarded as an excellent forage-plant by stockmen, quite equal in feeding value to alfalfa, and probably more palatable, because much less woody in character An analysis by the chemist of the Arizona Experiment Station shows it is quite equal to any clover for feeding purposes. It is being rapidly spread by the cattle in the extreme Southwest, for it is easily disseminated, and requires no particular cultivation. In this respect it resembles sweet clover; but animals do not have to be educated to eating it; on the contrary, they are fond of it from the start. As a honey and pollen plant it ranks very high, both as regards quantity and quality.

For the consideration of alfalfa, also a clover, see ALFALFA.

COLOR OF HONEY. See HONEY, COLOR OF.

COMB FOUNDATION. This is just what the term signifies—a base, midrib, or foundation, of the honey-comb. If we take a piece of comb and slice it down on both sides, nearly to the bottom of the cells, we get what is practically comb foundation.

The article originally consisted of nothing but the midrib, without any walls; but very soon after, there were added walls to stiffen and strengthen the sheet and to serve as the beginning of the cells.

Since the introduction of foundation, within the past few years, many difficult points have been solved completely; such as how to insure straight combs, how to insure all worker-comb or all drone-comb, as the case may be, and how to furnish the bees with the wax they need without being compelled to secrete it by the consumption of honey.

MACHINES FOR MAKING FOUNDATION.

There are two different and distinct classes of machines for doing this work.

One consists primarily of two flat plates, or dies,* operated by a press. The other is made up of a pair of rolls having embossed

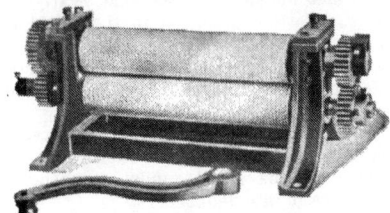

TEN-INCH FOUNDATION-MILL.

surfaces, and so adjusted, one above the other, that the die faces will mesh together. Through these the thin sheets of wax are run like clothes through a wringer. The first foundation-machines put out were presses with flat dies; but it was soon discovered that, in order to turn out foundation in a wholesale way, it would have to be

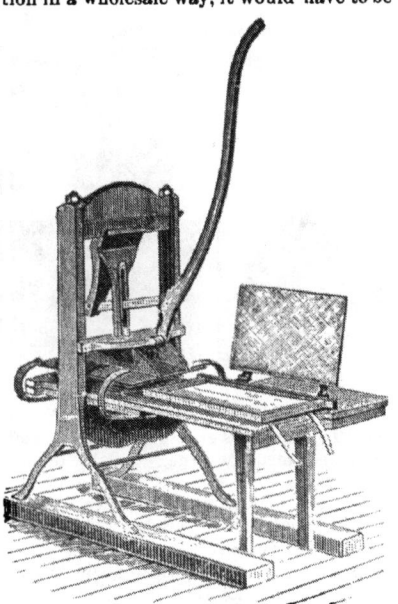

GIVEN FOUNDATION-PRESS.

done by means of rolls, for then the wax could be rolled out in continuous or long sheets, and the cost of production material-

*There is a machine sold in Germany that uses flat dies without a press. The dies are hinged together and open like a book. Hot melted wax is poured on the lower die, when the other die is brought down on to it like the closing of a book, before the wax cools. The resultant product is very crude compared with that made off from rollers or a good press.

ly reduced. While it is probable that the flat dies will make a more perfect foundation, the cost of making by means of them is so enormously increased that nearly all the foundation produced in the world is made on rolls. The best press that has been so far made is the Given; but it is not now offered for sale, and rolls are used almost exclusively.

The making of foundation is almost a trade by itself. As full directions are prepared by the makers of foundation-machines I will not go into details here.

FOUNDATION AND ITS ECONOMIC USES.

Comb foundation may be divided into two general classes: That designed for the brood-chamber and that for the surplus-apartment. Each of these general classes is subdivided still further. For instance, we have what we call "thin super," running 10 to 11 square feet to the pound; "extra thin," 12 to 13; "light brood," used only in the brood-nest,

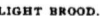

HEAVY AND MEDIUM BROOD. LIGHT BROOD.

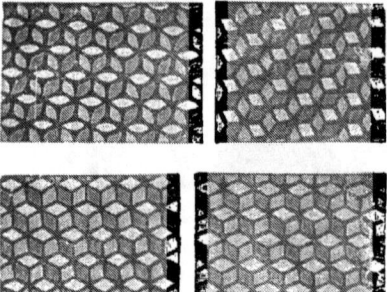

THIN SUPER. EXTRA-THIN SUPER.

running 8 to 9 feet; "medium brood," 7 to 8 feet. Thin super is generally used for sections, and medium brood for the brood-frames.

The four illustrations shown above represent the different grades. The medium has what is called the round cell. This foundation is generally used for the brood-nest, because of its tendency to resist sag while the bees are drawing it out into comb; stronger, because there is more wax in the corners of the hexagons. It has been found that bees will utilize all this wax in the walls, and draw it out into cells. The more wax we can give them in the wall, the quicker will they draw it out into comb. The light brood, running 8 to 9 feet to the pound, has what is called the regular hexagonal cell-wall. As will be seen by comparison of il-

lustrations, there is less of wax in the wall, and less strength to the sheet. On this account it is not recommended that light brood foundation be put into brood-frames that are not wired. The thin super has lighter wall still than the light brood; and the extra-thin super lighter walls still.

The ordinary thin super is generally preferred because the bees are less inclined to gnaw it down; and when they do begin work on it they draw it out more readily. The extra-thin is preferred by some because it is believed it makes less midrib, or what one or two have termed " gob, " in comb honey. When too heavy a foundation is used in the sections, especially when full sheets are used, the resulting comb honey, when eaten, is quite apt to show a midrib, or thickened center, and some go so far as to call it manufactured comb because they can not believe that it is as thin and friable as the comb honey they ate "on the old farm at father's." There is some truth in this, and for that reason only thin super or extra-thin should be used; and when one desires as little midrib as possible, and does not care how readily the bees may accept and work out the foundation, the extra-thin super is the one he should use.

Because of the tendency of foundation to cause midrib in comb honey, some have imagined that using a mere starter would remove the objectionable feature; because they argue that nearly all the comb would have to be natural, and it would, therefore, be delicate and friable like the old comb honey on the farm. But it has been shown in the majority of cases that the natural-built will be *store* or *drone*, the cells being larger so the bees can build them more readily. Some recent tests seem to show that natural - built *drone* comb has as much or more wax to the cubic inch than worker comb built from full sheets of thin worker foundation. If the bees, on the other hand, would make their natural comb *all worker*, then we should have a comb, the delicacy and friableness of which would be all that one could desire.

FLAT-BOTTOM FOUNDATION.

Flat-bottom foundation has been made, which some think is the best surplus foundation. It is nothing but a sheet of wax, embossed with hexagonal cells inclosing a flat base. While it makes very nice comb honey, yet the testimony of many of those who have tried it is to the effect that it is not readily accepted by the bees, and consequently valuable time is lost. We do know this much, that they remodel and rebuild the cells before drawing them out.

FASTENING FOUNDATION IN BROOD-FRAMES.

Some bee-keepers secure the foundation to the top-bar without using any stays or wires to hold the sheet in place; but the great majority seem to prefer to have all their frames wired—that is to say, strands of No. 30 wire stretched vertically or horizontally across the frame; these are then imbedded into a sheet of foundation which fills the frame. The resulting combs, therefore, are firmly

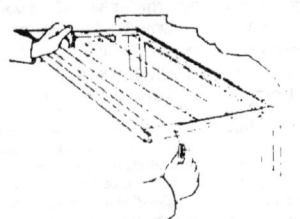

METHOD OF DRAWING UP THE WIRE PREPARATORY TO FASTENING.

anchored in place to stand the rough usage of the extractor, for shipment of colonies on them by express or freight, or hauling over rough roads to out-yards.

Most bee-keepers say that the expense of the wiring is so very slight in comparison with the great benefits secured that they

BROOD-FRAME HORIZONTALLY WIRED.

could not think of dispensing with it; and, what is of considerable importance, during the process of drawing out the foundation the wires tend to reduce materially the stretching of the wax; and such stretching, unless restrained by stays of some sort, results in elongated cells in which the queen will lay drone eggs. This one item alone, many aver, pays for the expense of wiring. The usual method is to pierce the end-bars about two inches apart, threading the wires through these holes back and forth as shown in the accompanying illustrations. The sheet of wax is then laid on wires, and imbedded with a spur tracing-wheel as shown in the opposite column.

While this is the usual method, some prefer *perpendicular* wiring, arguing that the horizontal strands are liable to sag to some extent, allowing a slight stretching of the wax. If the top-bars are thin the wires are threaded through the top and bottom bars, when the process of fastening the foundation is the same as before illustrated.

It is true that the vertical wiring permits of a thinner and therefore a cheaper grade of foundation; for when the horizontal strands are used, nothing lighter than those known as light brood should be used, running from 9 to 10 sheets, Langstroth size, to the pound.

But the difficulty in wiring perpendicularly is the thickness of the top-bars, which, according to modern practice, are from ⅝ to ⅞ thick. The only practical way to wire such frames is to use staples driven on a medial line on the under side of the top-bar; but as these interfere with the double-wedge-and-groove plan, to secure the foundation to the top-bar (described further on), the plan has not come to be very popular.

IMBEDDING THE WIRE.

Various methods of imbedding the wire have been used; but one of the simplest is the tracing-wheel to which allusion has already been made.

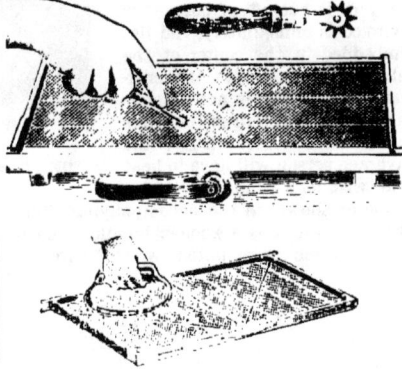

THE EASTERDAY.

A much better tool, because it has a much larger arc of contact, is the Easterday.

IMBEDDING WITH HOT WAX.

Mr. E. F. Atwater, of Meridian, Idaho, always waxes over the wire when it is imbedded with a tracing wheel. Since too much wax would be deposited along the wire if he used a spoon or regular wax-tube, and since a brush will not hold enough wax at a time to do fast work, he combines a brush and home-made spoon as shown in the following illustration.

IMBEDDING WIRE BY ELECTRICITY.

The following plan will give altogether the best results providing one is ingenious enough to handle an electric current, either from batteries or from electric-light wiring.

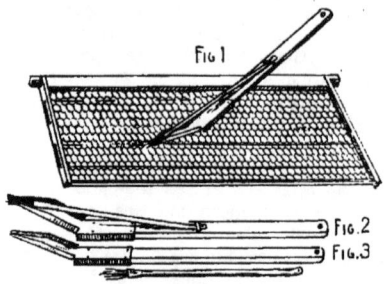

Fig 1

Fig. 2
Fig. 3

If a wire is too small to carry a given current of electricity, it will heat; and if the current is too great, the wire will melt. Taking advantage of this principle we can, with a proper amount of current, cause the wires to heat to a temperature of, say, 130 degrees Fahr., at which point they will, when properly applied, sink into the foundation; then when the current is cut off, of course the wire cools immediately, and lies imbedded in the center of the sheet of wax. With the ordinary batteries it is not practicable to heat all four of the wires at a time. Accordingly, the average person will have to heat one wire at a time, and this is done as shown in the accompanying illustration. Fig. 4 is a wooden handle, at each end of which are mounted two stiff wires. G

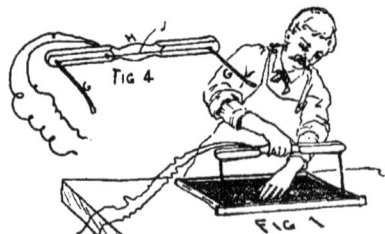

ELECTRIC IMBEDDER IN OPERATION.

G, flattened at the ends. To each of these is attached one pole of the battery. When the current is on, the points G G are pressed on

the extreme ends of one strand of wire, while the free hand presses the sheet on top of the wire until it melts its way half way through. The current is now broken by lifting up the handle H. The other four wires are in turn treated in the same way.

Where one has access to an electric-light current, by putting in sufficient resistance he can heat all four wires at a time, thus accomplishing the imbedding at one and the same operation.

THE WOODEN-SPLINT PLAN.

The scheme of a vertical support has been partially solved by the use of wooden splints, or strands of wood. Dr. Miller has used these very extensively according to the following directions which we take from his book, "Forty Years Among the Bees":

The splints should be about 1-16 inch square and about ¼ inch shorter than the inside depth of the frame. A bunch of them should be thrown into a square shallow tin pan that contains hot beeswax. They will froth up because of the moisture frying out of them. When the frothing ceases, and the splints are saturated with wax, they are ready for

IN SOME CASES WOODEN SPLINTS ARE GNAWED BY BEES

use. The frame of foundation is laid on the board as before. With a pair of pliers a splint is lifted out of the wax (kept just hot enough over a gasoline-stove), and placed upon the foundation so that the splint shall be perpendicular when the frame is hung in the hive. As fast as a splint is laid in place, an assistant immediately presses it down into the foundation with the wetted edge of a board. About 1½ inches from each end-bar is placed a splint, and between these two splints three others at equal distances. When these are built out they make beautiful combs, and the splints do not seem to be at all in the way.

A little experience will enable one to judge, when putting in the splints, how hot to keep the wax. If too hot there will be too light a coating of wax.

It must not be understood that the mere use of these splints will under any and all circumstances result in faultless combs built securely down to the bottom bar. It seems to be the natural thing for bees to leave a free passage under the comb, no matter whether the thing that comes next below the combs be the floor-board of the hive or the bottom-

bar of the frames. So if a frame be given when little storing is going on, the bees will deliberately dig
away the foundation at the bottom; and even if it
has been built down, but the cells not very fully
drawn out, they will do more or less at gnawing a
passage. To make a success the frames should be
given at a time when work goes on uninterruptedly,
until full-depth cells reach the bottom-bar.

Under some conditions the bees will gnaw
around the wooden stays, as shown by the
illustration, p. 100. This occurs more particularly when bees have not much to do; and
when they run across any thing which is
fibrous they will at such times show a disposition to remove the object.

The suggestion has been made that in no
case should the splints be allowed to project
beyond the edge of the foundation; or, better still, the sheet should reach clear to the
bottom-bar.

Other devices have been used, such as
paper imbedded in the center of the foundation; but this is very objectionable because the bees soon discover that this is a
foreign substance, and proceed to tear out
the paper bit by bit, utterly ruining the
foundation. They do not *always* do this;
but sooner or later they will; when they
have nothing else to do they will begin to
tear out the paper, imagining, perhaps, that
the fiber is a part of the silken gallery of the
moth-worm.

FASTENING FOUNDATION TO THE TOP-BARS OF BROOD-FRAMES.

After the wires have been imbedded in,
say, 100 frames, the top edge of the foundation is fastened to the top-bars, either with
the Van Deusen wax-tube or double-groove
wedge plan shown next. This makes use of
a top-bar with two grooves and a wedge.

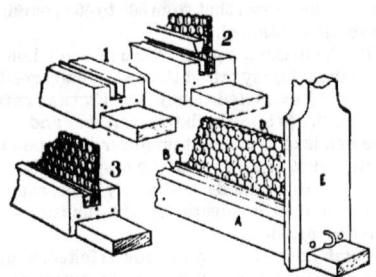

WEDGE TOP-BAR METHOD OF FASTENING FOUNDATION.

Most of the supply-factories furnish these
kinds of top-bars now because bee-keepers
generally prefer them. There is a double
groove, one of which is in the center of the

top-bar. In this groove is inserted the sheet
of foundation, as at D. The wedge-shaped
strip of wood B is then driven into the other
groove, crowding the central partition firmly
against the foundation. The foundation is
thus held firmly in place without any special
tools or the fussing with melted wax.

There are many who prefer the melted-
wax plan of fastening foundation. Where
the under side of the top-bar is plain without grooves or molded edge, this is perhaps
the best. In the case of sections using full
sheets, cut to a neat fit, it is the only
method.* The best tool for depositing a hot
stream of wax along the edge of the foundation is undoubtedly the Van Deusen wax-
tube fastener. It is simply a brass tube
half an inch in diameter, six inches long,
tapering, and at the apex a small hole. On
one side is bored another small hole which

VAN DEUSEN WAX-TUBE FASTENER.

may be opened or closed with the thumb.
When the tube is stood up in a cup of hot
wax the air will escape from the upper hole,
and the wax flow in at the other small hole
at the bottom. The thumb is closed over
the upper one; the instrument is drawn out
of the wax, and the point is then slowly
drawn along the edge of the foundation in
contact with the top-bar, leaving a fine
stream of hot wax to cement it.

Thus far we have described methods and
devices for fastening sheets of wax in brood-
frames. What follows relates to the fastening of foundation in section honey-boxes.

PARKER MACHINE FOR FASTENING START-ERS IN SECTIONS.

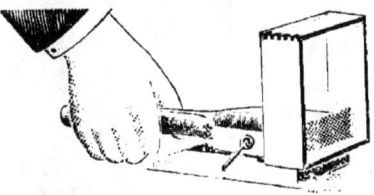

The idea is, to rub the edge of the wax
into the wood of the section. The motion of
the machine spreads the wax down, and
mashes it into the wood, as it were. It is
a very simple machine, and is used quite

*See COMB HONEY, under the discussion relating
to the use of full sheets of foundation in sections.

largely; in fact, many thousands of them have been sold. It does very nice work; but where thousands of starters are to be put in, it becomes a little tiresome on the hands, and besides is not as economical of foundation as the Daisy or Root foundation-fastener.

DAISY FOUNDATION-FASTENER.

The principle of the machine is this: A metal plate or tongue is kept heated by means of a lamp beneath. This plate, by a slight pressure of the hands while holding the foundation, is made to pass directly under and come in contact with the bottom edge of the starter. Instantly the edge of the foundation melts; the pressure of the hands being released allows the tongue or 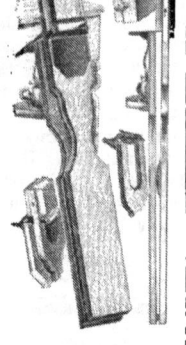 plate to withdraw, and the starter is allowed to drop on to the section, when it instantly cools and is held firm. This method of

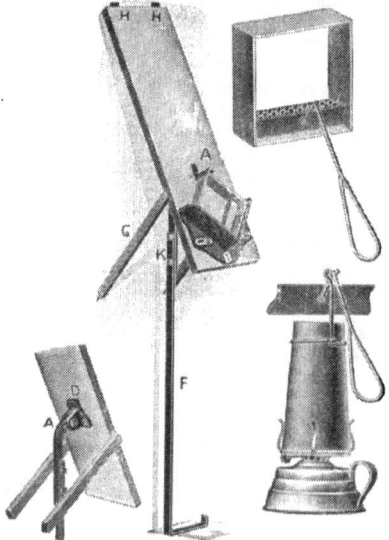

ROOT FOUNDATION-FASTENER AND SECTION-FOLDER.

fastening foundation is used very largely. Another method that seems to meet with a great deal of favor is a modification of the principles just shown; but in this case the heated plate is mounted on the end of a wire handle. The plate is heated over the lamp, then applied against the bottom edge of the foundation after it is folded and the starter is put in place. This makes the work more rapid, and, in the hands of the average person, it gives better results, for the complete outfit costs less than the others.

For a further consideration of this subject see COMB HONEY, sub-head FOUNDATION FOR SECTIONS.

COMB HONEY. No other subject (unless, perhaps, it be that of wintering) has been so much discussed and so much improved upon as the one now before us. Our forefathers, with their old straw skeps and box hives, thought they had done well when they had secured the paltry amount of ten or twenty pounds of box honey. With the mod-

ern appliances it is possible to secure, in a fair season, an average of forty or sixty pounds of section honey; and occasional reports have shown that from 300 to 400 pounds have been obtained.

By the masses, a good article of comb honey is more highly prized than an equally good article of extracted honey (see EXTRACTED HONEY). While the latter can be, and in the hands of the expert producer is, equal in body, color, and flavor to the best comb honey; yet, as extracted ordinarily runs, comb honey is a little superior in the qualities we have mentioned.

Comb honey can not be counterfeited, and, consequently, consumers are less suspicious of it. For these and other reasons, nature's sweet, in its original form, is in greater demand, and hence commands a higher price. To offset this, it also costs more to produce it, and requires, likewise, more skill and more complicated surplus arrangements to get a gilt-edged article. Years ago, all comb honey was produced in glass boxes. These were about five inches square, fifteen or sixteen inches long, glassed on both ends. They were not altogether an attractive package, and were never put upon the market without being more or less soiled with burr-combs and propolis. As they held from ten to fifteen pounds of honey each, they contained a

larger quantity than most families cared to purchase at once. To obviate these and other difficulties, what is popularly known as the "section honey-box" was invented.

It was what was wanted—a small package for comb honey. Thus was accomplished. not only the introduction of a smaller package for comb honey, but one attractive and readily marketable. The retailer was at once able to supply his customer with a small quantity of comb honey without daubing, or fussing with plates. The good housewife, in turn, had only to lay the package upon a plate, pass a common table-knife around the comb, to separate the honey from the section proper, and the honey was ready for the table, without drip.

WIDE FRAMES AND HIVE-SUPERS.

The next thing was something to hold the sections while on the hive and being filled. There was a score of different sorts of racks, frames, trays, boxes, clamps, all of which possessed some special features. It would

DOUBLE-TIER WIDE FRAME.

be impracticable to show all of these different devices; but for the sake of illustrating some principles it may be well to mention some of those that are used most largely.

What was known as the double-tier wide frame was perhaps the first device for holding sections in the hive. This consisted of a frame of the same depth and length as the ordinary brood-frame, but of the same width as the section, as shown in the illustration preceding. This was used very largely at one time; but in the course of time it was discovered that it had several objectionable features. First, a whole hiveful of them gave the bees too much capacity to start on; and, as a consequence, this discouraged them from beginning work. Second, they

DOOLITTLE'S SINGLE-TIER WIDE FRAMES.

did not permit of tiering up to any degree of advantage. Third, it was not convenient to get them out of the hive, and more inconvenient still to get the sections out of the wide frames. For these reasons wide frames, or crates holding only *one tier* of sections, were adopted.

The Doolittle surplus arrangement consists of a series of single-tier wide frames having no projections to the top-bars, although shallow wide frames have been made with such projections.

Both the single-tier and double-tier shown had tin separators nailed on one side of each wide frame; but in the arrangement shown below there is no provision for a separator. As the engraving shows, this is simply a shallow tray of the same depth as the section, plus a bee-space, and is divided off by transverse partitions—these very partitions preventing, of course, the use of separators; but those who did use this style of crate, and use it still, claim they can get along without separators; that they have no difficulty in crating for market all their honey. But the great majority of bee-keepers decidedly object to a non-separator crate, because, while one can dispense with the separators, he has to be very careful in handling the honey in putting it into the crate for market, or else there will be bruised and damaged faces to the honey. And then it is true that comb honey produced without separators is never as even and nice as separator honey. Commission men, for this reason, do not like

MOORE (OR HEDDON) CRATE.

it, and on this account the T super and other forms of separator-cases have the decided preference. If one should use a very narrow section, not wider than 1⅜-inch beeway or less, he could dispense with separators. But such sections are as yet hardly on the market. It might be a little risky to produce any considerable crop in them at the present, and consumers might not take to them.

T SUPER.

This, at one time, was one of the most popular forms of section-crates that was ever devised, and a very large number prefer it to any thing else. It is so named for the T tins that support the sections. The tins are folded in the form of a letter T

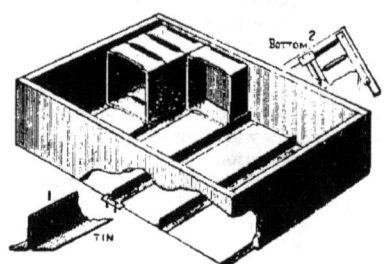

inverted, such construction making a very stiff and rigid support.

Some prefer, like Dr. Miller, to have the T tins rest loosely on a little piece of strap iron, both for convenience in filling the supers, and in emptying the same after the sections are filled. But there are others, like George E. Hilton, of Fremont, Mich., who

object to loose pieces, and prefer the super with stationary tins, the tins being nailed to the bottom inside edges of the super.

It will be noticed also that he prefers having compression—a feature which he accomplishes by means of wooden thumbscrews and a follower. There is no denying the fact that in any form of surplus arrangement the sections and separators should be squeezed together to reduce propolis accumulations. If there are open cracks or spaces between the sections the bees are sure to fill them with bee-glue.

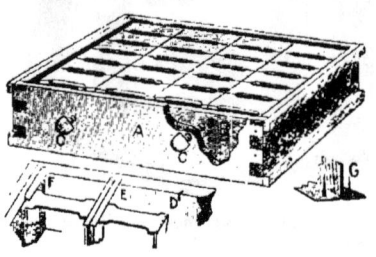

HILTON T SUPER.

With either form of T super one can use wooden separators, tin separators, or the fences described further along. The projection of the T is just high enough to support the separators at the proper point.

But the T super, perfect as it is, has its objections. If the sections are inclined to be a little out of square, or diamond-shaped, when folded, they will not be squared up in the T super unless an extra set of T tins or strips of wood are used to fill up the gaps between the rows on top. And, again, it is not practicable to alternate the several rows of sections. Sometimes, in a poor honey-flow, it is desirable to move the center row of sections to the outside, and the outside to the center. And still again, four-beeway sections, or plain sections, are not as advantageously used in these supers as in some other form which I shall presently describe.

THE J. E. HAND FORM OF SUPER

This is the one preferred by Mr. J. E. Hand, of Birmingham, Ohio, who uses plain sections and section-holders. A portion of one side of the super is removable. This is secured in position by means of the Van Deusen hive-clamps, that also bring about compression on the sections.

The objection to this form of super is that it is somewhat more expensive, is not as strong, and therefore not as durable. For further particulars concerning the J. E.

Hand system, see HIVES and also SWARM-ING.

DOV'D SUPER WITH SECTION-HOLDER.

This is the form of super that has been, perhaps, used more largely than any other. It is a sort of compromise between the

old-style wide frames and the T super. It consists of a series of section-holders that

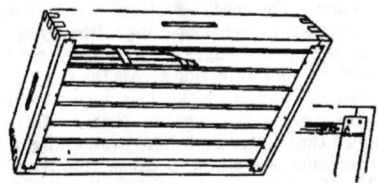

are open at the top. Each holder is supported at the end by a strip of tin nailed on the inner edge of the ends of the super, as shown in the accompanying illustration.

Four sections in each section-holder are held snugly and squarely in position with no spaces between the rows of sections as in the case of the T super. When beeway sections are used the bottom-bars of the sections are scored out to correspond with the beeways. Between each row of sections is dropped a wooden separator, as shown at D. After they are all in place, a follower-board, F, is shoved up against them, and the tightening-strip G, that is thicker one way than the other, is slipped in the narrow way between the follower and the super side, and given a quarter twist. This crowds the follower against the sections, causing compression.

This case is very popular with farmers. Four of them containing 24 sections without separators are placed on the hive. When they are filled they are taken off without removing the sections from the case, and are put on the market just as they left the hive. This is a sort of shiftless way, be-cause some sections will not be entirely filled; but it suits the farmer who has no time to do the sorting, scraping, and getting ready for market; and in some local markets this case does very well.

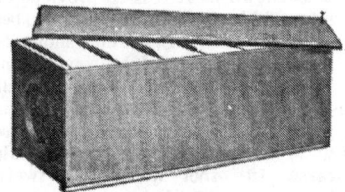

THE FENCE AND PLAIN-SECTION SYSTEM.

The sections and section-supers shown heretofore have all been of the beeway type. Brood-frames, when in hives, must be placed

a bee-space apart; so also must the sections. Almost the first honey-boxes that were introduced had the bee-space cut out of the top and bottom of the sections themselves, so that they could be placed directly in contact with each other or the separator. This kind of section continued almost up to the present, but in 1897 there was introduced a section without beeways, having plain straight edges all around. This had been used some ten or twelve years previously by various bee-keepers who found them to be in every way satisfactory. But plain sections (even width all around, without beeways) necessitate some scheme for holding them a bee-

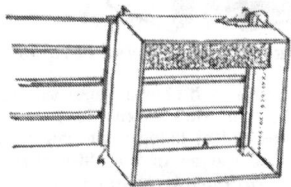

space apart while on the hive. Accordingly, a separator or fence was devised, having transverse cleats at regular intervals on both sides, binding the series of slats together—cleats so spaced as to come opposite the uprights in the sections. This will be shown more clearly in the annexed figure. It will be seen at once that the new system provides for a narrower section, and yet this same section holds as much honey as one ⅜ inch wider, because the extra width is taken up by the thickness of the cleats on the fences, as shown at A A A in previous cut or what would be in the old section two bee-ways of $\frac{3}{16}$ inch each. In the cuts shown below there are specimens of beeway sections and no-beeway, the last being generally termed plain sections. It will be seen that they save quite a little wood, and consequently take somewhat less room in shipping-cases. In other words, the twelve and twenty-four pound shipping-cases can be made somewhat smaller, because it is not necessary to have each comb bee-spaced apart in the marketing - cases, the same as while on the hive. Moreover, the plain straight edges of the new sections offer special advantages in the matter of scraping. There are no insets, often roughly cut (as in beeway sections), to work into and around with a scraping - knife. A single sweep of the knife on each of the four edges will remove the propolis or, better still, if the blade of the knife is long enough, one can scrape two edges at a time. Weight for weight, and of the same filling, a comb in a plain section looks prettier than one having beeways. The illustration on next page shows beeway sections in one shipping-case, and plain sections in the other. Compare also other cuts a few pages further on with these.

But there is one more point to be taken into consideration. The fences are made up of a series of slats having a scant bee-space between each slat; and as the cross-cleats,

ONE-PIECE V-GROOVE SECTIONS.

or posts, are ¼ inch shorter than the length of the section, the beeway is very much wider. Instead of being a narrow opening through the top as in the old section, the opening is *clear across* the top, and part way down and up each of the sides. This gives the bees much freer communication, and, in consequence, has a tendency to reduce the size of the corner holes in each section. Then there is that factor, namely, horizontal openings between each of the slats. This allows free communication from one section to another, not only *crosswise* but *lengthwise* of the super. Both theory and practice show that this results, under normal conditions, in a better filling of the boxes. A good many have already testified that they secure much better and more perfect filling of combs in plain sections than in the old style with solid separators: that the bees enter them sooner, and that in some markets better prices are secured. If the colony is not strong, the old-style super may be the better filled.

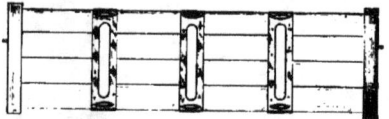

HYDE-SCHOLL SEPARATOR.

Another style of fence is shown in the accompanying engraving. It was introduced by Messrs. Hyde and Scholl, of Texas, some years ago. The special feature of it is that it provides transverse openings directly opposite the upright edges of the sections, thus affording communication across the faces of the several sections as well as across from row to row in the regular fences. It is claimed that better and more even filling of the sections is secured, because this fence makes the conditions more like those of a regular brood-comb, where there are no obstructions of any kind. The several slats are held together by strips of stamped sheet metal, having raised projections or bosses above and below the transverse openings to keep the sections a bee-space away from the slats or fence proper. There are many nice features about this fence if the expense of making can be overcome.

Under the same conditions the plain sections will be filled no better than the beeway. If there is any difference in the filling it is because the one offers special advantages in the way of freer communication; for in the ordinary old-style, with solid separators, each section, so to speak, is shut off in a little box by itself, and it has been proven that bees are disinclined to work in little compartments almost completely shut off from the rest. Open-corner sections, divided off by means of slatted separators, without cleats, ought to be and would be filled just as well as plain sections divided off by fences; for the conditions will be precisely the same, because the beeways, made part and parcel of these sections, exactly correspond to the beeways (cleats) on the fences.

But one would lose many of the advantages of plain sections if he were to adopt the open-corner boxes. They would not look, with even filling, as pretty as plain sections.

SUPERS FOR PLAIN SECTIONS.

In the main, these differ very little from the section-holder super already shown and described for the old-style sections. The section-holders themselves are the same width as the sections. Between each row of

speak, help to conserve the heat so they can draw out the comb and complete the sections on the outside as well as in the center. Both theory and practice sustain the proposition.

In the modern supers, and especially in those designed for plain sections, there are used, instead of wedges and thumbscrews, steel springs that bear against the center of the fence as well as against the two ends, as shown at B in the figure given on next page. The wedges, tightening-strips, or thumb-

SHIPPING-CASES WITH BEEWAY AND PLAIN SECTIONS.

sections in a section-holder is placed a fence, the end-posts of the fence resting upon the strip of tin nailed on the bottom inside edge of the end. There is a fence on the outside of each outside row of sections, because it was demonstrated by S. T. Pettit that a perforated divider, or what is exactly the same thing in principle, the fence, when placed between the outside rows and the super sides will result in having those outside rows of sections filled, in many instances, as well as

those in the center. The reason of this is, that it places a wall of bees on each side of the fence, between the comb honey and the super side; and these walls of bees, so to

screws, sometimes, owing to excessive dampness, cause trouble by every thing becoming swelled fast; but the springs at all times

present a yielding pressure; and, what is of considerable importance, they are not affected by propolis; at the same time they effectually close up all little air-gaps or interstices between the sections and fences.

FOUNDATION FOR SECTIONS; STARTERS V. FULL SHEETS.

In the illustrations on preceding pages, showing the supers, only narrow sheets of foundation (or starters) are shown in the sections. The expert comb - honey producer will never be content with a starter. He will buy his foundation of such size that he can cut it to suit his own individual notions. Some of our comb-honey producers cut it in nearly full sheets one-fourth of an inch narrower and half an inch shorter than the inside of the section. It is then fastened to the top as shown under the head of COMB FOUNDATION, with any one of the several styles of foundation-fasteners there shown. Others cut the sheets in the shape of a letter V; still others use half a sheet.

But the great majority of producers prefer to use two pieces—a large one secured to the top and a strip ¼ or ⅜ inch wide fastened to the bottom. The larger sheet is so cut as to reach within ¼ inch of the bottom starter when in place to allow for stretching.

During the subsequent process of drawing out, the bees will make one complete comb, the same being fastened to the top and bottom. Where only one large sheet or even a starter is put into a section, the fastening will be at the top and part way down on each side, but when the bottom starter is used in connection with a large sheet of foundation, there surely will be a fastening at the bottom as well as at the other edges. The result is a comb fastened to all four sides, one that is neater in its general filling, and, in consequence, will command a higher price; and last, but not least, a section that will stand shipping. A nice super of sections with combs not fastened at the bottom is liable to arrive at destination in

wax-tube here shown the sheet is then secured to all four sides by the stream of hot wax. See COMB FOUNDATION.

VAN DEUSEN WAX-TUBE

It has been found that very fine comb honey can be secured by this plan, the resulting sections having but few popholes. However, there are two disadvantages. For

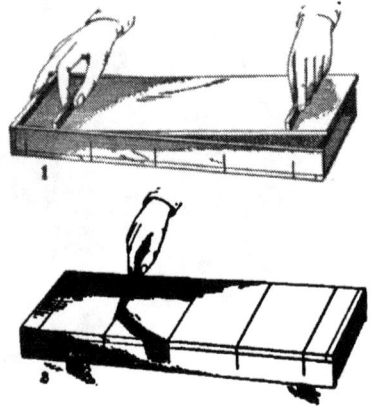

instance, some find it difficult to cut the foundation just the right size and still do the work rapidly. It can be seen at once that there must be but little variation in the size of the sheets. The best arrangement for

THE DIFFERENT METHODS OF CUTTING FOUNDATION FOR THE SECTIONS.

bad condition—many of the combs broken out; and it is, therefore, always advisable to use a bottom starter.

A few bee-keepers advise cutting the foundation so it will just neatly fill the section on all four sides. A section is then slipped over a block a little less than half its thickness so that when one of these just right-size sheets of foundation is laid on the block, the foundation will be perfectly centered in the section. With the VanDeusen

cutting the foundation that we know of is the miter-box shown above. This device can be quickly made by almost any one, the construction being plain from the illustrations. The box should be placed on a table with the saw-cuts down as in Fig. 1, and from five to twenty sheets of foundation laid in, care being taken to see that the ends are even. Then the cleated board should be put on top of the sheets of foundation, and the box turned over so that it rests on the cleats, as shown in Fig. 2. For cutting; a keen butcher knife should be used which need not be hot, if kept well lubricated with soapy water. The knife should be held at an angle as shown, and moved rapidly but slightly back and forth, cutting only on the drawing stroke. If the saw-cuts are carefully spaced and the whole box put together in a square, workmanlike manner, the sheets of foundation can be quickly and accurately cut.

Another disadvantage to the plan of fastening full sheets of foundation on all four sides is the tendency of such foundation to buckle, due to variation in temperature, etc. Mr. G. J. Yoder, of Meridan, Idaho, overcomes this buckling by fastening the full sheet of foundation only at the top and two-thirds of the way down each side. This plan has been tried quite extensively and found very successful. Mr. Yoder described his method fully in the April 1st issue of *Gleanings in Bee Culture* for the year 1908, and we herewith reproduce his directions as well as illustrations, which make it clear.

Cut a light board about three inches longer than the width of four sections, and just the width of the inside of the section. Now cut four square blocks of such a size that folded sections can slip over them and a fraction less in thickness than half the width of the section. Nail the first block 1½ inches from the end of the board, and place a section over it. Put block No. 2 with section over it, next to No. 1, and so on till all are nailed on. Make at least five or six of these forms with blocks on. Next make a trough the width of the board of the form without the section, and 2 inches deep, so the form will slip in easily to the depth of the blocks. I next melt some wax for fastening the foundation, using about one-tenth part of clean rosin, and have ready a wax-tube or teaspoon with the end bent in on both sides.

If possible, get the foundation cut by the manufacturer, so that all sheets will make a given number of uniform starters with as little waste as possible. The last three seasons I have been unable to buy starters cut just right, and so have had a loss of one-seventh of the foundation for the crop of 20,000 sections.

Put the sections on a form and spring the section-holder over them. This makes them square and tight. Place the foundation in clear to the top of the section. I prefer a ⅛ space between the lower end of the foundation and the bottom of the section, as this is just about the amount needed to take up any possible sagging, and to prevent the buckling of the foundation. Now grasp the form in such a way that the top part of the section is lowest, and apply the melted wax on the section at the edge of the foundation, turning the form so as to run the wax all around as far as wanted. If all four sides are waxed, the weather warm, and the honey coming in fast, there may be a bulge at the lower part of the section; so of late we prefer to cut the starter full size, ⅛ inch short at the bottom, and to wax the

THE YODER PLAN OF FASTENING FULL SHEETS AT THE TOP AND TWO-THIRDS THE WAY DOWN THE SIDES.

top and only two-thirds down each side. Lay this filled form down to cool, and take the next, giving the wax of the first four sections a few minutes' time to harden. Then place the form over the trough: press the tray down out of the sections and you will have the wide frame of sections, and with the foundation ready for the super without danger of buckling. One of our men filled 3000 sections in a day.

HOW TO PRODUCE COMB HONEY

A strong force of bees, of the right working age, should be in readiness just before the expected supply of nectar. It is penny wise and pound foolish to let the bees run short of stores in spring, just at the time of the year when brood-rearing should be stimulated to its utmost. If necessary, stimulative feed'ng should be practiced. If the weather is not cool, brood may be spread to advantage. This is done by inserting an empty frame of comb between one or more pairs of frames filled.* But this should not be done if there is a scant supply of bees, or if the weather is cool. If the bees need more room, as some of them undoubtedly will, then put on another story. If the colony is strong enough let them keep it, even after putting on a super of sections. If it is not strong enough take away the upper story, crowd all the frames of brood into the lower brood-

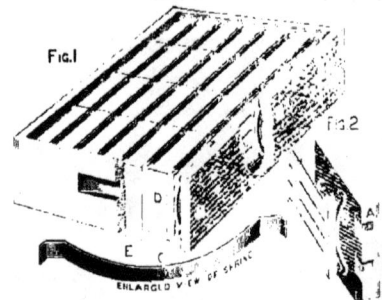

SUPER SPRINGS—HOW TO USE.

chamber, and then put on the comb-honey supers. If we can get a colony strong enough the bees will boil up into the super when it is put on.

Sometimes all the plans are brought to naught from inability to control swarming just as the bees are beginning or have begun to work on the sections. This inopportune swarming can generally be held in check by entrances on all four sides of the hive (see ENTRANCES) or by the "shake-out" or "brushing" plan spoken of under SWARMING, to which the reader is referred. He should read very carefully the means for preventing or controlling swarming before

* See SPREADING BROOD.

he goes any further with this subject, or he may lose a large part of his crop.

WHEN TO PUT ON SUPERS.

If the colony is in one story and the bees begin to come in from the field, and combs are whitened near the tops, frames fairly well filled with brood and with honey, we put on supers. If we have supers containing half-depth extracting-combs, we prefer to put these on first, even if we desire to produce comb honey, for the bees will enter them much more readily, and begin storing above. Then when they *are once well started* we raise the extracting super up and place under it a comb-honey super containing sections filled with *full sheets* of foundation. (See COMB FOUNDATION.)

The usual practice is to put the comb-honey super on at the start; but in our experience, Italians especially are loath to enter the boxes. If they *once get into the habit* of going above, they will keep it up, even if the super is changed. The extracting-super can remain on top of the same hive on which it was put in the first place, but we would put it on some other colony to give it the "upstair fever," after which it should be replaced by a comb-honey super. After a little there will be some filled extracting-supers as well as those of comb. By proceeding on this plan we have found that we can produce just about as much comb honey as we should if we put the comb-honey supers on in the first place, with the additional advantage that the extracted honey obtained is just so much clear gain.

Two of our correspondents sent to *Gleanings in Bee Culture* their method of using extracting-combs to bait the bees above. One uses a whole super of shallow extracting-combs, and the other uses both sections and extracting-combs in the same super. We have thought best to give them both here. The first mentioned writes:

I have been, for several years, very much interested in trying and comparing different methods of handling bees for comb honey. I have been in the business for eight years, and have had fair success. For the first five years I tried a different method each year. Three years ago I tried an experiment that succeeded so well I have followed it up, and have in a measure overcome the two greatest difficulties that I had to contend with—loafing and swarming. We use the eight-frame Dovetailed hives with section-holders for 4¼×4¼ sections. Our bees would always begin to loaf or hang out on the front of the hives when we put on the sections, and most of them would do but little in the sections until they had lost several days, and then would swarm, thus losing several days of the first alfalfa bloom.

I had sixty colonies of Italians in my out-apiary, and in trying my experiment I tried to be fair. I took 30 supers of half-depth extracting-frames full of comb from the home apiary, and put them on 30 hives in the out-apiary at the same time that I put sections on the other 30 hives. In four or five days the extracting-combs were full of new honey, and the bees excited and busy at their work, while most of those having sections were loafing, and some had swarmed.

I raised the combs by putting a super of sections between them and the brood-nest. At the end of two weeks from putting on the combs those sections under the combs were better filled than those on the hives that had no combs. As soon as the combs were sealed I put them away to extract, having that amount of honey extra, and the bees started nicely in their work. I had only about a third as many swarms from those hives as from the ones with sections and no combs

I liked the plan so well that last year I had enough of those little combs built to furnish a super of them to every colony that was to be run for section honey.

I tried the plan again this year, and from 75 colonies at the out-apiary I had 8000 fine white marketable sections, about 500 lbs of unfinished and imperfect sections, 1500 lbs. of extracted honey, and 60 lbs. of beeswax, and two barrels of vinegar. We got short of fixtures, and I had to cut out some of my little combs and have the bees build them again to keep them at work. I forgot to mention that we sell a lot of those combs to families for home use, as we can sell them cheaper than sections. When we cut them out we do so after extracting, and then the washings make good vinegar, and the wax goes into the solar extractor, and is of the best quality. We leave half an inch of comb at the top of the frame, to save putting in foundation. I do not believe we shall ever be able to overcome swarming entirely, but I believe my plan stops the loafing better than any thing else I know of. We had 57 swarms this year, but no loafing in the out-apiary. We have bought an extractor for that apiary, and will continue to run on that plan to start them to work. After the first super of sections is well started there is no more trouble about loafing My neighbor's bees loafed and swarmed through all the best of the season, while mine were hard at work.

MRS. A. J. BARBER.
Mancos, Col., Nov. 17, 1898.

Other correspondents to *Gleanings in Bee Culture* have reported good results from following the same methods. It is particularly applicable where both comb and extracted are called for.

Mr. E. D. Townsend, Remus, Michigan, the other correspondent. goes one step further than the Barber plan by producing comb and extracted honey *in the same super*. Instead of putting on a case of extracting-combs. and afterward substituting therefor one containing sections, he has a special super which contains *both* extracting-combs and sections.

The illustration shows an ordinary comb-honey super containing 4x5 sections. This

is equipped precisely the same as any other super for sections except that it has extracting-combs with closed-end frames on each outside. Where a super of this kind is placed on a hive the bees immediately occupy the drawn comb at the sides of the super and begin their storing. The comb being already drawn out, it is a very inviting place in which the bees can begin storing. Having made a nice start in the two side extracting-combs they work toward the center—that is to say, they begin to draw out the full sheets of foundation in 4x5 sections next to the combs, and store in them. When work is once in full progress in the side sections of the super, the center ones will take care of themselves, with the result that every section is finished about the same time, and of about equal fullness. When the super is completed, the two extracting-combs will be filled and capped as well as the section honey-boxes. The former can be extracted and used over again.

It will be seen that the extracting-combs serve the purpose of excellent baits; and Mr. Townsend draws attention to the fact that, when such baits are placed at the *sides*

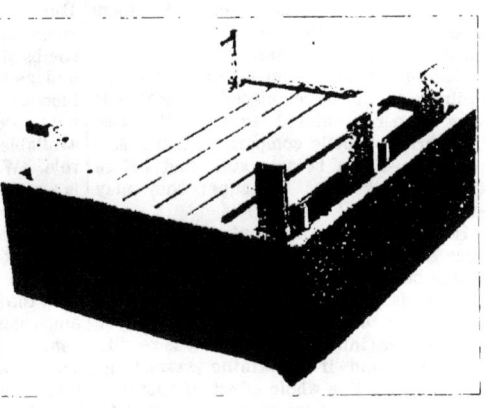

E. D. TOWNSEND'S SUPER FOR PRODUCING BOTH COMB AND EXTRACTED HONEY; ONE EXTRACTING-FRAME ON EACH SIDE.

instead of in the center, they cause an even filling of the entire super; whereas by the old plan of putting bait combs in the middle of the super the storing begins around the baits, gradually working from the center to the outside. This naturally brings about a better filling of the center sections, leaving those toward the sides at a much later stage of comb-building and filling. The result of

COMB HONEY IN 4¼ SQUARE PLAIN SECTIONS.

This honey would grade extra fancy according to the Eastern grading given further on The combs in such cases will not be capped over next to the wood like this in most cases.

this is that the center sections will be filled in advance of the outside ones; and by the time these latter are filled, all the former will be travel-stained, and may induce swarming in the meantime.

When Mr. Townsend first began this scheme of comb and extracted honey production from the same super he had in mind only baiting the bees up into the sections; but he incidentally discovered that, inasmuch as the bees would enter such supers without hesitation, he thereby almost entirely overcame swarming.

Comb-honey producers all know that the ordinary section-super placed on a hive is very often not entered readily by the bees. The series of little compartments (the sections) cause the bees to sulk, and before they actually enter the super they may swarm in disgust.

It is well known also that, after bees are once started going above, there is less inclination on their part to swarm. Mr. Townsend finds that the two side extracting-combs that he puts in every comb-super start the bees into the super about as readily as they would if containing extracting-combs only. The whole effect of this procedure is such that swarming is reduced to a minimum—almost brought under control.

For the local markets, the side extracting-combs can be cut out and sold for chunk honey at about the same price as that in the sections; so that there need be practically no loss; or when there is a call for liquid honey it can be extracted.

The Danzenbaker super, already described, with its 4x5 sections, section-holders, and Danzenbaker frames, is the best suited to carry out the Townsend plan.

Even the shallower supers using 4¼x4¼ sections can be similarly arranged.

WHAT TO DO WHEN BEES REFUSE TO ENTER THE SECTIONS.

At times bees will show a disposition to loaf, and consequently a disinclination to go into the sections. They will hang out in great bunches around the entrance, while the surplus-apartment is left almost entirely vacant, to say nothing of foundation not being drawn out. This condition may be wholly due to the backwardness of the season. During those years (which are not frequent) when the bees have not yet filled their brood-combs after the honey season is nearly over, and, as the days progress, make little if any increase in the quantity of honey, we can not expect the bees to go above until all the available cell room below has been filled, as a rule. When this is crammed full, and there is a rush of nectar, they will commence work in the sections. We will suppose you have a fair average season, and some colonies are storing honey in the supers, and others are not. In the latter, the trouble is clearly with the hive or with the bees. Some bees are much slower in going above than others. If honey is coming in freely, they can be baited, usually, by placing a partly filled section or two, of the year previous, in the center of the super. Or, better, give them a shallow extracting-super a la Barber; or, perhaps better still, give them a super of sections and a pair of extracting-combs as advised by Townsend. If none of these methods work go to a hive where the bees are already working in sections, if you can have access to such a one, and remove sections, bees and all, that are actually at work drawing out the comb, and place them on the hive that won't go in the supers. This will start any hive at work in the sections that contain bees enough to go above. The sections should contain full sheets of foundation, because it has been shown, over and over again, that bees are much more ready to accept full sheets than starters. If you have complied with this, perhaps the hive is not properly shaded, and, as a consequence, the surplus-apartment is overheated by the direct rays of the sun. In this event, if you can not extemporize some kind of shade, use a shade-board, and smoke the bees above. (See APIARY.)

If the methods given still fail to force your bees to occupy the sections, and you have followed faithfully the instructions, the trouble may be because honey is not coming in sufficiently rapid, because the brood-nest is not yet filled, or because the colony is too weak. It requires *strong* colonies under *any conditions* to do much work in the supers. The hive should be boiling over with bees.

TIERING UP.

If honey is coming in at a good rate, you may expect (if the bees have got started above) that the super, or case of sections, will soon be filled about half full of honey— with the sections in different stages of completion. When the super is about half filled with honey, raise it up and place another empty super under it. About the time this reaches the condition of about half completion, raise both supers and put under another empty one. This process of "tiering up," or "storifying," as it is called by the English, may be continued until three or four high, depending upon the length of the honey-flow and the amount of nectar coming daily. In the mean time the ripening process of the honey in the first super continues. It is not practicable to tier up more than two high.

CAUTION.

Care must be exercised in tiering up, or a lot of unfinished sections will be the result. When the honey-flow is drawing to a close, and you discover that there is an evident decrease in the amount of nectar coming in, give no more empty supers. Make the bees complete what they have on hand, which they will do if you are fortunate enough in your calculations as to when the flow of nectar will end. If uncertain whether another super is needed or not toward the close of the harvest, it is often advisable to put another super *on top*. The bees are not likely to commence on this till they really need it. It is impossible to give general rules on tiering up; but with the assistance of the foregoing you are to exercise your own discretion.

WHEN AND HOW TO TAKE OFF SECTIONS.

Usually it is not practicable to wait till every section in a super is complete; that is,

until every cell is capped over. Those sections most liable to be unfinished will be in the two outside rows, and these the bees will be long in completing. If the honey-flow is over we would not wait for them to be completed, but would take the whole super off at once. The longer it remains on the hive, the more travel-stained the honey will become, and the more it will be soiled with propolis. Bees have a fashion of running through their apartments with muddy feet, and in this particular are not so very much unlike their owners. However, if you desire a really fine, delicious article of comb honey, one more pleasing to the tongue than to the eye, and are not particular about the white marketable appearance of the cappings, leave the super on the hive for two or three months. Most bee-keepers agree that comb honey left on the hive acquires a certain richness of flavor not found in honey just capped over. Although such honey is really better, it is not quite so marketable.

HOW TO GET BEES OUT OF THE SECTIONS WITHOUT BEE-ESCAPES.

There is one danger in leaving honey on till after the honey-flow. As soon as you open the hive, the bees, especially hybrids, are apt to uncap and carry some of the honey down. Whether you leave it on the hive or whether you remove it as soon as capped, the methods of taking off and getting the bees out will be much the same. In the latter case, some supers may not be filled with honey, although a glance at the top may show nice white capped combs. Satisfy yourself by lifting one up and looking under. If capped below, it may be removed. To take off, blow smoke into the top of the super for a little while, to drive most of the bees down; lift off the super, and set it on end near the entrance (not as it sits on the hive, or you will kill bees). If honey is coming in freely, robbers will not molest, and in two or three hours the bees will have left the super and gone into the hive.

Until you have had some experience, perhaps your safest plan is, never to set a super of honey by the hive. Sometimes it may be safe to let it stand there all day when the bees have more than they can do on the flowers; but, again, all at once it may start the bees to robbing, and demoralize them generally.

If the honey flow has stopped or is tapering off, to avoid the possibility of robbing it would, perhaps, be better, after smoking the bees out as far as possible, to give the super a vigorous shaking in front of he

hive; then with the bee-brush clean off the bottom and top of the super; this will clean out nearly all the bees. The super should then be placed inside of a building. What few remain will desert, fly to the window screens, and get out through the bee-escape, which should be provided in all well-regulated honey-houses. But a better plan, perhaps, would be to shake out most of the

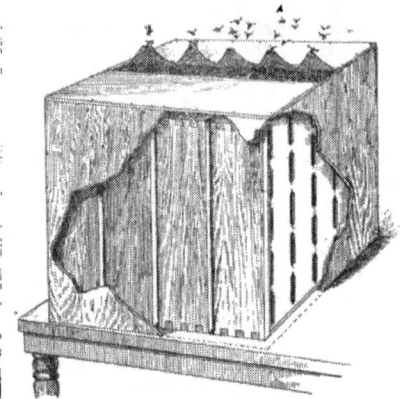

THE WHITNEY BEE-ESCAPE CASE FOR CLEARING THE BEES FROM COMB-HONEY SUPERS.

bees as before described, then stand the supers on end, and set over a case with bee-escapes on top, like that shown in the subjoined engraving. This is used by W. M. Whitney, of Lake Geneva, Wis.

MARTIN'S SUPER-JOUNCER.

Another very excellent plan for getting bees out of supers without a bee-escape is described by Mr. John H. Martin, under the *nom de plume* of "Rambler," in *Gleanings in Bee Culture*. It is simply a framework of suitable size bolted together, having four stout legs, braced and cleated in such a way as to hold a super of sections right over a cloth tray just beneath. Super, framework, and all, or "jouncer," as Mr. Martin calls it, are raised up and set down on the ground with a quick sharp jar. This "jouncing" is repeated in rapid succession until all the bees are shaken out on the cloth, from which they can easily be dumped in front of the hive. The work can be done more quickly than it takes to tell it.

There are those who are strong enough in their arms and back to shake nearly all the bees out with a tremulous motion without a jouncer; but it is back-aching work for the best of them.

MARTIN'S SUPER-JOUNCER.

By far the most satisfactory arrangement for getting bees out of supers is the regular Porter bee-escape. This is mounted on a board, cleated at the ends and sides, in such a way as to provide a bee-space on one side, so that it can be placed between the supers and the brood-nest beneath. But care should be taken that it be placed right side

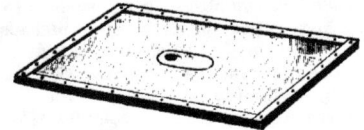

up—that is, the side up as shown in the illustration. If the device be put on toward night. or, better, along in the afternoon, by the next morning practically all the bees will be out of the super and in the brood-nest below; or in some cases will have gone from the finished super into one partly finished.

ing, prevents angering the bees, and saves killing them.

The best time to put on Porter escapes is at night. If thirty or forty of them are put on, the next morning about nine o'clock there will be about thirty or forty supers ready to come off, with hardly a bee in them. If there are three or four bees left, or say a dozen, they will usually take wing as soon as the super is uncovered. If not, one or two whiffs of smoke, and a shaking, will dislodge them.

SCRAPING SECTIONS.

In order to make sections present a clean marketable appearance, all propolis should be scraped off. Some prefer, for this purpose, a case-knife; others, an ordinary sharp jack-knife. But whatever implement you use, scrape the sections nice and clean. Be careful not to gash into the honey. Before you commence the operation you had better put on some old clothes. because the parti-

METHOD OF INSERTING THE ESCAPE-BOARD.

Our method of putting on one of these escape-boards is as follows: With a screwdriver, putty-knife, or pry, loosen the super so that propolis connections will be severed or broken. Now with one hand tilt up the super at one end enough to make a gap, and with the other hand take the smoker and blow in two or three whiffs of smoke to drive the bees back.

Next lift the same end of the super up a little further so that it will stand at an angle of about 45 degrees. With the free hand set down the smoker and pick up the escape-board, which should be leaning conveniently against your person. Slide this on top of the hive as far as it will go, bee-space side up. Let the super down on the escape-board gently, and, last of all, bring the escape-board and super so they will align with the hive.

You will find this method avoids hard lift-

cles of propolis will be almost sure to ruin good ones.

BOOMHOWER SECTION-SCRAPING TABLE.

Mr. Frank Boomhower, of Gallupville, N. Y., has a section-scraping table like the one shown herewith. As will be seen,

SECTION-SCRAPING TABLE.

two scrapers can work at a time, the sides of the box, or tray, being cut away in such a way as to allow a knife to scrape down clear past the edge of the section. Each section, as it is scraped, is put into the shipping-case. We have seen this table in operation and know that it is just the thing for hand scraping.

UNFINISHED SECTIONS.

The more carefully the apiary is manipulated in the matter of working for comb honey, the fewer will be the number of unfinished sections; but all such are not always the result of improper working of the colonies. With the best of care a sudden stoppage of the honey-flow will throw on the bee-keeper a lot of these sections; for such stoppages of the nectar supply, no one can foresee in some localities. In the alfalfa regions, and in some other places, it can be told within a few days when the honey will stop; it is then possible so to arrange the supply of sections on the hives as to leave very few of them unfinished when the season does finally close.

HOW DR. MILLER PREVENTS AN OVERSUPPLY OF UNFINISHED SECTIONS.

Dr. Miller takes off his supers as soon as a majority of the sections in the super are finished. These latter are set aside to be scraped and cased for market, while those unfinished are set back into the supers—the supers to go back on the hives immediately, consequently *before the honey-flow stops.* By proceeding thus he manages to have few unfinished sections at the end of the season. Those that are returned to the hive he fittingly styles "gobacks." These, as fast as they accumulate in the honey-room, are put into the regular hive-supers. Part of these goback supers may be placed on colonies that show a special aptitude* for finishing up work already begun in sections, and a part may be placed on the regular colonies already at work on their own sections. The great advantage of this plan is that it allows the sections to be taken off before all in the super are finished, consequently before any of the central ones have lost their virgin whiteness.

Such a plan of procedure is possible only in localities where the honey-flow lasts sufficiently long, not only to fill two-thirds of the sections full in the supers, but enough longer to finish out supers of gobacks placed on hives afterward.

---

* Some colonies are better at finishing up work already begun than at starting it from the raw foundation.

In any case, some unfinished sections will be on hand at the close of the season; for if the surplus be all stored in sections it is not possible to give the exact number of sections that will be finished.

FEEDING BACK AFTER THE HONEY-FLOW TO COMPLETE UNFINISHED SECTIONS.

The subject of feeding back is one that interests a large number of bee-keepers in the comb-honey class, the main object, perhaps, being to prevent unfinished sections. At the same time much can be done toward preventing swarming as well, if the sections are removed from the colonies before they are capped and finished up after the danger of swarming is over by the feeding-back process, for it is well known that a great amount of capped honey in the hives is very conducive to swarming.

Many who attempt to feed back, fail on account of the many difficulties encountered. Mr. J. E. Hand, of Birmingham, Ohio, has made a complete study of this subject, and he finds that, while the work can be profitably done, much attention must be given to the details, since there are many things to take into consideration.

He finds it more practicable to use a feeder in which the syrup can be given below the brood-chamber instead of on top, as this is the more natural way for the bees, and they take it more readily. The Quinby feeder has a tin tray, 2 inches deep, enclosed by a wooden frame of the same depth, which is the same width as the hive, but 2½ inches longer. The tin tray is exactly the same length as the hive, and when in use is pushed to the back end of the frame surrounding it, leaving a space of 2½ inches in front for the bees to pass out and in the hive. The other end of the tin tray projects the 2½ inches beyond the hive at the back to allow space for filling it. A framework of slats lengthwise of the feeder sits in the tray for the bees to travel over while working in the feeder so that they may not be drowned. The feeder rests square on the bottom-board, and the hive covers the feeder except the 2½ inches at the back end, which space is covered by a little board. The bees can not get into the place where the feed is poured in, and the honey (about six quarts) flows evenly under all parts of the hive, where it can be quickly taken up by the bees.

Many fail in their attempt at feeding back for the reason that they do not select the right time of the year. It is best to begin right after the main honey-flow has ceased before the work in the supers is over. At this time the bees naturally go right on as though the flow had not stopped. It is best to give about six quarts of thinned-down honey to each colony every other day. The interval between the feeding allows the bees time to remove the honey, which is first placed directly in the brood-cells, to the supers. No definite rule can be given for thinning down the honey, since the density varies so much. For average honey enough water must be added so that the syrup will be 75 per cent honey and 25 per cent water. Very thick honey needs more water, while thin honey needs less.

It is necessary to have the brood-chamber well occupied by brood, for bees never do well in supers over brood-chambers containing much capped honey. The first requisite, then, is a good queen, which will be able to hold her own against any amount of feeding. The brood-chamber must be contracted, furthermore, so that the queen will be able to keep every comb filled with brood. In this connection, the sectional hive is very convenient, for the reason that (ne section may be removed, thus contracting the brood section and still allowing brood in the shallow frames to be under the entire super. It is quite important, however, to have the combs in the brood-chamber as new as possible, for the bees are quite apt to carry up bits of the comb to be used in capping cells in the supers, and old dark comb will discolor the super-cappings to quite an extent.

The thinned-down honey should be put into the feeder just before sundown, so that there may be no uproar that may be likely to cause robbing. It is not desirable to have more than two supers of sections on the feeding colonies at a time. As soon as the sections in the super next the brood-chamber are nearly capped, this super should be raised up and the upper one placed under it next to the brood-chamber. Then as soon as the top super is finished and capped solid to the wood, it may be removed and an empty super placed next the brood-chamber. Of course it is not essential that combs be built out and capped solid to the wood. The combs all capped over, except the cells next to the wood, would grade No. 1.

WHAT TO DO WITH UNFINISHED SECTIONS.

Some prefer to dispose of unfinished sections by selling them around home for less money, or using them exclusively for home consumption. The honey, for eating purposes, is practically just as good; and it is the practice, in many bee-keepers' families, to consume all such sections if they can, reserving out those that are marketable and well finished, to be sold.

Some bee-keepers consider them very valuable for baits; that is, they place one of these in the center of a super to bait the bees above, as has already been explained. Others place them in stacked-up supers a few rods from the apiary. A very small entrance at the bottom of the pile, large enough for one or two bees to pass at a time, is provided. By this slow method of robbing, the bees will empty out the honey and carry it to the hives much more cheaply than the bee-keeper himself can afford to do it by means of the extractor. While this slow robbing may cause a little disturbance in the yard at the time, it does no particular harm. But mark this: Never give the bees a wide entrance at the bottom. It should be only wide enough to allow one or two bees to pass at a time. This is known as the Miller plan, having been, we believe, originated by Dr. C. C. Miller. Taking every thing into consideration it is the safer one to follow; but where one is an expert bee-keeper, and has a large lot of unfinished sections for the bees to empty out, a plan originated by the late B. Taylor is perhaps better. Dr. Miller, who now uses the plan, thus speaks of it:

For a number of years I have used the Taylor plan at the close of every season. All sections that are less than half filled are put in supers in the shop cellar, and the door kept closed till the whole business is over, and *all* that are to be emptied are in the cellar. The supers stand on end so as to be all open, or piled in piles crossing each other. When no more are to be taken into the cellar I open the door, and say to the bees, "Go in." They go in, I assure you. The air is black with bees at the door, and they do more or less sailing about in the vicinity. Sometimes they do a little tearing of the sections, but not much. There is too large a surface for them to cover. Gradually they give up the job as the supply ceases, but the supers are not taken away till a week or two after the bees have stopped working on them. They might as well be put in the open air, only they are safe from rain in the cellar. Please remember that this is what I do at the end of every harvest after the flow has stopped.

As a matter of fact, I use the Taylor oftener than the Miller plan. It depends on the number of sections to be emptied in proportion to the number of bees. Whether little or much is to be emptied, I am not afraid of a rampage. I will set a super of sections on top of a hive and let the bees rob it out, and there will be no rampage. But I will be exceedingly careful not to take away the super until all the honey is cleaned out, *and until at least 24 hours after the bees have stopped trying* to find any more honey there. Take away the super while the bees are at work at it, and wholesale destruction would follow.

HOW TO PILE UP THE SUPERS OF COMB HONEY IN THE HONEY-HOUSE AFTER TAKING OFF THE HIVES.

It is a very good practice, after the supers are taken off the hive, to pile them up crosswise as shown in the accompanying illustration, in a dry room that can be kept as warm as possible. If the room is kept tight, and the sun shines through the window, this will have a tendency to keep the honey dry, and to continue the process of ripening it. If allowed to stand this way for a month or two before shipping, the chances of its safe arrival at destination will be much improved.

Comb honey or honey in extracting-frames should not be piled up in a honey-room from which the bees can be excluded, one super squarely on top of another. No matter what the temperature of the room, honey shut up in this way from the air is in danger of souring. If it does not do so outright it will

METHOD OF PILING SUPERS.

have an acid taste—enough so that it will ruin its chances of bringing a good price.

We once had an experience of this kind with several thousand pounds of honey piled up solid, and a super cover placed on top. A good portion of the honey soured, and the flavor of the rest of it was very much impaired by reason of the acid taste.

If the honey be piled with the supers crisscross, as shown in the illustration, and the temperature of the room be kept as nearly as possible to that of the living-room, there will be but very little danger of candying or souring, and, what is more, the quality of the honey itself will be richer and riper.

SHALL WE USE SEPARATORS?

A few years ago there was considerable discussion among prominent bee-keepers as to whether separators could or could not be dispensed with profitably in the production of comb honey. Some stoutly maintained that they could, and others just as strenuously asserted that they could not. The former class urged that they could secure more honey without separators, and hence that they preferred to put up with the inconvenience of some few sections bulged out beyond the sides. While the latter class were ready to admit that *perhaps* a little more honey could be secured by the non-use of separators, they asserted that they obtained so much uncratable honey, and were put to so much inconvenience in trying to arrange the sections so as to have them built out evenly, that they never wanted to dispense with separators. It should be remarked right here, that, with the narrow beeway sections, 1⅜, 1⅝, or 1⅜, the separators are not so necessary as with the wide ones, such as 1⅞ or 1 15/16. Full sheets of foundation in either case greatly lessen the need of their use. How to dispense with separators entirely will be fully explained a little further on. But plain sections *should always* be used with fences or separators. At the present time, however, by far the greater majority of the producers of comb honey advocate and use fences, separators, or something of that sort; and as our experience in former years was so unsatisfactory without separators, we are compelled to agree with the majority.

WOOD OR TIN SEPARATORS.

Objection has been made to the tin separators, because of their metallic coldness. It is urged that the smooth sides of the tin are not congenial to the bees, and that, furthermore, the expense of separators made of tin is greater than most bee-keepers can afford, in consideration of the low price of their product. Partly for these reasons, and partly for others, wood separators costing an almost insignificant sum have been made. They are sometimes cut out on a slicing-machine, and are really thin veneer wood, cut to the size of the separator. Those cut with a saw are much better because the grain is not broken in shaving. The thickness varies from 28 to the inch up to about 16. The preference seems to be in favor of the thicker ones.

WHEN SEPARATORS MAY BE OMITTED.

It has been shown very conclusively that bees dislike a super divided off into a number of small compartments as is the case in the old-style supers with solid separators. Supers provided with *fence* separators, because they allow of a much freer communication, are more acceptable to the bees, for they dislike being shut off from one another by any obstruction, although some doubt this. This raises the question, "Why not dispense with separators altogether?" We can. But before we do so we must dispense with the present wide section altogether, for it has been demonstrated over and over again that it is impracticable to produce *thick* comb sections without separators if we desire to sell the honey away from home.

It may be asked why bee keepers have not adopted these narrow-width sections. The reasons are hard to give; but in a general way it is probably due to the fashion.

WHAT SIZE OF SECTION TO USE.

To answer this question intelligently for oneself, it will be well to consult the honey-market reports. As a general rule, sections holding an even pound of honey are preferred by consumers, and, of course, they bring a higher price. Notwithstanding this, few bee-keepers think that more honey can be secured in two-pound sections than in the smaller sizes. Most producers, however, are not so sure that it makes any difference to the bees; and while the fact remains that, in most markets, they sell for from one to two cents less per pound than the one-pound, it behooves every bee-keeper to think carefully before he decides on adopting two-pound sections. The size of section which seems to have the general preference is 4¼ inches square and 1⅞ inches wide for the beeway style, and 4¼x4¼x1¼ and 4x5x1¼ for the plain section

NARROWER SECTIONS.

Some markets demand a smaller package. Instead of going to the expense of making smaller sections, supply-dealers have been in the habit of making the regular 4¼ sections narrower—1¼, 1⅜, 7 to the foot, 1¼, 1⅜. The seven to the foot hold about three-quarters of a pound, while the 1¼ and 1⅜ hold about half a pound.

There is a very great advantage in diminishing the *thickness* of a section instead of the *size*, for this reason: They will fit most of the surplus arrangements in use, and can

be shipped readily in ordinary shipping-cases, with but little trouble. In Canada the narrow sections have the preference, and the tendency in this country is toward a narrower section of late.

FOUR-BEEWAY SECTIONS.

A few years ago these were talked of considerably; and it was stated at the time that the bees would enter them more readily; that they would be filled better, and have a better appearance for market. Very little attention was paid to them in this country, although they have been used continuously

COMPARATIVE SIZE OF TALL AND SQUARE SECTIONS OF THE SAME WEIGHT.

in Great Britain ever since; but since the plain sections and the fence have demonstrated the value of free communication crosswise and lengthwise of the super, the open-side sections are being talked of more now than they have heretofore; but, like

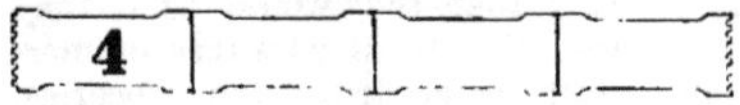

plain sections, they require a special kind of separator; and the cases for holding them would be just about as expensive. If one expects to make a change it would be as cheap, and better, for him to adopt the plain section.

TALL VS. SQUARE SECTIONS.

The standard section for a good many years is and has been 4¼ in. square; but, notwithstanding, during all this time, a good many bee-keepers, principally in New York, have been using a section taller than broad. Capt. J. E. Hetherington, who had the reputation of being the most extensive apiarist in the world, used a section 3⅞x5. Other bee-keepers in New York use them slightly larger or slightly smaller, but of the same proportion. (See HIVES.)

Some of the reasons that have been urged in favor of the tall section are as follows:

1. Weight for weight, and for the same thickness of comb, a tall section presents a bigger appearance than the average square one. In the 4x5 tall plain section, for example, 1⅛, we have about the same actual weight as the 4¼x4¼x1⅞ plain; and yet, as will be seen by the engravings the former

SAME WEIGHT OF HONEY IN SQUARE AND TALL SECTIONS.

looks to be the larger. As a result the tall box brings in some markets anywhere from one to two cents more per pound, but in other markets it brings no more. If this were the only reason why the tall box is preferred, we should say nothing about it here; but there are other reasons for this preference.

2. By long association we have come to like the proportion of objects all about us that are taller than broad. Doors and windows of their present oblong shape are much more pleasing than they would be if they were square. Nearly all packages of merchandise, such as of drugs and groceries, are oblong in shape — that is, taller than broad. To cater further to this taste, brought about by long association with the common objects round about us, the tall section was introduced: and outside of its relative appearance of bigness as compared with the square box, very many consider the tall one much more pleasing.

3. Mr. R. C. Aikin, one of the closest observers in all beedom, lays it down as a rule that " *in comb-building the downward progress exceeds the sidewise in the proportion of about three to two.* . . If, then, comb construction goes on in this way, a section as wide as deep will be finished down the center before it is at the outer edges." A tall section, then, more nearly conforms to the natural instincts of the bees.

4. A greater number of tall sections holding approximately a pound can be accommodated on a given hive surface.

5. A tall section will stand shipping better, because the perpendicular edges of contact of the comb itself are greater than in a square box.

GLASSED SECTIONS.

Glassed sections are simply sections of comb honey with squares of glass fitted in between the projecting sides of the section. The glass is held either by glue, tin points, or paper pasted over the top and bottom of the section, and lapping over on to the glass a little way. When the section is sold to the retailer, the glass is included in the price of the honey. Of course, the producer can afford to sell glass at from 12 to 15 cts. per lb.; but customers have sometimes objected, and justly, too. In spite of all this, glass sections have quite a rage at times in the New York and other eastern markets, and occasionally there is some sale for them in the West. In England such a section with a fancy border is sold quite extensively.

PASTEBOARD CARTONS FOR ONE-POUND SECTIONS OF COMB HONEY.

Mr. J. E. Crane, of Middlebury, Vt., formerly put nearly all of his honey into cartons. These were put into unglassed shipping-cases, the latter neatly stenciled with an old-fashioned straw hive, and lettered.

THE DANZENBAKER SECTION-CARTON.

This is somewhat cheaper than the others, and answers the purpose very nicely. They are shipped folded, and all one has to do is to crowd on two opposite corners, when the

THE DANZENBAKER CARTON.

package assumes a rectangular form as shown. This carton is specially adapted to use with a plain section, as will be seen from the illustration.

A new carton has been recently introduced to the trade that has a fancy engraved design on the front panel, and the whole is printed in two colors. The spaces on the top and two sides and bottom contain appropriate printed matter. On the back there is a recital of the contents of the package, and a denial of the oft-repeated canard that comb honey is manufactured. On the two sides is an explanation concerning honey and its flavors, and honey as a food. On the top

is a statement showing that the contents are pure under the national pure-food and drug act of June 30, 1906; and all over the package the caution is given not to store the honey in a refrigerator or cellar, but to put it in the warmest and dryest place available.

THE FRANKLIN CARTON.

Mr. Benjamin Franklin, of Franklinton, N. Y., uses a two-section carton, for he says he can sell two sections as easily as one. The illustration here given shows how it is put together.

GRADING COMB HONEY.

In order to get the largest price possible for comb honey, it will be necessary to grade it; and the more thoroughly and honestly it is done. the higher will be the price secured. If one is careless in grading there will be inferior sections mixed in with sections of a higher grade; and if the commission man or buyer discovers this he is likely to "knock down the price" of the whole caseful to the price of the inferior sections. It is very important to have every section in a case of the same grade.

Obviously not much will be accomplished if there be a dozen different systems or rules of grading. So far they have been reduced to two—one set for the Eastern bee-keepers and another for the Western. There is no reason why we could not have all adopted one and the same set of rules. It is unfortunate that a uniform grading is not universal over the country. The Eastern grading reads as follows:

GRADING RULES.

FANCY.—All sections well filled, combs straight, firmly attached to all four sides, the combs unsoiled by travel-stain or otherwise; all the cells sealed except an occasional one, the outside surface of the wood well scraped of propolis.

A No. 1.—All sections well filled except the row of cells next to the wood; combs straight; one-eighth part of comb surface soiled, or the entire surface slightly soiled; the outside surface of the wood well scraped of propolis.

No. 1.—All sections well filled except the row of cells next to the wood; combs comparatively even; one-eighth part of comb surface soiled, or the entire surface slightly soiled.

No. 2.—Three-fourths of the total surface must be filled and sealed.

No. 3.—Must weigh at least half as much as a full-weight section.

In addition to this the honey must be classified according to color, using the terms white, amber, and dark; that is, there will be "Fancy White," "No. 1 Dark," etc.

These are based on a set of rules originally adopted by the National Bee-keepers' Association in convention at Washington, D. C., in December, 1892. It will be seen that the question of color and source is taken care of very nicely in the last paragraph, so that we can have a No. 1 or fancy amber or a fancy buckwheat, the same as a fancy clover stock.

In the mean time the Colorado Bee-keepers' Association, the most influential organization west of the Mississippi, adopted the following set of rules:

No. 1 White.—Sections to be well filled and even'y capped except the outside row, next to the wood; honey white or slightly amber, comb and cappings white, and not projecting beyond the wood; wood to be well cleaned; cases of separatored honey to average 21 pounds net per case of 24 sections, no section in this grade to weigh less than 13½ ounces.

Cases of half-separatored honey to average not less than 22 pounds net per case of 24 sections.

HONEY SENT BY THE ONTARIO BEE-KEEPERS' ASSOCIATION TO KING EDWARD.
[Note.—This would grade as Extra Fancy by the Eastern grading rules.]

Cases of unseparated honey to average not less than 23 pounds net per case of 24 sections.

No. 1 Light Amber.—Sections to be well filled and evenly capped, except the outside row, next to the wood; honey white or light amber; comb and cappings from white to off color, but not dark; comb not projecting beyond the wood; wood to be well cleaned.

Cases of separatored honey to average 21 pounds net per case of 24 sections; no section in this grade to weigh less than 13¼ pounds.

Cases of half-separatored honey to average not less than 22 pounds net per case of 24 sections.

Cases of unseparatored honey to average not less than 23 pounds net per case of 24 sections.

No. 2.—This includes all white honey, and amber honey not included in the above grades; sections to be fairly well filled and capped, no more than 25 uncapped cells, exclusive of outside row, permitted in this grade; wood to be well cleaned, no section in this grade to weigh less than 12 ounces.

Cases of separatored honey to average not less than 19 pounds net.

Cases of half-separatored honey to average not less than 20 lbs. net per case of 24 sections.

Cases of unseparatored honey to average not less than 21 lbs. net per case of 24 sections.

Notice that these rules provide for no "fancy" nor No. 1 A. Some honey would pass for one or two grades higher than that provided for in the Colorado No. 1. Notice also that the rules discriminate against honey produced without separators. This is right.

GRADING BY PICTURES.

Some effort has been made to grade honey by means of pictures; but nothing definite has been accomplished, as it is difficult to make photos flexible enough to take in the various comb surfaces and cappings of honey that can be included in one grade. It is possibly true plates may be used *in connection* with the rules, to enable one to determine what section will grade No. 1, "fancy," or No. 2; for it must be understood that different persons would have a different idea as to whether one section should be graded as No. 1 or "fancy," and a set of pictures showing the idea of an expert on grading might be helpful to a novice. We have given here a few plates that may give an idea of what is meant. But it should be understood that in the pictures the unsealed cells show black—much more in contrast than in the actual combs themselves; or, to put it another way, any thing but an extra fancy, where no empty cells show, the pictorial representations do not show up as well as the real articles.

The honey shown on previous page would be what is called "extra fancy white," according to the Eastern grading, for it is white honey put up in plain sections, and, as the illustration shows, it is evenly and nicely

GRADING-RULES ILLUSTRATED.

the faces of such sections are examined carefully it will be found that the stain or discoloration goes *clear through*. These discolorations are due to the fact that the bees take up pieces of old black wax, propolis, or any thing that will answer as a substitute or filler for pure wax. We have seen the cappings of some sections of this sort filled with bits of old rope, lint from newspapers, small hard chunks of propolis, fine slivers of wood — any thing and every thing that is right handy. Sections of this class often look like those of the first class, hence the frequent confusion.

In the third class are those with soiled cappings. due to the pollen dust or possibly a thin layer of propolis stain.

The fourth and last class takes in all those that are

filled. When cells next to the wood are all sealed, or nearly so, it should be designated as "extra fancy;" but as such are the exception rather than the rule there will be very little "extra fancy" on the market, although such honey is generally shown at exhibitions when competing for a prize.

In the half-tone engraving above shown the honey in the top case, with its sample section opposite, would, by the Eastern grading rules, grade "Fancy;" that in the middle case "No. 1 A" or "No. 1," according to the amount of soiled surface, and that in the bottom case would be about "No. 2."

TRAVEL - STAINED AND OTHER SOILED SECTIONS.

There are really four classes of discolored sections, each due to a distinct and separate cause. First there is what is called the real travel-stained section. As its name indicates, the cappings are soiled because the bees have gone over the surfaces of the cappings with their dirty feet.

Then there is another lot that are stained **because the boxes are capped over in the vicinity of old comb, dirt, or propolis.** If

FANCY COMB HONEY IN 4x5 PLAIN SECTIONS.

called "greasy" or "water-soaked," having cappings that lie on the honey. The covering to each cell is more or less transparent, or water-soaked — the transparent part being half-moon shaped, or in the form of a ring encircling a white nucleus center that is not greasy or transparent.

If the reader will look over the unsold odds and ends of the grocer's he will be able to find samples of all these classes, and the fall of the year is a good time to find them, as they are the last to sell.

A knowledge of how to make dark or soiled sections No. 1 white, thus putting them at the top of the market, may be worth hundreds of dollars to some bee-keepers; and while it is probably not possible to make water-soaked and certain kinds of travel-stained sections white, there is a probability that a very large class of the soiled boxes can be rendered No. 1.

BLEACHING COMB HONEY.

Mr. Byron Walker, a honey-merchant of Chicago, had quite accidentally placed some yellow or pollen-stained sections in his show-window, where they were subjected to the direct rays of sunlight. A short time after, he noticed that the faces of these sections that were next to the light were bleached white, while those on the reverse side retained the old color. Instantly grasping at the suggestion he placed other sections of the same kind in the same window, and was gratified to learn that these were likewise bleached as were the first; but so far as I know, Mr. Walker was successful in bleaching pollen-stained or yellow-faced combs only. The real travel-stained and water-soaked ones he considered beyond redemption. The time required to bleach the yellow sections was anywhere from two to three days, depending on weather and sunlight.

Mr. A. E. White, of Pala, California, apparently goes one step further; for in connection with sunlight he uses sulphur, which is known to be a powerful bleaching agent. His method is described as follows:

"We first fumigate with sulphur, then place the combs where the sun will shine on them, and that is the whole process.

"I build a frame on the south side of my honey-house, and cover the same with cotton cloth. A door opens from the honey-house into this room. I place shelves on the side and ends of this room, the bottom shelf being a wide board to be used as a table. I place the combs on these shelves so that the sunlight will strike them. Dark combs will require several hours. This plan will whiten dark combs here in California. If you fumigate a few combs, then place them on a window-sill where the sun will shine on them, you will be convinced.

WHITE'S BLEACHING-HOUSE FOR SOILED COMB HONEY.

"In placing the sections on shelves in the morning, I find the following plan good: On the shelves at the east and west end of the room I place sections end to end lengthwise of the shelves, two rows on each shelf, one row on the outer and the other on the inner edge. The morning sun strikes one side, and the afternoon sun the other side.

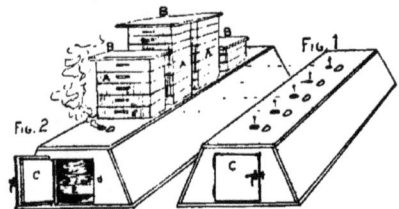

WHITE'S SULPHUR-BOX FOR BLEACHING.

On the front shelves I set them crosswise of the shelf, far enough apart so as not to shade each other.

"I pack them away every evening; all not white I put out again next morning. Some of them will bleach quite slowly, but I have been able to whiten the worst ones by perseverance."

SHIPPING-CASES FOR COMB HONEY

Just as soon as the crop of honey has been secured and the sections scraped, they should be put immediately into shipping-cases, provided there is no storage room that is bee-proof. The cases should be glassed on one side, in order that the fragile condition of the contents of the case when filled with comb honey may be apparent to freight-handlers, dealer, and consumer.

It is penny wise and pound foolish to try to make one's own cases. They will cost as much as or more than the factory-made articles, and will have an awkward and clumsy look. One prominent commission-man told me that these home-made affairs, in his market at least, "knocked the price of the honey down a cent or two" a pound.

NO-DRIP SHIPPING-CASE.

The standard size of shipping-case is a 24-lb. single-tier, shown in the middle of the cut given. Then there is the 48-lb., the same thing, only double-tier, having two glass with a strip of wood between. The 48-lb. cases formerly had one large glass; but besides the fact that these were much

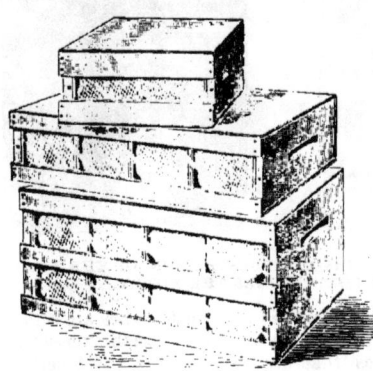

THE THREE STANDARD SIZES OF SHIPPING CASES.

more expensive, the honey actually shows off better when there is a strip of wood covering up the tops and bottoms of the sections, leaving only the best portion of the honey to show. Another very popular case is the 12-lb. single tier shown on the top of the pile.

Some bee-keepers and some markets prefer the three-row 12-lb. and the double-tier three-row 24-lb. But these are objectionable in that they will not tier—that is, not pile up on the floor as well as the flatter cases.

On account of the comb honey being broken in shipment, it used to be the practice, and is yet to a great extent, to put a paper tray in the bottom of the case, and at regular intervals wooden cleats from ⅛ to ¼ wide, and ⅛ thick, as shown in the cut opposite.

12 AND 24 POUND CASES.

The object of this is to keep the sections up high and dry, at the same time to leave room for the honey to drip, without sticking the sections to the paper tray, or, when the paper tray is not used, the bottom of the shipping-case. In that case the honey runs through, leaks on to the other shipping-cases, and, as a consequence, smears all the cases below it.

In 1908 and '9 the little strips of wood to hold the sections out of the honey drip were displaced to some extent at least by what is known as cellular or cushion paper. This is cut into sheets of the right size, and placed in the bottom of the paper tray. The corrugations of the paper serve a double purpose: First, they cushion the honey placed on them; and, second, the honey drip, if any, runs down between the grooves. The cushions of the paper, to a great extent, elim-

inate much of the breakage that takes place when honey is shipped in a solid wooden case on unyielding supports like wooden cleats. To provide for ready examination the case has a sliding cover—a little improvement very much appreciated by retailers and commission men generally.

During 1909 Mr. J. E. Crane, of Middlebury, Vt., devised a straw-board cellular shipping-case in which no wood at all is used. The corrugations of the material not only stiffen the package, but serve as an excellent cushion for the tops, sides, and ends, as well as the bottoms of the sections. By referring to the series of illustrations shown herewith, it will be seen that the case is made of several thicknesses of this cellular strawboard.

Apparently one would get the impression that a shipping-case or container for comb honey made out of paper could not possibly be as strong as one made of wood. To a certain extent this is true; but in another sense the strawboard cases with their cross-partitions are much stronger than the wooden ones without the cross-partitions. In one of the illustrations Mr. Crane himself is seen standing with the ball of his foot in the center of the case, his weight being sustained by the cross-partitions, which are a trifle taller than the sections themselves. From some preliminary tests, made by Mr. Crane and others, comb honey in these cases goes through to destination in very much better condition—that is to say, with less breakage and leakage—than takes place with the ordinary wooden cases. The reason of this is apparent from the fact that the wooden cases are stiff and unyielding, while the cellular strawboard containers not only cushion the whole case of sections but *each individual section* itself.

There are different ways in which these strawboard cases may be made up. The next set of illustrations shows a slightly different style. While these cost somewhat more than the Crane models they are rather stronger, because of the extra thickness and flaps that are used in the construction. Then there is the further advantage that they can be put up more compactly in the knockdown, and have only one joint.

Of course, it is perfectly evident that these light strawboard cellular cases of either pattern can not be secured by nailing. After the sections are put in place the cases are closed, and bound securely with strong cords; and these cords, by the way, serve as an additional cushion to the pile of cases, and at the same time they enable one to pick

CRANE'S CORRUGATED-PAPER SHIPPING-CASES. INSIDE ILLUSTRATION OF THE SAME. NO AMOUNT OF POUNDING ON THE FLAT SIDE INJURES THE HONEY.

up two cases, one in each hand, by running the fingers under the cord. For unloading and shipping they will be much handier than the wooden containers.

Where wooden cases are used we advise using carriers. These are nothing more nor less than large crates capable of holding from ten to a dozen cases of honey. Before they are put into the carrier, five or six inches of straw are strewn on the bottom of the crate, and the cases

ANOTHER STYLE OF CORRUGATED-PAPER SHIPPING-CASE.

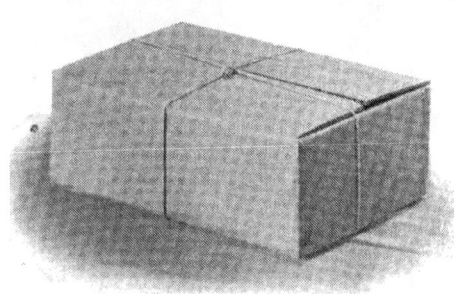

SHIPPING-CASE READY TO SHIP.

importance of using the carriers shown, page 129. However, when one ships a whole carload of comb honey it is not necessary to use a carrier, provided the producer does his own loading. In that case he will strew several inches of straw or hay on the bottom of the car, and then pile up his cases in rows. Between some of the rows it is advisable to jam in straw to afford an additional cushion to prevent the honey from being broken down when the car bumps.

piled on top. Two handles projecting from each end enable the freight-handlers to pick them up and load them in the car or on trucks. The object of the straw in the bottom of the crate is to cushion the honey piled on top of it; and by making this carrier large enough so that it will contain ten or twelve cases, it makes it impossible for the freight-handlers to toss or throw it.

When single cases of honey are sent by express they are almost sure to be broken down, no matter whether cellular or the old-style cases are used. We would urge, as a matter of necessity, the very great

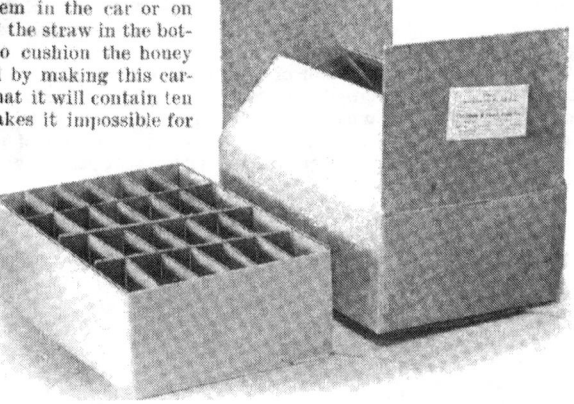

CORRUGATED SHIPPING-CASE; RIM AND PARTITIONS REMOVED.

In loading honey, always place the combs so that they will be parallel with the rail; and when on a wagon, parallel with the axletree.

MARKETING COMB HONEY.

There is nothing that can make a bee-keeper feel better than clean cash for his surplus honey at the end of the season.—Adam Grimm, page 86, Vol. I., —GLEANINGS IN BEE CULTURE.

Every thing, nowadays, depends on having goods neat, clean, and in an attractive shape, to have them "go off" readily; even our hoes have to be gilt-edged, for we noticed some once at a certain hardware store, and it seemed that those that were gilt, or bronzed, perhaps, were selling far in advance of the plain steel ones. We've been told of gilt-edged

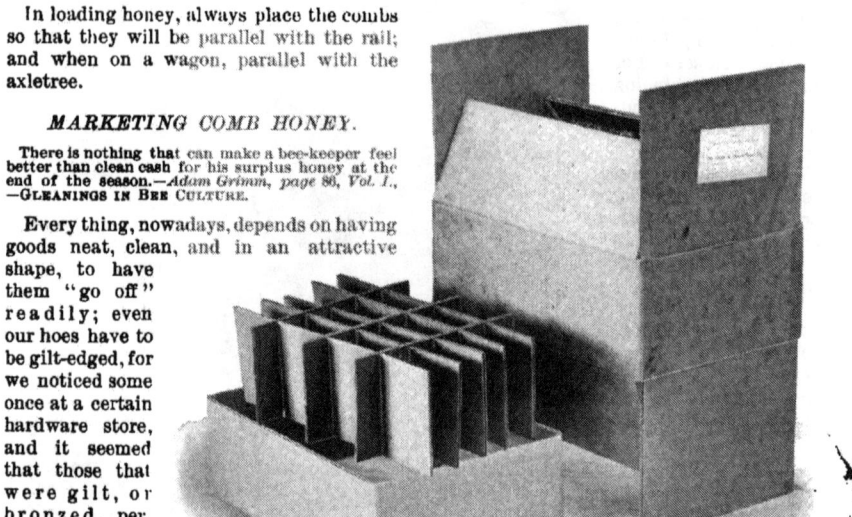

SHIPPING-CASE DISSECTED WITH ALL THE PARTS OPENED UP.

butter that sold for fabulous prices, but we hardly think it will be advisable to have our honey put up in that way, although we do wish it to look as well as any of the other products of the farm.

In order to get a fair price for your honey, you should watch the markets. To obtain this information, you should take one or more bee-journals. Through the medium of these you will learn whether the honey crop is going to be small or large. This you can not tell definitely from your own locality. If you have secured a good crop of honey, and you learn that the crop throughout the country is small, you must not be in haste to dispose of yours to the first buyer. In any case you must exercise judgment.

HOW TO MAKE HONEY SELL IN THE LOCAL MARKETS.

Supply your grocer with a lot of your choicest extracted, in tumblers and bottles; and also best comb in shipping-cases. Some of it should be set off in paper cartons, and some of it should be glassed. When customers come in, have in readiness strips of paper about 1½ by 2 or 3 inches. Dip one of these pieces of paper, curled in the shape of a trough, into the extracted. Twirl it around till all the drip is off, and pass it quickly to your customer, that he may sample. If he would like another taste, hand him another slip of paper, which he is to fold as nearly as possible in the form of a spoon. If the honey is ripe—that is, good and thick—your taster will want some. There is one thing that is very important. You want something to draw a crowd. Prepare a nucleus in a glass hive, and put it up near the window where the crowd can

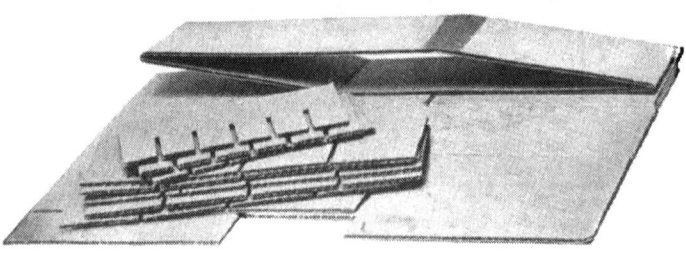

CORRUGATED-PAPER SHIPPING-CASE IN THE FLAT.

see the bees. Sometimes the crowd will be so great as to block the street to see the queen or "king bee;" but you will be the gainer, because *your* honey is inside.

COMB-HONEY CARRIER.

There should be on hand for a day or two an expert to explain about the honey, how it is produced, how good it is, etc., and to show that it is the most wholesome sweet in the world for children. He should then reinforce his arguments by handing out honey-leaflets that contain cooking-recipes, and that tell why the doctors recommend honey in preference to cane sugars, or why some invalids can eat honey when they can not eat other forms of sweet. Perhaps you yourself will be the best man to do the "talking;" and therefore you had better stay with your grocer for a day or two, or at least be on hand when he is likely to have a run of customers. Charge the grocer nothing for your services, telling him that you will take your pay out of the increased sales.

If you succeed well in one market, and the novelty of the thing wears off, try another one in a neighboring town, and so on complete the circuit of the towns roundabout. After you have done all this you will not need to ship much if any to the city markets, save commissions, save freight, and have your honey within a few miles of where you can look after it, without being at the mercy of a city commission house. See HONEY-PEDDLING; also EXHIBITS OF HONEY, sub-head SELLING HONEY AT COUNTY FAIRS.

SENDING HONEY TO COMMISSION HOUSES.

We believe commission houses throughout our cities are great aids to bee-keepers in disposing of their honey; notwithstanding, we want to enter a word of caution right here against being in too great haste to lump off your honey to these places. You may argue that you have not time to dispose of your product in small amounts; but many a bee-keeper has found to his sorrow the mistake he made in contributing to

the flood of honey at a certain commission house. The consequence is, that at that place honey is "a glut on the market," and must be sold at a very low price. As a general rule, we believe we would sell elsewhere before shipping it off to the city.

But it very often happens that one can get a higher price by sending to these commission men. The general trade looks to them for supply, and they make it their business to find a market.

Never send your honey on commission or outright sale to a new firm, no matter what it advertises, how big it talks of its financial standing, nor what promises it makes. Go to the nearest bank and find out regarding its responsibility. Then ask the commission house to send you the names of bee-keepers who have dealt with the firm. We would not advise you even then to consider this an evidence of good faith. We would take time to write to the parties and ask if their dealings were *entirely* satisfactory, and whether they

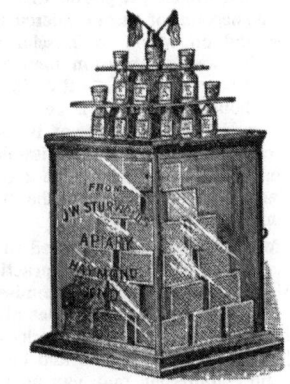

STURWOLD'S SHOW-CASE FOR HONEY.

would advise shipping to the commission house in question. The temptations in the commission business are very great; and if your man is not honest to the core he may take advantage of you. Commission men charge all the way from 5 to 10 per cent commission; and in addition to this the shipper is required to pay freight, drayage, and to stand all breakages.

Most commission houses will make advances in cash on receiving the honey; and a few of them will make payments as fast as it is sold; but a majority make no remittance until the honey is all sold, and sometimes not even then until the bee-keeper writes complaining, and inquiring regarding his honey or his money.

5

We have said that commission men should be strictly honest; but some of them yield to the temptation of quoting a higher price in the bee-journals than they are actually realizing in every-day sales. The bee-keeper complains when he receives his returns, and he is met with the statement that his honey was of poor quality, and had to be sold for less money; or that the honey came badly broken, and had to be lumped off as chunk honey; or he may be told that the "market suddenly fell" (which may be true), and it was not, therefore, possible for the house to realize quotations given in the bee-journals. It is a common trick on the part of dishonest commission men to quote high prices if they can get their names in the bee-journals, then sell for lower prices in order to "move off stock." But we've had reason to believe that sometimes, from complaints that have come in, and from certain evidence placed in our hands, honey has actually sold at several cents higher per pound than was shown by the account of sales rendered to a bee-keeper, and on which commission was based. In this way commission men practically take two commissions. Say, for instance, the honey sold for 12 cents. He makes returns to the bee-keeper of 10 cents, and then charges 10 per cent commission on this 10 cents. He thus makes the 2 cents which he actually steals, and then the 10 per cent which is rightfully his.

In the foregoing we've endeavored to set forth some of the tricks that are practiced by some of the unscrupulous commission houses. But we are glad to say that all, or nearly all, of the men who quote prices in the bee-journals are responsible and honest men; for no commission man can hold his name in the advertising columns of the average bee-journal to-day if there are complaints entered by bee-keepers against him. And right in this connection we wish to say that the mere fact that your bank says a certain commission house has good financial rating should not be considered as evidence that the house is also honest. we would rather trust the man who is honest and not responsible than the one who is financially good and yet "up to the tricks of the trade."

At the time you make shipment, send bill of lading to the commission house, and *name price below which the honey must not be sold.* A commission house has no right to sell at a lower figure until you give instructions. Before the honey is packed it should be carefully weighed so that you will know exactly how much honey you have sent. Do not send large shipments at first. If in any case you send honey, and the commission house fails to make returns, or refuses to do so, it is a criminal act. Such house has no right to appropriate your money without rendering to you some sort of returns; but never take a note in payment from an irresponsible firm or individual: if you do you will be powerless to help yourself; for legally a note is a settlement.

SELLING FOR CASH.

If you can sell for cash, and the party is responsible, by all means do so, providing you can get market prices. Look out for firms wanting to buy for cash with no rating, in Dun's or Bradstreet's commercial agencies. To make yourself secure ship the honey to *your* name at the point of destination, and then send bill of lading to some bank in the city with instructions to turn over bill of lading to purchaser on receipt of cash. Banks will charge you a small fee for doing the business, but you will be safe. The law gives the producer greater protection when his honey is sold on commission than when sold for cash, providing money is not received before honey is turned over. We wish to reiterate the point again: Never deliver honey to a firm on an outright sale or deal till the banks say your man is entirely responsible; *then* if every thing is in writing you are able to collect by due process of law; but if he is irresponsible you will be throwing away good money in trying to do any thing with him in a legal way.

KEEPING COMB HONEY.

It is sometimes desirable to keep comb honey for a better market, or that we may have a supply the year round, etc. Well, to keep it with unimpaired flavor it must not be subjected to dampness. If water condenses on the surface of the comb it soon dilutes the honey, and then it sours, etc. On this account the honey should never be put into a cellar or other damp room. Better put it upstairs; and that there may be a free circulation of air, without admitting bees or flies, the windows should be covered with painted wire cloth. We are accustomed to keeping comb honey the year round, and rarely have it deteriorate in the least. The same remarks will, in the main, apply to keeping extracted honey. During damp and rainy weather, the doors and windows to the honey-room or honey-house should be closed, and opened again when the air is dry.

Comb honey should under no circumstances be stored where it is likely to freeze, as freezing contracts the wax so as to break the combs and let the honey run. Mouse-traps should be kept set to catch the first mouse that appears.

Elsewhere under this heading we have drawn attention to the importance of keeping honey stored in a room kept, as nearly as possible, at the same temperature as the living-room. It should not go down to the freezing-point at any time—nay, rather, it should never go below 70 *if it is possible to avoid it.* Varying degrees of temperature have a strong tendency to make honey granulate; and nothing ruins comb honey quicker than this.

We made some experiments to see how hot we could keep the room and not have the combs melt down. We find the temperature must not go higher than 103 F. While this may seem excessively high, yet if the honey begins to candy the only way to arrest the process of granulation is to bring the temperature up to 103, and *maintain it there.* Aye, there is the difficulty. We accomplished it by putting steam-coils in the room with sufficient radiation so that the temperature can be held between 101 and 103. If it goes above the high point, an automatic regulator, something on the plan of an incubator-valve, allows the heat to escape. As the temperature drops, this valve closes.

We kept some 2000 lbs. of honey in this room for two months. Some of the honey had already begun to granulate, and it was our hope that we could not only arrest the granulation but bring the granulation back to a liquid condition. In this last we were disappointed, but we succeeded admirably in stopping the process that would have soon ruined this whole lot of honey.

We are not sure but a temperature of 100 F. might do as well, and possibly such a degree would be safer for the average person to use, because, if the thermometer shows higher than 103, there is great danger that the combs will be overheated, sag, and set the honey to leaking.

Perhaps one in a small way might be able to maintain a room hot by the use of a hardcoal stove, from which a regular heat will be given off. In some instances one might use furnace heat. This latter would, perhaps, be advantageous in that it would provide for ventilation and thus hasten the evaporation of any unripe or thin honey. But certain it is, there must be some sort of automatic regulation of the heat. While the heater can be controlled to a certain extent, it seems more feasible to let the surplus heat escape.

Under EXTRACTED HONEY will be found hints on peddling honey and marketing in general. See also PEDDLING HONEY.

CONTRACTION. A few years ago contraction of the brood-nest seemed to be all the rage. It was argued that most colonies, Italians especially, after they had put a little honey in the brood-nest, would be disinclined to go above into the supers; and to force them above, some bee-keepers took out three or four of the brood-frames below and contracted the brood-nest, and then placed supers on top. This was very pretty in theory, and in practice it *did* force things. It forced the bees into the supers, but more often forced swarming.

Another set of contractionists argued in favor of hiving *swarms* in a contracted brood-chamber. They did not believe in contracting the brood-nest in an established colony; and, therefore, when they contracted at all they did so only during swarming time. This form of contraction will certainly be better than the other; but as the years go by we hear less and less about contraction and more and more about expansion—how to get stocks strong—big, rousing, powerful colonies. An eight-frame brood-nest is usually small enough. Indeed, a ten-frame may be none too big. See HIVES, SIZE OF, elsewhere, for the further consideration of this subject.

COTTON. The cotton of the Southern United States is interesting to bee-keepers because of the fact that some years it is nectar-producing, the yield of honey being considerable at such times. It is of a light color, good body, but indifferent in flavor. As a rule it must be used for manufacturing purposes. Considerable quantities of it are offered in the market some seasons and none at others.

Cotton honey has the peculiarity, when confined, of bursting the receptacle in which it is held. Whether it ferments or generates gas has not yet been definitely determined. It can, however, be put into casks, providing there is plenty of air-space left to allow for expansion.

CRIMSON CLOVER. See CLOVER.

CROSS BEES. See ANGER OF BEES.

CYPRIAN BEES. See ITALIANS.

D.

DANDELION (*Taraxacum, dens leonis*) is undoubtedly an important honey-plant, not on account of the actual amount of the honey crop received from it, but rather from its great value to the bees in early spring as a stimulator of brood-rearing, and, later on, as a sort of tid-bit to keep the colonies from being fed when the main flowers have ceased to bloom. It flowers most in spring, no matter how cool may be the weather; but a small succession of bloom is kept up until late fall. It yields both honey and pollen, hence i s unique value as a bee-keeper's plant. All sorts of stock eat it more or less, but this seems to make no difference in the amo nt of bloom it will furnish. It is supposed to be especially good for milch cows, and in any case they are very fond of a dandelion pasture. In spite of this, many people are vigorously opposed to this plant, because it

A PART OF A FIELD OF DANDELION IN FULL BLOOM, AT MEDINA.

This, and other fields like it near Medina, furnish considerable honey and pollen in early spring—just when it can do the most good. We do not find that the plant hurts the hay or pastures in the least.

gets into their lawns, spoiling the green appearance so much desired, and crusades have been started in all parts of the country with a view to its eradication. The bee-keeper looks on with equanimity, because the methods usually taken only spread it further.

nishing early "greens," and for this use it is much appreciated by many.

In Europe the thick fleshy roots of several years' growth are ground and used to mix with coffee—not to make the latter cheaper, for the roots cost more than the coffee—but

A LARGE SPECIMEN OF DANDELION BLOSSOM, BUDS, AND LEAVES—LIFE SIZE.
The blossom here shown is larger than the average. The usual size is about two inches across.

Some farmers like to see it come, as it usually improves a pasture, and does not stay in land which is cultivated every year.

A large variety of the dandelion from France is now being cultivated by market-gardeners in the East for the purpose of fur-

it is understood that "taraxacum," the druggists' name for dandelion, is a very superior remedy for "liver trouble."

Usually the English people mix coffee with either chicory or dandelion, which are much alike.

To keep it out of a lawn, the lawn-mower ought to be sharp and close-cutting, and, in addition, a heavy roller should be used quite frequently. In any case one has to do this to get a fine lawn, even when dandelions are not present.

DAISY. See ASTERS.

DISEASES OF BEES. A few years ago it was considered that bees were freer from disease than perhaps any other class of animated nature, for the reason that individual members of the colonies were so constantly giving way to the younger ones. But this has been shown to be, to a great extent, a mistake; for apparently there are at least three or four distinct diseases with which the bee-keeper has to contend; and it is well for the beginner to have an idea, at least, of what they are like; for the time to cure a disease of a contagious character is to take it at the start, or, better still, take precautionary measures such as will prevent its making even a *beginning*.

HOW TO AVOID DISEASES.

Contagious diseases spread very rapidly among bees, just as they are inclined to make rapid headway in crowded centers of the human family. Unfortunately, bees are disposed to rob from each other during a dearth of honey; and if the germs of disease or infection reside in the honey they may be scattered over the entire apiary in a few days. An infected colony is naturally weakened and discouraged, and as a result the bees do not make the defense that they would under normal conditions. During a dearth of honey the healthy bees all over the yard are quite disposed to rob the weak or sick ones, so that the infection is scattered right and left.

One of the best precautions against disease is good food, and keeping all colonies strong. A healthy human being is much more able to resist the germs of infection than one who is "all run down." A person, for instance, is not likely to come down with typhoid unless his system is greatly reduced. Then it is that the typhoid germs, which may be ever present, take hold and begin their insidious work.

Another wise precaution is to keep all tools and clothing, and every thing that has been in contact with a diseased colony, away from the healthy ones. If one does not *know* what the disease is he should be on the safe side and proceed as if the sick colony were infected with the worst infection known to bee culture.

TWO CLASSES OF DISEASES.

The diseases with which the bee-keeper has to contend may be divided into two classes—those that affect the mature flying bees, and those that attack the brood.

Among the diseases that attack the mature bees may be mentioned "spring dwindling." This, perhaps, should hardly be considered a disease, but it is a malady with which we have to deal. For particulars regarding it, see WINTERING. Still another trouble is dysentery. This in some cases may be a germinal disease; and in most cases assumes the nature of an ordinary diarrhea. See DYSENTERY. The only disease of any account now remaining that affects adult bees is—

BEE-PARALYSIS.

This is a disease that is much more prevalent and virulent in warm than in cold climates. Almost every apiarist in the North has noticed at times perhaps one or two colonies in his apiary that would show bees affected with it. Yet it seldom spreads or makes any great trouble; but, unfortunately, this is not true in some parts of the South and West. In the South it is known to affect whole apiaries, and seems to be infectious. Unless a cure is effected in some way it will do almost as much damage as foul brood itself.

SYMPTOMS.

In the early stages an occasional bee will be found to be running from the entrance, with the abdomen greatly swollen, and in other respects the bee has a black, greasy appearance. While these sick bees may be scattered through the hive, they will sooner or later work their way toward the entrance, evidently desiring to rid the colony of their miserable presence. The other bees also seem to regard them as no longer necessary to the future prosperity of the colony. In fact, they will tug and pull at them about as they would at a dead bee until they succeed in getting them out in the grass, where the poor bees seem willing to go to die alone.

Another symptom is, that the bees often show a shaking or trembling motion. In the earlier stages, this peculiarity does not appear; but later on it manifests itself very perceptibly.

TREATMENT AND CURE.

In some cases destroying the queen of the infected colony, and introducing another from a healthy stock, effects a cure. This would seem to indicate that paralysis is constitutional, coming from the queen; but in the South, where the disease is much more prevalent and destructive, destroying the queen seems to have but little effect. Spraying the combs with a solution of salt and water, or of carbolic acid and water, has been recommended; but these do little or no good. One writer recommends removing the diseased stock from its stand, and putting in its place a strong healthy one. The affected colony is then removed to the stand formerly occupied by the healthy bees. He reports that he tried this in many cases, and found that an absolute cure followed in every instance. The *rationale* of the treatment seems to be that the bees of the ordinary colony having bee-paralysis are too much discouraged to remove the sick; as a consequence, the source of infection—that is, the swollen shiny bees—are allowed to crawl through the hive at will. But when the colonies are transposed, the healthy vigorous bees of the sound stock carry the diseased bees entirely away from the hive. The sick and the dying being removed, the colony recovers.

Mr. O. O. Poppleton, of Stuart, Fla., has had a large experience. One plan that he uses is as follows:

He sprinkles sulphur over the affected bees and combs, but not until all the brood in the diseased colony has been removed and put into a strong healthy one; for Mr. Poppleton says the sulphur kills all the unsealed brood and eggs; that no harm results in putting the brood among healthy bees, as he finds the source of the malady is not in the brood or combs; for he has put combs from paralytic colonies repeatedly into healthy ones, and never (but once) did the disease develop in any such colony, and that was a year afterward.

At first, says Mr. Poppleton, the disease seems to get worse instead of better. The colony will dwindle, but in two weeks there will be a decided improvement, and finally the colony will be cured and will stay cured. In many cases, he thinks, it may be necessary to repeat the application of the sulphur about ten days after the first time. This makes sure that every bee has received a curative quantity of the sulphur, even if it were not in the hive at the first dose.*

While the foregoing has worked well, yet because it is attended with a rapid reduction of the strength of the colony so treated, and because the disease has a tendency to run in certain strains that are very susceptible to it, Mr. Poppleton thinks that, in the long

* Always spray the sulphur on in the evening.

run, it may be better to use the following plan: He forms as many nuclei from strong healthy stocks as there are sick colonies to be treated. As soon as the nuclei have young laying queens, he gives to each, as fast as they can take care of them, one or two frames of the oldest capped brood from each of the paralytic colonies, and thereafter till all the brood of such colonies is used up. The diseased bees and queen he next destroys with sulphur fumes, fumigating the hives at the same time.

Repeated tests have shown that paralysis is never transmitted by the brood or combs, but that it is carried by the dead or sick bees. It is, therefore, important that, in giving the combs to the nuclei, there be no dead bees in the cells.

If not convenient then to use the nucleus plan, replace the old queen and use the sulphur.

FOUL BROOD* — AMERICAN AND EUROPEAN.

Probably many a bee-keeper is annoyed rather than otherwise that so much room is taken up in bee-journals on the subject of foul brood, all which matter he faithfully skips, feeling that it has no interest for him. But a day comes when something awakens his suspicion. Then he wants to know the symptoms.

SYMPTOMS OF THE AMERICAN, OR ROPY, FOUL BROOD.

The specimen shown next page is typical of an advanced stage of the disease, because it shows sunken and perforated capped cells, and those uncapped with the dead larvæ lying on one side. While we usually expect the larvæ to die in the case of old-fashioned or American foul brood after sealing, yet

* In referring to the principal forms of brood diseases, we have thought best to adopt the names used by the Bureau of Entomology of the United States government. Both the diseases, because they are much alike in appearance and effects, are designated as "foul" brood, and distinguished by qualifying adjectives. The foul brood that has been so long known in this country, as well as in Europe, will be here designated as "*American* foul brood," although it is not of American origin. The newer disease (black brood), first identified in Europe and later found in New York State, will be designated as "*European* foul brood." The old name for this disease, "*black* brood," is not descriptive of the disease it is supposed to name, for the brood affected is not black, although some shriveled specimens may take on that color. But this is also true of foul brood. Whether the selection of these qualifying adjectives is wise we will not discuss; and we therefore would refer the reader to Technical Series No. 14, Bacteria of the Apiary, and to Circular No. 79, by Dr. E. F. Phillips, of the Bureau of Entomology. Neither do we think it necessary in a practical work of this kind to discuss the bacteriology of these diseases, inasmuch as there seems to be a difference of opinion among scientific men as to the real microbe that is responsible for either.

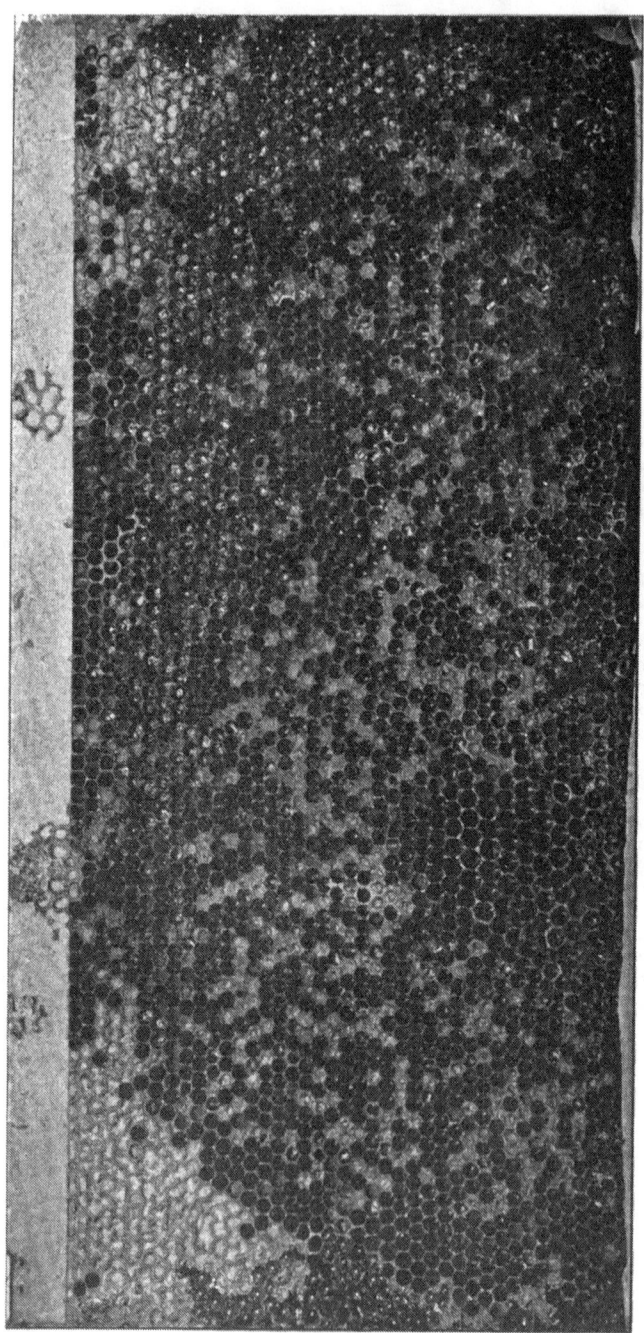

A COMB OF OLD-FASHIONED (AMERICAN) FOUL BROOD IN AN ADVANCED STAGE.

This is an excellent specimen of a comb badly affected with the disease. In this stage there are cells sealed and unsealed containing dead grubs. Notice particularly the rugged perforations of some of the capped cells. Notice also the unevenness of the cappings, some sunken, some flat, and others rounding, and probably containing healthy larvæ.

when the disease is very bad in the comb we find dead larvæ in almost all stages of growth, showing all gradations of colors, from a bright yellow to a deep dark brown. Just about as the larva dies it takes on a bright yellow. This turns darker and darker, showing next the color of the coffee we drink with milk in it. The shade deepens until it is of the color of strong coffee without milk. At this stage the larva loses its form, sinking down into a shapeless mass; and if a toothpick be introduced into this mass the dead matter will adhere to it, roping out some two or three inches like spittle. This has given rise to the term *ropy* foul brood, as distinguished from the type known as black brood, or, as the Bureau of Entomology has it, European foul brood.

The cappings of the cells of the old-fashioned foul brood are very apt to be sunken. Somewhere over the surface there may be a small hole as if it had been pricked with a pin. This hole may be very minute; but as it enlarges it is apt to be angular, with ragged edges. It would appear that the bees make an opening in the cells, knowing that something is wrong, and the mess within is so foul that they give it up in disgust. It would appear, also, that some of the bees go back, tear away the opening a little more, and then quit the job. By examining the engraving one may see the various sizes of openings in the cappings. Among the sunken cells and perforated ones will be found others that are perfectly normal. On opening up the same we find healthy grubs within.

It is very seldom that we find *all* the cells in a comb affected, even in an advanced stage. In the one before us, probably a tenth of them were in a healthy condition, and from them would emerge in the course of time healthy normal bees. Foul brood, then, seems to attack a comb in spots. This is due possibly to the fact that young larvæ are fed with the pap or honey containing the disease germs, and others may be accidentally fed by other bees a food that is in no way affected, and consequently they mature perfectly normal bees.

When the combs are badly diseased, like the one in the engraving, they will give off a strong odor like that of a glue-pot, such as one gets while the glue is boiling, except that it is worse. The stench is almost identical with that which emanates from a lot of dead bees piled up in a damp place in hot weather. Several times our men have been led to suppose there was foul brood in the yard by the peculiar odor, when examination showed that a lot of dead bees that had died during the winter were in front of the entrance.

But we have heard bee-keepers say that they do not regard the odor from foul brood as so foul as the books have stated. This all depends on the kind of nose one has. Some odors are sickening to one, but endurable to another. This is particularly true of the odor that emanates from foul brood.

When one finds a comb like the one shown in the engraving on the preceding page the colony is pretty badly diseased; and it is also probable that other hives in the immediate vicinity are likewise affected; because when a case is so far advanced as this, the probabilities are that several colonies in the yard are involved; and it would be well to make a general search through the apiary. Colonies with entrances pointing in the same direction, and near by, will be almost sure to show some diseased cells. Possibly one will not find more than three or four affected cells, and those in only one comb, for the disease has only started in that hive. Sometimes one will not be able to find a single cell containing a dead larva. In one case, where we could plainly smell foul brood, we could not find any dead specimen in any cell until we had looked over the combs for something like half an hour, opening up here and there a cell, until we finally located a dead larva whose tissue would rope out as we have before explained. But as a general thing, before there is any pronounced odor a comb will be quite badly diseased. In that case one is not likely to notice it, even at the entrance. Something will depend on the direction of the wind, if any, and whether the bees are ventilating the hive.

In the foregoing we have stated that a ropy condition of the dead matter was an important symptom of foul brood. We may say that it is the *most important* symptom, because it is the one test by which we distinguish American foul brood from all other brood diseases. While the dead matter of European (black) brood will rope slightly, perhaps ¼ of an inch or so, the dead matter of foul brood will stretch out like spittle anywhere from half an inch to a couple of inches. When it shows up like this, one can be very sure that he has before him the real foul brood. If he also finds the typical glue-pot odor is present and the cappings of the cells take on an appearance like those shown in the engravings, he does not need

ANOTHER COMB BADLY AFFLICTED WITH FOUL BROOD OF THE ROPY OR AMERICAN TYPE.

to go to the trouble of writing to the Bureau of Entomology of the United States government to find out whether he has foul brood, but had best begin his treatment at once.

There is a kind of pinhole perforation that is perfectly normal in healthy brood, and should not be confounded with the perforations for foul brood. Sometimes in hot weather the bees leave their young bareheaded, as it were; that is, there will be small openings in the cappings; but these openings are circular, and in the center of the cell; and if one peeps through he will see that the grubs are white, and that all is well. But beginners who have discovered this peculiar condition have jumped to the conclusion that it was foul brood, without due investigation. The matter is here mentioned so that they may not be confused.

TREATMENT AND CURE OF AMERICAN FOUL BROOD.

Years ago this disease got quite a start in our own apiary before we realized what it was; and had we at that time an engraving or photo like what we have already shown we should have discovered the disease long before we did. As it was we had to treat at a great disadvantage something like eighty colonies during that summer. Some of them we burned outright—hives, bees, frames, combs, and all. Others we treated with salicylic acid, carbolic acid, or phenol, but not with very satisfactory results. Indeed, if we had treated all colonies at the start by the McEvoy plan we might have had the disease under control, and probably would not have had to exceed two dozen affected colonies all told. The method that finally gave us relief was as follows: As soon as a colony was discovered having a cell or two of the diseased brood it was closed immediately, and a brick or stone was laid on the cover. Just before dark, and while all the bees of the apiary were in the hives, and all danger from robbers was past, we removed the hive from its stand, and put another one just like it in its place. This hive contained frames filled with full sheets of foundation. The bees were shaken off from the diseased combs, either on top of the frames or in front of the entrance of the new hive now on the old stand. The combs, as soon as free of bees, were put back into the old hive, and the whole thing was carried to the boiler-furnace, where the frames were burned in a hot fire. The hives were then disinfected by scorching out on the inside in a manner to be explained.

THE M'EVOY TREATMENT; DISINFECTING HIVES.

We said we boiled or burned the hives; but Wm. McEvoy, Woodburn, Ont., Can., foul-brood inspector for Ontario, and in the government employ, reports having treated successfully hundreds and perhaps thousands of colonies by putting the bees back into the *same hive from which they came.* His treatment is given thus in his own language:

In the honey season, when the bees are gathering freely, remove the combs *in the evening* and shake the bees into their own hive; give them frames with comb-foundation starters on and let them build comb for four days. The bees will make the starters into comb during the four days, and store the diseased honey in them which they took with them from the old comb. Then in the evening of the fourth day take out the new combs and give them comb foundation to work out, and then the cure will be complete.

Mr. McEvoy does not recommend treating the hive; but reports have been received by the publishers showing that the disease has returned in some instances where the hive had not been disinfected. It is advised, therefore, that one and all disinfect the hives as well as the combs. While they may be immersed in boiling water, yet completely disinfecting them would possibly require a boiling of two hours, as the spores of these brood diseases have been shown to be able to resist in some cases a temperature of 212° for two and a half hours, and still survive.

A far better plan, and one much simpler to apply, is to put a handful or two of dry straw in the empty hive that contained the affected colony, and touch a match to it. With a stick poke the straw around, so that every portion of the hive will be scorched or blackened by the flame. It is not necessary to char deep; for if the wood be burned to a light brown or black, the progress of the disease will be arrested. The flame can be quenched by throwing in a dipperful of water. Such a hive will be completely disinfected, and may be used again with entire safety. It should be noted, however, that the alighting-board of the hive, as well as the entrance itself, should be charred slightly. Where straw is not available a gill or two of kerosene may be thrown inside the hive and ignited. But straw is much cheaper, and when the job is done it leaves no odor clinging to the hive.

What shall be done with the frames and the combs? If there is only one colony in the yard that is affected, it is advised to burn them *at night*—combs, frames, brood, and all. In order to do this, a small bonfire should be made of old brush; then when the fire is at its height throw on the combs one by one. The ashes should afterward be raked up and buried, for sometimes the wax will melt and run down among the wood ashes, without coming in contact with the flame itself. The ashes may be rendered safe, however, without burying if they be put over live coals and reburned.

In case the disease gets a start through the yard it will be rather wasteful to burn the combs, and it is, therefore, advised to melt them up at night in a vat of boiling water, after extracting any honey they may contain. In this latter operation be careful not to spill any honey on the floor, nor let any come in contact with the tools or clothing where the bees can get at it the following day. Every thing about the room in which the wax is melted must be cleaned up, and

the old slumgum that may be left should be buried. Of course the process of rendering would ordinarily disinfect it; yet as there might be some carelessness in melting, the reader is advised to take the safer course and bury the refuse. Neither is it advised to put any diseased or supposed-to-be diseased combs in a sun or solar wax-extractor. Too many of these machines are not bee-tight. Very often they leak, allowing either honey or wax, or both, to run out on the ground. It is doubtful whether the sun heat alone would be sufficient to bring about a thorough disinfection of the affected honey or wax. Nothing short of a kettle of boiling water, a steam or hot-water wax-press, or boiling water and an open hand-press should be used for handling these old combs. The handle of the screw, if it be of iron, should be exposed to a flame from the stove after the work is done. Any thing else that might become contaminated during the process of extracting and melting of combs should be likewise disinfected. The extractor itself should be thoroughly scalded out with boiling water—not once but several times; *and do not put this off one single day.*

In case that foul brood breaks out in the yard, and continues to break out from time to time, the only thing that remains then will be to treat the whole apiary, whether diseased or not. As soon as brood hatches out of healthy combs, extract the honey and melt them up. The wax thus secured, if taken out with a modern wax-press, will pay for the foundation put back into the frames. Continue shaking every colony on frames of foundation as fast as brood hatches out. If in case of healthy colonies the disease shows up in only a mild form, one set only of frames and foundation need be given. In that case, use full sheets always.

A very good time to recomb the bees will be during swarming season. It will then be almost or quite time to practice "shook" swarming, as advised in the text-books. All combs as fast as extracted should be melted up and their place taken by frames of foundation. While the old frames may be used over again after boiling or subjecting them to the flame of a bonfire, many advise the purchase of new frames that will probably be stronger and better than the old things that were formerly in the hives. It probably would not be necessary to char out or burn out the old hives where the whole apiary is treated; but if one desires to be on the safe side he would do well to treat hives as well as combs.

A few may feel that they can not sacrifice good brood; for in the diseased combs there may be only a few affected cells. Such frames can be placed in an upper story over perforated zinc, while the bees and queens in the lower hive can be put on frames of foundation. As soon as the brood hatches out above, treat as before directed.

In describing the next disease we can not do better than to compare the two together.

EUROPEAN AND AMERICAN FOUL BROOD DIFFERENTIATED.

European foul brood (black brood) first manifested itself on this side of the Atlantic in New York, although, as already stated, it was first discovered by Cheshire and Cheyne in Europe, and hence the name, European foul brood. In several of the external symptoms it resembles foul brood, but lacks two or three very important characteristics of that disease. First, the European disease is seldom if ever ropy. The dead matter, does not, as in the American variety, become a shapeless gluey mass, leaving no semblance of the original grub, stretching out like glue when a toothpick is inserted in it; but, on the contrary, it is of a watery consistency, and seems to be confined mostly within the shriveled skin of the dead grub, which may vary in color all the way from a light yellow or dark brown, to black. A grub that dies with American foul brood seems to melt, as it were, into one mass of sticky stuff that adheres to the bottom or side of the cell; while a grub that dies from the European disease retains its general form, though shriveled up, and will remain in the *end* of the cell. It may, however, fall over on the side of the cell; but the shape of the grub in an elongated state will be practically the same except that it is shriveled brown or black. American foul brood smells like old glue. European foul brood, in the earlier stages, has a sort of soured or musty smell. In the *later* stages it takes on a foul odor something like that of the American disease, in which state the sour odor seems to be lost or obscured by the more pronounced odor of decay. American foul brood seems to affect both the sealed and unsealed grub, but more especially the sealed brood; and when the dead matter is allowed to dry, it adheres very tightly to the lower side of the cell wall. The European disease, on the other hand, seems to affect more particularly the unsealed brood, although much of the sealed brood dies, and has a perforated and sunken capping, very much like that of foul brood.

But a dead grub never adheres either to the side or the bottom of the cell. The larvæ of European foul brood when *first* affected have on the body a yellow spot; and before dying they move uneasily in the cell. After death they turn yellow, then brown, and finally black, ultimately drying down to a black scale or what appears to be an empty skin of the larva.

TO CURE EUROPEAN FOUL BROOD (BLACK BROOD).

The method of treatment is just the same as for foul brood in every particular. But Mr. E. W. Alexander, who has something like 700 colonies in one locality, reports that he was successful in eradicating this dreadful disease from his apiary by dequeening and putting in Italian blood; but before giving the new queen he keeps the hive queenless at least three weeks, during which time not a particle of brood is allowed to develop. The honey in the combs should be exhausted as far as possible; and during the three weeks the bees will have polished up and otherwise cleaned the combs in preparation for a laying queen, which they expect to get, but which is purposely kept from them until the alloted time has elapsed. A young vigorous Italian queen is then introduced. While we have received reports from some who have used this treatment, and have been successful, the foul brood inspectors of New York, from their experience of the disease, do not think that the treatment goes far enough. We would not advise this treatment except in cases where the disease seems to get a foothold and defies treatment—that is, lingers on. Then *all* colonies, whether showing the disease or not, should be treated by the dequeening process and afterward requeened.

PICKLED BROOD AND ITS CAUSE.

The name pickled brood has been applied to almost any form of dead brood that was not black or foul brood. In a general way, it seems to cover, then, any form of brood that is dead from some natural causes not related to disease of any sort. Pickled brood looks very much like European or black brood. The larva dies, lying on its side in the bottom of the cell, both ends of which begin to turn a little yellow, brown, and then black. The discoloration seems to creep along until the whole body is involved. About this time the larva begins to shrivel and finally dries up. The real pickled brood is probably nothing more nor less than starved brood. If there is a lack of stores the bees will neglect the brood, when it will die, as before described, But there may be a great abundance of honey or syrup in the hives, and still the larvæ will die. Some springs and early summers there is a lack of pollen. In order that brood-rearing may be carried on in the hive there must be nitrogenous food of some sort, either of natural pollen or of bean or rye meal which the beekeeper may set out. Sometimes malted milk powder is strewn over the combs; but as this is rather expensive, we would advise giving the bees bean or rye meal, or any meal that is obtainable from some grain. This should be put on boards in a sunny protected place outdoors.

During the early spring of 1909 considerable pickled or dead brood was reported from various sections of the country. Investigation revealed the fact that this was nothing more nor less than *starved* brood; starved, not because of a lack of honey or syrup, but because of the entire absence of pollen in the combs. A good deal of brood-rearing had started from pollen that was left over from the season before; but when this was exhausted, the poor bees, not being able to get any thing from natural sources, simply had to let the brood die. It is important, therefore, to see that all hives during the previous fall are supplied with pollen in one or two combs, for there can be no brood-rearing without it.

CHILLED, OVERHEATED, OR POISONED BROOD.

If the grubs all seem to have died about the same date, one may conclude some external change, probably a chilling atmosphere, or an exposure of the combs to a sudden change in the weather was the cause—particularly so if he discovers no odor of sourness or foulness. If the brood that comes on subsequently seems to be healthy, and continues to be so, then he may be sure he has no infectious disease. He may then conclude that his brood is probably chilled and possibly poisoned, as a large amount of brood dies every fruit-bloom season, as the result of poison sprayed on the trees by the orchardist. If he finds any such dead brood in his hives at that season he may conclude it died as the result of poison.

Overheated brood does not often occur except in the hottest weather, when the combs have been exposed to a hot sun without any bees over it, or when the same has been confined with a powerful colony with a closed entrance. When moving bees, and insufficient ventilation is given, many of the bees often die of overheating. In all cases of this kind much of the brood will be found dead. One will very often find that some of the brood looks suspicious from a shipment of bees just received by experts. Occasionally we have had reports from our customers of how they had received foul brood through a shipment of bees, not knowing that the nucleus or the hive of bees is often exposed by the expressman during shipment, to a hot sun or in a room with no air circulating.

SENDING SUSPECTED SAMPLES OF DEAD BROOD TO THE GOVERNMENT BACTERIOLOGIST.

We have taken pains to describe the various forms of dead brood, often called pickled brood, in order to enable the beekeeper to determine what he has in his yard; but if he finds a case of dead brood that smells quite strongly acid or sour, he had better send a sample, about 4x5 inches. wrapped in paraffine or oiled paper, the whole inclosed in a stout wooden or tin box, to Dr. E. F. Phillips, Bureau of Entomology, Washington, D. C. The report from the bacteriologists will soon determine what the trouble is. If the report comes back, "Not black brood nor foul brood," then the sender may rest easy. If the case looks like black brood, first smells a little sour and then afterward takes on a nasty decayed odor, we would advise treating the hive as if it were black brood.

BLACK BEES LESS ABLE TO RESIST FOUL AND BLACK BROOD.

It may be stated that black bees show less disposition to resist European or American foul brood than Carniolans or any of the new races. It follows, therefore, that all European foul brood should be eliminated from the apiary as soon as possible, as repeated tests have shown that the German bees do not resist any disease as well as the yellow races. But one must not rely entirely on a change of blood, as this of itself will not effect a cure in a great majority of cases.

A strong honey-flow always has a tendency to check the spread of both American and European foul brood. In the same way, heavy feeding will accomplish much the same result. But it often happens after a honey-flow, when stores are partly consumed, that the diseased matter is uncovered, when the dead larvæ, showing the effect of the microbe poison or disease, will begin to appear again.

PREVENTION.

It would be useless to effect a cure without extreme care not to have other colonies affected; and a little carelessness on the part of the bee-keeper may spread the disease throughout the whole apiary. A comb from a diseased colony or a single drop of infected honey is enough to carry the disease—hence the instructions to operate *in the evenings,* so bees from healthy colonies will not steal any of the diseased honey. A single bee from a diseased colony entering a healthy one will carry the disease in its honey sac.

CAUTION.

Do all work after dark, or at least when no bees are flying. Take every precaution not to start robbing, either of a diseased or a healthy colony. If there is *any* robbing, it endangers the whole apiary. If one suspects foul brood in any part of his apiary, he should by no means exchange combs. If it is in any colony, it may be in one that does not yet show the disease at all, but will give it to others. If one has extracted any honey he should not feed back without boiling. After handling a foul-broody colony he should not touch a healthy colony till his hands are thoroughly washed. Any knives, towels, or any thing daubed in the least with foul honey, must be religiously got out of reach of bees. One should be careful *from the first.* Caution at the start will be worth a hundred times later on.

FORMALIN, OR FORMALDEHYDE, FOR CURING FOUL BROOD.

In 1903 and '4 discussion arose in *Gleanings in Bee Culture* as to the possible value of formaldehyde (or formalin) for curing foul brood. Some of the experimenters who had subjected several combs of honey and brood from infected colonies to the fumes of the gas in a tight box reported it a success. Others tried the same thing only to find that such combs would transmit the disease the same as before. Experiments conducted in the Bureau of Entomology, Department of Agriculture, Washington, D. C., showed that, when combs were subjected to the fumes of the gas for 48 hours in a Novy's anaerobic jar, all germs of the disease would be destroyed; but as the average bee-keeper could not have the requisite facilities, skill, and knowledge to carry on such work, he had better not take his chances of transmitting any infectious disease through combs fumigated under conditions such as he is able to provide. In all probability the work would not be complete enough to make disinfection sure. If any infection at all were left, the disease would spread again, and so the work might just as well have not been done—or not attempted; because melting up the combs and boiling, or, better, burning up the frames, would remove all possible traces of disease.

DIVIDING. This term is usually applied to the operation of increasing the number of stocks by putting half the bees and combs into a new hive, just about swarming time: it is really one method of artificial swarming. If you have an extra laying queen to give the queenless portion, it may do very well; but otherwise it is a wasteful way of making increase, and has been mostly abandoned. See NUCLEUS and SWARMING, under subhead ARTIFICIAL SWARMING; also INCREASE.

DRONES. These are large noisy bees that do a great amount of buzzing, but never sting anybody, for the very good reason that they have no sting. The bee-keeper who has learned to recognize them, both by sight and sound, never pays any attention to their noise, but visitors are many times sadly frightened by their loud buzzing. We will commence as we did with the worker-bees, at the egg, and see how much we can learn of these harmless and inoffensive inmates of the bee-hive.

If our colonies are prosperous, we may find eggs in the drone-comb of some of the best hives as early as March, but not, as a general thing, until April. You can tell the drone cells from the worker at a glance (even if you have never seen them) by the size, as you will see by looking at HONEY-COMB. Whenever you see eggs in the large cells, you may be sure they are drone-eggs. I do not mean by this that the eggs that produce drones look any different from any other eggs that the queen lays, for in looks they are precisely the same. They are almost the same in every respect, for the only difference is that the eggs that produce worker-bees have been impregnated, while the others have not; but more of this, anon. The egg, like those producing workers, remains brooded over by the bees until it is about three days old, and then by one of nature's wonderful transformations is gone, and a tiny worm appears, a mere speck in the bottom of the cell. This worm is fed as before, until it is about a week old, and is then sealed over like a worker larvæ, except that the cap to the cell is raised considerably more; in fact, the cappings very much resemble a lot of bullets laid closely together on a board. The young drones will begin to cut the caps of these cells in about 24 or 25 days; the caps come off in a round piece, very much like those from a queen-cell.

The body of a drone is hardly as long as that of a queen, but he is so much thicker through than either queen or worker that you will never mistake him for either. He has no baskets on his legs in which to carry pollen, and his tongue is so unsuited to the gathering of honey from flowers that he would starve to death in the midst of a clover-field.

We presume the young drones are ready to leave their hive after they are about two weeks old, and they do this shortly after

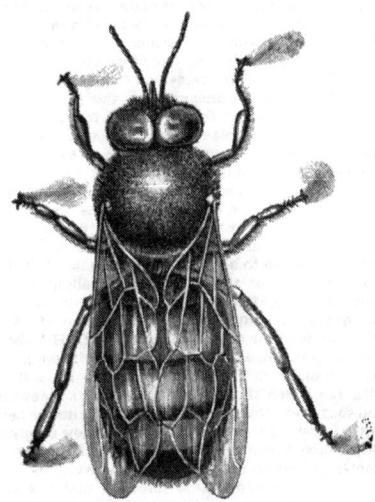

DRONE-BEE ENLARGED SEVEN TIMES.

noon, of a warm pleasant day. They come out with the young bees as they play, and first try their wings; but their motions are far from being graceful and easy, and they frequently tumble about so awkwardly that, as they strike against your face, you might almost think them either drunk or crazy. We do not know how we can very well decide how old a drone must be to fulfill the sole purpose of his existence, the fertilization of the queen, but should guess anywhere from three weeks to as many months. Perhaps they seldom live so long as the last period named, but we think they sometimes do. Many facts seem to indicate that they, as well as the queen, fly long distances from

the hive—perhaps two miles or more. We have now satisfactory evidence that the meeting between queens and drones takes place not very high up from the ground. Several observers, during the season of 1889, reported having seen this meeting not very far from the hives, during the swarming season. The queens and drones both sally forth during the middle of the day, or afternoon, and in from fifteen minutes to an hour, or possibly a couple of hours, the queen returns with a white appendage attached to the extremity of her body, that microscopic examination shows to be the generative organs of the drone. These facts have been observed by hundreds of bee-keepers, and are well authenticated. In attempts to have queens fertilized in wire-cloth houses, we have, after letting the queens out, seen the drones pursue them until both parties vanished from sight. Still another fact: If you take a drone in your hand some warm afternoon just as he has sallied from the hive, and press him in a certain way, he will burst open something like the popping of a grain of corn, extruding the very same organ we find attached to the queen, and dying instantly.

The manner in which the meeting of the drone and queen takes place has been witnessed a great many times. We give here the statements of a few observers.

The Rev. Mr. Millette, of Whitemarsh, Pa., appears to have been the first who witnessed the actual encounter. The following communication from his pen, which we copy from the *Farmer and Gardener* for November, 1899, settles the important fact, as it came under his observation in the preceding summer:

DRONE AND QUEEN BEE.

In the month of June, an old stock threw off a *second* swarm in which there were four queens. During the process of hiving, one of the queens was observed on the wing, and in a moment was seized by a drone. After flying about a rod they both came to the ground in close contact; the writer instantly followed them up; and as the drone was about departing (having broken loose), seized both the bees, the queen in one hand and the drone in the other. They were taken into the house, and left at liberty to fly, when the queen flew to the closed window; but the drone, after crawling about on the hand, was laid upon the window-seat, and in a very few minutes expired. Both the queen and the drone had a milky-white fluid upon the extremity of the abdomen, and upon pressing the drone there was no indication of his possessing the specialty of his sex.

To this we append the following extract of a letter written by Mr. S. B. Parsons (recently dead), of Flushing, New York, confirmatory of the foregoing. Mr. Parsons was well known as a man of probity and honor. He was the introducer of the Italian bee into this country.

He says (*American Bee Journal*):

One fact in our last summer's experience will interest the readers of the *Journal*. The copulation of an Italian drone and queen, upon the wing, was witnessed in my apiary by Mr. Cary and Mr. Otis. They saw the queen issue from the hive, and circle round, when the drone struck her (both being upon the wing). A sharp snap ensued; the drone fell to the ground, and was picked up dead. The queen fell in the grass, rose again, and entered the hive Mr. Cary soon searched for her, found the workers cleaning her off, and the male organs attached to her body.

Later Mr. Cary related his own account of the occurrence, which we submit in his own words:

About three o'clock P. M., on the 8th of July, I saw a young Italian queen enter her hive without any sign of impregnation She came out again in a few minutes, and I closed the entrance to the hive. During her absence, which lasted thirteen minutes, three drones came in front of the hive, and, finding the entrance closed, kept on the wing most of the time. When the returning queen was about three feet from the entrance, one of the drones very rapidly flew to her, and, clasping his legs about her, caused her to settle a little to come in contact with a long spear of grass. At the same time an *explosion* was distinctly heard, and they immediately separated—the drone falling to the ground perfectly dead, and having his abdomen very much contracted. The queen, after making a few circles in the air, entered the hive with the male organs of the drone attached to her. All these facts were witnessed by myself and Mr. R. C. Otis, of Kenosha, Wis., as we were seated on opposite sides of the hive, not more than six feet apart, so that there can be no possible ground of mistake.

In later times a correspondent in *Gleanings in Bee Culture* thus describes the act:

MATING OF THE QUEEN AND DRONE ON THE WING, AS SEEN BY AN EYE-WITNESS.

On June 21, 1888, I saw this mating take place. The queen issued from the hive, took two circles and came within five feet of my face, and was there met by a drone. They seemed to face each other, clinging by their fore legs, their bodies being perpendicular, and in this shape flew from my sight. It happened so unexpectedly that I hardly knew what was going on before it was too late to follow them. I could have easily kept up with them. I have described this because your book says they have not been seen, only as they were whirling about each other. I saw these fasten; and as they did so they turned and came together, square up and down; and as they flew away their bodies inclined about like this /, and each bee was using its wings.

Myrtle, Pa.   E. A. PRATT.

Shortly after this another correspondent reported the one thing yet unobserved; viz., the manner of separation of the queen and drone. He described it as follows:

AN EYE-WITNESS TO THE QUEEN'S SEPARATION FROM THE DRONE AFTER MATING.

I was going out to my bees one day, when two bees came whirling down in front of me and fell on to a pumpkin leaf. It proved to be a queen and drone. The drone acted as if he had been stung by a worker. He held fast to the leaf with his feet, and the queen kept whirling over and over, about as a fly would if caught in a spider's web, until she freed herself, then she flew out of sight in an instant, and the drone remained where he was on the leaf, but showed life for only about three minutes.

Onawa City, Iowa.   S. R. FLETCHER.

The late E. L. Pratt, of Swarthmore, Pa., a queen-breeder of note, in *Gleanings in Bee Culture* for 1904 thus wrote:

I have this day witnessed the act of copulation between a queen and a drone. About 2:30 o'clock on the afternoon of Thursday, July 21, I was standing near a fertilizing-box filling a feeder when my attention was attracted by an unusual commotion in the way of extra loud buzzing, as of drones on the wing. I looked and saw a queen rapidly flying toward the fertilizing-box, evidently her home. She was closely followed by two drones, one of which turned and flew off, but the other remained in pursuit. They were flying not six inches from the ground, and were not over eight feet from the fertilizing-box when the act took place. It was done so quickly that I marveled at it, and I wish here to record the facts as I witnessed them. I could not see that the queen was flying in any but the usual way when returning to her hive, but the drone was unusually swift of wing. They were both flying rapidly; and as they flew the drone made two circles about the queen as though to head her off; and as these circles were made about the queen she rose slightly each time. Directly after making the second circle about the queen the drone flew at her as a worker flies with the intention of stinging in earnest. His abdomen was curved, and his wings rattled in about the same manner. Directly the drone was in contact with the queen there was a sudden lurch sidewise, and they went together some distance into the field until I lost sight of them. As they flew together they much resembled workers when they attempt jointly to bear off their dead. I remained by the fertilizing-box perhaps three minutes, and saw the queen return and enter, bearing the marks of having met a drone. I still lingered by the box, and soon saw a worker bear out the tell-tale white speck. I later opened the box, and saw the queen bearing the usual thread from male contact. A queen-bee is very swift of wing; but I am convinced that a drone is ten times swifter; for to be able to encircle the queen in the manner this one did, such must be the fact.

In the fall of 1876 we saw a swarm of black ants sporting in the sunshine. A close look showed them to be both males and females; and as pair after pair fell to the ground, we had ample opportunity of noting all circumstances. In this case the drones at first seemed paralyzed; but after the queens flew away, they revived and subsequently flew away also. One point here particularly impressed me: The ants of both sexes were in such countless thousands that they must have come from all the ant-hills for, we should say, miles around; the result was, as you see, that there was hardly a possibility of insects from the same family meeting. Now, is there any other way in which the strain of blood could be so effectually crossed with that of some distant colony as by this huge jubilee of both sexes?

Queen-ants, like queen - bees, seldom if ever come out of their homes at any other time, and, as if by some preconcerted arrangement, they meet and mix up apparently for the very purpose of effectually preventing "in-and-in breeding," as it is usually termed when applied to stock. Do queens and drone-bees meet in the same way, in vast numbers? There seems to be no doubt about it, as all known facts point that way. Drones have been seen in places in larger numbers than we would think could possibly come from one hive; and many have heard their loud humming who have not seen them. The fact that a queen should become fertilized in so short a time after leaving the hive seems strange, unless it really is a fact that she is called to the swarm of drones by their loud humming, which she would instinctively recognize from a long distance. Flying among them she meets the drone face to face, falls to the ground, tears herself loose from her dead mate by whirling, and then returns to her hive, having been absent only a few minutes.

DOES THE DRONE HAVE ONLY ONE PARENT?

One of the most wonderful things about the drone, or male bee, is that it is hatched from an egg that is unimpregnated. So wonderful indeed is this that the matter was for ages disputed, and is even now, by many who have not looked into the matter and examined the evidence. What we mean by unimpregnated is, that queens that have never met the male bee at all will lay eggs, and these eggs will hatch, but they always produce drones, and never workers. Those who have had the care of poultry are well aware that the hens will lay eggs right along, if no cock is kept in the yard at all; and, if we are not mistaken, a pullet would commence and lay her full quota of eggs, if she had never seen a male bird. Now, nearly the same is true with regard to the queen-bee. If she fails to meet a drone during the first thirty days of her life, she usually begins to lay eggs; but she seldom lays as many, or with the same regularity, as a fertile queen. The eggs a hen lays, if she is allowed to sit, never produce any chicks at all. The eggs laid by a queen, under the same circumstances, as we have said before, always produce drones. There is one more fact connected with the common fowl: If a male bird is put into the yard with the hen for one day only, good fertile eggs will be laid for many days, possibly a whole laying. If a Black-Spanish cock should get among a flock of white hens for only a single day, all the eggs laid for many days afterward will produce chicks with more or less black feathers on them. We give these statements from actual facts. The point we wish you to observe is, that the eggs of even the common fowl are fertilized as they are laid by the hen, or possibly a few days before. With the fowls, one meeting with the male bird suffices for the fertilization of an egg daily, for a week or more; with the queen-bee, for her whole life of three or even four years.

We do not know whether the hen has the power of laying fertile or unfertile eggs at will or not; probably not; but we do know that a queen-bee lays both fertilized and unfertilized eggs, alternating from one kind to the other in rapid succession. Ski lful microscopists have carefully dissected eggs from worker - cells, and found the living spermatozoa in numbers from one to five. These living spermatozoa were precisely identical with those found in dissecting a mature drone. Again: Every egg a queen lays passes a little sac containing a minute quantity of some fluid; the microscope shows that this fluid contains thousands of these spermatozoa. Is it not wonderful that these spermatozoa should live four years or more in this little sac, awaiting their turn to be developed into a higher life whenever they should be required to fertilize the egg that is to produce a worker-bee? Very well; now the egg that is taken from a drone-cell contains no trace of spermatozoa. Therefore it, like the unimpregnated egg of the common fowl, should never hatch. Strange to say, it *does* hatch, and produce the drone. The first glimpse we get of the little bit of animated nature is the tiny speck alive at the bottom of the cell. Does he grow out of nothing, without parentage, at least on the paternal side? If his mother was an Italian, he is also an Italian; if a black queen, he is also a black. We shall have to conclude, perhaps, that he is the son of his mother, and nothing more. The egg that has never been impregnated in the usual way, must, after all, have some living germ incorporated in its make-up, and this germ must come only from the mother. The great skill and proficiency with the microscope, required to make these minute examinations, is such that but one or two have ever succeeded in exploring as far as we have mentioned, and it is somewhat like our investigations in the polar regions. Who among us will educate himself for the work and carry it along?

Drones are also hatched from eggs laid by worker-bees. These drones are usually smaller in size than those from a queen because they are generally reared in worker-cells, and the question as to whether they are capable of fertilizing queens, so as to be of some value, like other drones, is one that we believe has never been decided. Some facts have been brought to light that seem to be pretty good evidence on both sides of the question; but, so far as we know, nothing very definite. We confess that we should not want to make use of them, even if they were good, for we want the strongest, healthiest, and largest drones we can get. For a further account of the mothers of these queer drones, see LAYING WORKERS.

After what we have said, you will perhaps see how clear it is that the drones are in no way affected by the fertilization of the queen; or, in other words, that all daughters of a purely fertilized Italian queen produce drones absolutely pure whether they have been fertilized by a black drone or not.

Until the invention and general adoption of foundation we had no easy way of repressing the production of drones in far greater numbers than could ever be desirable. Since the introduction of foundation, however, it is found to be quite an easy matter to make almost every cell in the hive a worker-cell. On the other hand, if we choose we can have a hive filled entirely with drone comb, and a good queen could, we think, be induced to raise nearly, if not quite, a full quart of drones at one time. By this means we can have our drones raised from such stock as we choose, and we can save the vast amount of honey that has so long been wasted by rearing and feeding drones that we do not need. While extracting, we have found as many as several pounds of drone larvæ in a single hive; and, to save the honey they would consume as soon as hatched, we used to shave their heads off with a very sharp knife. This is certainly rather expensive business, for it must take more than a pound of honey, to say nothing of the value of the pollen, to get up a pound of sealed brood. If all this labor and material had been utilized in the production of worker-brood, it would doubtless have been equivalent to a swarm of bees. All-worker comb would have insured this without trouble.

This general subject is covered in a more technical article entitled PARTHENOGENESIS elsewhere in this book, and also under head of QUEENS.

HOW TO MAKE BEES BUILD ALL WORKER COMB WHEN ONLY STARTERS ARE USED.

Where one can not afford the expense of full sheets of foundation it is well to know how to make the bees eliminate all drone comb. Mr. E. D. Townsend, of Remus, Mich., tells in *Gleanings in Bee Culture* how this may be accomplished.

The secret seems to be in having just the right number of workers and just the right amount of honey coming in, so that the bees will draw out the combs no faster than the queen can occupy them with brood. As long as this condition lasts we should expect the bees to build worker combs. From this we see that, in order to get good results in comb-building from a natural swarm, this swarm should be of just the right size, and there should be a honey-flow of, say, three or four pounds a day.

We will suppose a large swarm is hived during a period when honey is coming in freely. At this time there is too much honey coming in for the best results in comb-building in the brood-nest, if the whole force of workers is compelled to do all their work in the brood-nest. The remedy is to put most of the workers at work in the supers. Most beginners fail in doing this; but the principle is to make the surplus receptacles more inviting to the workers than the brood-nest, and the bees will immediately go up into the supers on being hived. Our comb-honey super with extracting-combs at the sides make an ideal arrangement for this very thing.

It is plain to see that, if most of the honey being carried in is placed in the sections, where it should be, the queen will not be hurried to keep pace with the workers, consequently nearly all worker comb will be built. The brood-nest should be filled with comb during the first 28 days after the swarm is hived, for the queen must keep up with the workers and lay in nearly every cell as fast as it is drawn out, or the bees will begin to store honey in the cells. When this condition arrives, the bees, on the supposition that the queen has reached her limit, and that the rest of the combs will be used for storing honey, begin to build the storage size or the drone-cells in the brood-nest. This is likely to occur in about 28 days after the swarm is hived; for by this time the brood is beginning to hatch out in that part of the hive where the laying began. From this time on the queen has nearly all she can do to keep the cells filled with eggs where the young bees are hatching. This means that the comb-building part of the hive is neglected, and that the bees build store or drone comb to a great extent until the hive is filled.

There are artificial ways of handling bees so that they will build good worker combs. I refer to the plan of shaking the bees into an empty hive, in the same way that a swarm is hived. If a colony is divided into nuclei of, say, two or three combs each, and each nucleus given a young queen reared the same year, such little colonies will build very nice worker combs; but the beginner will not be interested in this artificial way of making increase, for he should stick to the natural-swarming plan for his increase until such time as he has had experience and made a success of getting a crop of honey. In fact, there are many things to be learned before a beginner should take up artificial ways of making increase.

RESTRAINING UNDESIRABLE DRONES.

Drones undesirable for breeding purposes may be prevented from going out to meet the queens, by keeping them from going out of the hive, or by letting them go out into a cage through which workers can pass and they can not. This is done by taking advantage of the fact that a worker-bee will pass readily through slots in perforated metal where a drone can not. In the figure shown we give the form of the perforated metal.

Zinc is the material generally used, because it is cheap and will not rust. Some attempt was made to perforate tin as above, but it proved to be very unsatisfactory.

THE PROPER SIZE FOR THE PERFORATIONS.

The oblong holes, as shown below, must be of such a size as to permit the easy passage of workers, but exclude not only drones but even queens (see COMB HONEY and SWARMING). It is no great task to make the perforations drone-excluding; but to make them *queen*-excluding at the same time, and yet not hinder the easy passage of workers, requires a very nice adjustment in the width of the perforations. The first sheet of perforated zinc was cut in England, and imported to this country. This had perforations ₁⁶₄ of an inch in width. While this answered a most excellent purpose, a few claimed that queens would occasionally get through it. To obviate this, zinc was made with the perforations a little narrower.

The width of this was ₁ or ₁₆₄ of an inch. While no queen succeeded in getting

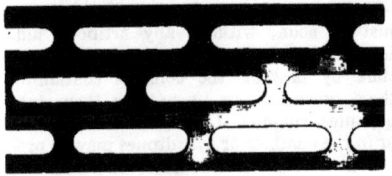

TINKER ZINC.

through this, reports, as well as our own experience, convinced us that this size was too narrow. It not only proved to be a great hindrance to the workers when their honey-sacs were empty, but, when gorged with

honey, they were scarcely able, if at all, to pass through. More recently, perforated zinc has been made in this country on a different pattern, but with perforations exactly ₁⁶₄ of an inch in width, or a *trifle*

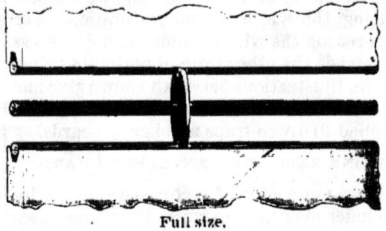

Full size.

smaller than the foreign. The reports, as well as our own experience in regard to the perforated zinc as so made, have led us to believe that this size of perforations is about right.

In 1908 there was put on the market a new form of queen-excluder consisting of wire bars held at the required distances apart by means of soft-metal cross-ties at every two or three inches. These bars consist of No.

WOOD AND WIRE HONEY-BOARD.

14 hard drawn galvanized wire that has been straightened in a wire-straightener so that it is true as a die. Contrary to what one might expect, the spaces between these bars are more exact than the width of the various perforations in sheet metal. In the process of making, the bars are laid in metal forms having grooves that are spaced exactly right, and then a soft metal in a molten state is made to flow in certain cross-grooves of the metal form. As the metal cools almost instantly, the wires are held at the exact right intervals. The smooth, rounding edges of the bars afford less obstruction to the bees passing and repassing, and it is be-

lieved that this form of excluder is superior to the old perforated metal.

Regarding the latter, unless the dies are very sharp there will be a slight rough burr edge on the under side of the sheet. It is impossible to remove this edge without reducing the width of the perforation. For this reason the wire excluder will doubtless supersede the other form of perforated zinc.

The illustrations herewith shown give one an idea of how the new excluder has been applied to drone-traps and honey-boards.

DRONE-EXCLUDING ENTRANCE-GUARDS.

If we put a strip of perforated zinc or wire excluder over the entrance, the worker-bees can go out, but the drones can not; but as a simple excluder is liable to get clogged if if there are many drones in the hive, an arrangement shown below is usually used.

ZINC ENTRANCE-GUARD.

This is simply a strip of perforated metal, 3¾x14 inches long, folded at right angles, as shown. Each end is then closed with a block 1⅜ x 1⅜ x ⅜, fastened in place with a couple of double-pointed tacks. To use, place tight up against the entrance as represented in the cut.

When it is desirable to get the drones *all* out of a hive without permitting any to get back again, we put the guard over the entrance and then shake all the bees in front of the hive. The workers will, of course, crawl back on the combs; but the drones

ALLEY'S DRONE-EXCLUDER.

will have to stay out, and the queen too, unless we watch for her and put her into the hive. In the morning, when the drones are stiffened with cold, they may be fed to the chickens or otherwise destroyed.

If one objects to this method as being too much trouble, he can try another way. On a sunny day a very large part of the drones

will be out for a fly about 1 P. M., or a little later. He is then to place the drone-guard at the entrance; and when the drones return a little later they will be shut out. In the evening they may be disposed of as before.

The drone-excluder just described is not automatic. Accordingly, the late Henry Alley, of Wenham, Mass., devised the one shown at the bottom of the first column.

It is to be observed that this is similar to the one just described, only it has a wire-cloth cone in the top. The drones, after making a fruitless attempt to pass the metal, will enter the wire-cloth cone in the top,

WIRE ALLEY TRAP.

and escape; but none will have sense enough to go back the way they came, but will huddle together outside and await their fate.

If it is desirable to get the drones into a box, so they may be carried to some other apiary, for instance, a cage is made with an upper story, and a couple of these wire cones conduct the drones "up stairs." If any worker-bees should go up too, they can readily go up through the perforated zinc. This latter arrangement is shown in the cut above.

As to how this trap may be used for catching swarms, see SWARMING, elsewhere.

REARING DRONES OUT OF SEASON.

This is quite a difficult matter to accomplish, especially in the spring; and although we have many times fed colonies with this end in view, we have always found some other colony that would have drones flying just as soon, without any artificial aid. Drones may be kept almost any length of time by making the colonies containing them queenless, or by putting them into queenless colonies. During warm dry weather in the summer or fall, drones may be procured by feeding, but the feeding must be regular, and given every day for several days or weeks. By feeding one colony a barrel of sugar in the fall, we succeeded in getting a nice lot of drones in October. Of course, their combs were taken away and empty ones given them, to give the queen room. Before we can raise drones, we must get worker-brood under good headway, and then, if we put a drone-comb right in the center of the brood-nest, the queen will, if all things are favorable, begin at once to fill it with eggs. The feeding must be kept up, however, for bees are very easily discouraged; and if a stoppage occurs in the daily supplies, they will not hesitate to pull the young drones out of their cells and sacrifice them without mercy.

A queen will seldom produce drones until she is nearly or quite a year old, even though drone comb may be placed in the very center of the brood-chamber.

DRONES FROM DRONE-LAYERS.

Queen-breeders find that one or more drone-layers of good stock rearing fully developed drones, if supplied with plenty of worker brood, will furnish a fine lot of nice drones in and out of season; but drones from laying workers, or from queens that have never been fertilized, are to be avoided. Drones from queens that have once laid worker eggs, and then failed, are as good as the drones from any queen.

DESTRUCTION OF DRONES IN THE FALL.

This does not necessarily occur in the fall, but may take place at any time in the summer; and we have several times known the drones killed off between apple-bloom and white clover, only because supplies ceased, causing the bees to become discouraged and give up swarming for the time being. We know of no way in which one can tell so well that the yield of honey has ceased, as by the behavior of the bees toward their drones. When, in the midst of the honey season, we see a worker buzzing along on the back of a drone that seems to be doing his best to get away from the hive, we may take warning that the yield of honey is failing, and that we had better stop making artificial swarms, and prepare for feeding, if it is our intention so to do. We do not know that we ever saw bees sting drones, but they sometimes pretend to do so. It is probable that it is only a feint to drive them away. The poor drone, at such times, after vainly trying to go back into the hive, will sometimes take wing and soar away off in the air, only to return after a time to be repulsed again, until, through weakness perhaps, and want of food, he flutters hopelessly in the dust, and so submits to the fate that seems to be a part of the inexorable law of nature and of his being.

To preserve drones for late queen-rearing, we have been in the habit of carrying all frames containing drone-brood to some queenless hive, knowing they would be safe there as long as wanted, even if it were all winter. We believe drones have been, under such circumstances, wintered over; but whether they are of any value in the spring or not, we are unable to say. We should fear they would not be by the time queens could be reared. We usually have drones in some of our colonies as soon as April, and that is as early as we should care to undertake to rear queens, in ordinary seasons. We have several seasons reared queens and had them successfully fertilized, even after all the drones had been gone some time, so far as we could discover; and as they proved to be purely fertilized, we have been not a little perplexed.

DRONES WITH BRIGHTLY COLORED HEADS OF DIFFERENT COLORS.

This is a queer feature in natural history. Almost every summer some one writes or sends us specimens of drones with heads of different colors. The matter has been reported and commented on at different times in *Gleanings*. Not only do we occasionally find drones with white heads, but we find them with heads of a cherry-red color; again, of a bright green, and at other times yellow. We confess there is something very wonderful and mysterious to us in this matter. Why queer old dame nature should decide to single out the heads of drones to sport with in this way will, it seems to us, be a pretty difficult matter to explain. Why should this peculiarity show itself in the drones more than in the queens and workers? Again, why should *heads* be the subject of these bright rainbow colors? Is there really any purpose or design in it? or is it just because it *happened* so? We presume there are very few among our readers but will say there is a purpose and a design in it; and the next thing is to decide why it should be so. Here is a conundrum.

DYSENTERY. When we see our bees covering the entrances to their hives with a brownish yellow, disagreeable-smelling excrement or stain, we may say they have the dysentery, or what is usually known as such. If the weather becomes very warm and pleasant, they will usually get over it after they have had a full flight. If, on the contrary, the symptoms show themselves before warm weather, and no opportunity is given them to fly, they may get so bad as to cover their combs with this substance, and finally die in a damp filthy-looking mass.

CAUSE OF DYSENTERY.

The real cause is long-continued low temperature, further aggravated by bad food. In order to keep up sufficient animal heat, the bees have to overeat, surcharging their intestines. The long-retained fecal matter results in purging or dysentery. We can hardly think that any food alone would produce the disease, because we rarely, if ever, find the bees suffering from any thing they will gather, in warm summer weather. Honey gathered from rotten fruit, if we may call it honey, is very productive of this complaint, and cider from cider-mills is almost sure to kill bees at the approach of cold weather. We knew a lady who boiled up a mash of sweet apples and fed to the bees, because they were short of stores, and she could not afford to buy sugar for them. They all died of dysentery, long before spring. Where dampness accumulates from their breath, and settles on the combs, diluting the honey, it is very apt to cause these symptoms. Sorghum syrup has brought on a very aggravat. ed form, and *burnt* candy or sugar is almost sure poison to bees during cold weather, al. though it may be fed them with impunity in the middle of the summer.

While it is very certain that no such symptoms are found in warm weather, it is also certain that a strong colony in a hive with soft, warm, dry porous walls, will stand an amount of bad food that a weak one, or one exposed to drafts of cold air, will not. We have known bees having considerable stores of cider, to winter very well if the colony were strong enough to keep the whole interior of the hive dry and warm. A powerful colony, if left with their hive uncovered during a rain storm, will soon dry themselves; and while they are doing this they remind one of a sturdy cart-horse as he shakes the water off his hide and dries h mself by his internal animal heat. While they have the health and numbers to repel moisture in this way, they are safe against almost any thing. But to help them to keep this internal strength, they should have close and comfortable quarters, very much such as we would need for ourselves to enable us to pass a severe winter's night in health and comfort. The hives often used are so large and barn-like, in respect to the winter's brood-nest, that comfort is almost out of the question, for it does little if any good to pile straw, corn-fodder, etc., over the outsides of the hives while the cluster within has no sort of protection at all. If they were in a hollow tree, the diameter of which was so small that they could fill it completely, they would be in a much better place, especially if the sides were lined with soft dry rotten wood. We have seen icicles nearly as large as the arm, in box hives that were tight and large; these had all formed from the condensation of the breath of the bees. Now, should they melt during a thaw, in such a way that this water would run down on the bees and their unsealed stores, it would be very apt to produce unhealthiness, to say nothing further.

THE AGENCY OF THE APHIDES IN PRODUCING DYSENTERY.

The very worst winter food is, without doubt, the honey gathered from the aphides (see HONEY-DEW); or, at least, most complaints have been made of this honey. As bees seldom touch this, except during drouths or unfavorable seasons, it no doubt has been the cause of much of the mischief. If the early honey is all extracted from the brood-combs, and the bees left with nothing but this bad honey, gathered late in the fall, the matter is much worse; and many cases have been reported of colonies dying where the extractor had been used, while those untouched had been free from the disease. The moral is, refrain from extracting too closely from the brood-apartment. We would at least let the bees fill their brood-chamber with clover or linden honey, just before the yield ceases, extracting toward the close of the harvest, only from the combs in the upper story, unless we choose to feed them up for winter on sugar or candy. We have had one or two favorable reports of wintering on the aphidian honey, from which we may conclude it is not always deleterious.

PREVENTION OF DYSENTERY.

From what we have said, one will probably infer that we would make the colony larger or the hive smaller, during the winter season. If we say, also, have the walls of the hive of some warm porous material that will absorb moisture and afterward dry out readily, we have the idea so far. Perhaps the chaff cushions and division-boards are the readiest means at our command of accomplishing this. A dry cellar is excellent.

While bees might get along on almost any kind of food when thus prepared, we would by no means fail to give them good wholesome stores, as far as possible. Honey gathered in the middle of the season is generally wholesome; for by the time winter comes, it is thoroughly ripened by the same drying-out power we have spoken of. Honey gathered in the fall, if sealed up, is generally good; but some of the fall flowers produce a honey that seems to separate into a thin watery liquid, and a granular substance, something like candied honey. We are not quite sure this causes dysentery, but it looks in some seasons very much as if it does. A syrup made of white or granulated sugar, is always wholesome, and when bees are short of stores it is probably the cheapest and safest of any thing for feed.

We once wintered a colony on sugar stores, that came out so healthy in the spring that they did not even spot the white snow visibly, when they voided their excrement at their first flight in the spring.

A good many are asking if some other form of sweet will not give just as good results for feeding in winter. In reply we always say that a cheaper sugar has no more actual food value than granulated sugar, if as much.

CURE FOR DYSENTERY OUTDOORS.

If the affected colonies are outdoors, about the only real remedy is settled warm weather. Even one good warm day will often serve to alleviate the trouble, as it gives the bees a chance to void their excrement out in the open air, away from the hives and the combs. Otherwise the continued confinement during an extended cold spell sometimes compels the bees to retain their fæces or excreta so long that they are finally forced to void it over the combs and over the hives. In such cases, where one has good nice clean combs of sealed honey he may take out the combs and replace with the clean ones. At the same time the brood-nest should be contracted down to a space the bees can fill. This work should never be done on a cool day—only when it is warm and balmy, as we have explained. But the practical beekeeper of to-day does not make it a rule to fuss with colonies affected with dysentery; for he knows that, as soon as warm weather comes on, the trouble will disappear of itself, in all such colonies as are not too far gone and too weak to recover.

DYSENTERY IN BEE-CELLARS.

After a very long and cold winter, if the temperature in the cellar goes much below 40° Fah., or if the stores are of poor quality, there is a liability of some colonies being affected with dysentery. The best remedy is prevention. The cellar should be dry, and the temperature should be as near 45 as possible. It should never go below 40 for a longer period than ten or twelve hours. If the temperature of the cellar can not be kept up a coal-oil stove, or a small stove with a connection to a chimney, should be used to keep the temperature up to the requisite point.

Some authorities think that dampness has nothing to do with causing dysentery in the cellar; but dampness in combination with a temperature below 40° for several weeks, we are satisfied, is the most potent cause of dysentery in cellar repositories. We have one cellar that is perfectly dry, and where we control the temperature. In this we have very little dysentery—in fact, almost none. At our outyards we have damp cellars, and where, too, the temperature goes down below 40°. It is a most noticeable fact that in these cellars we have so much dysentery we have about decided to abandon them.

But what are we going to do if the bees do get the dysentery? Suppose the food is bad, and the cellar one where it is not practicable to use artificial heat, say at an outyard. If there are days during mid-winter when the bees can fly (and most localities do afford such weather for one day and possibly two), take the diseased colonies out on one such day and let them have a flight, then at night put them back in the cellar. A cleansing flight will do a world of good. We are well aware that some authorities disagree with us here; but our own experience has shown conclusively, over and over again, that it does pay. If the bees are suffering from an over-accumulation of poisonous fecal matter, why will there not be almost instantaneous relief as soon as it can be voided? It stands to reason that there should. If the food is bad, give the bees better next year. Some recommend taking away all fall stores and feeding sugar syrup. For further consideration of this subject, see WINTERING.

E.

ENEMIES OF BEES. King-birds and bee-martins, and a few other insectivorous birds, prey on bees. We once saw a single king-bird capture six or eight bees in as many trips, on the wing. It would alight on the peak of the barn near the apiary, and then make a dive through the air, grab one bee on the wing, return to its perch to dispose of its morsel, and then catch another.

There have been a number of conflicting reports as to whether king-birds do or do not swallow their victims. Some have asserted that they do, and afterward expelled the ball of bees. At one experiment station a number of king-birds were shot, and the conclusion, after examining their crops, was that they did not eat bees; but from observations that have been made since it appears that the king-bird does not generally swallow worker-bees. It grabs the bee, flies away, and, after it alights on some perch with its victim in its beak, bites away until it absorbs the honey or juices, when it drops the carcass, and flies away for another, which it treats in the same way. Observers have reported seeing these carcasses of bees below the birds' favorite perches.

The loss of a few bees which the birds might kill would amount to nothing: but in large queen-rearing yards, if the birds are allowed to go unmolested there is quite likely to be a loss of young queens: for no doubt the birds select the largest and slowest-flying bees, and these, of course, will be *queens* and drones. If such be the case, the owner of a queen-rearing yard would do well to use his shotgun until every thing in the way of bee-killing birds is destroyed.

MICE.

Mice do harm only when they get into the hives, and this part of the subject will be sufficiently noticed under the head of ENTRANCES. It may be well to remark, that mice sometimes make sad havoc among surplus combs, when stored away with small patches of honey in them. The combs will be completely riddled during the winter time, if they are left where mice can get at them. On this account, the honey-house should be mouse-proof; and for fear that a stray one may by accident get in, it is well to keep a trap ready, baited with toasted cheese. If you have not a tight room, make a tight box, large enough to hold all the surplus combs which have honey in them. See ENTRANCES.

PARASITES.

The only parasite we have ever seen is the *Braula*, or Italian bee-louse, and we have never seen them except on bees just imported from Italy. We feel safe in saying no fear need be anticipated from them if the bees are kept in strong colonies, and in clean tight hives, with no old refuse and rubbish accumulating about them. One or two reports have been received of bee-lice in our own country, but they were exceptions.

SKUNKS.*

Skunks have been known to approach the hive at night time, and by scratching on or near the alighting-board, entice the bees out where they could "gobble them up." It would seem a little strange that these animals have no fear of stings, but they, doubtless, are guided by a sort of instinct that enables them to divine how to get hold of the bee with its sweet morsel of honey in its honey-sac, without receiving harm from the sting.

SPIDERS.

Spiders as well as toads seem to have a rare appreciation of a heavily laden bee as it returns to the hive; we should therefore be careful that all spider-webs be faithfully kept brushed away from the hives, and that they have no corners or crevices about them to harbor such insects. Be sure there is no place which the broom will not clear out at one sweep; for where we have a hundred hives we can not well spend a great amount of time on each single one.

We are inclined to think that many of these so-called enemies take up the destruction of bees only as a chance habit, and that it is not always to be looked for nor expected. Common fowls sometimes get a habit of eating their own eggs; but it is so unusual

---

* A lady correspondent in *Gleanings in Bee Culture,* page 866, Vol. XV., writes that she effectually got rid of skunks by the use of Rough on Rats stirred in an egg. This mixture was placed at the entrance of hives previously visited by skunks. After the doses had been repeated two evenings in succession the skunks never again paid their visitations.

an occurrence that we can hardly regard it as a matter of any very serious importance. It may be well at times to look out for the enemies that prey on bees; but, as a general thing, we think they are quite capable of fighting their own battles if we give them the proper care and proper hives.

It was Mr. L. L. Langstroth, just before he died, who showed how spiders may be of value to the bee-keeper. If, he said, they have access freely to the combs stored in stacked-up hives in the apiary, there never need be any fear that the moth-worm or moth-miller will be able to do any damage, for the spiders will very shortly destroy them.

WASPS.

Wasps and hornets sometimes capture and carry off honey-bees; but unless they should take part in the work in great numbers, we would have no solicitude in regard to them.

A large fly, called the bee-hawk, or mosquito-hawk, has been mentioned by our Southern neighbors, but it is said to be easily frightened away by opening a vigorous warfare with whips and sticks.

THIEVES.

Thieves are sometimes troublesome at outyards, and once in a long while at the home yard. The best way to put a stop to their depredations is to put up a sign or two offering fifty or a hundred dollars reward for the arrest and conviction of the guilty parties. The thief is immediately warned that a price is put upon his head, and that he had best, if he knows when he is well off, stop his stealing. It is seldom that the reward money is ever called for, and further annoyance is stopped.

ENTRANCE-GUARDS. See DRONES.

ENTRANCES TO HIVES. We do not know that it makes any very great difference to the bees, or with the amount of honey gathered, where the entrance is; whether at the very lowest part of the hive, or right in the top. We have had them do well with their entrance in almost all positions. On many accounts, an entrance even with, or a little below, the bottom-board of the hive would be most desirable. This gives the bees every facility for removing dirt or dead bees that frequently clog the hive and combs in cold weather; also bits of refuse comb, cappings from the cells, dust, etc., for this all falls to the bottom of the hive, and is naturally carried toward the entrance by the passage, out and in, of the inmates. Also, if the upper part of the hive is close and

warm, the warm air generated by the cluster, rising by its lightness, compared with the colder air outdoors, has a much less chance for escape than if the entrance were nearer the top of the hive. If the entrance is a little below the bottom-board, cold winds and storms are not so readily admitted.

It has been said that an entrance part way up is not so liable to become clogged with dead bees. This is probably true; but, on the other hand, the live ones will not be able nearly so easily to remove the dead if they have to tug them up the perpendicular sides until they reach the opening; neither can the apiarist himself assist in the process. Where the entrance is on a level with the bottom of the hive, he can reach in with a hooked wire and rake out all the dead bees that may have accumulated during the winter. Indeed, he should, if the accumulation is enough to clog the entrance, clear it out once or twice during the winter, with a wire.

There is still another objection to a high entrance. During cool weather many of the flying bees on returning will become chilled in their efforts to crawl up the perpendicular side, and thus fail to get into the hive; so, all things considered, an entrance that is handy for the bees is also best for the bee-keeper.

On account of the tendency of returning bees to chill in cool weather, there should be a large alighting-board if the hive is raised off the ground; or if on the ground, there should be a nice easy slanting grade or doorstep to the entrance. All grass and weeds should be kept down within at least a foot of the front of the hive; and it would be better if there were a good full yard of clear space. Bees that come in heavily laden are often knocked down by bumping into tall weeds or sprigs of grass. While they ultimately take wing, making another attempt, finally landing in the hive, such obstructions, if hindering to the bees, are wasteful to the bee-keeper.

It is impossible to estimate just how much the loss in honey is; but if the actual figures could be secured the producer would be surprised. When it is such an easy mat ter to cut away the weeds, or keep them away from the entrance with a little sprinkling of salt or with a wide board, it is "penny wise and pound foolish" to wear out the wings of our little servants trying to pass this obstruction, at the same time delaying them when every moment counts. Farmer

laid directly on the ground, abutting up close to the bottom-board if it rests on or close to the ground. No grass or weeds can grow, of course, where these boards are laid; and general practice shows it is cheaper and better to use such boards than to be compelled to use salt or cut down the obstructions every few weeks in front of the hive.

The cut in the opposite column contains a suggestion which can be very easily applied to the cleated boards just described. Bend some iron wires, about No. 8, as shown with hook at each end. Drive one of the

bee-keepers especially seem to have the idea that bees will work for nothing and board themselves, and in three cases out of five one will find the entrances of their hives, what few they may have, all tangled up with grass and weeds. On mornings when there is a heavy dew such obstruction is very considerable.

Very many use a scythe, lawn-mower, or a common sickle, to cut down the grass. Others keep it down with a small handful of salt scattered around the front of the hive.

Still others prefer to use a piece of board about a foot wide or more, and as long as the hive is wide. Rough unplaned lumber of the cheapest kind would be better than clear planed stuff, as the bees can cling to it better. The boards should be cleated, and

hooks into the board as here illustrated, and secure in position by means of a common blind-staple near the other edge. If the wires are cut right, this alighting-board can be easily hooked into the entrance and make a nice easy grade from the ground up to the hive. At any time these alighting-boards can be unhooked so that the grass can be cut down with a lawn-mower and then replaced.

SIZE OF ENTRANCES.

This depends on the season of the year, the size of the colony, and whether the bees are wintered indoors or out. During the height of the honey-flow the aperture should be as large as the bottom-board or hive will permit — not less than ⅜ inch deep by the width of the hive. Experience has shown that a contracted opening does not give the bees sufficient ventilation; and the result is, the great mass of bees are forced out of the hive, where they will loaf day after day, doing nothing. When they once get into the loafing habit they will be much inclined to swarm, to say nothing about wasting valuable time during that part of the season when, if ever, they should bring in money in return for all the labor expended on them.

Where one uses hives of the loose-bottom type, he can usually cure this clustering out and loafing by raising the brood-chamber off the bottom, placing four blocks ⅜ of an inch thick on the bottom-board and setting the brood-chamber back again. This will provide an opening on all four sides. While the bees will use the front or main entrance mainly, they will fly out from the others. With so much ventilation the bees, unless the colonies are extraordinarily strong, will

HIVE RAISED ON FOUR BLOCKS TO PROVIDE VENTILA-
TION AND TO SOME EXTENT KEEP
DOWN SWARMING.

go back into the hive and go to work. Some bee-keepers go so far as to claim that the procedure will almost entirely eliminate swarming. For further particulars on this subject see "Prevention of Swarming" under head of "Swarming."

Nuclei or weak colonies must have no larger entrances than they can easily defend. They should be as small as possible after the regular honey - flow, for then it is that robbers are liable to rush in pellmell and overpower the guards of the little colony, depriving it of the scanty stores it may have. See Rob-bing. A two-frame nucleus should not have an opening larger than will admit two or three bees at a time if it is during the robbing season. When the honey-flow is on, it may be larger; but it should be contracted as soon as it eases up.

When cool weather comes on, the entrances of all colonies should be contracted, both strong and weak, and kept so during the entire winter if bees are left outdoors. Formerly the practice was to allow the full

size; but experience has shown that this is a serious mistake. There is no more reason why the bees should have their doors wide open in mid-winter, letting chilling drafts blow in, than that we should leave our doors open. But a bee-hive is supposed to be hermetically sealed at all points except the entrance, and, unlike the dwellings we live in, it should have at least a small opening at the entrance, otherwise the bees will be sure to die before the following spring. An ordinary eight - frame Langstroth hive should have an entrance not much larger than 8 inches wide by ⅜ deep. During very severe weather it might be still further closed. Some of the very strongest colonies may have an opening of 8 or 10 inches; but with this contracted entrance it may be necessary for the apiarist to hook the dead bees out with a wire once during the winter, and possibly once more in the spring; for in no case must the opening be clogged up.

It is customary to have some sort of cleat to reduce a wide entrance to a small slot on one side ⅜ by 5 or 6 inches. This, when inserted slot side down, reduces the opening to the proper size for outdoor-wintered bees. In cleaning out the dead bees the entrance-stop should be removed entire-

A COLONY WITH AN ENTRANCE TOO SMALL WHERE THE
BEES HAVE FORMED THE LOAFING HABIT.

ly, making the entrance itself the full size. Any dead ones that may have accumulated should be raked out and the stop put back.

If it is discovered that the colony is weak, the slot should be reduced to one inch in width. At the same time, the frames should be contracted to the number that the bees

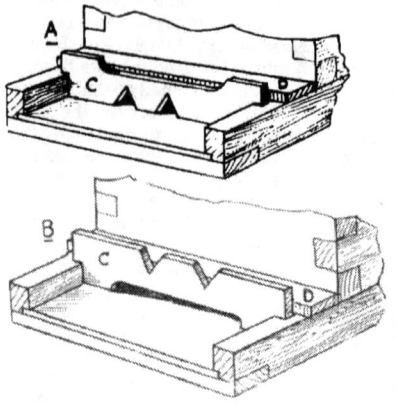

can reasonably occupy or cover. If they are compelled to keep a large room warm, much above their present needs, they may die from c ld.

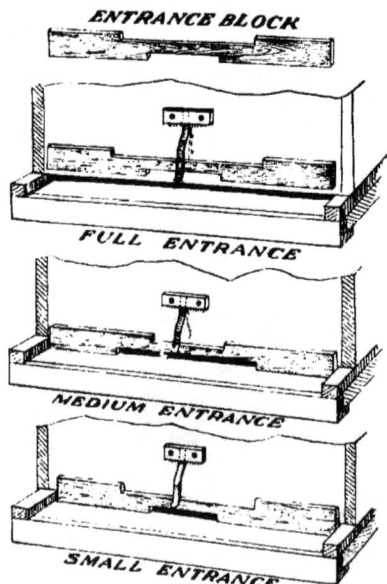

ENTRANCE BLOCK

FULL ENTRANCE

MEDIUM ENTRANCE

SMALL ENTRANCE.

The illustrations show very simple cleats which can be made at any planing-mill, or can be cut at home, using nothing but a common hand-saw and a chisel. These cleats give various-sized entrances accord-

ing to the way they are attached. When the cleats are removed entirely the full opening of the hive is given.

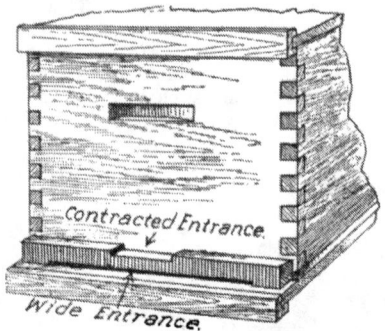

Contracted Entrance.

Wide Entrance.

If a cool or cold spell suddenly comes on in the spring after a stretch of warm weather, during which the bees have a large amount of young brood started, some of the brood is liable to be lost unless the entrance is c n-

*ALIGHTING-BOARD G PROPERLY PLACED.

tracted or closed temporarily. W. L. Coggshal', of West Groton, N. Y., the most extensive bee-keeper in the world, owning somewhat over 3000 colonies, recommends closing the entrances at such times with a handful of sawdust. This he carries around in a pail; and as he walks up and down the rows of hives he throws a handful here and a handful there in front of each hive. The heaped-up sawdust confines the heat of the cluster, thus making it possible to save bees and brood. When it warms up, the bees will push the loose dust away themselves, without any time or effort on the part of the apiarist. Possibly this same method might

* This entrance is too large for winter use, but just right for summer.

be practiced to advantage in winter during a very cold spell. As soon as it has warmed up, the bees could push the obstruction away.

ENTRANCES PROPERLY CONTRACTED FOR WINTER.

The accompanying illustrations will show the modern Dovetailed and Danzenbaker alighting-boards having cleats nailed on

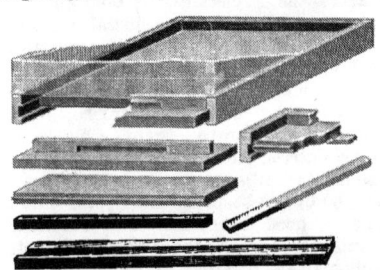

DETACHABLE ALIGHTING-BOARD AND HOW IT MAY BE USED TO VARY THE SIZE OF THE ENTRANCE.

them permanently. When the board is pulled out entirely it gives an entrance 1¼ inches deep by the width of the hive. When the plain side is inserted, the entrance is reduced to 8 by ¼ inch; and this may be further reduced, if necessity requires it, by putting in a ¼-inch strip of wood of sufficient length to bring the entrance down to the point required.

PLURAL ENTRANCES AND SWARM CONTROL.

While it is true that a plurality of entrances may be a detriment in a brood-chamber, it does not necessarily hold good during the honey season when the hive is tiered up two or three stories high. It then becomes difficult, and wasteful of bee energy that might be better employed, to ventilate the whole hive from one entrance, however large it is in the lower story, for the bees have to maintain a current of cold air rushing in, and another going out at the same aperture.

If queen-excluders are used the case is made worse. It almost goes without saying, that, during the period in which the honey is evaporated while in the combs, there ought to be more than one entrance to the hive— at least two, and, during very hot weather, more, one to each story, with the cover or roof slightly raised at the back to furnish additional means for the fetid air to escape at the top of the hive.

It is said by those who have tried this method of air control that it is a great preventive of swarming, and this looks reasonable; for the brood-chamber is far less crowded, since the field workers arrive and depart from the upper entrance to a great extent, saving overcrowding of the brood-chamber, which surely leads to swarming.

On the other hand, it may be said that there is danger of the honey-chambers being rendered too cool by so many entrances; but against this may be stated that, if this is the case, it is also too cool for honey-gathering, and the upper stories should be removed. If the colony is weak, upper entrances are unnecessary; and in that case, also, the honey-chambers should be removed, as such a colony does not gather a surplus of the honey in any event. It is too weak.

Some of our well-known writers on bee culture heartily commend upper entrances— notably so Dr. C. C. Miller, C. P. Dadant, R. F. Holtermann, W. K. Morrison, and, in early times, Adam Grimm, who, with the money he made with his bees, established a bank.

Dr. C. C. Miller, writing in *Gleanings in Bee Culture* for June 1, 1907, writes: " Prof. Cook says, p. 312, that bees ventilate so effectively at the entrance that it is best to have only one opening to the hive, evidently meaning at all times; and W. K. Morrison, page 686, asks if I subscribe to that doctrine. Emphatically, no. If running for extracted honey I would generally have one more opening than the number of stories in use—the regular entrance and an opening at the top of each story. Each year for years I have had one or more piles thus ventilated, and none has ever swarmed. Many years ago I learned from Adam Grimm to have an opening for ventilation at the top of the brood-chamber at the back end when running for comb honey. I gave it up because it interfered with the finishing of the sections near such openings. But I have gone back to it again, believing that such disadvantage is overbalanced by the gain in ventilation. You can't make me believe that it is not easier for the bees to have one hole for the air to go out and another for it to come in than to make the air go both ways in the same hole." The practical bee-keeper will soon discover for himself when and how to use a plurality of entrances, for much depends on the climate. Evidently it does not work so well with comb-honey production as it does extracted; yet even this may be satisfactorily arranged. It looks now as if plural entrances were a long step toward swarm prevention by causing the field workers to leave the brood and confine their energies to storing honey in the upper chambers. See SWARMING.

ENTRANCES FOR INDOOR WINTERING.

Authorities differ as to the size of entrance that should be used for indoor wintering. Some argue that, the larger the openings,

the better. A few go even so far as to urge that the bottom-boards be removed entirely, one hive piled upon two others, leaving an opening between the two lower hives of about one-third of the size of the entire bottom of the hive. Others advise a regular bottom-board, but an entrance two inches deep by the full width of the hive; while others recommend no larger entrance than the bees have during the summer.

The preponderance of evidence seems to be in favor of the last-mentioned size. Too much ventilation, even in a cellar where the temperature is reasonably under control, has a tendency to induce too large a consumption of stores. Over-feeding causes dysentery; and when that happens in a bee-cellar the colony is doomed unless it can be given a flight on a warm day, as recommended under the head of WINTERING in the latter part of this work.

Our practice has been to use the same entrance that we have in the summer for our indoor-wintered hives; and so long as we used that size we had excellent results in wintering. But one winter, for the purpose of experiment, we raised each individual hive off its bottom-board and inserted a rim three inches deep and of the same outside dimensions as the hive. The sides of these rims were open, but covered with wire cloth. The result was that we lost over 100 colonies out of the 230 odd put into the cellar, and the rest came out in a very weakened condition.

The bee is essentially a warm-blooded animal. Experience has shown that a temperature of 45 degrees Fahrenheit in a cellar gives the best results. An ordinary colony with ordinary summer entrance in such cellar temperature will be able to warm the interior of its hive without too much expenditure of animal heat. When the bees are too cold they will eat largely of their stores, and in doing so bring on disease.

EUCALYPTUS. There are something like two hundred species of eucalypti recognized in Australasia by scientific botanists. Baron Mueller, who is the chief authority on this genus, noted that nearly all the eucalypti are honey-yielders, but some are much better than others. Redgum (*E. rostrata*) seems to be the leader, though others may take the leadership when the Australian bush becomes better known. The most famous of the gum trees of Australasia is the *E. globulus*, the blue gum of Tasmania, and this also is a liberal producer of bee nectar. For its valuable properties as a first-class lumber-producer, and as an anti-fever plant, it has been introduced into many countries—California, Mexico, West Indies, South Europe, Egypt, Chili, and other countries; and as it is a fair producer of honey its further propagation can be encouraged by bee-keepers. *Eucalyptus gunni* is also a good honey-tree, and excellent for lumber. Indeed, the whole eucalypti family may be regarded as honey-yielders. Any one desirous of gaining more information relative to these extremely useful trees may consult with profit Baron Mueller's "Select Extra-tropical Plants for Industrial Culture." It is a book well worth perusing in any event by bee-keepers. Attempts have been made to introduce the honey of the eucalypti into England, but without success. Eucalyptus honey has a peculiar flavor which the English people do not like, and there the matter ends.

EXTRACTED HONEY. Liquid honey, taken from the comb with the honey-extractor, has been before the world since the year 1865, and much has been the discussion, pro and con, in regard to its merits, and its desirableness compared with comb honey for table use.

If all the extracted honey put upon the market were as good as some we have raised and purchased, there would, we are sure, be no trouble at all in deciding that it would drive honey in the comb almost out of the question. Much has been said about adulteration, and there has been some ground for it. Glucose has been used very largely, but it can readily be detected by chemical analysis and by the taste. Pure glucose, that is, such as is used for adulterating, has a strong metallic taste that is almost nauseating. One who has once tasted the "stuff" will readily recognize proportions exceeding 25 per cent in honey. See HONEY ADULTERATION.

Since the new national pure-food law has gone into effect there will be very little adulterated honey on the market, especially so as over two-thirds of the States have pure-food laws also. We may safely conclude, therefore, that all extracted honey so labeled will necessarily be pure.

A really nice article of extracted honey will bring 8 or 10 cts. quicker than a poor one will bring 4 or 5; and we have seen some, aye, and have offered it for sale too, that we do not honestly think was worth over 2c., if it was worth anything at all, unless to feed bees. Is all this difference on account of the source from which it was gathered? Not at all; for all the honey we get here, in the great majority of seasons, is from clover and linden. Then where is the great difference? It is, so far as my experience goes, simply because it is taken from the hive before it is ripe. We have never seen any honey we thought was fit to extract until it was all sealed over. Still further, we do not believe it is nearly as nice, even when it is all sealed over, as it will be if left in the hive three or four weeks *after* it has been all sealed. We will tell you some of our experience to illustrate the point.

In 1870 we extracted, from our apiary of less than 50 colonies, over 3 tons of honey. It was put up in 1-lb. bottles, and more than half was sold for 25c per pound when prices were high on extracted honey. During the fore part of the season the honey was allowed to get pretty well capped over; but during basswood bloom, we, bees and all, got somewhat crazy, we fear, and they brought in what was but little better than sweetened water; we extracted and put it into bottles, and hurried it off to fill orders, hoping it would all get "good" as soon as the weather got cool. It candied when the weather became cold, for almost all honey will candy, or at least one portion will candy, leaving a thin watery part, which, if it does not sour, acquires in time a disagreeable brackish flavor, like that acquired by liquids standing in an old barrel. At about this stage it shows that peculiar qual-

ity of pushing the bungs out of the barrels, and the corks out of the bottles, running over on the shelves and tables to the discomfiture and disgust of everybody who likes to be cleanly in his habits. When we tasted some of the honey in one of these bottles, six months afterward, we did not wonder it had stopped selling, and we made up our mind it should no more be offered for sale. We believe it was all poured out of the bottles, and sold to a tobacconist. The contents of the jars were not all alike, for the thin watery honey has quite a tendency to swim on top. We, one season, commenced to retail from a barrel of what all pronounced fine clover honey. One day a customer returned some, saying it was not like what he bought before. We assured him it was drawn from the same barrel, and went and drew some, to convince him. Behold! it was sweetened water, compared with the first. The thin honey having risen to the top, it was the last to be drawn out.

Again, new honey has, many times, a rank, disagreeable odor and taste. We have been told that in the Eastern States much honey is sometimes obtained from the fields where onion seeds are raised for the market, and that this honey, when first gathered, is so strong of onions that it can not be used. In a few weeks, however, this rank and disagreeable flavor has all gone, and the honey is very fair. Few persons can tolerate the strong, aromatic flavor of basswood honey when first gathered, and some of the jars we have mentioned, when opened, gave one the impression that something akin to turpentine had been mixed with the honey. This was because it had been closely corked when first gathered; had it been left in the comb until sealed, the unpleasant taste would have mostly disappeared. We say mostly, for even sealing does not seem to remove entirely the rank flavor, until the combs have been some weeks in the hive. We remember we once took a beautiful-looking piece of comb honey out of a jar that was found in the market. On opening the cells we found the honey had such a rank basswood flavor that it was, to us, quite disagreeable, and yet we are fond of the basswood honey. Very white new comb honey is seldom of the fine, pure, sweet flavor of honey that has been a long time capped over, such as is found in the dark-looking comb. To which shall we give the preference — looks or taste? We once were so busy that we could not attend to extracting, and so we raised the filled stories up, and put some filled with empty combs just under them over the brood. This occupied little time, and the bees were not hindered in their work a single moment. We have never seen bees amass stores faster. Some colonies filled four stories to repletion, and the whole was left on the hives until the latter part of the summer. In fact, we left them on so long to be safe from the depredations of the moth, intending to cut out the honey and sell it in the comb, or to extract it, whichever form should prove most marketable. This honey was cut out of the frames and sold the following winter; and it was the nicest and richest honey we ever saw or tasted. To our astonishment, the liquid portions, that ran out when the combs were cut, would not candy at all, even when exposed to zero weather. The honey was so thick that a saucer full could be turned over without spilling

Extracted honey, if taken out while "green" (as we have often termed the unripened state), has a greenish tinge, which well-ripened honey has not.* Some specimens have a turbid or cloudy look, and we believe such honey is never really fine-flavored. We are well aware that we are condemning the very honey we once sold, by these remarks, but we can not help it. If we had now some extracted honey such as was taken from those well-ripened combs, we would feel that it was preferable, at 12 cts., to that which sells at 5 or 6 cts. Properly ripened basswood or clover honey has a sparkling clearness, of a slightly yellowish tint, and the flavor is pure and exquisite. We have never seen any nice-looking comb honey equal to it, for the market always demands comb honey that is white, and has not remained on the hive a long time. We do not mean to say that extracted honey should be without color, like water, for it usually has a transparent pale yellow tint, or it may be quite yellow. After it has candied, if it does candy, it should be hard, and free from any liquid portion, like that in unripened honey. This thin liquid portion is the part that usually changes and gives it the bad taste. In fact, if the liquid portion be drained off, the solid portion may be melted, and it will be found very nearly like that ripened in the hive.

RIPENING HONEY BY ARTIFICIAL MEANS.

The most that is done in the way of evaporating honey that is not entirely ripe is to put it in large tanks, covering the top with a semi-porous cloth tightly tied down over the edge of the can to prevent robber bees from getting in. In California these tanks hold anywhere from 20 to 30 tons. In some cases the tanks are contracted toward the top, leaving an opening of about 18x24 inches. In other cases the tank has a large diameter of about eight feet, and only four feet high. This presents a large surface of honey, and the evaporation, therefore, would go on more rapidly. These great honey-reservoirs are usually set down outdoors, and covered as before explained. As it seldom or never rains in California during the dry season the honey will evaporate down to a good thick body, even if it was a little green when taken out.

Mr. E. W. Alexander, of Delanson, N. Y., uses oblong tanks in small buildings painted a dark color to draw the sun's rays. In these he stores his partially ripened buckwheat until it thickens up.

Whether such evaporated honey is equal to that which has been ripened entirely in the hives, we have our doubts. We have sampled both kinds, not knowing which was which, and we believe that in every case we have been able to tell the natural from the evaporated article. Commission men and producers strongly urge that no honey be extracted except that which has been capped over; that while a few experts may practice artificial ripening, the average bee-keeper should leave that wholly to the bees.

HOW TO KEEP EXTRACTED HONEY.

Unless the crop has been secured early it is best to dispose of it at once, when the market is at the highest; but it is sometimes advisable to hold the honey until the price again goes up, which it is likely to do after the berry season is over, when every one is thinking of the holidays, Christmas and New Year's : for it is then that honey comes into fresh demand again, and the market becomes firmer.

Extracted, or comb honey either, for that matter, should be kept in a room about as near summer temperature as possible. The mercury ought not to drop below 65, and it may go as much higher as ordinary summer weather will permit—even 90 or 100 in the shade. Extracted, if kept, should be stored in big tin cans, or, better still, in a large tank—one capable of holding eight or ten barrels, if the apiarist is so extensively engaged in bee-keeping that he is likely to have that amount of honey on hand at one time. Where the cans hold more than 500

---

* Pure sweet clover and cleome are exceptions.

lbs., it is customary to have them made of galvanized iron; and while some objection has been made to this metal because of its alleged poisonous quality, yet in the large-sized cans no injury to the honey has ever been noted; for it is the custom in California, Arizona, Colorado, and other States of the West, where great quantities of extracted honey are produced, to have the honey stored in large galvanized storage-tanks, some of them practically good-sized cisterns above ground. In those hot climates the

ever it is used it may be liquefied by the directions that go with the package.

Ordinarily we would not advise the storage of honey for any considerable time in barrels: but when no other storage room is admissible, barrels may be used, but they should be watched to see that they do not start to leaking in the honey-room; and occasionally the hoops should be driven down to compensate for the slight shrinkage that may take place; for it is a fact that the staves of barrels, even when filled with

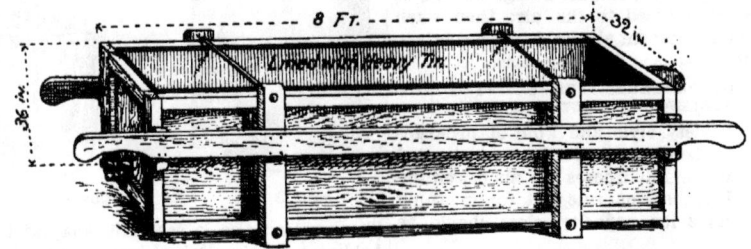

ONE OF ALEXANDER'S STORAGE AND EVAPORATING TANKS FOR EXTRACTED HONEY.

honey will remain liquid for some time, and can be kept perfectly clear until cool or cold weather comes on. If the honey has a tendency to granulate very soon after extracting, it would not be advisable to have it stored for any great length of time in these large tanks. It should be drawn off into the marketing tin pails we have described under CANDIED HONEY, and allowed to candy hard. It may be kept in this condition for a year or two, without detriment; and when-

honey, will shrink somewhat in dry hot rooms, with the result that there will be a leakage, and possibly robbing on the part of the bees. If honey be stored in barrels they should be waxed on the inside as described under BARRELS. The bungs should be left out, and the barrels be kept in a hot dry room. When ready to ship, the bungs should be driven in, and hoops driven tight.

In California, ten to twenty ton galvanized tanks, as shown under the head of EXTRACT-

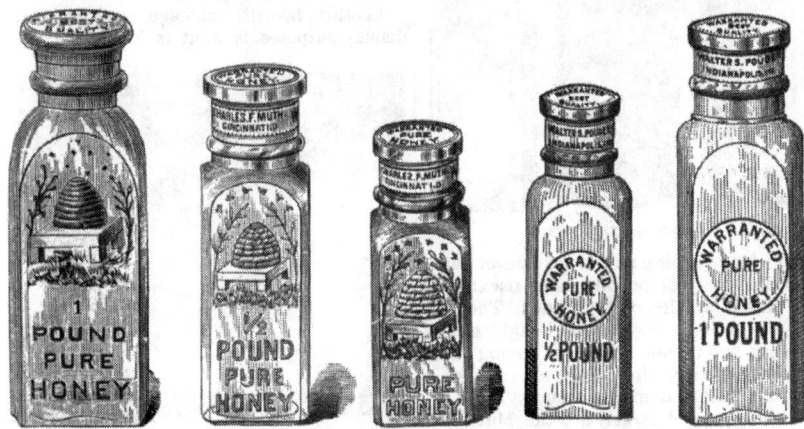

SEVERAL STYLES OF THE GLASS PACKAGES FOR SELLING AND SHIPPING HONEY.

6

OR, are used very extensively. These are covered with cheese-cloth to prevent insects from getting in. While honey is in storage it should always be exposed to the air, providing, of course, that the atmosphere is not heavily charged with moisture.

Some bee-keepers in the East use an oblong shallow tank like an ordinary cheese-vat, covered with cheese-cloth. The Alexander tank, shown in the drawing above, is a type. Others store their honey in square cans with the screw tops left off; then when ready to ship, the caps are put on. This plan is excellent, because a large surface of honey is exposed to the air; then when ready for shipment all that is necessary is to put on the caps and box the cans.

VARIOUS PACKAGES FOR SHIPPING AND SELLING EXTRACTED HONEY.

The variety, style, and kind of packages that have been used in putting up extracted honey for retail purposes are almost unlimited. It is the usual rule that, for any thing less than 3 lbs. capacity, glass should be

HERSHISER JARS.

used; for any thing larger, tin cans or pails. Perhaps the most popular glass package is the Mason jar, already mentioned. They are popular because they can be bought at any grocery, and no one objects to buying them with the honey, since they are always a useful article in domestic economy.

Packages used largely are the Muth and Pouder bottles that are made especially for

holding honey. Molded right into the glass itself is the image of an old straw bee-hive and the words "Pure Honey." These bottles are square in shape, and very nice for shipping and for retailing small quantities.

NO. 25 JAR.   JELLY-TUMBLER.

The smallest size is especially adapted for holding a dime's worth of honey, and, all in all, it is a very pretty size.

The Hershiser jar is of the same general style, but with an aluminum screw-top. It is made of clear heavy glass and is especially adapted for shipping and exhibition.

Another package much used is the jelly-tumbler, and this, like the Mason jar, has the advantage that it is useful in the house.

With each one there is usually a little circular piece of paraffined paper. After the tumbler is filled with honey this paper is placed on top, after which the tin cap is crowded down over the whole, making an almost hermetical sealing.

Another favorite package, especially for display purposes, is what is known as the

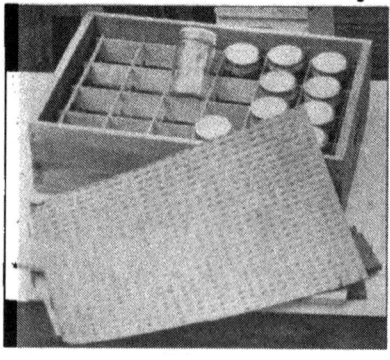

HOW THE NO. 25 JAR IS PACKED.

No. 25 jar. It is self-sealing, somewhat on the order of the Mason can. It is handsome in appearance and cheap in price. These are used very largely.

Still another style of jar with a quick-fastening top is known to the trade as the Tiptop, as shown in the accompanying illustration. In putting up honey in glass it is important to have a variety of packages, as this helps to make a display of honey in grocery windows. In all cases it is desirable to use a jar that can be used for something else when empty. For that reason the Mason jars, jelly-tumblers, and all self-sealing packages, have the advantage over others using only corks, which may be lost.

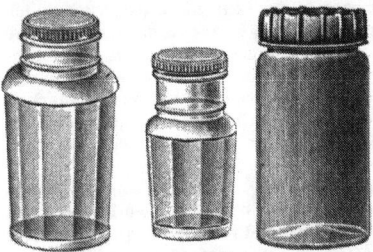

The styles of jars shown above were introduced in 1908 and 1909. When a combination of these different styles are used on shelving, for exhibiting purposes, they help to set off the honey in a general display. See EXHIBITS elsewhere.

WILLIAMS' STAND FOR SELLING EXTRACTED HONEY.

But one who does a large business in putting up honey in glass should not confine himself strictly to one size or kind of package. For purposes of display at groceries he should have an assortment of Muth bottles, Mason jars, jelly-tumblers, and some of the No. 25. An assortment of these can be very tastily arranged in the grocery show-window. Sometimes a little honey-stand may be used to advantage. The one shown above is the one that was used by George F. Williams, of New Philadelphia, Ohio. So much for glass packages. See HONEY, PEDDLING.

TIN PACKAGES FOR HONEY.

While cans holding ½, ⅓, ¾, 1, or up to 5 lbs., have been used for holding honey they are not nearly as desirable as glass. Crystal-white honey itself is beautiful, and to conceal it from sight by tin and a fancy label is a mistake. The purchaser of a small quantity requires to see what he is buying; and when the tin package and the glass package of equal size are put side by side on the counter, it is quite generally admitted that tin should not be used for quantities less than 5 lbs., to say the least. Above this size lard-pails and nested pails are used. The former have sloping sides and can be nested together in so small a compass

SLOPING-SIDE PAIL.

that 100 7½-lb. size can be put in a barrel; but such pails are not adapted to shipping extracted honey unless it is candied. See CANDIED HONEY. They do very well for retailing around home and at local groceries. The same is true of the nested pails below.

A NEST OF FIVE RAISED-COVER PAILS.

The smallest one holds a pint, and the largest four quarts. One reason, perhaps, why these pails are sold for the purpose in such enormous quantities is, that they are of just such sizes as to be extremely convenient for household purposes. The pails shown above are short, so as to be handy for a little girl's or boy's dinner-pail, or other like purposes. Such a pail does not give the greatest economy of tin, however, nor is it suited for a graduated measure like those next shown.

The picture explains the great point in their favor; that is, that they will measure

FORMS OF PAPER MILK-BOTTLES THAT MIGHT BE IMPROVED SO AS TO USE FOR HONEY.

accurately any liquid, going down to as small a quantity as half a pint, and as large a quantity as a gallon, where one has a complete nest. Of course, suitable labels are to be used on these pails when they are full of

GRADUATED TIN PAILS.

honey; and, furthermore, none of these pails can be turned upside down without leakage, unless, indeed, the honey is candied so solid that it will not run in cold weather, as is often the case with a well-ripened article. These packages are used principally by retailers who purchase their honey by the barrel, and put it into pails about as fast as their customers want it. They are to be carried about, however, rather than to be shipped long distances.

The packages thus far shown for holding or retailing honey are made of glass or tin. In most cases when the honey is emptied out of them they are useful for some other purpose. The Mason jars, or any of the screw top cans, can be used for the preserving of fruit, the honey tumblers for jelly, and the tin pails for general culinary purposes around the home. But sometimes the good

housewife has too large a supply of these very articles already in the house, and does not care to buy any more packages which she can not use. For this class of trade we know of nothing better than the different forms of paper milk bottles, which, during recent years, have been put on the market. They are self-sealing, and if tight enough to hold milk, ought to be good enough to hold honey.

They are very cheap, for a box of them containing two dozen bottles or packages can be purchased for the insignificant price of 25 cents. A quart of honey, or a pint, could be sold in such packages very cheaply, and if the purchaser objects to the more expensive glass and tin containers, furnish these.

For large quantities of from 200 to 500 lbs., kegs and barrels may be used. All such should be perfectly tight and *bone dry*; and to prevent the honey from soaking into the wood and wasting; or to prevent the taint of the wood from going into the honey, the barrels should be coated on the inside with paraffine or wax, as explained under BARRELS. But wooden packages can be used only in the Eastern or Middle States. In the Western States, especially Arizona, Colorado, New Mexico, and California, square tin cans holding about 60 lbs. of honey are about the only shipping-package that can be used ; for the dryness of the climate will cause the wooden packages to shrink so as to be entirely useless with any kind of treatment.

The square tin cans of the West have come to be so popular that they are now, to some extent, displacing barrels in the East ; for the wooden packages have a fashion of leaking, and running out on the bottom of the car, causing commission men and honey-merchants no end of trouble; and there is danger that the wood will give the honey a taint unless waxed on the inside, as explained; but the trouble is, many bee-

60-LB. HONEY-CAN AND HONEY-GATE.

keepers won't take the trouble to do this, and the honey therefore sells at a lower price. If the tin packages are tight in the first place, they will remain tight; and no degree of dryness will in the least affect them; and while they are somewhat more expensive per pound of honey, yet this disadvantage is offset by the convenience in retailing or wholesaling any amount less than 100 lbs. If a honey-merchant buys a carload of extracted honey in square cans he can parcel it out in 60-lb. or 120-lb. or 1000-lb. lots, just as he likes, without breaking or opening a package.

There is still another point in favor of the square cans; namely, there is never any loss of honey by its soaking into the package. In the case of barrels or kegs, this loss of honey sometimes runs up to two and even five per cent of the total amount of honey, and this is considerable. When it is borne in mind that wooden packages must be bone-dry, and well coopered, one can see that a large amount of honey might soak into the pores of the wood. This, of course, can be overcome by paraffining inside; but that involves considerable labor.

Of course, the square cans have to be boxed — usually two in a box—as shown. They are sometimes boxed separately.

A honey-gate is shown in an enlarged view at the right, below the large cut. It is made of a piece of stout charcoal tin, 2¼ x 3 inches. A bit of heavy leather is fastened by four rivets to this tin. The leather is 2 x 3 inches, so that we have ¼ inch of the tin projecting on two sides. Fold this tin which projects, in such a way as to take in the tin slide, as shown in the cut. With a tinner's punch, cut a hole through the leather and tin. In like manner make a hole through the screw cap, and solder to the tin, as shown in the cut. This gives us a honey-gate that will fit on any of our square honey-cans, so the grocer need have but one honey-gate, which he can attach to his square cans as fast as he retails from them. These gates should not cost over 15 cts. each.

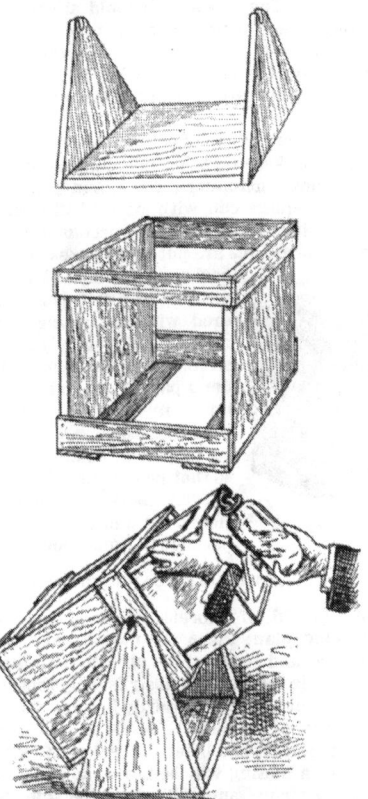

A HANDY DEVICE FOR EMPTYING SQUARE CANS.

An ordinary 60-lb. square can full is a rather awkward thing to handle when it is desired to get a small quantity of honey out of it for a customer who comes with a pail and wants only " a little." In tipping it over at an angle to let the honey run out, it is so heavy that it is difficult to keep it at the right balance so as not to run out too much, or daub the can or the pail. Mr. G. C. Greiner, of LaSalle, N. Y., sent a sketch of a very handy device, and so simple that anybody can make one out of the material in an ordinary drygoods box. The illustration will make its method of construction as well as its manner of use perfectly plain. When a can is pivoted on its centers on each side, it can be tipped to the proper angle very easily. When the package is full, the can may be instantly tipped up to a perpendicular. When one can is empty, another one can be put in its place, and the operation repeated. The screw top should always be on the upper right-hand corner to let the air in as fast as the honey flows out—otherwise the honey will come out with a gurgling sound. A honey-gate can be used or not as desired.

More recently, to meet the wants for a smaller package on the same plan, manufacturers have introduced a 1, ½, and ¼ gallon capacity square can with sizes of 12, 6, and 3 lbs. of honey, shown in the accompanying cut. The gallons are put up in boxes of ten

each, and are sold at $1.50 per box, or $12.00 per hundred without boxing. In many cases it may be desirable for the dealer to order a part of his extracted honey in the 60-lb. square cans and kegs, and a part in the 12-lb. square cans, so that he can distribute to his customers according as they want a large or small package of liquid honey.

ONE-GALLON　12-LB. SQUARE CAN.

HOW TO TEST SQUARE CANS FOR LEAKS.

A. J. Hill, of Florida, recommends the following plan: Place the mouth over the aperture, and suck out the air into the lungs and exhale through the nostrils. By repeated draughts, that necessarily become shorter, a partial vacuum is made in the can. Stop a minute, and listen for leaks. If there are any, a hissing will be heard, and the decreasing air-pressure will allow the sides to crack back into place. These cans should be discarded, and repaired later.

SECOND-HAND CANS, AND HOW TO CLEAN.

Square cans are used exclusively for sending gasoline and kerosene to the Pacific coast. After they are emptied they are sold for about half what new ones cost, and in many cases bee-keepers have used them, almost ruining their honey. Some of the more careful ones have washed them out. The one who has succeeded the best, and claims that second-hand cans are exactly as good when so treated, at about half the cost, is Mr. S. S. Butler, of Los Gatos, Cal. He writes:

I melt off the four faucets by setting four cans, with the corners that have the faucets, together, putting a shovel of hot coals on them A good worker can clean about 100 in a day by putting in a handful of unslacked lime in each, with 3 or 4 quarts of boiling water. After it is slack-ed, rinse it well, and afterward rinse out twice with cold water, washing them twice with lime. In that way it will clean them perfectly.

During 1909 there was considerable discussion in Gleanings in Bee Culture as to whether even the new tin cans are clean enough to put honey in without washing out. Some have claimed that they are more or less dusty inside and should be rinsed out with hot water. The difficulty comes of drying out the cans on the inside, afterwards, for if any drops of water are left in the can they will make rust spots, resulting in leaks or the discoloration of the honey. As to whether new cans should be washed out, or not, will depend very greatly upon the cans themselves. If they appear to be bright and clean we should say that one would be running a risk to attempt to wash them out again.

BOTTLING HONEY.

Under BARRELS we have given some general directions on how to put up the honey in wood so that it may be sent to market. But right here we will devote a little space to telling how to put it up in glass so it will not candy. Under CANDIED HONEY we have already given some general hints; but here we wish to give some details which, while insignificant of themselves, yet, taken collectively, are sufficiently important to make all the difference between success and failure. One who can bottle honey and put it up in neat and attractive form so it will not candy for at least a year can get good prices and do a first-class business.

Steam from a boiler is by a long way the most convenient of any thing for heating that we can employ; but as the average reader of this book probably can not get it he must use something else. While the ordinary cooking-range or cook-stove, using either coal or wood, may be used for heating honey preparatory to bottling, a gasoline-stove with three burners is far better — better because the heat *can be perfectly controlled.* A wood or coal fire is apt to burn too strongly at one time or go down at another. If the honey be overheated it will ruin it — that is, it will have been scorched or the flavor so impaired that it will sell at a moderate price; in fact, it will be absolutely unfit for bottling, and would, therefore, have to be barreled up and sold at a low price to the large baking concerns which can use an inferior or off grade of honey. Then it should be said that, on account of the danger from overheating from a coal or wood stove, *use a gasoline-stove by all means* if you can not get steam.

There are two methods in vogue for heating honey to be put in glass. One is, to draw it off from a large can, while cold, into cans or tumblers, and heat while in the bottles. The other is, to heat the honey in bulk, all at once, in the filling-tank. Draw it off into the bottles while hot, and seal. Where one does or is expecting to do a good business in bottling, this is the method to follow; yet, on the other hand, if he has only a small trade, the other plan of heating the honey in bottles, the bottles standing up to their necks in hot water, is the one to follow, and cheaper in the first cost, for the entire outfit need not consist of more than a large shallow pan to set on top of the cook-stove, and to hold the bottles while heating. But if one desires to keep the honey liquid in the hands of the retailer for a considerable length of time, the heating-in-bulk method is the better way. A large quantity of honey in a tank can be kept hot for five or six hours, at a temperature of 120 to 130 degrees. This low temperature long continued will keep honey in a liquid condition longer than a higher temperature for a shorter period. But, on the other hand, it may be said that a long-hot honey will not have quite as fine a flavor as the quick-heated article; but this difference will be noted, not by the ordinary consumer, but by the bottler or honey connoisseur. As the consuming trade is one to which he is catering, the long-hot plan will, perhaps, be preferable, because it is better to sacrifice slightly on the flavor in order to secure a better appearance; that is, to keep the honey liquid until sold and consumed. Honey that candies quickly or clouds in the bottles on the grocer's shelves is likely to have a slow sale, and to kill the sale of other

honey. The public is suspicious of honey that begins to show granulation, classing it as "sugared" or adulterated.

There are two methods of heating the honey in bulk that we will here describe, either one of which has its special advantage; and the reader, after going over them can determine which is the better one for him to adopt. The question of first cost of the apparatus will have some bearing on the proposition. The one used by Mr. Fowls is cheaper but not quite so efficient as that of Mr. W. S. Pouder.

MR. FOWLS' MELTING-TANKS, SIPHON, AND GASOLINE-STOVE.

In the accompanying cut Mr. Chalon Fowls makes use of a gasoline-stove already referred to, and puts a couple of large cans on each of the top burners. These are partially filled with water, then a square can of honey is let down in each until it is completely submerged. After the honey is all melted, a thermometer is let down as will be seen; and when the mercury rises to about 150 (not higher than 160), the honey is drawn off by means of a siphon into a filling tank that stands on a lower step of the stove. This siphon may be of glass, as shown in the illustration, or it may be of common rubber tubing, such as can be obtained at the drug-store. The latter is to be preferred because it is more convenient to handle. While the honey is hot the tubing should be let down entirely into the honey until it is filled. To do this, attach a string at both ends and submerge it in the honey. Draw out one end and run it over into the filling-tank, which is lower down. The hot honey will now immediately run out; and as the can is emptied the water surrounding the can should be drawn off or else the can will float and tip over. From the filling-tank the honey is drawn off while hot, or about as near 160 as possible, into honey-tumblers, Mason jars, Muth jars, or any of the packages already described. As soon as filled they should be sealed while hot; after which, as soon as they are sponged off in warm water, they may be labeled, when they are ready for market.

The apparatus shown in the next two illustrations can be made at any first-class tin-shop, provided a quantity of half-inch copper or block tin pipe can be secured. If this is not obtainable locally, the tin-smith can send away and get it.

The pen-drawing next page represents first a small tin boiler standing on a gas or gasoline stove; and, second, a melting-tank in which the honey is heated and drawn off into the retail packages. Boiler E can be made from any two or three gallon syrup-can with a screw top. The water-gauge on the side to indicate the level of the water is not absolutely essential, and may be omitted. If gas is not obtainable it is better to get a gasoline-burner of large dimensions, for the ordinary single burner would hardly generate steam fast enough for the purpose. If the tinsmith can not get an oven gasoline burner, he can put two common gasoline-burners close together. The boiler will then have to be constructed with a larger bottom, but shallow in depth; for too large a quantity of water should not be used at a time. The heating-tank should be mounted on a level, above the boiler, and a connection made with a common hose as at G.

The tank used by Mr. Pouder is 30 inches deep, 12 inches in diameter, holding 12 gallons. While his is made of copper, and is nickel-plated, yet one made of tin would be just as good if kept clean, and cost a good deal less.

Five or six feet of half-inch copper pipe tinned on the outside is coiled and inserted inside of the heating-tank, as shown; but instead of a portion of it lying in a flat coil at the bottom, the spirals of the pipe should rise one above the other like a bed-spring, gradually spreading further apart near the

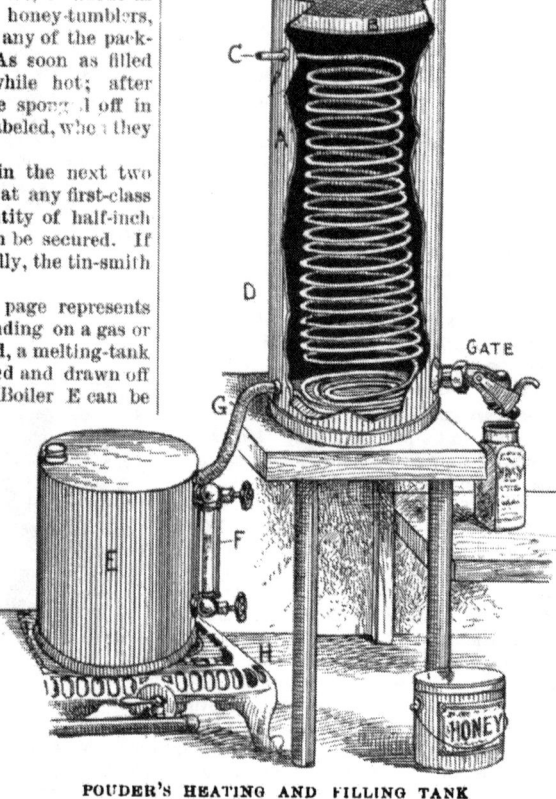

POUDER'S HEATING AND FILLING TANK

top. One end should have an opening at C and the other with G. Steam is generated in the boiler E, and finds its exit at the tube C. But when the honey is first poured into the tank to be heated, all the steam will be condensed and run back into the boiler E. After the honey is hot the steam will come out at the tube C.

Contrary to what might be expected, Mr. Pouder does not find that hot steam does any damage to the flavor of his honey. The apparatus is really very simple, and occupies but a small amount of room. He keeps his outfit right in his retail store on the counter where his customers can see it and its method of working, and this helps to advertise his goods.

After the honey has been run out, the heating-tank should be left just as it is, without washing out unless the outfit is to stand for some months before being used again, for the honey will prevent the rusting of the tin.

The question might arise as to why it is necessary to have the height of the tank nearly three times its diameter. Mr. Pouder explains this by saying that, in pouring honey from one receptacle to another, air-bubbles will accumulate. The deeper the tank the greater the pressure on the honey at the drawing-off point. This pressure will force the bubbles to the top. It is very important, in bottling honey, that the air-bubbles be all expelled, as they have a tendency to cause granulation.

The two outfits already shown for heating honey in bulk illustrate principles that may be applied to various kinds of tanks.

HEATING HONEY IN BOTTLES, OR BOTTLING FOR A SMALL TRADE.

There is a class, as already intimated, who do not care to go to any great expense in a bottling-apparatus, since they have in view only a small trade. In brief, all that is needed is a shallow pan just deep enough so that the deepest bottles can be submerged in hot water up to their necks and no further.

We now need a square or oblong galvanized-iron pan as large as the whole top of the stove, with perpendicular sides, and about six or seven inches deep. If a gasoline-stove is used, the pan should be as long and as broad as the top: and if the three burners are on the same level, all the better. The pan should be just about the depth of an ordinary Mason jar; or, rather, the depth of the deepest package to be used for bottling purposes. A false bottom of coarse wire cloth should be secured about half an inch above the bottom proper by means of proper stays. This is for the purpose of providing a circulation of water under the bottoms of the bottles of honey, for otherwise they might break. Fill the pan about half full of water, and set it on the stove. When the water registers about 180 according to the thermometer, set into the tray, on the false bottom of wire cloth, the bottles of honey that have just been filled from the large filling tank above referred to. When the pan is full of bottles placed close together the water should be raised to within about an inch of the top of the bottles. Let them stand in the hot water until the honey in one of the bottles registers about 160. They may now be taken out and corked or sealed. A fresh supply of filled bottles of honey should next be put back to replace the

first lot, and the operation of heating and sealing can be continued indefinitely.

There are several advantages of this method, aside from the one of first cost for apparatus. viz.:

1. One can fill a small order at any time ; and it is not necessary to heat a great bulk in order to put up a dozen bottles or so of honey. In heating a large quantity of honey one necessarily has to keep it hot a great length of time. The longer the honey is kept hot the greater the liability to discolor and impair its flavor.*

2. Bottles that are submerged in hot water can be easily wiped off with a cloth ; and as soon as they are corked or sealed they are ready for labeling.

3. Any honey that has been poured into the vessels, either cold or hot, will have collected a large number of air-bubbles ; and it is these particles of air that have a tendency to hasten granulation. When the honey is

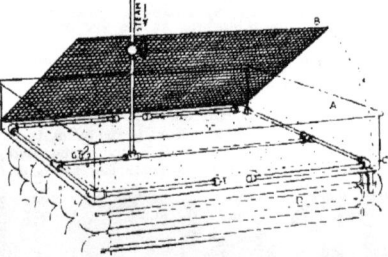

HEATING-TRAY AS USED AT THE ROOT CO.'S FACTORY.

Instead of using a gasoline-stove to heat the water in the tray we use ¾-inch steam-pipes connected as in the manner shown. The outside pipes are perforated with holes that blow a jet of steam transversely across the bottom of the pan. The wire cloth rests on the pipes. The coil of steam-pipes below serves no purpose· but to keep the large filling-tank of honey w·rm

heated gradually in the bottles after filling, the process expels the air-bubbles; and by the time the honey is clear it is ready for sealing and labeling.

If any honey should candy one can unseal, and set the bottles in the tray of hot water, and reheat and seal without emptying.

COVEYOU'S METHOD OF FILLING BOTTLES.

Mr. E. E. Coveyou, of Petoskey, Mich., one of the most extensive bottlers of honey in the United States, has a very fully equipped plant. The accompanying description,

*The longer it is kept hot, the longer it will be before it candies again. I advise erring on the side of good flavor, even if it does candy more quickly. The same honey can be remelted in precisely the same way.

FIG. 1.—E. E. COVEYOU'S HONEY-BOTTLING ROOM.
The bottles are filled by means of a short piece of hose connected to the honey-tank. A quick-working stop at the end controls the flow of honey into the bottles.

together with the half-tones, will give a very fair idea of how he operates.

Fig. 1 shows at the right the boiler and pipe leading to the different tanks. Next is the filling-tank in front of which are the glasses ready to be filled with the hose hanging at the bottom of the tank.

At the left the glasses are piled up with galvanized wire screen between each tier. This makes a very good way to dry.

Fig. 2 shows our liquefying-tank partly filled with 60-lb. cans of honey. There is a partition through the center, so that 1000 lbs. of honey can be heated in each side. A lower temperature can be main-

FIG. 2.—COVEYOU'S LIQUEFYING-TANK.
This is divided into two parts, each of which will hold a thousand pounds of honey. The temperature of the water in each part is controlled by a separate steam-pipe.

FIG. 3.—FILLING AND LABELING BOTTLES.

The method of filling the bottles is here shown. The top label in the bunch is pasted, and the bottle
rolled over it. Thus the labels are put on without being handled at all.

tained in one side than the other, should it be thought advantageous to heat the honey slowly for the first twelve hours.

The steam-pipe in the middle is divided with valves close to the partition, so that the steam can be turned on or off to keep the temperature uniform. I am standing with a thermometer in my hand, not ing the temperature. This should be done quite fre, quently until the right degree of heat is reached when the valve practically does the work.

In Fig. 3 the lady at the right is my sister, Mary Coveyou, filling glasses with what Mr. Townsend has named our "wild goose bill." This is attached to a hose, and fills the glasses right in the cases, which saves handling. We find this is one of the very best methods we have ever tried. One person can fill 4000 half-pound glasses with honey in less than a day's time, in this way.

The lady in the center is my wife, showing our new way of labeling glasses. In the first place the labels are not gummed. We take one end of the package of labels and paste it, which keeps the pile together. Then the bunch of labels is also pasted upon the table, face down, which holds them securely in place. The young lady at the left does the pasting. As soon as the top label is pasted, the glass is simply rolled over it, which picks it up and at the same time presses it firmly in place. Thus the work is done without any handling of sticky labels. By this method we can label with the ungummed papers just as fast as we could with the gummed.

Mr. Coveyou's scheme for filling his honey-bottles is very unique. It is, in fact, the same general scheme that is uses by bottlers of pickles and other canned goods in large canning-factories. A rubber hose is attached to the filling-tank, and on the other end is an arrangement something similar to the cover on a syrup-pitcher to shut off the syrup without drip; indeed, it opens and closes much like a goose-bill. A pressure of a little hand-lever opens the beak of the bill, as it were, and allows the honey to run into a bottle. Just the moment the honey reaches the desired level the beak or goose-bill is closed, chopping off the honey without a particle of drip.

A quantity of the empty bottles are placed up on a table or tray within reach of the hose. The operator grasps it, holds the beak over one of the bottles, opens it and then closes it at just the exact moment when the bottle is filled. In like manner all the others are filled without touching a single bottle until that entire lot are full. The whole tray of them is removed, when another lot is put in place.

There can be no doubt that this method of filling the bottles is much more rapid than the old way of placing the bottles one at a time under a honey-gate, filling it, removing it, and filling another. It can readily be seen that the handling of the bottles necessarily consumes a large amount of time, whereas the rubber hose, with its goose-bill or beak can be moved to any one of the bottles where they stand, and fill them one by one in the shortest space of time.

WASHING AND CLEANING BOTTLES.

Prepare several tubs of water — one of them with strong suds — and then have on hand a few ounces of shot — No. 6 is about right. If particles of glass or dirt cling to the inside of the bottles, pour in four or five ounces of shot and give the bottle a shaking. This will dislodge all particles, when the shot may be poured into another bottle, to be similarly treated. In rinsing, use clear soft water. Hard water is liable to leave traces of sediment. Any glass package used for honey designed for table purposes should be spotlessly clean.

HOW TO INSERT CORKS IN BOTTLES.

Two or three methods are employed. One is, to use a rubber mallet, which can be purchased at any of the rubber-stores. The ends of the mallet being soft, a cork that is barely entered can be driven into the bottle with a blow.

Another plan is to use a lever, as shown at D, in cut. This lever should have a projection on the under side so the cork can be forced down into the bottle about a sixteenth of an inch. It is important, after corking,

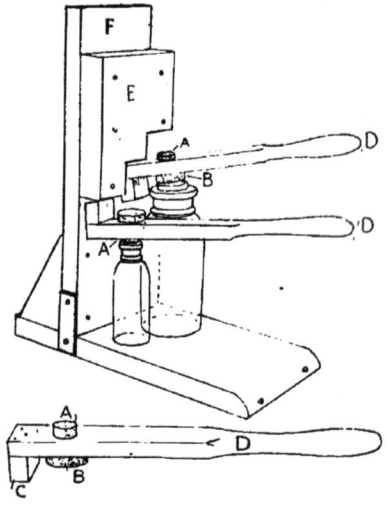

to pour a layer of paraffine or wax over the top of the cork. Some go so far as to dip the corks into hot paraffine, then pour a hot layer on top after they are inserted in the bottles. Nay, some go even further. After the corks have been paraffined they put on a neat tinfoil top. If the honey has been heated above 160, and sealed while hot, and the cork is made impervious, it will remain liquid for months; as we have seen samples of honey put up in Muth jars that have been kept in a refrigerator six months, and yet it would remain perfectly clear all the time. But do not advise your grocer customers to put honey in a cold place. The bottles should not be handled more than is necessary, but be kept in a warm place at as uniform a temperature as possible.

Assuming that no directions are necessary for sealing packages using rubber rings, we would only say this: That you must be sure you make the sealing as tight as possible. In the case of Mason jars, screw the tops down with a wrench, and *screw them down tight.*

In sealing jelly-tumblers, cut squares of paper (preferably paraffined paper) about the size of the top of the tumbler. When the jar is filled, put the paper on top of the jar, and squeeze the top down with the palm of the hand, putting a large part of the weight of the body on it. If the top goes down too easily, use thicker paper or two thicknesses.

A BLEND OF SEVERAL KINDS OF HONEY FOR BOTTLING PURPOSES.

The seasons for honey production are so uncertain at times that one finds himself unable to supply his trade with the honey he produces from his own yard. If, for example, his honey is almost exclusively from clover, with little or no basswood or fall flow, the trade will become educated to like that particular flavor, and will reject all other honeys of other flavors on the ground that they are impure. To provide against a contingency of this kind it is advisable to use from the start for bottling purposes a honey that can always be furnished year after year. We make a blend of white clover, basswood, and alfalfa. These are fine table honeys; and if the trade is supplied with this blend from the very start it will become accustomed to it. Such a blend can be made up of honeys that one can purchase when local honey fails; whereas if one puts up only white clover at the beginning, he will find it difficult to purchase a strictly pure clover except at highest prices. Where one lives in a clover locality he will do well to make up a blend of 50 per cent of clover, 25 per cent of basswood, and 25 per cent of alfalfa. We will assume, for example, that he has a season of failure, and yet the bottling trade keeps up just the same. He can usually buy a mixture of clover and basswood. His taste will become educated so he can determine the percentage of the one to the other. Then by putting in a small amount of alfalfa, which he can always procure, he will be able to supply his trade with the proper blend.

If one lives in a locality where alfalfa is produced exclusively, there will be no need of having a special blend, because the pure alfalfa can usually be obtained in most of the irrigated regions.

REQUIREMENTS OF THE LAW AS TO LABELS.

It will be well to state that the national pure-food law, and in some cases State laws, requires that the label shall indicate the exact contents of a package; and therefore it would not be advisable to call a blend, such as we have described, a *pure* clover. It will be perfectly proper to say " pure extracted honey bottled by John Jones;" but John Jones must not say " pure extracted honey from the apiary of John Jones" unless such honey actually did come from his apiary.

LABELING BOTTLED HONEY.

As a general rule, use small circular labels. The big ones that cover up the whole jar do not usually afford as pretty an effect as the small neat tasty labels that give the customer a good chance to see the honey. It is the honey that sells; and if it is a fine quality, get the grocer to display it in such a way in his window that the light will sparkle through it, and we will guarantee it will sell.

EXTRACTOR. The extractor, like the movable frame, is one of the things that have made a revolution in bee-keeping. It was invented in the year 1865 by Major Francesco de Hruschka, of Venice, who died at the good old age of 75, in the year 1888. Like a good many other inventions, its discovery was made by accident. His little boy chanced to put a piece of comb in a basket to which was attached a bit of rope. With rope in hand, the boy began to whirl it. The centrifugal force caused a few drops of honey to be thrown out of the basket around in the air, and the father, seeing it, was keen enough to see that in this was a *principle*, and the nucleus of a big invention whereby it became unnecessary any longer to smash the combs up and strain the honey out in the old-fashioned way. He very soon constructed a rude extractor that demonstrated the practical utility of the discovery; and, shortly afterward, perfected the machine.

Among the early extractors brought out in this country was one made by J. L. Peabody. This was so constructed that the whole can revolved, and the honey ran out through a hole cut in the center. But this was poorly adapted to the wants of the bee-keeper. In 1869 A. I. Root constructed what he called the "Novice" honey-extractor.

This was so great an improvement over all those that had preceded, that it found a ready sale at once. The inside baskets for holding the combs, in order to combine lightness with the greatest strength, were made of folded-tin bars and tinned wire cloth, four meshes to the inch. The crank was geared so that one revolution made three revolutions of the baskets.

REVERSING EXTRACTORS.

The basket in the Novice extractor requires the pulling-out of the combs in order to present the unextracted sides next to the can. This wastes time, as well as being awkward. About the time A. I. Root was

EXTRACTOR WITH SPACE FOR HONEY BELOW REVOLVING FRAME.

experimenting with extractors, Thos. Wm. Cowan, editor of the *British Bee Journal*, constructed what was then known as and is still called the Cowan reversible extractor. To obviate the necessity of removing the combs, the pockets, or wire-cloth cages, were hinged, like an ordinary door, to a reel without a center-shaft. Combs could be put into these pockets; and after one side was extracted the pocket could be swung on its hinges the other side to, door fashion, without even stopping the machine, by merely slowing up so the left hand could catch the edge of each pocket, throwing it around. The cut next shown, while it does not represent the original extractor made by Mr. Cowan, shows the Americanized machine.

The mechanism has been greatly improved in workmanship and design.

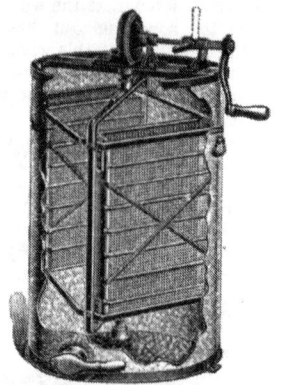

TWO-FRAME REVERSIBLE EXTRACTOR.

Shortly after the two-frame Cowan was introduced in this country (1890), there came a demand from the bee-keepers of the West, who produce honey by the carload, for machines that would do the work in a still more wholesale way than even the two-frame reversible Cowan. In response to

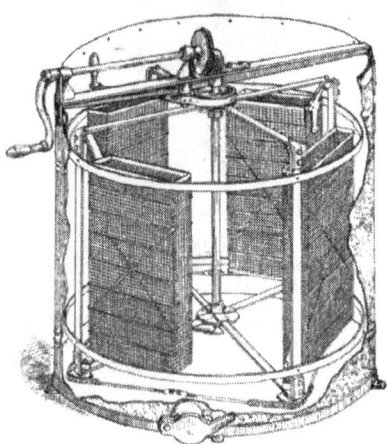

INSIDE OF THE FOUR-FRAME COWAN.

this, four and six frame Cowan machines were made. The same principle of the swinging pockets was used in a large revolving reel, as in the two-frame machines, with this difference, that all the pockets were geared together so that when one was swung around all would be moved at the same time. In late years this has given way to the

ROOT AUTOMATIC REVERSIBLE EXTRACTOR.

This is an improvement over the old original Cowan because of the fact that it is

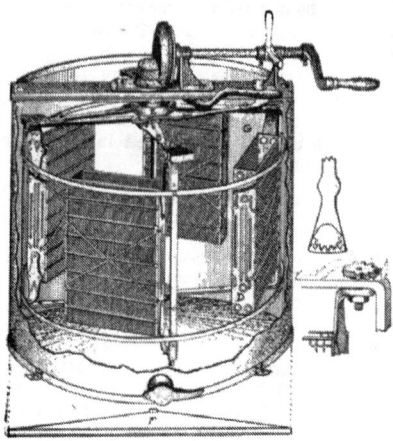

ROOT'S AUTOMATIC FOUR-FRAME HONEY-EXTRACTOR—SIDE VIEW.

an automatic reversible machine. The reversing mechanism, the invention of Frank G. Marbach, is situated on top of the reel, and is actuated by a slight pressure on the brake-lever. This action is always positive and reliable. Other automatic reversing-devices have been put on the market at various times; but they were so complicated in their action, and so likely to get out of order, that they have never become popular.

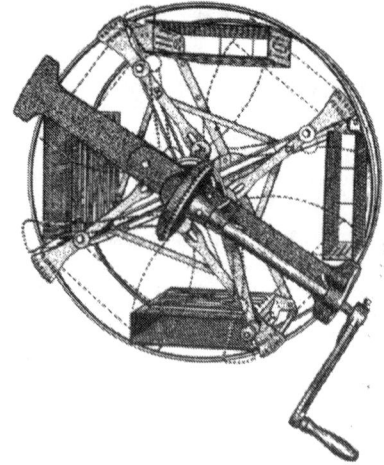

ROOT'S AUTOMATIC FOUR-FRAME HONEY-EXTRACTOR—TOP VIEW.

ONE ENGINE DRIVING TWO LARGE FOUR-FRAME EXTRACTORS.

The advantage of this arrangement is that one extractor can be emptied and filled with combs while the other is extracting. In this way the work of extracting can proceed without interruption.

Moreover, they required a reversal of the crank-handle in order to bring about a change in the position of the combs. This placed a heavy strain on the gearwork, causing breakdowns, and very often stripping the cog-wheels of their teeth. This has all been overcome in the Marbach device, because the strain incident to reversing is placed entirely on the brake-lever, relieving all stress on the gears. Another feature of this machine is that it can be reversed while in motion; a pressure on the brake lever slows down the reel, when, presto! the combs are flopped the other side to in the fraction of a second—so quickly, indeed, that it seems like a sleight-of-hand performance.

POWER-DRIVEN HONEY-EXTRACTORS.

In some localities, where a large amount of extracting has to be done, the extractors are driven by water-motors, gasoline-engines, or any other small power. Little gasoline-motors have now arrived at such a state of perfection that they are exceedingly reliable and efficient, and in view of the fact that a steam-engine is expensive, and that a water-motor is out of the question for most localities, the internal-combustion engine, driven by the force of an explosion, is the most available power for this purpose. Small air-cooled engines of this type are now made in one-horse-power sizes that will drive a honey-extractor with a consumption

of gasoline of only one quart for a run of ten hours, and the cost of the engine is only from $50.00 to $75.00 at the factory, and they are so simple in construction that any child capable of reading and understanding directions can manage them.

The method of transmitting the power of the engine to the machine is shown in the accompanying illustrations. In view of the

ONE-HORSE-POWER AIR-COOLED GASOLINE-ENGINE CONNECTED TO EIGHT-FRAME EXTRACTOR.

fact that it is not practicable to stop and start a gasoline-engine every time the combs are taken out of the extractor, and replaced, a loose belt with idler is employed so that the extractor can be stopped and started—in fact, any speed desired obtained—simply by a pressure on the lever that holds the idler used to increase the tension on the belt. This form of transmission of power has been tested thoroughly, and found to be a success in every way.

Where a large amount of extracting is to de done, this gasoline-outfit, together with an eight-frame extractor, will almost pay for itself in one season. On the other hand,

DETAIL OF DRIVING MECHANISM — IDLER RELEASED AND BELT LOOSE.

an extractor run by hand power takes a good strong man, whose services can not usually be had for less than $2.00 a day.

But experiments have shown that a honey-extractor driven by power will do quicker and more thorough work. It is impossible by hand power to do a clean job of extract-

DETAIL OF DRIVING MECHANISM — IDLER IN POSITION AND BELT TIGHT.

ing; and the result is, the combs go back into the hive very wet. While a good portion of this honey will be stored back, experience shows that a large part of it will be consumed by the bees.

RIGHT AND WRONG PRINCIPLES IN EX-TRACTORS.

Some of the earlier machines sold in this country, notably the Peabody, made use of a revolving can without gearing. This was a mistake. For the last twenty years extractors have been built with *stationary* cans, inside of which the comb-pockets, reversible or non-reversible, revolve, motion being imparted by gearing so that one turn of the crank-handle makes two or three turns of the baskets.

MORE EXTRACTED THAN COMB.

Some of the advantages and disadvantages of using a honey-extractor in the apiary are considered under the head of Ex-TRACTED HONEY. That more honey can be obtained by the use of the machine than by having it stored in section boxes in the shape of comb honey, all are agreed; but all are not agreed as to *how much* more. If it is nicely sealed over as it should be before being extracted, we do not think more than half as much more will be obtained, on an average, although the amount is placed by many at a much higher figure. A beginner will be likely to get more extracted than if he relies upon having the bees work in sections; he will also be much more apt to take away too much, and to cause his bees to starve. This last is a an unfortunate feature attendant upon the use of the machine, especially where the bee-keeper is prone to carelessness and negligence. To secure the best results with the extractor, plenty of empty combs should be provided. that ample room may be given, in case the hives should become full before the honey is ripe enough to remove. If a second story does not give room sufficient, add a third for a heavy stock, during a good yield of honey.

HOW TO EXTRACT.

Much will depend on whether one has a large amount of honey to be extracted, or whether he is only a novice and wishes to use the simpler and cheaper methods. If he keeps bees in only a small way, and probably will not extract to exceed a thousand pounds in a season, the ordinary Novice extractor will answer his purpose; but as he seldom foresees that he may go into the business extensively, it would be better to purchase the two-frame reversible extractor, as the difference in cost is very slight. One of these will save labor, do quicker work, and more of it.

Having selected the machine, it should be placed on a box or hive-body about as large as the bottom of the can, and about as high as an ordinary water-pail: that is to say, the extractor should be elevated high enough so that the honey-gate may empty into a common pail, something as shown in the above illustration. Both box and extractor should be securely anchored down. As fast as the honey is extracted it is to be drawn off pailful after pailful, and then poured into kegs, square cans, or any large receiving-vat for holding the honey. This filling and empty-

EXTRACTOR ELEVATED ON A HIVE-BODY.

ing of the pails may seem to involve quite a little labor; but one of the largest honey-producers in the world, Mr. W. L. Cogg-shall, uses identically this method.

Some prefer to have the extractor on a higher box so that the honey-gate can stand just over the bunghole of a barrel, thus allowing the honey to go directly from the comb into the marketing-package. But this necessitates raising the extractor to a point so high in the air that it is inconvenient to work, and awkward to put in and remove the combs. It is, therefore, desirable that the machine should be as close to the floor as possible on a low box, low enough so we can run the honey into the pail, or direct into square cans; but if the honey is first run into an open tin pail, its quality, and whether or not there are dead bees floating in it, can be seen before it is emptied into the regular marketing-packages.

For a strainer a cheese-cloth sack attached to the honey-gate will answer very well in a small way, although something more elab-

orate will have to be used where the extractings are conducted on an extensive scale. It is then customary to run the honey through a strainer having a large surface, not less than three or four square feet. Or the honey may be conducted into large tanks, where all particles of comb can rise to the top and be skimmed off. The honey is then drawn off from the bottom into square cans and barrels.

Mr. E. W. Alexander takes an ordinary ten-quart milk-pail, cuts out the sides and bottom of it, leaving a top and bottom rim. These are united by upright tin braces as shown. The open spaces are next filled in with a fine mesh of brass wire cloth, secured to place by solder. A good tinner should be employed to do the job When finished it makes a large pail seive. This he hangs over the discharge-pipe of his extractor, and he finds it ample to take care of the output of a four frame machine run to its fullest extent. He advises, however, having

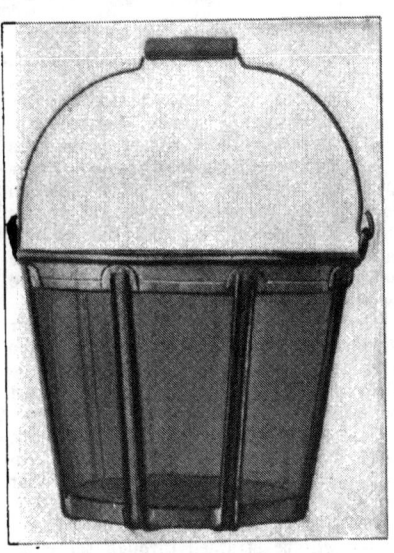

THE ALEXANDER HONEY-STRAINER.

two pails, so that when one is clogged up another one can be put in its place; then, after the day's extracting is over, both can be cleaned.

S. T. Pettit, of Alymer, Ontario, Canada, has devised a strainer, which we consider superior to any thing else that is here shown. The accompanying illustration will make its manner of construction clear. It consists of a large tin funnel with perpendicular sides, having oblong V-shaped pieces of tin soldered across the bottom and up and down the sides on a perpendicular line and at regular intervals, so that when the wire-cloth basket is put inside it will be held

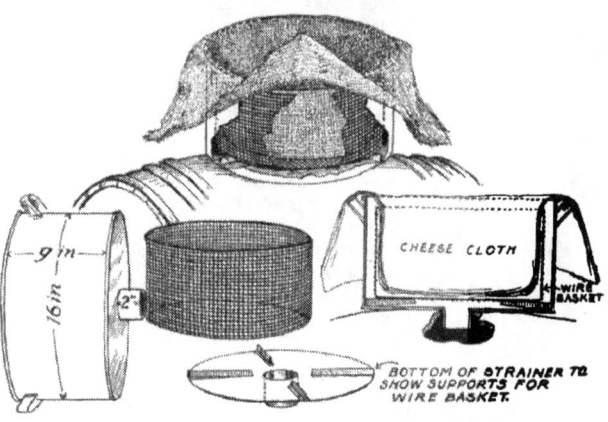

PETTIT HONEY-STRAINER.

away from the sides of the funnel by a distance equal to the pieces of V-shaped tin. Inside the wire-cloth basket is hung a square of cheesecloth, that practically does all of the straining. This cloth comes in contact with the wire-cloth basket, and as this has a space of practically half an inch between it and the walls of the funnel, the honey can run down between through the two-inch pipe into the barrel.

The special feature of the Pettit strainer is that extra squares of cheesecloth can be substituted when the one already in shall be clogged with refuse. These can be rinsed out later on and be used again.

One can, if he chooses, modify the shape of the funnel, using the ordinary form with tapering sides, but it is our judgment that the one shown in the illustration is better, because of its *vertical* sides, for most of the honey will be strained through the cloth that hangs on the perpendicular line rather than that laying horizontally on the bottom. Mr. John Baily, of Brrcebridge, Ontario, made an Alexander strainer, but he uses sloping sides. This can readily be put inside of an ordinary large funnel that can be purchased at almost any large hardware store; but in our judgment the Pettit idea in using coarse-mesh wire-cloth and cheesecloth for the strainer material would be better than using a fine milk-strainer gauze only.

EXTRACTING IN A LARGE WAY.

Where the production of extracted honey goes up into the carload, or the tens of thousands of pounds, it is advisable to have an extracting-building located on a side hill, the first floor of which should be on a level with the top of the hill, and the basement floor even with the base of the hill. The combs from the hives are then to be run on a comb-cart on a direct level with the extractor, which in this case will stand on the floor. In the room or basement below, just beneath the extractor, and communicating directly with it through a hole or pipe, should be a large storage-tank that will hold from 5000 to 10,000 lbs. of honey at a time. Into this the honey runs direct from the extractor as fast as it is taken. From this the honey will be drawn off into square cans, the latter to be loaded on a wagon at the base of the hill. The illustration next page shows somewhat

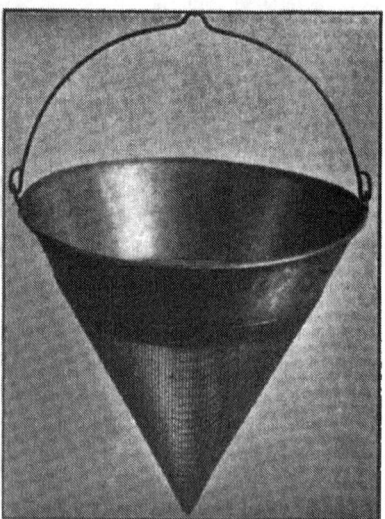

BAILY'S HONEY-STRAINER.

ALEXANDER'S EXTRACTING-HOUSE; PUTTING THE COMBS IN.

ALEXANDER'S EXTRACTING-HOUSE; TAKING THE COMBS OUT.

how such buildings are used in California. Others use a pipe connecting directly with the honey-gate of the extractor, and leading directly to a storage-tank that is on a lower level, and off at one side. In either case the extractor is, of course, secured to the floor, and the operator is thus enabled to exert his power to the best advantage.

As to the building itself, some put up a cheap structure as shown in the illustrations; but in every case it should be well

HONEY-TANKS ON A LEVEL LOWER THAN EXTRACTING-TANK, NEAR BUR-BANK, CALIFORNIA.

battened, and bee-proof. The doors should swing outward, so as to let the bees escape that get inside. The windows should be provided with wire screens having bee-escapes.

Mr. E. W. Alexander, of Delanson, N. Y., one of the most extensive bee-keepers in the world, uses a small extracting-house that certainly has some features to recommend it. It is just large enough to receive a four-frame extractor, a man to operate it, an uncapping-box, and space to receive the fresh combs as they come in and those that go out. The combs are carried in comb-carriers, which are nothing more nor less than hive-bodies rigged up with a convenient iron handle as shown. Mr. Alexander has something like 700 colonies, all in one apiary, and his crops of honey annually go up into

the carloads. While the carrying-boxes may seem very crude, yet, used in the manner in which he uses them, in connection with this small building, they give excellent results with a minimum of labor.

Two men take the combs out of the hive, and shake or brush off the bees. While one is putting in fresh empty combs from which the filled ones have been taken, closing up the hive, and opening up another one, the other carries the combs just removed in the carrier to the man in the extracting-house. The sliding door at the right is lifted, and the combs, carrier and all, are pushed inside and the door drops, shutting out all possible robbers. In the same way the empty combs are removed in another carrier from the other door at the left, and so on the process continues. The quick opening and closing of the slide doors prevents robbers from getting at the work inside. The three men thus working, changing place every now and then to relieve the monotony, are able to take out several thousand pounds of honey in a day. As the ground is very hilly and rough at this yard, a wheelbarrow would be out of the question.

It will be noted that the tin pipe going down through the floor, connecting with the honey-gate (see cuts page 178) passes down through the yard and communicates with a large open honey-tank inside of a small building not shown. The whole arrangement, from start to finish, is unique and perfect for the conditions mentioned.

Where the ground is comparatively level, and no steep grades, a wheelbarrow or hand-cart, preferably with pneumatic tires, as described a little further along, would, perhaps, be better. Other bee-keepers make a very small extracting-house that can be lifted up on wagon-wheels, and carried from one yard to another. It sometimes happens that localities change, and then it becomes desirable to move the extracting-house.

E. F. Atwater, of Meridian, Idaho, uses a building which he can take down, load on a wagon, and set up at any spot desired.

Still others prefer a genuine portable extracting-house—that is, a house permanently on wheels; such as the one shown in the next illustration, used by W. D. Jefferson, of Safford, Arizona. Low wide-tired iron wheels are used, and a platform wide enough to extend out over and even with the outer edges of the wheels, and long enough to give sufficient room for extracting purposes, is mounted just high enough to clear the wheels. Beneath the platform is a long shallow galvanized tank, hanging between the front and rear axle-trees, that will hold 200 gallons. On the top of it is built a light skeleton-like structure, the upper portion of which is screened with wire cloth. This house on wheels is equipped with extractor, uncapping-knives, uncapping-tank, and all. The extractor is placed just over the tank; and as fast as the honey is thrown out it runs down into it.

JEFFERSON'S PORTABLE HOUSE.

The screen door is made to open outward, and the building is provided with Porter bee-escapes. The structure is large enough to take care of an ordinary day's extracting; but to provide for emergency, another wagon has a tank holding 200 gallons mounted low so that the honey can run from the tank of the extracting-house into another tank. This extracting - wagon is drawn from yard to yard; and the honey, as fast as taken, is hauled home, leaving none at the yards where thieves can molest. On the whole, the Jefferson outfit has many features to recommend it; and in some localities, where roads are reasonably good, but where light-fingered people exist, it is the very best arrangement.

TAKING THE COMBS TO THE EXTRACTOR.

We next come to the matter of getting the combs out of the hives, transporting them to the extractor, and uncapping them. We shall need a wheelbarrow or handcart—preferably latter, for the wheels are large, and the burden is sustained entirely by the cart.

COGGSHALL'S EXTRACTING-CART.

This, as will be seen, is nothing but a handcart without a box. The tray or bot-tom has cleats around the outer edges, to hold the hive bodies or supers that are placed thereon from sliding This cart, with the supers, is run close to a hive. Over the whole four, or over each one individ-

ually, may be pla ed a wet cloth or cloths, the purpose of which is to shut out robber bees that may be hovering around: for bees are disinclined to push up under wet cloth.

Some prefer a light spring wheelbarrow holding one or two empty hive-bodies. Mr. William Lossing. of Arizona, makes use of a foot-lever closing device over the hive.

A PNEUMATIC-TIRED CART FITTED WITH A TIN-LINED BOX FOR CARRYING EXTRACTING-COMBS.   - -;

Mr. L. E. Mercer, of California, uses a sort of two-wheel barrow with pneumatic tires, and a long box in which to receive the combs. The bicycle-tires and wheels make the vehicle much better for carrying the combs over ordinary rough ground.

GETTING THE BEES OFF THE COMBS.

We next open the hive, pull out one comb and give it a rapid shaking motion in front of the entrance. The Coggshall or the German bee-brush attached to our person by means of a string will brush off the remaining bees. The frame should be held by one corner and one side and then the other be brushed as shown in the views below. Or, if preferred, the comb

HOW TO HOLD THE COGGSHALL BEE-BRUSH.

MANNER OF USING GERMAN BEE-BRUSH.

may be rested on the hive, and brushed. We then place the frame in one of the supers on the cart or barrow. The next comb is then removed; but instead of being shaken in *front of the entrance* it is shaken in

the hive. The few remaining bees are then dislodged with the brush, as before explained. In this way one or more supers on the carrier are filled with combs, and are then wheeled to the extracting-house. Arriving here they are taken care of by a couple of helpers. We then take back with us on the cart four other empty supers, which are filled as were the others; but where one carries on bee-keeping in a limited way, an ordinary wheelbarrow with two supers on would answer. In that case one operator might take off combs, run them into the extracting-house, extract them, bring them back, and put them on the hive again. Or he might put in the house a dozen or so of supers and then extract. The method or methods can be varied to suit the individual conditions that may exist; but in any case the importance of having pants tucked in the tops of boots, or, if shoes are worn, in the tops of the stockings, is urged: for, during the operation of shaking, the combs the bees will almost surely try to crawl up one's trousers legs. It would also be a wise precaution to have long

PORTER BEE-ESCAPE.

sleeves, on the ends of which are sewed gloves having the finger-tips all cut off. These, when put on over the coat or shirt sleeves, will prevent the bees from crawling up the sleeves or attacking the wrists. But all this annoyance of bees crawling up the trousers legs, and shaking and brushing off the bees, stings, and robbers, may be avoided by the use of the bee-

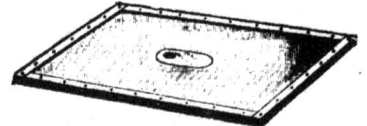

escape. If there are a hundred supers to extract the next day, a hundred bee-escapes can be placed under the supers the night before; then during the afternoon of the day following one can go to the hives and take off super after super, and find scarcely a bee on a comb; nor does it in any way anger any of the colonies. A little smoke at the entrance will prevent the guards from flying out and attacking while the honey is being removed. These hundred supers, six or eight at a time, can then be taken to the extracting-house, on the hand-cart, with never a robber in sight, even during the robbing season; and if the extracting-house is as tight as it surely ought to be, the extracting can be done at any time with ease and pleasure. But at out-yards it is sometimes impracticable to use escapes unless two trips are made—one to put on them and the other to take off the honey. Some apiarists think the extra trip more than offsets the inconveniences of the brushing and shaking of the combs.

UNCAPPING-CANS.

In dry climates the combs may be taken out of the hive when they are half capped over; but it is a much safer rule to wait till the cells are pretty well covered before attempting to extract. The honey will be

DADANT'S UNCAPPING-CAN.

thicker and richer, will sell better, and the product will always be in demand from that time on.

The outfit shown in the next column is something like an ordinary extractor-can, only it is made in two pieces—the upper one slipping into the other. A wire-cloth partition, as shown in the cut, catches the caps as they fall, and the honey drips down, to be drawn off through the gate. The very finest of the honey will come from this uncapping-can, as it has all been ripened and sealed. A wooden cross-arm extends across the top on one side. A scraping-stick (to clean the knife on) extends at right angles, and is at a convenient height. Centrally through the intersecting piece at one end passes a screw which may be lowered or raised and the end of which is sharpened to a point. On this point the frame to be uncapped is pivoted, so that one side or the other can be turned very readily for the knife. The cappings, as they fall, easily pass down between the two side arms, dropping on to the screen below. The honey-knife can be readily scraped on the wooden scraping-stick in the manner shown in the illustration, without dulling the edge.

M'INTYRE'S UNCAPPING-BOX.

The cut above shows the device used very successfully by Mr. J. F. McIntyre, one of those extensive bee-keepers in California who produce honey by the carload, and the following is his description, taken from *Gleanings*, page 770, Vol. XVIII.:

It is 2 feet wide, 2 deep, and 6 long outside, made of ¾ lumber dressed on both sides. The bottom is 2 inches lower in the middle than at the sides, and is lined with tin to keep it from leaking. Eleven pieces of wood, 1x1x22 inches, are laid across the bottom about 6 inches apart to support the screen which the cappings fall on. This leaves room below the screen for the honey to run to one end, where it passes out through a tin pipe. Two pieces, ¾x3x72 inches, are nailed on the top edge, one on each side, to contract the top of the box to the same width that a Langstroth hive is long inside.

One piece, ¾x3x22¼, is fixed across the top of the box about 14 inches from one end, with an iron pivot sticking up through it, 1½ inches high to rest the combs on. When uncapping you set one end of the comb on this pivot, uncap one side, whirl it around, and uncap the other side, and set the comb in the end of the box, as in the diagram. When we have a surplus of combs we often hang them in the other end of the box, in the diagram. C is cappings, and D the space for the honey to run out.

The bottom of the box is 7 inches from the floor, which leaves room for the honey to run into the strainer arrangement below. This makes the top of the box about 32 inches from the floor, which is about the right height for me to uncap easily. A shorter person might make the box a little shallower, or lay a plank on the floor to give the right height, which is the way I do when my wife uncaps.

I know many will think this box unnecessarily large. I will tell you why I think it is not. When uncapping over a round can like Dadant's, the cappings fall on top of those taken off earlier in the day; and when the can is half full the honey has to pass through such a pile of cappings that it takes a long time for all to run out; and when you put the cappings in the sun extractor they are heavy with honey. With this box, when a pile of cappings accumulates under the knife we take a four-tined fork and pitch them over to the other end, where they may drain for 4 or 5 days. There is a small stream of honey running out of the box all the time, day and night, during the extracting time; and when the cappings go into the sun extractor they are almost dry. I think it pays well for the extra space in the box, because all the honey which goes into the sun extractor is spoiled for the market.

J. F. McIntyre.

THE TOWNSEND UNCAPPING-BOX.

Mr. E. D. Townsend, of Remus, Mich., has made an improvement in the McIntyre uncapping-box, and we hereby submit a cut and description of it as well as a cut and description of his honey-strainer and weighing-machine:

Our McIntyre uncapping-box is made of galvanized steel, and is 4 ft. long, 2 ft. high, 2 ft. wide, as shown in the engraving. The slatted frame work at the bottom is made a little smaller than the can so that it may be easily removed to be washed. As there is only a 1½-inch space under this frame for honey storage, we leave the gate open all the time so that nearly all of the room in the tank is available for the storage of cappings, as it should be.

The engraving does not show the frame at the top correctly, for the long side-pieces should be close enough together so that the frames can hang between them as though they were in the hives. After the honey is extracted, the combs may be placed back in this rack; but the principal value of the arrangement consists in providing a place where the uncapped combs may be hung to drip before they are extracted, for in this way no extra apparatus is needed.

The two short pieces of the framework at the top should be nailed on the bottom of the long side-pieces about 1¼ inches from either end. It can be seen that, when the long side-pieces rest on top of the tank, the short cross-pieces fit just inside, keeping the framework from sliding either way, and yet allowing it to be easily removed when the cappings are taken out. The metal pieces containing nail-points can be tacked on in any position to suit the convenience of the operator.

We have used many different designs of uncapping-boxes, but none seem to me quite so convenient as this McIntyre box. It will hold all of the cappings from one extracting in a yard of ordinary size. We use a six-tined short-handled fork for handling the cappings, and each morning the dry cappings from the day before are pitched up toward one end of the tank, and in this way the honey from the new cappings does not have to drain through the dry ones over and over again as it would if we were to uncap on top of the cappings left from the day before. In one instance we had more cappings than we could keep in the tank, and a sugar-barrel with a perforated bottom was set over a galvanized steel washtub, and the dry cappings pitched into it. In this way the capacity of the tank may be said to be unlimited. The advantage of the large area of the bottom is that the honey drains out of the cappings much better if they are spread out in a thin layer than it could in a deep tank where the bottom is comparatively small.

The strainer-can is elevated in order to run the honey from the gate into a 60-pound can set on the scales. The gate is open all the time except when

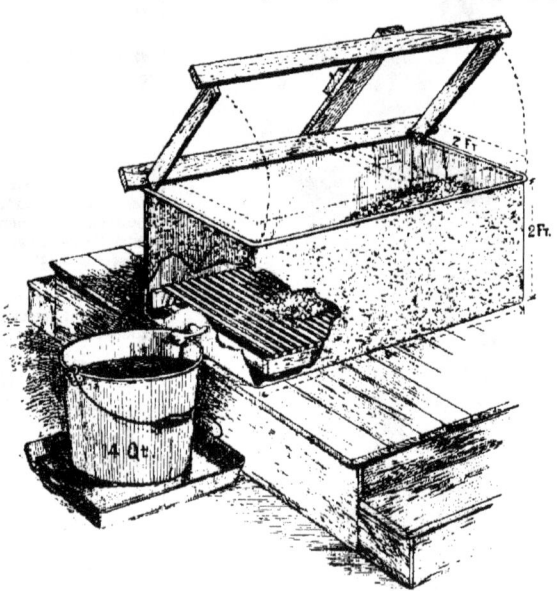

THE McINTYRE UNCAPPING-BOX AS IMPROVED BY
E. D. TOWNSEND.

the cans are changed. An electrical alarm, as first described by Mr. Hutchinson, is used to give us warning when the can is full—see Fig. 2. No one should hesitate about trying one of these alarms, for they are very simple. The engraving shows the method of connecting the bell to the battery. In brief, two wires run from the two posts on the battery to the two posts on the bell; but one wire is broken, one of the ends being fastened to the scale-beam at the pivot, and the other being located just above the outside end of the beam. It can be seen that, when the can is full, the scale-beam rises and the circuit is completed so that the bell rings. It is necessary to have all of the connections tight, as the bell may fail to ring if there are any loose contacts. We set the scales as usual at the 62½-pound mark to allow for the 60 pounds of honey and the weight of the can, and then lay a two-pound weight on top of the can and turn on the honey and go on with our work. It can be seen that, when the scale-beam goes up and rings the bell, there will be 58 lbs. of honey in the can. We then remove the weight and weigh the honey as usual.

W. Z. Hutchinson uses a form of uncapping-box (or barrel) that is about as cheap as any thing that has yet been devised. His description is as follows:

It is possible that the California plan of

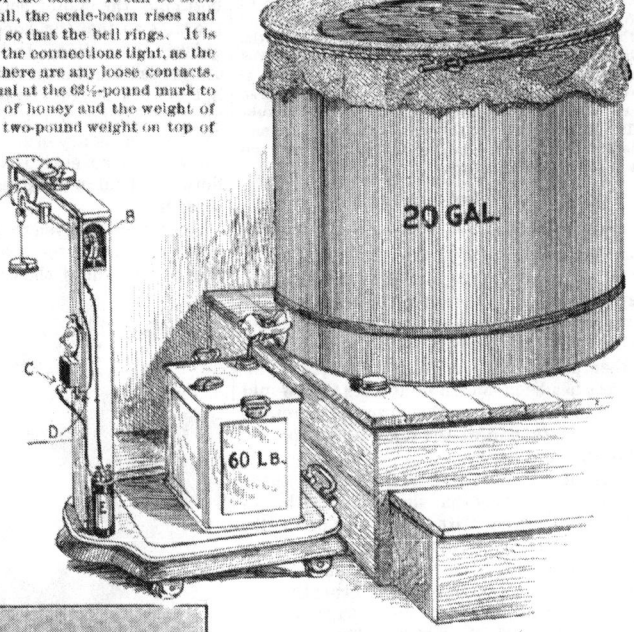

FIG. 2.—E. D. TOWNSEND'S ARRANGEMENT OF STRAINER AND SCALES, ILLUSTRATING THE HUTCHINSON AUTOMATIC ALARM.

melting the cappings as fast as shaved off may prove the most desirable plan ; but, so far as my experience goes, I have found nothing better than letting the cappings drop into a cracker-barrel set over a tub. Some grocers give the barrels away, if you are a customer ; some ask five cents apiece for them, and I never paid over ten cents. The cappings can be allowed to stand and drain for weeks and weeks—no hurry about the barrel ; simply pay ten cents for another one.

I bore three or four holes in the bottom of the barrel for the honey to run out. This may not be necessary, as such barrels are not water-tight ; but it is a wise precaution to be sure there is a place for the honey to get out. Then I nail a wooden cross-piece just inside of the top of the barrel ; but before nailing the cross-piece in place I drive through it a ten-penny nail ; and when putting the cross-piece in place I turn the point of the nail upward.

In uncapping a comb the end of the frame is rested upon this nail-point, which comes as near being a universal joint as any thing with which I am acquainted. The frame can be turned "every which way," and it will not slip about. The barrel is supported over the tub, or slightly below the top, by means of double hooks made of heavy wire. In the accompanying engraving one of these hooks is hung outside, upon one of the handles, to show its shape and make-up. Four hooks are used, placed equidistant around the edge of the tub, and the barrel lowered down upon them, the hooks catching just inside the "chime." There is still another plan of supporting the barrel that has the advantage of furni-hing handles with which to lift the barrel, and that is to nail two slats of wood to the sides of the barrel, about four inches from the lower end. The slats are nailed to opposite sides of the barrel, at right angles to the staves, and are long enough so that the ends rest upon the upper edge of the tub. The only objection to this plan is that the ends project out slightly beyond the edges of the tub, and are just a little in the way.

CAPPING-MELTERS.

The uncapping arrangements so far described have been merely receptacles for holding the cappings and allowing the honey to drain out, the cappings themselves being rendered into wax at some later time. During the last year or two in California and other parts of the country considerable interest has been shown in devices that would melt the cappings as they dropped from the honey-knife and at the same time separate the wax and honey.

One of the most practical forms of these capping-melters is that shown herewith. As will be seen it consists simply of a can within a can, the space between being filled with water kept hot by means of a gasoline or blue-flame kerosene-burner underneath. At the bottom of the inner can is a tube extending out through the water-jacket to a te on the outside, and around this exit, on one side of the inner can, semicircular screens are arranged to prevent the unmelted cappings from passing out of the gate—a coarse one to catch the heavier particles and a fine one to stop smaller particles not caught by the other. There is room for one or more uncapping-knives to hang down into the hot water between the two cans, as shown, so that if one desires to use the hot knife he may do so with no extra attachment for heating. When in actual use a cross-arm with a nail-point as shown or a large wooden box may be set over the top of the can with flaring bottom through which the cappings drop into the can beneath. This box provides a somewhat more convenient place to work and gives more room besides, and is to be preferred to the cross-arm.

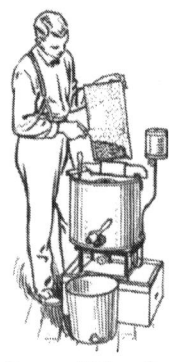

Manner of Using a Capping melter over a Small Gasoline-stove.

Experience has shown that the gate at the bottom of the melter should be left open all the time so that the honey may pass out as quickly as possible. In this way the danger of overheating it is greatly lessened; in fact, if the work is properly done, there need be no overheating of the honey, the temperature of the honey ordinarily running from the gate being such that the finger is not burned if held in the stream for ten or fifteen seconds.

Many have believed that such an apparatus in an extracting room would be objectionable on account of the heat, but it has been

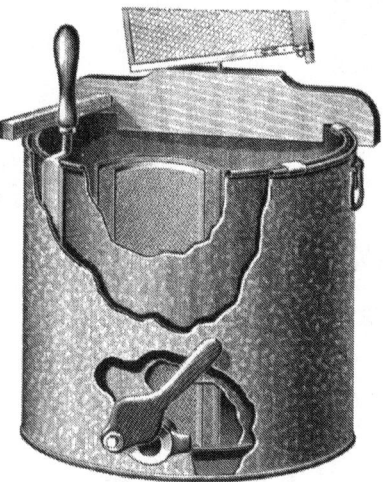

CAPPING-MELTER, A DEVICE FOR SEPARATING THE HONEY FROM THE CAPPINGS AS FAST AS THEY DROP FROM THE KNIFE.

shown that the heat is so largely used in warming the honey and melting the wax that but little radiates out into the room.

The stream of honey and wax from the melter may be run directly into a pail or can; and as soon as this one can is full it may be set aside and an empty one put in its place. In a few hours' time the layer of wax on top of the honey will have hardened enough so that it may be lifted off and the honey poured through the regular strainer together with that from the extractor. Or, the receiving can may be provided with a gate at the bottom so that the honey may be drawn off at intervals as fast as the can becomes full. In this way the layer of wax remains permanently in the can until the next day, when it is lifted out before beginning work.

The most convenient plan, however, for disposing of the hot honey and wax that run from the melter is to have the stream pass directly into an Aikin honey and wax separator, a diagram of which is shown herewith. The wax being lighter than honey floats on the top of it and may be drawn off when it reaches a certain level, if desired. The honey being heavier than the wax settles to the bottom and runs down under the division in the can and from thence up and out of the honey outlet as indicated.

We have found that this separator works well in every way except that the wax has a tendency to chill somewhat, and to overcome this difficulty we enclose the separator in a wooden box having a tight cover with a

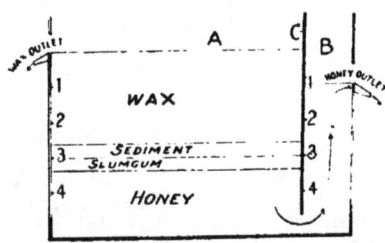

funnel through one end to allow the honey and wax to run in from the melter. The wooden box confines the heat enough so that there is no chilling of the wax, and by the next morning all the wax may be lifted off in one solid cake, which needs only scraping on the bottom to make it in good shape for market. The quality of the wax secured in this way is very good, being practically equal to that secured from a solar wax-extractor

The capping-melter shown in the engraving is 15 inches in diameter and 16 inches high, and the water-jacket holds about a pail of water. This is about as large a melter as can be operated over a single-burner gasoline-stove. If more capacity is needed it would be advisable to use an oval-shaped melter, perhaps of the size of a large washboiler, and a two-burner stove.

The value of a capping-melter is at once apparent, for it is impossible with ordinary methods to get *all* of the honey out of the cappings; and besides the honey saved, there is a great saving in time and labor, the wax being automatically rendered in good shape for market as fast as the honey is extracted. In an apiary of any size this saving of honey and labor will soon pay for an outfit of this kind. Almost any tinsmith can construct a melter as described, of heavy tin, or

the machines can be obtained direct from dealers.

Besides melting cappings, these double cans are excellent for liquefying candied honey on a small scale. On account of the water-jacket there is no danger of burning the honey, and that which liquefies runs out immediately so that it is not subjected to the heat longer than is really necessary.

UNCAPPING-KNIVES.

There are two forms of uncapping-knives used. One, the Novice, has a thin flexible blade, made of steel. The other, the Bing-

THE NOVICE HONEY-KNIFE.

ham, has a thick flat trowel-shaped unyielding blade having edges beveled on the under side. The first mentioned will do uncapping, and is very handy for scraping bottom-boards or removing burr-combs on the inside of the hive. Being thin and flexible it will fit curved surfaces; but for uncapping only it is in no sense to be compared with the Bingham.

An improved form of the Bingham knife is shown in the next illustration. The shank connecting the knife and the blade has circular projections on each side forming a part of the shank, and folded at right angles so as to afford a good solid grip to the thumb and fore finger. As the blade is on a different plane from the handle, one can get a better grip, and a closer one to the blade, if

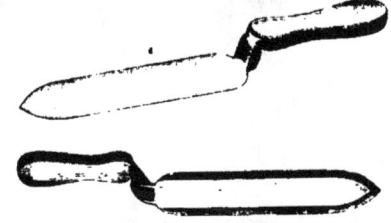

BINGHAM IMPROVED UNCAPPING-KNIFE.

he can grasp the shank itself. Experience also shows it is an advantage to have the handle flattened in such a way as to give a good solid hold.

HOW TO USE UNCAPPING-KNIVES.

The blade should have a keen edge and be frequently sharpened to get the best results. Grasp the knife as shown in the illustration following. Bring the fingers as close to the blade as possible, but not far enough to interfere with the cutting of the cappings. The comb should be placed upon some sort of a projection, a nail point supported over the uncapping-box or can. It then should be leaned forward when the knife by a sawing movement begins cutting at the bottom edge. When particles of wax and honey

cling to the blade so as to interfere with the work, it should be scraped on a wooden edge of some sort. See illustration on preceeding pages, showing Dadant's uncapping-can in use.

Some prefer to work with *hot* knives, and where the honey is very thick there is no question but that they will do faster and nicer work with less strain on the wrist. For this purpose it is customary to use two knives. A sort of bread-pan is made or provided, having a wooden cross-partition as

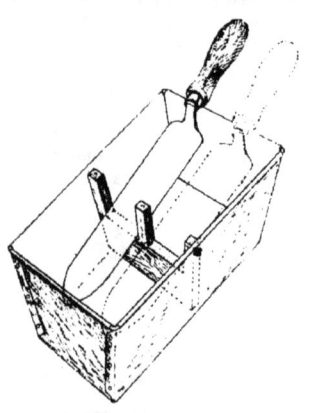

shown in the accompanying sketch. This is filled with water and placed on a single-wick kerosene-stove. The whole outfit should then be placed within easy reach of the uncapping-box, so that the operator can use one knife and then the other as fast as either cools.

There are some who claim that there is no advantage in using hot knives, but our experience leads us to believe that when honey is very thick, as it often is in some locali-

ties, it is economy, both in labor and time, to use them. Indeed, if the combs are new a hot blade is indispensable.

In Europe, and to some extent in this country, uncapping-knives have been kept continuously hot by the use of electricity or of steam. As the former will not be available to most bee-keepers located on their ranches, steam has the preference. A thin sheet of copper is soldered on the top side of the blade of an ordinary uncapping-knife in such a way as to make a chamber over the entire top surface of the knife. This chamber should have a small hole at the end for the exit of steam, and a tube at the other to which is attached a quarter-inch rubber hose, three or four feet in length. This is secured to the spout of an ordinary small tin tea-kettle by winding bicycle-tire tape around the tube and the spout until a tight connection is made. A common rag, after the kettle is filled with water, is placed over the opening of the kettle when the cover is crowded into place. This makes almost a tight steam joint, or tight enough for the purpose for which we wish to use it. The kettle is next placed upon a kerosene or gasoline stove; and when the water boils, the knife is ready for use.

In operation a small jet of steam will be forced out from the small orifice at the end of the blade. If a good circulation of steam is provided the knife can be kept continuously hot, and, while hot, it is to a great extent self-cleaning, as the honey and the cappings will melt off from it about as fast as they accumulate.

Some have tried these steam-heated knives, and say that there is no advantage in using them, as they would prefer to work with a cold keen-edged blade rather than a hot knife with all its attendant heat. The attachment of the tubing somewhat interferes, of course, with the free action of the knife; but for all these objections there are others who feel that a steam-heated uncapping-knife is a long way ahead of the cold one.

While it is customary with any knife to use the upward stroke, there are some few who prefer the *down* stroke. Experience will have to determine which is the better for the individual user.

SHALL THE COMBS BE SPACED WIDE OR
CLOSE FOR UNCAPPING?

The majority of extracted-honey producers space the combs 1¼ inches, or 1½ inches from center to center. Hoffman frames can be spaced as wide as this as well as any. The thick combs have more honey to the comb, and, consequently, fewer need be handled. If the uncapping-knife cuts deep there will be more wax, and wax always has a good market. The thick combs should always be cut down to normal thickness in uncapping before returning them to the bees.

After one day's uncapping, the cappings should drain dry. They should be removed before letting a fresh lot of cappings drop on to them. To get the cappings perfectly dry, some put them in a cheese-cloth bag to hang behind the stove over a pan for a few days. This will do for a small extracting business. Where the business is carried on more extensively, the cappings, after draining for one day, shou'd be put in a wax-press and squeezed dry while cold; or, better yet, they should be melted up as fast as they accumulate. See WAX-PRESS, under WAX.

Caution.—After an extracting, do not make the mistake of returning the combs to the hives as fast as extracted lest you start robbing, and make the work of extracting very disagreeable. Return the combs the last thing, or toward evening, and by morning all will be quiet.

SHALLOW OR FULL-DEPTH EXTRACTING-COMBS.

The question is often asked, whether one should use the shallow extracting-frames that are advertised in most of the dealers' catalogs. This depends a good deal on the honey-flow and general conditions. If the frame is as deep as a Quinby, the shallow frame for extracting purposes is almost a matter of necessity, as it is very inconvenient to handle these large combs, both in uncapping and extracting. But shallow combs have the special advantage that bees will enter a super containing them quicker than they will one of full depth. There is not so much room in the shallow supers for them to keep warm at one time; and they will, therefore, fill a set of shallow combs when they would hardly deign to enter an upper story containing full-depth ones. It is a common practice with a good many practical bee-keepers to have both shallow extracting-combs and full-depth combs. After the bees are well started to going above, the full-depth supers may be used. They may be also used on all strong colonies; but in the case of weaker ones only the shallow ones should be given. We can thus get extracted honey from weak stocks.

THE QUEEN-EXCLUDER FOR EXTRACTING.

As a general rule, in hives run for extracted honey, the queen will occupy one or more supers containing extracting-combs, unless she is confined to the brood-nest by means of a queen-excluding honey-board; see DRONES. When one is used, the extracting-combs will

contain nothing but honey and perhaps a little pollen, while the brood will be confined where it should be, in the lower story or brood-nest.

When running for *comb* honey it is usually not necessary to use the excluders.

Some objection has been raised by some to the effect that zinc boards hinder the passage of bees loaded with honey, and that, therefore, they have a tendency to restrict the amount stored in the supers. This is denied by the great majority of users. However, a few provide an entrance to the upper story or supers, placing the same at the bottom of the first super and above the excluder. This allows the bees in the super to escape directly into the air, without passing through the honey-board from the brood-nest below and out into the regular entrance. It is argued that this extra entrance to the super saves time and permits incoming bees to go directly into the supers and store the honey without any waste of time.

In order to catch the bees that are going into the lower entrance, Mr. B. Walker, of Clyde, Ill., has a long wide board connected with the upper entrance and slanting downward at an angle of 45 degrees in front of the lower hive entrance. The incoming bees strike this inclined plane, crawl upward and enter the supers just above the zinc, as shown on next page.

The entrance to these supers may be through one or more holes bored near the bottom edge of the super, or the wooden rail at the front end of the honey-board may be left out, so that the bees can pass into the super and above the perforated zinc.

HOW TO EXTRACT DURING A DEARTH OF HONEY WITHOUT THE ANNOYANCE OF ROBBERS.

As explained under FEEDING and FEEDERS, and under ROBBING, it is possible to create a little artificial honey-flow during a dearth of honey so that the bees, instead of pouncing upon the hives and on the combs that are being extracted, will be otherwise engaged, making extracting easy and pleasant without a robber in sight. One can put the whole apiary in good humor for such work by putting out two or three outdoor

WALKER'S PLAN OF USING AN UPPER ENTRANCE IN CONNECTION WITH AN ALIGHTING-BOARD.

feeders a hundred yards from the apiary, and suspending them in the air under trees as explained under FEEDING and FEEDERS. These feeders should contain a good grade of honey diluted with water to about the consistency of raw nectar. When the feeders are first set out it will take some time before the bees will discover them, even during the robbing season; but when they get to visiting them they begin carrying in the feed. If one or two feeders thus set out do not restore good humor on the part of the bees, it may be necessary to put out more until all the would-be robbers are kept ousy.

This outdoor feeding should be practiced a couple of days before the time set for the regular extracting, and then, of course, the feeders on the morning or the afternoon when the work is to be done should be well filled and kept so during the entire time that the hives are opened and combs exposed in extracting.

Once the bees get nicely started on the outdoor feeders there will be no trouble from robbers, provided that extracting-combs are not left lying around loose for any length of time. The extracting should be done inside of a screened building; and when such precautions are taken in connection with outdoor feeding there will not be a robber in sight, no matter if the fields are barren of nectar of any kind.

One may have to feed in outdoor feeders anywhere from 25 to 50 pounds of honey a day while such extracting is going on; but that amount of honey so given goes back into the hives; and while some of it may be lost, yet a good portion of it is saved to the bee-keeper. The saving in labor, annoyance, stings, and the general uproar in the apiary, will pay for the cost of the honey so fed many times over.

In this outdoor feeding to divert the robbers during extracting we would recommend feeding nothing but honey. Sugar syrup ought never be given during the extracting season, for it would very probably go into the combs and then be taken out again and mixed with the honey; but when one is attempting to do other work with bees, such as queen-rearing, it is perfectly legitimate to use sugar syrup instead. See FEEDING AND FEEDERS.

MANAGING A SERIES OF EXTRACTING-YARDS BY MAKING ONLY FOUR VISITS IN A YEAR.

The general treatment of this subject of extracting would hardly be complete were we to omit mention of the remarkable success attained by Mr. E. D. Townsend, of Remus, Mich., in handling a series of outyards by making only four trips a year to each yard. As he makes no secrets of his methods, it may be well to describe them.

He believes primarily in strong colonies, and a brood-nest not smaller than ten Langstroth frames. In the fall of the year he makes one trip to feed up and pack in winter cases. Colonies a little short are given enough to furnish them from 25 to 30 lbs. of stores all told. The bees are then left until the first of June following. As his fall visits are made some time in October, there is a period of seven months when no one goes near them.

He says he has practiced fussing with bees in the spring to equalize stores, and reduced the brood-nest to a size that the bees can readily occupy; but colonies so treated have averaged no better than those that had no care whatever. When he next visits them (in June) he gives each of the strong colonies two ten-frame supers of empty extracting-combs; but instead of putting ten combs in a super he puts in eight, spacing them apart equally to fill out the room. The bees are not seen again until he makes a third trip (in July). This is for the purpose of extracting all honey, as he does not wish his basswood mixed with clover. Except for this he would let them go entirely until the end of the season for the final extracting, managing the outyards with only three trips in a year. As it is, he separates his clover from his basswood by making a fourth trip. On his third visit the combs are extracted of all clover, and put back on the hives again. Last of all, he makes one more (a fourth) trip, removes all the filled combs, and extracts them of the basswood. The bees are then left until he puts them away for winter in the fall, which will be the first trip of the next year.

His secret of success lies in the fact that he is a skillful bee-keeper and has a large number of drawn combs — enough to give every strong colony two extra supers. The combs being spaced wide apart, eight frames to fill the ten-frame capacity, they are drawn out thick and capped over. As the bees have an abundance of room at all times, there is little or no swarming; and such swarming as there is does not amount to much. In fact, Mr. Townsend argues it does not pay to keep a man at the yard to look after that, for he can buy more bees, if he needs them, at $3.00 a colony, to make up for any losses; and this will be far less cost to him than to keep a man looking after the swarms.

In uncapping he runs the knife deep, planing the combs down to a normal thickness. This gives him a surplus of wax that always finds a good market, and an extra amount of honey in the cappings; but as this drains off he gets all the honey, and finally melts all the cappings up into wax.

He thinks bees in the height of the honey-flow are bound to build comb; and if no provision is made they will stick in burr and brace combs; when, if the frames are spaced wide, their natural instincts for comb-build ng can be satisfied, and the extra depth of comb can be converted into wax, which is as good as cash.

Of course, when he makes his visits to the yards he takes helpers along. Cheap help, with a good manager, can do as much or more work than expensive men without the boss along.

Another fact worth recording is that Mr. Townsend gets two cents above the market for his honey. The fact that it is left on the hives till after the season, where it *can ripen thoroughly*, gives it a richness and quality that the consumers demand and want more of when they have tasted the first lot.

EXHIBITS OF HONEY — *How they may be used in the development of the bee and honey industry.*—Of late, very much indeed has been accomplished by the exhibits of bees, honey, and apiarian implements at State and county fairs. Several of the larger societies have had very pretty buildings erected on the fairgrounds for these displays, and often the bee-keepers who meet at such places have very interesting conventions.

Such exhibits have a decidedly educational influence on the public. They show *how* honey is produced; and not only that, but that it can be produced by the ton and carload. On account of newspaper yarns, there seems to be a general impression among people that comb honey is manufactured, and that the extracted article is adulterated with glucose. It is absolutely impossible to manufacture comb, fill it with honey, and cap it over with appropriate machinery—just as impossible as it is to manufacture eggs. We have had for several years a standing offer of $1000 to any one who would show where comb honey was manufactured, or even procure a *single manufactured sample* which could not be told from the genuine. Although this offer has been published broadcast in the daily papers, no one takes it up. We have also had the conditions of this offer printed on a neat little card, the same distributed by bee-keepers at fairs and other honey-exhibits, so that, if such a thing were possible, there would be a bonanza for somebody. As to extracted honey, there was a time when it was adulterated somewhat, but owing to the action of State and national laws there is very little of it now. See HONEY ADULTERATION.

A SUGGESTION FOR A BEESWAX EXHIBIT AT STATE FAIRS.

THE APIARIAN EXHIBIT AT THE COLUMBUS STATE FAIR IN SEPTEMBER, 1906.

Bee-keepers, besides educating the general public as to the *genuineness* of their product, can create a larger demand for honey. As a usual thing, exhibitors are allowed to sell their honey, distribute circulars, and do a great deal of profitable advertising. This not only helps the individual, but helps the pursuit in general.

The preceding engravings will give an idea of how a model exhibit should be arranged.

There should be shelving arranged in the form of pyramids, octagons, semicircles, etc. The honey should be put up in tin and glass, in large and small packages, and the whole should be neatly " set off " with appropriate labels. As a general thing, glass packages should have a very small label, so that as much of the liquid honey as possible will show. Tin receptacles should have labels to go clear around the can. Comb honey should be put up in cartons and shipping-cases ; and yellow cakes of wax should be shown in a variety of shapes.

In one of the illustrations will be seen a large pyramid of beeswax, supporting on its several shelves packages of honey, the whole surmounted by the bust of a goddess. Make a series of square shallow boxes of such varied sizes that, when piled one on top of another, they form a perfect pyramid. These are to be completely covered with sheet wax having the edges that come in contact nicely cemented together with a hot iron. The next thing to make is the goddess of liberty, or the bust of a prominent man. These in plaster can usually be purchased at any of the stores for a small sum of money, and, after being dipped in hot wax, give a very fine wax figure.

A correspondent has suggested dipping a teddy bear in melted wax. It might muss up his fur a little, but he ought to look like a bear; and as this animal is known to be a connoisseur of good honey, his presence surmounting the pyramid would be very appropriate.

The bust of a woman on top of the pyramid, shown in the illustration, was made of plaster, and came with a box of soap. It struck the exhibitor that this would make a fine wax bust; and, as you will note, it shows up well.

Besides the exhibit of honey in various styles of packages, there should be a moderate collection of bee - supplies, so that, when the eager public come along with their string of questions, they can be shown step by step the process of producing honey,

7

and its final putting-up for market. A good many questions will be asked in regard to the extractor. It will be called a churn, a washing-machine, and every thing else except what it really is. And last, but not least important, there should be one or more observatory hives to show folks how bees behave when at home. A good many will want to see the " king-bee." Tell them it is not a *king* but the *queen* that reigns.

Very much can be done by having a glass hive and live bees, with an entrance communicating outdoors through the sides of the building where the exhibit is made. What is equally good, or perhaps better, is a one-frame nucleus having glass sides, making, as we call it, an observatory hive. This should contain one frame of nice healthy brood, regular and perfect comb, finely marked bees, and a bright-yellow queen. Hundreds of people will stop and examine, and ask a variety of questions about the bees and the queen. By this means one can convey to the consumer some knowledge of the habits of bees, and how honey is produced, thus indirectly creating a demand.

It should be stated in this connection that bees in an observatory hive will stand confinement for two or three days or even a week. Ordinarily at fairs and other places, where the show lasts only two or three days, the confined bees will do very well. But at

expositions, where they are shown week after week, it is absolutely necessary to give them a flight every two or three days. Some arrangement should be made with the management by which these glass hives may be placed next to the wall of the building, the entrance communicating with a hole through the building.

The usual plan is to have two or three observatory hives, and keep one or two on exhibition all the time while the other is being

DEMONSTRATION WORK AT THE OHIO STATE FAIR, COLUMBUS.

THE A. I. ROOT COMPANY'S DEMONSTRATING-CAGE AT THE MEDINA COUNTY FAIR.

CHARLES MONDENG AND HIS SON NORMAN DEMON-
STRATING ADEL BEES AT THE MINNE-
SOTA STATE FAIR.

Mr. Mondeng and his son were awarded the first prize for bee
demonstration; first prize on golden Italian bees; first
prize on leather-colored Italian bees.

LIVE - BEE - DEMONSTRATION WORK TO ADVERTISE HONEY AT THE FAIRS.

In connection with an exhibit
inside of the building, there should
be a placard directing the visitor
to a bee-show outside, as near the
building as possible. This should
be a demonstration of the method
of handling live bees inside a wire
cage, the operator taking them up
by handfuls and forming artificial
swarms. Where the two exhibits,
one of honey and bee-supplies, and
the bee-show itself, can be located
outdoors, it will be better. The
former should then be in a temporary booth or tent, since it would
not do to have the exhibits of wax
and comb honey exposed to the
direct action of the sun. The
bee-demonstrating cage should be
located close by, within ten or
twenty feet, and, as we have explained, it consists of a wire-cloth
structure large enough to take in
man, a hive of bees, and leave
room enough to practice ordinary
bee - manipulation. This cage
should be elevated on a stand four
or five feet above the ground—the
higher the better, because there
will be a great jam of people
around to see the man inside pick
up live bees by the handful.

freshened up by a
flight outdoors. Af-
ter these latter have
had two or three
days in which to
cleanse themselves
the entrance should
be closed at night,
when the hive can
be put back on its
stand, and another
observatory hive
take its place. So
in alternation each
one of the two or
three lots of bees
can be freshened
up.

It goes without
saying, that, if
there is no honey in
the fields, the bees
should be fed occa-
sionally.

Norman Mondeng is only eleven years old, yet he handles bees without fear.
His entire clothing was a bathing suit.

THE A. I. ROOT COMPANY'S EXHIBIT AT THE OHIO STATE FAIR.

Announcement should be made from outside of the cage that, during certain hours, an operator, bareheaded and barearmed, will perform some wonderful stunts in handling bees. When the performance begins, the people will surge around the stands, and that is just what is desired in order to sell honey at the other stand a few feet away.

The operator begins his performance by stepping inside the cage of live bees, and shutting the door behind him. He then tells the crowd that he is going to handle live bees, every one of which is armed with a sting; and if any one doubts it to come forward and he will furnish the "proof." He then proceeds to take off his coat and vest and roll up his sleeves, take off his collar, and tuck down his shirt-band. It will then be necessary for him to put on bicycle pants-guards, or slip his trousers into his stockings. The crowd will quickly appreciate this part of the performance, because the operator tells them the bees will sting if they get inside of his clothing. With a lighted smoker he opens up the hive. After pulling out the frames he shows the bees and queen on the comb; then he calls out for everybody to wait and see the next stunt, for he is going to make a swarm. With a large dishpan, which he has previously provided, he shakes two-thirds of the bees off the combs into this pan. Then he takes it up and turns to the crowd, saying, "The bees are not real mad yet, so I'll begin to shake them up to make them so." The

people wonder what he is going to do, seeing him barearmed and bareheaded. He keeps on shaking until he has the bees all in one big ball, and to the uninitiated it *looks* as if they would sting him to death. But, no! the continual shaking is the *very thing* that makes them gentle instead of cross. He now runs his hand under the ball of bees, pushing it under gently, being careful not to pinch any. The movement must be very deliberate—so slow indeed that the hand scarcely seems to move. He picks up a handful and holds them up for the crowd to look at. If he has good nerves he can shake the handful on top of his head, and in the mean time pick up another handful.

At the next performance there will be big crowds around to see the work. While the man is doing his stunts with the bees he tells what honey is, saying that it is a wholesome sweet, and that there is no such thing as manufactured comb honey, and that he will pay $100 for a single sample of it; then he draws attention to the fact that he has some good honey at the stand opposite or in the building yonder. The crowd will then go round to the stand and buy the honey.

The preceeding illustrations show the exhibits of bees and honey, the exhibit of the live bee cage, and the crowd that assembled around it, both at the Ohio State Fair, held at Columbus, and the Minnesota State Fair.

After the exhibitor gets his questioner interested, he can hand out one of his adver-

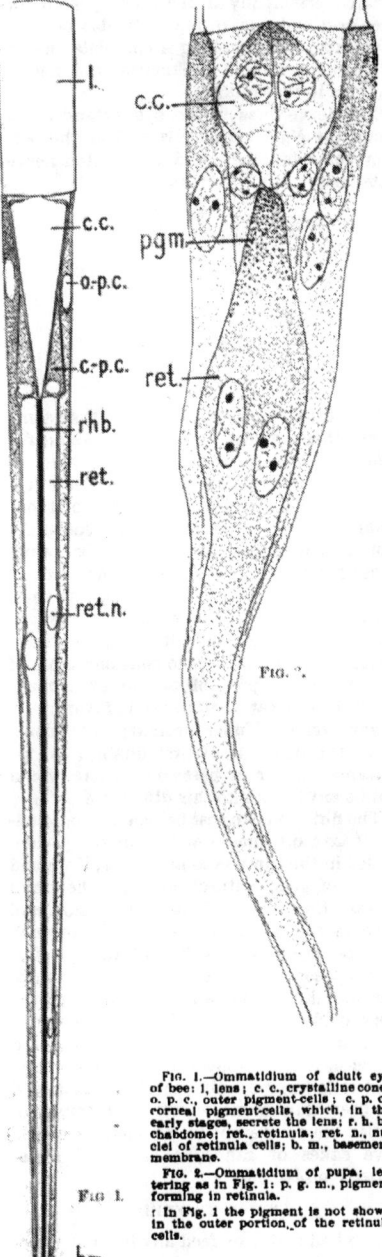

l.

c.c.

c.c.

pgm.

o.-p.c.

c.-p.c.

ret.

rhb.

ret.

ret.n.

FIG. 2.

FIG. 1.

bm.

FIG. 1.—Ommatidium of adult eye of bee: l, lens; c. c., crystalline cone; o. p. c., outer pigment-cells; c. p. c., corneal pigment-cells, which, in the early stages, secrete the lens; r. h. b., rhabdome; ret., retinula; ret. n., nuclei of retinula cells; b. m., basement membrane.

FIG. 2.—Ommatidium of pupa; lettering as in Fig. 1: p. g. m., pigment forming in retinula.

† In Fig. 1 the pigment is not shown in the outer portion of the retinula cells.

tising cards, and at the same time give him a little sample of honey to taste. This can be done very readily by handing out some strips of strong manila paper, which are to be dipped in the honey and then transferred to the mouth.

EYE, COMPOUND. An examination of the large compound eyes of a bee will show that the outside is made up of hexagonal areas, thousands in number. Each of these hexagons is the outside of one of the elements of which the compound eye is composed; and, since they are all constructed alike, a description of one will serve for all. Each of these elements is called an ommatidium. If, then, we take a section through one of the compound eyes parallel with the top of the head of the bee we shall get some of them cut lengthwise, thereby showing best the structure, although it is also necessary to cut other sections at right angles to this plane in order to get the shape of some of the parts. The figures which accompany this show the ommatidium cut lengthwise. Another figure shows an ommatidium from the *pupa* stage.

The outside portion, already mentioned, is the lens layer *l*, and is composed of chitin, as is all the rest of the outside covering of the bee. The section shows this cut open, so that only two sides of the hexagon are shown.

The next lower structure is the crystalline cone *c, c,* which is composed of four cells, of which only two show in the long section. In the pupa stage the boundaries are much clearer, and the nuclei larger than they are in the adult eye. This cone is clear, and, like the lens above it, gathers in the light rays so that they can act on the nerves below just as the lens in the human eye gathers together rays of light so they can affect the nerves behind it.

Directly in line with the cone is a long rodlike structure which runs clear to the bottom of the ommatidium, called the "rhabdome," *rhb.* This probably contains the end of the nerves, which are sensitive to light.

Around the rhabdome are eight retina cells *ret,* which have poured out a secretion while in the pupa state to form the rhabdome.

Around the cone and retina cells there are pigment cells *o. p. c.* and *c. p. c.,* that keep the light from passing from one ommatidium to the other, and thus making a confused image, just as the inside of a camera is painted black to avoid reflections. In the human eye we also find pigment, which is also located just behind the nerve-endings, and answers the same purpose. There are two kinds of these pigment-cells. The ones at the base of the cone, *o. p. c.*, are two in number, and do not extend below the base of the cone. The other pigment-cells, *c. p. c.*, extend from the lens to the base of the ommatidium, and are generally twelve in number. The pigment in these cells is located principally at the outer portion of the eye; and the retina cells also contain a pigment, thus making a complete sheath of pigment around the nerve and nerve-endings in the middle.

The nerve lines in the eye extend down along the eight retinacells, and at the bottom come together, and the united nerve extends toward the brain.

F

FEEDING AND FEEDERS. Feeding is practiced for one of two purposes—to stimulate brood-rearing at times of the year when no honey is coming in from natural sources, or to supply with food colonies that are short at the approach of winter. Whenever possible, feeding should be avoided; for at best it is a messy job, expensive, and, in the case of the beginner, liable to cause robbing. In a good locality it may be possible to avoid feeding altogether. Especially would this be true in those places where there is plenty of buckwheat or fall flowers. To buy sugar by the barrel every fall is very expensive, and the bee-keeper should lay his plans to avoid it as far as possible. In many cases fall feeding is made necessary by extracting too close, in some cases even from the brood-nest. This is bad practice and decidedly poor economy. But there are times when it is absolutely necessary to give the bees food either to keep up and stimulate brood-rearing or to prevent actual starvation.

When the honey already in the hives at autumn is of good quality and nicely sealed, it would be penny wise and pound foolish to extract it, put it on the market, buy sugar, make syrup, and feed it to the bees. There would be very little gained by it, even if the honey sold at a higher price, and the sugar syrup were cheaper. Where the natural stores are dark, of poor quality, or bad honey-dew, it might be advisable to extract and put in their place the syrup. Yet of late years it has been our practice to let the bees have every thing of their own gathering, provided it is nicely ripened and sealed in the comb, no matter what the source; and it is very seldom we lose bees in outdoor wintering by reason of poor food.

Of course, sugar syrup is better than some honey that the bees gather; and, pound for pound, it will go further in the hive as food. Some experiments were made a few years ago which went to show that of those colonies fed on honey, the average consumption in winter was from 14 to 18 lbs., while those fed on sugar syrup consumed from 1 to 7 lbs. The inference drawn was that, while the pound of honey had less strength than the pound of sugar, it was more stimulating, causing the bees to consume more of it. But in all probability this experiment showed too great a difference in favor of the sugar syrup. Under ordinary conditions, when the honey is of first quality, as, for instance, clover or basswood, there would not be any thing like this difference.

The difference in cost between a first quality of extracted honey and sugar syrup when sealed in the comb is so little that, if we had combs of good natural stores, rather than extract them we would set them aside, and then in the fall give these combs to such colonies as had an insufficient supply. But in any case we would not use all such combs, because, during midwinter, it is sometimes very handy to have them ready, as they can be placed right down in the center of a brood-nest of a colony, for the simple reason that it is impracticable to give liquid food to bees during midwinter. If combs of sealed stores are not to be had, we would give cakes of candy, as described under CANDY elsewhere.

WHAT TO FEED.

It is bad policy to feed any form of sweet that is cheaper than any of the very best granulated-sugar syrups. There are certain grades of molasses and sorghum that may be used;

but, as explained, they have a tendency to be unduly stimulative—that is, make the bees restless during winter. It seems to be generally agreed that, dollar for dollar, granulated sugar, when converted into first-class syrup, is as cheap a food for the bees as can be had; and not only cheap, but comparatively safe. Unbleached West India crystallized cane sugar of a pale straw color is said to be excellent—but we do not find it as good, nor any cheaper.

HOW TO MAKE THE SYRUP.

Something will depend on whether the bees are to be fed for the purpose of inducing brood-rearing or to give a supply for winter. For stimulating, a syrup made of one part of sugar to one of water by bulk is about right. If the water is hot the sugar will dissolve more readily. For a winter food given early in the fall the proportion should be about two parts of sugar to one of water. For late feeding, just before cold weather comes on, the ratio should be about two and a half to one. When made as thick as this the syrup is liable to go back to sugar to some extent, and sometimes it is necessary to put in about a teaspoonful of tartaric acid to every 20 lbs. of sugar. Others find it better to use honey. The proportion then of honey will be about one-third by bulk of the amount of water used. In our own practice we have never found it necessary to use either honey or acid.

A syrup made by mixing sugar and water in equal parts does not necessarily require heat. The water may be poured into a receptacle cold, and sugar stirred in until the volume of the sugar equals that of the water. The stirring will have to be continued until the sugar is dissolved. If there is any quantity to be mixed in that way, an ordinary honey-extractor serves as a very excellent agitator. The machine is filled nearly half full of water, when the sugar is stirred in little by little while the reel is being turned. It will have to be revolved until the sugar is all dissolved. After a vigorous turning of the crank, even after the sugar is thoroughly mixed, there will be a number of small air-bubbles. These will all disappear if the syrup is allowed to stand for a while. When the proportion of the sugar is two to one or two and a half to one, it is advisable to use hot or boiling water.

Syrup can be mixed in a common wash-boiler where heat is employed. In that case the boiler is put on the stove and filled with the requisite quantity of water. After it has come to a boil, the sugar is slowly stirred in, a little at a time. While on the stove the mixture *must be kept thoroughly stirred* to prevent the undissolved sugar from settling on the bottom and burning. Care should be taken about that, because burnt sugar or syrup is liable to be fatal to the bees.

In many cases syrup has to be prepared at the outyard. Or perhaps the good wife objects to having her stove messed up. While an oil or gasoline stove will heat the water, either one is very slow. The Hutchinson brothers use and recommend a good-sized common galvanized wash-tub, such as can be obtained at any hardware store at a comparatively low price. This is placed on four or five stones of suitable size outdoors when the right proportion of water is poured into the tub. A fire is then built under, and when the water comes to a boil the granulated sugar is slowly stirred in. After it is all dissolved, the fire should be scraped out from under the tub to prevent overheating or burning. This work should be done on a cool or rainy day when the bees are not flying; otherwise one would have a mess of robbing on his hands.

FEEDING TO STIMULATE BROOD-REARING.

During spring or summer we *may* use a cheaper grade of sugar, if we happen to have it on hand, or cheap off grades of honey that would ordinarily be unsalable. If honey,[*] we would thin it down slightly with warm water; but if the sweet has to be *purchased*, then, as we have already said, we would recommend only granulated sugar, for the reason that it is just as cheap as any other sweet, and the very best. Nuclei, as a rule, require stimulative feeding before or after the honey-flow, in order to make them do their very best, for a queen will seldom lay much after the honey season unless the bees are fed a certain amount daily. Where colonies lack sufficient strength for the harvest it is customary to practice stimulative feeding.

FEEDERS.

There have been hundreds of feeders invented and put on the market. Some of them are very complicated, and the more so the less useful. If one desires to keep down his investment he may use common tin pans. These can be placed in the upper story of the hive, and filled with syrup. On top of the syrup should be laid carefully a strip of cheese-cloth that has been dampened in

---

[*] If the honey is purchased it should be boiled for at least 20 minutes, to kill any possible germs of disease.

water. The bees will crawl up on the cloth, and appropriate the syrup, without danger of drowning. One objection to pans is that it litters them up; and after the feed is all taken, the cloth is likely to be stuck

SIMPLICITY BEE-FEEDER.

down by the dried crystals. Boiling water will, however, very soon clean them.

A feeder that has been used very largely is the Simplicity trough feeder. It is an excellent feeder, cheap in price, and occupies very little room on top of the brood-frames.

Another feeder that has been used very largely consists of a common wooden tray, such as one gets at the grocery when he buys butter. A hundred of these can be nested together so as to take up but very little room, and the price is insignificant. It is not necessary to use cheese-cloth with the butter-tray. Set them on the top of the frames, and fill them with syrup.

Another feeder is the pepper box. It is a can, of pint or quart size, with a perforated

PEPPER-BOX FEEDER.

top. This is filled with syrup, inverted, and set right over the brood-frames in the upper story.

Still another feeder is the Boardman. This makes use of a Mason jar—something that is a common commodity in every household. The jars are filled with syrup; and with the

THE BOARDMAN ENTRANCE FEEDER.

special cap that is furnished by the manufacturers of bee-keepers' supplies, one can

feed a large number of colonies with a supply of these jars at once.

The cans themselves when inverted are set down through a hole in a sort of box. The two side pieces of this box are made in such a way as to leave projections which extend clear into the entrance, thus barring robbers from dodging into the box. The top of the box has a hole just large enough to let the Mason jar be supported ⅛ inch from the inside of the bottom. When one has a supply of Mason jars, all he requires from his manufacturer will be the box and a special cap that permits the bees to get the syrup in small quantities at a time. As this is an entrance feeder it is always in sight, and one can see at a glance whether the jars are empty or not.

A wheelbarrowful of filled cans with the special caps may be run through the apiary; and whenever a can is discovered that is empty, it is taken out of its box and replaced by another jar filled with syrup. The special feature of this feeder is that one can see by a glance at a row of hives those colonies that have emptied their cans, and a fresh supply given without disturbing the bees or opening the hives. But there is one objection—it has a tendency to incite robbing; yet where one is careful, and sees that the caps to the cans are properly adjusted, there will be little or no trouble.

ALEXANDER FEEDER.

The Alexander is another outdoor feeder that is very popular with many bee-keepers. It is nothing more nor less than a trough feeder on the principle of the Simplicity, previously described. secured under the back end of the hive when the bottom-board

is shoved forward as shown. To feed, it is only necessary to lift up the block with one hand and pour in the syrup. So convenient is it that a hundred colonies can be fed up in a few minutes. No robbers can molest, for the food is clear back away from the entrance. For stimulative purposes this is one of the best feeders sold. The only objection is that it is sometimes difficult, owing to the unevenness of the ground, to adjust the feeder to the back end of the hive in such a way that it will fit up tight to the hive, shutting out all robbers.

DOOLITTLE DIVISION-BOARD FEEDER.

The illustration given below shows that it is nothing more nor less than a large brood-frame paneled on each side. Down through the center runs a partition reaching almost to the bottom. This feeder, from the very nature of its construction, can be set down in the brood-nest like an ordinary division-board, or brood-frame, for that matter; and as it is confined wholly within the brood-nest, not even requiring an upper story or super, it is the most convenient and

most satisfactory of any thing we ever used —fully as handy as the Boardman. All that is necessary is to slide the cover about an inch; then with a coffee-pot pour in the feed. Close the hive up and treat the next one the same way. For stimulating *weak* colonies or nuclei for the purpose of queen-rearing, our people unhesitatingly pronounce it by all odds the best feeder in the whole list, and if a colony does not require more than five or six pounds it is the best winter feeder.

There is still another feeder, and a very excellent one, and that is the Miller. We

THE MILLER FEEDER

use it almost exclusively for feeding up colonies for winter. This has a large capacity, and one can feed from 10 to 25 pounds at one time. When for any reason feeding has

been deferred till late, this feeder is the one to use. The small feeders before described are adapted to stimulative purposes, and will hold only a couple of quarts at most; but we use only the Miller feeder when we may desire to feed a large amount of syrup at once.

The first cut shows the feeder adapted to an eight-frame Langstroth hive, and its capacity is 25 lbs. of syrup. The accompanying cross-section shows that there are two feed-reservoirs. On the principle that liquids always seek their level, the syrup passes under the raised partition B; and the bees, to get access to the syrup, start from the arrow E, and take the feed from the inner chambers under the cover-board A. With most feeders of the kind, bees are obliged to pass through the two ends or the outside, and sometimes, in cool weather, refusing to leave the center of the brood-nest,

they fail to take the syrup. The great feature of the Miller feeder is that the passage-way to the feed is located directly *over the center* of the brood-nest, and the warmth of the cluster rising is confined in the passage-ways and chambers under A. This feature, coupled with the fact that it is made of wood, renders it possible to feed bees during quite cold freezing weather.

FALL FEEDING: FULL DETAILS ON HOW TO DO THE WORK RAPIDLY AND EASILY.

If colonies are to be wintered on sugar syrup mainly, the general practice is to feed some time in September, and, as a rule, this is, perhaps, the best time to feed. Still, in many localities in central United States, there is warm weather in October sufficient to start brood-rearing, and much of the stores fed in September may be consumed so that what is left is not sufficient to last until the new honey-flow. For this reason it is often unsafe to feed in September and give no further attention to the bees. There are other cases when, for one reason or another, feeding may be delayed until cold weather begins; for instance, if one is running a number of outyards it is impossible, without hiring a large force of men, to feed all these yards at once, and by the time the last yard is reached it may be rather late.

But before we begin the actual work of feeding we make a preliminary canvass of the whole apiary. This we do by "hefting" each hive; that is, we lift up either the front or back of the hive. A little practice will enable one to determine approximately the amount of stores in each hive, provided there is not too large a force of bees. In that event, we must allow for a corresponding increase. As we go over each hive we mark on the cover with a piece of chalk the number of pounds that will be required. If the colony is a strong one we allow for a total of 25 lbs. if it is to be wintered out-doors; for indoors, about two-thirds that. We aim to have each colony strong enough so that it will require an average of about 20 lbs. for each outdoor wintering. After all the hives are marked up we proceed to the actual work of feeding.

For this late fall feeding we know of no better feeder than the Miller. This will hold at least 25 lbs. of feed at a time, and it can be quickly put on and taken off without much disturbance to the brood-nest. On the other hand, if the colonies are not quite as strong as they should be, so that some contraction is necessary in the winter any way, it is probably just as well, and perhaps even better, to use the Doolittle division-board feeder holding about 6 lbs. of thick feed at a time. During the season, any combs which are found that are too old, or which, for some reason or other, are not perfect, whether due to drone-cells or irregularities, can be gradually pushed to the outside of the brood-frames; then in the fall, when it is time to put in the feeder, provided the division-board feeders are used, these defective combs can be very easily gotten rid of with a very small amount of labor, and with no loss of brood. Furthermore, if the colonies need feeding, these outside combs will not contain much honey. On a cool day an out-yard can be looked over very quickly, and the old combs that are on the outside of the brood-nest removed with very little trouble. If a follower is used, the removal of one comb and the follower makes room for the feeder; but if the combs completely fill the hives, two combs must be removed. It is rather bad practice, if sealed covers are used, to break the propolis sealing around the covers of the hives after cold weather has set in; but, as we said before, there are many instances where the feeding must be done late; and there is this advantage—that, in cold weather the feeders may be put in in a very short time, and with but little shaking of bees from the combs that are removed.

The best time of day for putting feed into the feeder is toward the close of the after-noon. It is not advisable to do the work in the morning or early in the day, for the reason that the bees are always excited, and robbing might be started, especially if it were warm enough for the bees to fly. Right here is a point in favor of the chilly-weather feeding, for there is no such danger of robbing, of course, when the bees can not fly on account of the cool temperature. With the cans of feed distributed at regular intervals throughout the yard we have found that 100 colonies may be fed in an hour's time providing the work is rapidly done. Everything must be right, so that no stops need be made for anything.

We fix the feed at home and carry it to the yards in the regular five-gallon honey-cans, as these are about the largest-sized cans that can be handled conveniently by one person. If two were doing the feeding a larger can might be used.

While the syrup is still hot we load it into the wagon, six or eight cans at a time, and carry it rapidly to the yard. When we reach the edge of the apiary, we take the cans, one at a time, and locate them throughout the yard where the markings on the hives show that we shall need them. If the cans have good strong handles we are able to carry two at a time, one in each hand; but the difficulty is that the handles are liable to tear loose from the can at one end and drag through the hand, cutting the fingers and allowing the heavy can to fall on the feet. For this reason we prefer to carry one can at a time in the arms. If a small rope sling were used, two cans could be carried without danger.

When we are ready to commence feeding we fill a large sprinkling-can, with the rose removed, and then proceed at once to pour the syrup into the division-board feeders in every hive. Each feeder, as mentioned before, will hold about six pounds of thick syrup. By the time we have emptied one of the five-gallon cans we have reached a point in the yard where a new full one is waiting for us and we can proceed without stopping to run for more cans. On the covers of the hives are marked the number of pounds of syrup which each hive is to receive. It is likely that not all of the hives will need feeding a second time, so the second day the work can be done even more quickly than the first time. When it is not too cool the bees will have taken the syrup in one feeder in 24 hours' time; but if the weather is very cold they will require 48 hours; but this time can be materially reduced if the syrup is given hot. We would always give it hot if it is cold enough so that the cluster is contracted. After all the hives have been fed up we go over the hives again, this time making a careful examination of the brood-nest. If more syrup still is required we mark the hive again and later on feed it and all others that may be short.

FEEDING IN FREEZING WEATHER.

Though colonies have been wintered well when fed after cold or freezing weather, we think much the safer plan is to have it all done during fall not later than October, that they may have the syrup ripened and entirely sealed. If the weather is not too cold you can feed with the Miller feeder as previously intimated. If you have been so careless as to have bees that are in need of stores, at the beginning of winter, we would advise frames of sealed honey if you can get them; and if you can not, use candy.

If the candy is covered up with warm chaff cushions or something equivalent, it may be fed at any time, although it does not seem to be as satisfactory under all circumstances as stores sealed up in their combs.

When feeding in cool or cold weather, you are very apt to uncover the cluster, or leave openings that will permit the warmth of the cluster to pass off. We have several times had colonies die in the spring after commencing feeding, and we imagined it was from this cause alone. When they first commence raising brood in the spring, they need to be packed up closely and snugly. Making a hole in the quilt or cushions above the cluster, and placing the feeder over this so as to close it completely, does very well, but is not, after all, as safe as giving the feed from below. For feeding in early spring, especially where the colony is weak, we would prefer candy or well-filled combs of sealed stores.

FEEDING IN THE SPRING, OR FEEDING ENOUGH IN THE FALL TO LAST TILL THE NEXT HONEY-FLOW.

Some years ago it was the general practice to feed in the spring to stimulate brood-rearing, such feeding taking place as soon as settled warm weather came on. The purpose of this was to get a large force of young bees for the harvest when it came; but in later years the tendency on the part of our best bee-keepers has been toward feeding copiously in the fall enough to last not only all winter but during the spring and until the honey-flow. Experience seems to show that spring feeding very often does more harm than good by over-stimulation. Brood is expanded beyond the capacity of the bees to hover and keep warm. Robbing is often induced. Beginners especially are apt to overdo it; and even a veteran will sometimes get his colonies so strong before an extra supply of nectar comes in, that swarming will be brought on prematurely.

This question of feeding heavily in the fall to last until the next honey-flow the following year, or feeding moderately in the fall and stimulating the following spring, depends somewhat on the locality, and very largely on the man himself. Many bee-keepers of experience, especially in some localities, can doubtless practice spring feeding to advantage; but as a rule beginners will do better to give all their colonies enough in the fall so that they will have about 25 lbs. of sealed stores about the time cold weather begins to come on. In most of the northern States this will be about the first or middle of November. In our more northern States and in Canada the stores should be sealed about the first of October.

SPRING FEEDING A LA BOARDMAN.

After what we have just said on the advantage of fall feeding it may at first seem a little contradictory even to suggest spring feeding, but Mr. H. R. Boardman, of Collins, Ohio, does it for a different purpose. In brief his plan is this : He feeds as soon as it becomes settled warm weather, whether the bees need stores or not. The syrup is given them slowly to stimulate brood-rearing. This feeding is continued clear on to the honey-flow, when, of course, it is discontinued. The result is that the hives are overflowing with bees and brood, and all available space in the brood-nest is filled clear full with sealed sugar stores. Just as soon as the honey-flow commences, supers are given ; and with a tremendous force of bees secured by stimulative feeding, and with a brood-nest already filled to its utmost capacity with sugar stores, the honey, when it *does* come, is *forced* right into the supers, because there is no place for it in the brood-nest.

Our friend was driven to this mode of procedure because of a series of very poor honey-flows one year after another. Figuring that sugar syrup cost only about a fourth as much as the first quality of comb honey, he reasoned that, if he could make a legitimate trade with the bees, he could take *their* product in exchange for his sugar, and almost quadruple his money.

While it costs considerable to feed bees in this way, we believe that Mr. Boardman's experience has been such that he feels warranted in continuing it; and then if the year proves to be a good one he will get a tremendous crop of honey. One year when we visited him he had secured a fair-sized yield from each colony, and a poor year at that, while his neighbors round about him had no surplus, while all they did get was brood-nestfuls of honey, and nothing more. He also had his brood-chambers full; but instead of being honey it was sugar syrup, and the honey was in sections worth at least 12 or 15 cents per pound while we believe the sugar syrup cost him in the hive only about 4 cents. Clearly, he had made a good trade.

The feeder that is best adapted to this kind of feeding is the Boardman, already illustrated, because it is assumed that all colonies so fed are strong, and can make a proper defense at the entrance.

We would advise one who has not tried the plan to do so on a small scale. Feed up, say, 25 or 30 per cent of the colonies in the yard, and let the others go on in their own sweet way. Keep a careful account of the net proceeds after deducting expenses; and if those fed show a *larger* balance on the right side of the ledger than those not fed, then next year one would be warranted in feeding the whole apiary *a la* Boardman.

But, of course, it must be understood that feeding should not be continued long enough to force the sugar syrup into the sections, as that would be a fraud on the public. Nothing but the nectar of flowers ripened by the bees should be sold as honey.

WHEN ROBBERS ARE BAD, FEEDING AT NIGHT.

During the early fall of 1887 we found our apiary almost on the verge of starvation, the previous summer having been very dry. Robbers were unusually vigilant, and it was almost impossible to perform any manipulation with the hives without getting a perfect storm of robbers in the brood-nest. Feeding during the day was out of the question, and yet the colonies must be fed in order to prepare them for winter. Accordingly, to circumvent the robbers we fed at night by the light of lanterns. Contrary to what we might expect, the bees gave us but very little trouble by flying against the lanterns. As the bees took up all the feed in the feeders during the night, and the robbers had had no opportunity to investigate during the feeding, every thing was comparatively quiet next morning, and during the following day. We fed successfully in this way some three or four barrels of sugar. Although I have

recommended feeding *toward* night, in the preceding paragraphs, in the case above mentioned we fed from about 7 P.M. in some cases until 10:30 P.M. Perhaps I should also remark, that, if it is inconvenient to work at night, feed on the first rainy day. Put on your rubber hat, coat, and rubber boots. As long as it rains, bees will not bother you.

For particulars regarding feeding back to fill out sections, see COMB HONEY.

OPEN-AIR FEEDING—ITS POSSIBILITIES.

After what has been said by our best authorities regarding the danger of exposing sweets in the open air during the robbing season it may seem foolhardy to recommend the very thing that we under some conditions condemn. But under ANGER OF BEES, under EXTRACTOR, we show how one may stop or prevent robbing by feeding bees outdoors—that is to say, we bring about artificially, as nearly as possible, the conditions of a natural honey-flow. It is well known that, when bees can be kept busy in the field, hives can be opened without any trouble. Now, then, if we can keep the bees equally busy by making them go after food at a distance from the yard, we shall accomplish the same results.

This outdoor feeding is attended with some risk, and the reader is cautioned to go over this matter very carefully. Let him follow our instructions closely and he will experience no difficulty.

A good deal depends on circumstances or what one desires to accomplish by outdoor feeding. If he wishes to extract, or in any case to put bees in such good humor they will not rob, he should make a syrup or honey thinner than if he intends to feed up the entire yard for winter. For checking the robbing tendency, a syrup two parts water and one of sugar is just sweet enough to draw away all would-be robbers, and yet not make them crazy for it. Too sweet a syrup is apt to make them wild. But weak syrup must not be made up ahead before being given to the bees, as it will be likely to sour. If there is any likelihood that it will not be taken up inside of 48 hours it had better not be made weaker than one part of sugar to one of water. But for the prevention of robbing, a weaker syrup serves an altogether better purpose, for it is then of about the consistence of raw nectar.

HOW TO MAKE THE OUTDOOR FEEDER.

About the best thing we have found for the purpose is an ordinary 60-lb. square tin can. It would be well to prepare three or four such, as one might need them all at one time. Melt off the handle that is on *top* and then solder it to the *bottom*. The reason for this will be apparent later. If you have not the proper facilities, take the cans to the tinsmith. Now with a wire nail punch a lot of holes in the *top* of the can. The smallest holes that you can make are better than large ones. These holes should be about a quarter of an inch apart, and cover the whole surface of the top. Perforate the tops of the two other cans, and your feeders are ready. Fill each can with a thin syrup, *clear full*, and then screw on the cap. Procure some good strong clothesline; then put the cans on a wheelbarrow and wheel them out to a tree or grove about 200 yards away from the apiary. Select some limb about 20 feet from the ground, without any branches or obstructions beneath. Tie a stone to the end of the rope that you brought along, and throw it over the limb and draw the end down. Hitch it to the wire handle in the bottom of one of the feeder-cans. Now haul the can up in the air, upside down, until it is 16 or 18 feet above the ground. At first the syrup will leak out a little; but it will soon stop dripping if the screw top has been put on tightly.

This can, elevated in the air, will not be discovered by the bees, probably, for two or three hours; but the next day a good many will be found working at it. If there are many bees in the apiary, say one or two hundred hives, it may be necessary to hang up another feeder. When the bees are eagerly at work on the cans one may see strings of them going up and down to the feeder. Just as soon as a bee gets a good sip, one or more bees will grab hold to get at the same hole, when the two or three will fall together; but before they strike the ground they take wing and fly up again, and so on the process continues. Sometimes whole bunches of bees will fall at a time, only to take wing before they strike the ground. Up they go, and at it again. It takes a bee almost as long to take a load from one of these feeders as it does from a field of clover, because it has to spend a lot of time up and down, up and down, before it can get enough for a load. And herein is the secret of its success: If the syrup were fed thick in open cans, thousands of bees would be drowned; or if it were put into receptacles where they could get at it rapidly and not drown, they would fill up immediately, and in the course of half an hour all the syrup would be gone, and then robbing would be worse than ever. But a feeder put up in the air as explained makes it necessary for the bees to spend a lot of time in order to get the syrup, and consequently they are kept busy all day in emptying the cans. During this time one can extract, rear queens, and open up hives generally, with scarcely a robber showing up.

We would not advise this outdoor feeding generally for supplying the colonies with winter stores, or for stimulating only, because it involves considerable waste of bee life and energy.

For feeding up for winter, or for general stimulating, it is far better to feed within the hive, with any one of the good feeders just described. The long flight to and from outdoor feeders is apt to wear out the bees prematurely; and their hard struggles against each other to get a sip causes the fuzz to wear off, making them look like old bees very soon. Outdoor feeding is advised only to stop or prevent robbing, while important work like extracting after the honey-flow, or queen-rearing, is going on. If it is necessary to feed up the bees, and robbers are inclined to be meddlesome, we would advise doing so by night or during rainy days, as previously explained.

FENCE. See COMB HONEY.

FERTILE WORKERS. See LAYING WORKERS.

FERTILIZATION OF FLOWERS BY BEES. See FRUIT-BLOSSOMS, also POLLEN.

FIREWEED. See WILLOW-HERB.

FIXED FRAMES. See FRAMES, SELF-SPACING.

FOUNDATION. See COMB FOUNDATION.

FRAMES, SELF-SPACING. By these are meant frames held at certain regular distances apart by some sort of spacing-device, forming either a part of the frame itself or a part of the hive. Under SPACING OF FRAMES, elsewhere, and under EXTRACTOR, we have discussed the distances that frames should be apart. Some prefer 1½ inches from center to center; but the majority, supported by the best of reasons, prefer 1⅜ inches. Self-spacing frames, then, are those that, when put into the hive, are spaced automatically, either 1½ or 1⅜ inches from center to center. Loose frames differ from them, in that they have no spacing-device connected with them, and are, therefore, when placed in the hive, spaced by eye—or, as some have termed it, "by guesswork." Such spacing results in more or less uneven combs ; and beginners, as a rule, make very poor work of it. The advocates of self-spacing frames claim that they get even perfect combs, no burr-combs, and that, without any guesswork, the combs are spaced accurately and equally distant from one another. Self-spacing frames are always ready for moving the hives, either to an out-yard, to and from the cellar, or for ordinary carrying around the apiary. Loose frames, on the contrary, while they are never spaced exactly, often can not be hauled to an out-apiary, over rough roads, without having sticks between them, or something to hold them in place. It is contended by some, also, that spaced frames can be handled more rapidly. See FRAMES, MANIPULATING. On

Heddon, the Hoffman, the thick-top staple-spaced, metal-spaced Hoffman, and the nail-spaced.

The closed-end Quinby is, as its name indicates, one whose end-bars are wide their entire length. The top and bottom bars are one inch wide. These closed uprights, or ends, when they come in direct contact, cause the combs which they contain to be spaced accurately from center to center. Fig. 1, A, shows one such frame. Several of the closed-end frames are made to stand, and have very often been called "standing frames." Mr. Quinby, in order to keep such frames from toppling over, invented the strap-iron hook on one corner, as shown in Fig. 1, re-engraved from Cheshire. *h* is the hook that engages the strap iron *i*, in the bottom-board; *gr* is a groove to admit

FIG. 1.—HOW THE QUINBY FRAME HOOKS ON TO THE BOTTOM.—*From Cheshire.*

the other hand, the advocates of the loose frame urge, as an objection to the self-spacers, that they kill bees.

This depends. The careless operator may kill a good many bees. If he uses a little common sense, a little patience, applying a whiff or two of smoke between the parts of the frames that come in contact, he will not kill any bees. All this talk about self-spacing frames—Hoffman and closed-end type—killing bees emanates from a class who have never used them, and are therefore incompetent to render judgment. The fact that some of the most extensive bee-keepers of the world are using self-spacing frames, and the further fact that the number of self-spacing-frame users are constantly increasing, shows that this supposed bee-killing is more fancied than real.

There are a good many styles of self-spacing frames. We will describe, first, those most commonly used in this country and then show some of the others that are or have been used in Europe. Among the first mentioned we might mention the closed-end Quinby, the Danzenbaker, the

of the hook, and at the same time render it possible to catch under the strap iron.

These hooks are on the outside of the hive proper, and hence they do not kill bees, nor are they filled with propolis as they would be if made on the inside of the hive. A and B are respectively the frame and the follower, although they are drawn somewhat out of proportion. With a panel on each side, a cover and a bottom - board, the Quinby-Hetherington hive is complete, the ends of the frames forming the ends of the hive; although, for additional protection in the spring, Mr. Elwood and Mr. Hetherington both use the outside case to set down over the whole. This makes a very cheap hive, and has many desirable features in it. For fuller details in regard to this frame, and its manner of construction, the reader is referred to "Quinby's New Bee-keeping."

DANZENBAKER CLOSED END FRAMES.

The closed-end frame that promises to displace all others of this kind, and which, perhaps, is to-day the most extensively used of any of its class in the United States, is the

Danzenbaker, as described under HIVES, and shown under FRAMES, MANIPULATING. The end-bars are pivoted at the center, the pins resting on hanger cleats secured to the ends of the hives. These pins make a very small line of contact, whereas the ordinary

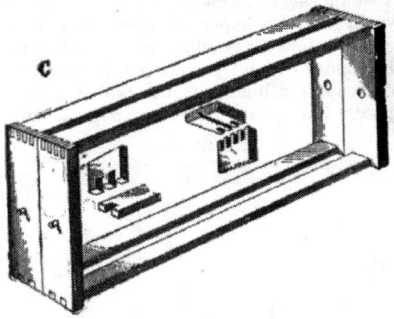

standing closed-end frame resting on tins secured to the bottom edge at the ends of the hive will crush a good many bees. They have the further advantage that, if there is

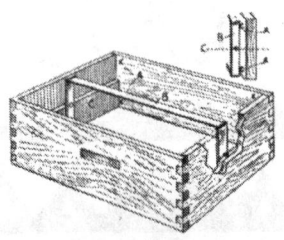

any reduction in the depth of the hive due to shrinkage, the bee-space above and below the frames will be affected only half as much as if the frame were standing.

Many bee-keepers prefer what is known as the "hanging frame." This has many very decided advantages over the standing frame; and there is no doubt that, for this reason, the loose frame is used so generally; but the hanging frame is also used as a fixed frame.

IMPROVED HOFFMAN FRAMES.

It will be observed that this frame can be used in an ordinary Langstroth hive (see HIVE-MAKING); and the end-bars are closed-end only a couple of inches from the top. The rest of the frame, two-thirds of the way down, is narrowed to 1⅛ inches. The top-bars of the original Hoffman were made 1⅜ inches wide with the middle scored out so as to measure one inch wide.

After having for a time Hoffman frames with top-bars widened at the end, and no

rabbets, we began the use of top-bars with the ends notched (see cut) and resting on the tin rabbets, as shown in HIVE-MAKING. After several seasons' use of the latter we much prefer them. The lateral feature is more perfect, and there is very much less liability of bee-killing. Indeed, with proper care there need be practically none.

Another feature of this frame is the end-spacing staple that abuts against the tin rabbet shown at 6, in the cut. The ends of the top-bars are cut off so as to leave a

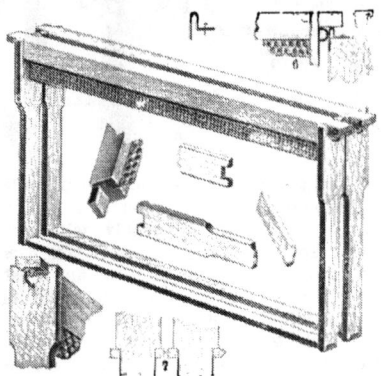

bee-space around them. With the old-style frames the bees can sometimes glue the ends of the top-bars to the rabbet. This has all been done away with in the style shown.

When the top-bar is long enough to reach and almost come in contact with the ends of the rabbets, the bees will chink in bee-glue between the ends of the top-bars and the rabbets. After the ends of *all* the frames have been thus glued, it is somewhat difficult to remove any one comb, because the fastening of each frame must be loosened before the combs sought can be lifted out: but when the top-bar is shortened, as at 6 in the illustration, and the staple is used, there is none of this kind of gluing, the only fastening being that between the upright edges of the end-bars themselves; and this fastening, for the majority of localities, so far from being a disadvantage, is helpful in that it holds the frames together while the hives are being moved, and yet does not hold them so as to prevent easy handling.

This is by all odds the most extensively used self-spacing frame in the United States. In fact, most of the hive-manufacturers supply it as a part of the regular equipment of their standard hives.

For details concerning its use, see FRAMES, HOW TO MANIPULATE.

METAL-SPACED HOFFMAN FRAMES.

All that has been said in favor of the regular Hoffman will apply with equal force to the metal-spaced frame here shown. In some localities where propolis is very abundant, sticky, and hard, the wooden projections of the regular Hoffman sometimes split off when the frames are pried apart.

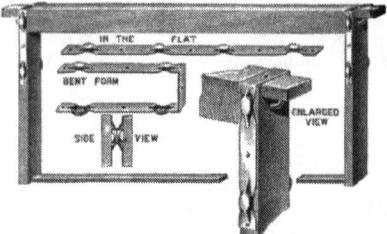

For localities where this condition prevails we recommend the metal-spaced, which can be used interchangeably with the regular Hoffman. The spacers on this new frame are stamped out of metal and must necessarily be accurate. The form of its construction in the shape of a letter U bending over the top-bar projection prevents the latter from breaking through careless handling.

STAPLE-SPACED FRAMES.

There are some others who prefer frames with staples for side-spacers, as here shown. Others use nails in place of staples; but the

STAPLE-SPACED FRAMES.

latter with their rounding edges allow the frames to slide past each other worse.

OTHER SELF-SPACING DEVICES.

Various spacing-devices have been suggested at different times. A few of these we present here, leaving the reader to judge of their relative merits. It will not be necessary to describe them in detail, as the engravings make plain their manner of construction and use.

It will be noted that there are two kinds of spacing-devices. One is made a part of the frame and the other a part of the rabbet. It would seem at first glance that the latter would be a very happy solution of the problem of automatic spacing, as it would leave the frames without projections in the way of uncapping; but the fact is, rabbet or hive spacers have never been very popular, and

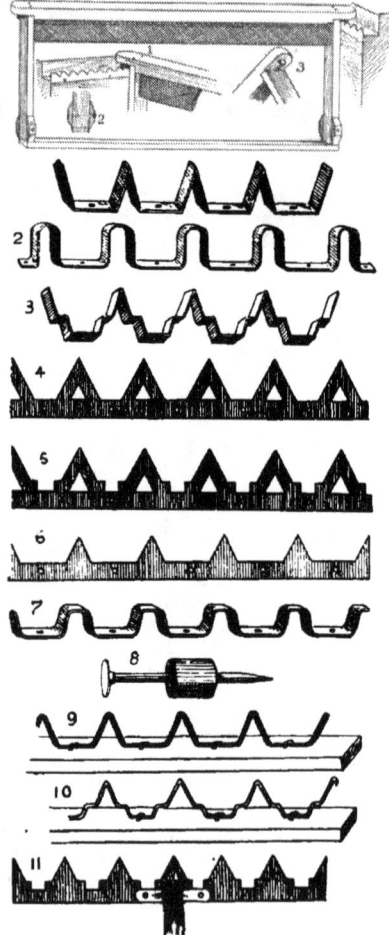

HIVE-RABBET SPACERS.*

---

*These are nailed on the side of or in the wooden hive-rabbet—the top-bars or frames resting between the notches or bends of the sheet metal or wire.

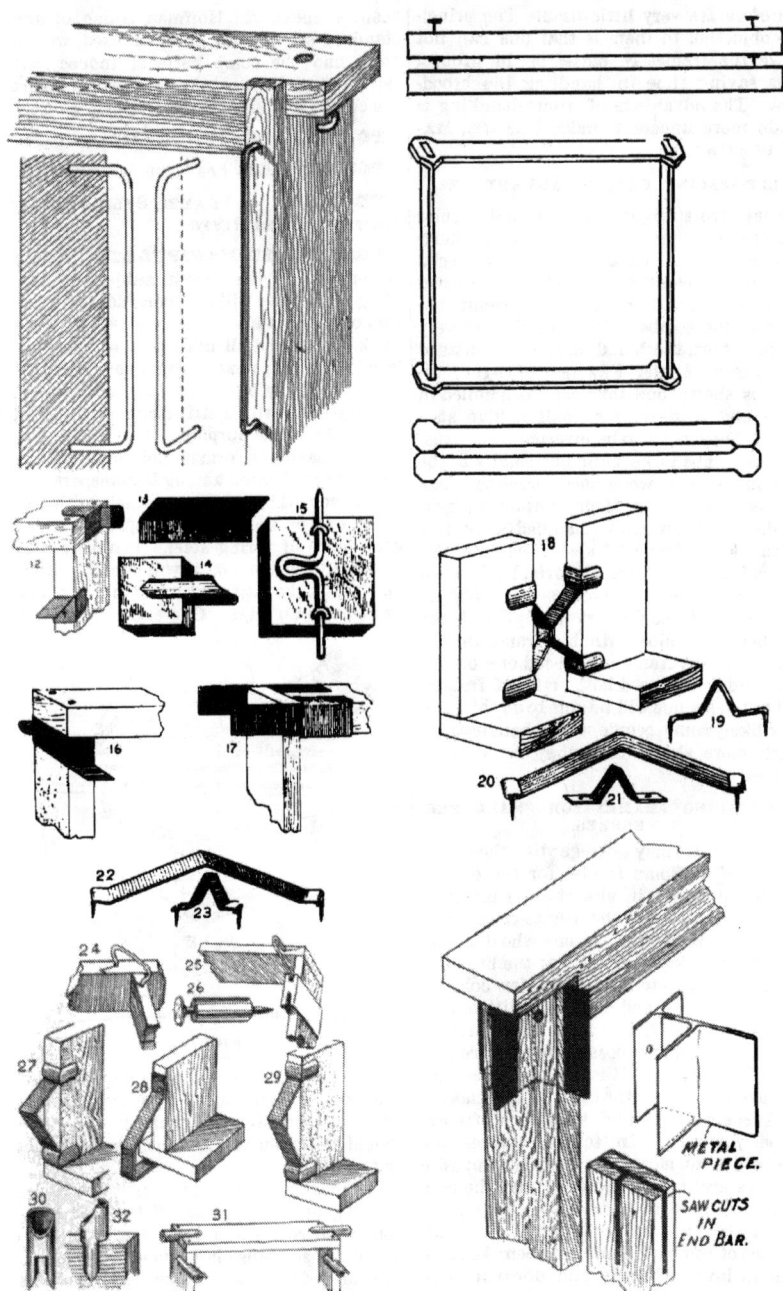

VARIOUS FORMS OF FRAME-SPACERS.

therefore are very little used. The principal objection to them is that one can not move the frames *en masse* or in groups, thus saving time in handling the brood-nest. The advantage of group handling is made more apparent under FRAMES, MANIPULATING.

SELF-SPACING FRAMES—ADVANTAGES.

They give straight beautiful and regular combs; are practically free from burr-combs; can be hauled without any special preparation over the roughest roads, turned upside down, and rolled over without disturbing the combs. They permit, to a very great extent, the handling of hives instead of frames. Under FRAMES, MANIPULATING, is shown how they can be handled in pairs and trios—in fact, half a hive at a time. They can also be inverted, thus causing the combs to be built out solidly to the bottom-bar; and, when once completed, they can be restored to their normal upright condition. They can be handled as rapidly as the loose frame. Indeed, the late Mr. Julius Hoffman, of Canajoharie, N.Y., when owner of some 600 colonies on Hoffman frames, said he could work nearly double the number of colonies with his frame that he could with any frame not spaced or close-fitting, and he had used both styles of frames. But not every one will be able to do this; and very likely some people would handle them much more slowly than they could loose frames.

SELF-SPACING FRAMES FOR SMALL BEE-KEEPERS.

Whatever we may say regarding the adaptability of Hoffman frames for the expert, we feel sure that, in almost every instance, they are better for the beginner, average farmer bee-keeper, or any one who does not propose to make a specialty of the bee business, but desires to keep only a few colonies to supply himself and neighbors with honey. Such persons are apt to be a little careless, and, with ordinary loose unspaced frames, make bad spacing. It is seldom indeed that we have looked into the hives of this class of bee-keepers and found their loose frames properly spaced. In some instances the combs are so close together that opposite surfaces are gnawed down to give the bees sufficient space to pass between; and in others they are so far apart that small patches of comb are built between; because it is an invariable rule laid down in hive economy, on the part of the bees, not to leave more than proper bee-spaces. Now,

then, whenever the Hoffman frame, or any standard self-spacing kind, is used, we always find the comb perfect; indeed, the self-spacing feature shows how far apart the combs should be placed.

FOUL BROOD. See DISEASES OF BEES.

FOUNDATION. See COMB FOUNDATION.

FRAMES. See FRAMES, SELF-SPACING, REVERSING, and HIVES.

FRAMES; TO MANIPULATE. Before we proceed to the general subject of handling frames, we will first consider the question of hive-seats and tools necessary for the work. First and all important is a smoker (see SMOKERS); next is some sort of hive-tool, which may be an ordinary screwdriver, a putty-knife with a stiff blade, or a special tool made for the purpose. The subjoined illustrations show a form of tool that has given general satisfaction among bee-keepers.

It is something that any blacksmith can make out of an old buggy-spring or any good piece of spring steel. It must not be tempered too hard or it will break. Each end should be flattened out while hot, and brought to an edge. One end is bent to a

FIG. 1.

right angle, and the other is left straight. The tool is then taken over to an emery wheel or grindstone and finished up. Care should be taken to have the edges *straight and square.*

The hooked end is ordinarily used for scraping propolis or wax off the frames or bottom-boards, while the other end (also useful for scraping) is pushed between the two parts of the hive; but the drawing shows the tool held improperly. The bent or curved end should be placed directly against the palm in order that sufficient pressure may be exerted to shove the other or straight end between the two hive parts.

Either end of the tool may be used for separating Hoffman frames, or, in fact, any style of frame that one happens to use; but our men prefer the hook end. This is inserted between the frames to be separated, as shown in Fig. 2, when a side

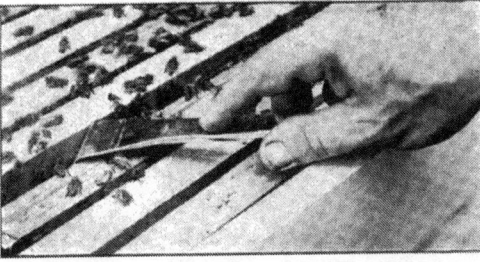

FIG. 2.—A side twist of the tool affords a strong leverage by which the frames are separated easily, and without jar.

Fig. 4 shows how the tool may be used for crowding all the frames over to one side in one block, as it were; or one can, if he prefers, use the plan shown in Fig. 2; but it will generally be found that the one shown in Fig. 4 is more convenient. In Fig. 5 the curved end is used to good advantage in lifting the division-board out of the hive. See also, in this connection, Fig. 9.

FIG. 3. — Another method of using a hive-tool when prying the frames apart.

twist of the wrist will exert considerable leverage, forcing apart the frames very gently. But there are some who prefer to use the straight

end of the tool in the manner shown in Fig. 3; but the method given Fig. 2 exerts more of a leverage, and, at the same time, is less liable to crush bees.

FIG. 4.—The proper way to pry all the frames over at one operation.

Some prefer a hive-tool having a narrowed end like a screwdriver; but the continuous use of a tool like this abrases the edges of the hives so that, after a time, it leaves bruise marks and cracks, inviting winds and storms, and robbers when they are prowling about. For separating two hives heavy with honey there is nothing better than a *wide thin blade* made of good spring steel, tempered just hard enough to have the resillient qualities of a buggy-spring.

HOW TO WORK OVER THE HIVES.

Many yard men prefer to work with a sort of stool and hive box combined; others wish to have nothing to lug around except the bee-smoker and the hive-tool. As most hives are placed on or near the ground, one must either sit down on some object or kneel in

FIG. 5.—How the hook end is useful in fishing out frames and division-boards.

FIG. 6.—Making a gap between the frames so that one can be easily removed.

hives, sitting down on the hive-cover or hive-stool, he finds it convenient to vary occasionally the position by resting on the knees close to the hive; and still again he may find it comfortable to vary the monotony by standing upright, bending over only when it is necessary to remove a frame.

FIG. 7.—A comfortable position for all-day work. Note that the left arm that supports the weight of the frames rests comfortably on the knee.

front of the hive, to bring himself to the proper working distance. We usually use a hive-cover as shown in Figs. 6, 7, 8, 9. It is always handy, and has the further advantage of a milk-stool in that one can shift his body back and forth on the hive-cover in order to reach frames toward the near or far side of the hive, as the case may be. A seat that does not allow one to shift his body back and forth, necessarily requires more stooping or bending of the back.

Occasionally it will be found desirable to turn the cover up lengthwise, and we always use it in that manner when we desire to place the weight of the body against the frame that we are crowding over against its fellows. See Fig. 8. In pulling out a division-board, one has a little more leverage if he sits high rather than low. See Fig. 9. But if he merely wishes to separate the frames, then spend several minutes hunting for the queen or looking over the brood, as shown in Fig. 7, one should sit on the narrow side rather than on the end. In this the operator assumes a very natural, easy, and comfortable position. The left arm rests upon the knee, supporting the weight of the frame, while the right arm merely holds it in a position for examination.

A change of position is often restful. After one has been working over a number of

Perhaps it may seem that the operator in Fig 9 is taking things easy. There are times when only one hand can do good work. If one can assume a comfortable attitude, even though it be only momentary, he ought to do so.

We are well aware that some of our apiarists will say they have no time to sit down, much less "loaf on the job," as might appear in Fig. 6. It is our opinion, however, that the more one can save his legs and arms the more he can actually accomplish in a day. In hunting for a queen we can not afford to stand up on the job, but should get right down where the eyes can do their best work, as seen in Fig. 7, always holding the frame in such a way that the sunlight will strike it squarely. In looking for eggs this is very important, especially if the operator is getting toward the shady side of life when eyesight is not at its best.

Where one is working over bees day after day, a special hive-seat is a great convenience. The illustration at the bottom of the page shows what we have used in our bee-yard for nearly thirty years. It was shown in one of the early editions of this work, but was dropped out because we thought it of hardly sufficient importance to occupy space. During all the years that have intervened, our apiarists have

FIG. 8.—A higher seat is better when one wishes to place his weight against the frame to be shoved over.

FIG. 9.—Pulling out a refractory division-board that resists removal.

ments on each end usually hold the smoker fuel, hive-tools, hammer, bee-brush, queen-cages, and other articles of like nature. The smoker has a hook on the bellows so that it can be carried in the manner shown. With this whole outfit one has practically all the tools he needs, including smoker fuel, for a day's work.

seemed to find it very handy. In fact, they seem to consider it almost indispensable; so if you come to any one of our yards you will find the men carrying one around as they go among the hives. The top is made of ⅜ lumber, having two oblong holes in the center to provide a handle by which to carry the box. The legs are also of ⅜, while the sides, ends, and bottom are of ⅜. The compartment in the side, reached by the oval hole, is very handy for holding broken section pieces for record work, and other small articles, while the two compart-

The exact dimensions of the seat are not important. The one we use is 13 inches high by 22 long, outside measurement.

FIG. 1.—A handy seat and tool-box for bee-yard work.

Fig. 9.—Method of inserting the hive-tool under the cover : blowing smoke in the gap thus made.

HOW TO OPEN A HIVE.

Having considered the necessary tools and appliances for working with bees as well as the manner of sitting or standing over the hives we will now turn our attention directly to the method of handling the frames themselves. Approach the hive that is to be opened and blow a little smoke into the entrance. This latter procedure is not always necessary, but it will be found to be a very wise precaution on the part of a beginner. After he learns the individual temperament of his different colonies, and also discovers that on certain days and certain times of days, the bees can be handled much better than others, he will of course use his judgment in the matter. If he has reason to believe that a colony would be irritable he should send two or three whiffs of smoke into the entrance. He will now push the screwdriver, or special hive-tool already shown, under the cover. He should do this very gently, working the thin edge of the blade between the two hive parts until the cover is raised about the thickness of the blade, but not wide enough to allow any bees to escape. Through the gap thus made

he will blow three or four whiffs of smoke. He then shoves the tool a little further, increasing the gap, following it up with some more smoke. He now lifts or lowers the hand holding the tool so that the cover is raised an inch above the hive. The smoker is next set down upon the ground, when the cover is gently lifted off. Sometimes much more smoke will be required than others. If the atmosphere is a little chilly, or if it be immediately after a rain during a honey-flow, much more smoke will be needed than on a warm balmy day when bees are at work in the fields. If they are at all nervous the smoker should be brought into play again ; indeed, at such times we would advise putting it between the knees, as shown in the illustration at the top of the next page.

This nervousness may not immediately be recognized by a novice, but for his special benefit we may say that when bees are subdued and require no more smoke they will be down between the frames almost out of sight; but if they are inclined to "resent the intrusion," dozens and dozens of them will have their heads sticking up, and as the apiarist proceeds to lift out a frame, he may meet with a "warm reception." But before this takes place, he will usually see on the part of the bees a nervous, quick movement, their bodies turning either to the right or

FIG. 10.—Holding a smoker between the knees while manipulating frames.

to the left, apparently ready to take wing. When they do so, it will be a quick sharp dart, without warning, for any exposed part of the bee-keeper's anatomy. But even if the bees do make a general onslaught, and

smoker while the operator proceeds to handle the frames.

HOW TO HANDLE UNSPACED FRAMES.

To get at the center frame, crowd the frames, one at a time, adjacent to it, toward the sides of the hive. This will give room to lift out the desired frame. Beginners are very apt to pull the frame out without spacing the frames apart. This rolls the bees over and over, enrages and maims them, besides running a pretty good chance of killing the queen. Lift the frame out carefully, and be careful not to knock the end-bars against the sides of the hive. If it is one's first experience he may be nervous, and do things a little hurriedly. As a reward, the bees will quite likely sting him and make him still more nervous. To avoid this, proceed very cautiously and make the movements deliberate. Having removed the frame, hold it up as shown in Fig. 1, which we will call the first position.

Perhaps the queen is not to be seen on this side so it may be necessary to turn it over and see the other side. If the comb is not heavy with honey, it can be turned right over with the bottom-bar resting horizontally. But a better way and a good habit to fall into, and one that bee-keepers usually adopt, is to raise the left hand until the top-bar is perpendicular, as shown in Fig. 2.

Now revolve the frame like a swinging door, or the leaf of a book, so that the opposite side is exposed to view (see Fig. 2).

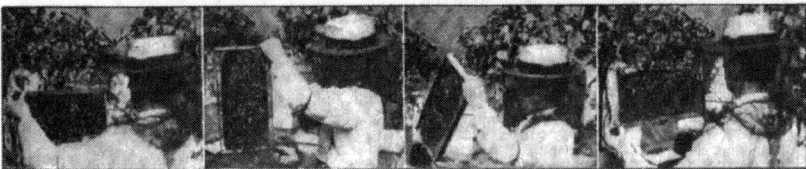

FIG. 1. FIG. 2. FIG. 3. FIG. 4.

grab as if about to strike, the sting may be averted if the operator is quick enough to brush the bee or bees off. There is an interval of a fraction of a second, not very long it is true, in which, after the bee shoves its claws into the flesh, that it can be brushed off, before the sting gets into action, for a bee, when it stings, must have a good strong hold, and it is while it is taking this hold that the apiarist can often save himself many a wicked jab.

If, then, the bees seem inclined to fly up, smoke them just enough to keep them down. If an attendant is present, let him use the

Lower the left hand as in Fig. 3 until it reaches the position as shown in Fig. 4. To examine the other side follow the exact reverse order.

Having examined this frame, lean it up against the side of the hive, and remove another frame next to the one already taken. Examine this in like manner. Lean this also against one corner of the hive, or return it to its place; lift out another, and so on until all have been examined. Now, should the queen not yet have been found, look the frames all over again, being careful to examine the bottom edge of the combs.

If a colony is not populous it may be advisable to go over the frames once more; but very often it is better to close the hive and wait an hour or two, after which we can go back and search the frames as before. By this time the colony will have recovered itself, and the queen, in all probability, have shifted her position from the bottom or sides of the hive to one of the combs. Nine times out of ten she will be found at the second going-over of the frames, without any trouble. When the queen can not be found the first time going over, as a rule we would not advise hunting longer, because one is liable to waste a good deal of valuable time; and it is, therefore, better to wait till the queen comes out of her hiding-place back to the brood-frames themselves.

In the case of black colonies, especially where very populous, it is sometimes necessary to lift the hive off the stand and put it down at one side. On the old stand place an empty hive, affixing an entrance-guard. See DRONES. Now take the frames one by one out of the old hive, and shake them in front at the entrance of the empty hive on the old stand. Black bees fall off very readily; and as they crawl toward the hive the queen can be very easily seen; but if she eludes scrutiny she will be barred by the perforated zinc, so she may be very readily discovered trying to make her way through. After all the frames are shaken, if she can not be found, take the old hive, now empty, and dump it, causing the bees to be thrown before the zinc. She will soon be seen trying to pass the guard.

We have told how to find the queen; but do not imagine that it is going to be as difficult as this every time. She is usually to be found on the center frames; and especially with Italians, she will likely be found on the first or second frame handled.

When we put back loose frames we must space them carefully, 1⅜ in. from center to center. We fail to do it exactly, but try it the best we can. With loose frames we shall be obliged to space each one in position individually. If we do not space our frames carefully we will have some combs bulged, and some thinned down; and, again, between others bees will be likely to build spurs of comb. All this nuisance may be avoided by the use of fixed frames or the Hoffman, which we now tell how to handle.

HOW TO MANIPULATE HOFFMAN FRAMES.

The manner of opening hives containing the Hoffman or any other self-spacing frame

is precisely the same as that for hives of loose unspaced frames already described; but the manner of handling the combs is somewhat different.

With the hive-tool we pry apart the first pair or trio of frames, if the combs are not too heavy, and lean them against one corner of the hive as shown below. In so doing we pretty nearly handle the brood-nest by halves and quarters.

We shall discover that these frames are held together by propolis, and that the bees

FIG. 5.—Handling Hoffman frames in pairs and trios.

on the two inside surfaces are hardly disturbed. Loose frames, on the contrary, when out of the hive, must be leaned on one or two corners of the hives, against each other—in fact, be scattered all around, inviting the depredations of robbers. This is quite a point in favor of the Hoffman frame. If we do not find the queen on one of the combs, we next pry off the outside frame of the trio leaning against the corner of the hive. If she does not appear on that one, we pry off the next, and so on.

Where combs are heavy with honey, we may lift out only one frame. Having seen the surfaces of two or three combs, the practiced eye will get a very fair idea of the condition of the colony and what the queen is doing. When we see eggs and larvæ in all stages, including sealed brood, we do not usually stop to hunt up the queen; accordingly we put back the second pair removed, and return the trio, as shown. We do not generally crowd these frames together at once, but blow a little smoke down between the end-bars, and then with a quick shove we close them all up again.

There is no cut-and-try spacing as with loose frames—no big and little fingers to get

ABOUT TO INSERT A DANZENBAKER FRAME INTO THE PLACE FROM WHICH IT CAME.

the distances at wide and narrow spaces. There is no need to instruct the beginner just how far to space combs, and there is no finding the apiary afterward, with any of the combs spaced so far apart that spurs of comb are built where they ought not to be. With the regular Hoffman frames the spaces must necessarily be exact, so the combs may have a fixed and uniform thickness; and we do not hesitate to say that one can alternate them just as well as or better than he can many of the loose or unspaced frames. We will explain. Space the loose frames during the honey-harvest, anywhere from 1⅜ to 1½ or even 1⅝ inches from center to center, and then, after the honey-harvest, try to alternate them with other frames spaced a little closer, and see where you are. You may say you can space frames near enough right. Although we have visited many large apiaries, we seldom see a loose-frame apiary spaced correctly.

To go back, we will replace the follower, and crowd the frames tight together. If there are any bees on the tops of the frames, a whiff of smoke will usually drive them down and then the cover is replaced with a sliding motion, which we have already explained.

Perhaps from the description about manipulating the hive with Hoffman frames, it may appear like a long operation; it is a very short one. Mr. Hoffman said he could handle nearly double the number of colonies on his frame that he could on any loose frame; and we will add right here that he used loose frames for years, until necessity, the mother of invention, caused him to bring out this style.

There is another good feature; namely, by removing two or three frames in a trio, the rest of the combs in the hive need not be lifted out. They can be slipped back and forth, and each surface examined; but if the tin rabbet is covered with pieces of propolis, this lateral sliding is not easily accomplished.

There are some localities where propolis is very much worse than in others. In such places the Hoffman frame is not as satisfactorily used as the staple-spaced shown in FRAMES, SELF-SPACING. With perhaps one exception this can be handled like the Hoffman; and that exception is that it can not be handled in pairs or trios. Each comb must be manipulated individually. In this respect it is quite a little behind the Hoffman.

HOW TO HANDLE DANZENBAKER FRAMES.

As shown under HIVES, the frames are pivoted in the center, and rest on hanger-cleats in the ends of the hive. When opening up for inspection, keep the frames together in one solid body, without any spaces between them. It is not advisable to loosen all the frames with a screwdriver at the start. Break the propolis connections only

SLIDING A DANZENBAKER FRAME DOWN BETWEEN TWO OTHERS.

on the frame or frames to be handled, leaving the rest glued together so they can be lifted out in blocks of two, three, or four, as at top page 219. If it is desired to examine the comb surface of one frame, break the propolis connections on each side of it, as before explained, and pull it out as in cuts here shown. Usually the examination of the brood in one frame will suffice to give to the practiced eye some idea of the laying capacity of the queen, of the amount of brood in the hive, and the amount of stores. If it is necessary to examine another frame, set the one first taken out down by the side of the hive; loosen another frame, and remove that. In this way all the frames in the hive can be exam'ned; but when the frames are reinserted, if the end-bars are covered with bees they should be slipped back into place *by sliding the edge of one end-bar against anoth-*

METHOD OF GRABBING DANZENBAKER FRAME WHEN REMOVING IT FROM THE HIVE.

HANDLING CLOSED-END FRAMES IN GROUPS OF THREE AT A TIME.

er, beginning at the top, and working downward. By so doing the bees are pushed or shoved out of the way without crushing or pinching. With a little practice and experience this can be done without killing a single bee. When all the frames are in place except the last one, there will be a space just wide .enough to admit it. Slide it into position, pushing the bees off the end-bars on both edges at once.

Be careful not to get the frames loosened up so that they will tumble over against each other in a bad mix-up. If t:ey are separated about two or three inches apart they are so nearly on a balance they will topple one way and the other. The bees will naturally crawl between the upright edges of the end-bars; and now to crowd the frames all together with a slam would smash the bees by the scores, and at the same time anger them into stinging fury. *Bear in mind that Danzenbaker frames must be kept together in groups of twos and threes. Never let one frame hang by itself on the pin supports.* It is important to remember also that when they are all in place they must be shoved up together tight without any spaces between them.

For many manipulations like giving brood to another hive, or for the purpose of extracting, it becomes necessary to dislodge the bees from the frames. This can be done by brushing them off as shown under EXTRACTING, or they can be pounded off with a blow of the fist on the back of the hand, grasping the end-bar as shown.

Or one may grasp the end-bars of the frame solidly, and with a quick downward

HOW TO BUMP THE BEES OFF A COMB.

DR. MILLER'S METHOD OF JARRING BEES OFF THE COMBS.

DETERMINING THE FILLING OF THE SUPERS AND WHETHER READY TO COME OFF.

jerk remove all or nearly all of the bees. When more convenient one can swing the frame, pendulum fashion, with one arm, letting the corner drop violently against the ground while the other end is held in the hand. See the two illustrations at the top of page 220. See HIVES.

HOW TO ASCERTAIN THE CONDITION OF THE HIVE WITHOUT HANDLING FRAMES.

A good many, in working for extracted honey, operate on the tier-up principle, leaving the supers all on the hives until the season is over. By that time it is important that robbers be given no opportunity to help themselves to sweets, when the honey is taken off; but before doing so the condition of the supers should be determined in advance. In order to keep ahead of the bees it is necessary to make an examination from time to time. Toward the early part of the season it is customary to place the empty supers under those partly filled. As the season began to draw toward its close, the process is reversed—that is to say, the empties were put on top of those partly filled.

In order to determine the amount of honey in any super, it is not necessary to take off the cover and pull the hive apart. If it is tiered up four and five stories high, it involves a large amount of labor and considerable lifting to pull the supers off one by one, inviting the attention of robbers in the operation. If one is supplied with a good strong steel hive-tool and a smoker, he can get a fair idea of the filling of any super, without even removing the cover from the hive. In the series of snap-shots shown herewith, the reader will be able to gather, almost at a glance, the exact method to be used in determining what the bees are doing.

Let us take an example. We will start with the hive shown in Fig. 5, opposite page. It has three supers. The middle one is the one on which the bees began work first, and at the time of this examination it should be completely filled. The bottom super was placed under after the middle one was about half filled. The third super was put on top because there would probably not be more than a week more of honey-flow.

At this time we desire to know what the bees have actually done; so, without removing the telescope cover on top nor the super cover directly beneath, we extend the thin blade of the hive-tool, broad end, between the two lower supers *at the back end of the*

LEARNING CONDITION OF HIVE WITHOUT REMOVING COVER OR PULLING TO PIECES.

FIG. 14.—SHAKING BEES OUT OF A SUPER.

hive; for one should always endeavor to keep out of the flight of the bees. This is gradually shoved in until the blade has been pushed in anywhere from ½ to a full inch. A gap is now formed, of approximately $\frac{1}{16}$ inch just wide enough so that a little smoke will drive back the bees. A slight pressure downward separates the two upper supers about an inch at the back end, when more smoke is blown in. The tool is pushed down a little further, making the gap a little wider. See Fig. 6, p. 220. But we are not quite satisfied as to the condition of the supers, so we push the tool and supers upward, as shown in Fig. 7, until we have the hive-tool in position as shown in Fig. 8. Here it acts as a prop, when, with the intelligent use of the smoker, we can drive back the bees enough so that we can see the condition of the two supers, or enough to determine whether the bees need more room.

But suppose we are not quite satisfied. We turn to the position as shown in Fig. 9, disregard the hive-tool, and lift the two supers higher, the hive-tool falling on the ground. When doing this we slide the two supers about an inch forward so that the back end will fulcrum on a safe bearing. If the super is slipped back, as shown in Fig. 7, it can readily be seen that it can not be tilted up very high without sliding off back. See Figs. 9, 10, 11.

Usually an examination of this sort is quite sufficient. If the supers are not filled they are quietly let back into place, using sufficient smoke to drive the bees away so they will not be crushed as the hive parts come together again. The operation as shown in Figs. 5, 6, 7, 8, 9, 10, 11, is then repeated with other hives, taking from 30 to 60 seconds per hive. At no time have we lifted only a part of the dead weight. When the supers are held at an angle the load is on the fulcrum point of contact, while the hand sustains only a small part of the weight.

Fig. 12 shows the method employed when supers are apparently well filled and ready to come off. The top super is removed and leaned up against the leg of the operator. The middle super that has been filled can now be taken off; but before doing so a second examination is made as shown. It is set off, when the bottom super may also be removed if ready. If not, the top super is put back, the idea being to confine the bees to as small a super capacity as possible as the season draws to a close, in order to make the bees finish their work.

Fig. 13 shows a slightly different pose from that indicated in Fig. 8. While the position of the operator is somewhat cramped, it is true, yet it is much easier than tearing down the hive, super by super, and replacing the same.

In Fig. 14, page 222, we have a case where the season is closing abruptly. The bees have only partially begun work in the top super. To leave it on would mean that all the supers would have honey in, and none of them quite completed. Accordingly we shake the bees out of the top super, place a

FIG. 13.—HOW A SMOKER AND A HIVE-TOOL WILL ENABLE ONE TO LEARN THE CONDITION OF THE SUPERS AT ONE GLANCE.

thin super cover on the two lower supers, place the super just shaken on top, and the regular cover on it. The hive is now left until we can determine a little more about the season. If there should be some good rains and warm weather, the season may take another start. In that case the super cover that was placed between the top super and the two below is removed, when work will be resumed in the third super. If we were sure that the season was drawing to a close, the top super should be removed in the first place.

HOW TO PUT ON ESCAPE-BOARDS.

In going through bee-yards we have noted the fact over and over that some bee-keepers have an awkward way of putting on escapes. They will pull the hive apart, super

by super, place the escape on the brood-nest or on a super partly filled, then one by one put back the supers. If no honey is coming in, this will probably mean that robbers will get started.

There is no need of removing any super, nor a cover, for that matter. All that is necessary is to apply the principles illustrated in Figs. 5, 6, 7, 8, 9, 10, 11. See also illustration under COMB HONEY on page 115.

FRUIT-BLOSSOMS. In the northern portions of the United States, where much fruit is grown, especially apples, pears, and peaches, there will be an occasional spring when quite a little honey is gathered from the blossoms. Nearly every season fruit-trees yield a little honey, if not too cold, just when it is most needed to stimulate brood-rearing; and although the bees may not store much, they will gather enough to give the whole apiary a new impetus, so that, where fruit is grown extensively bee-keepers often receive considerable benefit.

As to its quality, the honey from fruit-blossoms is among the very best. It is light in color, of good body, and in flavor not unlike the beautiful aroma one enjoys when going through an orchard in full bloom. Such honey, if it could be gathered in sufficient quantities, would doubtless have an extensive demand; but it is very seldom that bees are able to get enough to store any in the supers or sections.

SPRAYING DURING BLOOM DESTRUCTIVE TO BEES AND BROOD.

Now that spraying with various poisonous liquids has come to be almost universal among fruit-growers, the question arises, "Shall such spraying be done during the time the trees are in bloom, or before and after?" If it is administered when the petals are out, bees are almost sure to be poisoned, much brood will be killed, and many times valuable queens are lost. About the first thing one notices during fruit-blooming time, if trees are sprayed while in

APPLE-BLOSSOMS.

bloom, is that a good deal of the brood dies, until the bee-keeper begins to wonder whether his bees have foul brood, black brood, or pickled brood—unless the truth dawns upon him that they have been carrying in poisonous liquids from the trees that have just been sprayed. Experiment stations all over the United States have shown that it is quite useless—indeed, often decidedly harmful to the young fruit — to spray during the time the trees are in full bloom ; and they have shown over and over again that just as good and better results can be secured by spraying both *before* and *after* blooming, when there is no danger of bees visiting the trees in quest of pollen and nectar. Some experiments that were conducted at the Cornell and Geneva experiment stations, New York, are particularly conclusive in showing that to spray in full bloom is decidedly injurious to the blossoms themselves, to say nothing about the great damage done to the bee-keeper. The poison as ordinarily used is very harmful to the growth and development of the pollen. Again, the delicate organs of the flowers (stamens and pistils) are either killed or injured. Some of the pollen in the experiments above mentioned was taken into the laboratory and mixed with a thin syrup of about the consistency of raw nectar, and to this was then added a quantity of the spraying-liquid of the strength that is ordinarily used on fruit-trees. In every case it was found the pollen failed to develop. In short, those in charge of these experiments gave any amount of proof to the effect that, irrespective of any interests of the bee-keeper, the fruit-grower himself *could not afford to spray during fruit-blooming time, because spraying-liquids that are sufficiently strong to kill insect pests are decidedly harmful to the delicate reproductive organs and to the pollen of the flowers themselves.*

Some prominent fruit-growers who once were of the contrary opinion, and who sprayed during full bloom, have since found their mistake to their sorrow. In some instances they confessed to losing nearly one thousand dollars.

Some spraying-fluids are not poisonous. Take, for example, the lime-sulphur washes, the kerosene, and other emulsions of crude oil; but even these should not be sprayed when the trees are in bloom. Hellebore, or any of the Bordeaux mixtures, especially if they contain Paris green, or any of the arsenites, will be poisonous, of course; such fluids are too strong for the delicate pistils and stamens of the flower.

Spraying is practiced to kill the fungi and injurious insects. The codling moth that is responsible in the main for wormy apples lays its egg in the bark of the trees. As soon as the larva hatches, it seeks out the blossoms about the time the petals fall and begins to burrow into them. If they have a coating of poison it dies before it can do any mischief. Otherwise it makes its temporary home in the maturing fruit.

THE STATEMENT OF A HIGH AUTHORITY IN FRUIT CULTURE.

"The American Apple-orchard" is the title of a book by F. A. Waugh, published by the Orange Judd Co., of New York. It contains over 200 pages of interesting and valuable matter. Price $1.00.

Those fruit-growers in the vicinity of our bee-keeping friends, who insist on spraying at the wrong time in spite of the advice of experiment stations all over the United States, and up-to-date fruit-growers, should be shown a copy of this work. If they are so behind the times as to spray while the trees are in bloom they have a lot to learn, and it would be dollars and dollars in their pocket to purchase a copy of this work and read it carefully. We are not sure but that bee-keepers can afford to buy it and loan it out to their fruit-growing neighbors. We copy a portion of chapter 11, entitled "The Insect Campaign." Under the head of "Codling Moth," the worm that so often turns one's stomach as he bites into an apparently sound apple he says:

This is one of the best known and most widely distributed enemies of the apple. Newly settled districts have nearly always enjoyed a temporary im-

8

munity from this pest, but experience has shown that the moth can not long be kept out of any commercial apple-growing district. Apparently the ravages of the codling moth are more serious in central and southern latitudes, where two or three, or even as many as four, broods are hatched in a year. However, the campaign against this insect is an annual one, and has to be fought in practically all the commercial orchards in the country.

The principal preventive of damage is the spray-pump, using poison sprays. Paris green is largely used at the present time, but is being generally supplanted by lead arsenate. Thorough spraying at the right time with these insecticides will very greatly reduce the percentage of damage. Indeed, in many cases the work of the insect is practically eliminated. As in dealing with every other insect or fungous pest, thorough spraying at the proper time is highly essential. The proper time in this case is within one week to ten days after the falling of the blossoms. A longer delay can not be made with safety. After about 10 days the calyx, or blossom leaves of the young apple, close and the apple turns to a pendant position. Before this time the newly set fruit stands erect with the calyx lobes open. A poison spray properly distributed falls into this calyx cup and the poison lodges there. As many of the young larvæ enter the apple by eating in at this blossom end they secure with their first meal a taste of poison which usually prevents any further apple-eating on their part.

Special attention should be called to the fact that apple-trees should not be sprayed while in blossom. Spraying at this time is not always totally without value, but in many instances it is not only unnecessary, but even highly dangerous to the crop. Under all circumstances it is very likely to poison the bees working on the apple-blossoms. This sort of damage is far-reaching in many cases; and as the bee is one of the fruit-grower's best friends we can not afford to murder whole swarms in this way.

This early spraying, just after the blossoms fall, will not usually catch quite all the codling moth, even all the first brood. When the second or third brood hatches later in the year a still smaller percentage can be poisoned by the arsenical sprays. Nevertheless it pays to give additional sprayings for this purpose in case the second and third broods appear to be large.

Note the special paragraph in italics, which are ours.

The average manufacturer of spraying-outfits usually gives directions for making the spraying liquids; and so far as we know there is only one who advocates spraying when the trees are in bloom. We respectfully suggest that our readers investigate very carefully, and be sure that they do not buy from parties who give such advice. We do not usually advocate the boycott, but we do think in this case that it is entirely proper to—buy of the other man.

In a number of States, laws have been enacted making it a misdemeanor to spray during blooming-time; but there are many ignorant fruit-growers—stubborn as well—who persist in administering the poisonous mixtures to the very flowers from which bees are gathering pollen and nectar. The result is, many bees are killed, also a great deal of brood. The only thing that can be done when there is no law in force is to labor with neighbors and friends who may be ignorant of or indifferent to the rights of others. Show them that the use of arsenites during the flowering of the trees is both a waste of chemicals and time, and a very great damage to the bees and to the bee-keeper, if not a menace to human beings who might eat honey tinctured with the poisons that bees gather from the trees. Much more can be done through moral suasion than by big talk and bluff, threatening suit for damages.

The first thing for the bee-keepers of any State to do, where there is no anti-spraying legislation, is to have a law enacted at the next session of the legislature.

AGENCY OF BEES IN FERTILIZING FRUIT-BLOSSOMS.

At various times bee-keepers and fruit-growers have come into conflict, the latter affirming that bees puncture ripe fruit, besides interfering more or less during its packing; and the consequence is, that bee-keepers have in some cases been asked to remove their bees, on the plea of being a nuisance. But fruit-growers little realized that they were trying to drive away something necessary to the proper fertilization of fruit blossoms. We are happy to say, however, in later years the two factions are beginning to realize that their industries are mutually interdependent. If any thing, the fruit grower derives very much *more* benefit from bees than the bee-keeper himself; for it is now known, as we shall presently show, that certain kinds of fruit not only depend very largely for their proper development upon the agency of the bee, but in many instances will fail to come to fruitage at all without it. Some years ago a bee-keeper in Massachusetts was obliged to remove his bees to another locality, on complaint of the fruit-growers that they were a nuisance; but after a year or two had passed they were very glad to have the bees back again, because so little fruit set on the trees in proportion to the amount of blossoms appearing. The bee-keeper was recalled; and, as was to be expected, not only more fruit but more perfect fruit development followed.

It is also related that red clover, after being introduced into New Zealand, failed to bear seed. Finally bumble-bees were imported, and then there was seed.

In more recent years, very careful and elaborate experiments have been conducted by scientific men, as well as by bee-keepers and fruit-growers together; and the combined testimony shows almost conclusively that the two industries depend more or less upon each other.

Much has been written in the back volumes of *Gleanings in Bee Culture* on this question; but in the journals for January 15 and February 15, 1894, there appeared a symposium in which a few of the facts were collated. It would be impossible for us to give space to the whole; and we will, therefore, refer only to a few paragraphs. It may seem almost unnecessary to give evidence of that which we already *know* to be true; but many a time ignorant prejudice on the part of fruit growers causes trouble, because they can not, or think they can not, afford to read the papers Let the bee-keeper present to them a few *facts and figures* and they will, if disposed to be fair, acknowledge their mistake.

Well, here are the facts: In *Gleanings in Bee Culture* for Sept. 15, 1891, there appeared a most valuable article from the pen of Prof. A. J. Cook, professor of entomology, then of the Michigan Agricultural College, detailing the experiments that had been made at that place on the subject of fruit-fertilization. He goes on to say that, while there are solitary insects that help to do pollen-scattering, the work they perform is infinitesimal as compared with that of bees, because, unlike the bees that live over winter, they are not present in early spring, when the fruit-trees are in bloom. After calling attention to the fact that it is important, by definite experimentation, that we learn just how necessary the bees are in the pollination of plants, he says :

I tried many experiments last spring. I counted the blossoms on each of two branches, or plants, of apple, cherry, pear, strawberry, raspberry, and clover. One of these, in the case of each fruit or each experiment, was surrounded by cheese-cloth just before the blossoms opened, and kept covered till the blossoms fell off. The apple, pear, and cherry were covered May 4th, and uncovered May 25th and May 19th. The number of blossoms considered varied from 32, the smallest number, to 300, the largest. The trees were examined June 11th, to see what number of the fruit had set. The per cent of blossoms which developed on the covered trees was a little over 2, while almost 20 per cent of the *uncovered* blossoms had developed. Of the pears, not one of the covered developed, while 5 per cent of the uncovered developed fruit. Of the cherries, 8 per cent only of the covered developed, while 40 per cent of

APPLE-TREES IN BLOOM—A. I. ROOT'S ORCHARD.

the uncovered blossoms set their fruit. The strawberries were covered May 18th, and uncovered June 16th. The number of blossoms in each experiment varied from 60 in the least to 212 in the greatest. In these cases, a box covered with cheese-cloth surrounded the plants. The plants were examined June 2d. Eleven per cent of the covered blossoms, and 17 per cent of the uncovered had developed. To show the details, in one case 60 blossoms were considered, 9 of which in the covered lot, and 27 in the uncovered, had developed. That is, three times as many flowers had set in the uncovered as in the covered. In another case of 212 blossoms, the fruit numbered 80 and 104. In a case of 123 blossoms, the number of fruit was 20 and 36. * * * *

Our experiments with clovers were tried on both the white and alsike. While the uncovered heads were full of seeds, the covered ones were entirely seedless. This fully explains the common experience of farmers with these plants.

In the symposium referred to at the outset, the first article of the series was from J. C. Gilliland, who, in the summer of 1893, in a large field of medium red clover that came within 30 feet of his door, covered some blossoms with netting, and around others *not* covered he tied a small thread. During the following August he gathered seed from the covered blossom, and also some from the plants not covered; and by careful counting he found that the latter

gave 21 per cent more seed. His experiments were repeated again, with like results. As bumble-bees visited the field very profusely that year, it seems pretty evident that the larger amount of seed came as a result of cross-fertilization by bees. But this only shows what bumble-bees may do. When it comes to the ordinary *honey*-bees, the per cent in favor of uncovered blossoms as against the covered is very much larger. Witness, for instance, the extract from Prof. Cook's article just given.

Mr. J. F. McIntyre, a bee-keeper, and a delegate at the California State Fruitgrowers' Association for 1893, reports that:

A gentleman stated that he had a friend in this State who started into fruit-growing several years ago, locating 35 miles from any fruit-growing section, or where any bees were located. The first year that his trees blossomed, and in expectancy of at least some returns from his orchard, what should be the result but complete failure! He was advised to procure some bees to aid in the fertilization of the blossoms. He did so, and since then his orchard has been productive.

C. J. Berry, one whose fruit-orchard contains 440 acres, and who is Horticultural Commissioner for Tulare Co., Cal., an inland county that has made great progress in the fruit-industry, gives this valuable testimony:

Bees and fruit go together. I can't raise fruit without bees. Some of the other cranks say I'm a crank; but I notice there is a pretty good following after me, hereabouts, and they keep a-comin.'

Yes, sir, 'e. I have bees all about my big orchard. *Two years in succession I have put netting over some limbs of trees; and, while they blossomed all right, nary fruit; while on the same tree, where limbs were exposed to the aid of bees, plenty of fruit.*

Some three or four years ago, in the State of Michigan, a convention of fruit-growers and bee-men assembled together for the purpose of discussing their common interests; and the fruit-men acknowledged generally that the keeping of bees in the vicinity of their orchards was an important factor in the production of fruit. At the various conventions of the Michigan State Bee-keepers' Association, it has been shown quite conclusively by the bee-keepers who were fruit-growers, that not only greater quantity but more perfect fruit is secured by having the bees in the vicinity of orchards.

Again, Chas. A. Green writes for the *Fruit Grower*, published at Rochester, N. Y., an article from which, for lack of space, we shall be able to quote only a couple of paragraphs:

It has now become demonstrated that many kinds of fruits, if not all kinds, are greatly benefited by the bees, and that a large portion of our fruit, such as the apple, pear, and particularly the plum, would be barren were it not for the helpful work of the honey-bee. This discovery is largely owing to Prof. Waite, of the Agricultural Department at Washington. Prof. Waite covered the blossoms of pears apples, and plums, with netting, excluding the bees, and found that such protected blossoms of many varieties of apple and pear yielded no fruit. In some varieties there was no exception to the rule, and he was convinced that large orchards of Bartlett pears, planted distant from other varieties, would be utterly barren were it not for the work of the bees, and even then they could not be profitably grown unless every third or fourth row in the orchard was planted to Clapp's Favorite, or some other variety that was capable of fertilizing the blossoms of the Bartlett. In other words, he found that the Bartlett pear could no more fertilize its own blossoms than the Crescent strawberry. We have already learned that certain kinds of plums will not fertilize their own blossoms, such as the Wild Goose, etc.

The fruit-growers of the country are greatly indebted to Prof. Waite for the discovery he has made. The lesson is, that fruit-growers must become interested in bees, *and I do not doubt that within a few years it will be a rare thing to find a fruit-grower who does not keep honey-bees,* the prime object being to employ bees in carrying pollen from one blossom to another in the fields of small fruits as well as for the large fruits.

Mr. F. A. Merritt, of Andrew, Ia., testifies as follows:

THE TWO SIDES OF A TREE.

Our apple-orchard is situated in such a way that it is exposed to both the north and south winds About four years ago, as the trees on the south row (Transcendents, that throws out a heavy growth of foliage at the same time it blooms) began to open its bloom, a heavy south wind prevailed for about five days. I noticed, during this period, that the bees could not touch the bloom on the south side of these trees, but worked merrily on the more sheltered limbs of the north side. What was the result? Those limbs on the north side were well loaded with fruit, while on the south side there was almost none to be seen. Does this prove that these trees depend on the aid of insects to fertilize the bloom? I leave it to the judgment of the reader.

Mr. G. M. Doolittle, in winding up his article for the symposium above referred to, says:

Again, I wish to note, as a matter of history, that, during the past season of 1883, very little buckwheat honey was secured from the buckwheat regions of the State of New York—so little that we have had, for the first time in my remembrance, buckwheat honey selling in our markets for nearly if not quite the same price as No. 1 clover honey, while it usually sells for about two-thirds the price of clover honey. And what has been the result? Why, the unheard-of thing of buckwheat grain bringing 75 cts. a bushel, on account of its scarcity, while the best of white wheat is selling at only 62 cts.! As a general thing, buckwheat brings from one-half to two-thirds the price of wheat. That it now brings nearly one-fourth more than the best of wheat tells very largely, under the circumstances, on the side of the bee.

Mr. H. A. March, of Puget Sound, Wash., one of the most extensive seed-growers of the Pacific coast, testifies that he found bees very valuable, and that seed was very much more abundant when bees were allowed to work on the flowers; and he says that stone fruits seemed almost incapable of self-fertilization, as he had fully proved by trying to grow peaches under glass.

The editor of the *Rural New-Yorker* put in his paper, unsolicited, this short pithy paragraph:

In those great greenhouses near Boston, where early cucumbers are grown, it is always necessary to have one or two hives of bees inside to fertilize the flowers. No bees, no cucumbers, unless men go around with a brush and dust the pollen from one flower to another.

Mr. J. F. Becker, of Morgansville, N. J., has eight greenhouses where he grows cucumbers, and, attached to each one of them, with an entrance on the inside as well as outside, he has two colonies of bees. He found that, without them, he could not successfully fertilize the blossoms of the vines, and, consequently, could get no cucumbers. With them he is entirely successful in growing the finest of cucumbers for the early market, where he gets fancy prices. While the bees do their part of the work, many of them are lost in the attempt to find their way back to the hive. They fly against the glass, where, of course, they worry themselves to death. This makes it necessary to supply fresh colonies every now and then: but even this expense is made up many times over in the crop of cucumbers.

In the spring of 1892 the late Allen Pringle, of Selby, Ont., one of the leading bee-keepers of Canada, testified that he was summoned to appear before a legislative committee of the House of Assembly of Ontario, to give evidence of the agency of bees in scattering pollen. The Minister of Agriculture summoned not only the leading bee-

INTERIOR OF CUCUMBER - GREENHOUSE ; HIVE WITH ENTRANCE INSIDE.

men, but those engaged in growing fruit, to present the facts, experiences, and the pros and cons on both sides. Not only this, but the scientists were also summoned from Ottawa and Guelph. Mr. Pringle goes on to say, that "the horticulturists, with one single exception, admitted the valuable and indispensable offices performed by honey-bees in the fertilization of our fruit-bloom. And this was corroborated and confirmed by the entomologists. . . . Prof. James Fletcher, the Dominion Entomologist, said bees did ' not visit in dull weather, and then we have but little fruit in consequence.' . . As to bees injuring fruit, there is no direct evidence." Mr. Pringle also says :

I have kept bees for 30 years, and have grown fruit and clover alongside for the same period. I have

also studied and experimented somewhat in this line as well as many others. As to some kinds of fruit — notably apples — I have observed that if, during the bloom, the weather was such that neither winged insects nor the wind (being wet and cold) could perform their function with the flowers, the fruit was lacking. When the weather at other times was favorable and the bloom abundant, I have excluded the bees from certain portions of the tree, only to find the fruit also excluded — but only from those reserved portions. . . .

The fruit-growers agreed that the "bees play a very important part in cross-fertilization, and, therefore, should not be destroyed;" that "we are very generally dependent upon insects for the fertilization of our orchard. To destroy them to any extent would be very injurious to fruit-growers."

The consensus of the meeting was, that "bee-keepers and fruit-growers are of great help to each other, and even indispensable, if each class is to obtain the best results in their work."

Mr. Frank Benton, lately in the employ of the Department of Agriculture, Washington, D. C., in one of the Government Bulletins for 1894, page 254, commenting on the agency of bees in the fertilization of fruit-blossoms, says :

The facts they have brought forward are gradually becoming more widely known among fruit-growers and bee-keepers, and additional evidence accumulates. A case illustrating very clearly the value of bees in an orchard has recently come to the notice of the writer, and its authenticity is confirmed by correspondence with the parties named, who are gentlemen of long and extensive experience in fruit-growing, recognized in their locality as being authorities, particularly in regard to cherry culture. The facts are these: For several years the cherry crop of Vaca Valley, in Solano Co., Cal., has not been good, although it was formerly quite sure. The partial or complete failures have been attributed to north winds, chilling rains, and similar climatic conditions; but in the minds of Messrs. Bassford, of Cherry Glen, these causes did not sufficiently account for all the cases of failure.

These gentlemen recollected that formerly, when the cherry crops were good, wild bees were very plentiful in the valley, and hence thought perhaps the lack of fruit since most of the bees had disappeared might be due to imperfect distribution of the pollen of the blossoms. To test the matter they placed, therefore, several hives of bees in their orchard in 1890. The result was striking, for the Bassford orchard bore a good crop of cherries, while other growers in the valley who had no bees found their crops entire or partial failures. This year (1891) Messrs. Bassford had some sixty-five hives of bees in their orchard, and Mr. H. A. Bassford writes to the Entomologist: "Our crop was good this season, and we attribute it to the bees;" and he adds further: "Since we have been keeping bees our cherry crop has been much larger than formerly, while those orchards nearest us, five miles from here, where no bees are kept, have produced but light crops."

Again, J. E. Crane writes in this same symposium an article so full of pith and point that we can not forbear publishing the whole of it here in permanent form:

HOW BLOSSOMS ARE FERTILIZED; WHY SOME FLOWERS ARE MORE GAUDY THAN OTHERS; EXPERIMENTS OF CHARLES DARWIN.

Many volumes have been published in several different languages upon the fertilization of flowers—the first by Christian Conrad Springel, in 1793; yet the subject attracted but little attention until thirty or forty years later, since which time many botanists have given the subject much attention. Our most eminent botanists now classify flowering plants in their relation to fertilization into two classes: *Anemophilous* and *Entomophilous*—literally, wind-lovers and insect-lovers. The flowers fertil-

them, and thus be carried from flower to flower. In this class of plants or flowers many ingenious arrangements are provided to secure cross-fertilization. One sex is found in one blossom, and the other in another, sometimes on the same plant, as in the squash and melon families. In other species the sexes are found upon separate plants, as the willow-trees. In some plants the pistils appear first, and become fertile before the stamens ripen their pollen. In others the stamens shed their vitalizing dust before the stigma of the pistil is ready to receive it.

The common red raspberry matures its pistils first, so that, unless the bees or other insects carry the pollen to it from other earlier blossoms, the fruit is imperfect.

CUCUMBER-BLOSSOM WITH A BEE ON IT; CAUGHT IN THE ACT.

ized by the wind are dull in color, and nearly destitute of odor or honey. The sexes are frequently separated, either on the same or on separate plants. They produce a superabundance of pollen, light and dry, easily transported by air or wind.

Pines, firs, and other conifera, are familiar examples, which sometimes fill a forest with "showers of sulphur" when shedding their pollen. Our nut-bearing trees are examples among deciduous trees. The grasses and grains are familiar to all. A kernel of corn will grow as well alone as with other plants; but "the ear will not fill" unless it can receive the wind-wafted pollen from neighboring stalks. On the other hand, those plants which seem to have need of bees or other insects to carry their pollen from one flower to another have more showy blossoms, with bright colors, or white, which are showy at dusk, else they give out a strong perfume or nectar, or both. The pollen grains are moist, glutinous, hairy, or otherwise so constructed as to adhere to the insects that visit

The partridge-berry is very interesting. The blossoms upon about half of the plants produce their stamens first; the other half, the pistil. In a week or ten days the order is reversed in the same flowers.

Many flowers that invite insects appear to be capable of self-fertilization, and often are; yet the pollen from a neighboring plant of the same species seems more potent. Some flowers are constructed with stamens so placed that their pollen can not fall upon the stigma of the same flower, and have special adaptation for the transport of pollen by insects from one flower to another. One curious plant produces small inconspicuous flowers early in the season, capable of self-fertilization; later in the season it produces more showy flowers that can become fertile only through the agency of insects.

Many plants remain constantly barren unless they receive the visits of insects. Some of your readers have doubtless observed how the fuschia or begonia never produces seed in a closed room; yet, when set out of doors in summer, they seed abundantly. Still other plants never produce seed because the insects that feed upon their blossoms have not been imported with the plants.

But this is a large subject, and to me one of great interest, as I study the many ways the Author of nature has provided for the best good of all his works. A large number of examples have been given of bees as agents in the production of fruit and seed, and I will give one or two more.

Mr. H. A. March, of Puget Sound, while here last summer, informed me that he produced large quantities of cauliflower seed, and found bees very valuable, as the seed was much more abundant when bees were provided to work on the flowers.

the Creator has desired cross-fertilization among plants, and has wisely provided for it in a multitude of ways; and the chances of such fertilization appear to be as great among plants as among our bees, for which such special arrangement has been made. We might assume it to be valuable or necessary, even if we could see no good reason for it. We all know that birds or domestic animals will prove fruitful for one or perhaps several generations in spite of the intermarriage of near relations; but it is, I believe, the universal experience that such unions are most unwise, and, as a rule, prove injurious.

Some twenty-five or thirty years ago Charles Darwin, in studying this subject, and noting the provisions of nature for the cross-fertilization of

FRUIT-TREES IN BLOOM IN THE AUTHORS' ORCHARD.

The stone fruits seem almost incapable of self-fertilization, as is often proven by trying to grow peaches under glass, success seeming to come only when bees are provided while the trees are in bloom. A curious problem has presented itself to the horticulturists of this country for a number of years past, in the refusal of some varieties of the Chickasaw plum to produce fruit in the Northern States unless set near some other variety or species of plum, that insects might carry the pollen from one to the other. Such a tree I can see from my window as I write, that is a bank of bloom every spring, but has never, to my knowledge, produced a crop of fruit.

Now, suppose it were true that all trees or plants that produce fruit or seed of value for the use of man would become fertile without the aid of bees or other insects, would it prove them of no value? Not at all. Enough has been written to show that

flowers, became so much interested in it that he began a large number of experiments to test the value of insects in cross-fertilization, and the effects of cross and self fertilization upon plants. His experiments were conducted with great care, and continued through several years; and his book on the effects of "Cross and Self Fertilization," describing these experiments, containing several hundred pages, is very interesting reading to say the least.

Of some 125 plants experimented with, more than half were, with insects excluded, either quite sterile or produced less than half as much seed as when insects were allowed to visit them. Among his catalog of these plants I notice the white and red clover. His experiments with these are very similar to those of Prof. Cook, late of Michigan Agricultural College. He says, page 361, of red clover, "One hundred flower-heads on a plant protected by a net did not produce a single seed, while 100 heads on plants growing outside, which were visited by bees, yielded 68 grains weight of seeds; and as 80 seeds weighed two grains, the hundred heads must have yielded 2720 seeds." His experience with white clover was nearly the same.

Another most interesting result of his experiments was that plants grown from seed of self-fertilized flowers were, as a rule, when grown side by side with seed of cross-fertilized flowers, much less vigorous, although in other respects the conditions were as nearly alike as it is possible to make them. On page 371 he says, "The simple fact of the necessity in many cases for extraneous aid in the transport of the pollen, and the many contrivances for this purpose, render it highly probable that some great benefit is thus gained; and this conclusion has now been firmly established by the superior growth, vigor, and fertility of plants of crossed parentage over those of self-fertilized parentage."

In *Gleanings in Bee Culture* for June 1, 1894, Prof. Cook furnishes this additional:

Prof. Bailey, the very able horticulturist of Cornell University, writes: "Bees are much more efficient agents of pollenation than wind, for our fruits; *and their absence is always deleterious.*"

The Division of Vegetable Pathology, of the Department of Agriculture, has just issued a most valuable bulletin on "Pollenation of Pear-flowers," by Norman B. Waite. Mr. Waite says: "Incidental mention has been made of insect-visitors. We should not proceed without laying some stress upon the importance of these visits. The common honey-bee is the most regular, important, and abundant visitor, and probably does more good than any other species." He says, further, that cool or rainy weather interferes *seriously* with insect-visits. Many varieties (22 out of 364 of those he experimented with), says Mr. Waite, *require* cross-pollenation; and the pollen must be from a different variety. Bees and other insects are the agents of the transportation of pollen. In summing up, Mr. Waite says—and this from crucial decisive experiments: "Plant mixed orchards, or, at least, avoid planting solid blocks of one variety. *Be sure* that there are sufficient bees in the neighborhood to visit the blossoms properly. When feasible, endeavor to favor insect-visits by selecting sheltered situations, or by planting windbreaks."

Again, E. C. Green, of the Ohio Experiment Station, for June 1st writes:

Quite an interesting fact came under my observation this winter in tomato-forcing, along this line. We had in one house about 200 Dwarf Champions that were planted in August; and by the time winter set in they were as fine and thrifty plants as one could wish to see, and setting their fruit nicely. We felt glad to think what a nice crop of tomatoes we should have; but when January came, and they began to ripen up their fruit, the bulk of it was about the size of hickorynuts, and *without any seeds.*

The tomato, as you know, is a bisexual flowering plant, but in this case it is evident that the pollen from the same flower was what is called "self-irritant." If bees or some other cause had carried the pollen from one flower to another, or one plant to the other, there would have been a good crop. I have been doing something in cross-fertilizing tomatoes this winter, and have been surprised at the case with which they crossed, having used the Potato-leaf, Dwarf Champion, Ponderosa, Peach, and several of the common kinds, making in all about 40 crosses. I do not think I shall fail to get seed except in a few of them. I expect that from the seed I shall get a lot of "mongrels," as one writer in GLEANINGS calls such crosses; but I prefer to call them crossbreeds, as "hybrid" has a different meaning.

Still again, Prof. V. H. Lowe, of the Geneva Experiment Station, New York, in 1899 covered a certain set of small pear-trees, as it was not practicable to use large ones in a hood of sheeting. This hood was large enough to sit down over the whole tree, something in the form of a bag, and the lower end of it was tied around the trunk of the tree. The object of this was to keep out insects, ants, bees, and any thing, in fact, that might assist in pollenizing the blossoms. On all of these trees so covered, there was a large number of buds, and all the conditions were favorable for a good crop, except that the flight of insects was entirely cut off. Now, then, for the results: Out of the whole lot of trees covered, there was just one fruit. On another set of trees of the same sort and size not covered, there were 145. In the other case, where it was not practicable to envelop the whole tree, one large limb, for instance, would be enclosed in the bag, the mouth of the bag being tied around the trunk of the limb. In one such instance there were 2483 buds on an apple-tree that were thus covered with the sheeting. Out of that number just one fruit matured. There was plenty of fruit on other portions of the tree where the limbs were not covered. In one case, where the sheeting broke open so that insects could get in, there were 13 perfect fruits from 818 buds. It was clearly shown that bees or other insects play a most important part in the pollenation of average fruit-trees.

Prof. Bailey, the very able horticulturist of Cornell University, writes: "Bees are much more efficient agents of pollenation than wind, in our fruits, and their absence is always deleterious."

The Division of Vegetable Pathology, of the Department of Agriculture, Washington, D. C., has issued a most interesting bulletin on "Pollenation of Pear-flowers," by Norman B. Waite. Mr. Waite says: "Incidental mention has been made of insect-visitors. We should not proceed without laying some stress upon the importance of these visits. The common honey-bee is the most regular, important, and abundant visitor, and probably does more good than any other species."

At a joint meeting of the National Pomological Society and the National Bee-keepers' Association, occuring on Sept. 12, 1901, at Buffalo, a number of valuable papers were read—all of them testifying to the invaluable office of the bee in pollenating fruit-blossoms. Space will permit us to give only two references. Prof. James Fletcher, of the Ottawa Experiment Station, among other things said :

It will be found that not only are flowers absolutely necessary to bees as the source of their food —nectar and pollen—but that bees and other insects are no less necessary to most flowers, so that their perpetuation may be secured.

This fact should be recognized by the fruit-grower above all others; for were it not for insects, and particularly for the honey-bee, his crop of fruits would be far less than they are every year, and even in some cases he would get no fruit at all.

Failure in the fruit crop is more often due, I think, to dull or damp weather at the time of blossoming, which prevents insects from working actively in the flowers, than to any other cause.

At the same joint meeting of bee and fruit men, H. W. Collinwood, already mentioned, editor of the *Rural New-Yorker*, said :

We can easily forgive the bee his short working days when we consider the good he does. There is no question about the debt fruit-growers owe him. People talk about the wind and other insects in fertilizing our flowers; but I am confident that any man who will really take the time and pains to investigate for himself will see that the bee is nearly the whole story. I have seen the certain results of his good work in a neighbor's orchard. Those bees broke the trees down just as truly as though they had climbed on the trees by the million and pulled on them. The appearance of those trees after a few years of bee-keeping would have convinced any fair-minded man that our little buzzing friends are true partners of the fruit-grower.

In addition to all this we may state that there has been a demand of late on the part of a large number of extensive fruit-growers of Wisconsin, Michigan, New York, and Pennsylvania, asking bee-keepers to locate a few colonies in orchards near which there have been no bees. Indeed, the fruit-growers have offered to furnish the space and the buildings necessary to accommodate the bees and appliances, free of charge to the bee-keepers. It is needless to say that the latter have availed themselves of the opportunity, for honey from fruit-blossoms is some of the very finest ever produced, and the fruit-grower profits immensely in his turn.

In one of the leading fruit-journals of the country, *Better Fruit*, for July, 1909, appears a very strong article from the Oregon College Experiment Station, showing the almost indispensable service performed by bees in pollenating fruit-trees. It is shown conclusively that many varieties are sterile to their own pollen; that wind itself is not a very important factor in carrying it from one tree to another; that the bee is practically the *sole agent* in doing this important work.

If any one desires to secure more facts relative to flower-fertilization, he may consult " Mueller's Fertilization of Flowers," an authority on the subject; also see POLLEN, in this work. See also "Bees and Fruit," issued by the publishers.

G.

GALLBERRY. (*Ilex glabra*). This produces quite a quantity of honey in the South, of light color and high quality. It is a species of holly, which grows to the size of a scrubby bush. It is abundant in North Carolina, Georgia, South Carolina, and adjacent States, and is growing more to yield a crop, for the reason it blooms in May, when the weather is settled and fine.

The quality of the honey is excellent, being classed as white. Though a considerable quantity of it is actually produced in the South, it is seldom shipped, on account

GALLBERRY, OR HOLLY.

and adjacent States, and is growing more plentiful, for it springs up wherever the forests have been cut off. Mr. J. J. Wilder, of Cordele, Ga., states that there are thousands of gallberry bee-locations wholly unoccupied at present, and that it seldom fails of an active local demand. Shakespeare asks, "What's in a name?" but in our opinion "holly" would be a much better name than "gallberry," which rather suggests bitterness. "Holly honey" would sound romantic.

GLOVES FOR HANDLING BEES. Although a good many apiarists work with bare hands and bare wrists, there are a few who prefer to use gloves with long wrists, and quite a large number who use them with fingers and thumbs cut off. If the bees are hybrids, and extracting is carried on during

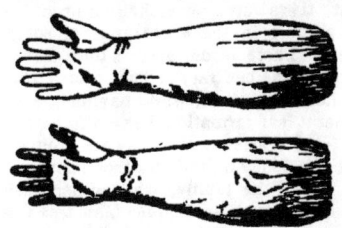

the robbing season, it is a great convenience to use something that protects the back of the hands and wrists, leaving the fingers bare, so that, for all practical purposes of manipulation, one can work as well with protectors as without. See EXTRACTING.

Lady bee-keepers and men who are at all timid, and a very small number who seem to be seriously affected by even one sting, might use gloves to great advantage — especially the last-mentioned class, where two or three stings might prove to be serious if not fatal.

As to the kind of gloves, some use buckskin or dogskin with loose flowing sleeves sewed on at the wrists, with a rubber cord gathered in the end to fit over the elbow. Then there is a kind of glove made of heavy drilling soaked in linseed oil or white-lead paint, made specially for the purpose, shown in the illustration. As sent out by the supply-dealers they are not coated, as some prefer to use them plain; but where the bees are especially cross, the fabric will need to be further reinforced with paint or linseed oil.

For further particulars regarding bee-dress, see VEILS.

GLUCOSE. This name is applied to the thick viscous liquid obtained by the concentration of a solution coming from the incomplete hydrolysis of starch. The word is mis-applied by a great many, especially in the sugar-cane belt, for the reducing sugars present in the cane. From a purely chemical side, glucose means the sugar dextrose, so with these various applications of the word some little confusion exists. In the commercial world, however, the first is the accepted meaning of the word. In the United States the source of glucose is corn starch, with a little made from potato starch, but in Germany all is made from potato starch.

Its manufacture consists in the heating of the freed starch with water, and a small percentage of hydrochloric acid under pressure. The process is carefully conducted, and stopped at the proper point of hydrolysis. The liquid is neutralized with soda, and concentrated to the desired consistency, which is a liquid of about 15 to 20 per cent water. Formerly sulphuric acid was the acid used for conversion; but on account of its carrying arsenic its use was stopped. The solids of commercial glucose consist of about one-third dextrose and two-thirds dextrine. The dextrins present in commercial glucose are of a different character from those present in floral honey or honey-dew, and on this property its presence in honey can be easily detected.

By increasing the amount of acid, and also lengthening the time of heating, products are made which contain more dextrose and less dextrin. These are known commercially as "70, "80, and "anhydrous "starch sugar." They are, for the most part, solid. Their use in honey adulteration is very rare, and, if used, their detection is comparatively easy for a trained chemist.

Commercial glucose is sometimes known as corn syrup.

The ease with which commercial glucose can be detected when mixed with honey has led to its disuse except in mixtures so labeled. See HONEY, ADULTERATION OF.

GOLDENROD. This is one of the most important sources of honey during the fall months in many localities in the United States—important, not for any great amount of honey, for there is never enough so that

THREE SPECIES OF GOLDENROD.

it gets into the market, but important because it comes at a time of the year when it helps to keep the bees busy, and at the same time serves to make up for the loss in stores during the late summer.

There are something like 80 distinct species of goldenrod in the United States. Of these, some forty odd are found in the northern part of the country. All of the species have yellow flowers, save one, a slender wandlike plant (*S. bicolor*) that has whitish or silverlike flower-heads—a departure from the general family habit. This species appears to be comparatively rare, and even when discovered is not readily recognized as

GOLDENROD (*Solidago Canadensis.*)

belonging to genus *Solidago*, or golden-rod. The number of species is so very large that botanists have made no attempt to classify all of them. Indeed, some of the species seem to merge so gradually from one into the other that it is difficult to distinguish them readily. Even botanists are confused. But there are, nevertheless, pronounced differences in the appearance of some of them. There is one species that grows all through the central-northern States, *Solidago lanceolata,* that, while having the same general leaf-formation, has a different flower from that shown. They are grouped in flat top clusters, unlike other members of the family, while other species such as *Solidago Canadensis* have flower-clusters that terminate in a point.

At one time there was considerable talk about making goldenrod the national flower, for the reason that the general family is more widely scattered over the country than almost any other flower.

The honey is usually very thick, and of a rich golden color much like the blossoms. When first gathered, it has, like the honey of most other fall flowers, a rather rank weedy smell and taste; but after it has thoroughly ripened, it is rich and pleasant. On getting the first taste of goldenrod honey, one might think he would never like any other; but, like many kinds, one soon tires of the peculiar aromatic flavor, and goes back to clover honey as the great universal staple to be used with bread and butter.

GRANULATED HONEY. See CANDIED HONEY.

GUAJILLA. See HUAJILLA.

H.

HANDLING BEES. See FRAMES, TO MANIPULATE; ANGER OF BEES; also STINGS, and HIVES.

HAULING BEES. See MOVING BEES.

HEARTSEASE (*Polygonum persicaria*). This is one of a large family of honey-bearing plants of which the common buckwheat is one. Heartsease, sometimes known as knotweed or heartweed, and (perhaps incorrectly) smartweed, is scattered over certain portions of the West, particularly in Illinois, Kansas, and Nebraska. In the last named it reaches a height of from three to five feet, and grows luxuriantly on all waste and stubble lands. The flowers in clusters are generally purple, and, in rare instances, white. It yields in Nebraska, and other States in that section of the country, immense quantities of honey. One bee-keeper, Mr. T. R. Delong, at the North American convention held in Lincoln, Neb , in October, 1896, reported that two of his colonies yielded each 450 lbs. of extracted, and that the average for his entire apiary was 250 lbs. per colony—all heartsease. While perhaps these yields were exceptionally large, quite a number of other bee-keepers reported at the same convention an average of 200 lbs. from the same source. When we visited Nebraska last there were acres and acres of this honey-plant over the plains as far as the eye could reach ; and as it yields honey from August till frost, one is not surprised at the enormous yields.

The extracted honey varies in color from a light to a dark amber; and the flavor,

A FINE FIELD OF HEARTSEASE.

while not quite up to that of white honey, is very good. Heartsease comb honey, in point of color, is almost as white as the clover. The extracted granulates in very fine crystals, and looks very much like the candied product of any white honey. Care should be taken in liquefying, as heartsease honey is injured more easily, and to a greater extent, by overheating, than any other kind.

HIVE-MAKING. Unless one is so situated that freights are high, and unless, also, he is a mechanic, or a natural genius in "making things," he had better let hive-making alone. Hives can be bought, usually, with freight added, for a great deal less than the average bee-keeper can make them himself, if we consider spoiled lumber, sawed fingers, and the expense of buzz-saws; and, besides, hives made in the large factories, where they are turned out by the thousands, by special machinery run by skilled workmen, are much more accurately cut, as a general thing.

The following letter from a practical planing-mill man, who ought and does know what he is talking about, sets forth the actual facts as they are:

ELIAS BAMBERGER
Manufacturer of
SASH, DOORS, BLINDS
Contractors' and Builders' Supplies,
including all Kinds of Window Glass.
Cor. Exchange and Adams Sts.
Estimates Furnished on Application.
Freeport, Ill., June 11, 1907.
The A. I. Root Co., Medina, Ohio.
Gentlemen:—I received five of your A E525-10 hives yesterday, and find that I can not make my own hives and supplies as cheap as yours and use the same quality of lumber. You can see by the head of this letter that if any one can make hives cheaper than your prices or any of the so-called "trust hive" manufacturers, I ought to be able to do it; but, using the same quality of lumber, I can not.
(signed) JOHN H. BAMBERGER.

But there is lots of fun in making things, even if they are not so well made; and there are some rainy or wintry days in the year, when, if one is a farmer, for instance, he can as well as not, and at little or no expense for time, make a few hives and other "fixin's." Again, if one lives in a foreign country he may not be able to get the hives that we shall recommend.

REQUISITES OF A GOOD HIVE.

While it is very important to have good well-made hives for the bees, we would by no means encourage the idea that the hive is going to insure a crop of honey. As the veteran Mr. Gallup used to say, "A good swarm of bees would store almost as much honey in a half-barrel or nail-keg as in the most elaborate and expensive hive made, other things being equal." This is supposing we had a good colony in the height of the honey-season. If the colony were small, it would do much better if put into a hive so small that the bees could nearly or quite fill it, thus economizing the animal heat, that they might keep up the temperature for brood-rearing, and the working of wax. Also, should the bees get their nail-keg full of honey, unless more room were given them at just the right moment a considerable loss of honey would be the result. The thin walls of the nail-keg would hardly be the best economy for a wintering hive, nor for a summer hive either, unless it were well shaded from the direct rays of the sun.

P. H. Elwood, of Starkville, N. Y., who owns over 1300 colonies, said in *Gleanings in Bee Culture*, April 15, 1891, "A good hive must fill two requirements reasonably well to be worthy of that name. 1. It must be a good home for the bees; 2. It must in addition be so constructed as to be convenient to perform the various operations required by modern bee-keeping. The first of these requirements is filled very well by a good box or straw hive. Bees will store as much honey in these hives as in any, and in the North they will winter and spring as well in a straw hive as in any other. They do not, however, fill the second requirement; and to meet this, the movable-frame hive was invented."

Under the subject of HIVES, a little further on, will be shown styles and the special features that belong to each. But there is only one hive that is used largely throughout the United States, and that is the Langstroth—that is, it embodies the Langstroth dimensions. We start first with the frame, 17¼ long by 9¼ deep. This establishes the length and depth of the hive. As to width, that depends upon the number of frames used. Some bee-keepers prefer eight, perhaps the majority of them; others ten, and still others twelve frames. Where one runs for extracted honey the ten-frame width should have the preference, especially in the South. If one produces only comb honey the eight-frame-hive width should be the one selected, particularly in the North, where the honey-flow is of short duration and is principally from clover and basswood. The selection of the frame, and the number to the hive, then, determines the dimensions of the hive itself.

We said the Langstroth is the standard throughout the United States; but of late there has been a tendency toward a frame of the same length, but two inches deeper. There is also a tendency to go to the other extreme in adopting a frame of Langstroth length, but two or three inches shallower, using two stories of such a hive for a single brood-nest.

On account of the diverse notions of bee-keepers, and the peculiarities of locality, it would hardly be worth while to give general directions for the manufacture of any one hive; and, besides, no printed directions will give as good an idea of the construction of a hive as the very thing itself. For these and other reasons it would be far better for the one who intends to make hives to send to some manufacturer for a sample in the flat, all complete. With the several pieces for patterns he will then know exactly the shape and dimensions, how to make the rabbets, and in general how the hive is constructed in every detail. If one does not find on the market just such a hive as suits his notion, of course he sees, or thinks he sees, " in his mind's eye" just what he wants to make; but in that case we would advise him to make a sample or two before he makes very many of them; for nine times out of ten — yes, ninety-nine times out of one hundred — he will discard the one of his " own get-up," and adopt some standard made by manufacturers generally.

HIVES based on Langstroth dimensions are the standard. Some thirty years ago there were in use the American, Gallup, Langstroth, Adair, and Quinby frames. All of these required, of course, hives of different dimensions. Between the Adair, the Gallup, and the American there was but very little difference, comparatively, as they were square, and very nearly of a size. The Langstroth was long and shallow—the shallowest frame that had then been introduced; and the Quinby, having about the same proportions, was the largest frame in general use. By consulting the diagram containing the different sizes of frames it will be seen that there are practically two classes—the square and the oblong. As there would be but very little difference, theoretically and practically, between the results secured with a Gallup, American, and Adair, we will consider the arguments for the square frame.

The Jumbo frame will be considered later on under the head of LARGE HIVES.

In nature, bees have a tendency to make a brood-nest in the form of a sphere; patches of brood are more inclined to be circular than square or oblong. Theoretically, then, a circular frame would be the best; but as that would not be practicable, owing to the difficulty in the construction of the frame and hive, obviously the square frame would come the nearest in conforming to nature and a perfect cube for the hive. The square frame, as a rule, called for a hive in the exact shape of a cube. If, for instance, the frame was 12 inches square, outside di-

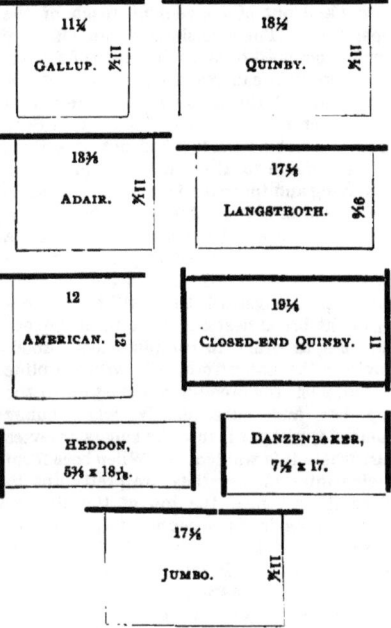

mensions, then the hive, if the combs were spaced 1¼ inches apart, and 12¼ inches wide inside, should take in just nine American frames. Such a hive, it was argued, would conserve the heat of the bees to the best advantage, would give the greatest cubical contents for a given amount of lumber—barring, of course, the perfect sphere. As it economized heat in winter, it would winter bees better than a hive having oblong frames.

All of this seemed to be very pretty in theory; and there are some users of square frames who insist that the theory is borne out by actual experience. But the great majority of bee-keepers, after having tried the square and the oblong frame, finally decided in favor of the Langstroth for the following reasons:

THE LANGSTROTH FRAME AND HIVE, AND WHY THEY BECAME THE STANDARDS.

1. A shallow frame permits the use of a low flat hive that can easily be tiered up one, two, three, and four stories high. This is a great advantage when one is running for extracted honey, as all he has to do when the bees require more room is to add upper stories as fast as the bees require them, and then at the end of the season extract at his leisure. Square or deep hives can not be tiered up very high without becoming top-heavy and out of convenient reach of the operator. 2. The long shallow frame is more easily uncapped because the blade of the uncapping-knife can reach clear across it. 3. The shape of the Langstroth frame favors an extractor of good proportion. 4. A deep frame is not as easily lifted out of a hive; is more liable to kill bees in the process of removing and inserting frames. 5. The shallow frame is better adapted for box honey. It is well known that bees, after forming a brood-circle, are inclined to put sealed honey just over the brood. In a frame as shallow as the Langstroth, there will be less honey in the brood-nest and more in the boxes; for bees, in order to complete their brood-circle in the Langstroth, will, with a prolific queen, push the brood-line almost up to the top-bar, and, consequently, when honey comes in, will put it into the supers or boxes just where it is wanted. 6. When bees form their winter cluster they are pretty apt to place it very near the top of the hive or cover. This is on account of the greater warmth at that point, for heated air has a tendency to rise. It sometimes happens, in case of the square frame, that the bees will eat all of the honey or stores away from near the top of the hive; and as the cold weather continues, the bees simply starve, not being able to move the cluster down into the colder part of the hive where the stores are. In the case of the Langstroth, the cluster may be either at the front or rear. As the stores are consumed it will move toward the stores, and still keep within the warmest part of the hive.

But in actual experience bees seem to winter just as well on one frame as another; and as the shallow frame is better adapted to box honey, bee-keepers naturally turned toward the shallower frame, with the result that now probably three-fourths of all the frames in the United States are of Langstroth dimensions; and whatever advantage there may be in favor of the square shape, the bee-keeper is able to buy standard goods so much cheaper that he adopts the standard Langstroth frame.

FRAMES SHALLOWER AND DEEPER THAN THE LANGSTROTH.

Of late there has been a tendency toward a frame still shallower than the Langstroth, and what is called the Heddon; but as eight or ten of these frames, or one section, make too small a brood-nest, two sets of such frames are used to accommodate a whole colony. Of the Heddon hive we shall have more to say later on.

There is another class of bee-keepers who feel that the Langstroth is not quite deep enough, and who, therefore, prefer the Quinby. They argue that ten such frames, or frames Langstroth length, and two inches deeper, are none too large for a prolific queen, and that these big colonies swarm less, get more honey, and winter better. Of these latter, we shall have more to say under the subject of "Large vs. Small Hives."

THE ORIGINAL LANGSTROTH HIVE.

The old original Langstroth hive that father Langstroth put out contained ten frames 17⅞x9¼. Each hive had a portico, and cleats nailed around the top edge to support a telescoping cover, under which were placed the comb-honey boxes, or big cushions, for winter. There was a time when this style of hive was the only one used; but owing to the fact that it was not simple in construction, that the portico was a splendid harboring-place for cobwebs, and gave the bees encouragement for clustering out on hot days instead of attending to their knitting inside of their hives, a far simpler form of hive was devised. The Simplicity, first brought out by A. I. Root, having Langstroth dimensions, was the result. Instead of having telescoping covers the contiguous edges of the hive were beveled so as to shed water and give in effect a telescoping cover. The cover and bottom of this hive were exactly alike, the entrance being formed by shoving the hive forward on the bottom, thus making an entrance as wide or narrow as seemed most desirable. The upper story was exactly the same as the lower one or brood-nest—so, taking it all in all, the hive was simplicity itself. But it had one serious defect, and that was the beveled edge. It was found to be practically impossible at times, on account of the bee-glue, to separate the upper story from the lower one without breaking or splitting the bevel. Finally there was introduced a hive very much the same, having straight square edges, and along with it came the feature of dovetailing or locking the corners, as shown in the hive below.

This hive was introduced in 1889, and seemed to meet with the general approbation of bee-keepers. It embodied in the

main the Langstroth dimensions, but used eight instead of ten frames; for at the time it was introduced, nearly every one preferred

eight frames. The original Dovetailed hive had a flat cover, and a bottom-board made the same as the cover, except that there were side-cleats to raise the hive off the bottom-board.

Since that time there have been modifications of the hive, and it is now made in eight, ten, twelve, and sixteen frame sizes. The cover is made of six pieces. The body is locked at the corners, and the bottom-board is made in several styles. See ENTRANCES.

The Hoffman self-spacing frame, described under FRAMES, SELF-SPACING, and FRAMES, MANIPULATING, is used in the Dovetailed hive almost exclusively. The usual width of the hive is eight-frame, although there seems to be a tendency toward the ten and twelve frame sizes. The supers for this hive are the same as those shown under COMB HONEY.

As now constructed the hive embodies the very latest developments in hives and hive-construction. It can be handled rapidly, and is especially adapted for out-apiary work, where frequent moving from one field to another is necessary. It is standard, being made by all the supply-manufacturing concerns, and is for sale everywhere. The

lock corner is especially well adapted for hot climates; and for any place it is far superior to work depending on nails alone. The ordinary miter or halved joint is inclined to pull apart in parts of California, Texas, Florida, and other portions of our country subject to extremes of heat, or hot dry winds.

A very important requisite of a good hive is a good cover. While the flat cover—one making use of one flat board and two cleats —was a good one, yet, owing to the width of the single board, and increasing scarcity of such lumber, something made of two or three narrow boards had to be used. Accordingly, the Excelsior was devised. It consists of boards not exceeding 6 inches in width, for narrow boards will not shrink and check from the influence of the weather like the wide ones. The two side boards, B, B, are beveled or chamfered on one side so that one edge is left only about one-half the thickness of the other edge, but the ends are

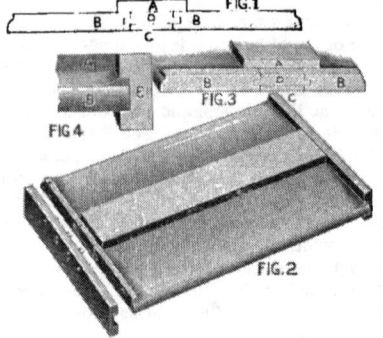

left full thickness of the boards to shed water away from the ends and to give more nail-grip for the grooved end-cleats, E,

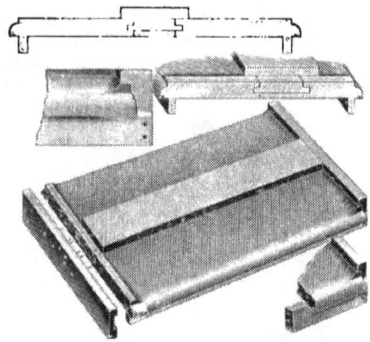

that slip over and bind the whole together. The purpose of the chamfering is to shed water to the sides of the hive and away

from the center-piece, AD, which is tongued and grooved to fit a corresponding tongue and groove edge of the two side-boards that were beveled to shed water. The space

under D is filled with a thin board ¼ inch thick, the ends of which project into the ⅛-inch groove of the end-cleats, E, where it is securely held in place.

In very hot climates a beveled or gabled cover is used. The lower part of the cover is flat, and the upper part gabled, as shown in the accompanying illustration.

HIVES THAT WE RECOMMEND.

The hives we have thus far shown are those that we use and recommend ourselves, because we have tried them on a sufficiently large scale so that we know that we are recommending no experiment. But there are other good hives that are not standard, that may be just as good or better; but as they illustrate certain principles of hive-construction, and as each one of them has some valuable feature, we will endeavor to explain their general construction and points of merit, as fairly and carefully as we know how, without in any sense giving them an indorsement. We will first take up

HIVES WITH CLOSED END FRAMES.

Under FRAMES, SELF-SPACING, we have spoken of the Quinby, as that is the one used in Central New York, especially in Herkimer and Otsego counties. But in this department we shall have more to do with the subject of closed-end frames, certain principles of their construction, and their adjustment in several of the best hives.

Closed-end frames may be divided into two classes—the standing and suspended. The Quinby, already spoken of under FRAMES, SELF-SPACING, the Bingham, and the Heddon, are of the first-mentioned class; the Danzenbaker, to which we shall soon refer, belongs to the latter class. It is generally considered that frames with closed uprights, while not as convenient, perhaps, for general manipulation, are better adapted to wintering. Frames partly closed end, like the Hoffman, or open all the way up, like the ordinary loose hanging frame, permit of currents of air around the ends of the frames, and, (it is claimed) as a consequence, that bees are not so inclined, to bring their brood clear out to the end-bars as they do when closed ends are used. Experience shows in our apiaries that there is something in this. See DANZENBAKER HIVE under this head.

THE BINGHAM HIVE.

Mr. Quinby was the first to apply Huber's principle of closed-end frames in this country (see HIVES, EVOLUTION OF). This he introduced shortly after the appearance of the Langstroth hive. Almost contemporaneously Mr. Bingham in 1867 brought out his hive with closed-end frames with a narrow top-bar and no bottom-bar, but still embodying the chief features of Huber's hive of 1789. But the peculiar feature of this hive was that it made use of shallow frames only 5 inches deep, a series of them being lashed together by means of a wire loop and stretcher sticks, said loop drawing on the follower-boards in such a way as to bring tight compression on frames inclosed in manner shown. Seven of these brood frames in the present hive make up a brood-nest, and an entire brood-nest may consist of one or two sets of frames. The top-bar is dropped down from the top of the end-bars a bee-space, while the bottom-bars are flush with the bottoms of the end-bars. With a bottom-board having a $\frac{4}{8}$ in. strip on each side, the ordinary bee-space is preserved through the several divisions of the hive.

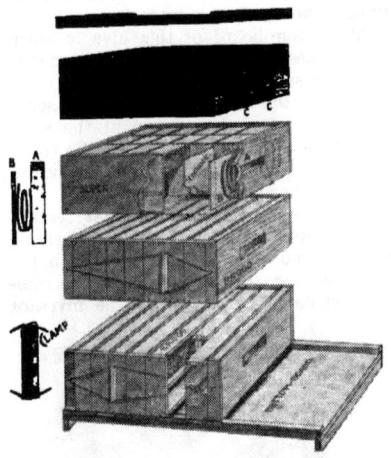

The super is like any ordinary one adapted to comb honey, except that it uses coiled springs to produce the necessary tension.

Although Mr. Bingham has used this hive for a great many years, and quite successfully too, no one else seems to have done much with it; but a modification of the hive is shown in the Danzenbaker and the Heddon, both of which, in some sections, have come to be favorites.

THE DANZENBAKER HIVE.

The Danzenbaker hive, with closed-end frames, is one of the very best; certainly it is slowly working its way into the confidence of bee-keepers. It consists of a brood-chamber of the same length and width as the 10-frame Langstroth Dovetailed hive, but only

deep enough to take in a depth of frame of $7\frac{1}{4}$ in. The rabbet, instead of being near the upper edge, is dropped down about midway; or, more strictly speaking, there is a cleat or board nailed on the inside of the ends of the hive, as shown at F F in the accompanying

diagram of the hive. On this support hang the closed-end brood-frames, pivoted at the center of the end-bars by means of a rivet driven through from the inside, as shown at I in the diagram. Ten of these frames fill the hive; and when they are crowded together with a follower-board on the side, we

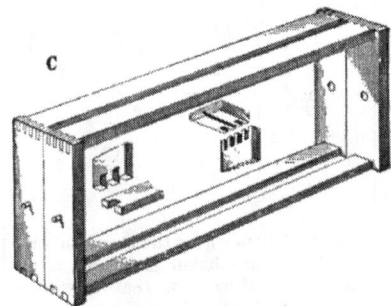

have practically a double-walled hive—the ends of the frames with closed uprights forming one wall, and the ends of the hive the second or outer wall; the follower on one side wall, and the side of the hive the outside or secondary wall. These frames being pivoted in the center, as shown at C, can be reversed, and this feature, while it costs nothing, is something to be desired, as it enables us to have all frames filled solid with comb.

The bottom of these hives is the same as that shown for the Dovetailed, already described; or, to be more exact, the Dovetailed hive has appropriated the bottom-board of the Danzenbaker. The super for comb honey takes in the 4x5 plain section, and makes use of the fence-separator system. The sections are supported in section-holders; indeed, the whole arrangement is the same as the section-holder super already described in COMB HONEY.

This hive is especially adapted to the production of comb honey, and Mr. Danzenbaker prefers to use only one brood-chamber at a time, although in some localities it might be better to use two. The ordinary Langstroth frame is just deep enough to permit of the bees building from an inch to an inch

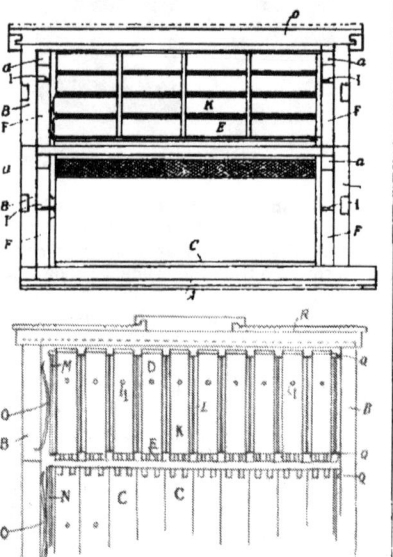

and a half of honey over the brood in each frame. Mr. Danzenbaker makes his frame just enough shallower so that it will be almost solid with brood, and the honey that would otherwise be put in the brood-chamber is forced into the sections just where we want it, and where it will bring the highest market price.

ITS GOOD WINTERING QUALITIES.

Under FRAMES, MANIPULATING, will be found a description of how the frames of this particular hive may be handled without killing bees — to this the reader is referred.

The Danzenbaker hive has recently been coming into prominence as one that seems to be especially adapted for wintering and springing bees. It is, to a great extent, double-walled, and the closed-end frames make the hive a warm one.

But the claims for good wintering and springing of the bees in this hive will apply with almost equal force to bees in the next hive to be described.

THE HEDDON HIVE.

This hive was patented and introduced by Mr. James Heddon, of Dowagiac, Mich., in 1885. Its peculiar and distinguishing feature is in the use of one brood-chamber divided into halves horizontally, each half containing a set of eight closed-end close-fitting brood-frames, $5\frac{3}{4}$ in. deep by $18\frac{1}{8}$. The end-bars, as already stated, are close-fitting—that is, the brood-frame slides into the hive with just enough play to allow of its easy removal and insertion. On the bottom inside edge of the ends of each case are nailed strips of tin to support the frames, and the whole set of eight are squeezed firmly together by means of wooden thumbscrews as shown. Under the head of COMB HONEY we have already spoken of the value of compression for squeezing sections or section-holders or wide frames. The more tightly the parts are held together, the less chance there is for bees to chink propolis into the cracks.

The bottom-board of this hive is much like that used on the standard hives, in that it has a raised rim on the two sides and ends, to support the brood-chamber a bee-space above the bottom-board, and at the same time provide for an entrance at the front. The cover is the ordinary flat one-board, cleated at the ends.

As already stated, the peculiar feature of this hive is the divisible brood-chamber, not two shallow hives one upon the other, but two *halves* composing one complete whole. The purpose of the inventor

in having the hive divided in this way was to afford more rapid handling, and to accomplish contraction and expansion by simply taking from or adding to the brood part of the hive one or more sections. This divisible feature of the hive, according to its advocates, enables them to handle *hives* instead of *frames*, to find the queen by shaking the bees out of one or both of the shallow sections. The horizontal bee-space through the center of the brood-nest is considered an advantage in wintering, in that the bees can move up and down and laterally through the combs.

HAND DIVISIBLE-BROOD-CHAMBER HIVE.

Mr. J. E. Hand, of Birmingham, O., uses a hive embodying some of the basic principles of the Heddon, but with some improvements which, in his opinion, render it simpler, cheaper, and more practicable and workable. In the first place, he simplified it

J. E. HAND'S SECTIONAL HIVE.

by making the brood-chamber of the same depth and general construction as the super for containing sections. In doing this, instead of making the brood-chamber deeper than the super, as did Mr. Heddon, he cheapened the hive by making each division or section of it one and the same thing in every respect. Instead of using thumb-screws, which will very often swell in damp weather so as to become immovable, making it impossible to remove the frames, he made one side of his super or brood-chamber with a removable follower-board, the same being secured in place with a pair of ordinary Van Deusen hive-clamps. By consulting the engravings herewith one may readily under-

stand the principle; but the removable follower-board is only three-fourths as wide as one side of the brood-chamber, the remain-

SIDE OF UPPER SECTION DETACHED TO SHOW CONSTRUCTION.

ing space being taken up by a permanent wooden strip which securely holds the two ends and the sides in position. The follower-board, as will be seen, is cleated on the inside; and on the opposite side are two super springs, just opposite the uprights of the brood-frames or section-holders, as the case may be. When sections or frames are in place, the follower-board closes up the open

LOOKING THROUGH A SECTION FROM THE BOTTOM, SHOWING THE VERY NARROW BARS.

space, where it is secured in place by two Van Deusen clamps that crowd it up against the brood-frames or sections which, in turn, bear against the springs. No matter what the weather conditions may be, the yielding springs will cause a pressure on the frames or sections, and yet allow removing them with the greatest of ease. The brood-frame is 4½ inches deep by 17¼ long. The section-holders are the same size, containing 4¼ plain section with fences.

Mr. Hand finds it quite important to have the top and bottom bars of the brood-frames narrow, so that he may look through the comb surfaces. The ordinary wide thick bars would not answer for a hive of this description. While it is possible to handle the frames, and absolutely necessary under some conditions, he emphasizes the importance of handling hives, or brood - sections, rather, instead of individual frames. He says that practically all the necessary manipulations, even to the finding and catching of queens, can be accomplished without handling a single frame.

A WIDE FRAME FOR THE SECTIONS AND A REGULAR BROOD-FRAME.

Mr. F. J. Miller, of London, Ont., Canada; Louis H. Scholl, of New Braunfels, Texas; J. E. Chambers, Vigo, Texas, and quite a number of others who use the divisible-brood-chamber hive, have so far demonstrated the feasibility of handling hives instead of frames that they claim they are able to dispense with from one to two men, doing all the work alone, because there is no handling of the frames, and little or no time lost in hunting for and catching the queen and clipping her wings.

THE DADANT HIVE.

Almost the very opposite of the Heddon in principle and general construction is the Dadant hive. While Mr. Heddon divides up the brood-chamber into one, two, or three separate portions, Mr. Dadant would have it all in one large complete whole. His frames are 18⅜x11¼—that is to say, they have the Quinby dimensions, and he uses nine or ten to the hive. Such a hive has about the equivalent capacity of a twelve-frame Langstroth, regular depth. The Dadants have always insisted that their ten-frame Quinbys, when compared with the ten - frame Langstroths, averaged up year after year, would give far better results, both in honey and in economy of labor. This opinion is not based on the experience of two or three years, but on a period covering a good many years. The large hives, they claim, swarm less, produce more honey, and winter better. If we are correct they do not, at their home yard at least, have to exceed two per cent of swarming, and this average has been maintained year after year. Apparently the colonies in these large hives have very little desire to swarm; but when they *do* swarm the swarms are enormous. In regard to this point, in an article that was published in *Gleanings in Bee Culture*, Nov. 1, 1898, C. P. Dadant says:

Don't understand me to say that, with large hives, you will have no swarms, for this is incorrect; but if you want to prevent swarming, to the greatest possible extent, you must, first of all, have large hives. Other things are required, such as the removal of the excess of drone combs, plentiful ventilation, a supply of surplus combs, etc.; but the *sine qua non*, in our eyes, is large hives.

With a little care it is not difficult to keep swarming down to such a point that the natural increase will barely make up for winter losses. In our case we find it insufficient, and we resort to artificial swarms, or dividing, which we find much more satisfactory, for we can breed from the queens that we prefer, and, at the same time, keep our best colonies for producing honey. Every practical bee-man will agree that it is the large colonies that give the large crops, whatever may be his opinion as to the size of hive needed.

But if we *must* have swarms, with large hives they will be large, take my word for it.

The Dadants have claimed that the ordinary eight and ten frame hives are not large enough for good prolific queens; that a brood-frame of Langstroth depth is too shallow; that we never know what a good queen can do till we give her a large hive and a large frame. Again, in one of their articles for Oct. 1, 1898, in *Gleanings in Bee Culture*, Mr. C. P. Dadant says:

With the large hives we found queens that had a capacity of 4500 eggs per day. Exceptions, you will say? Certainly, but it is a very nice thing to give a chance for those exceptions. And I hold that you can not do this as fully with a two-story eight-frame hive as with a hive that may be enlarged, one frame at a time, till it contains all the room that the queen may need. Your eight-frame hive gives her too much room at once when it is doubled in size. If the season is a little cool, there is a chance of delaying the breeding by chilling the combs. The bees will then concentrate themselves upon the brood and keep it within narrow limits, for the queen will seldom go out of the cluster to lay.

As to the matter of wintering, these jumbo hives seem to offer exceptional advantages. Mr. Dadant, in one of his articles, says :

The facts upon which I base my conclusion are those which we have seen under our own eyes, of better success in wintering the large deep hive. . We have thus stronger colonies for winter, which is in

the preference. There can be no sort of doubt that these large hives, for *extracted* honey, have some advantages over the smaller ones; but when it comes to the production of *comb* honey, then there is a question, and a big one too—Is such a large hive as good as a smaller one ? In some localities the bees might fill only a brood-nest in such a hive ; whereas if a shallower one were used, like the Danzenbaker or Heddon, the available comb space below would be filled with brood ; and the honey, when it did come in, and what little there was of it, would be forced into the supers. In the selection of a

DADANT–QUINBY HIVE.—*From "Langstroth on the Honey-Bee, Revised," by Dadant.*

itself a great advantage, as the number of bees has much to do with their ability to keep warm, and their ability to retain the heat has also much to do with their honey consumption. A weak colony suffers much from the cold, and is compelled to eat more. But to me the greatest advantage of the deep large frame is the greater ease bees have in reaching the honey while preserving a more compact cluster.

LARGE HIVES ; WHERE AND UNDER WHAT CIRCUMSTANCES USED.

The Dadants have a considerable following in their vicinity ; and in France the Dadant - Quinby has become almost the standard hive. But it should be remembered that the Dadants are extracted - honey men ; and in France liquid honey has rather

large hive, then, a good deal depends on the locality, and whether one proposes to run for comb or extracted honey.

THE LARGE HIVES NON-SWARMERS.

There is one very important feature in favor of the Dadant hive, and, in fact, any large hive ; and that is, the reduction or almost entire control of swarming. There has been no satisfactory method proposed to accomplish this result with the single-story eight-frame Langstroth when run for the production of comb honey ; and a great many give up the problem, stating that it is better to let the bees swarm once, and then somehow afterward control the after-swarms, arguing that more actual comb honey will be produced from the parent colony and its swarm than where other methods are employed. But if swarming is to be allowed, what is to be done at outyards ? If an attendant has to be constantly on hand during the swarming part of the day, it means a big expense, and this might, in a poor season, balance the entire proceeds of the honey crop. If, on the other hand, swarms are allowed to go to the woods, then there is a loss. It is true that swarms will not escape if the queens' wings are clipped ; and to a very great extent clipping does prevent this waste.* But better—far better—is it to take away the desire for swarming altogether, *if* it can be done. In the production of extracted honey, at least, the Dadants have demonstrated that, with their large hives, they have practical control of swarming, because their hives are so large that the bees and the queens rarely feel cramped for room. But Mr. Dadant argues that he would use large hives, even if he were running for *comb* honey ; for with a division-board he can reduce the brood-chamber to any size desired. And then when he has a prolific queen that can fill a whole Quinby hive he is that much ahead, because the colony has more working bees to its size than a smaller one ; and there is no use in denying the fact that these jumbo colonies have a certain vim and energy—a day-after-day "stick-to-it-iveness"—that we do not find in the smaller ones. Personally we believe in large colonies; and we are hopeful that the time will soon come when we shall learn how to make these big colonies produce comb honey as well as, at the same time, remaining practically non-swarmers. At the present time (January, 1910) shallow hives, Langstroth or Danzenbaker, have the general preference for comb honey throughout nearly all the territory in the northern portion of the country—the territory where the main honey supply is almost entirely from clover and basswood.

LARGE COLONIES IN TWO-STORY EIGHT-FRAME LANGSTROTH HIVES.

We have experimented a little with two colonies in eight-frame Langstroth hives tiered one above another, raising brood in both bodies. · When we have a good queen, such colonies in these double chambers grow

* See CLIPPING QUEENS' WINGS TO PREVENT SWARMING, under head of QUEENS; also SWARMING.

to be tremendously strong, and they show less inclination to swarm—no sort of doubt about that ; and, what is more, in a few instances we have placed comb-honey supers on top of these same colonies, and had them fill two and three supers. But in a majority of cases the colonies will not be strong enough to fill two stories and go into the supers besides ; so, after getting the colonies up to good strength, and just at the approach of or during the honey-flow, we take away one story and place on one or two comb-honey supers. Such a large force of bees, of course, rush right into them ; then if there is any honey in the fields the supers are filled and completed in short order. We have thus far succeeded in getting stronger colonies in this way than in a single eight-frame brood-nest alone. By thus breeding in double stories, and having prolific queens, or, perhaps, what may be better, working colonies on one eight-frame full-depth story, and one eight-frame half-depth story, we can get the bees into the sections at once. For particulars regarding this last, see the Barber plan spoken of under COMB HONEY.

OBJECTIONS TO LARGE HIVES.

Their size renders them both heavy and unwieldy. They cost more money—about twice as much if made as shown in the engraving of the Dadant hive. It is difficult, in the first place, to get good clear lumber wide enough to make these deep hives ; and then when they are made, and are full of bees and honey, it is not practical to move them about much. The Dadants, for instance, leave these large hives on their stands all summer and winter, both at the home and out yards. They find it more practical to do so. Even when wintered on their summer stands in single-walled hives, the loss, we understand, just about equals the slight increase they have in swarming.

These large frames are not nearly as easy to manipulate as the shallow Langstroth. It takes longer to get them out of the hive, and during the operation there is more danger of killing bees. The Dadants and others having the Quinby hive find it necessary to use another size that they call their shallow or half-depth frame, 5⅜x18½, for extracting. These are placed on top of the brood-nest, and are tiered up one, two, three, or four high. One is led to wonder why a compromise between a deep Quinby and these extracting-frames would not be better — a frame adapted for breeding as well as for extracting — as, for instance, one like the Langstroth ; then when one wants a large hive he can tier up one brood-chamber on top of the other.

THE TEN-FRAME LANGSTROTH HIVE OF EXTRA DEPTH.

It was suggested by A. N. Draper, of Upper Alton, Ill., one of Mr. Dadant's followers, that, in order to reduce cost, instead of making a hive after the Quinby dimensions, and on the Dadant pattern—the former being odd-sized and the latter expensive to construct—a hive be constructed after the pattern of the regular ten-frame Dovetailed, having Langstroth dimensions save in one measurement — that of depth. He would add to the hive and frame 2½ inches. As the Dadants ordinarily use nine frames in their Quinby hives, ten frames 2½ inches deeper, with Langstroth top-bar, would give the hive equal capacity. Such a hive would take regular Langstroth ten-frame bottom-boards, cover, supers, honey-boards, winter-cases — in fact, every thing adapted to the regular ten-frame Langstroth Dovetailed hive. As the ten-frame hive is one of the standards, it seems reasonable to suppose that, if the large hive is really better, such a hive would be more simple, and cost less, than to adopt regular Quinby-frame dimensions, and make the hive as the Dadants show it in the cut, p. 247. Indeed, we have been told that the Dadants would favor such a hive rather than the one they have adopted, if they were to start anew. Your supply-dealer will make the brood-chamber for about 25 per cent more than the regular ten-frame Langstroth Dovetailed; the super, covers, and bottom-boards would, of course, cost no more. Where one by reason of locality or preference desires such large hives, the Jumbo ten-frame Langstroth of extra depth, suitable for taking standard ten-frame fixtures and fittings, is the hive to select.

CLEATS V. HAND-HOLES.

By referring to the illustration of the original Langstroth hive on page 240, and also to the illustration of the Dadant hive, page 247, one will see that they have cleats or rims running all around the hive near the top edge. These serve the double purpose of supporting the telescopic cover and affording convenient handles by which to lift the hives; but on account of the expense, these cleats running around the hive

were in later years abandoned, and hand-holes, made by means of a wabble-saw, were used. But these hand-holes, while very neat and cheap, did not begin to afford the excellent grip that one secures when getting hold of a seven-inch cleat. But a far better arrangement than either is a combination of cleat and hand-hole, as shown in illustration of the Dovetailed hive, p. 241, and the cuts below. A short strip of ⅜-inch molding is nailed just above the hand-hole so that the fingers get a double grip. In the accompanying diagrams the reader will see the advantage of this arrangement. Referring to the diagram at D, when one lifts by the hand-

THE COMPARATIVE DIFFERENCE IN SIZE BETWEEN A REGULAR EIGHT-FRAME HIVE AND A TEN-FRAME JUMBO.

holes alone he lifts by the tips of the fingers only; and when the hive is heavy, the strain on the fingers is severe and often painful. But if he can get the greater part of the weight on the middle joints of the fingers, as shown at A, and on a rounding edge, he

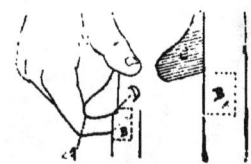

can lift all his back will stand. The cleat alone would not give room enough for the fingers to permit of the grip on the middle joints, as shown at A; but when the side of the hive is recessed by the hand-hole, it allows of the fingers being shoved to a point to get the best possible grip. If one expects to use heavy hives, then he needs some such arrangement as this. The cost is insignificant, and the advantage great.

DOUBLE - WALLED OR CHAFF HIVES.

The hives that we have thus far described are what may be called single-walled hives; that is, the outer shell or case consists of a single-board thickness of lumber. Such hives, as a rule, unless as large as the Dadant, can not very well be wintered outdoors on their summer stands. They either have to be carried into the cellar at the approach of cold weather, or else have to be put in outside packing-cases, as the single walls hardly afford sufficient protection to enable the average colony to go through the winter safely, or without great loss both in bees and in stores. The poorer the protection, the greater the consumption of winter food. A colony poorly protected outdoors will probably consume twice as much as one adequately protected.

In the South, of course it is not necessary to carry the single-walled hives into the cellar or winter repository; but north of latitude 40, hives of single - board thickness either ought to be housed or protected with winter - cases. Where one from choice or necessity has to winter outdoors, what are known as double - walled or chaff hives should be used. These have the same inside dimensions as the single-walled hive, and are generally made to take the same supers and the same inside furniture. The first double-walled hives that we used were two-

HILTON'S TWO-STORY CHAFF HIVE.

story; but they were awkward and unwieldy things compared with the hives of to-day. The one shown in the illustration next following represents an eight-frame Langstroth single-story double-walled hive; and as it represents the simplest form of

wintering hive, we will describe this only, leaving the reader to adapt it to the dimensions of whatever frame he is using.

EIGHT-FRAME DOVETAILED DOUBLE-WALLED HIVE.

It can be made large or small; so also the distance between the walls may be increased or diminished in accordance with the demands of the locality in which one lives. The outer wall consists of a shell of $\frac{7}{8}$-inch lumber, locked at the corners. This outer shell should be made just large enough to give two inches of space between the walls for packing material. In our locality a packing of two inches seems to answer very well. The inner wall is simply a hive made of $\frac{7}{8}$-inch lumber, and is let down in the outer

case, and secured to the same by means of a water-table or picture-frame, as we may call it, to shed water. Between the outer and inner walls there is a boxed passageway, as shown, for an entrance.

The raised projection of the water-table is made to fit the upper story of an eight frame Dovetailed hive, or any of the supers or covers of that hive; and in summer the hive may be tiered up as shown in the illustration next; and in winter it may be prepared as described under WINTERING, which see.

At our own home apiary we prefer this double-walled hive to the single because it is nearly as light, and because, in our locality, we can leave the colonies in these hives winter and summer. There is no lugging into and out of the cellar; and after the colonies are fed up for winter the preparations for their long winter's sleep and housing are

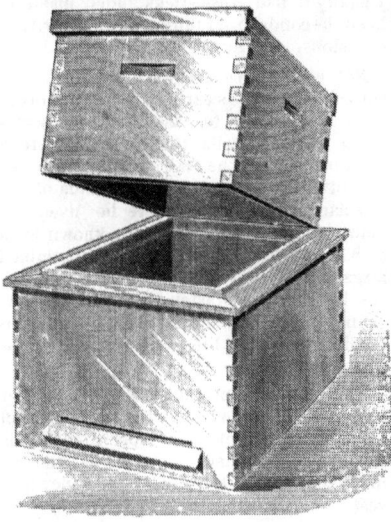

EIGHT - FRAME DOUBLE - WALLED HIVE WITH AN EIGHT-FRAME SINGLE-WALL UPPER STORY.

very short, occupying two or three minutes to a hive. Then the double walls also afford excellent protection in hot weather, in the same way that the two walls and packing material between the walls of a refrigerator prevent a too rapid melting of the ice within.

PACKING MATERIAL FOR DOUBLE-WALLED HIVES.

We formerly used wheat or oat chaff; but as we could not secure this readily we gradually began to use planer-shavings, which we can get more easily. These, we find, answer every purpose, and we now use them exclusively. Forest leaves, if good and dry, would doubtless do just as well, and they have the advantage that they make the hive, when packed, lighter—that is, easier to lift and handle.

There are a great many who, having in use a large number of single-walled hives, prefer to winter on their summer stands, if that can be done. For such there has been devised a winter-case made of ⅜-inch lumber, and just enough larger than the hive to be protected to give one or two inches of packing-space all around the hive. This is

placed over and around the smaller hive, the space at the bottom edges between it and the inner hive being closed up with ⅜-inch cleats padded so as to fit the hive closely, as shown in the diagram. Packing material is then poured in and around the hive and on top, when the telescope cover is placed over the whole.

OUTSIDE WINTER-CASES.

Colonies in such packing-cases winter almost perfectly, and I have no hesitancy in recommending them. But when it comes to unpacking in spring, they are very inconvenient, to say the least. The packing material has to be scooped out and poured into baskets, when the cover is removed to see if the bees are alive. The loose stuff tumbles down between the frames, much to the annoyance of the apiarist and discomfort of the bees. For that reason we greatly prefer

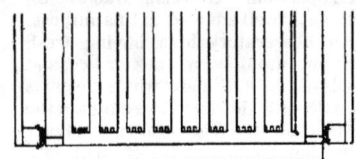

the regular double-walled hive pure and simple. If the locality is cold enough to warrant wintering in the cellar, we should, of course, use single-walled hives exclusively.

OBSERVATORY HIVES.

These are simply hives having glass sides and ends. They usually have only one comb, so that both sides as well as the ends of it can be readily examined. With more than one comb the queen can not be readily found. At exhibitions for the purpose of showing a full-sized colony, an eight or ten comb glass hive is often shown, as well as the one-comb nucleus in glass. The super also has glass sides and ends so that the work of the bees on the combs in the sec tions can be readily examined without opening the hive.

The hive shown in the illustration has a floor board and cover of wood. The corner-posts are 1¼ inches in diameter, having longitudinal saw-grooves at the proper angles to receive the glass—at the ends and also at the sides. The ends of the posts are reduced in diameter, thus leaving a

shoulder. These shanks are then set down into holes bored in the floor-board at the right points. The glass is slipped into the grooves in the post, when the frames are supported on wire staples driven into the floor-board. It would not be practicable to use tin rabbets in a hive with glass ends, so none are used. As the frames stand, they are secured together at the top so as to hold their position. Hoffman frames are eminently well adapted to this purpose.

An observatory hive having fresh bees put into it every week or two, and displayed in a window where honey is on sale, will do much to stimulate the demand for it. When shown at county fairs they are the means of eliciting a great amount of interest and questions. If the exhibitor hangs out his business card, giving prices of honey—genuine bees' honey—it will do much to help his trade. See EXHIBITS.

HIVES, EVOLUTION OF.

Primitive hives were simply the trunks of trees in which bees were lodged, cut down, and carried wherever the beekeeper desired. This plan of bee-keeping is still practiced in some parts of Europe, and is common enough in Africa. The stingless-bee apiaries of South America are made in this way.

The next step was to construct a cylinder resembling the trunk of a tree, either of wood or earthenware. In northern climates

straw came into use, but had to be fashioned in the shape of a bell to make it easy of construction. This is the kind of hive which was so highly praised by poets, probably because it was the least practical. It has the merits of extreme simplicity and cheapness. Usually it had cross-sticks added inside to keep the combs from falling down on critical occasions. See SKEPS.

Not all bee-keepers were satisfied with these hives; and as early as the 17th century some few began to cast about for something better. Della Rocca, who wrote a book on bees in the 18th century, mentions bar hives as in vogue in the islands of the Grecian Archipelago, where he lived for many years. Such hives were known even to the ancient Greeks. They resembled large flower-pots with wooden bars on which the bees were to fasten their combs. The shape of the hive made it practically impossible to cause a breakdown of the combs except by heat.

The plan of a movable roof was another step in advance, as it gave the bee-keeper an opportunity to put on a super to hold the surplus honey where it should be, and remove the same at the end of the honey harvest.

Mewe, in Great Britain, constructed hives of wood on somewhat the same plan as early as 1652, and these were gradually improved by various inventors.

FIG. 1.—HUBER'S OBSERVATION HIVE, SHOWING HOW COMBS COULD BE REMOVED FOR STUDY.—FROM CHESHIRE.

Maraldi, about the same era as Mewe, invented a single-comb observation hive made with glass sides, which contained the germ of the movable-comb frame. He allowed too much space for one comb, and frequently the bees built their comb crosswise. Still there was in the Maraldi hive the important idea of handling one comb at a time, and by this means to get a far better conception of what was going on inside the hive. Huber extended this idea by his improvement, Fig. 1, which came very near to the hanging movable frame invented by Langstroth sixty years later.

To Huber belongs the credit of inventing hives with movable frames*, and it was by

Examining the illustrations of Huber's hive makes evident he had a clear idea of what was required in a hive for practical purposes. Fig. 3 shows how he increased his apiary by artificial means. In this case he divided a strong colony by slipping a board between the frames, thereby splitting it in two. His plan of providing a part of each frame for surplus honey is excellent.

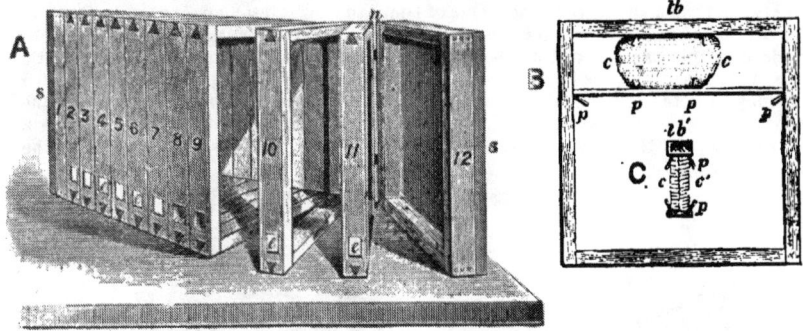

FIG. 2.—HUBER'S LEAF HIVE, 1789.—FROM CHESHIRE.

the use of these that he was able to make the discoveries in apiculture which so astonished and delighted the scientific world. Huber invented these hives about 1789, or perhaps a little earlier, Fig. 2. It has been contended by some writers that Huber's hive was not practical; but some of the most

It is very evident from this that Huber invented some of the principal features of our movable-comb hives. The Heddon and Bingham hives are on the Huber plan.

About 1819 Mr. Robert Kerr, of Stewart Town, Scotland, invented a bar hive of considerable merit, shown in Fig. 4. This hive

FIG. 3.—HUBER HIVE, SHOWING HOW HE ARTIFICIALLY INCREASED THE NUMBER OF HIS COLONIES. E, E, E, ARE ENTRANCE-HOLES.—FROM CHESHIRE.

practical bee-keepers the world has yet produced used modified Huber hives, notably Quinby and Hetherington, bee-keepers of New York State, whose names are revered by American bee keepers.

was used very successfully, and is still, but with movable frames instead of mere bars. It was still further improved by Howatson, also of Scotland, about 1825. The Stewarton hive looks outside not unlike our modern improved dovetailed Langstroth hives. Here we have the tiering principle clearly comprehended; and had this author and inventor grasped the idea

* This honor is usually ascribed to Langstroth, for, indeed, he was the first one to invent an all-round practical hive and frame—a frame that provided a bee-space all around it; but, strictly speaking, he did not invent the first movable frame.

of movable-comb frames instead of bars he would have solved the great problem of inventing a practical hive equal to all emergencies.

Prokopovitsch, a Russian, about 1835, invented and made in large numbers a movable-comb hive of great merit, Fig. 5. In his own apiaries, of which he had many, were over 3000 of these hives in actual use. His pupils (for he established a school of bee-keeping) had many more in use. One of the features of this hive was the bee-space, provided by thin bars of wood on the back, sides, and ends of the hive-box.

It may be noted that his surplus frames bear considerable resemblance to our bee way sections, and that his hives were dove-

the hive, all the other combs had first to be removed. Evidently his hive was far inferior to those we have already mentioned. When he adopted frames he did not change the construction of his hives in the least.

Next came Langstroth with his epoch-making movable-comb hive with movable roof, which combined the essential requirements of a hive. All the combs in the Langstroth hive are readily removable without the slightest annoyance either to the bee-keeper or the bees. Langstroth did his work so well that he left very little for future inventors to do. Many have tried to improve his hive, but in most cases the so-called improvement has proven to be a backward step. The striking feature of the

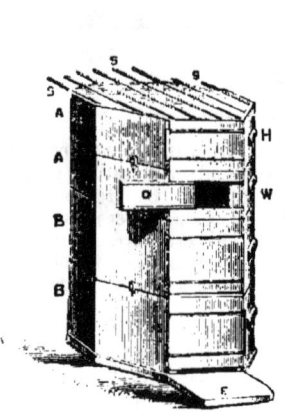

FIG. 4.—THE STEWARTON HIVE. 1819; SHALLOW-BAR HIVE WITH GLASS STRIPS BETWEEN BARS.— FROM CHESHIRE.

FIG. 5.—PROKOPOVITSCH'S HIVE, 1830.—FROM FRARIERE.

tailed. Prokopovitsh was certainly a bee-keeper of remarkable abilities, and employed means and methods far ahead of his time.

It has been claimed by some writers that Dzierzon, of Germany, invented movable frames in 1845; but it is evident he has no claim whatever to this distinction. As a matter of fact, according to his own statements he used bars until 1855, when he was persuaded by Baron Berlepsch to use movable frames, which had just been introduced from America. Dzierzon's bar combs were removed by using a long knife to cut the attachments from the back of the hive one by one; for, to reach the comb at the front of

Langstroth hive is the provision for a bee-space on all sides of the comb. This bee-space can not be less than one-sixth of an inch nor more than one-third. This alone was a great discovery, and placed Langstroth far above the mere inventor.

From his writings it is evident that Langstroth knew nothing about what others had done before him in this line; and it is apparent that his invention was the result of a very profound study of the bee and its habits. To some extent he was misled by others into thinking that the principle of the Langstroth hive had been discovered by Dr. Dzierzon independently, whereas there is no manner of doubt that the German bee-keeper had no claim to the invention of the hanging movable comb, to say nothing of the bee-space and the movable roof, which are essential features of the hive.

Langstroth's invention, accompanied by an excellent treatise on the art of keeping bees, created a revolution in bee-keeping in a short time, linking his name with that of Huber as the two founders of modern apiculture.

HIVES, MANIPULATING. See FRAMES, TO MANIPULATE.

HIVE-STANDS. See APIARY.

HOARHOUND (*Marrubium vulgare*). This is quite an important honey-plant in Texas. It begins yielding some time in February, and continues to furnish nectar until quite late in the summer, or until hot dry weather sets in. The honey is of a golden color, and good body, but not a nice table honey. It has been said that it is not fit to eat, being very bitter; but Louis H. Scholl, of Texas, declares this is hardly the case in his locality ; that the honey has a very sweet taste, liked by some but nauseating to others. It is said to have pronounced medicinal qualities, and we believe is described in the pharmacopœia as a medicine.

HOLLY. See GALLBERRY.

HOLY-LAND BEES. See ITALIANS.

HONEY. Every reader of a work of this kind is supposed to know, of course, what honey is; and yet there may be a good many who have only a superficial idea of it, and perhaps a very brief statement should be made.

According to the Century Dictionary, " Honey is a sweet viscid fluid collected from the nectaries of flowers, and elaborated for food by several kinds of insects, especially by the honey-bee (*Apis mellifica*)." An accepted German definition is, " Honey is the nectar obtained from flowers by worker bees, which, after modification in the honey-stomach of the latter, is stored in the cells of the comb for the nourishment of the young brood." In this country the food standards consider " honey as the nectar and saccharine exudations of plants gathered, modified, and stored in the comb by honey-bees (*Apis mellifica* and *Apis dorsata*)." In the latter definition there is included, besides the nectar of flowers, also saccharine exudation of plants. This comes about in that many plants contain sugar in their saps, and, when an exudation of sap takes place, and the water in the sap is evaporated, a saccharine residue remains, which is gathered by the bees. Also, many trees exude a sweet sap when stung by some insect, and this is also gathered by the bees (see HONEY-DEW).

Honey in itself is approximately a pure saccharine substance, naturally flavored, and containing aromas imparted to it by the flower and the bee. Its chemical composition shows it to contain, for the greater part, two sugars, dextrose and levulose, in about equal quantities, also generally (but not always) sucrose. The other substances, in order of their quantity, are dextrins, acids, ash, and a number of substances whose nature and composition have not been thoroughly worked out. An average analysis of American honey given by Brown in Bulletin 110, Bureau of Chemistry, United States Department of Agriculture, shows—

Moisture	17.70 per cent.
Levulose	40.50 per cent.
Dextrose	34.02 per cent.
Sucrose	1.90 per cent.
Ash	0.18 per cent.
Dextrin	1.51 per cent.
Undetermined	4.19 per cent.
Total	100.00 per cent.

Under the national pure-food law, "A honey should be lævorotatory, and should contain not more than twenty-five per cent of water, not more than twenty-five hundredths per cent of ash, and not more than eight per cent of sucrose." All floral honeys are lævorotatory—that is, turn the plane of polarized light to the left, while honey-dew is dextro-rotatory—that is, turns the plane of polarized light to the right. In mixtures of floral honey and honey-dew, honey which bees often collect together, the polarization is about the only means of determining whether the product deserves the name of pure honey.

For the further consideration of this subject see CANDIED HONEY, EXTRACTED HONEY, HONEY-DEW, HONEY AS FOOD, and NECTAR.

HONEY, ADULTERATION OF. Until the passage of the national pure-food bill by Congress, June 30, 1906, liquid or extracted honey was quite often adulterated, it being safe to buy only comb honey; but with the passage of the bill, and the careful work of the Department of Agriculture inspectors, besides the work of the individual State food commissions, this has been brought to a minimum. The label on the bottle must tell the composition of the contents. Honey can bear that label only when it is pure; but if mixed with other substances these must appear on the label in as large type as the honey.

The most common forms of adulteration which are practiced at present in the sophistication of honey are the addition of commercial glucose, cane sugar, and invert sugar. The adulteration of honey by dilution with water is less commonly practiced; such addition is easily recognized by the increased fluidity of the honey, and, there is, besides, the increased danger that the product will spoil through fermentation.

Since the food standard requires the product to contain less than 25 per cent water, the bee-keeper can determine the water content of his product by accurately weighing a gallon of his product. The net weight should be over 11¼ pounds, or, by means of a Beaume hydrometer ranging from 0 to 50 degrees, which can be obtained from any chemical house, and a glass cylinder 12 inches high and 1½ inches in diameter, he can ascertain the weight of his product. By filling the cylinder with the honey, allowing the air-bubbles to come to the top, and cooling to 70° Fahr., the hydrometer is allowed to float in the liquid. It should float at the mark of 42° for a product of less than 25 per cent water.

Commercial glucose is not used so much now as formerly. Its presence is easily detected by the chemist. For a description of this product see GLUCOSE.

The addition of cane-sugar syrup is also easily detected by the experienced chemist. The standards allow 8 per cent sucrose to be present, which is far in excess of what is ordinarily found in pure honey; and, while this may seem an arbitrary amount, it is certainly to the honey-producer's advantage to have a standard provided. Any excess of 8 per cent would surely be called an adulteration.

The adulteration of honey with invert sugar syrup is being practiced to some extent in this country, though not so widely at present as in certain parts of Europe. This syrup has in many respects the same composition as pure honey; it is deficient, however, in ash, albuminoids, and other constituents which occur in honey in small amounts. It is recognized by the expert chemist on account of some of its ash constituents and other chemical constituents, while not with the ease that the presence of glucose is told, but with sufficient accuracy to determine its presence in mixture.

HONEY AND ITS COLORS. The various kinds of honey differ very much in color, flavor, and density. One variety may be practically colorless, while another produced in the same locality, under the same conditions, by the same bees, but from different flowers, may be a dark brown. One kind may contain less than one-sixth of water, while another may contain a third. The proportions of dextrose, levulose, and sucrose vary considerably; but as the extent of the variation is known to chemists they are compelled to take this into account and analyze it differently from the way they would other foods.

Ordinarily honey is judged by its color, flavor, and density. There is an almost endless variety of flavors, making it practicable to suit the most exacting connoisseur. Color is a fair guide, but not always so, for the famous heather honey of Europe is quite dark, and yet no honey stands higher in popular esteem on that continent.

The best honeys of this country are usually spoken of as " water-white;" and, though this is not quite correct, still it is near enough for all practical purposes without coining a new word.

Clover honey may be taken as the typical white honey by which others may be conveniently judged. For the purpose of comparison some may be a little lighter, and others a little darker shade; but these nice points of distinction are visible only to an expert.

Taken by this standard, in the North we have all the clovers—white, alfalfa, crimson, mammoth, alsike, sweet—and the European sainfoin, basswood, raspberry (wild), willow-herb (or fireweed), Canada thistle, apple, cucumber (pickle), and Rocky Mountain bee-plant. In the South we have white honey from the following: Gallberry (holly), sourwood, tupelo, mangrove, cotton, palmetto, guajilla, catclaw, huisache, mesquite, California sage, and some others of less importance. From the American tropics the chief white honeys are logwood, or campeche; campanilla (Cuba), and the mangrove (courida), on all tropical seashores.

Amber-colored honey comes from many sources. Among them, only the more familiar ones can be noted in a popular book of this kind; namely, goldenrod, wild sunflower, heartsease, aster, Spanish needle, sumac, milkweed, poplar, gum, magnolia, lima bean, marigold, horsemint, horehound, carpet-grass, and the hog plum (hobo), rose-apple, and royal palm of the West Indies.

Of dark honeys we take two great examples — the buckwheat of the United States and Europe, and heather, which is confined to Europe alone. The latter, though dark, is a rich, strong-flavored, thick honey, so dense that the extractor is not used to take it from the combs. That produced in Scotland commands a very high price, while that of England is cheaper, being gathered from another species of heather. In North Germany the heath or heather honey commands a good figure. It is largely produced by migratory bee-keepers, their bees existing on white clover during summer, and in the fall being moved to the heaths.

Buckwheat honey is not nearly as good as clover, either in flavor, density, or color; but it is so liberally produced in buckwheat localities that it is a paying crop to the bee-keeper. It blooms late, hence the bees can be prepared in ample time to profit by its bloom. This feature alone makes it very valuable to the bee-keeper who is fortunate enough to live in a buckwheat-growing section. In those parts of this country where buckwheat is grown largely, consumers are willing to pay as much, or almost as much, as they will for fine white honey. Indeed, many prize it more highly.

In France there is a great demand for buckwheat honey from bakers of a kind of bread which has been made for centuries. No other sort of honey is desired by these bakers, who derive nearly all their supply from Brittany, where buckwheat is commonly sown. Attempts have been made to get the bakers to use other dark honeys, but without success.

In Europe there are some prominent honeys which are almost or quite unknown in this country. Heather has been mentioned. Sainfoin is another which is quite common, being almost the same as alfalfa honey with us. Narbonne honey belongs to this class. In southern Europe romarin (rosemary) is very highly spoken of; and in Greece there

9

is the classically famous honey of Mount Hymettus, from wild thyme. In Australia the honey of eucalyptus is highly appreciated, but attempts to sell it in England have always ended in failure, although it ought to be useful for persons suffering from coughs and colds. Instead of the eucalyptus flavor proving to be an attraction it proved a drawback. In California, eucalyptus honey has a limited demand.

HONEY AS FOOD. The American nation consumes an enormous amount of sugar, averaging nearly 80 pounds per head of population, and the British Isles surpass us by 10 pounds or more. The increased consumption of sugar during the last few years has been phenomenal, and even the poorest use a large amount. This, of course, is due to the great fall in the price of sugar, which now sells within the reach of all.

Honey has not fallen in like proportion, though it sells in some States for very little more than good cane sugar. It is very much superior to sugar in several respects, having more flavor and aroma. For baking certain fancy cakes it has no equal, and for this reason will always command a higher price than sugar. We know fastidious people are always willing to pay high prices for foods having fine flavors, and all physiologists are agreed that flavor has much to do with the dietetic value of a food by inducing a free flow of saliva and promoting digestion by pleasing the palate.

Honey is an excellent food in the prevention of fatigue, owing to the fact that, while it builds up the body, or, rather, makes up for the loss of tissue, it does not tax the system. The latter is not called upon to throw off or get rid of a mass of perfectly useless material, for it is undoubtedly true that not more than one two-hundredth part of honey is actual waste. Practically the human system uses up almost every particle of honey placed in the stomach. This can be said of no other food except sugar, which must undergo a process of *inversion* before the system can utilize it. Honey, on the other hand, is in a state of partial digestion before being eaten; and this, in addition to the very free flow of saliva induced by the flavor, causes it to be completely used up in the digestive system without straining it at all—so much so, in fact, that many invalids and infants can use honey when sugar would be prejudicial.

Honey, it is believed, after passing through the stomach, becomes glycogen by the action of the liver, and in this way is converted into heat and work. It differs from sugar in two important particulars. First, it does not require to be "inverted," or converted into natural glucose (it is that already), a process which frequently leads to diabetes (kidney trouble); and, again, it possesses an aroma and flavor which granulated sugar does not. It is a purely natural production, requiring neither cooking nor preparation.

There is an almost infinite variety of flavors in honey, so that the peculiar palate of every one can be suited. In dealing with children and delicate people this is important. In countries where the consumption of sugar is large, as in the United States, Canada, and the British Islands, a kidney disease (diabetes) generally spoken of as a "kidney trouble," is quite common. This is due to the fact that the system of those afflicted is so constituted that they are unable to convert ordinary sugar into glucose. There is always a certain number of such people in every community. *Diabetes*, as the doctors term it, bears considerable resemblance to Bright's disease of the kidneys, which is, however, due to excess of albumen—not sugar.

Children generally crave something sweet, a perfectly healthy and natural longing which ought to be satisfied in some way. This is generally done by giving confectionery and sweetmeats, which frequently are rather indigestible. Honey can be made to take their place with most children if allowed in the regular dietary. In this way the craving for sweets is effectively met. In France and other parts of Europe the doctors recommend honey and cream, or honey and butter, for the treatment of consumptively inclined children. They say this combination is better than cod-liver-oil emulsion, for the reason it is much more palatable and satisfactory to the patient's stomach.

Honey is very effectively used in summer drinks, and should take precedence of sugar in this respect, more particularly where workmen are employed in hot fatiguing work such as in glass and iron factories.

Immense quantities of honey are used by bakers, both in America and Europe. In this country alone the National Biscuit Co. uses an amount which seems staggering to a man unacquainted with the industry. This concern recently purchased in one lot 70 carloads of good honey, and is always in the market for honey in big lots. There are no means of knowing just how much honey the baking industry uses in this country; but it is very large indeed. The best bakers

have discovered that honey is far superior to sugar as a sweetening agent. The latter causes the cakes and bread made with it to dry up and become unpalatable in a few days; whereas honey, on the other hand, causes them to remain sweet and moist for a long period. Cases are reported of honey-jumbles remaining moist for twelve years; and in France nobody thinks it is any thing very wonderful to keep honey-bread a year or eighteen months, and yet remain perfectly good and satisfactory. If hard, it is simply put into a damp place for a few days, when it returns to its original condition.

It is perfectly clear that, where bread and cakes are made in factories, they must have some "keeping" qualities; and by experience the managers have found honey the only acceptable agent for this purpose. At Dijon, in France, from time immemorial a kind of honey-bread (*pain d'epice*, or *Leb Kuchen*, as the Germans call it) has been made and has a wide fame. It is also made in other parts of Europe, but that place seems to excel in its production. The bakers there are fastidious, and can not be induced to use any but buckwheat honey. They say they can not risk their reputation by using any other. The honey is obtained in Brittany; and when it is used up the bakers simply stop baking rather than use a substitute.

Honey-bread is now made and sold in New York, and what we have used of it here in Medina proved to be very fine eating indeed. The general opinion of it was, it would be very acceptable to dyspeptics or persons of impaired digestion, being very open and porous, and easily masticated.

Honey-cakes and jumbles have attained a very large consumption of late years. showing that consumers appreciate a really nice and satisfactory article, no matter if it seems somewhat higher priced than similar foods.

A considerable amount of honey has been used in confectionery, and this demand is increasing; in this connection beeswax is also used to some extent. The beeswax is used in about the same proportions that we find it in a piece of comb honey, and some actually buy comb honey for making confectionery. Honey-candies coated with chocolate are much consumed in Europe.

Honey is largely used as medicine and as a vehicle for carrying nauseous doses. It is so soothing in action that it is used effectively for many purposes in the sick-room. In continental Europe the doctors often recommend and use honey. For some unexplained reason our medical men are not so favorable to honey as their European *confreres*, possibly because they are afraid of its adulteration. Since the passage of the national pure-food law there need be little fear of this, and honey can be freely recommended.

Honey has an excellent effect on the skin; for this reason much is used in soaps and similar preparations by ladies for softening the cuticle and improving the complexion. Salves are also improved by the use of honey and beeswax; in fact, the latter is considered the only proper substance for forming the base of ordinary salves.

Very many of the so-called honey cooking-recipes are apt to be worse than nothing; for when the ingredients are put together and made into a cake, the result is simply vile. The recipes given below have been tested, and every one is guaranteed to be good. The honey-jumble recipe, for instance, is especially good, as is the honey-cake recipe by Maria Fraser.

HONEY COOKING-RECIPES.

HONEY-GEMS.—2 qts. flour, 3 tablespoonfuls melted lard, ¾ pint honey, ½ pt. molasses, 4 heaping tablespoonfuls brown sugar, 1½ level tablespoonfuls soda, 1 level teaspoonful salt, ½ pint water, ½ teaspoonful extract vanilla.

HONEY-JUMBLES.—2 quarts flour, 3 tablespoonfuls melted lard, 1 pt. honey, ¼ pt. molasses, 1½ level tablespoonfuls soda, 1 level teaspoonful salt, ¼ pt. water, ½ teaspoonful vanilla.

These jumbles and the gems immediately preceding are from recipes used by bakeries and confectioneries on a large scale, one firm in Wisconsin alone using ten tons of honey annually in their manufacture.

HONEY-CAKE OR COOKIES without sugar or molasses.—2 cups honey; one cup butter; four eggs (mix well); one cup buttermilk (mix); one good quart flour; one level teaspoonful soda or saleratus. If it is too thin, stir in a little more flour. If too thin it will fall. It does not want to be as thin as sugar-cake. I use very thick honey. Be sure to use the same cup for measure. Be sure to mix the honey, butter, and eggs well together. You can make it richer if you wish by using clabbered cream instead of buttermilk. Bake in a rather slow oven, as it burns very easily. To make the cookies, use a little more flour, so that they will roll out well without sticking to the board. Any kind of flavoring will do. I use ground orange-peel mixed soft. It makes a very nice ginger-bread. *Maria Fraser.*

HOWELL HONEY-CAKE.—(It is a hard cake.) Take 6 lbs. flour, 3 lbs. honey, 1½ lbs. sugar, 1½ lbs. butter, 6 eggs, ½ oz. saleratus; ginger to your taste. Directions for mixing.—Have the flour in a pan or tray. Pack a cavity in the center. Beat the honey and yolks of eggs together well. Beat the butter and sugar to cream, and put into the cavity in the flour; then add the honey and yolks of the eggs. Mix well with the hand, adding a little at a time, during the mixing, the ½ oz. saleratus dissolved in boiling water until it is all in. Add the ginger, and finally add the whites of the 6 eggs, well beaten. Mix well with the hand to a smooth dough. Divide the dough into 7 equal parts, and roll out like gingerbread. Bake in ordinary square pans made for pies, from 10 x 14 tin. After putting into the pans, mark off the top in ¼-inch strips with something sharp. Bake an hour in a moderate oven. Be careful not to burn, but bake well. Dissolve sugar to glaze over top of cake. To keep the cake, stand on end in an oak tub, tin can, or stone crock—crock is best. Stand the cards up so the flat sides will not touch each other. Cover tight. Keep in a cool dry place. Don't use until three months old at least. The cake improves with age, and will keep good as long as you will let it. I find any cake sweetened with honey does not dry out like sugar or molasses cake, and age improves or develops the honey flavor. *E. D. Howell.*

AIKIN'S HONEY-COOKIES.—1 teacupful extracted honey, 1 pint sour cream, scant teaspoonful soda, flavoring if desired, flour to make a soft dough.

SOFT HONEY-CAKE.—1 cup butter, 2 cups honey, 2 eggs, 1 cup sour milk, 2 teaspoonfuls soda, 1 teaspoonful ginger, 1 teaspoonful cinnamon, 4 cups flour. *Chalon Fowls.*

GINGER HONEY-CAKE.—1 cup honey, ½ cup butter, or drippings, 1 tablespoonful boiled cider, in half a cup of hot water (or ½ cup sour milk will do instead). Warm these ingredients together, and then add 1 tablespoonful ginger and 1 teaspoonful soda sifted in with flour enough to make a soft batter. Bake in a flat pan. *Chalon Fowls.*

FOWLS' HONEY FRUIT-CAKE.—½ cup butter, ¾ cup honey, ⅓ cup apple jelly or boiled cider, 2 eggs well beaten, 1 teaspoonful soda, 1 teaspoonful each of cinnamon, cloves, and nutmeg, 1 teacupful each of raisins and dried currants. Warm the butter, honey, and apple jelly slightly, add the beaten eggs, then the soda dissolved in a little warm water; add spices and flour enough to make a stiff batter, then stir in the fruit and bake in a slow oven. Keep in a covered jar several weeks before using.

MUTH'S HONEY-CAKES.—1 gallon honey (dark honey is best), 15 eggs, 3 lbs. sugar (a little more honey in its place may be better), 1½ oz. baking-soda, 2 oz. ammonia, 2 lbs. almonds chopped up, 2 lbs. citron, 4 oz. cinnamon, 2 oz. cloves, 2 oz. mace, 18 lbs. flour. Let the honey come almost to a boil; then let it cool off, and add the other ingredients. Cut out and bake. The cakes are to be frosted afterward with sugar and white of eggs.

FOWLS' HONEY LAYER-CAKE.—¾ cup butter, 1 cup honey, 3 eggs beaten, ½ cup milk. Cream the honey and butter together, then add the eggs and milk. Then add 2 cups flour containing 1½ teaspoonfuls baking-powder previously stirred in. Then stir in flour to make a stiff batter. Bake in jelly-tins. When the cakes are cold, take finely flavored candied honey, and after creaming it spread between layers.

FOWLS' HONEY-COOKIES.—3 teaspoonfuls soda dissolved in 2 cups warm honey, 1 cup shortening containing salt, 2 teaspoonfuls ginger, 1 cup hot water, flour sufficient to roll.

HONEY NUT-CAKES.—8 cups sugar, 2 cups honey, 4 cups milk or water, 1 lb. almonds, 1 lb. English walnuts, 3 cents' worth each of candied lemon and orange peel, 5 cents' worth citron (the last three cut fine), 2 large tablespoonfuls soda, 2 teaspoonfuls cinnamon, 2 teaspoonfuls ground cloves. Put the milk, sugar, and honey on the stove, to boil 15 minutes; skim off the scum, and take from the stove. Put in the nuts, spices, and candied fruit. Stir in as much flour as can be done with a spoon. Set away to cool, then mix in the soda (don't make the dough too stiff). Cover up and let stand over night, then work in flour enough to make a stiff dough. Bake when you get ready. It is well to let it stand a few days, as it will not stick so badly. Roll out a little thicker than a common cooky, cut in any shape you like.

This recipe originated in Germany, is old and tried, and the cake will keep a year or more.

Mrs. E. Smith.

Honey Drop-cakes.—1 cup honey, ½ cup sugar ½ cup butter or lard, ½ cup sour milk, 1 egg, ½ tablespoonful soda, 4 cups sifted flour.

Honey Short-cake.—3 cups flour, 2 teaspoonfuls baking-powder, 1 teaspoonful salt, ½ cup shortening, 1½ cups sweet milk. Roll quickly, and bake in a hot oven. When done, split the cake and spread the lower half thinly with butter, and the upper half with ½ pound of the best-flavored honey. (Candied honey is preferred. If too hard to spread well it should be slightly warmed or creamed with a knife.) Let it stand a few minutes, and the honey will melt gradually and the flavor will permeate all through the cake. To be eaten with milk.

Honey Tea-cake.—1 cup honey, ½ cup sour cream, 2 eggs, ½ cup butter, 2 cups flour, scant ½ teaspoonful soda, 1 tablespoonful cream of tartar. Bake thirty minutes in a moderate oven.

Miss M. Candler.

Honey Ginger-snaps.—1 pint honey, ¾ lb. butter, 2 teaspoonfuls ginger. Boil together a few minutes, and when nearly cold put in flour until it is stiff. Roll out thin, and bake quickly.

Honey Fruit-cake.—1½ cups honey, ⅔ cup butter, ½ cup sweet milk, 2 eggs well beaten, 3 cups flour, 2 teaspoonfuls baking-powder, 2 cups raisins, 1 teaspoonful each of cloves and cinnamon.

Honey Popcorn Balls.—Take 1 pint extracted honey; put it into an iron frying-pan, and boil until very thick; then stir in freshly popped corn, and when cold, mold into balls. These will specially delight the children.

Honey Caramels.—1 cup extracted honey of best flavor, 1 cup granulated sugar, 3 tablespoonfuls sweet cream or milk. Boil to "soft crack," or until it hardens when dropped into cold water, but not too brittle—just so it will form into a soft ball when taken in the fingers. Pour into a greased dish, stirring in a teaspoonful extract of vanilla just before taking off. Let it be ½ or ¾ inch deep in the dish; and as it cools cut in squares and wrap each square in paraffine paper, such as grocers wrap butter in. To make chocolate caramels, add to the foregoing 1 tablespoonful melted chocolate, just before taking off the stove, stirring it in well. For chocolate caramels it is not so important that the honey be of best quality.

C. C. Miller.

Honey Apple-butter.—1 gallon good cooking-apples, 1 quart honey, 1 quart honey vinegar, 1 heaping teaspoonful ground cinnamon. Cook several hours, stirring often to prevent burning. If the vinegar is very strong, use part water.

Mrs. R. C. Aikin.

Honey and Tar Cough-cure.—Put 1 tablespoonful liquid tar into a shallow tin dish and place it in boiling water until the tar is hot. To this add a pint of extracted honey and stir well for half an hour, adding to it a level teaspoonful pulverized borax Keep well corked in a bottle. Dose, teaspoonful every one, two, or three hours, according to severity of cough.

Summer Honey-drink.—1 spoonful fruit juice and 1 spoonful honey in ½ glass water; stir in as much soda as will lie on a silver dime, and then stir in half as much tartaric acid, and drink at once.

Honey Cereal Coffee.—Fresh wheat bran, 5 lbs.; mix with 2 lbs. of rye flour, 2 lbs. of alfalfa honey. Mix the honey with 3 pints of boiling water. After the honey and water have come to a boil, pour into the bran mixture. Stir thoroughly, and knead to a very stiff dough. Put them through a domestic meat-grinder to separate them. Dry in a warm oven. Brown the same as coffee. For a coffee flavor, add 2 lbs. best Mocha and Java. Have it all ground and put in air-tight cans for future use.

W. L. Porter.

Honey Paste to put Labels on Tin.—Take two spoonfuls of wheat flour and one of honey. Mix the flour and honey, and add boiling water to make it the right thickness. This is fine for labels or wall paper where paper will not stick with ordinary paste.

W. L. Porter.

FOREIGN HONEY RECIPES.

Alsatian Gingerbread.—1 lb. honey, 1 lb. flour, ginger to suit, 2½ drams bicarbonate soda. The honey is first brought to a boil, preferably in a double boiler. It is then removed from the fire, and the flour well stirred into it, and then the soda (or baking-powder; bake. If sweet gingerbread is wanted, add the white of an egg, well whipped, and more honey. The above will keep well for a year if kept in a cellar.

Swiss Cookies.—Prepare some dough as for the gingerbread, and mix with it ½ lb. crushed almonds, orange and lemon juice, and cinnamon; and, if desired, cloves to suit the taste.

Honey Fruit-cakes.—4 eggs, 5 teacups flour, 2 teacups honey, 1 teacup butter, 1 teacup sweet milk, 3 teaspoonfuls baking-powder, 1 lb. raisins, 1 lb. currants, 1 teaspoonful cloves, 1 teaspoonful cinnamon, 1 teaspoonful nutmeg. Then bake in slow oven. The above will keep moist for months.

French Honey-muffins.—1½ pints flour, 1 cup honey, ½ teaspoonful salt, two teaspoonfuls baking-powder, 2 tablespoonfuls butter, 3 eggs, and a little over half a pint milk or thin cream. Sift together the flour, salt, and powder; rub in the butter cold; add beaten eggs, milk, and honey. Mix smoothly in batter as for pound cake; about half fill sponge-cake tins, cold and fully greased, and bake bread in good steady oven for eight minutes.

Remedy for Constipation.—Dr. Vogel, of the University of Dorpat, one of the greatest authorities on the subject of children's diseases, recommends giving the juice of well-stewed prunes, sweetened with honey, to very small children, and not give castor oil or other remedies. This is also a remedy which can be used by adults with good results. Try it.

HONEY TAFFY.—Boil honey until it hardens when dropped into cold water. Pull until it becomes white. Any quantity may be used. A pound requires 20 minutes' boiling and stirring. Great care must be exercised not to burn the honey. It makes very fine taffy.

DYSPEPSIA REMEDY.—Dr. McLean, San Francisco, Cal., recommends this for the cure of dyspepsia. Mix a drink of honey and water to suit the taste, then add a small quantity of myrrh (just a few drops), and drink every morning as you first get up.

HONEY-DROPS.—Blend ½ cup honey, 1 teaspoonful butter, 1 egg well beaten, ⅔ cup flour, sifted with half a teaspoon of baking-powder, and a pinch of salt. Drop by teaspoonfuls on a tin, and bake in a quick oven. These proportions will make about 20 cakes.

PICKLED GRAPES IN HONEY.—7 lbs. good grapes (wine grapes if possible) on the stalks, carefully packed in a jar without bruising any of them. Make a syrup of 4 lbs. of honey, a pint of good vinegar with cloves, etc., to suit the taste. Then boil the syrup, carefully skimming it, for 20 minutes. While boiling hot, pour the syrup over the grapes and seal up. This will keep perfectly for years, as the honey is a preservative.

HONEY COLD CREAM.—1 cup of honey; ¾ of a cup of beeswax; 1 cup of cottolene. Melt all, take off the fire, and stir till it is cool; rose or violet perfume may be added. It should be well protected from the air. The blending should be well done. This is fine for chapped or rough hands, if they are slightly wetted before applying.

HONEY-CAKES (pain d'epice or Leb Kuchen).—The following recipe will be much appreciated by cake-makers. The cakes are excellent, and will keep indefinitely. If they get dry, simply put them for a few days into a bread-tin. Use 3 lbs. of honey, 3 lbs. of flour, 1 oz. powdered ammonia, a small teacupful of ground cinnamon, half-teaspoonful of ground cloves, 6 oz. orange peel (or citron) cut very fine; 4 oz. sweet almonds cut very small. (The ammonia evaporates in baking.) Directions. Pour the honey in a graniteware or copper sauce-pan, and set on the stove. When it boils, draw it aside and remove the scum (as honey boils and burns very quickly, great care must be used). Then pour the honey into the vessel in which the paste is to be made; leave it to cool; then add flour and other ingredients, except the ammonia, which latter must not be added till the flour and honey have been mixed up and the paste has become cold. In preparing for use, place the ammonia in a cup; pour on a few drops of cold water, and stir it well, so as to form a thick paste, then mix it up with the rest. Then take a piece of the paste, roll it out into a cake not over ¼ inch thick, and cut up into convenient sizes. Put these on a flat tin and bake in a hot oven 12 to 15 minutes. The above is made by the monks of Buckfast Abbey, England.

HONEY VINEGAR.—The best vinegar produced anywhere is made from honey. Any one who understands how to make cider vinegar can easily make honey vinegar, only substituting water sweetened with honey for the apple juice.

BAR-LE-DUC PRESERVES.—These preserves are believed to be the finest of their kind, and have hitherto been imported at extravagant prices. Other fruits besides currants may be treated in this way, as honey is of itself a preservative. These preserves do not require to be kept absolutely air-tight.

Take selected red or white currants of large size, one by one; carefully make an incision in the skin ¼ of an inch deep with tiny embroidery scissors. Through this slit remove the seeds with the aid of a sharp needle; remove the seeds separately, preserving the shape of the fruit. Take the weight of the currants in honey, and when this has been heated add the currants. Let it simmer a minute or two, and then seal as for jelly. The currants retain their shape, are of a beautiful color, and melt in the mouth. Care should be exercised not to scorch the honey, then you will have fine preserves.

HONEY-PASTE FOR CHAPPED HANDS.—An excellent paste for chapped hands is made as follows: The white of one egg, one teaspoon of glycerine, one ounce of honey, and sufficient barley flour to compose a paste. It may not be generally known that honey is a prime ingredient of cosmetics; for its action on the skin is always agreeable.

HONEY FOR CLEANING THE HANDS.—Honey is an excellent cleanser of the skin, though few are aware of the fact. Try this: Rub a little honey on the dry skin; moisten a little, and rub again: use more water, and rub. Wash thoroughly, when it will be found the hands are as clean as the most powerful soap can make them.

HONEY TOOTH-PASTE.—Eight ounces precipitated chalk, 4 oz. powdered castile soap, 4 oz. orris-root powder, 40 drops oil of sassafras, 80 drops oil of bay, and honey to make a paste.

This is really a first-class tooth-paste.

FRENCH HONEY-CANDIES.—In an enameled-ware sauce-pan melt one part of gelatine in one part of water, stirring well. When arrived at the state of a soft paste, add 4 parts of honey previously warmed, stirring lively. Take from the fire; add the desired flavor and color, mixing carefully, and pour into a shallow lightly greased dish. Let it dry for a few days.

HONEY AS A SOFTENER OF THE HANDS.—A good many ladies are unaware that the very best cosmetics are made with honey as a prime ingredient. Here is one for the hands, which is said to be very fine. Rub together 1 lb. of honey and the yolks of 8 eggs; gradually add 1 lb. oil of sweet almonds, during constant stirring; work in ½ lb. bitter almonds, and perfume with 2 drams each of attar of bergamot and attar of cloves. Of course, the quantities may be reduced if necessary.

HONEY SOAP.—Cut 2 pounds of yellow soap in thin slices and put into a saucepan with sufficient water to prevent the soap from being burnt. Place on the fire, and as soon as all the soap has dissolved add one pound of honey and stir until the whole begins to boil. Then remove from the fire, add a few drops of essence of cinnamon, pour out into a deep dish to cool, and then cut into squares. It improves by keeping.

HONEY FOR FRECKLES.—Half a pound of honey, 2 oz. glycerin, 2 oz. alcohol, 6 drams citric acid, 15 drops ambergris. Apply night and morning.

HONEY CHOCOLATE.—Chocolate sweetened with honey rather than with sugar is excellent. Here is how it is made: Melt 1 lb. of gelatine in a pint of water; add 10 lbs. of honey, thoroughly warming

the same, and then add 4 lbs. of cocoa. Flavor with
vanilla when taken off the fire, and then pour into
greased dishes or molds.

HONEY BROWN BREAD.—One cup corn meal, 1 cup
rye meal, 1 cup sour milk, ½ cup or less of honey, a
teaspoonful of salt and a teaspoonful of soda.
Steam four hours, and then dry in the oven fifteen
minutes. It may be added that most of the molasses now sold is not fit to eat, and in any case honey
is much better.

HONEY-BOARDS. See COMB HONEY,
and HIVES.

HONEY-COMB. For many years all
theories as to wax-production were far from
the truth. Somewhere between 1744 and
1768 it was discovered that wax is produced
between the plates on the lower side of the
worker bee's abdomen. The honor of this
discovery is usually ascribed to a Lusatian
peasant of unknown name. But Thorley, a
quaint writer of 1744, speaks of "six pieces
of solid wax, white and transparent like
gum within the plaits." *

Wax is produced at the will of the bee,
and when called for by the necessities of the
hive. The wax-producing bees obtain a
somewhat high temperature, usually by
close clustering, although they sometimes
hang in slender festoons and chains.

"Wax is not chemically a fat or glyceride,
hence those who have called it ' the fat of
bees' have grossly erred; yet it is nearly allied to the fats in atomic constitution, and
the physiological conditions favoring the
formation of one are curiously similar to
those aiding in the production of the other.
We put our poultry up to fatten in confinement, with partial light; to secure bodily
inactivity we keep warm and feed highly.
Our bees, under Nature's teaching, put themselves up to yield wax under conditions so
parallel that the suitability of the fatting-
coop is vindicated."—*Cheshire.*

On the inner side of the eight plates lining
the lower side of the abdomen are about
140,000 glands (Cheshire), from which the
wax is secreted as a white liquid, which
hardens on exposure to the air. When first
formed it is white and very brittle, and is
pulled out from between the plates by the
pincers on the hind legs. The pieces of wax
are then passed to the front legs, and thence
to the mouth, where they are made plastic
by the addition of various materials in the
saliva and by thorough mastication.

* It was the celebrated anatomist John Hunter
who discovered just how the bees secrete wax, and
thereby settled a vexed question. He communi-
cated his discovery in a paper read before the Royal
Society of London, Feb. 23, 1792, and subsequently
published in Philosophical Transactions.—W. K. M.

From this raw material the sculpture bees
make three kinds of cells. First, at certain
times of the year, when a new queen is
needed, they build a few large, almost perpendicular, peanut-shaped cells. The two
other kinds, drone-cells and worker-cells,
are practically the same in form, the drone-
cells differing in being larger. As their
names imply, they are used for rearing
drones (male bees) and workers (undevel-

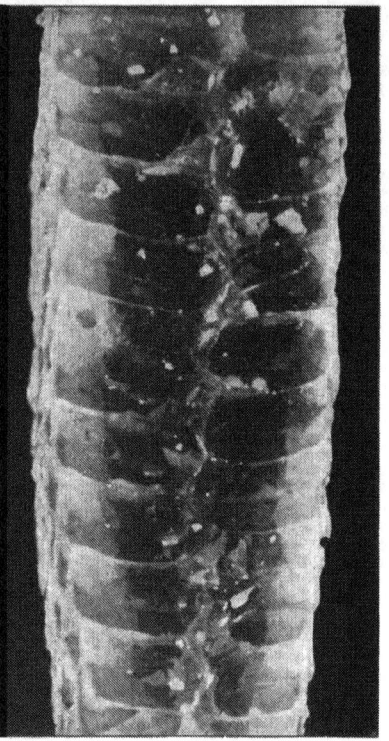

FIG. 1.—EDGE OF HONEY-COMB BUILT NEXT
TO GLASS—ENLARGED VIEW.
The cells are partly filled with honey. This illustration shows that the cells are not straight and
horizontal, but curved and slanting upward.

oped females). Both kinds of cells are
nearly horizontal, slanting upward slightly
from the center to the exterior of the comb.
Both kinds are utilized for the storage of
honey, and this slight inclination facilitates
the filling of the cells by preventing the
honey from running out before the cap is
added. See Fig. 1.

All three forms are *primarily* cylindrical.
The queen-cells, isolated from the others,
always remain cylindrical. All solitary bees

(not honey-bees) make such cells. The hexagonal form is due largely to mutual pressure, and partly to optical illusion. Cells near the edge of the comb, where it is at-

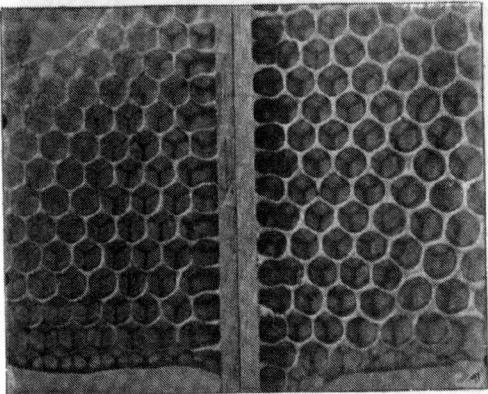

FIG. 2.—CIRCULAR CELLS.

tached to some support, are either circular or elongated circular. See Fig. 2.

Worker-cells seem more closely crowded together than drone-cells, and thus have their angles, in most cases, more sharply defined. In drone comb some cells are almost without angles, the spaces between the tubes being filled in by a thickening of the cell walls greater than is customary. See Figs. 4 and 5. In such parts a casual glance shows them to be almost as hexagonal as the usual type. But close examination or magnifying shows many cells that are cylindrical tubes. The more one studies comb, the more firmly is he impressed with the belief that the original "intention" of the bee is to produce a hollow cylinder, and that the hexagonal result is due solely to a force of circumstances, and is entirely "unintentional."

Much has been written about the mathematically exact angles of honey-comb. Some philosophers have stoutly maintained that the bees have solved difficult problems, and that their work is an example of the wonderful perfection of nature or natural instinct. Many of these claims make interesting reading. Ab-

struse theories and complex formulæ have been contributed to sustain these claims. But they lack one essential feature, and in this they do not stand alone, even in the productions of writers on natural history—*they are not true.*

Actual measurements of the angles show that they greatly vary. But, notwithstanding the fact that the cells vary in size and form, comb is none the less a wonderful structure, with all its parts arranged for the greatest strength, the largest storing capacity, and most perfect adaptation to circumstances. Wax is produced by the bee at a great expenditure of labor, material, and strength. Well-informed investigators say that "The costliness of wax to the bee, since it can be produced only at the expense of many times its own weight of honey or sugar, has led to great economy, one pound of it being molded into 35,000 worker-cells," while still others have observed 50,000 made from that amount. To help the bee in this economy, apiarists

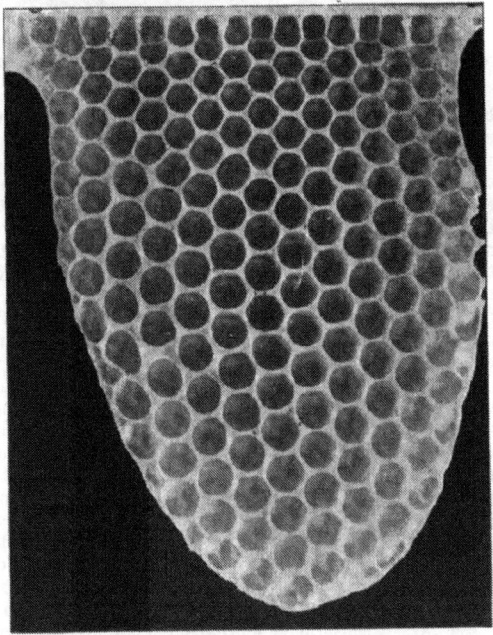

FIG. 4.—A COMBINATION OF WORKER AND DRONE CELLS. None of the angles are sharp, and most of the cells are circular.

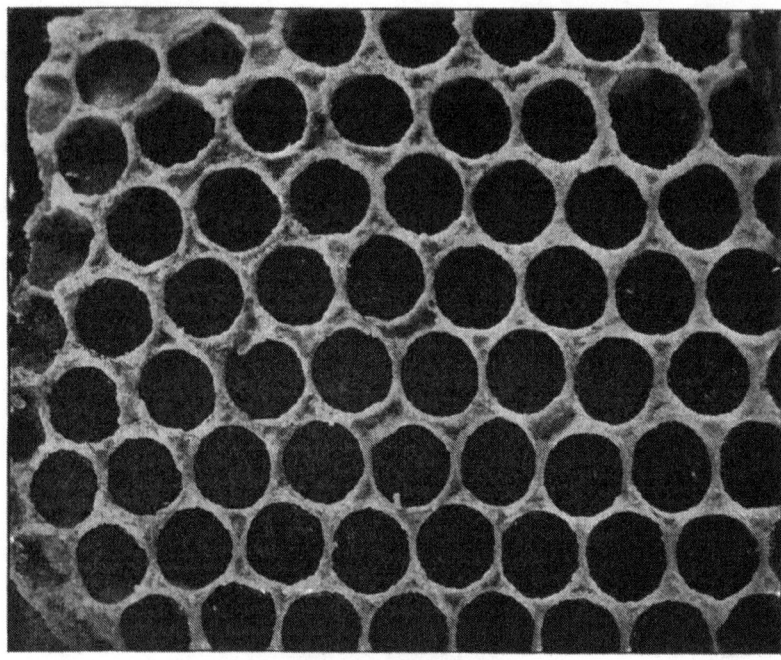

FIG. 5.—A STUDY IN CELL-MAKING.

Note that the cells are made independent of each other, and that it is the refuse wax, like droppings of mortar in brick-laying, that seems to tumble into the interstices to fill up.

have found it advantageous to use machinery by which the same material can be
worked over and over. As the combs become old they are melted, the pure wax tak-
en out and remodeled into thin comb-building foundation. But this is in no sense the
manufacture of a new product, but an extracting, purifying, and remodeling of the
bees' own choice material. It simply saves
the bees much arduous labor that machinery
can do easier and at less expense, when we
consider the effect on the bee.

No one is so foolish as to claim that a suit
of clothes made on a machine is any more
"artificial" than one sewed by hand. It is
simply economy of labor. Yet hundreds of
persons have the incorrect notion that there
is a honey-comb made from wood pulp,
punk, putty, paraffine, or perhaps material
other than wax. We say "foolish enough"
advisedly, because a wise man changes his
mind (when it becomes necessary); but a
fool, never. It would not be surprising in
these days of sensational journalism and of
false nature-stories if one should get the
notion that artificial comb honey really

exists; but the foolish part comes in when
a person, totally inexperienced with bees,
stoutly and smilingly maintains that there is
such a thing as manufactured honey in the
comb. We feel sure that the inimitably
foolish expression of such a person is the
origin of the colloquialism, "The smile that
won't come off." No use. Do not argue.
It won't come. "Why, I've seen it at the
stores. Grocer told me all about it—was
several cents cheaper. I tried it; we didn't
like it as well as the genuine." And then
the bee-keeper goes away, not a wiser but a
madder man, and wonders why the fool-
killer doesn't do his duty, and why every
one except the bee-keeper knows all about
bees and their products.

It is, however, true that there are many
interesting problems about comb-building
that even the experienced bee-keeper doesn't
know. To us one of the most interesting of
these problems has been the fact that bees
carry along at the same time the comb and
the storage work in the sections in all stages
of progress. If an empty super were put on
a colony so strong that the bees "boiled"

up into all parts of the super until there would be no vacant "standing room" left, one would suppose that the work of comb-building would begin in all sections at the same time, and progress with almost equal rapidity. But it doesn't. A few sections in the center will be completed before work has been started in some of the outer sections, and nearly all gradations may be observed between the extremes. From two supers on a ten-frame hive we selected one-half, that is, 32, as shown in Fig. 7, that exhibited seriatim every part of the progress from the first extension of the suggestive nest-egg starter to the completed fancy comb. Another series, almost as well graded, could have been made up from the other 32 sections. Now, why was it that there were not 32 or more one-eighth filled, then one-quarter filled, then one-half filled, and so on gradually, *all* advancing "right dress," and about equally in a uniform line of progress till all had been brought to completion?

Drone-cells and worker-cells are made from new wax and are at first of pearly whiteness, which soon becomes yellowish. Queen-cells are made mostly from surrounding comb, so a queen-cell just completed is aged in appearance if on old comb. Almost any material is used, yet not extravagantly. So economical are the bees that they "pit" the cell till it has the roughness of a peanut. This arrangement of material gives greater strength than the same amount would give in a layer of uniform thickness—on the principle that a certain amount of material is stronger in a large hollow cylinder than in a smaller one that is solid.

Bees change readily from the building of worker-cells to drone-cells. They seem to have no trouble in making correct adjustments and angles. It is not at all uncommon to see a group of drone-cells near adjoining worker-cells on the same comb. One wonders why the bees change the size of cells. When capped over for honey, both are of the same height; but when over brood, drone-cell cappings stand above the surrounding worker-cells. The cappings of the drone-cells are made stronger by six bracing ribs or buttresses, Fig. 6. This gives the whole capping a most beautiful appearance when viewed as an opaque object under the microscope. The cappings of both cells, though extremely thin, are not air-tight. It is wonderful to observe how the bees adapt the comb to the form of the hive, often curving it, and sometimes making it cylindrical. In the arrangement of the several combs in a hive there is wonderful provision for the ventilation of every cell, and for the convenience of the workers in the various depart-

FIG. 6.—DRONE-CELLS USED FOR HONEY-STORAGE.

It will be seen that the lower part of the opening is capped first. This, with the slant of the cell, keeps the new honey from running out.

ments of labor. What a wonderful coincidence (or shall we say purpose?) is it that honey-bees do not make their cells of paper as do wasps, yellow-jackets, bumble-bees, and hornets! If they did so, the luxury of comb honey would be unknown. Honey-bees place their combs perpendicularly. All paper combs with which I am familiar are horizontal.

SIZE OF DRONE AND WORKER COMB.

We have said bees build two distinct, regular sizes—drone and worker. Worker comb measures very nearly five cells to the inch,

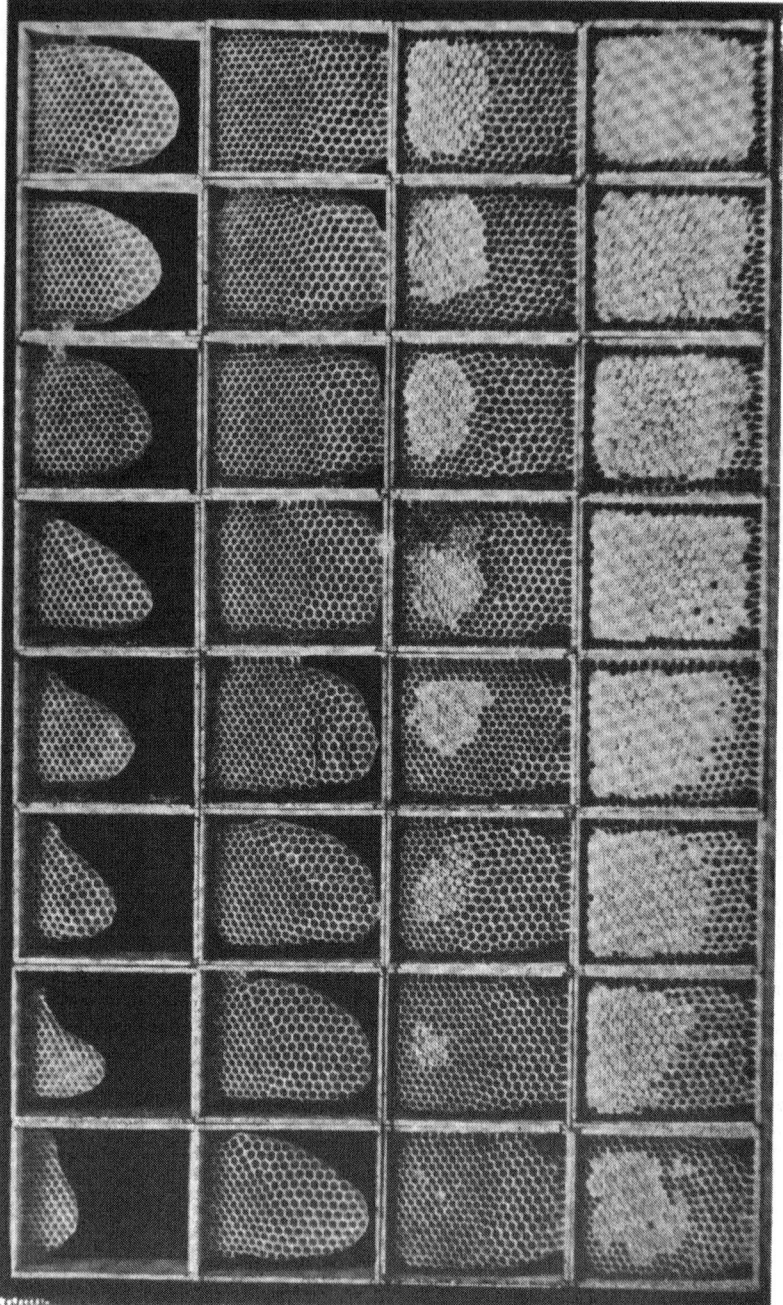

FIG. 7.—THE DEVELOPMENT OF COMB HONEY.

Note.—These sections were selected from two supers of 28 sections each.

on an average. Some specimens are a little larger, and some a little smaller; but when the comb is at all irregular, it is quite apt to be a little larger. The best specimens of true worker comb generally contain 5 cells within the space of an inch, and therefore this measure has been adopted for comb foundation. If there are five cells to the inch, a square inch would give, on an average, about 25* cells, and 25 on the opposite side would make 50 young bees that can be hatched from every square inch of solid brood. As foundation is so much more regular than the natural comb, we get a great many more bees in a given surface of comb, and here, at least, we can fairly claim to have improved on nature.

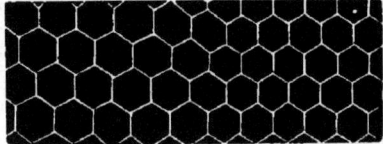

DRONE COMB.   WORKER COMB.

Drone comb measures just about four cells to the inch, but the bees seem less particular about the size of it than with the worker. They very often seem to make the cells of such size as to fill out best a given space; and, accordingly, we find them differing from worker size all the way up to considerably more than ½ of an inch in width. Drones are raised in these extra-large cells without trouble, and honey is also stored in them; but where they are very large, the bees are compelled to turn them up, or the honey would flow out. Now, as honey is kept in place by capillary attraction, when cells exceed a certain size the adhesion of the liquid to the wax walls is insufficient, of itself, to hold the honey in place. Where drones are to be reared in these very large cells the bees contract the mouth by a thick rim. As an experiment, we had some plates made for producing small sheets of foundation, having only 3½ cells to the inch. The bees worked on a few of these, with these same thick rims, but they evidently did not like the idea very well, for they tried to make worker-cells of some of it, and it proved so much of a complication for their little heads that they finally abandoned the whole piece of comb, apparently in disgust. Bees sometimes rear worker

* The exact mathematical calculation makes these numbers 29, 29, and 58, respectively, but ordinarily the numbers we have given in the context are more nearly correct.

brood in drone comb, where compelled to from want of room, and they always do it in the way we have mentioned, by contracting the mouth of the cells and leaving the young bee a rather large berth in which to grow and develop. Drones are sometimes reared in worker-cells also, but they are so much cramped in growth that they seldom look like fully developed insects.

Several times it has been suggested that we enlarge the race of honey-bees by giving them larger cells; and some circumstances seem to indicate that something may be done in this direction, although we have little hope of any permanent enlargement in size unless we combine with it the idea of selecting the largest bees to propagate from, as given a few pages back. By making the cells smaller than ordinarily, we get small bees with very little trouble; and we have seen a whole nucleus of bees so small as to be really laughable, just because the comb they were hatched from was set at an angle so that one side was concave and the other convex. The small bees came from the concave side. Their light, active movements, as they sported in front of the hive, made them a pretty and amusing sight for those fond of curiosities. Worker-bees reared in drone-cells, if we are correct, are sometimes extra large in size; but as to whether we can make them permanently larger by such a course, we are inclined to doubt. The difficulty, at present, seems to be the tendency to rear a great quantity of useless drones. By having a hive furnished entirely with worker-comb, we can so nearly prevent the production of drones that it is safe enough to call it a complete remedy.

HOW BEES BUILD COMB.

In this day and age of bees and honey it would seem that one should be able to tell how our bees build comb, with almost as much ease as they would tell how cows and horses eat grass ; but for all that, we lack records of careful and close experiments, such as Darwin made many years ago. In our house-apiary there are dozens of hives where the bees are building right up close to the glass, at this very minute ; and all one has to do, in order to see how it is done, is to take a chair and sit down before them. But the little fellows have such a queer sleight-of-hand way of doing the work that we hardly know how they do accomplish it.

If we examine our bees closely during the season of comb-building and honey-gathering, we shall find a good many of them with

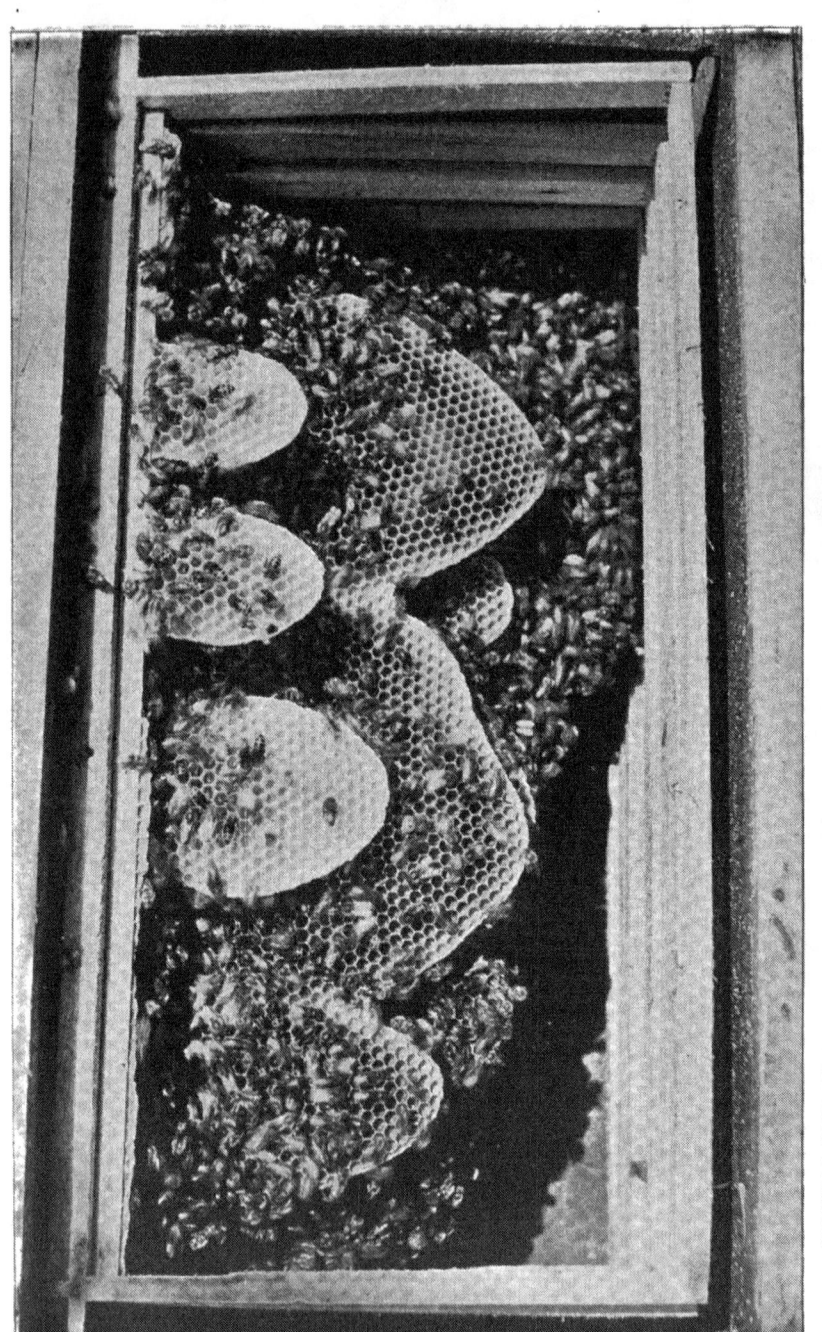

NATURAL COMB-BUILDING.—PHOTOGRAPHED BY W. Z. HUTCHINSON, EDITOR "BEE-KEEPER'S REVIEW," FLINT, MICH.

NATURAL-COMB BUILDING IN A HIVE MADE ENTIRELY OF GLASS.

wax scales protruding between the rings that form the body, and these scales are either picked from their bodies or from the bottom of the hive or honey-boxes in which they are building. If a bee is obliged to carry one of these wax scales but a short distance, it takes it in its mandibles, and looks as business-like with it thus as a carpenter with a board on his shoulder. If it has to carry it from the bottom of the honey-box, it takes it in a way that I can not explain any better than to say it slips it under its chin. When thus equipped, you would never know it was encumbered with any thing, unless it chanced to slip out, when it will very dextrously tuck it back with one of its fore feet. The little plate of wax is so warm from being kept under its chin as to be quite soft when it gets back; and as it takes it out, and gives it a pinch against the comb where the building is going on, one would think it might stop a while, and put it into place; but, not it; for off it scampers and twists around so many different ways, you might think it was not one of the working kind at all. Another follows after it sooner or later, and gives the wax a pinch, or a little scraping and burnishing with its polished mandibles. then another,

and so on; and the sum total of all these manœuvres is, that the comb seems almost to grow out of nothing; yet no *one* bee ever makes a cell.

The finished comb is the result of the united efforts of the moving, restless mass; and the great mystery is, that any thing so wonderful can ever result at all from such a mixed-up, skipping-about way of working as they seem to have. When the cells are built out only part way they are filled with honey or eggs, and the length is increased when they feel disposed, or "get around to it," perhaps. It may be that they find it easier working with shallow walls about the cells, for they can take care of the brood much easier, and put in the honey easier too, in all probability; and, as a thick rim is left around the upper edge of the cell, they have the material at hand to lengthen it at any time. This thick rim is also very necessary to give the bees a secure foothold, for the sides of the cells are so thin they would be very apt to break down with even the light weight of a bee. When honey is coming in rapidly, and the bees are crowded for room to store it, their eagerness is so plainly apparent, as they push the work along, that they fairly seem to quiver with excitement;

BEES LIVING ON COMBS BUILT IN THE OPEN AIR.

but for all that, they skip about from one cell to another in the same way, no one bee working in the same spot to exceed a minute or two, at the very outside. Very frequently, after one has bent a piece of wax a certain way, the next tips it in the opposite direction, and so on until completion; but after all have given it a twist and a pull, it is found in pretty nearly the right spot. As nearly as we can discover, they moisten the thin ribbons of wax with some sort of fluid or saliva. As the bee always preserves the thick rib or rim of the comb it is working, the looker-on would suppose it was making the·walls of considerable thickness; but if we drive it away, and break this rim, we shall find that its mandibles have come so nearly together that the wax between them, beyond the rim, is almost as thin as tissue paper. In building natural comb, of course the bottoms of the cells are thinned in the same way, as the work goes along, before any side walls are made at all.

When no foundation is furnished, little patches of comb are started at different points, as shown in the engraving, p. 268. Then as these patches enlarge, their edges are united so perfectly that it is sometimes difficult, when the frame is filled solid, to determine *where* the pieces were united, so perfect is

the work. At other times there is, perhaps, a row of irregular or drone cells along the line of the union.

The midrib of natural comb becomes thicker as it approaches the line of support and tapers toward the bottom. Why this is so is evident. That there should be a gradual gradation in thickness from top to bottom seems wonderful when we remember the hap-hazard, skip-about work on the part of so many different bees.

HOW TO GET BEES TO BUILD WORKER COMB OFF FROM STARTERS OF FOUNDATION.

While we always recommend bee-keepers to use full sheets of worker foundation because the raising of drone comb and drone brood is an unnecessary waste, yet it very often happens that a bee-keeper runs short of foundation just when it is impossible to get another shipment in time, and therefore the knowledge of how to get the bees to build all worker comb from mere starters is important. Mr. E. D. Townsend, of Remus, Mich., to whom reference has been made elsewhere in this work, in an article for *Gleanings in Bee Culture* for Aug. 1, 1909, which we here reproduce, explains the conditions under which bees will build all-worker comb, and when they will build worker and drone comb both.

It is a fact that bees under certain conditions build almost all worker comb; and it is also true that, under other conditions, a great deal of undesirable drone comb is built. For instance, a new medium-sized swarm, placed in a hive of a size that may be filled with combs and brood in about 23 days or less, ought to build worker comb mainly, though some of the last combs built may contain a few drone-cells. The secret seems to be in having just the right number of workers and just the right amount of honey coming in, so that the bees will draw out the combs no faster than the queen can occupy them with brood. As long as this condition lasts we should expect the bees to build worker combs. From this we see that, in order to get good results in comb-building from a natural swarm, this swarm should be of just the right size, and there should be a honey-flow of, say, three or four pounds a day.

We will suppose a large swarm is hived during a period when honey is coming in freely. At this time there is too much honey coming in for the best results in comb-building in the brood-nest, if the whole force of workers is compelled to do all their work in the brood-nest. The remedy is to put most of the workers at work in the supers. Most beginners fail in doing this; but the principle is to make the surplus receptacles more inviting to the workers than the brood-nest, and the bees will immediately go up into the supers on being hived. Our comb-honey super with extracting-combs at the sides makes an ideal arrangement for this very thing.

It is plain to see that, if most of the honey being carried in is placed in the sections, where it should be, the queen will not be hurried to keep pace with the workers, consequently all-worker comb will be built. The brood-nest should be filled with comb during the first 23 days after the swarm is hived; for the queen must keep up with the workers and lay in nearly every cell as fast as it is drawn out, or the bees will begin to store honey in the cells. When this condition arrives, the bees, on the supposition that the queen has reached her limit, and that the rest of the combs will be used for storing honey, begin to bu ld the storage size or the drone-cells in the brood-nest. This is likely to occur in about 23 days after the swarm is hived; for by this time the brood is beginning to hatch out in that part of the hive where the laying began. From this time on, the queen has nearly all she can do to keep the cells filled with eggs where the young bees are hatching. This means that the comb-building part of the hive is neglected, and that the bees build store or drone comb to a great extent until the hive is filled.

It sometimes happens that a very late swarm will issue; and since the season is nearing its close, it is not possible for such a swarm to build more than five combs before the honey ceases coming in. We hive such swarms as usual, and in about two days five of the frames having the least combs built are removed and a division-board placed up against the remaining five frames, this five having been shoved over to one side of the hive. If a super is given such a swarm at the time of hiving, it must be a nearly finished one, as the bees will need most of the r time to finish up the five combs in the brood-nest. If one has two of such five-comb colonies they can be united at the close of the season, so that there will

be none but full-sized colonies to winter. A better plan than this for late swarms, or for any small after-swarms that one may have, is to hive them on full sets of combs taken, possibly, from hives in which colonies died the previous winter. This is a very good way to get such combs filled with bees, but some swarms hived in this way may need feeding for winter.

There are artificial ways of handling bees so that they will build good worker combs. I refer to the plan of shaking the bees into an empty hive, in the same way that a swarm is hived If a colony is divided into nuclei of, say, two or three combs each, and each nucleus given a young queen reared the same year, such little colonies will build very nice worker combs; but the beginner will not be interested in this artificial way of making increase, for he should stick to the natural-swarming plan for his increase until such time as he has had experience and made a success of getting a crop of honey. In fact, there are many things to be learned before a beginner should take up artificial ways of making increase.

SOME CONDITIONS WHERE BEES BUILD MOSTLY DRONE COMB.

Any colony found rearing drone brood in the brood-nest will, if a comb is removed and an empty frame put in its place, build drone comb. It can be depended upon, moreover, that a colony of bees wintered over, containing a queen reared the season before, or one older, will build drone comb until the time that it swarms. By this it can be seen that it is necessary to replace any combs, removed from a colony before it swarms in the spring or early summer, with an empty comb or with a frame containing a full sheet of foundation, or else drone comb will be the result. To be sure that a colony will build a large per cent of worker comb it is necessary to remove all the brood and to cause the bees of that colony to begin all over again, as in the case of natural swarming; or, as mentioned before, the colony can be broken up into nuclei, each nucleus containing a young queen.

For the consideration of the thickness of combs and how far to space them apart see FRAMES, SELF-SPACING; also SPACING OF FRAMES; also COMB FOUNDATION.

HONEY-DEW. So named because it was formerly supposed to come down from the heavens in the form of a saccharine spray, settling on the leaves of trees and low-growing shrubbery. It is now known to be almost, if not entirely, the product of aphides, or plant-lice, and coccids, or scale insects. These are sometimes found on the topmost limbs of a tree, and the honey-dew which they secrete is thrown out as a spray, which falls on the lower limbs and on the sidewalk* or grass. Observers, seeing the leaves of the lower limbs of trees and the grass covered with a sort of saccharine varnish, naturally came to the conclusion that this substance was a real honey-dew, and hence the name.

---

* Sometimes the sidewalks in our vicinity, in July and August, are spotted all over near the trees.

There are certain plants which, under certain conditions. it is said, exude a sort of saccharine substance from the leaves, but, strictly speaking, this is not honey-dew. The ordinary " stuff " that is gathered by the bees, commonly called honey-dew, is nothing but a secretion from plant-lice. There are several species of honey-dew lice, among which may be named *Lecanium tiliæ*, that attack the basswoods; *Lecanium tulipifera*, of the tulip-tree, often called " poplar," and the scale or bark louse that attacks maple-trees, *Pulvinaria innumerabilis* (Rath.). Prof. Cook, formerly of the Michigan Agricultural College, now of Claremont, Cal., professor of entomology, and a bee-keeper of long experience, thus describes these lice :

The maple-tree scale or bark louse (*Pulvinaria innumerabilis* Rath.) consists at this season (1884) of a brown scale about five-eighths of an inch long, which is oblong, and slightly notched behind. On the back of the scale are transverse depressions, marking segments. The blunt posterior of the insect is raised by a large dense mass of fibrous cotton-like material, in which will be found about 800 small white eggs. These eggs falling on to a dark surface look to the unaided eye like flour; but with a lens they are found to be ob-

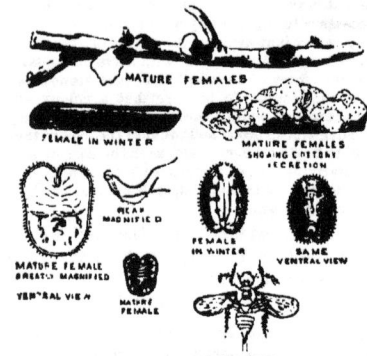

long, and would be pronounced by all as eggs, at once. This cotton-like egg-receptacle is often so thick as to raise the brown scale nearly a fourth of an inch. The scales are found on the under side of the limbs of some trees, and are often so thick as to overlap each other. Frequently there are hundreds on a single main branch of a tree. I find them on basswood, soft and hard maple, and grapevines, though very much more abundant on the maples.

Another feature, at this mature stage of the insect, is the secretion of a large amount of honey-dew. This falls on the leaves below, so as fairly to gum them over, as though they were varnished. This honey-dew is much prized by the bees, which swarm upon the leaves. If such honey-dew is pleasant to the taste, as some aver, I should have no fear of the bees collecting it.

From the middle to the last of June, the eggs begin to hatch, though hatching is not completed for some weeks after it begins, so we may expect young lice to hatch out from late in June till August.

The young lice are yellow, half as broad as long, tapering slightly toward the posterior. The seven abdominal segments appear very distinctly. The legs and antennæ are seen from the other side. As in the young of all such bark-lice, the beak, or sucking-tube, is long and thread-like, and is bent under the body till the young louse is ready to settle down to earnest work as a sapper. Two hair-like appendages, or setæ, which soon disappear, terminate the body.

The same writer, in the *American Bee Journal* for January, 1899, gives his reasons for doubting the plant origin of honey-dew. He says :

1. I now have carefully examined this secretion for years, whenever seen, and have always found either aphides — plant-lice ; coccids — scale insects ; other hemipterous bugs ; or else larvæ of insects (these are reported to me) often working in scores—to be the source of this nectar. This gives strong presumption that such is always the source of honey-dew.

2. We have reason to believe, in the economy of Nature, that energy is never expended by plant or animal that does not in some way benefit by such outgo. We are easily able to see how the insects profit by the secretion of this nectar. They thus lure bees, ants, wasps, etc., to their immediate presence, and these in turn repel the birds which else would feed on and destroy the insects.

I once noticed an exhibit of this function in Michigan, so palpably displayed that to doubt it was impossible. The *Lecanium tiliæ* — a large bark louse— was thick on a linden-tree close beside my study window. In early spring the beautiful song sparrow commenced to feed on the young scale insects which thickly dotted the leaves. Suddenly the bees and other sweet-loving insects commenced to visit the same leaves for the honey-dew which dropped from the coccids, and the birds at once ceased to come. In a few days cold, or, preferably, nectar in other places, kept the bees and their companions from the place, and the birds again commenced their good work. This alternation of bird and bee visits occurred several times. Such observations make the value of the expensive secretion to the insects clearly evident.

On the other hand, the honey-dew always becomes foul with the black smut or fungus that attacks sweet substances on tree or bush. We can hardly doubt that it is a serious evil to the plants, and are unable to see any good that comes to the plant from it. I fully believe it is always harmful to vegetation, and I feel certain that plants do not originate it to their own hurt.

I referred above to certain acorn-infesting larvæ that secrete nectar. I have never seen them, but have often heard of such—principally from Missouri— so often that I think they may be more than a myth. Yet I am free to say that I should feel more certain if I actually saw them. I can see how oak-tree plant-lice, which are by no means rare, might lead to an erroneous conclusion.

Ergot—a fungus which attacks rye and other plants —is also said to secrete honey-dew. If this be true, then I feel sure that the sweet in some way benefits the fungus. If it does the fungus no good, then I be- lieve it, too, has other origin.

In California, where scale insects and aphids are so common, it is very easy to study the honey-dew, and the black repulsive fungus, which our orchardists denominate " smut." The walnut-tree, this season, has been infested generally with an aphid, and honey-dew and smut have always attended it.

It is not to be inferred that this honey-dew is unwholesome. It is a secretion, and not an excretion. It has a similar origin to honey, and may be as delicious. Much aphid honey-dew is deliciously wholesome, and the honey from it is superior. Most if not all of the coccid honey-dew, on the other hand, is dark and of ill flavor, and its presence in honey, or as honey, is greatly injurious, and can never be sold for the table. I have sold it by the barrel for manufacturing. This was used to make cookies, and was said to be all right by the manufacturer. I explained all to him, yet he gave the ruling price.

Often this honey-dew is produced in exceeding quantities, and I have known it to crystallize on plants, especially on pine and larch trees, so as to encrust them with white, and become very conspicuous.

Another authority, Prof. H. A. Surface, President of the Pennsylvania State Beekeepers' Association, and State Zoologist, has this to say on the subject of the origin of honey-dew:

Honey dew in this State is never found excepting on plants that are infested with certain scale insects, plant lice, or similar insects. It is true that it will be seen on the lower leaves of a tree before the insects get there; but this is because they often leave the trees by flying through the air and commence to feed on the tender new leaves of the upper part and drop their sweet secretions on the leaves below. Later they drop to the leaves below or crawl down the tree, and may be seen on the lower leaves. This does not mean that honey-dew was on the leaves before the insects were there.

Honey-dew attracts ants, wasps, bees, and other insects that feed on sweets; but the plant-lice do not feed on the honey-dew nor on sweets, as they draw all their living from the sap of the trees or plants that are infested. No one has ever seen plant-lice feeding on the sweet liquid called honey-dew; but, on the other hand, we have frequently observed this liquid coming from the cornicles or honey-tubes of plant-lice, as well as from the vent or digestive tract. No one can watch plant-lice during the summer without seeing the honey-dew appear first in small globules, and then increase to larger drops on the cornicles or honey-tubes, especially when ants are stroking the plant-lice with their antennæ. There can be no possible doubt about the source of this liquid.

As to whether the honey-dew is a benefit to the bee-keeper depends upon how he winters his bees, and upon locality. If the bees can be wintered on their summer stands, or where they have flight as frequently as they need it, and the locality and season are such that they can fly frequently, say once every two or three weeks, they will winter all right on honey-dew; but if they are to be put into a cellar, or otherwise kept from flying for six weeks or two months, they will doubtless perish with dysentery. Honey-dew makes far more waste material to be voided from the system than any other food that the bees can take, and it is known that this voiding is done only when in flight. This explains why bees must be given an opportunity for flight if they are forced to feed on honey-dew. If such opportunity be not given, it is better to feed the bees abundantly as soon as possible with sugar syrup, after having removed the honey-dew, and save this for stimulative feeding next spring.

THE UNPRECEDENTEDLY HEAVY YIELD OF HONEY-DEW DURING THE SUMMER OF 1909.

The year 1909 was remarkable for the immense quantities of honey-dew produced in almost every section of the country outside of the irrigated region where alfalfa and sweet clover are grown. In the eastern portions of the United States there was almost a failure of clear white clover or basswood. What little there was produced was so mixed with honey-dew that much of it was not suitable for table use.

Most of the honey-dew for 1909 came from the leaves of the hickory and oak. Contrary to what many have supposed, this saccharine matter found on the leaves came from aphides located higher up on the trees. But the ordinary observer not finding the insects, even after a search, might naturally conclude that they were not present, and that the sweet, sticky, gummy stuff on the leaves was an actual exudation from the leaves themselves; but in every case a more careful and scientific search has shown somewhere the aphides.

Oddly enough, the honey-dew of 1909 made the bees unusually cross. They worked heavily on the dew during the early morning hours, and as soon as the sun dried the gummy substance down toward noon, so they could get no more of it, they became furious; in fact, they would act very much as if they had been robbing, and the supply of stolen sweets had suddenly given out. For further particulars regarding this, see ANGER OF BEES.

QUALITY OF HONEY-DEW.

Prof. A. J. Cook says that much of the honey-dew is "deliciously wholesome." While there are samples that are fairly palatable, the great majority of them, according to our experience, are dark and of very poor flavor, and in some cases positively nauseating. There is almost no market for them. Even the large baking concerns will not have them, for, as a matter of fact, they require good table honey, even though it be of very strong flavor.

We do not know what to do with honey-dew of poor quality but to hold it over and feed it out to the bees in the spring for stimulating brood-rearing—see FEEDING. It is positively unfit to use as a winter food; but for raising bees it is as good as the best honey known.

HONEY EXHIBITS. See EXHIBITS.

HONEY ON COMMISSION. See COMB HONEY.

HONEY-PEDDLING. Under Ex-TRACTED HONEY, which see, we have already told something about selling direct to consumers. But there are many who say they "haven't the gall or cheek to go around and ask folks to buy," and prefer to be excused from any such disagreeable experience. But there are ways in which one does not need to lose either his dignity or self-respect. A peddler may, it is true, call at unseasonable hours, or steal valuable time from a prospective customer in trying to force a sale. In such ways one may make himself very obnoxious, and render a second visit utterly useless. Dan White, of New London, Ohio, a progressive and practical bee-keeper, has hit upon a novel plan that entirely eliminates all objectionable features. As he has succeeded so well we will let him tell his plan in his own way:

PEDDLING MADE EASY.

I packed my grip and took two 12-pound cans of honey and started out. About all I had in my grip was a good supply of those leaflets published by The A. I. Root Co.; also 50 postals addressed to myself.

I got into the town just before dinner time; and after eating a good meal at a boarding-house I filled my pockets with leaflets and took one honey-can and commenced business. I started down a street and did not miss calling at every house. After ringing the bell, or rapping, a lady would open the door and look at me with more or less suspicion. I would say, "I made the call to ask you if your family were fond of honey."

They generally answered yes, but believed they would not buy any.

"Well," I would answer, "but I am not selling honey to-day. I am giving it away, and should be glad to give you some in a sauce-dish."

Some would look astonished, others would smile, and say, "That's funny," but in *every* instance I was invited in. I would pour out the honey, then hand out a leaflet, telling them to read every word of it. "You will find it very interesting; it will tell you all about honey — how and why we extract it, etc. Then here is a postal addressed to me; and should you decide to want a 12-pound can, put your name, street, and number, on the card; drop it in the office; and when I deliver in about ten days you will get a can of honey."

Well, there were enough cards put in the mail within five days to take thirty cans of honey. I promptly made the delivery on time, taking along twenty extra cans that sold about as fast as I could hand them out; and since then I have received orders for 50 more cans from the same town. I tell you, it has got all over town that a honey-man had been there selling *real* honey, 12 pounds for one dollar. I am certain that this one place will take over 2000 pounds, all in one-gallon cans. Now, then, 18 pounds of honey given away from house to house, 50 postal cards, 200 leaflets left at houses and handed to people on the street, and one day walking over a very small portion of the town, has found a place for at *least* 2000 pounds of honey. Then think what I can do next season should I secure a good crop.

All I shall have to do is to take a big load and go up there and hand it out. By the way, the honey sold there was thrown out of clean white combs, over every inch of whose surface the uncapping-knife had to go. It weighed strong 12 pounds to the gallon—just as good as the best comb honey, *only* it was out of the combs. Of *course*, I can go back just as often as I choose; yes, and the people will be glad to see me. DAN WHITE.

New London, Ohio.

It would appear that one of the prime requisites is a first-class article of well-ripened extracted honey. Very many make a mistake right here, and, of course, if the honey is poor, one is not likely to make a second sale. Mr. White's scheme is to have the honey taste *so good* that, when it is gone, the good people will drop that postal for more, and not haggle over the price, even if the "store stuff" does cost less.

In a similar way Mr. Herman F. Moore, then of Cleveland, O., now of Chicago, retailed large amounts of honey. His plan, like that of Mr. White, was to go around and solicit orders. In the cities of Cleveland and Toledo, or even those of smaller size, he would start out on foot, exhibiting a sample of his honey in a quart Mason fruit-jar. His reason for using this package was that almost any family would be willing to take a household article of this kind, for the simple reason that it would not have to be thrown away when it had served the purpose of holding the honey.

With this jar of honey Mr. Moore would call at private houses, one after another, and ask for a dish and spoon, saying that he had some very nice honey, and that he would like to give the women-folks a sample to taste. He then held up the beautiful transparent goods to the light, told them he was a bee-keeper, and dealt only in pure honey; explained how it was produced, and finally named the price. If the lady of the house cared to take any he would take her order and deliver the next day. As a rule he took an order.

In this way he would make the rounds of a certain section of the city. When he first began he would take the orders one day and deliver the next; but his business grew so rapidly that he was finally obliged to take on a helper, his brother, and, a little later on, two more men and a man and his wife. The two last named would wash the jars and fill them. Two of the men would deliver while he and his brother took orders. In this way they sold enormous quantities of honey; and as it was always of the finest quality, and guaranteed to be pure, they built up a large trade. Mr. Moore has since

SELSER, HIS HONEY-PEDDLING WAGON, AND HIS HONEY-BOTTLING SHOP.

removed from Cleveland; and although now a practicing attorney he does considerable at selling honey, either direct to consumers or to the grocers.

Here is another plan, providing one can trade honey for other useful articles too numerous to mention. Even if one did not sell much he would get a day of royal sport. Well, here is the Vinal plan:

TRADING HONEY FOR DUCKS, PIGS, PUPS, ETC.

In all the literature on bees and honey, we are urged to develop the home market. Acting on the advice, after I had traveled over my regular route this fall I went into an entirely new locality. After enjoying the scenery and the sunlight for about a five-mile drive I called at a farmhouse and inquired of the good lady if she would like some honey.

"Well, yes. I should like some, but I have no money."

Seeing some ducks, I offered to trade honey for ducks; and for a pair I gave four pint jars of honey.

Calling at another house, I sold $2.00 worth for cash; and while I was talking with the man one of the ducks gave a quack, which led to an inquiry as to what I had. I told them I had traded honey for ducks.

"Well, now, look here; can't I trade you some hens for some honey?"

I traded for half a dozen, and made the children, I hope, happy (I was). In this way I passed the day, and on my drive home I was trying to figure out my profits. I had disposed of two gross of pint jars, and 120 pounds of comb honey. For the pint jars I received 25 cents; also 25 cents each for the sections of comb. I had had a royal day's sport; and as I listened to the quack of the ducks and geese, the cackle of the hens, and squeal of the pigs, and looked at the large box of eggs that I had in the wagon, I thought I would have to send for some of Dr. Mason's egg-preservative. After getting home I took account of stock. I had $54.40 cash, 108 dozen eggs, 8 ducks, 1 goose, 2 pigs, 24 hens, and 1 bullpup. The pup is for sale.)   GEO. L. VINAL.
Charlton City, Mass.

Another experience is thus given by G. C. Greiner, of La Salle, N. Y.:

Peddling honey has, like every thing else, its ups and downs. We don't always strike it rich. Some days it may seem like terribly steep uphill business while other days the money may roll in by the handfuls. As an illustration, and a proof that the latter sentence is almost literally true, let me give you one day's experience.

Late last fall I chanced to take a trip to Niagara Falls with the intention of making a display of my goods at the city market. At first, things looked a little gloomy. Purchasers did not flock in as I had hoped, until after some minutes of patient waiting. One passing lady, in looking at my honey, asked, "Is your honey *pure?*" The reply I made must be imagined, for it would fill more space than the editor would be willing to allow. But let me emphasize — here is where the blabbing came in. In answering her question I delivered a good half-hour lecture in less than two minutes, trying to convince her of the purity and all the good points of my honey. In the mean time, passing people had stopped to listen; and by the time my lady friend was ready to buy one of my quart cans

I had quite a crowd around me. To cut the story short, for quite a few minutes I handed out cans, mostly quarts, as fast as I could make the change, many of the purchasers promising to buy more the next time I attended the market, if the honey proved to be what I had recommended it to be.

When the market closed, at 11 A.M., I had a few cans left. With these I drove to Main Street and tied my horse in front of one of the stores, where I had a little business to transact. A few minutes later, while I was conversing with the storekeeper inside, some one opened the door and inquired:

"Hello! where is this honey-man?"

After introducing myself he requested me to show him what I had to sell. It did not take very long to convince him that I carried the genuine article; and what pleased me still more was the fact that he ordered two cans to be left at the corner drugstore across the street.

When I delivered the cans they were closely scrutinized by the clerks and some other parties who happened to be present, and one of the clerks asked:

"What guarantee have we that this is pure honey?"

Here another lecture-like conversation, too long to be repeated, took place, the substance of which may be concentrated in my reply:

"First, pure honey and my name and address are on every package; and, second, back of this is the New York State law that prohibits all honey adulteration."

Before I left the place I sold two more cans to those other parties.

A great help in selling honey on the road is a proper traveling-outfit, which enables us to present our products in clean, neat, and inviting appearance. I know from experience that at least one-fourth of my sales of honey can be traced back directly to this feature.

PEDDLING HONEY AT GROCERIES AND OTHER RETAIL STORES.

Mr. W. A. Selser, of 10 Vine St., Philadelphia, is not only a practical bee-keeper, but he is also a large buyer of honey. In addition to the amount he produces in his own apiaries, he buys up every year the product of several large yards. All of this, mostly extracted, he peddles out from a honey-wagon to the retail trade.

The secret of his success in selling and in getting good prices is in putting up always a first-class article in a neat and attractive form. He advertises liberally, and every one knows him about Philadelphia as "the honey-man." In connection with his apiary he has a bottling-shop shown in the top view of the engraving. In a room in this building (see view at the right) he puts up all of his extracted honey in Muth jars. See EXTRACTED HONEY. In this room is a large steam-caldron that will hold perhaps two or three barrels of honey at a time. Into this he pours several choice grades of extracted whether candied or not. A gentle heat is applied until it is all brought to a liquid condition. It is then heated to about 150 or 160 degrees Fahr., after which it is bottled and sealed while hot. This, as is well known, will prevent the honey from candy-ing for a considerable length of time. The corks, before being put into the bottles, are dipped into a mixture of beeswax and resin, and inserted, making a perfectly hermetic sealing.

After several gross, perhaps, are put up, Mr. Selser loads all he can carry in a special wagon shown at the left, and in the central view at the bottom. He then visits the city stores and replenishes their stock. After he has supplied all the city retail places he then goes into the country, visits the suburban towns, and even drives as far as the city of New York, supplying some stores in that metropolis.

HONEY-PLANTS.—Not every flower that blooms helps to fill up our hives. The beautiful flowers of the garden, made double by cultivating them, yield no nectar at all. They produce no seed, so there is no nectar to invite the bees to come and fertilize them. If you will read the article about pollen you will understand this better. Some yield plenty of pollen with little or no nectar. Others yield immense quantities of honey, but the plants are so few in number that they are not worth considering. The poinsettia is an example. We have seen large drops of nectar on one of these plants, which had evaporated to the consistency of honey; but what does it matter how much honey can be obtained from a single plant, if there are no plants except a single one here and there in a greenhouse? Some yield nectar, but the flowers are so constructed that the honey-bee can not obtain it, although some other insect can.

In spite of all this, the list of flowers that are of more or less value to us is a very large one—so large that it is not desirable to give a full list. Throughout the book, in their proper alphabetical places, will be found some account of the principal plants that specially interest bee-keepers. It may be desirable, however, to be able to tell at a glance what they are, so a list is here given.

Words in small capitals means the subject is treated in the body of the work. " Which see " means the subject is treated of under another name.

Acacia dealbata, or silver wattle; California, from Australia; commercially important.

Acacia decurrens, black wattle; California; similar to the above.

Acacia farnesia (huisache); along the Rio Grande; much grown in Europe as a florist's flower.

Acacia Greggii (catclaw, or uña de gato), Southwest Texas, New Mexico, and Arizona—see CATCLAW.

Actinomeris squarrosa, golden honey-plant.

Agave Americana, pulque, CENTURY PLANT; Mexico, Southern United States

Aguinaldo(Ipomea sidœfolia),Cuba—see BELLFL W-ER.

Alders (*Alnus*).

Alfilaria (Erodium cicutarium), or pin clover; Arizona and California; an excellent honey and forage plant from Europe—see " pin clover " under head of CLOVER.

Alfalfa, or lucerne (*Medicago sativa*), see ALFALFA.

Algarroba (*Inga dulcis*), and other species.

Alsike or Swedish clover (*Trifolium hybridum*)—see ALSIKE CLOVER.

Anchusa tinctoria, dye-plant. All the anchusas are excellent bee-plants.

Antigonon leptopus, Mexican rose, or coralita; California, Florida, West Indies, and Mexico; an excellent honey-plant.

Apple (*Pyrus*). The whole apple family is here meant—see FRUIT-BLOSSOMS.

Apricot (*Prunus Armeniaca*), California.

Archas sapota, sapodilla; fruit-tree of the tropics; Florida.

Ash (*Fraxinus ornus*) or flowering or manna ash; planted south for its beauty.

Asters (*Aster*) of many species almost everywhere —see ASTERS.

Asparagus (*Asparagus officinalis*), cultivated.

Artichoke, true or globe artichoke (*Cynara scolymus*).

Avocada pear (*Persea gratissima*), Florida.

Banana (*Musa sapientum* and *M. Cavendishii*), Florida and the tropics generally.

Berberry (*Berberis vulgaris*).

Basil, or mountain mint (*Pycnanthemum lanceolatum*).

Basswood, or American linden (*Tilia Americana*), also *T. heterophylla*, Southern Kentucky, and Allegheny Mountains—see BASSWOOD.

Beans (*Phaseolus lunatus*), lima beans in California; horse beans (*P. nanus*) in British Isles and Holland.

Bee balm (*Melissa officinalis*), garden flower.

Beggar-tick, or burr marigold (*Bidens frondosa*), United States—see SPANISH NEEDLE.

Bellflower, Christmas bells, Christmas pop, aguinaldo, campanilla, etc. (*Ipomea sidœfolia*), of Cuba, Jamaica, and other West India islands and Mexico.

Bergamot (*Monarda fistulosa*), a kind of mint; United States.

Bignonia radicans, south—see NECTAR.

Blackberry (*Rubus*), of many species; Europe and United States.

Black gum—see NYASSA or TUPELO.

Black mangrove (*Avicennia nitida*); Florida and the coasts of all tropic seas; generally known as mangrove except in British Guiana, where it is known as "courida"—see MANGROVE.

Blackheart, or water smartweed (*Polygonum acre*), closely related to buckwheat; Illinois.

Black mustard (*Brassica nigra*)—see MUSTARD.

Black sage (*Ramona stachyoides* and *R. palmeri*), California— see SAGE.

Bladdernut (*Staphylea trifolia*), north and west.

Blue gum (*Eucalyptus globulus*), Tasmania and California—see EUCALYPTUS.

Blue thistle (*Echium vulgare*) viper's bugloss; a weed from Europe; Virginia and Pennsylvania.

Boneset, or thoroughwort (*Eupatorium perfoliatum*), a honey-plant of considerable importance.

Borage (*Borago officinalis*), Europe, but now well known in the United States.

Box-elder, or ash-leaved maple (*Acer negundo*), Northern States.

Boxwood (*Buxus sempervirens*), the tree box of the Balearic Islands and Turkey; produces much honey but it is very bitter; introduced into the U. S.

Buckbush (*Symphoricarpus vulgaris*)—see BUCKBUSH.

Buckeye (*Æsculus glabra*), Ohio and similar States.

Buckthorn (*Rhamnus catharticus*), Southern States

Buttercup, oxalis of Bermuda (*Oxalis Bermudiana*), fine for those who wish to hunt for bees.

Buckwheat (*Polygonum fagopyrum*) — see BUCK-WHEAT.

Buckwheat, wild (*Polygonum acre*), also black-heart.

Burdock (*Lappa major*), has white pollen.

Burr marigold (*Bidens frondosa*), a near relative of Spanish needle, which see.

Bush honeysuckle (*Diervilla Japonica*), cultivated, Japan.

Button-bush (*Cephalanthus occidentalis*); important on the overflowed lands of the Mississippi.

Butterweed (*Senecio lobatus*), South and Southwest.

Cabbage (*Brassica oleracea*) common cabbage: see also colza, rape, turnip, charlock, white and black mustard, belonging to the Cabbage family.

Campanilla (*Ipomea sidæfolia*), Cuba—see BELL-FLOWER.

Canada thistle (*Cirsium arvense*), in Canada.

Cardinal flower (*Lobelia cardinalis*).

Cardoon (*Cynara cardunculus*); good where grown for seed; very common in Argentina.

Carob bean (*Ceratonia siliqua*)—St. John's bread for the Southwest; similar to catclaw.

Carpenter's square—see FIGWORT.

Cassia (*Cassia chamæcrista*). Probably all cassias are honey-plants.

Catalpa (*Catalpa speciosa*), hardy catalpa, planted for its timber and shade.

Catclaw (*Acacia Greggii*), important in the Southwest—see CATCLAW.

Catnip (*Nepeta cataria*), an important honey-plant in Europe and North America.

Ceratonia siliqua, or St. John's bread, now introduced into the United States from Europe, will probably become important.

Chaste-tree (*Vitex agnus castus*) introduced from Europe into parks, cemeteries, etc. This and the New Zealand species, *Vitex littorales*, are excellent.

Chayote (*Sechium edule*), grown as a vegetable around New Orleans; a good honey-plant.

Cherry (*Prunus cerasus*), the cultivated cherry.

Chick pea (*Cicer arietinum*), known in the West as coffee pea; grown very largely in Mexico—"garbanza."

Chicory (*Cichorium intybus*), cultivated in Europe —a common weed here.

Chinquapin (*Castanea pumila*), of considerable importance to the South.

Cleome integrifolia, also *C. spinosa*, same as Rocky Mountain bee-plant, which see.

Clovers—see article under this head; also ALFALFA, ALSIKE, SAINFOIN, SULLA, CRIMSON CL., SWEET and PEAVINE CL.

Clover, alsike (*Trifolium hybridlum*), Swedish clover—see CLOVER.

Clover, crimson *Trifolium incarnatum*)—see CRIMSON CLOVER.

Clover, red (*Trifolium pratense*)—see CLOVERS.

Clover, yellow (*Trifolium procumbens*), New England, Eastern and Middle States to Tennessee.

Cocoanut (*Cocoa nucifera*) Florida and the tropics.

Coffee (*Coffea Arabica* and *Liberica*); honey clear, but season very short; sometimes grown in Florida.

Coreopsis (*Coreopsis aristosa*)—see SPAN. NEEDLE; Illinois and Missouri.

Corn, Indian (*Zea mays*); under certain conditions maize, or corn, is a good honey-plant.

Cotton (*Gossypium herbaceum*); south; some say it compares with clover.

Cowpea (*Vigna sinensis*); Southern States.

Crab apple (*Pyrus coronaria*) New York; west and south.

Crocus (*Crocus*), of many species; both spring and fall varieties are good.

Crowfoot (*Ranunculus repens*).

Cucumber (*Cucumis sativus*). In the vicinity of pickle-factories this plant yields quite a harvest of honey after clover is over.

Culver's root (*Veronica Virginica*); north.

Currant (*Ribes rubrum*), from Europe; cultivated *Cytisus proliferous alba* — tree alfalfa; grown a little in California; a great honey-plant in the Canary Islands.

Dandelion (*Taraxacum officinale*).

Date (*Phœnix dactylifera*) ; a great honey-plant now being planted in Arizona and California.

Duranta plumieri, or pigeon-berry, recently introduced into Florida and California ; an exquisite honey-plant.

Ebony (*Zygia flexicaulis*), Southwest Texas—not the true ebony.

Echinops spherocephalus, also *E. ritro* — excellent plants for introduction—see CHAPMAN H. P.

Elms (*Ulmus*), of various species. Where plentiful the elms are of considerable importance on account of their aid in early brood-rearing.

Eriobotrya Japonica—loquat fruit of Japan; excellent honey-plant; Florida, Gulf Coast, California, Georgia, and Arizona; known in some sections as Japan plum.

Esparcette—see SAINFOIN.

False indigo *Amorpha fructicosa*), Ohio, Pennsylvania; south and west.

Figwort (*Scrofularia nodosa*).

Fireweed, or willow-herb, which see (*Epilobium angustifolium*), the great fireweed of the North; Ontario, Quebec, Northern Michigan, and the Hudson Bay country.

Fog-fruit (*Lippia nudiflora*), California (carpet weed); Texas and the West Indies; a great honey-plant, but little known. See CARPET GRASS.

Freesia refracta alba, an exquisite honey-plant grown in California for its bulbs; also in Florida and the Gulf Coast.

Gallberry, or holly (*Ilex glabra*), south; important.

Genip (*Melicocca bijuga*), in South Florida; heavy yielder where common.

Germander, or wood-sage (*Teucrium Canadense*).

Giant hyssop (*Lophanthus*) — species, chiefly north and west.

Giant mignonnette (*Reseda grandiflora*)—see MIG.

Gill-over-the-ground, or ground-ivy (*Nepeta glechoma*).

Golden apple (*Spondias dulcis*), Florida.

Golden honey-plant (*Actinomeris squarrosa*).

Goldenrod (*Solidago*), — species.

Gooseberry (*Ribes grossularia*).

Grape (*Vitis labrusca*).

Ground-ivy (*Nepeta glechoma*).

Guajilla—see HUAJILLA.

Heal-all, or figwort, which see (*Scrofularia nodosa*).

Hibiscus esculentus—okra, or gumbo, of the South.

Hibiscus sabdariffa—Jamaica sorrel of Florida.

Hawthorn (*Cratagus Oxycantha*), Great Britain, Ireland, and North Europe; introduced here.

Hazelnut and filbert (*Corylus avelana* and *C. Americana*), valuable in early spring for pollen.

Heartsease, which see, or large smartweed (*Persicaria mite*), on the overflowed lands of the Mississippi River.

Heather (*Erica vulgaris*); a prolific source of honey in Europe and the British Isles. The honey is thick, with a rich flavor. In the same latitude on this continent its place is taken by the "fireweed," which see—an excellent yielder also.

Hemp (*Cannabis sativa*, also *C. Indica*), ganja of the East.

Hercules club (*Aralia spinosa*).

Hoarhound (*Marrubium vulgare*). Good yields of honey have been reported from this plant; but it is so bitter as to be worthless except as medicine. It might improve with age.

Hog-plum (*Spondias lutea*); Florida; a splendid yielder of honey. Known as hobo in Cuba.

Holly, American (*Ilex opaca*).

Honey-locust (*Gleditschia triacanthos*), also known as white locust.

Honeysuckle (*Lonicera caprifolia*), and some other species not so well known.

Horse-chestnut (*Æculus hippocastanum*), European species.

Horsemint, which see (*Monarda fistula*).

Hoya carnosa, or wax-plant—see NECTAR.

Huajilla (*Zygia brevifolia*), Texas and adjacent countries.

Huisache, Mexican name for *Acacia Farnesiana*, a beautiful tree of the Southwest, similar to catclaw.

Indian currant, coral-berry, buckbush, which see (*Symphoricarpus vulgaris*).

Ironwood, or hornbeam (*Carpinus Americana*).

Japanese buckwheat—see BUCKWHEAT.

Japan plum; south; same as "loquat."

Japan privet *Ligustrum Japonicum*), all Southern States and California; hedge-plant of the best.

Judas-tree, redbud (*Cereis Canadensis*).

June-berry, service-berry, shad-berry (*Amelanchier Canadensis*).

Knotweed, or heartsease, which see (*Persicaria mite*).

Lantana (*L. nivea* and *L. mixta*), Florida, Bahamas, and Bermuda.

Lemon (*Citrus limonum*), Florida and California.

Lentil (*Ervum lens*), or pulse of the East; much used in Europe to make soup. Italians grow it in this country.

Lime (*Tilia Europea*), English name for linden or basswood; now much planted as an avenue tree in the United States.

Lime (*Citrus limetta*); Florida, California, and the West Indies.

Limnanthes Douglasii, or marsh-flower; native of California; cultivated in England for bees.

Linden (*Tilia Europea*), or European basswood; famous in Berlin and other places as a street tree; now popular in the United States.

Liquid ambar Styraciflua, sweet gum; very important, particularly south.

Locust, which see (*Robinia pseudacacia*); now being planted for its timber in Ohio and other States. See LOCUST.

Logwood (*Hæmatoxylon Campechianum*); the various states bordering on the bay of Campeche; introduced into Florida, Jamaica, West Indies, and South America. See LOGWOOD.

Loquat (*Eriobotyra Japonica*); sometimes wrongly named Japan plum; south; valuable because it flowers very late.

Lucerne (*Medicago sativa*); the English name for the Spanish *alfalfa*.

Lupine (*Lupinus perennis*).

Madrona (*Arbutus Xalapensis*), southwest.

Magnolia (*M. grandiflora* and others); south.

Malva (*M. alcea*).

Mammoth red or peavine clover—see CLOVER.

Manzanita (*Arctostaphylos*), California.

Maples (*Acer*), — species. The different species are of much value, yielding well for early brood-rearing.

Marigold, which see (*Gailardia p lchella*).

Marjoram (*Origanum vulgare*).

Marsh sunflower (*Helianthus strumosus*).

Matrimony-vine (*Lycium vulgare*).

Meadow-sweet, or spiræa (*Spirea salicifolia*).

Melilot (*Melilotus alba*), or honey lotus—see SWEET CLOVER, white and yellow.

Melons (*Cucurbita melo*). Melons of all kinds are valuable to apiarists.

Mesquite, which see (*Prosopis pubescens* and *juliflora*); southwest and New Mexico.

Mignonnette (*Reseda odorata*).

Milkweed (*Asclepias cornuti*).

Milk-vetch (*Astragalus Canadensis*).

Motherwort (*Leonurus cardiaca*).

Mountain laurel, sheep laurel, rhododendron (*Kalmia latifolia*), famous for producing honey which has sickening properties—see POISONOUS H. P.

Mustard (*Brassica arvensis*), charlock of England.

Okra, or gumbo (*Hibiscus esculentus*).

Onion (*Allium cepa*)' There are reports of yields of honey from fields of onions cultivated for seed, having very strongly the peculiar onion odor, which, however, disappears after a time.

Orange (*Citrus aurantium*); considered valuable in some places.

Oxeye daisy (*Bellis integrifolia*); Kentucky and southwest.

Palmetto.

Parsnip (*Pastinaca sativa*), from the common parsnip run wild.

Partridge pea (*Cassia chamæcrista*).

Peach (*Prunus Persica*)—see FRUIT-BLOSSOMS.

Peavine, or mammoth red clover (*Trifolium pratense*)—see CL.

Pecans (*Hicoria Pecan*). Good South.

Pepperidge—see TUPELO.

Peppermint (*Mentha vulgaris*).

Pepper-tree (*Schinus molle*), California and Florida; fine shade-tree; excellent for honey.

Persimmon (*Diospyrus Virginianum* and *Texana*); known as "lotus" in Europe.

Phacelia tanacetifolia, a beautiful garden plant from California.

Phormium tenax, New Zealand flax; sometimes grown south; good yielder; may become very important commercially.

Pin-clover, or alfilarila (*Erodium Cicutarium Geranicæ*).

Plane-tree (*Platanus orientalis*), also known as sycamore or buttonwood; good in Europe, and introduced here; similar to our sycamore; a fine shade-tree.

Plantain, or rib-grass (*Plantago major*), has white pollen.

Plantain fruit (*Musa paradisica*), similar to the banana, but extensively used as a vegetable in all tropic latitudes, Florida, and Porto Rico.

Pleurisy-root (*Asclepias tuberosa*); highly praised by James Heddon.

Plums. All kinds of wild plums yield honey.

Poinciana regia, Florida.

Poplar, or WHITEWOOD, which see (*Liriodendron tulipifera*).

Poplar (*Populus*), south.

Prairie clover (*Petalostemon candida*), good in Texas.

Protea mellifera alba, South Africa; a wonderful yielder of honey. See NECTAR.

Pumpkin (*Cucurbita pepo*); cultivated; the original, *C. ovifera*, runs wild in Texas.

Rape (*Brassica campestris*).

Raspberry (*Rubus strigosus*), Northern Michigan and similar localities; *R. idæsis*, European raspberry, and *R. rosæfolius*, Porto Rico and West Indies.

Rattan (*Berchemia scandens*); Texas; a heavy yielder.

Rattlesnake root, or white lettuce (*Nabalus altissimus*).

Rattleweed, or figwort.

Redbay (*Persea Carolinensis*), south.

Redbud, or Judas-tree (*Cereis Canadensis*).

Red gum [*Eucalyptus rostrata*], California and native of Australia.

Rhododendron, species; rosebays, azaleas, species; and sheep laurels, or mountain laurels; important in the mountains of the South; known in England as American plants. *Rhododendron pontica* was the source of the honey which poisoned Xenophon's army of ten thousand.

Rocky Mountain bee-plant, which see [*Cleome integrifolia*].

Rose apple [*Eugenia jambos*], Florida; very important in Cuba and Porto Rico.

Royal palm [*Oreodoxa regia*], Florida, Cuba, and Porto Rico.

Sage, black (*Ramona stachyoides* and *R. palmeri*); very important in California—see SAGE.

Sage, white (*Ramona polystachis*); California.

St. John's-wort [*Hypericum*]. — species.

Sage, button, same as black sage, which see.

Sainfoin, [Onobrychis sativa]; a great plant, similar to alfalfa. See CLOVER.

Saw palmetto [Sabal serrulata]; Georgia and Florida.

Serradella clover [Ornithopus sativus]; a fine honey-plant, similar to sainfoin, which see.

Shadbush [Amelanchier Canadensis], also known as June-berry and service-berry.

Shaddock, pumelo, or grape fruit [Citrus decumana]; Florida and California.

Simpson honey-plant.

Smartweed, same as heartsease, which see.

Sneezeweed [Helenium autumnale].

Sorrel-tree, same as sourwood, which see.

Sourwood [Oxydendron arboreum]; Pennsylvania, Ohio, and south.

Spanish needle, which see [Coreopsis aristosa and C. aurea], better known as tickseed.

Spider-flower or spider-plant, [Cleome pungens].

Square-stalk, same as figwort.

Squash [Cucurbita maxima].

Stone crop [Sedum pulchellum], south.

Strawberry [Fragaria vesca]; cultivated.

Sulla clover [Hedysarum coronarium], or Spanish sainfoin; a good honey plant for the Gulf States.

Sumac [Rhus venenata].

Sunflower [Helianthus major].

Sweet clover [Melilotus alba]—see Cl.

Sweet gum—see Liquidambar styraciflua.

Sweet potato [Ipomea batata].

Tea (Thea Bohea).

Thistle [Cirsium arvense], Canada.

Thyme [Thymus vulgaris]. The classical honey of Mount Hymettus was from this.

Tickseed, or Spanish needle, which see.

Ti-Ti [Cliftonia monophylla]; Georgia and Florida principally.

Touch-me-not, or swamp balsam [Impatiens pallida]—see POLLEN.

Trefoil, or clover, which see.

Tulip tree, or whitewood, which see [Liriodendron tulipifera].

Tupelo [Nyssa multiflora], common tupelo, or sour gum; N. aquatica, water tupelo or gum; N. uniflora, large tupelo; N. capitata, Ogeechee lime; very important south.

Turnip [Brassica depressa].

Valerian [Valeriana edulis]; Ohio and westward.

Varnish-tree [Ailyanthus glandulosa]; south from Japan; honey bad.

Vervain [Verbena officinalis].

Vetch [Vicia], — species.

Viper's bugloss, or blue thistle, which see [Echium vulgare].

Virginia creeper [Ampelopsis quinquefolia].

Vitex agnus castus, chaste-tree in Europe and United States; introduced; V. littoralis, important in New Zealand.

Vitus bipinnata, south.

White mustard [Brassica alba].

TEXAS HORSEMINT.

White sage [*R.m out polystachya*], California.

Whitewood, which see [*Liriodendron tulipifera*].

Wild buckwheat [*Polygonum*]; produces a light-colored honey.

Wild cherry [*Prunus Pennsylvanica*], north.

Wild rose [*Rosa Carolina, lucida, blanda, canina, rug sa*].

Wild senna [*Cassia chamæcrista*].

Wild sunflower [*Helianthus*]. – species.

Willow [*Salix*]. All species form an important class, coming as they do early in the season, and yielding both honey and pollen.

WILLOW-HERB, which see [*Epilobium angustifolium*], northern parts of the United States and Canada.

Wistaria [*Wistaria chinensis*].

Yellow-wood [*Virgilia lutea*]. Virginia. One of the finest native ornamental trees.

HONEY VINEGAR. See VINEGAR.

HORSEMINT (*Monarda fistulosa*). This plant was first brought to notice several years ago, and at that time the seeds were sold quite extensively as a honey-bearing plant. It was dropped and almost forgotten, until reports of large crops of honey, said to be from this source alone, began to come in. It first attracted attention on the alluvial low lands bordering on the Mississippi River; afterward, wonderful reports came of it, from different parts of Texas—one man reporting as high as 700 lbs. gathered by a single colony in a single season. The bees that did this wonderful feat were Cyprians, or, at least, were crossed with Cyprian blood.

Horsemint in Texas begins to bloom in May or June, and the honey is of good color and body, and fair flavor. It is a little strong, and on that account has been compared with Northern basswood. It is one of the very best honey-plants of Texas. One peculiarity of the flower is that it has very deep corolla-tubes—even deeper than those of red clover, so that bees with long tongues are a desideratum in Texas as well as in red-clover regions of the North.

HOUSE-APIARY. See APIARY.

HUAJILLA. (*Zygia brevifolia*, Sargent). This is a very important honey-plant, or tree, rather, in Texas, for the dry arid portions where there is little or no irrigation, and where nothing, in fact, grows except mesquite, catclaw, sage-brush, and other desert plants. The fact that it does not depend on irrigation, and needs only a scanty amount of rain early in the season, makes it most valuable to the bee-keeper in those regions where it grows and yields large quantities of beautiful water-white honey. Indeed, it is the finest produced in Texas, and is so nearly water white as to be almost as clear as pure water. It is at its very best in the region of Uvalde, Texas.

The leaves look like a small delicate fern, and partake somewhat of the nature of the sensitive plant, for when touched they immediately close. The view of leaf is life size.

HUAJILLA.

HYBRIDS. Strictly speaking, there is no such thing as a true hybrid in bee culture, because the term applies only to a cross between different *species*. We obtain many crosses between *races* of bees. As these were early called hybrids in bee-literature, the term has been permanent. Everybody who has had Italians very long probably knows what hybrids are, especially if they have kept bees when the honey crop was suddenly cut short during a very severe drouth in the fall of the year. The term hybrid has been applied to bees that are a cross between the Italians and the common bee.* If one buys an Italian queen that is pure, he can at once set about rearing queens if he chooses, for it matters not how many common bees there are around him; and if he rears all his queens as we direct under NUCLEI and QUEEN-REARING, he may have the full benefit of the Italians so far as honey-gathering is concerned, just as well as if there were no other bees within miles of him. This seems a paradox to most beginners, for we have letters almost daily, asking if it will be of any use to purchase Italians when other bees are kept all around them. If you are keeping bees for the honey they produce, and for nothing else, we do not know but that you are better off with other bees in the neighborhood. The queens that you rear will be full-bloods like their mother; but after meeting the common drones, their worker progeny will of course be half common and half Italian, generally speaking. These are what we call hybrid bees. In looks they are much like the Italians, only a little darker. Sometimes a queen will produce bees all about alike; that is, they will have one or two of the yellow bands, the second and broadest being about as plain and distinct as in the full-bloods. Other queens will produce bees variously striped, from a pure black bee to the finest three-banded Italian. We have had black queens fertilized by Italian drones, and these seem to be hybrids just the same as the others. We have not been able to distinguish any particular difference.

As honey-gatherers, these bees that have the blood of the two races are, we believe, taking all things into consideration, fully equal to the pure Italians. There are times, it is true, when the full-bloods seem to be ahead; but we think there are other times and circumstances when the taint of black blood gives an advantage, in respect to the amount of honey gathered, that fully makes up the difference; and we would therefore say, if honey is your object, and nothing else, you are just as well off to let your queens meet such drones as they may happen to find. Why, then, do hybrid queens find slow sale at about one-fourth of the price of pure Italians? It is because of their excitability and vindictive temper.

Italians, as they generally run, are disposed to be quiet and still when their hive is opened, and to remain quietly on their combs

while they are being handled, showing neither vindictiveness nor alarm. Black or common bees, on the contrary, are likely to become frightened, and either make a general stampede, or buzz about one's head and eyes in a way quite unlike the Italians. Italians do not stand still because they are afraid to make an attack, for, let a robber approach, and they will sting it to death in a way so cool as to astonish one who has seen only common bees under similar circumstances. A race of bees so prompt to repel intruders of their own kind, it would seem, would also be prompt to repel interference from man; but such is not the case. They do not seem to be at all suspicious when their hive is opened and a frame lifted out. Well, these half-bloods inherit the boldness of the Italians, and, at the same time, the vindictiveness of the blacks; and to raise the cover from a hive of hybrids, without smoke, during cool or chilly weather, is a bold operation for even a veteran. Without any buzz or note of alarm, one of these daughters of war will quietly dart forth and inflict her sting before you hardly know where it comes from; then another, and another, until, almost crazed with pain, you drop the cover, and find that they are bound to stick to you, not only out into the street, but into the house or wherever you may go, in a way very unlike either pure race of bees. Sometimes, when a hive is opened, they will fix on the leg of one's trousers so quietly that you hardly dream they are there until you feel them stinging with a vehemence that indicates a willingness to throw away a score of lives if they had so many. This bad temper and stinging is not all. If you should desire to introduce a queen or queen-cell to these bees they would be very likely to destroy all you could bring; while a stock of either pure race would accept them without trouble. During extracting time, when taking off surplus honey, you will find little trouble, providing you work while honey is still coming in; but woe betide you if you should leave it on the hives until the honey-flow is past.

In preparing hybrid stocks for wintering, we have seen them so cross that it was almost impossible to get in sight of the hive after they had once been roused up; and when we attacked them suddenly with smoker in excellent trim, they charged on us as suddenly, took possession of the smoker, buzzed down into the tube in their frantic madness, and made us glad to beat a retreat, leaving them in full possession of not only the "field," but the "artillery" as well. This was a very

* For test as to what constitutes a hybrid, see ITALIAN BEES.

powerful colony, and had been unusually roused up. Although it was then quite cool weather, they hung on the outside of the hive watching for us, we suppose, until next morning. We then came up behind them with a great volley of smoke, and got them under and kept them so until we could give them chaff cushions and put them in proper wintering trim. The queen was extremely prolific, and we do not know that we ever had one single queen that was the mother of a larger family of bees. Many of these hybrid queens are extraordinarily prolific.

Hybrids are more disposed to rob than Italians, but not as much so as the common bees. We decide thus, because, when at work among them, the bees that buzz about the hives, trying to grab a load of plunder if chance offers, are almost invariably full-blood blacks. They may have a dash of hybrid blood, but we judge not, because hybrids and Italians will often be at work when the blacks are lounging about trying to rob, or doing nothing. We have known a strong hybrid stock to be slowly accumulating stores in the fall when full-bloods, in the same apiary, were losing day by day. See ITALIAN BEES.

HYBRIDS OF CARNIOLANS AND CYPRIANS WITH ITALIANS.

In this country, at least, we have as yet done very little to determine with accuracy the value of different crosses which can be made very easily. The Italian-Carniolan has been highly praised by some bee-keepers as being very tame, and capable of great results in honey-gathering. A cross between Italians and Caucasians is well spoken of. A hybrid of Cyprian and Italian is very good. Though not as vindictive as pure Cyprians, yet they are quite cross.

It may be well to observe there are two ways of making all bee-crosses; for example, in the cross just mentioned the mother may be Cyprian mated with an Italian drone, or an Italian mated with a Cyprian drone. It must undoubtedly make a difference which way the cross is effected.

Other hybrids may be considered by the bee-keeper who has in mind to produce a superior strain of bees for some particular purpose. We know that crossing, as a general rule, increases the size, courage, and stamina of our domestic animals; and it is probably so in bees, yet we have made but little progress along this line, because it is so difficult to distinguish between the crosses and pure breeds in many cases.

We have an imperfect control over bees when mating, hence it is very difficult to effect mating just as we desire to have it. In this connection there is a grand field for practical experiments, such as would prove useful to bee-keepers.

A SLOW BUT SURE WAY OF MOVING BEES.

I.

INCREASE. Under head of NUCLEUS several methods of forming nuclei are explained, but under this head we shall deal with the subject more from the standpoint of the honey-producer who actually desires increase and at the same time produce a crop of honey. One can divide up a strong colony into three or four nuclei; but in doing so he would probably destroy all his chances of securing a crop of honey, and might possibly cause some brood to die. It should always be borne in mind that the field bees will go back to the old stand. The nucleus left will necessarily receive more than its proper proportion of bees, while those moved to the other locations may or may not (depending upon circumstances) have too few bees to take care of young brood. The loss of brood may be minimized somewhat by putting most of the sealed b ood on other stands and a large part of the unsealed at the old stand; but if the division be made during cold weather even the sealed brood may die from chilling.

The plan that we are about to describe avoids all this loss of brood, and at the same time enables one to make a moderate increase as well as secure a honey crop. It was practiced and recommended by one of the most extensive bee-keepers in the United States, Mr. E. W. Alexander, who has been recognized as an authority on general practical apiculture, for indeed his crops of honey have gone up into the carloads. He first made the plan public in 1905, after having tested it many years. So many favorable comments were received of bee-keepers who had tried it and found it to be a success that we republished it with some slight modifications in 1906. We here present the plan as it was given in *Gleanings*, page 423, 1906:

When your colonies are nearly full enough to swarm naturally, and you wish to divide them so as to make two from one, go to the colony you wish to divide; lift it from its stand and put in its place a hive containing frames of comb or foundation, the same as you would put the swarm in providing it had just swarmed. Now remove the center comb from this empty hive, and put in its place a frame of brood, either from the hive you wish to divide or some other colony that can spare one, and be sure to find the queen and put her on this frame of brood in the new hive; also look it over very carefully to see that it contains no eggs or larvæ in any

queen-cells. If it does, destroy them Now put a queen-excluding honey-board on top of this new hive that contains the queen and frame of brood with their empty combs, then set your full queenless colony over the excluder; next put in the empty comb or frame of foundation, wherever you got your frame of brood, and close the upper hive except the entrance they have through the excluder into the hive below. Now leave them in this way about five days, then look over the combs carefully, and destroy any larvæ you may find in the queen-cells unless they are of a good strain of bees that you care to breed from, for they frequently start the rearing of queens above the excluder very soon after their queen was placed below the excluder. If so, you had better separate them at once; but if they have not started any queen-cells above, then leave them together ten or eleven days, during which time the queen will get a fine lot of brood started in the lower hive, and every egg and particle of larva that was in the old hive on top will have matured, so it will be capped over and saved; then separate them, putting the old hive on a new stand. It will then be full of young bees mostly, and capped brood, and in about twenty-four hours they will accept a ripe cell, a virgin, or laying queen, as they will then realize that they are hopelessly queenless. I would advise you to give them a laying queen, as I never like to keep my full colonies for even a day longer without a laying queen than I can help. In this way you have two strong colonies from one, as you have not lost a particle of brood nor checked the laying of your queen; and with me it almost wholly prevents swarming. This is the way we have made our increase for several years, and we like it much better than any other method we ever tried. In doing so you keep all your colonies strong during the whole summer, and it is the strong colonies that count in giving us our surplus.

The mere fact of having a large number of colonies does not amount to much unless they are strong in bees and are *well* cared for at all times. This is a fact that many have sadly overlooked; and when the season comes to a close, giving them a small surplus, they feel disappointed and lay the fault on many things that have had but little to do with their failure.

In making your increase in the above way your new swarm on the old stand is in fine shape for a clamp of sections, as it has a large working force backed up by having its hive nearly full of brood, and but little honey, as the bees have been in the habit of storing their honey in the old hive that was on top, so they will soon go to work in the sections and have no notion of swarming. Then the old hive that has been set away can usually spare 15 or 20 lbs. of honey, which can be taken with the extractor, giving its new queen plenty of room to lay, and in a short time will be one of your best colonies, and also have no desire to swarm.

Now, if you have done your duty by your bees since taking them from their winter quarters, as I have recommended in the above, keeping them snug and warm, and feeding them a little thin warm syrup nearly every day for the first thirty days after they have commenced to fly, you can have two good strong colonies in the place of one ready to commence work on your clover harvest, which here commences about June 15.

From an extensive experience along this line I find I can get nearly twice the amount of surplus by dividing as above stated over what I was able to acquire either by letting them go undivided or dividing in a way that caused the loss of a greater part of their brood. This losing of brood we must guard against at all times if we expect to secure a fine surplus. It costs both time and honey to produce it, and it is the principal factor in obtaining those strong colonies that give us tons of honey.

Far too many bee-keepers think that the value of their apiary consists in the number of colonies they keep. This is so only to a certain extent; for if you had 1000 colonies and they were all weak in bees, so they would give you no surplus, they would not be worth as much as one good strong colony that would give you 200 or 300 pounds of honey.

Several years ago one of my sons bought nine colonies of bees in common box hives, about the first of June. He brought them home and transferred them at once to movable-frame hives, and in about three weeks divided them, making 20 colonies of the 9 he bought, using some queen-cells I had on hand for his surplus colonies. He then attended to those 20 colonies so they were all strong at the commencement of our buckwheat harvest. I then lent him 20 hives of empty combs to put on top of his colonies to extract from. He took 2849 lbs. of extracted honey from those 9 colonies and their increase, and left them in good condition so every one came out the next spring in fine order.

Another son, the same season, took one colony, divided into three, and received 347 lbs. of extracted honey. They also came through the following winter in good condition. I speak of these cases simply to show that it is not necessary to keep hundreds of colonies in order to get a little honey. If you will keep only strong colonies and give them the best of care you will soon find both pleasure and profit in bee-keeping.

Now, in regard to the criticism on this way of making our increase, which has been published in GLEANINGS. I find that nearly all who have made a failure of the method have taken colonies that had already made some preparations for swarming by having eggs or larvæ in their queen-cells, as did J. D. Ronan, of Chesterville, Miss., and also Don Mills' of Highland, Mich.

During the summer I received a few letters from parties who had made a failure of this method in about the same way. Some had taken colonies that had capped queen-cells in their hives at the time they put the queen in the under hive, and, of course, they swarmed in a day or two. I can not see that these failures are any proof of fault in the method. When we work with our bees we must always use some discretion in such matters. If a colony is very strong in bees it certainly requires different management from one rather weak.

INTRODUCING. Under normal conditions only one queen will be tolerated in a colony at a time. Should there by accident be two, when they meet there is likely to be a royal battle, until one of them is killed. So it happens that queens are, as a rule, jealous rivals; but there are exceptions. Under certain conditions (as when an old queen is about to be superseded) when the young daughter may be tolerated in the hive along with her mother—both laying side by side; but in the course of a few days or weeks the mother will be missing. Whether she dies of old age or the daughter kills her we do not know. There are other conditions where two and sometimes a dozen queens will be permitted to stay in the hive, but under circumstances which seem to be abnormal.

Again, it may be stated that a normal colony of bees will not take a strange queen, even though they have no mother of their own, much less will they accept an interloper when there is already a queen in the hive. We may, therefore, lay it down as a rule that has exceptions,[*] like all other good rules, that we can not introduce any queen, young or old, to a colony that already has one. Moreover, bees that have been suddenly deprived of a queen will not. under ordinary conditions, accept another, no matter how much they may need one, until she has been "introduced." It follows, then, in the process of requeening we are compelled to put a new queen in a wire-cloth cage and confine her there (where the other bees can not attack her) until she has acquired the same colony odor or individual scent as the bees themselves. This usually takes two or three days, at the end of which time the queen may be released and they will treat her as their own royal mother. We do not know how bees recognize each other, or how they can tell a strange queen from their own, except by scent factor.

It is a fact well recognized that a dog can pick out his master from hundreds of others through the agency of scent; nay, further, he can track him if he loses sight of him by catching the scent of where he has walked, in spite of the fact that hundreds of other people may have gone over the same ground. This scent that is so acute in a dog is undoubtedly highly developed in the bee, otherwise we should be at a loss to account for some of the phenomena in the domestic economy of the hive. See SCENT OF BEES.

---

[*] If a virgin queen, on returning from a mating-trip, enters by mistake a hive where there is an old laying queen she may, and very often does, supplant the old queen. The virgin is young and vigorous, and more than a match for the old queen full of eggs. Even though the colony odor be lacking, the bees in this case accept the supplanter.

Hence we naturally conclude that, by the sense of smell, bees recognize their own mother from a new or strange one.

Again, we learn that, if two queens have exactly the same colony odor after being caged for two or three days in a queenless hive, either one may be liberated and the bees will accept one just as readily as the other. If both be liberated at the same time, one in one corner of the hive and the other in the opposite corner, both will be tolerated by the bees; but once the queens come together themselves there is danger of a royal battle* resulting in the death of one. From this fact we infer that the bees, providing a queen or queens have the requisite colony odor, will accept at any time one or more such queens under many conditions; that, further, when two queens have the same colony odor, if they can be kept apart by means of perforated zinc both will continue to lay eggs in the same hive without let or hindrance. This condition will be allowed so long as the colony prospers, until a dearth of honey comes; then the bees show a disposition to rob, and they may destroy one of the queens.

Bees that have been thrown into a box or pan, and then shaken or bumped again and again until they are demoralized or frightened, are much more tractable than those not so disturbed. Such bees if made queenless just prior to the shaking, and confined without combs or brood in a cool place for a few hours, will usually accept a queen at once. The factor of colony odor then apparently does not operate, for the bees are put out of their normal condition.

Young bees just hatched will at any time accept any queen. Therefore, it comes about that, when one desires to introduce a valuable breeder on which he desires to take no chances whatsoever, he causes her to be released on a frame of very young or hatching bees; but consideration will be given to this later.

Virgin queens, if just hatched, will usually be accepted by a colony, if not too long queenless, without the process of introduction or even of caging; but when one of these queens comes to be four or five days old she is very much more difficult to introduce than a normal laying queen. Why this should be so, we do not know.

When but little honey is coming in, it is much easier to introduce and unite bees than during a dearth.

---

* We say "danger" of a battle. Queens will not always fight when so put together.

A queen in the height of her egg-laying will be accepted far more readily than one that has been deprived of egg-laying, as in the case of one that has been four or five days in the mails.

Some colonies are more nervous than others. To open a hive of such on an unfavorable day might arouse the inmates to a stinging fury. Indeed, such colonies will often ball and sting their own queen when the hive is opened if the day is unfavorable.

It is easier to introduce toward night, or after dark, than during the day. The reason of this is that after dark the excitement of the day has subsided. There is no chance for robbing and no reason for vigil. In short, bees are not *expecting* trouble and are not inclined to make any.

A fasting queen, or, rather, a queen that is hungry, will usually ask for food, and hence will generally be treated more considerately than one that shows fear or fight.

Having stated, therefore, the basic principles governing the relation of the queen to the bees we can now more intelligently proceed to the methods of introduction, most of which are based on the theory that the queen to be introduced must first have acquired the colony odor of her new subjects.

The cages are supplied with bee candy (see CANDY), so that, in case the bees do not feed the queen, she will not starve. In some cases the bees release the queen by eating away the candy and letting her out. In other cases the apiarist himself liberates her after she has been confined the requisite length of time, or until such time as she has acquired the colony odor.

Most of the cages are sent out by queen-breeders with directions how to perform this operation; and it is usually safer for the beginner to follow these directions implicitly.

The mailing and introducing cage that is ordinarily used over the country is called the Benton, and is shown in the accompanying illustration. This consists of an oblong block of wood with three holes bored nearly through, one of the end holes being filled with Good candy (see CANDY), and the other two are left for occupancy by the bees and queen. On the back of the cover are printed full directions for introducing, and at each end of the cage is a small hole bored through lengthwise the grain of the wood. One hole (next to the bees) is covered with a piece of perforated metal, secured in place with two small wire nails driven through the perforations. The other hole (that is, at the candy end) is covered over with a piece of pasteboard perforated by a line of holes run-

BENTON MAILING-CAGE.
Postage on this cage is one cent. A larger size for longer distances, as shown below, requires two cents.

ning through the center. The object of these perforations is to give the bees an opportunity to taste the candy through the holes of the pasteboard; and once having gotten a sip they will gnaw the holes larger, and finally eat away the pasteboard entirely.

Very often, after the cage has been through the mails, and been on the journey for several days, the bees in the cage will have consumed two - thirds or three - fourths of the candy. If those in the hive to which the queen is to be introduced gain access to the candy direct they would eat out what little there is of it in five or six hours, liberate the queen, and probably kill her. In order to accomplish introduction safely the cage should be on the frames (where the bees can get acquainted with the queen) for at least 24 hours, and longer wherever practicable. As it takes anywhere from 12 to 24 hours for the bees to gnaw away the pasteboard before they can get at the can-

dy, and from 6 to 24 hours to eat out the candy, we are assured of at least 18 hours before the bees can release their new mother; and generally the time is longer — anywhere from 24 to 48 hours. The pasteboard has another advantage, in that it makes the introduction entirely automatic. The one who receives the queen pries off the cover protecting the wire cloth, and then by the directions which he reads on the reverse side of this cover he learns that all he has to do is to lay the cage wire cloth down over the space between two brood-frames of the queenless colony, *and the bees do the rest.* It is not even necessary for him to open the hive to release the queen; indeed, he had better let the colony entirely alone for three or four days, as opening the hive disturbs and annoys the bees to such an extent that very often they will ball the queen, seeming to lay to her door what

HOW BEES AND QUEENS ARE PUT UP IN A MAILING-CAGE.

must be to them a very great disturbance in having their home torn to pieces.

There are several sizes of these Benton cages—the larger ones being used for longer distances. The one shown at top of page 287 is good for 1000 miles through the mails, although very often used for twice that distance. This may be called a combination mailing and introducing cage. Ordinarily, if we have much introducing to do we prefer something especially adapted to the latter purpose alone; we have, therefore, used with a great deal of satisfaction the Miller introducing-cage.

As many of the readers of this work may possibly do something at mailing queens, it might be well to add a word about making

PUTTING QUEEN AND BEES IN EXPORT BENTON MAILING-CAGE.

the candy for Benton cages. This should be prepared as directed under CANDY, which see. It should be made several days in advance of the time it is expected to be used; for after it has been made it will soften down and become quite sticky. If put in cages in this condition it will result in the death of the bees and queen before accomplishing half their journey. After the candy has stood several days it is likely to become soft again, when more sugar should be kneaded in. It would be better then to let it stand two or three days, and then, if necessary, knead in more sugar until it holds its consistency so that the dough is *stiff, moist, and mealy*. This is important. It should then be crowded into the candy hole or candy end, as we call it, and then the hole in the end over which the pasteboard is to be tacked should be plugged full of candy, after which the pasteboard may be nailed on.

The manner of filling a cage for mailing is to pick it up with the left hand in such a way that the thumb covers the hole over which the perforated metal has been nailed, but which, before the time of filling, should be revolved around on one side or taken off entirely. The queen is first to be picked up by the wings, her head pushed into the hole as far as possible. After she runs in, place the thumb over the hole. Worker-bees are next picked up in a similar manner, and poked in, selecting those that are filling with honey from open cells until there are a dozen bees. If the cage is larger, two dozen may be used; and if it is extra large, four or five dozen. When cages are mailed during cold weather there should be more bees put in, to help keep up the animal heat. During hot weather a dozen bees are quite sufficient in the smallest Benton cage, which is ordinarily mailed for a cent.

MILLER'S INTRODUCING-CAGE.

It is very convenient to have in the apiary small special cages for introducing and holding queens that come out with swarms until they can be introduced or disposed of. The one below illustrated is the best of any. It is especially handy for introducing young virgins. The cage is so flat it can slide in at the entrance without even removing the cover of the hive, and the bees will release the queen by the candy method. Yet for introducing fertile or valuable queens we recommend inserting it between two combs and drawing them together until they hold the cage. The queen thus acquires the scent of the combs, brood, and the cluster, and hence when released will be more likely to be accepted.

This cage, like the Benton, will give very much better results if a piece of pasteboard is nailed over the end. This the bees will

gnaw away, gaining access to the candy, which they eat out. Since we discovered the value of the pasteboard used in the manner stated, with either the Benton or the Miller cage we are able to introduce 99 per cent of all queens, providing, of course, the colony has not been queenless more than four or five days. One that has been without a mother longer may get to depending on cells; and when the work has so far progressed they are liable to destroy the introduced queen and await the hatching of one of the virgins.

We copy its manner of construction from Dr. Miller's own words:

Take a block 3 inches long, 1¼ wide, and ⅝ thick; two blocks 1 inch by ₇₁₆x⅝; two pieces of tin about an inch square; a piece of wire cloth 4½x3½; two pieces of fine wire about 9 inches long, and four small wire nails ⅝ or ¾ long. That's the bill of material. Lay down the two small blocks parallel, ⅜ of an inch apart, one piece of tin under, and one over them. Nail together and clinch. These two blocks, being ⅝ inch apart, make the hole to fill with Good candy, through which the queen is liberated

Another feature of this cage, of great importance to beginners, is as a queen-catcher. It can be put down over the queen after the wooden slide is removed, and when she crawls upward the plug is replaced.

M'INTYRE'S CAGE.

Another excellent introducing - cage is the one devised by J. F. McIntyre. How it is managed, we copy from Mr. McIntyre's article in *Gleanings in Bee Culture*, page 880, 1890 :

I take a piece of wire cloth 5¼ inches square, cut little pieces ¼ of an inch square out of each corner, and bend the four sides at right angles, making a box 4 inches square and ½ inch deep. In one corner

I fasten a tube of wood or tin ⅜ inch in diameter, and two inches long, which is filled with Good candy, for the bees to eat out and liberate the queen.

I use this cage altogether in my apiary, for changing laying queens from one hive to another. I kill my old queens when they are two years old, and introduce young laying queens in their places. My practice is to go to the nucleus having the young laying queen; lift out the comb with the queen on, and press one of these cages into the comb over the queen, and what bees may be around her. Carry this comb to the hive which held the old queen. After finding and killing her place the comb with the young queen caged on it in the center of the hive, taking one comb from the hive back to the nucleus. In a week I go and take the cage out and find the young queen laying. When I receive a valuable queen from a distance I liberate her at once on a comb of hatching brood, with some young bees; and when she commences to lay I introduce her as above.

Fillmore, Cal., Oct. 21.   J. F. McINTYRE.

A cage that is very popular with many bee-keepers, and somewhat similar to the foregoing, is shown in the two illustrations
10

next following. From a piece of wire cloth perhaps 6 inches square a piece 1¼ inches is cut out of each corner, as shown in Fig. 2. Several strands of wire are then raveled out, and it is then folded as shown in Fig. 3.

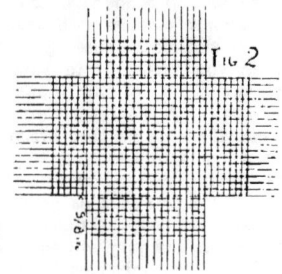

To introduce, the queen is placed on a patch of hatching brood with a few cells of honey. When she is at the right point the cage is clapped over her, and the strands are forced clear up to the cross-wires. The young bees, as they hatch, will treat her kindly, and in the mean time she will begin laying in the cells vacated by the bees. If the outside bees seem to be favorably disposed. in two days the cage may be pulled off; and if the bees still treat her kindly, the comb can be put back 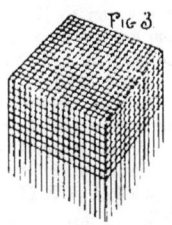 into the hive, which is then closed up. If the bees show any disposition to ball her, she should be caged again as before, but this time all combs with unsealed larvæ should be removed, and care must be taken that there be no queen-cells of any kind. In from three to five days more she may be released again. By this time the bees will be almost sure to accept her.

The difference between this and the McIntyre cage is that the apiarist has to release the queen himself, whereas by the McIntyre plan the bees eat out the candy and liberate her automatically. The latter plan is to be preferred, because sometimes opening the hive will so disturb the bees as to cause them to attack the queen.

A SURE WAY OF INTRODUCING.

There is one perfectly sure way of introducing a very valuable queen, such as an imported one, if we only observe the conditions carefully. Remove frames of hatching brood from several hives, shaking off every bee and put them into an empty hive closed down to a small space ; and unless the weather is very warm, place the whole in a warm room. Let the queen and her attendants loose in this hive, and the young bees, as they hatch out, will soon make a swarm. As several who have tried this plan have been so careless as to leave the entrance open and let the queen get out, we would warn you especially to have your hive so close that no bee can by any possibility get out.* If the frames you have selected contain no unsealed brood, you will have very little loss; but otherwise the larvæ, having no bees to feed them, will mostly starve. As soon as a few hundred bees are hatched, the queen will be found with them, and they will soon make a cluster. When the combs have been taken from strong colonies, where the queen is laying hundreds of eggs in a day, in a week or two the swarm will become strong. Three frames will do very well at first, and one or two more may be added in the course of a week or two. Remember, *no live bee* is to be given to the queen. A queen is seldom lost, even by the first plan given, if you are careful, and watch them until they are safely received.

There is another way that has a little the preference. In order to describe it we can do no better than to make an extract from an editorial in *Gleanings in Bee Culture*, page 539, Vol. XXI. :

We have just received a consignment of 30 imported Italian queens, direct from Italy, by express. Every queen came through alive and in good order, and they are now introduced into the apiary without the loss of one. Our method of introducing with this lot was something we had not tried before on so large a number of queens. We took four or five strong colonies, and divided them up into 30 one-frame nuclei. This was done in the forenoon. In the afternoon we transferred the imported queens, without any attendants, to Miller introducing-cages, placing one in every nucleus above mentioned. Most of the queens were out at the expiration of two days, in good order, and they are now all out.

You see, the point is here: These newly divided nuclei will have old and young bees, and more or less hatching brood. Before the imported queen is released, the *old* bees will have returned to the old stand, and it is these old fellows that always make trouble in introducing. By the time the queen is released, there are none but *young* bees, including those that were brought to the nucleus-stand and those that are hatched out in the interim. These, of course, all being young, will accept their new mother, without any trouble. The plan has proved to be so satisfactory that we shall employ it hereafter for all valuable queens.

------

* They can be set out and allowed to fly in two or three days.

DIRECT METHOD OF INTRODUCTION.

Where it is desired to introduce a queen from a nucleus to a queenless colony, both in the same yard, the operation can usually be performed with safety and with very little labor, as follows: The colony to receive the queen should be made broodless a few hours in advance. Go to the nucleus and lift out two frames, bees and all, with the queen in between. Put these down in the center of the queenless colony; close up the hive and don't go near it for several days. The bees that have been queenless and broodless are crying for a mother. When she is given them with a large force of her own subjects, she seems to be protected, even if she does not have the odor of the new colony which, by the way, has been modified by the bees and brood given them from the other hive.

This is a modification of the Simmins direct method of introducing. It could not be used in the case of a queen sent through the mails.

THE SIMMINS FASTING METHOD.

While this has been discussed to a greater or less extent in the bee-journals, the plan, while very simple, is not one that we would recommend in the case of a valuable queen, or in any event to a beginner. It is as follows: The queen to be introduced should be put in a cage at night without attendants and without food. She should thus be confined for thirty minutes when she must be released by lamplight over the frames of the queenless colony, and the hive closed up for 48 hours. This will work safely in many cases, but we are sure there are some conditions where it does not.

DUAL PLAN OF INTRODUCING.

Another plan is to introduce two virgins or laying queens at one operation to save the necessary time it takes for the bees to get acquainted with the queen. This is described in detail under the head of QUEEN-REARING, to which the reader is directed.

HOW SOON WILL AN INTRODUCED QUEEN BEGIN TO LAY ?

As a general thing, we may expect her to begin laying the next day; but sometimes, especially if the queen has been a long time prevented from laying, as in the case of an imported queen, she may not lay for three or four days, or even a week. If introduced in the fall of the year, she may not commence laying at all until spring, unless the colony is fed regularly every day for a week or more. This will always start a queen that is good for any thing.

HOW TO TELL WHETHER A COLONY IS QUEENLESS OR NOT.

Having discussed mailing and introducing cages, it may be pertinent at this point to give one of the prime essentials in successful introducing. The very first thing to be determined before you attempt to introduce at all, is that your colony is *certainly* queenless. The fact that there may be no eggs nor larvæ in the hive, and that you can not find the queen, is not sufficient evidence that she is absent, although this state of affairs points that way. But during the earlier part of the summer there should be either brood or eggs of some kind if a queen is present. Yes, there should be eggs or brood clear up until the latter part of summer. In the early fall, queens generally stop laying, and shrivel up in size so that a beginner might conclude that the colony is queenless, and therefore he must buy a queen. In attempting to introduce the new queen, of course he meets with failure, as she is stung to death, in all probability, and carried out at the hive-entrance. If you can not find eggs or larvæ at any season of the year when *other* stocks are breeding, and the supposedly queenless colony builds cells on a frame of unsealed larvæ that you give them, you may decide that your colony is surely queenless, and it will be safe to introduce a new queen. But when you find eggs, larvæ, and sealed *worker* brood, the presence of queen-cells simply indicates that the bees are either preparing to supersede their queen or making ready to swarm. See SWARMING.

HOW LONG SHALL A COLONY BE QUEENLESS BEFORE ATTEMPTING TO INTRODUCE?

The worst colony to introduce a laying queen to is one that has been queenless long enough so that there is a *possibility* of one or more virgin queens being in the hive. It is hard to decide definitely in all cases when such colonies are queenless. Most young virgins, after they are three or four days old, are very apt to be mistaken for workers, especially by a beginner. It is not always practicable to wait until they have built queen-cells, especially if you happen to have a nice surplus of laying queens for which you wish to find room. We prefer colonies that have not been queenless more than a couple of days — just long enough to see cells start, and just long enough so the bees begin to recognize their loss, but not long enough for them to get cells under way. Cells nicely started or capped over are quite apt to make the colony feel as if it wanted something of its own ; and when a laying queen is introduced to them they take a notion sometimes that they *won't* have a strange mother.

WHAT TO DO IF BEES BALL THE QUEEN.

When we introduced queens in the old-fashioned way—that is, before cages were constructed so as to release queens automatically — we used to experience much trouble by bees balling queens. If the bees were not ready to accept her when she was released by the apiarist, they were pretty sure to ball her. But here is a point that it is well to observe : When the *bees* let out the queen they very rarely ball her. But when it is necessary for the *apiarist* to perform the work, opening the hive, accompanied by general disturbance, is apt to cause the bees to ball her as soon as released. Well, suppose they do ball her. Lift the ball out of the hive and blow smoke on it until the bees come off one by one. When you can see the queen, get hold of her wings and pull the rest of the bees off from her by their wings. Do not be nervous about it, and you can get her loose and cage her again. Put more candy in the opening, and give her another trial. Some one—we do not remember who—advised dropping the queen, when she is balled, into a vessel of water. The angry bees will immediately desert the queen when, she can be easily taken out of the water, and recaged. We have never tried it, but we believe we should prefer the method first described.

WHAT TO DO WHEN THE QUEEN FLIES AWAY.

Sometimes a beginner is very nervous, and by a few bungling motions may manage to let the queen escape from the hive where he expects to introduce her. Or this may happen: The queen may take wing right off from the frame—become a little alarmed because there are no bees about her, and fly. In either case, step back immediately after opening the hive, and in fifteen or twenty minutes she is quite likely to return to the same spot, and you must not be surprised if you find her again in the hive. If you do not discover her in the hive near where you are standing, in about half an hour look in other hives near by. If you see a ball of bees somewhere down among the frames, you may be quite sure that here is the queen that flew away, and that she has made a mistake, and entered the wrong hive.

INTRODUCING VIRGIN QUEENS.

As previously explained, a young virgin just hatched, generally weak and feeble, can usually be let loose in a queenless colony without caging, and be favorably received; but one from two to six days old is, as a rule, much more difficult to introduce than a laying queen; and one ten days old, more than old enough to be fertilized, is most difficult. Such queens can be introduced, however, but generally it is a waste of time to attempt it in a strong vigorous colony. Better by far give them a cell or a virgin just hatched, thus saving time and vexation; for even should the old virgin be accepted, she may be minus a leg, or be so deformed from rough treatment as to become in a large measure impaired for usefulness. Under head of QUEEN-REARING we describe "baby nuclei;" and, as already stated, it is much easier to introduce any queen, either virgin or laying, to a nucleus or weak force of bees than to a strong vigorous colony; so if we would attempt to introduce four or five day old virgins, give them to nuclei—the smaller and weaker the better; but, as we shall direct under QUEEN-REARING, it would be much better to give queen-cells or young virgins.

INVERTING. See REVERSING.

ITALIAN BEES. At present the Italians, and even hybrids, have shown themselves so far ahead of the common bee that we may safely consider all discussion of the matter at an end by the great majority of bee-keepers. Many times we find colonies of hybrids that go ahead of pure stock; but as a general thing (taking one season with another), pure Italians, where they have not been enfeebled by choosing light-colored bees to breed from, are ahead of any admixture. There has been a great tendency with bees, as well as other stock, to pay more attention to looks than to real intrinsic worth, such as honey-gathering, prolificness of the queens, hardiness, etc.; and this may have had much to do with the severe losses we have sustained in winters past.

Even if it were true, that hybrids produce as much honey as pure Italians, each bee-keeper would want at least one queen of absolute and known purity; for although a first cross might do very well, unless he had this one pure queen to furnish queen-cells he would soon have bees of every possible grade, from the faintest trace of Italian blood, all the way up. The objection to this course is that these blacks, with about one

band (with the exception of the Eastern blood), are about the worst kind of bees to sting, being very much more vindictive than either race in its purity; they also have a very disagreeable way of tumbling off the combs in a perfectly demoralized state whenever the hive is opened, except in the height of the honey-season, and of making a general uproar when they are compelled, by smoke, to be decent.

Our pure Italian stocks can be opened at any time and their queens removed, scarcely disturbing the cluster, and, as a general thing, without the use of any smoke at all, by one who is fully conversant with the habits of bees. A good many hybrids will not repel the moth as do the half-bloods and the pure Italians. For these reasons and several others, we would rear all queens from one of known purity. If we do this, we may have almost if not quite the full benefit of the Italians as honey-gatherers, even though there are black bees all about us.

The queens, and drones from queens obtained direct from Italy, vary greatly in their markings, but the worker bee has one peculiarity that we have never found wanting; that is, the three yellow bands we have all heard so much about. Unfortunately, there has been a great amount of controversy about these yellow bands; and to help restore harmony, we have been to some expense for engravings.

Every worker-bee, whether common or Italian, has a body composed of six tubes, or segments, one sliding into the other, telescope fashion. When the bee is full of honey these segments slide out, and the abdomen is elongated considerably beyond the tips of the wings, which are ordinarily about the length of the body. Sometimes we see bees swollen with dysentery spreading the rings to their fullest extent, and in that condition they sometimes would be called queens by an inexperienced person. On the contrary, in the fall of the year when the bee is preparing for its winter nap, its abdomen is so much drawn up that it scarcely seems like the same insect. The engraving on the left shows the abdomen of the bee detached from the body, that we may get a full view of the bands or markings that distinguish the Italians from our common bees. Now we wish you to observe particularly that all honey-bees, common as well as Italian, have four bands of bright-colored down, J, K, L, M, one on each of the four middle rings of the body, but none on the first and none on the last. These bands of down are very bright on young bees, but may be so worn off as to be almost or entirely wanting on an old bee, especially on those that have been in the habit of robbing very much. This is the explanation of the glossy blackness of robbers often seen dodging about the hives. Perhaps squeezing through small crevices has thus worn off the down, or it may be that pushing through dense masses of bees has something to do with it; for we often see such shiny black bees in great numbers, in stocks that have been nearly suffocated by being confined to their hives in shipping, or at other times. These bands of down differ in shades of color, many times, and this is the case with characteristic of the Italians; for, after this has worn off, the yellow bands are much plainer than before. A, B, C, are the yellow bands of which we have heard so much, and they are neither down, plumage, nor any thing of that sort, as you will see by taking a careful look at an Italian on the window. The scale, or horny substance of which the body is composed, is yellow, and almost transparent, not black and opaque, as are the rings of the common bee, or the lower rings of the same insect.

The first yellow band, A, is right down next the waist; now look carefully. It is very plain, when you once know what to look for, and no child need ever be mistaken about it.

 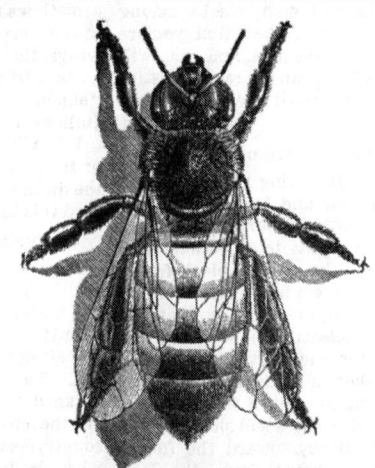

HOW TO TELL HYBRIDS FROM PURE ITALIANS.

the common bee as well as with the Italian. Under a common lens the bands are simply fine soft hair, or fur, and it is this principally which gives the light-colored Italians their handsome appearance. You have, perhaps, all noticed the progeny of some particular queen when they first came out to play, and pronounced them the handsomest bees you ever saw; but a few months after they would be no better looking than the rest of your bees. This is simply because they had worn off their handsome plumage in the " stern realities " of hard work in the fields. Occasionally you will find a queen whose bees have bands nearly white instead of yellow, and this is what has led to the so-called albino bees. When the plumage is gone, they are just like other Italians. Now, these bands of down have nothing to do with the yellow bands that are

At the lower edge is the first black band; this is often only a thin sharp streak of black.

The second, B, is the plainest of all the yellow bands, and can usually be seen in even the very poorest hybrids. The first band of down is seen where the black and yellow join, but it is so faint you will hardly notice it in some specimens.

We have at the lower edge of the scale, as before, a narrow line of black; when the down wears off, this shows nearly as broad as the yellow band.

When we come to hybrids, we shall find a greater diversity; for while the bees from one queen are all pretty uniformly marked with two bands, another's will be of all sorts, some beautifully marked Italians, some pure black, others one or two banded. Some will sting with great venom, while others with only one or two bands will be as peaceable as your best Italians. Without a doubt, many queens have been sent out as pure that produced only hybrids; but since our recent studies in the matter we are quite well satisfied that we have sold several queens as hybrids that were really full-bloods. A very slight admixture of black blood will cause the band C to disappear on some of the bees, but we should be very careful in such matters to be sure that the bees in question were really hatched in the hive; for bees of adjoining hives often mix to a considerable extent. If you examine a colony of blacks and one of hybrids that stand side by side, you will find many Italians among the blacks, and many blacks among the Italians. Take young bees that you are sure have hatched in the hive, and you will be pretty safe, but you can not readily distinguish the third band until they are several days old.

FOUR AND FIVE BANDED ITALIANS.

In 1890 and the following year there was quite a rage for four and five banded Italians. These are nothing more nor less than Italians bred for *bands* by selection. For instance, we may take a lot of black fowls, and from one having a few white feathers we can, by selection, breed fowls that are entirely white by selecting the whitest fowls to breed from for successive generations. Some Italians show a tendency toward the fourth band. Perhaps some of the daughters of the mother of these bees will show in their bees a *greater* tendency toward the fourth band. Again, we breed from the last named queen, and select from her another breeding queen whose bees show quite clearly the fourth band with a glimmering of the fifth. By continued selection we may be able to get the fifth. But after all, when we have bees with four and five yellow bands, we are liable to have bees for color and not for business. It is possible to develop any trait that we may wish to have characteristic of our bees. In the same way it is possible to breed bees that are very energetic. But as a general rule we shall have to lose sight of fancy colors.

HOLY-LAND AND CYPRIAN BEES.

In 1882 considerable excitement arose over two new races of bees brought over from the Old World by D. A. Jones, of Beeton, Ontario, Canada, who was the leading bee-keeper across the line. They were called Cyprian and Holy-Land bees, from the places where he found them. The former, from the Isle of Cyprus, seem to have been for many years isolated, and are a very distinct and uniform race.

While they look like Italians, and might be classed as such by bee-keepers not familiar with their peculiarities, yet they have a few distinct characteristics. Holy-Land bees show whiter fuzz-rings, and the bodies are slimmer than those of the ordinary Italians. They are more like the ordinary albinos. In fact, most of the albinos formerly sold were of Holy-Land extraction. The Cyprians look very much like the four and five banded Italians. The yellow bands are of a deeper orange than those of the Italians, slightly wider, and sometimes more than three in number. Just at the base of the thorax, and between the wings, there is a little yellow spot that is quite distinct and prominent, called the "shield." This may be seen on some yellow Italians, but it is less pronounced.

When Italians are crossed with Cyprians or Holy Lands it is a little difficult to detect the difference except by their nervousness. And this brings us to the

TEMPERAMENT OF EASTERN BEES.

They are more nervous, especially the Cyprians. Sometimes smoke seems to have no power over them. They will fly up twenty or thirty at a time without warning, and sting the moment they touch the apiarist. The more smoke is used, the more enraged they become. Cyprians especially are the crossest bees ever brought into this country—so cross, indeed, there is scarcely a breeder in the United States who has them for sale. The same objection, though to a less extent, applies to the Holy Lands.

We once sold an imported Cyprian queen; and our customer, after he had kept her for a while, returned her, saying that her bees were so vicious that on one occasion they stung every thing in sight, and drove even the family down cellar. We bought the queen back; but after we had had her for a few weeks and her bees had begun to hatch out we found it would hardly be safe to keep them in the yard. They would become so enraged at times that the whole colony would rush out in battle array. While the progeny of this queen was exceptionally cross, the general run, both of Cyprians and Holy Lands, is so disagreeable to handle that they are now well nigh discarded by the bee keepers of the United States.

The only possible redeeming feature is that they are good brood-rearers; but they breed to excess after the honey-flow, using up all their available stores in raising bees, when Italians would conserve their energies and leave enough honey for winter.

In the matter of rearing queen-cells, either the Cyprians or Holy Lands will rear more queens than any Italians, Carniolans, blacks, or hybrids we ever saw. We have known as many as a hundred natural cells on one frame; and we also had one instance where 25 cells from a Holy Land queen hatched within a few minutes of each other; and so vigorous were these young queens that some of them actually flew the moment they popped out of their inclosures.

ITALIANIZING. Few questions are asked oftener than, "How shall I Italianize? and when shall I do it?" There is always a loss in removing a queen and substituting another, even where we have laying queens on hand; and where we are to use the same colony for rearing the queen, there is still greater loss. Under the heads of NUCLEI and QUEEN-REARING these points will be found fully discussed. Where one has an apiary of black bees, his cheapest way, especially if he has plenty of time to devote to the subject, is to purchase three or four choice tested breeders, and rear his own queens from them after the honey-flow. He should then put drone-traps on all his black and hybrid colonies, leaving only the Italian drones the freedom of the air. See DRONES. If the breeders are bought in the spring or summer months, we would not remove the old queens until the summer crop of honey is over; only, instead of allowing natural swarming, take two or three frames from each old stock about swarming time, and make nuclei, giving them queen-cells from the breeding stock.

When these queens are hatched and laying, build the nuclei up, with frames of brood given one at a time until they are full stocks. By such a course you have the full benefit of your old queens during the honey-season, until the new ones are ready to take their places. After the honey-yield has begun to slack you can remove the old queens, and give the now small colonies queen-cells, as you did the nuclei at first. This does the

swarming for the season, and the Italianizing, at one and the same time. See INCREASE; also NUCLEUS.

If you have more money than time to spare, and wish to have the work done up quickly, purchase as many queens as you have colonies, and introduce them at any season of the year, as directed in INTRODUCING QUEENS. You can purchase all tested queens if you wish, but we would advise taking untested Italian queens during the months of July and August, when they are the cheapest, as this is also the best time of the year to Italianize. If done in the spring it is liable through change of queens to cut off brood-rearing, and, hence, cause few worker-bees when the harvest comes on. Some find it more convenient to change queens *during* the *swarming* season, first for the purpose of stopping swarming, and, second. because there are plenty of cells usually at this time from choice stocks. See West's queen-cell protector under QUEEN-REARING.

After your stocks have all been provided with Italian queens, by either of the plans given above, if you wish your bees to become pure Italians you are to commence replacing all queens that prove to be hybrids, as soon as the young bees are hatched in sufficient numbers to enable you to decide. See ITALIAN BEES. Now, if honey only is your object we would not replace these hybrids until they are one or two years old; for they will average nearly if not quite as good honey-gatherers, and will raise just as pure drones as pure Italians. If you should find the bees of any particular queen too cross to be endurable, replace her with another, at any time. Be careful, however, that these hybrid colonies be not allowed to swarm naturally; for if they raise a queen she will produce hybrid drones*; and this is something we wish most scrupulously to guard against. It will be better to raise all the queens yourself, and make nuclei while seeking to Italianize.

*To get rid of black and hybrid drones, see DRONES.

L.

LABELS FOR HONEY. See EXTRACT-ED HONEY.

LAWS RELATING TO BEES. Blackstone, the great exponent of common law, says: "Bees also are *feræ naturæ* (wild by nature); but when hived and reclaimed, a man may have a qualified property in them by the law of nature as well as by civil law." And Bracton says: "Occupation, that is, hiving or including them, gives the property in bees; for, though a swarm alights upon my tree, I have no more property in them till I have hived them than I have in the birds which make their nests thereon, and, therefore, if another hives them he shall be their proprietor; but a swarm which flies from out of my hive is mine so long as I can keep it in sight and have power to pursue it; and in these circumstances no one is entitled to take them. But in respect to such animals as are in the habit of going and returning, as pigeons and bees, which are accustomed to go into the woods and fields, and come again, we have this traditional rule that, if they cease to have the intention of returning, they also cease to be ours, and become the property of the first taker, because they cease to be what are termed *animus revertendi* when they have discontinued their habits of returning."

QUALIFEID PROPERTY RIGHTS.

In case a swarm fly from the owner's hive, his qualified right continues only so long as he can keep them in sight and possesses the power to pursue them where he has a right to pursue, or otherwise positively and distinctly identify them. The difficulties in reclaiming bees after taking flight are many. The decisions of our courts furnish numerous peculiar circumstances, and unfold the difficulties in reclaiming bees that have escaped from the hives or soil of their original owner. In the case of Goff vs. Kiltz, 15 Wend, N. Y. 550, the New York Supreme Court held that, where a swarm of bees left the hive of the plaintiff, and went into a tree on the land of another, as he followed the bees and marked the tree into which they went, while he had no right to enter upon the property to recover them without the consent of the owner, yet he could maintain an action of trespass and damage against a third party who did enter the land, cut the tree down, kill the bees, and take the honey away.

REPLEVIN.

Bees may be recovered by the issuance of a writ of replevin.

TROVER.

If the claimant simply requires damages for the loss of the bees, trover is the remedy.

ANIMUS REVERTENDI.

This, Blackstone says, "extends this possession further than mere manual occupation; for my tame hawk that is pursuing his quarry in my presence, though he is at liberty to go where he pleases, is nevertheless my property, for he hath *animus revertendi*. So are my pigeons and bees that are flying at a distance from their home, and likewise the deer that is chased out of my park or forest, all which remain still in my possession, and I still preserve my qualified property in them. But if they stray without my knowledge and do not return in the usual manner, it is then lawful for any stranger to take them."

IDENTITY.

It is practically impossible to prove the identity of a swarm of bees in a court of law, even if they possess peculiar characteristics.

TRANSPORTATION.

Though it may be optional with railway companies whether they will accept the full responsibility of transporting bees, yet if they do so without any express restriction they are liable as common carriers. For a given reward they proffer to become his carrier; for a less reward they proffer to furnish the necessary means that the owner of the bees may be his own carrier; and if the owner and shipper agrees to this arrangement the railway is not liable.

LARCENY.

Bees may be the subject of larceny if they are in some person's possession. Much depends on what constitutes possession; but it is generally assumed the owner of the land is also the owner of the bees (in hives) situated thereon. Bees are likened unto wild animals, belonging to no one so long as they are in their wild state, and property in them is acquired by occupancy, hiving and reclaiming only, and are not the subject of larceny unless they are in the owner's custody, as in a hive or bee-house, or otherwise confined and within control of the possessor or owner.

FINDING BEE-TREES.

The Supreme Court of New York in the case of Goodwin vs. Merrill said: "A man's finding bees in a tree standing on another man's land gives him no right, either to the tree or bees; and a swarm of bees going from a hive, if they can be followed and known, are not lost to the owner, but may be reclaimed."

RECLAIMED BEES.

If bees temporarily escape from the hive of their owner, who keeps them in sight and marks the tree into which they enter, and is otherwise able to identify them, they belong to him and not to the owner of the soil. In such a case the property draws after it possession sufficient to enable the owner of the bees to maintain trespass and recover damages against a third person who fells the tree, destroys the bees, and takes the honey, notwithstanding the owner of bees himself is liable to trespass for entering on the land of another for similar purpose without authority.

LICENSE.

Where one discovers bees in a tree, obtains a license from the owner of the soil to take them, and thereupon marks the tree with his own initials, he gains no property till he takes possession of the bees, that is to say, he must take them out of the tree.

WHEN BEES ARE OR ARE NOT A NUISANCE.

Strictly speaking, a trade or occupation, a business or industry lawful in itself, and which becomes a nuisance because of its location, or the manner in which it is conducted, or the character of the animals or thing is not a nuisance *per se*, though it may be a *prima-facie* nuisance.

Whether bees are a nuisance or not depends on the evidence submitted to the court, and in a broad way it may be stated that bees are a nuisance when the plaintiff can claim damages for injury either for himself or his business.

WHERE BEES MAY BE KEPT.

This has been very clearly decided by the courts. In case of Olmsted vs. Rich, before the Supreme Court of New York, the evidence showed that the plaintiff and defendant were neighbors, the latter keeping a large number of hives of bees in a lot immediately adjoining the plaintiff's dwelling, and at certain seasons they were a source of great annoyance to him and his family, and also that they could be removed without material difficulty to a place on the defendant's premises where they would not disturb the neighbors. The action was in the nature of an injunction to prevent defendants from maintaining their apiary at the place above named. The court held that the case was a proper one for a permanent injunction. In such action the issue was not as to defendant's motive in keeping bees, nor whether he had any knowledge of any vicious propensities of the bees, but simply whether the condition of things as then and previously existing constituted a nuisance. The court held affirmatively, and the bees were ordered removed in order to abate the nuisance.

WHEN NOT A NUISANCE.

The most celebrated case of this kind on record is that of Clark vs. City of Arkadelphia, Arkansas (52 Ark. 23). The evidence in this case showed that Clark, who had kept bees in that city for a number of years, was not in political harmony with those in power, and the latter sought to punish him and get rid of his presence by prohibiting the keeping of bees within the corporate limits of the city. Clark was ordered to move his bees, but refused to do so, and his arrest and conviction by the city court under the ordinance followed. He appealed to the Circuit Court, the latter dismissing the prosecution, and the State appealed to the Supreme Court wherein it is held that, "Although bees may become a nuisance in a city, an ordinance which makes the owning, keeping, or raising of them within the city limits a nuisance, whether it is in fact so or not, is too broad and is not valid."

BEES MAY BE KEPT IN CITIES.

In April, 1901, the council of the city of Rochester, N. Y., passed an ordinance prohibiting the keeping of bees within the city limits. W. R. Taunton, who refused to remove his apiary, was arrested and brought before a police court. The judge set aside the ordinance and the defendant was discharged. The latter was defended by the counsel of the National Bee-keepers' Association.

In the Butchers' Union Co. vs. Crescent City Co. (111 U. S. 746), Justice Fields says: "The common businesses and callings of life, the ordinary trades and pursuits, which are innocent in themselves, and have been followed in all communities from time immemorial, must, therefore, be free in this country to all alike on equal terms. The right to pursue them without let or hindrance, except that which is applied to all persons of the same age, sex, and condition, is a distinguishing privilege which they claim as their birthright." In the same case Judge Bradley says: "I hold that the liberty of pursuit, the right to follow any of the ordinary callings of life, is one of the privileges of a citizen of the United States, of which he can not be deprived without invading his right to liberty within the meaning of the constitution."

It may be well to state in this connection that the National Bee-keepers' Association frequently undertakes to defend its members in a court of law where the circumstances warrant the assistance of this influential body.

FOUL-BROOD LAWS.

BEE-DISEASE LAWS; THEIR ENFORCEMENT.

In controlling bee diseases in a community, past experience has shown that it is necessary that every bee-keeper do his part; otherwise the work done by individuals is largely nullified by the carelessness or neglect of a few. Where all the bee-keepers are progressive, a simple plan of co-operation would be enough; but, unfortunately, there are in almost all communities some bee-keepers who are either ignorant, careless, or willfully negligent. If, therefore, they will not voluntarily care for their bees as they should, there must be some legal means of compelling them to abate a public nuisance when disease appears among their colonies. Without such a law for regions where disease exists, progressive bee-keeping is difficult and nearly impossible.

Laws providing for inspection of apiaries with the object of controlling disease are, therefore, drafted primarily for the bee-keeper who does not voluntarily treat diseased colonies. The progressive bee-keeper needs no such law to compel him to do his duty. The inspector of apiaries, however, in actual practice, is much more than a police officer; in fact, his police duties are but a small part of his work. However the law may be worded, the good which an inspector does is due in the greater part to his work as an educator. It is the duty of the inspector, specified in the law in most cases, to instruct the bee-keepers how to know dis-

ease and how and when to treat. The great good which has been done by the various inspectors in the past has been due almost entirely to this phase of their work.

It is, however, most unwise to set the inspector to work merely as an educational officer without any power to enforce his orders. This has been tried, and appears to be a failure. There are, unfortunately, in almost all communities, bee-keepers who, from obstinancy or spite, must be driven to their duty. Most men, however, when once they learn that they must treat disease will accept the teachings of the inspector.

The following States and Territories now have laws of some kind providing for inspection: California, Colorado, Connecticut, Hawaii, Idaho, Illinois, Indiana, Iowa, Kansas, Michigan, Minnesota, Missouri, Nebraska, Nevada, New Mexico, New York, Ohio, Oregon, South Dakota, Texas, Utah, Washington, Wisconsin. Somewhat similar laws exist in New Zealand, some states in Australia, Ontario, Ireland, and parts of Europe. The bee-keepers in several other States are now agitating the passage of similar laws.

These laws may be divided into two groups —those in which the work is done by men employed by the State, and those in which, by a State, Territory, or county law, the county authorities may appoint inspectors for the county only. Of these the work by State officers has proven much more effective. In States where the counties are small, as in the East, county inspection is of practically no value (e. g., Ohio). In States where the counties are small it is practically impossible to get competent inspectors in every county; and, furthermore, there is not enough work or enough money available to induce a good man to take the work, unless he is doing it merely for the good of the industry. In the West, where some counties are as large as some of the Eastern States, there is more reason for county inspection; but even in these cases the results are, as a rule, not equal to those obtained in States having State inspection.

The chief weakness in county inspection is the lack of co-operation among the inspectors in neighboring counties. There is in most cases not only a lack of co-operation, but too often a jealousy between them which results in a loss of co-ordination in the work. This might be remedied by the appointment of a competent State inspector to whom the county inspectors would be responsible; but county officials would probably object to the appointment of officers over whom they had nว direct jurisdiction. A much better plan would be the appointment of enough State inspectors to do the work (e. g., New York), removing all appointments by county officials from consideration.

A special tax on colonies to bear the expense of inspection is sometimes made. When this tax applies to every bee-keeper in the State, no objection can be found to it. The plan of requiring each bee-keeper to pay for the work of the inspector in the actual inspection of his own apiary is most unjust, however (e. g., Nebraska). Inspection is instituted for the benefit of all bee-keepers in the State, and they should pay for it. To compel the bee-keeper who is unfortunate enough to have disease among his bees to pay for work, the object of which is to protect other bee-keepers in the community and State, is unwise, unjust, and shows lack of foresight on the part of the framers of the bill.

In nearly all the laws now in force, there is a provision that the bee-keeper shall not sell, give away, or barter honey from diseased colonies. This is a just provision, but seems to be rarely enforced. Inspectors too often hesitate about enforcing it, either from pity for their brother bee-keepers or from fear of pressure being brought to bear which will cause their dismissal, or perhaps bring about a repeal of the law. The result is that both diseases are being spread to new localities, and other bee-keepers suffer because of this neglect of duty. A bee-keeper has no legal or moral right to endanger the property of others by shipping contaminated honey, yet it is being done every year. An inspector who allows this is not only remiss in his duty but becomes party to the crime. Because of this neglect to enforce the provision under discussion, the bee-disease situation in the United States is becoming worse instead of better; and the good done by the inspectors by education seems to be more than nullified by the harm done by this neglect.

Inspectors and bee-keepers are more careful about shipping diseased colonies to new localities. This is probably because they can see the harm which will result from this procedure more clearly than in the case of shipping honey from diseased colonies. The danger in such cases, while great, is probably much less as a whole than that resulting from the shipping of contaminated honey.

As was pointed out in the discussion of county inspection, the lack of co-operation between the various inspectors is a weak point in our present method of control. While an inspector may now in most cases prohibit the shipping of diseased colonies and contaminated honey to another State, he rarely does so, nor do State inspectors usually report such shipments to each other. If there had been some provision prohibiting interstate shipments of contaminated material, it is probable that we should not now have European foul brood in twenty States, and American foul brood in practically every State in the Union in which progressive bee-keeping is found. If there is no more rigid inspection, our future work on disease control can consist only of the educational work of the inspector. Quarantine regulations will, of course, be valueless when disease is present practically everywhere.

A form of law which, if rigidly enforced, would seem to be the most desirable is given. This must be changed to cover local conditions.

AN ACT FOR THE SUPPRESSION OF CONTAGIOUS DISEASES AMONG BEES IN —— BY CREATING THE OFFICE OF INSPECTOR OF APIARIES, TO DEFINE THE DUTIES THEREOF, AND TO APPROPRIATE MONEY THEREFOR.

Be it enacted, etc.

SECTION I. In addition to the duties heretofore assigned to him, the State Entomologist (or officer in charge of entomological inspection) is hereby appointed State Inspector of Apiaries, and he is empowered to appoint one or more assistants as needed, who shall carry on the inspection under his supervision.

SEC. 2. The inspector or his assistant shall, when notified in writing by the owner of an apiary, or by any three disinterested tax-payers, examine all reported apiaries, and all others in the same locality not reported, and ascertain whether or not the diseases known as American foul brood or European foul brood, or any other disease which is infectious or contagious in its nature, and injurious to honey-bees in their egg, larval, pupal, or adult stages, exists in such apiaries; and if satisfied of the existence of any such diseases he shall give the owners or care takers of the diseased apiaries full instructions how to treat such cases as, in the inspector's judgment, seems best.

SEC. 3. The inspector or his assistant shall visit all diseased apiaries a second time, after ten days, and, if need be, burn all colonies of bees that he may find not cured of such disease, and all honey and appliances which would spread disease, without recompense to the owner, lessee, or agent thereof.

SEC. 4. If the owner of an apiary, honey, or appliances, wherein disease exists, shall sell, barter, or give away, or move without the consent of the inspector, any diseased bees (be they queens or workers), colonies, honey, or appliances, or expose other bees to the danger of such disease, or fail to notify the inspector of the existence of such disease, said owner shall, on conviction before a justice of the peace, be liable to a fine of not less than fifty dollars nor more than one hundred dollars, or not less than one month's imprisonment in the county jail, nor more than two months' imprisonment.

Sec. 5. For the enforcement of he provisions of this act the State Inspector of Apiaries or his duly authorized assistants shall have access, ingress, and egress to all apiaries or places where bees are kept; and any person or persons who shall resist, impede, or hinder in any way the inspector of apiaries in the discharge of his duties under the provisions of this act shall, on conviction before a justice of the peace, be liable to a fine of not less than fifty dollars nor more than one hundred dollars, or not less than one month's imprisonment in the county jail, nor more than two months' imprisonment.

Sec. 6. After inspecting infected hives or fixtures or handling diseased bees, the inspector or his assistant shall, before leaving the premises or proceeding to any other apiary, thoroughly disinfect any portion of his own person and clothing and any tools or appliances used by him which have come in contact with infected material, and shall see that any assistant or assistants with him have likewise thoroughly disinfected their persons and clothing and any tools and implements used by them.

Sec. 7. It shall be the duty of any person in the State of ——— engaged in the rearing of queen-bees for sale to use honey in the making of candy for use in mailing-cages which has been boiled for at least thirty minutes. Any such person engaged in the rearing of queen-bees shall have his queen-rearing apiary or apiaries inspected at least twice during each summer season; and on the discovery of the existence of any disease which is infectious or contagious in its nature, and injurious to bees in their egg, larval, pupal, or adult stages, said person shall at once cease to ship queen-bees from such diseased apiary until the inspector of apiaries shall declare the said apiary free from all disease. On complaint of the inspector of apiaries, or of any five bee-keepers in the State, that said bee-keeper engaged in the rearing of queens is violating the provisions of this section, he shall, on conviction before a justice of the peace, be liable to a fine of not less than one hundred dollars nor more than two hundred dollars.

Sec. 8. The inspector of apiaries shall make annual reports to the ———, giving the number of apiaries visited, also the number of diseased apiaries found, the number of colonies treated, also the number of colonies destroyed, and the expenses incurred in the performance of his duty. He shall also keep a careful record of the localities where disease exists; but this record shall not be public, but can be consulted with the consent of the inspector of apiaries.

Sec. 9. There is hereby appropriated out of any moneys in the State treasury, not otherwise appropriated, a sum not exceeding ——— per year, for the suppression of contagious bee diseases among bees in ———. The salary of the deputy inspectors shall be determined by the State Inspector of Apiaries.

Sec. 10. All acts and parts of acts inconsistent herewith are hereby repealed.

Sec. 11. This act shall take effect immediately.

LAYING WORKERS. These queer inmates, or, rather, occasional inmates, of the hive are worker-bees that lay eggs. Aye, and the eggs they lay hatch too; but they hatch only drones, and never worker-bees. The drones are rather smaller than the drones produced by a queen, but they are nevertheless drones, in every respect, so far as we can discover. It may be well to remark, that ordinary worker-bees are not neuters, as they are sometimes called: they are considered undeveloped females. Microscopic examination shows an undeveloped form of the special organs found in the queen, and these organs may become, at any time, sufficiently developed to allow the bee to lay eggs, but never to allow of fertilization by meeting the drone as the queen does. See QUEENS.

CAUSE OF LAYING WORKERS.

It has been over and over again suggested, that bees capable of this egg-laying duty are those reared in the vicinity of queen-cells, and that by some means they have received a small portion of the royal jelly necessary to their development as bee-mothers. This theory has, we believe, been entirely disproven by many experiments; and it is now pretty generally conceded that laying workers may make their appearance in any colony or nucleus that has been many days queenless, and without the means of rearing a queen. Not only may one bee take upon herself these duties, but there may be many of them; and wherever the bee-keeper has been so careless as to leave his bees destitute of either brood or queen for ten days or two weeks, he is liable to find evidences of their presence, in the shape of eggs scattered about promiscuously; sometimes one, but oftener half a dozen in a single cell. If the matter has been going on for some time, he will see now and then a drone larva, and sometimes two or three crowding each other in their single cell; sometimes they start queen-cells over this drone larva: the poor motherless orphans, seeming to feel that something is wrong, are disposed, like a drowning man, to catch at any straw.

HOW TO GET RID OF LAYING WORKERS.

Prevention is better than cure. If a colony, from any cause, becomes queenless, be sure it has unsealed brood of the proper age to raise a queen; and when this one is raised, be sure that she becomes fertile. It can never do any harm to give a queenless colony eggs and brood, and it may be the saving of it. But suppose you have been so careless as to allow a colony to become queenless, and get weak, what are you to do? If you attempt to give them a queen, and fertile workers are present, they will be pretty sure to get stung; it is sometimes difficult to get them to accept even a queen-cell. The poor bees get into a habit of accepting one of the egg-laying workers as a queen, and they will have none other until she is removed; yet you can not find her, for she is just like any other bee; you may get hold of her, possibly, by carefully noticing the way in which the other bees deport themselves toward her, or you may catch her in the act of egg-laying; but even this often fails, for there may be several such in the hive at once. You may give them a small strip of comb containing eggs and brood, but they will seldom start a good queen-cell, if they start any at all; for, in the majority of cases, a colony having laying workers seems perfectly demoralized, so far as getting them into regular work is concerned.

It is almost impossible to introduce a laying queen to such colonies; for as soon as she is released from the cage she will be stung to death. No better results would follow from introducing a young virgin; but the giving of a queen-cell, if the colony has not been too long harboring laying workers, will very often bring about a change for the better. In such case the cell will be accepted, and in due course of time there will be a laying queen in place of the laying worker or workers: but often cells will be destroyed as fast as they are given. The only thing then to be done is to scatter brood and bees among several other colonies, perhaps one or two frames in each. From each of these same colonies take a frame or two of brood with adhering bees, and put them into the laying-worker hive. The bees of this hive, which have been scattered into several hives, will for the most part return; but the laying worker or workers will remain and in all probability be destroyed in the other hives. Of course, the colonies that have been robbed of good brood will suffer somewhat; but if it is after the honey season, no great harm will have been done. They will proceed to clean up the combs; and if they do not need the drones as they hatch out they will destroy them.

Sometimes a laying worker may be disposed of by moving the combs into an empty hive, placed at a little distance from the other; the bees will nearly all go into their old hive, but the queen, as she thinks herself to be, will remain on the combs. The returning bees will then accept a queen or queen-cell. After all is right the combs may be returned, and the laying workers will be—well, we do not know just what does become of them, but we suspect they either attend to their legitimate business or get killed.

See that every hive contains, at all times, during the spring and summer months at least, brood suitable for rearing a queen, and you will never see laying workers.

HOW TO DETECT THE PRESENCE OF LAYING WORKERS.

If you do not find any queen, and see eggs scattered around promiscuously, some in drone and some in worker cells, some attached to the side of the cell, instead of the center of the bottom, where the queen lays them, several in one cell and none in the next, you may be pretty sure you have a laying worker. Still later, you will see the worker-brood capped with the high convex cappings, indicating clearly that the brood will never hatch out worker-bees. Finding two or more eggs in a cell is never conclusive, for the queen often so deposits them in a feeble colony where there are not bees enough to cover the brood. The eggs deposited by a fertile queen are in regular order, as one would plant a field of corn; but those from laying workers, and usually from drone-laying queens, are irregularly scattered about.

LAUREL. See POISONOUS HONEY.

LINDEN. See BASSWOOD.

LOCALITY. This has a great influence in bee-keeping. Many of the manipulations recommended in one locality will not answer for another. A hive well adapted to one place might give indifferent results in another having different conditions. The length of the honey-flow, the time it comes on, whether the nectar comes in a rush for three or four weeks at a time as it does in the East, or whether the flow extends over a period of three or four months, coming in very slowly, are all conditions the bee-keeper must study and be able to meet as they are. A slow honey-flow, continuing over a period of four or five months, may require an altogether different hive. It may render the production of comb honey impracticable, for the reason the combs will be travel-stained, and therefore not fit to compete with honey from other localities. On the other hand, a short rapid honey-flow, as in the basswood regions, and where the honey is mainly white, and of good flavor, makes the production of comb honey more profitable than extracted as a rule. Then locality, too, has a bearing on the kind of treatment the bees should receive. If there is no honey after the first or middle of July, and the bee-keeper is located in a region where snow falls in winter, and where cold winter weather prevails for five or six months, he will have to make some plans to keep down brood-rearing after the honey-flow, and arrange to get the bees in the best possible condition for cold weather. He will probably have to feed, and then in the spring he will be compelled to stimulate brood-rearing to a high pitch as soon as the bees can fly, thus getting the colonies strong at the beginning of the honey-flow. If, however, one is located in the South he must see that his bees have a large amount of stores; for in a warm climate they will consume more than in the North, where it is cold. While the bee-keeper of the colder regions tries to prevent his bees from dying during the winter, he who is located in the South endeavors to prevent his bees from starving until the next honey-flow.

THE BEST STATES FOR KEEPING BEES.

We are very often asked the question as to the best location in the United States for keeping bees as a business. We usually advise the inquirer to stay right where he is. While bee-keeping in good seasons may be very profitable in California, yet experience has shown that the honey-producers of the Golden State have only one good year in from three to five. Taking every thing into consideration they do not average any better than their brethren of the East where the market is certainly better. Colorado, Arizona, New Mexico, Utah, Idaho, *in the irrigated portions*, sometimes show wonderful results in honey; but in all the States named, where the bee-range is at all good, the country is overstocked with bees and bee-keepers, and one can scarcely get into one of the places without buying out somebody already in the field.

Texas as an all-around bee proposition is one of the best bee States in the Union. It is not over-populated yet, and there are very many desirable bee-ranges within its borders. The same may be said of Idaho and Utah. Kansas and Nebraska are good bee States, having usually good fall flows; but sometimes either or both have fearful drouths that kill down nearly all vegetation, rendering farming as well as bee-keeping, for that season, almost a failure. Among the eastern States, New York is one of the best because it has, in addition to clover and basswood, immense acreages of buckwheat, which on those hills yields immense quantities of honey. Wisconsin and Minnesota were formerly good localities for basswood; but that desirable tree for timber as well as honey is now being rapidly cut off, and the main stay will be,

as with the other States, white clover, with a large sprinkling of sweet clover along the roadsides and railways. Most of the north-central States have conditions that are practically the same, reaching away from Minnesota to Maine, and continuing down the Ohio River and Chesapeake Bay. While the amount of honey secured in these localities is less per colony, the price it brings is higher, because in this portion of the United States the centers of population are located. Throughout the South, east of the Mississippi, the honey secured is very good, mostly extracted, and the flow covers a long period; but the quality is not quite equal to the honey of the North.

LOCUST, HONEY (*Gleditschia Triacanthos*) is one of the best honey-yielding trees in the United States, but, unfortunately, it is nowhere abundant. It is not so valuable as the black locust for timber, and is seldom planted for that purpose except for posts. It is frequently planted as an avenue tree, and in Europe it is very popular for that purpose — much more so than it is with us. It is also planted sometimes for a hedge, and does well as a high windbreak.

It blooms when quite young, and the odor of the blossoms suggests honey, of which the bees must extract a goodly amount, as it comes between fruit-bloom and clover, just when the weather is likely to be favorable. It has been suggested that, when grown in large masses for fence-posts, and where climate and soil are suitable, it might be possible to make its culture pay. It is frequently planted in pleasure-grounds and parks, and in such position renders good service to the bee-keeper. Probably the honey locust will be more extensively planted in the future than it has been in the past.

LOGWOOD (*Hæmatoxylon Campechianum*) is the English name of a tree extensively used by dyers. The French term it campeche, from the country of its nativity; and the Spanish, "palo pinto," the paint or dye-wood tree. The wood obtained from it is very valuable, hence it has been naturalized throughout the West Indies, notably in Jamaica and Haiti, where it has become quite common. It grows well in Antigua and St. Lucia islands. It has been naturalized in British, French, and Dutch Guiana, and in Trinidad. Where tried, it grows well in Florida. It is closely allied to the catclaw and guajilla of Southwest Texas. Considering both the quantity and quality of the honey produced by it, no plant can be said to excel it. The honey obtained from logwood, in point of color, body, and flavor, is equal to the finest table honey in the world; indeed, it is almost water-white, and the bouquet is of the best. It blooms after a season of rains, hence it may give four crops in a year, and frequently gives three where the climate admits of it. When the conditions are favorable it yields enormously. It is a common tree over the whole peninsula of Yucatan, including British Honduras; and were the people of that country to engage extensively in apiculture, logwood honey would cut quite a figure in the European and American markets. When in a pure state, unmixed with other flavors, the price obtained for it is so high that the tariff duty does not interfere with its sale in New York. However, much of it is mixed with honey from other sources, or perhaps is not properly handled, hence it does not cut much of a figure in the honey markets of the world at present. Probably the bulk of it goes to Hamburg, Germany, and Antwerp, while Jamaica ships her output mostly to London. The principal exporting countries of logwood honey are San Domingo, Haiti, Honduras, and Jamaica.

LUCERNE. See ALFALFA.

M.

MANIPULATING FRAMES. See FRAMES, HOW TO MANIPULATE; also REVERSING.

MANGROVE (*Avicennia Nitida*). On the list of honey-producing plants and trees of Southern Florida the black mangrove stands at the head. Whether or not this is a true mangrove seems an open question among good authorities. The tree has the appearance and characteristics of lignum vitæ, and is said to be of that family. It is an evergreen, designed by nature to follow the red mangrove (not a honey-producer) in the building up of land along tropical and semi-tropical tide waters. For this purpose it is provided with a great number of slender spicules that grow straight up from all parts of the root system to the height of a foot or more above ground, that catch and hold debris and mud washed there at high tide.

The tree, which often resembles that of the apple in form, varies in size from a mere bush at its northern limit, just above the 29th parallel, to a monarch five to seven feet in diameter of trunk on the banks of the lower Indian River and along the coasts of all tropic seas. The bark is of a dark color, the leaves thick, of a dark glossy green above, lighter beneath, and oval in outline, with smooth edges that turn slightly toward the under side. The blossoms are small white four-petaled flowers growing in clusters of from 10 to 30 at the extremity of three inch-long flower-stems that terminate the extremity of each twig. These flowers, in bloom from about June 15 to August 1, where growth is fairly plentiful, often show large drops of nectar all day long within easy range of large apiaries. In fact, it seems almost impossible to overstock a good range of this tree at that time, and the crop rarely fails, yet some failures have been experienced, which appears the more remarkable when it is known that the roots of this tree are mostly under water twice a day, at high tide—a fact which would seem to preclude the possibility of its suffering from drouth.

In 1895 and 1899 the mangrove met with serious disaster from cold through fifty miles south from its northern limit, where it seems more prolific and constant in its secretion of nectar than further south; but it rapidly recovered, and soon gave full crops as of old. In 1894, the season before the big freeze, 20½ tons of extracted honey was secured in one apiary of 116 colonies, at least 15 tons of it being from the black mangrove. Of 200 tons taken within a range of 15 miles of the same yard, at least 130 tons was from this source, gathered from a narrow strip along the coast rivers.

Pure mangrove honey is white, clearer than that from white clover, and of a light pleasant flavor without any "minty twang." It is not of as heavy body, however, and inclined to ferment if not thoroughly cured and then carefully sealed from moisture.

In the form of comb honey it is as handsome as the world produces, but must be kept in a dry warm room to prevent sweating and blistering when cool weather comes.

Its quality has been very highly extolled by Messrs. Langstroth, Hasty, Ch. F. Muth, and others, who have classed it as one of the three table honeys of America.

MARIGOLD (*Gailardia pulchella*). This is found all over the United States, but, so far as we know, it does not yield any great amount of honey except in Texas, where it is considered one of the main honey-producing plants. It begins to yield in May or June, giving a rich golden honey. While it is praised greatly by many connoisseurs in the South, it would not rank well with clover and basswood of the North. The comb honey is golden yellow, not white.

MESQUITE (*Prosopis glandulosa* and *Juliflora*). A leguminous tree common in Southern Texas, New Mexico, and Arizona, and important in old Mexico, more particularly in Sonora, where it grows to the dignity of a fine timber tree in the valley of the Yaqui River. Growing in a semi-arid country it is always possible to get a yield of honey from the mesquite except where it grows so far north that the cold injures it. In Uvalde Co., Texas, it is looked on by the bee-keepers as a great tree for honey. There, it is little more than a shrub; but further south in Mexico, around Monterey, it becomes of far more economic importance. The Texans class the mesquite honey high; but we should be inclined to rate it second-class among the ambers. There are several species of mesquite, but the foregoing is the

MARIGOLD, GREAT HONEY-PLANTS OF TEXAS; BUT FOUND ALL OVER THE UNITED STATES.

MESQUITE LEAF.

one usually referred to by bee-keepers. The others are probably equally good for honey.

MIGRATORY BEE-KEEPING. Experience has shown that the secretion of nectar in a given locality varies sometimes, even within a distance of only a few miles. For example, it will happen that the home-yard bees will be gathering no honey when an outyard eight or ten miles away will be securing a fairly good crop. This is due to the fact that the character of and moisture in the soil, makes possible the growth of some plants that will not take root in other locations only a few miles away. For example, a

bee-yard may be situated in a valley close to a stream, along which there will be a heavy growth of honey-yielding plants. Within a few miles from there, perhaps on higher ground, and soil less productive, there will be nothing.

Sometimes we find conditions like this—in one locality a large amount of buckwheat will be grown; ten miles away from there, there will be none whatever. The same is true of red clover, alsike, and a number of other artificial-pasturage crops.

Again, it will happen that in one year when there is an excess of rainfall the location in the valley will be too wet for the proper growth of plants yielding nectar, while on the higher ground, a few miles away, conditions will be just right for a fine flow of honey.

The knowledge of these varying conditions in localities only a few miles apart has led some bee-keepers to practice what is known as migratory bee-keeping. For example, in one yard it is evident that bees are not getting any honey, and there is no flora of any sort that gives any promise of any. On the other hand, there is another yard that is doing well, and there are still other locations without bees where there are immense quantities of alsike or red clover, or of buckwheat. Evidently it is a part of wisdom and business sense to move the yard that is yielding no returns to the location in which the honey can be secured.

While migratory bee-keeping is not practiced to any considerable extent in this country, largely because of the expense of moving, yet there are some sections in the country that make the practice exceedingly profitable. In Germany migratory bee-keeping is carried on somewhat more extensively than in this country, and occasionally we hear reports of a whole bee-yard being put on an immense raft on a river. This raft is secured near the shore, and when the honey crop is taken the raft is let loose, when the raft, bees and all, are towed to pastures new. These floating apiaries have never been much of a success. Too many bees appear to drop in the water and drown. Mr. C. O. Perrine, many years ago, tried out this experiment on the Mississippi River, but the experiment was a financial failure.

MILKWEED (*Asclepias Cornuti*). This plant is celebrated, not for the honey it produces, although it doubtless furnishes a

POLLEN OF THE MILKWEED, ATTACHED TO A BEE'S FOOT.

good supply, but for its queer winged masses of pollen which attach themselves to the bee's feet, and cause it to become a cripple, if not to lose its life. Every fall we have many inquiries from new subscribers

in regard to this queer phenomenon. Some think it a parasite, others a protuberance growing on the bee's foot, and others a winged insect-enemy of the bee. We give here an engraving of the curiosity, magnified at *a*, and also of a mass of them attached to the foot of a bee.

It is the same that Prof. Riley alluded to when he recommended that the milkweed be planted to kill off bees when they become troublesome to the fruit-grower. The folly of such advice—think of the labor and expense of starting a plantation of useless weeds just to entrap honey-bees—becomes more apparent when we learn that it is perhaps only the old and enfeebled bees that are unable to free themselves from these appendages, and hence the milkweed can scarcely be called an enemy. The appendages, it will be observed, look like a pair of wings, and they attach themselves to the bee by a glutinous matter which quickly hardens, so that it is quite difficult to remove if not done when first attached.

MOTH-WORMS. See BEE-MOTH.

MOVING BEES. Young bees, when they first start out, or old ones on the first flight of the season after a winter's confinement, hover in the air, about the hive-entrance, take a careful survey of surroundings, making wider and wider circles, each time taking in new objects by which they may familiarize themselves with the home. When the location is once carefully marked they will go back and forth without taking any note of distinguishing objects. But when the hive is moved only a few feet there is apparent consternation and confusion.

One can not, therefore, move his bees a few feet or a quarter of a mile without having the great majority of them go back to the old spot unless treated by the plans we shall describe. They would perish, or possibly get into some other hive near their old location, with the result that there would be a fight, and many bees killed.

If one desires to move his bees, and wishes to take them at least a mile and a half or two miles away, the problem is quite easy; for then they will stay wherever they are placed. As soon as they are liberated in their new position they will mark the location as thoroughly and carefully as when taking their first flight. After that they will go to and from the same spot as if it had always been their home.

But to move our bees from the front to the back yard, or, we will say, from a fourth to half a mile, is not so easy. They are familiar with the whole range of flight within a mile of the old stand; and when they go over their old hunting-ground, so to speak, instead of returning to the hive from which they have just come they will return to the old location. How, then, shall we make them stay where placed? One way, and the very best one, is to wait till fall or winter. After they have quit flying for the season, move them to the spot desired. If they are confined for several weeks by cold weather, or longer, they will mark their new location and go back to it as their regular and permanent home. It will be better still if they can be confined for several months in the cellar; then when they are put out again in the spring, place them in the new location; for it is well known that cellared bees can be placed anywhere the following spring without reference to their old stands. Wherever they are placed they will mark their location, and that must be their fixed position for the season.

But suppose it is the midst of summer, and for some reason the bees must be moved a few rods from their old location. Perhaps complaint is made that the bees in the front yard are interfering with passersby, and to avoid trouble it seems desirable to move them to the back yard. In an emergency of this kind the following plan may be used:

Tack wire cloth over the entrances, carry the hives down cellar, and keep them there for at least five days, and longer if they appear to be quiet. While the bees are in the cellar, change the surroundings in the front yard or in the old location as much as possible. After the bees have served out their allotted time of confinement, put them in the back yard in the same order as before if it can be done conveniently. While some of the bees may, perhaps, go back, the great majority will stay in their new location. Those that do return should be given a frame of brood in a hive ; and when they have clustered on it take them to the new location and dump in front of the entrance to the hive. If the bees are confined during cool or rainy weather, when they can not fly, there will be no loss of honey that might possibly be gathered from the field; but while the bees are confined in the cellar, keep a watch on them to see that they do not suffocate; and, if practicable, cover the whole top of the hive with wire screen.

In cool weather it is not necessary to put the bees in the cellar; but after the wire cloth is tacked on at the entrance the hive

may be moved immediately to its new location. The bees should be kept confined at least five days, or as long as they are apparently quiet. If they crowd around the entrance so as to cause suffocation they should be released at once. But do not think of confining a strong colony in warm weather without putting it in the cellar where it is cool, and giving it plenty of ventilation.

Ordinarily, weak nuclei can be readily moved from one location to another without danger of suffocation. As explained under the head of NUCLEI, further on, we always make it a practice to confine the bees for at least three days. At the end of that time they are usually content to stay in their new location without returning to the old spot. This plan is not to be used if it be at all practicable to leave the bees till fall or winter.

There is still another method; and wherever it is practicable to carry it out we would recommend it in preference to carrying them into the cellar; that is, move the bees to a point a mile and a half or two miles from the old location. Let them stay there two or three weeks, then move them back. But this involves considerable labor, so that the average person would not think it practicable.

There is danger that bees confined in the cellar, and then released, may go back to the old location. This is especially true of black bees; and it becomes, therefore, advisable to do all short-distance moving in the winter. As a general thing we would advise against moving full colonies short distances in mid-summer; but in case of necessity or emergency they may be confined in the cellar as explained.

HOW TO MOVE BEES A DISTANCE OF SEVERAL MILES.

The remarks that have been made heretofore apply to moving bees only a short distance; but when they are to be carried a considerable distance, and jolted over rough roads, the bees require more ventilation than can usually be afforded by an ordinary entrance. If they are shut up during the middle of the day, those in the field are liable to be lost. Ordinarily they should be confined at night or in the early morning — better at night.

If you wish to move bees during the day time, while many are in the fields, you can get them nearly all in by smoking them at intervals for about half an hour. This will give those that are out time to come in, and the smoking will prevent any more goin

THE ROOT CO.'S MEN READY TO MOVE BEES TO ONE OF THE OUTYARDS.

out. If the colony is very strong, leave a hive with a comb of brood on the old stand, and the owner can start a nucleus very conveniently with the returning bees.

Most bee keepers fasten the bottoms to their hives permanently, so all that is necessary in such cases is to secure the cover and put a wire-cloth screen over the entrance. A very good plan is shown in the next engraving, consisting of two cords or ropes.

One rope is drawn around as tight as possible at one end, and the other is put on the other end. The cords are then drawn together at the top in such a way as to produce a strong tension.

FASTENING BOTTOM-BOARD AND COVER.

Another plan, somewhat similar, is to use one cord or rope. It is drawn around the hive, and tied loosely. A stick is then slipped into the cord and given a half-twist in such a way as to draw the loop up very tight.

But by far the most satisfactory plan, certainly the safest, and the one that we adopt

in our own moving, is that of using a special staple (obtained at the hive-factories) shown in the accompanying illustrations. One leg of the staple is driven into the bottom-board, and the other into the hive-body. One staple on each side and one at

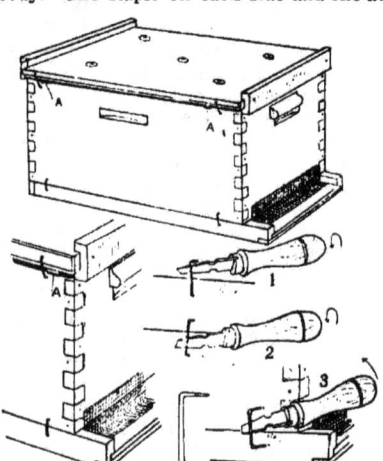

the rear will be sufficient to hold the bottom-board. For the cover there should be four staples—two on each side.* The staples are very easily removed with a screwdriver

* All our bottom-boards are permanently fastened in this way, and when necessary the staples can be removed without turning the hive upside down to remove nails.

MOVING BEES BY BOAT.

driven in, leaving a gap of ¼ inch between the hive and cover. This, together with the entrance-screen, usually affords sufficient ventilation providing one does not have to be too long on the road. But even in that case one can prevent smothering the bees by dashing a pint of water over the entrance-screen. This will drive the bees from the wire cloth when smoke would not. Smoke, on the other hand, would only tend to aggravate the trouble, whereas water affords instant relief. It cools the bees and drives back those that are shutting off ventilation.

If the water does not succeed in keeping the bees from the wire cloth, remove the screen and let them come out. If the hives have been jarred at least half a mile on the

at least a foot long, if they are not driven down too tight. The tool is shoved under one side, close to a leg of the staple, and given a quarter-twist, and then it is moved over to the other side, and twisted again. When the staple is raised high enough so the screwdriver can get under and give it a good pry it can be easily removed.

TO PREVENT BEES FROM SMOTHERING.

Provision should be made to prevent the bees from smothering. Even in the hottest weather we do not now use wire-cloth screen

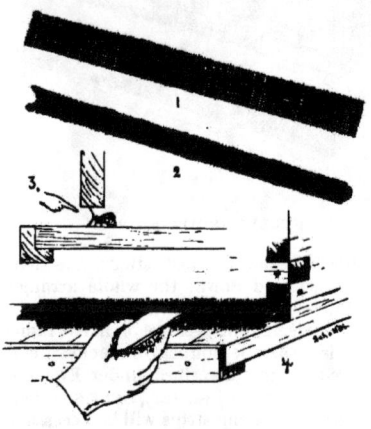

on top. Four pieces of wood about ¼ inch wide, and not more than ¼ inch in thickness, are put between the cover and the hive at the four corners. The staples are then

UNDER WAY.

ourney there is very little fear of their flying out.

For closing the entrance nothing is simpler and better than a plain strip of wire
cloth as long as the inside length of the entrance and two or three inches wide. This
is bent at right angles lengthwise, and then
pushed in the entrance, in the manner
shown, so that it wedges fast. On arrival
at destination the wire cloth can be quickly
jerked out.

In moving our bees to outyards we generally use a two-horse team with an ordinary
hay-rack. Hives with bees are put on
the bottom; those on top are only empties One should take along a quantity of
rope, a hammer, tacks, screwdriver, and a
lighted smoker. Be sure it does not go out
on the road. A little smoke at *just the right
time* may save the lives of valuable horses,
a whole load of bees, and possibly the life of
the bee-keeper and of the driver as well
While on the route, be sure to give the
smoker a " whiff " or two to make sure it is
still going. We would also carry along a
pail of water and a big sponge. If any of
the colonies seem to be suffering from lack
of ventilation, dash a little water over the
wire screen. As a general thing, avoid moving bees by day during very warm weather.
Do it at night, when the atmosphere is a
little cooler.

SHIPPING BEES LONG DISTANCES BY EX-
PRESS.

During hot weather great care should be
exercised that the bees be not smothered,
nor their combs melted down by the intense
heat that is generated where they have an
insufficient quantity of air during shipment·

THE DOVETAILED HIVE, PREPARED FOR
SHIPPING BEES.

We always tack a wire screen on to a
frame about 1½ inches deep, and of the same
width and length as the hive. This is secured on top of the hive by means of two
wood screws. Nails can be used when preferred, but screws are much more easily re-

moved. The cover should be secured about
two inches above the wire cloth so it will act
as a shade-board for the bees in case the
hive should be put in the sun. The cover so placed may be the means of saving the
lives of the bees.

To secure the frames so that they will not
shove about, we use a notched stick, as
shown at A A, of the accompanying cut, the
notches passing down between the frames
just over the rabbet in the hive.

A couple of wire nails hold it secure. A
similar notched stick is nailed to the bottom-board, notches upward, transversely
through the center. This keeps the bottoms
of the frames from jarring against each other. After the wire cloth has been tacked to
the entrance, the combs put in the hive and

NUCLEUS SHIPPING BOX.

secured by the notched sticks, the wire
screen screwed down, the whole arrange·
ment is ready for shipment.

Of course, if your bees are on fixed frames
—that is, either the Hoffman or the closed-end,
referred to and described under FRAMES,
MANIPULATING ; FRAMES, SELF-SPACING,
no notched spacing-strips will be necessary,
the frames being already fastened for moving
or shipping; and the beauty of it is, no time
need be lost in preparing them for that purpose.

It is almost absolutely necessary that the combs themselves be wired, or at least that they be old, tough, and securely attached to the bottom-bar if not wired. It is always risky, however, to ship in combs not wired, because it is impossible to tell what sort of rough usage they will receive at the hands of careless or indifferent express agents; and while we should not be too hasty in condemning railroad officials for careless handling, we should take every precaution. The bees buzzing around the wire cloth is usually enough to guarantee safe handling.

Quite an extensive business is carried on in shipping bees in one, two, three, and four frame nuclei. The illustration, p. 310, shows a light shipping-box, the sides and top of which are made of good strong lumber only ,⅜ inch thick. The ends are ⅝. The bottom is covered with wire cloth, then two cleats are nailed across the ends to raise the nucleus off the floor. For the sake of convenience the wire cloth is secured on the special cover shown above, which, when set down in place, leaves a space of an inch between the cover proper and the wire cloth. The thin board over the wire cloth protects it from the direct rays of the sun, and from sharp projections of any object. It also affords a convenient place to attach the address, and to put on the caution, "With Great Care."

Bees go at a rate and a half by express, hence it is very necessary that the packages be as light as possible; and for that reason the combs should hold no more honey than just enough to carry them through to their destination. Neatly printed directions on the outside will explain stimulative feeding so that a nucleus may be made into a strong colony.

HOW TO PREPARE A CARLOAD OF BEES.

If you use loose hanging frames, fix them with the spacing-strips illustrated on a previous page. Frames of the self-spacing type, of course, require no preparation. Remove the top, and cover the hive with wire cloth. The best way is to make a two-inch rim and nail the wire cloth on this, as explained on a previous page. There should be about two inches between the brood-frames and the wire cloth. Put four or five inches of loose straw on the car floor and then place the colonies upon this. After the car bottom is covered put some 2x4 pieces (four-inch way vertical) across the tops of the hives, and then the next tier of hives on top of these. For convenience in loading, leave a passageway through the center of the car, and then, if you accompany your bees, you can easily get at any of the colonies. The purpose of the straw is to give a spring to soften the heavy concussions. One thing more is important: Be sure to load the hives so that the frames are parallel with the rails; and don't pile them up more than two or three tiers high. After the hives are in place they should be securely stayed with suitable braces. Long strips of wood two inches wide, one on each side, should be nailed on the hives, thus tying all the hives in a row together so that they can not be disturbed when the car is bumped. In loading on a wagon, have the frames parallel with the axletree.

When bees are to go any great distance it is imperative that some man go along with them—either the owner himself or some competent apiarist. Every now and then the tops of the wire cloth should be sprinkled with water; and on hot days, especially where the car is a closed one, and not a cattle-car, the water should be administered several times a day. If the bees are found in any particular hive clustering on the wire cloth, spray water on them at once. For this purpose a small spray-pump and several five-gallon square cans filled with water should be taken along.

It is not practicable to ship strong colonies any distance. Attempts to do so almost surely result in the loss of the bees. Where one has, say, 100 strong stocks he is advised by all means to divide them into halves, using 200 hives instead of 100 in which to ship the bees. The division should take place several days before hauling to the car, if possible, and the queenless portion supplied with a cell or virgin, or, better still, a laying queen, because bees on a journey are likely to worry. A queen will do much to keep them contented and quiet on the combs.

The question is often asked, "Shall a cattle-car or a closed one be used for the purpose?" If the shipment is made in hot weather, or through a hot section of country, a cattle-car is advised. In this case a piece of canvas large enough to cover one side or end of the car should be taken along. This will be needed only when a stop is made for a few hours to protect the sunny side of the car. If it is very warm, the canvas should be thoroughly wetted down with water. When shipment is made in cool weather a box-car would be preferable.

In moving bees a long distance the shipper should first have them thoroughly examined by a competent inspector to see if any bee disease, American or European foul brood, is present; otherwise the shipper would be liable to the action of the State law in any State into which he might ship the bees. He would lose his bees, and be out his freight and other expenses.

CAUTION.

Before closing, let us add a caution. In moving bees, be sure that you have fixed all the entrances so that not a bee can by any possibility escape. Do not have your wire cloth too short, and then splice it out with leaves. Be sure to have it cut exactly the right length. For further particulars, see OUT-APIARIES.

MUSTARD (*Brassica arvensis*). This belongs to the same family as the turnip, cabbage, rape, etc., all of which, we believe, almost invariably furnish honey while they are in bloom. We have a good opportunity of testing these plants, because acres of them are raised for other purposes besides the honey. It will be a hard matter to determine which is best for your locality, without trying some of every kind. Find out what market you have for your seed, and then proceed to raise it as if you were going to depend on the seed alone to pay expenses. Should you secure a good crop of honey from it, you will then be so much ahead, and there is little chance of any great loss.

The honey from these plants is said to be very light, equal to any in flavor, and to command the highest price in the market. The seed should be sown very early in the spring, either in shallow drills so far apart that the cultivator can be used between them, or broadcast. The former plan is, of course, the better one for nearly all honey-plants, but is more trouble. From 6 to 10 lbs. per acre will be needed, sown in drills, and from 15 to 20 when sown broadcast. If you wish to save the seed, it should be sown not later than July 1st.

N.

NECTAR. Many times has honey been analyzed by competent chemists, but very seldom has there been an attempt to analyze nectar, owing to the difficulty of securing a sufficient quantity for experimental purposes.

The only satisfactory experiments of the kind which have yet appeared are those of Prof. Planta, of the university of Zurich, Switzerland, who was not only one of the best chemists in Europe, but also a competent bee-keeper besides.

It will be noted he experimented with the nectar of two American plants, *Agave Americana* (century plant) and *Bignonia Radicans* (trumpet-creeper). The former is a prodigious yielder of honey, far excelling any plant we know of in the North, and excelled only by some tropical trees such as *Protea mellifera*, *Hakeas*, and *Leucodendron*, and perhaps others not yet known. It grows in the southwest part of the United States and is common in Mexico.

Several translations of Dr. Planta's article on nectar analysis have appeared, and we give one which we deem best for our purpose.

Probably nectars do not all analyze alike; but Dr. Planta's analysis will be found sufficiently near an average to satisfy all practical requirements.

In the *Zeitschrift fuer Physiologische Chemie*, Band X., Heft 3, Dr. A. de Planta describes his researches on the chemical composition of some of the nectars in plants. He says it was a great pleasure for him during his researches on the life of bees to have established the relation which exists between nectar and honey, nectar serving for the preparation of honey. There was a great difficulty in getting a sufficient quantity of nectar, as plants yield it usually in small quantities, but there are some exceptions. Among these are *Protea mellifera*, *Hoya carnosa*, and *Tacoma radicans*, or trumpet-creeper, which contain such large quantities of nectar that it is easily collected. Thunberg says in his "Flora Capensis" of *Protea mellifera (Zuykerbosches, Zuykerboom, Tulpboom)* that it flowers in autumn; that is to say, in March and the following months. The flowers are often half filled with watery honey which furnishes an excellent syrup after it has been filtered to rid it of insects and impurities, and slightly evaporated by gentle heat.

This syrup is an article of commerce at Cape Town. Two bottles of it were produced, the specific gravities being 1.375 and 1.372. It had a slight acid reaction, but contained no albuminoids or nitrogenous matter. It contained 73.17 per cent solids, 70.08 being glucose and 1.31 per cent cane sugar. By glucose is meant a mixture of crystallizable grape sugar (dextrose) and uncrystallizable grape sugar (levulose), both having a similar chemical composition. This glucose may already be formed in the nectar by the action of the ferments it contains upon the cane sugar, transforming it into glucose; and this inversion can be continued in new honeys, owing to the action (which he had already demonstrated in 1879) of the saliva of bees which also transforms cane sugar into glucose.

Grape sugar from the syrup was also obtained in a crystallized form. No trace of formic acid could be detected in the syrup, though quantities of pollen were found in suspension, determined by Professor C. Cramer to be that of *Protea mellifera*, testifying to its genuineness.

Wishing to compare this with fresh nectar, he succeeded, after great difficulty, in getting three bottles. The specific gravity was 1.078, 1.079, and 1.077. These contained 17.66 per cent of solids, of which 17.06 was grape sugar. They contained no cane sugar. There was not the least trace of formic acid. A comparison of the two shows that the difference was due only to the extra quantity of water contained in the fresh nectar.

Besides these he also examined the nectars of *Hoya carnosa* and *Bignonia radicans*, both in the fresh and evaporated states. The following table gives the results:

Nectar of	Sugar.	Cane sugar.	Grape sugar.
Protea mellifera, fresh,	17.06		17.06
" " dry,	96.60		96.60
Hoya carnosa, fresh,	40.64	35.65	4.99
" " dry,	99.68	87.44	12.24
Bignonia radicans, fr.,	15.27	.43	14.84
" " dry,	99.85	2.85	97.00

Dr. de Planta has also made aqueous extracts of various flowers, among others those of *Rhododendron hirsutum* and *Onobrychis sativa*. In order to obtain 1 gram of sugar (equal to 1.3 grams of honey) the bees must visit at least 3129 flowers of *Rhododendron hirsutum* and 5530 of Sainfoin (*Onobrychis sativa*).

As honey is almost entirely formed from nectar, he gives the following table, comparing the quantity of water he has found in nectars and also in old and new honeys:

Nectar of	Nectar.	Water in Old honey	New honey
Protea mellifera,	82 34		
Hoya carnosa,	59.23		
Bignonia radicans,	84.70		
Fritillaria imperialis,	93.40		
Honey from			
Department of Landes,		19.09	
Senegal,		25.59	
Melipona,		18 84	
Canton Grisons (alt. 600 m.),		18.61	21.74
Sainfoin,		19.44	
Canton Grisons (alt. 1395 m.),		17 52	20.41
(high Alps).			21.68
Buckwheat,			33.36
Acacia from Ingoldstadt,			20.29

Whereas the nectars vary between 59 and 93 per cent, the quantity of water contained in old honeys varies only between 17 and 21 per cent, and that in new honeys 20 to 21 per cent, with the sole exception of buckwheat honey, in which he found 33 per cent.

From these observations he thinks that the bees throw off a considerable quantity of the water while it is in their stomachs. He does not admit that it is evaporated entirely in the cells, for the analyses he has made of honey newly deposited in the cells show that it already reaches them considerably concentrated. The following table shows the relative proportions of sugar contained in different honeys:

A—Old honeys from—	Present.	Quantity formed by inversion.
Department of Landes,	87.00	1.00
Senegal,	85.40	3.70
Canton Grisons (alt. 600 m.),	80.60	1.70
Sainfoin,	88 70	0 00
Canton Grisons (alt. 1395 m.),	84.10	0.50
B—New honeys from—		
Canton Grisons, Alpine region,	81.60	10.60
" " (alt. 600 m),	81.60	9.30
" " Alpine region,	87.20	00.80

Although most of the nectars contain a considerable quantity of cane sugar it is found in very few of the honeys of the Alps. Some honeys contain a little, while in others it is entirely absent. It is clear that, during the formation of honey, the cane sugar in the nectar is converted into grape sugar by the saliva of the bees, which contains a ferment endowed with this property (see his researches on this subject in *Deutsche Bienenzeitung*, 1879, No. 12).

Another difference between honey and nectar consists in the former containing nitrogenous substances and formic acid. Mullenhof has shown how this last is deposited in the honey, and E. Erlenmayer has proved its antiseptic properties.—*British Bee Journal*.

It will be observed Dr. Planta attributes the inversion of nectar to the saliva of the bees. It seems on the face of this to be only a "guess," and yet it has been repeated by many writers on the honey-bee ever since. We know inversion is taking place even while the nectar is still in the corolla of the flower, and it occurs long after the honey has been made and deposited, for new honey contains quite a large percentage of sucrose (sugar) whereas old honey contains little or none. We are very sure this change is caused by minute microorganisms similar to those in soft sugar or rum. For this reason the composition of honey is quite variable—so much as to baffle the best chemists to make a true standard by which to judge honey. Old honey therefore is actually superior to new, for the process of inversion is complete. If kept in a dry place it also contains less water, and, besides, loses the ethereal essential oils or essences of the flowers from which it was gathered; therefore nectar collected even from poisonous plants may become quite innocuous if allowed sufficient time to ripen. See HONEY.

NUCLEUS. This word, applied to bee culture, signifies a small colony of bees, perhaps from one-fourth to one-tenth of a full colony. The plural of the word is nuclei; it were well to bear this in mind, for there is much confusion in the use of the terms, even in printed circulars. If you remove a dozen bees from the hive, take them so far away that they are homeless, and then let them fly, they will after a time come pretty nearly back to the place from which you released them; but they will soon wander away and be lost, unless you give them a queen to which they will come back and probably remain if *she* does not stray away. She, like the rest, must fulfill her destiny, or disappear; we shall, therefore, have to provide her a comb wherein to lay eggs. The bees would build the comb themselves, provided they were numerous and had plenty of food. A dozen would never build any comb, nor make any attempt to rear and hatch her eggs if the comb were given them. Perhaps a hundred bees put in a suitably small box, with a fertile queen, might start a colony, and this is what we call a nucleus. It is the center, about which a colony of bees may in time be formed. Should they develop a full colony, the building-up would be done by the queen filling her combs with eggs, which, when cared for by the nursing bees (see BEES), would be converted into larvæ, and in 21 days hatch out perfect bees. These bees would then help the original hundred, and the queen fill a still larger area with eggs, which would hatch in the same way, and so on. The difficulty in the way of building up from such small beginnings seems to be that the queen will lay all the eggs a hundred bees can care for, perhaps in an hour or two, and then she has to sit or loaf around for the whole 21 days, until she can have another "job." Before the 21 days are up, she will be very likely to get disgusted with such small proceedings, and swarm out, or at least induce the bees with her to do so. See ABSCONDING SWARMS. If we should increase the number of bees to 500 or 1000, we could get along then very much better, and there would be little danger of swarming out unless the hive given them were too small. A very spry and ambitious queen might fill all the cells the bees had prepared for her, then set about filling them the second time, as they sometimes do, and then swarm out; but with a quart of bees—about 3200, if I have figured rightly—things will generally go along pretty well.

To have this quart of bees work to the best advantage, something depends upon the sort of hive they occupy. A single comb, long and narrow, so as to string the bees out in one thin cluster, is very bad economy. Two combs would do very much better, and three a great deal better still. It is like scattering firebrands widely apart.

One alone will soon go out; two placed side by side will burn very well; and three will make quite a fire. It is on this account that we would have a nucleus of three, instead of one or two frames. Bees seem to seek naturally a space between two combs; and the queen seldom goes to the outside comb of a hive unless she is obliged to for want of room.

FORMING NUCLEI FOR INCREASE; HOW TO DO IT.

Dividing colonies into nuclei for the sake of increasing the number of hive tenants is usually very bad practice, especially in the hands of beginners. When running for honey, colonies can not be much too strong. Yet there are times, especially after a severe winter, when many colonies have died, that some form of artificial increase is desirable. Here is one of several plans we have practiced with success. We will start with one colony:

As soon as settled warm weather comes we would divide our colony into four two-frame nuclei, introducing an untested Italian queen to every division as formed; confine them at least three days (72 hours), tacking wire cloth over the entrance. At the end of this time remove the wire cloth, when the bees will stay contentedly without returning. If honey is not coming in we would feed a little every day.

When the queen fills the frame or frames with eggs, and there are bees enough to cover, we would put in another frame on the *outside*. As the weather warms up it might be advisable to put in still another frame, putting this one in the *center* of the cluster, in the mean time keeping up gentle feeding daily. A very good feeder for this purpose is the Boardman. See FEEDERS. This can be slipped into the entrance, and by screwing the can tightly or loosely into the cap the flow of feed can be regulated for the daily needs.

Make the syrup by mixing together sugar and water in equal proportions by measure. Stir thoroughly, and pour into feeder-cans.

As soon as the nuclei have four or five frames of sealed brood, larvæ, and eggs, take out one or more frames from each, and form another. This plan can be continued till one has 15 and possibly 20 little colonies; but he should stop dividing at least 60 days before the setting-in of cold frosty nights.

If one can not afford to buy queens he will have to raise them and then the increase will be cut down more than a half, probably.

In 1892 the writer, without any special effort, reared all the queens, and increased an apiary from 10 colonies, some of which were almost nuclei, to about 85 good colonies that went into winter quarters. They had no empty combs, but they were given full sheets of foundation. They were not fed, but made to depend entirely on natural sources for their supply. Had he fed after the honey season, and given empty combs, he might have made double the increase.

CONFINING TO KEEP THE BEES IN.

Another method, first introduced to the bee-keeping world by Mr. W. W. Somerford, is reported to give such good results that we are glad to place the plan before the readers of this work.

To begin with, remove the queens or cage them in all your fancy stock, after getting the brood-nest well filled with brood (the more brood the better—8 or 10 frames in a hive if possible). Wait ten days after removing the queen, when the bees will generally have cells on each and every comb, and be in a broody or listless condition, waiting for cells to hatch. Divide and remove the frames quietly, giving each new hive two frames of brood and all adhering bees, and one good frame of honey, using it for a division-board (and, by the way, such division-boards are to my notion the best in the world); put the two frames of brood and bees next to the wall of the hive, and let the honey-frame be the third from the side of hive. Be sure to see that you have at least one good ripe-looking cell in each new hive, or division, and don't forget the frame of honey. As soon as each division is made, stop the entrance of the hive by stuffing it full of green moss. If you haven't any green moss, use green grass or leaves, and be sure to stuff them in tight—as tight as though you never intended the bees should gnaw out, and be sure there are no cracks or holes that a single bee could get out at; for if there are, your division will be ruined by all, or nearly all, the bees that can fly leaving it. Each parent colony should make four or five good divisions that will make boom-

ing colonies in 40 or 50 days, and I have had them the best in the apiary in less time. Leave or loose the old queen on the old stand (if not too old), and the bees from it will work straight ahead, as they don't have to be confined to make them stay at home.

Don't be uneasy about the divisions that are stopped up, unless you failed to stuff the entrances well, for they *will not* smother, but busy themselves gnawing at the moss or grass for two or three days, possibly four or five, if you have done an extra good job at stuffing the entrance. At the end of that time you will find they have all gnawed out so as to secure egress and ingress. Then you can move enough of the grass or moss to give them a clean entrance, 1½ or 2 inches wide; and by looking into them you will be astonished at the quantity of bees you have in each hive (and they, too, well satisfied), having consumed so much time in gnawing out that the queen had time to hatch and kill off her rivals and be ready for the wedding-trip by the time the entrance is cleared. So, instead of, in a week's time, having a worthless weak division with a *chilled* inferior queen, as is the case in the old-style way of dividing, where nine-tenths of the bees return to the old hive, you have a strong vigorous queen and a nice little *satisfied* swarm of bees, ready for business in the way of pulling foundation before they are three weeks old.

I have succeeded with nineteen out of twenty divisions made in the above way, when I did not even see them until the third week, after dividing as above; and for the average bee-keeper who has out-apiaries I think there is no better way in the world to make increase. If there is I'd like to see or hear of it while the expansion question is being aired.

In the above method of increasing, you have no queens to buy, no robbers to bother with, and but little time lost, as an expert can make 20 divisions an hour.

Navasota, Tex.

For particulars regarding the use of small nuclei for mating queens, see QUEEN-REARING.

Another plan of making two colonies out of one is given under the head of INCREASE, which see. For full consideration of the subject of BABY NUCLEI, see QUEEN-REARING.

A PORTION OF MR. STEWART'S APIARY, CONTRA COSTA COUNTY, CALIFORNIA.

O.

OBSERVATORY HIVE. See HIVES.

ORANGE-BLOSSOM HONEY has come to be known as a commercial article; but, unfortunately, a great deal of the honey that masquerades under that high-sounding name never came from the orange-tree at all.

Pure orange-blossom honey is exquisite in flavor, light in color, and of heavy body. While its quality is superb, its quantity is somewhat limited. The pure article is obtained in only very limited regions, while a mixture of orange-blossom and other Southern honeys is often obtained.

ORANGE-BLOSSOMS.

Bees seem to work busily on the blossoms of orange-trees, without gathering any very great quantity of nectar. It would seem that nature had intended that the delicious sweetness which the tree is capable of yielding should be left for the golden fruit that follows later. For that reason, pure orange-blossom honey scarcely ever finds its way to remote markets, for what there is of it will be consumed where it is produced.

ORGANIZATIONS OF BEE-KEEPERS. The reader of this work ought to ally himself with some local organization of bee-keepers if there is one, and with the National Bee-keepers' Association. This society has already a membership of over 2000, and is composed of the most successful bee-keepers in the United States and Canada. At the present rate of growth its membership will run up into the thousands. Its object is to protect bee-keepers in their rights, to secure pure-food laws, to disseminate useful information, to fight adulteration—in short, to look after the interests of bee-keepers as a whole. It has secured many valuable precedents in law, and has shown that bees are not a nuisance *per se;* that they can be kept in incorporated villages and towns, and that they are like any other property.

The annual membership fee in the Association is $1.00. This secures to the member all the rights and privileges of the society, the right to vote at its annual meetings and at the annual election of officers; the annual report of the work done, and a stenographic report of the three-day conventions that are held in all the principal cities of the country. This report contains verbatim discussions by the most successful bee-keepers in the United States. A report alone is well worth the membership fee.

The Association consists of a President, Vice-president, Secretary, General Manager, and a Board of twelve Directors. These latter, as nearly as possible, represent the various sections of the United States where the honey business is most prominent.

One who has very many bees can not afford to do without one or more bee-journals, neither can he afford not to be a member of the National Association. He may never know when he may be sued for damage on an alleged trespass by his bees, or notified to move them out of the town or city. The small membership fee of $1.00 entitles him, under certain conditions, to the protection of the General Manager, who, when circumstances warrant, will employ an attorney and fight the case to a finish. One can not secure protection by joining the Association *after* he gets into trouble.

The General Manager's address can be ascertained in any of the bee-journals.

OUT-APIARIES.—Within late years this term has been used to apply to bee-yards remote or distant from the home yard by some two or three miles. It is a well-known fact, that only a limited number of colonies, comparatively, can be accommodated in any one locality, different places being able to support widely different numbers of colonies.

NUMBER OF COLONIES IN AN APIARY.

The number of colonies of bees that can be profitably kept in one locality is limited by the amount of pasturage. Of late years quite a number of bee-keepers have established one or more out-apiaries, for the sake of keeping more bees than the home pasturage would support. Just how many bees can be supported in a single locality has probably never been ascertained, and it is just as probable that it never will. One field may support five times as many as another, and the same field may support five times as many this year as last. Most bee-keepers, however, think it inadvisable to keep more than 75 to 100 colonies in one apiary, while a few think their locations so good that 200 or more can be profitably kept together. The man who has only a few more colonies than he thinks best to keep in one apiary may find it better to have his bees *just a little* crowded at home before he goes to the extra expense of an out-apiary. Indeed, it depends somewhat upon the man, whether, having been successful with one apiary, he will find any profit in the second. But having gone so far as to have one or more apiaries away from home, it is not best for him to have any crowding in the least. If 100 colonies will do well in each apiary, the probability is that 75 will do better; and while there is unoccupied territory all about him he had better keep on the safe side and have so few in each place as to feel sure of not overstocking. His own convenience should have much to do in deciding. For instance, if he has, in all, 300 colonies, and thinks that 100 can find enough to do in a place, but can get through the work of only 75 in a day, then he will keep the 300 in 4 apiaries of 75 each, rather than in 3 apiaries of 100 each. For it will make one less travel to have in each apiary just

what he will do in a day's work. If he can do 50 in a day, then he may just as well have 100 in two apiaries as in one, for in either case he must make two trips to get through with them.

DISTANCE BETWEEN APIARIES, AND LOCATION THEREOF.

A location for an out-apiary must, of course, be far enough distant from the home apiary not to interfere much; but just how far is best, it is not easy to decide. Perhaps, all things considered, a good distance is something like three miles apart. As the area of flight is a circle, the ideal plan of locating out-apiaries so as to occupy fully all adjoining territory is to put them in hexagonal form, in which case a circle of six will surround the home apiary.

In the diagram, A represents the home apiary, and B, C, D, E, F, G, the out-apiaries, at equal distances from A and from

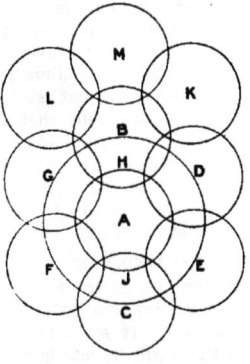

each other. If more than seven are needed then a second series may be started, as at K, M, L, indicated by the letters. The circles representing the area of flight from each apiary are seen to overlap each other; but this is at the outer parts, where the ground is more sparsely occupied, and the doubling on the same ground is compensated by the convenience of the shorter distance to go from one apiary to another. But this ideal plan, although a good thing to work from as a basis, is not likely ever to be fully carried out. Many reasons will make it desirable to vary. The roads may run in such directions as to make a difference; no good place may be found for an apiary at some of the points, etc. It may be remarked that the area of flight is not always a circle. An apiary placed in a valley between two ranges of hills might have an oblong area, the bees perhaps flying twice as far along the line of the valley as in the other direction. If only a single out-apiary is to be planted, it is probably best to go in the direction of the best pasturage—a thing not always easy to determine. Sometimes one location proves to be better than another, year after year, although no apparent reason for it can be seen. It may even be worth while to vary a location a mile or more for the sake of having it where pleasant people live. But you can do much toward making the people pleasant by being pleasant yourself. See to it that you make as little trouble as possible, and be still more careful than at home to avoid every thing that may incite robbing, for robbing begets cross bees on the place.

RENT FOR OUT-APIARIES.

The agreement between the bee-keeper and his landlord, for rent, is as varied as the cases that occur. Some pay a fixed sum, five or ten dollars per year; others agree to pay a per cent of the crop; some make a bargain to pay so much for every swarm hived by some one of the landlord's family, and so on, while some can not get the landlord to agree to take any rent whatever. In this latter case it is only right to make sure that the landlord has a good supply of honey for his family to use during the coming year. In any case, be sure to do *a little better* than is expected of you.

HAULING BEES.

Whenever you decide to start a second apiary, you must give some attention to the matter of hauling. If you winter on summer stands, there will be less hauling than if you bring all your bees home to winter in the cellar and then take them back again in the spring. If you use chaff hives you can have light cases made to carry merely the brood-frames with the bees. The first thing to see to is to make *very sure* that no bees can get out to sting the horse or horses. Of course, you think you are careful, and that there is no need of anxiety in your case; but, wait and see. The probabilities are that, with all your care, one of your first experiences in hauling bees will be to get your horse stung; and you may be thankful if you get off without a runaway and a general smashup. Some little leak evaded your notice, from which the bees escaped, or you drove your horse too close to the apiary, or in some other way you may find yourself in such a scrape that you may wish you never had any thing to do with bees. A. E. Manum used on his horses a sheet of cot-

ton cloth which completely covered head and body, and kept it on until some half a mile distant from the apiary.

You can haul bees on almost any kind of vehicle. Some use wagons with springs; some use a hay-rack with two or three feet of hay on it, while others use a common lumber-wagon, or a hay-rack with neither hay nor springs, leaving the frames with no other fastening than the propolis and brace-combs. With smooth roads this latter plan is very satisfactory. With good level roads it may be best to have the brood-combs run across the wagon, as most of the shaking comes from the wagon rocking from side to side, while a road very rough may make it best to have the combs running parallel to the line of travel. Where combs are secure enough, it will matter little how they are placed. To carry colonies of bees to advantage, some sort of rack is necessary. As we are not farmers we had to extemporize a rack for our one-horse wagon.

Whatever the kind of hive you may decide to use, some plan must be adopted for fastening in the bees, so that they may have abundance of ventilation while being hauled. As, however, the hauling is done in spring and fall, less ventilation is needed than during hot weather. The ordinary entrance, say 14 inches by ⅜, covered with wire cloth, will answer, as that gives a ventilating surface of about 5 inches, although more would be better, and it might be bad to have so little if the day should be warm. Of course, the bees must be shut in when not flying, and in spring it is a good plan to shut up in the evening all that are to be hauled the next day. In the fall the weather may be such that bees will not fly at any time in the day, otherwise you must get to the out-apiary early enough in the morning to shut in all the bees you will haul that day. If you are to take bees to an out-apiary in the spring, the sooner it is done the better, as pasturage is then apt to be rather scarce at best. Where bees are to be brought home in the fall to be cellared, they may as well be brought just as soon as heavy frost occurs, or as soon as they stop gathering; at least, they should be brought early enough to have a good fly before going into winter quarters. After being unloaded from the wagon the bees may be liberated at once by blowing in a little smoke or dashing in some cold water; or, if loaded too late in the evening to fly, they may be left till the next morning when they will be quietly settled down; and if carefully opened, no smoke need be used.

TOOLS FOR OUT-APIARIES, AND WHERE TO KEEP THEM.

Whatever tools you use in the home apiary, you are likely to need the same in each out-apiary. If a different person is in charge of each apiary, then each one must have his own set of tools ; and even if the same force go in succession from one apiary to another, it may be the more convenient to have a separate outfit kept at each place. We do not think just now of any thing in the line of

WESLEY DIBBLE'S TOOL, SMOKER, AND FUEL HOUSE.

tools needed for an out-apiary, different from those that are needed at home, unless it is a robber-cloth. We should not like to be without one of these in the home apiary, but they are specially valuable in out-apiaries where, sometimes, notwithstanding robbers are troublesome, your plans are such that you want to force through a certain amount of work. By having two or three robber-cloths we have sometimes been able to go on with our work when, without them, we should have been obliged to desist. We'll tell you how to make one. Take about a square yard of stout sheeting or cotton cloth ; if your hives are small, less will do. Lay one of the cut edges on a piece of lath, about the length of your hive. Lay a similar piece of

lath on top of it, and drive wire nails through both, at a distance of perhaps three inches apart. Let the nails be long enough to reach through and clinch. Then treat the opposite edge the same way, and your robber-cloth is complete.

This robber-cloth is exceedingly convenient to throw quickly over any hive or super that you want to cover up temporarily. You can grasp a lath at the side with one hand, and, with a single fling, throw it over a hive making it instantly bee-tight. It does not kill bees, if any happen to get under it. If you have one hand occupied with something else, you can very quickly uncover and cover with the other. We have sometimes worked with a colony when robbers were so bad they would pounce into every opening ; but a robber-cloth on each side covering the frames allowed us to make an opening at the frame we wished to take out. As a general rule, of course, we would try to manage not to work the bees at such times.

But, to return. It would be ery convenient, as you go about from one apiary to another, to have a little tool-house at each yard. We are not sure, however, that it would pay. A hive or box covered over water-tight (we use a tin hive-cover) answers very well. We would have one or more of these at each apiary in any case, for there are some things you want to be sure of having on hand, as smoker fuel. Matches should also be kept under cover in such a place, in a tin box. A baking-powder box does well. Bee-hats, smokers — in fact, a full set of every thing can be kept in the same way.

It is possible, however, to get on very well by always taking your tools with you, provided you never forget them. One day we went to the Hastings apiary, without any smoker, and we realized then how important a smoker is. Don't trust to memory. In your record-book have a list of the things you generally need to take ; and after you are all ready to get in, read aloud the list and be sure that every thing is in the wagon, as : Hats, smokers, dinner (we never forgot our dinner), chisel, etc. Our own practice has been a sort of compromise between having a full kit of tools at each apiary and taking every thing along. If a buggy is used, it is not convenient to have very much bulk. By the way, a bad season is not without its compensations. We have had two years of such dead failure that we could make almost every trip the entire season in a buggy, for there was no honey to haul, and little in the way of supplies.

GENERAL MANAGEMENT OF OUT-APIARIES.

The ways of managing out-apiaries will be just as many as the men who manage them; but the general treatment should be about the same as at the home apiary. There will always be the advantage of moving at any time a colony or part of colony from one apiary to another, and feeling sure that the bees will stay where they are put. The more you are interested in out-apiaries the more you are apt to be interested in the prevention of swarming; and if you have been in the habit of wintering in the cellar, an out-apiary will make you debate somewhat the question whether you can not find any way of safely wintering outdoors. Some practice having a competent assistant in charge of each apiary, remaining there all the time; while others take a sufficient force of helpers to go from one yard to another doing the work of each apiary regularly—every six days or oftener.

In *Gleanings in Bee Culture* appeared an article from Mr. E. France, of Platteville, Wis.; and as it contains so many valuable suggestions, we reproduce it here entire, with the diagram.

gether more than I had supposed. The accompanying diagram will show how they stand, and I will give some facts and figures that will make quite an interesting study about setting out out-apiaries and overstocking our pasture. Of course, it is impossible to locate a set of out-apiaries just so far from the home apiary, in a circle, each one in its proper place, just as nicely as we could make it on paper. We have to take such places as we can get, and many of the places that we can get won't do at all, for some reason or other; and when you have six or eight yards planted you will be likely to find, as in our case, some of them badly crowded—too much so for profit.

The circles in the diagram are three miles each, or 1½ miles from center to the outside, which is a very short distance for a bee to go in search of honey. If the bees fly three or four miles, as I think they do in poor seasons, it is plain to see how it works in a poor season. The outside apiaries may be getting a fair living, while the inside yards are nearly starving. In first-class seasons, when honey is plentiful everywhere, and very few bees go over one mile, there is enough for all. I here give the number of bees in each yard this spring, the amount of honey taken, and the amount of feeding this fall to put the bees in trim for winter.

Atkinson yard.	Colonies, spring count,			100
Cravin "	" "	"	"	90
Kliebenstein yard. "	" "	"	"	96
Waters "	" "	"	"	88
Jones "	" "	"	"	80
Gunlauch "	" "	"	"	90
Home "	" "	"	"	105
		Total		649

No increase to speak of

Honey extracted:

Atkinson yard	....	190
Cravin "	....	200
Kliebenstein "	....	740
Waters "	....	497
Jones "	....	600
Gunlauch "	....	350
Home "	....	540
	Total	3125

Fed back:

Atkinson yard	....	000
Cravin "	....	336
Kliebenstein "	....	000
Waters "	....	000
Jones "	....	210
Gunlauch "	....	486
Home "	....	900
	Total	1932
	Surplus after feeding,	1193

Now, notice the Kliebenstein yard, how it is located away by itself, as, for distance, from other yards. It has a great advantage; and then there is plenty of basswood all around it. It has no bees belonging to other parties on its territory. It gave the most honey, no feeding, and is in the best condition of any yard for winter stores.

We will now notice the Atkinson yard. It is pretty well hemmed in on the north and east sides by the other yards, but it has an unlimited field on the west, of good pasture. We took but little honey there, but it is in good condition for winter, without feeding.

Now, away over on the east side we have the Waters yard. It is two miles from basswood, but a splendid white-clover range — plenty of basswood two miles north and east. This yard gave some honey, and required no feeding for winter.

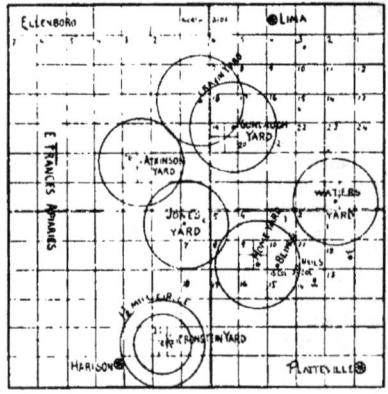

E. FRANCE'S SYSTEM OF OUT-APIARIES.

I have taken pains to make a correct diagram of the territory that we occupy with our bees; and I must say that I was surprised myself when I saw the exact position of each yard. They are clustered to-

Then there are the Cravin and the Gunlauch yards, each 90 colonies in spring, only 1¼ miles apart—too close, with very little basswood north of them. Both of these yards were fed more honey than we took from them. There were a few acres of buckwheat near them that helped them a little. The Jones yard did fairly well, considering its surroundings. It had the least number of bees, an abundance of basswood near, and then had eleven acres of buckwheat just over the fence.

We will now notice the home yard. There were 105 colonies. The Jones yard is rather too close. Then there is an apiary of 20 colonies a little over half a mile east, at a point marked Beihls; another apiary 1½ miles east, 30 colonies, marked Nails; another apiary southeast, marked W, about 40 colonies. Another apiary still further to the east, and a little to the north, marked W, about 40 colonies. So you see the home-yard territory is overstocked the worst of all, and had to be fed 360 lbs. more than was taken from them. The home yard has the best clover field of any, but basswood is scarce within two miles. In looking at the diagram, one not acquainted with the ground would naturally ask, "Why don't you use that open space southeast of the home yard?" It is all prairie land. Corn and oats don't yield much honey.

We will now just look back to the record of a year of plenty, 1886, and see how the yards averaged up then.

COLONIES, SPRING OF 1886.

Atkinson yard, 72 cols.; average lbs. per col., 106
Cravin   " 80 "   "   "   "   "   106¼
Kliebenstein" 60 "   "   "   "   "   109
Waters   " 72 "   "   "   "   "   107
Gunlauch " 50 "   "   "   "   "   100½
Home   " 61 "   "   "   "   "   117

Jones yard not planted then.

FOR 1885.

Atkinson yard, 56 cols.; average lbs. per col., 90
Cravin   " 53 "   "   "   "   "   74
Kliebenstein" 46 "   "   "   "   "   62
Waters   " 57 "   "   "   "   "   57
Gunlauch " 46 "   "   "   "   "   77½
Home   " 62 "   "   "   "   "   71½

FOR 1884.

Atkinson yard, 51 cols.; average lbs. per col., 107
Cravin   " 41 "   "   "   "   "   113
Kliebenstein" 51 "   "   "   "   "   109
Waters   " 41 "   "   "   "   "   130
Gunlauch " 41 "   "   "   "   "   106½
Home   " 61 "   "   "   "   "   113½

FOR 1883.

Four yards, average for the whole............105 lbs.
Number of colonies, 35, 43, 33, 60.

In 1887 we kept no record. It was a very poor season, and we got but little honey.

The year 1888 was a very poor year also.

		Cols. in spring.	Average per col.
Atkinson	yard,	76	23
Cravin	"	75	20
Kliebenstein	"	67	31
Waters	"	69	32
Gunlauch	"	77	21½
Home	"	66	37½

FOR 1889.

		Cols. in spring.	Average per col.
Atkinson	yard,	72	40
Waters	"	79	40
Kliebenstein	"	87	63
Gunlauch	"	79	47
Cravin	yard,	78	49
Whig	"	52	40
Home	"	84	52

Now, friends, you have the figures and the map of the ground that our bees are on. Study it for your-

selves. But if you plant out-apiaries, don't put them less than five miles apart if you can help it. If you are going to keep help at the separate yards, to run the bees, six miles apart is near enough; then, if the pasture is good, you can keep from 100 to 150 colonies in each place. If you go from home with your help every day, then you want to gauge the number of colonies so as to work one whole yard in one day; or if you have but three or four apiaries in all, you will have time to work two days in each. But don't go over the roads for less than a full day's work when you get there; and remember, when you are locating an apiary, that, when you are hitched up and on the road, one or two miles further travel will pay you better than to crowd your pasture. Don't overstock your ground.   E. FRANCE.
Platteville, Wis.

Soon after the appearance of Mr. France's diagram, there appeared in *Gleanings* another valuable article from the pen of C. P. Dadant, of the firm of C. Dadant & Son. It substantiates what Mr. France has said, and shows the relation that apiaries bear to each other along the banks of the Mississippi.

The very interesting article of Mr. France, on out-apiaries, has induced us to give you our experience in this matter, not because we can throw any more light on the question, but because our practice, which extends back to 1871, in the matter of out-apiaries confirms the views of both Mr. France and Dr. Miller, and will add weight to their statements.

Under ordinary circumstances it is not advisable to place apiaries nearer than four miles apart; but Dr. Miller is undoubtedly right when he says that the configuration of the land has a great deal to do with the greater or lesser distance that bees travel in certain directions.

In the accompanying diagram you will perceive that these apiaries are all located on land sloping toward the Mississippi River, and are separated from one another by creeks, and groves of timber land. The Grubb apiary is owned by D. W. McDaniel, who has had charge of our apiaries also for a few years past. Of all these apiaries, the Sherwood is the best in the product of both spring and fall crops, although there are seasons like the past when the fall crop fails there altogether.

The Villemain apiary has the poorest location, to all appearances; but it is located near the only basswood grove there is in the country, and has also quite a fall pasture from blossoms that grow on the islands near it. But what will you think of the Sack apiary, which is located a little over two miles south of the Lamet apiary, with another apiary close to the latter, but not shown on the diagram, and only one mile and a quarter north of another apiary of 60 colonies, owned by A. Dougherty? Yet this Sack apiary gives us the best average of honey of all, excepting the Sherwood apiary. The reason of it is, that the pasturage is all west of it on the river bottoms, and very abundant. It is probable that the bees in this apiary go as far west as the river, about three miles, while they perhaps do not travel over a mile east on the bluffs. Their course north and south, in the direction of those other apiaries, is over a hilly country covered more or less with timber which makes their flight more difficult.

11

The two small circles in the northern part of the diagram show the spots where we had apiaries formerly, and which, you will perceive, were further away from home than the present. At that time the Sherwood apiary did not exist, nor did the Grubb apiary; and yet we must say that we can see no difference in the yield of the home apiary. We are satisfied that the Grubb bees go east, the Sherwood bees and the home bees northeast, for their crop. When we say the bees go in a certain direction, we do not mean all the bees, but the greater part of them We can give you one convincing instance of the correctness of this opinion.

By glancing at the diagram you will notice that the home apiary is just about a mile and a half from the north point of an island in the river. In certain seasons the islands are covered with water in June; and after the waters recede they become covered with luxuriant vegetation, and the yield of honey from them is very large. In one of these seasons we found a colony, belonging to a neighbor, located

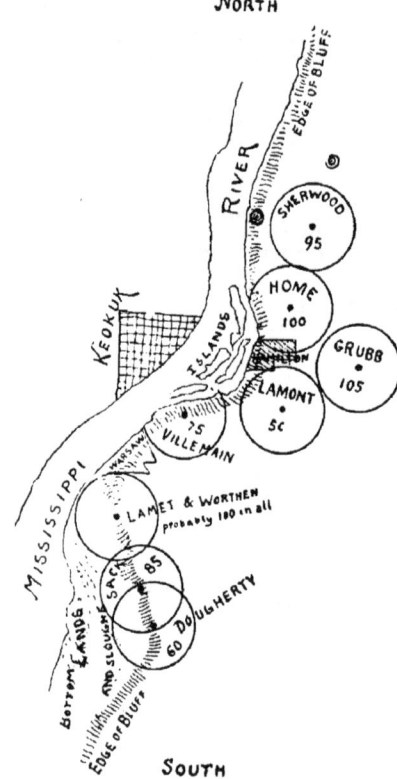

NORTH

SOUTH

THE DADANT SYSTEM OF OUT-APIARIES ALONG THE MISSISSIPPI RIVER.

half way between us and the river, harvesting a large yield of honey from this source, while our bees harvested nothing. Is it not evident that our bees

had not gone that far? Yet we have seen them two miles and more from home in another direction.

Hamilton, Ill. C. P. DADANT.

In 1890, and also 1897, we visited a number of extensive apiarists in the States of New York and Vermont. Among others whom we called upon was Mr. P. H. Elwood, who occupies a territory for his system of out-apiaries not many miles from that formerly occupied by Mr. Quinby. Mr. E. runs about 1000 colonies in a series of eight or ten out-yards, and they are located in the valleys in the midst of those York State hills. These hills are anywhere from 500 to 1000 feet high, and are covered with basswoods and clover. The former, scattered over the hills from top to bottom, prolong the duration of the honey-flow very considerably. Instead of there being only ten days or two weeks of basswood, it sometimes lasts a whole month. The first basswoods to blossom are at the foot of the hills; and as the season advances, those higher up come in bloom; so the flow does not entirely cease until the trees at the very top of the hills have gone out of bloom. The bees will first commence flying on the horizontal; and as the season progresses, they keep flying higher and higher, until they have scaled the top of the hills. Bee-keepers who are situated in such a country, or in swamp land, are in the best localities for honey. It might be well to observe in this connection, that these hills form excellent windbreaks for apiaries in the valleys. In Vermont, a colder climate, this feature cuts quite a figure. Mr. A. E. Manum's apiaries were located among the hills, in some cases on the sides of the mountains; but, unlike Mr. Elwood, he had no basswood there.

MOVABLE APIARIES.

Experience has shown, in many instances, that a yard which in years gone by has furnished tons of honey is now practically worthless, or so nearly so that the moving of the bees to some more favorable location is a necessity. For instance, four or five years ago an apiary furnished an abundance of basswood honey; but the basswoods have all been cut off; there is no clover and the field is worthless. Again, a locality has once furnished immense quantities of white clover; but intensive agriculture has set in, and clover pasturage has given way to immense wheat-fields. The inroads of civilization sometimes cut off the honey-resources of a locality, at other times; augment them very considerably. There are a few locations in York State that formerly gave very little honey until the farmers, in recent years, introduced buckwheat to such an extent that these are now splendid buckwheat countries; and the yield of this dark rich honey plays a considerable part in the net profits of the season. In a word, we want our apiaries so we can load them up at a moment's notice, and move them at practically little expense to any new field that may be more inviting. We can not always tell at first whether it will be a favorable location. If it does not come up to our expectations, we can "pull up stakes" and again try elsewhere. How are we to make our apiaries movable? Keep them on fixed frames, to be sure. Neither Mr. Elwood, Captain Hetherington, nor Mr. Hoffman fusses with fastening frames. When it becomes desirable to move a yard, all that is necessary is to close the entrance and load up the bees. See FRAMES, SELF-SPACING.

A SCALE HIVE AT AN OUT-YARD.

It is a well-known and established fact, that one yard may yield quite a crop of honey while another, only a few miles distant, requires to be fed. It is highly important to be able to tell just what the bees are doing at stated periods during the season. Mr. Manum kept a hive on scales at each yard; and every time he visited one he consulted the scales. If they indicated an increase of several pounds, he knew the bees in this apiary needed more room, and were also liable to swarm; but if they indicated a loss of several pounds, he inferred that the whole yard was losing likewise, and that some colonies needed to be fed. Of course, the hive on the scale should contain a fair average colony. In many cases it is not always possible to visit yards at regular periods, and so Mr. Manum had some resident near the apiary to watch the scale, and report by postal card any unexpected developments.

A CAUTION ABOUT ENTERING INTO THE OUT-APIARY BUSINESS.

We have already gone over the ground of the general subject of out-apiaries, and what contributes toward making their management a success. While there are many bee-keepers who have brains and capacity enough to manage a series of out-apiaries, there are also more who had better never think of entering into the project. To be a keeper of several out-apiaries means great perseverance and a good deal of system, besides ability to manage not only the bees, but the help who are to take care of them. If you can not make fifty or sixty colonies pay in one location, do not delude yourself by the idea that you can make bees pay by establishing a series of out-apiaries. The man who can not make a small business pay probably will not make a large one do so. When you can manage successfully your home apiary, it may be profitable, as soon as the increase is sufficient, to take a part of it to an outyard.

OVERSTOCKING. By this term we mean having more colonies in a given place than the locality can support. Our treatment of the question under OUT-APIARIES (which see) hints at benefits of restriction to 75 strong stocks in any one apiary. While, doubtless, better to retain at home unavoidable increase to the limit, perhaps, of 20 or 30 swarms, still, when 50 more than the requisite number is reached, a new yard should be started two miles away, or, better, even four.

A given locality with only ten colonies to gather the nectar in it may show a wonderful average per colony—perhaps 200 or 300 pounds. When the number is tripled or quadrupled, the average will be cut down a half. The locality should be carefully studied, and only that number of colonies be used which on an average, one year with another, will give the largest results in honey, with a minimum of labor and capital. If 75 hives during an average season would furnish an average of 150 pounds to the hive, then, obviously, the number might be increased to 100 or even 150. When, on the other hand, the average is, say, only 50 lbs. of extracted honey, and there are only 50 colonies in the apiary, then, clearly, 50 would be all there could be kept with profit in that spot; and it could be questioned whether or not 35 might not be just as profitable, and at the same time save a little in the investment and some labor in gathering and harvesting the crop.

But in some locations, notably California, Colorado, Cuba, and in some portions of Florida, one can have as many as 300 or 400 colonies, and in some rare instances 500 colonies in one apiary. The late E. W. Alexander, of Delanson, N. Y., had some 700 colonies in one bee-yard; but he had immense acreages of buckwheat and goldenrod. The celebrated Sespe apiary, in Southern California, owned by J. F. McIntyre, has, in one yard, some 600 hives of bees; but the great mountains on either side, the fertile valley, and the great abundance of honey flora, make such a number possible. See APIARIES.

OVERSTOCKING AND PRIORITY RIGHTS.

A new phase of overstocking has been developing within recent years, bringing up a rather difficult and serious problem. In good localities such as, for example, the irrigated regions of Colorado, the keeping of bees is much more profitable, or at least once was, than in some of the less favored localities in the central and northern States of the Union. It has come to pass that, in recent years, certain bee-keepers, learning of the wonderful yields in Colorado, in the irrigated alfalfa regions, have started apiaries within less than a mile of some other bee-keeper having 100 or 200 colonies in that locality. When the new comer establishes another apiary of 100 colonies, the place becomes overstocked, with the result that bee-keeper No. 1 has his average per colony cut down very materially. There is only a certain amount of nectar in the field to be gathered; and if all the colonies get a proportionate share, then bee-keeper No. 2 practically robs bee-keeper No. 1 of a large percentage of honey that he would have obtained had not other bees been brought into the locality to divide the spoils. But there is no law against such a procedure, the only protection that the original squatter has being an unwritten moral law that is observed among the better class of bee-keepers, to the effect that no bee-keeper should locate an apiary so close to another as to rob him of a certain amount of nectar in the field which is his by priority of location. In a good many localities in Colorado, we are sorry to say that this unwritten moral law is only loosely observed. Locations that once afforded an average of 100 or 150 pounds per colony now afford, owing to this species of overstocking, only about 50 or 75 pounds.

For the other side, on this question of priority of right it may be said that the first-comer bee-keeper has in no sense leased, bought, or borrowed the land growing the plants from which the nectar is secreted; that any and every one has a right to the product from the flowers. Legally the second comer has just as much right to the field as his neighbor.

We will not attempt to define moral distinctions which may be involved in this question, any more than to state that, if a bee-keeper has by luck, careful observation, or at great expense, discovered a locality that yields large amounts of honey, he ought to be left in the peaceful enjoyment and free possession of his discovery, to the extent that no one else should locate an apiary nearer than a mile and a half from any of his apiaries; and right here it seems to us the principle of the golden rule ought to be used to settle such little problems; for it is practically certain that bee-keeper No. 2, who comes into an already occupied field to divide the profits, would not regard with very much favor such action on the part of another if he were in the position of the one having prior rights.

P.

PALMETTO (*Sabal chamerops*) is frequently an excellent yielder of good honey, but only on the peninsula of Florida. There are numbers of these trees in the Carolinas and Georgia, but not in sufficient numbers to be valuable to the bee-keeper. There are two palmettos in Florida which yield honey —viz., the creeping palmetto (*Sabal Adansonii*) and the saw palmetto (*Sabal serenoa*), also a creeper. The leaves of the latter are very sharp, and serious impediments to walking through the woods in some parts of Florida, hence the popular name. In some seasons a very heavy honey-yield is obtained from the Florida palmetto, of a quality considered excellent by connoisseurs.

The palmetto grows to a height of 70 feet or more in Southern Florida, where it succeeds best, and where, too, the landscape is greatly beautified by many specimens of it. It generally blooms in June, just before the rainy season, sending out great racemes of creamy-white flowers that form a mass four to seven feet long and two feet wide.

The honey can scarcely be distinguished from that collected from black mangrove; and it frequently happens that both flower simultaneously, and the bees, therefore, mix the nectar.

PARTHENOGENESIS. In the great majority of cases the sex cells disintegrate unless they unite with the products of the opposite sex of the same species; but in some cases of the animal kingdom cells are given off from the ovary, which, without fertilization, are able to undergo development. That these cells are true eggs is evident from their origin, appearance, behavior, and fate, while the only difference between these eggs and eggs requiring fertilization is that the former are able to divide and grow without receiving the stimulus given by the male sex cell. To this phenomenon the name " parthenogenesis " is applied.

The word parthenogenesis (virgin development) was first used in this sense by Professor v. Siebold in his classic paper, "Parthenogenesis in Lepidoptera and Bees," in 1856.

However, earlier writers described the phenomenon under various other names.

In 1745 Charles Bonnet described the parthenogenetic development of plant-lice; and Prof. Oscar Hertwig, the great German embryologist, designated this work as marking one of the milestones in the history of the science of development.

Just one hundred years later the Rev. Johannes Dzierzon, of Carlsmarkt, Germany, put forth the theory that the drone or male bee is produced from an egg which is not fertilized. This work, published in the *Eichstadt Bienenzeitung*, may well be looked on as the starting-point of the theory of parthenogenesis, since it began a very important discussion, and marks the origin of a host of works along similar lines. Dzierzon based his views on the following facts observed by him and since confirmed by many others: 1. An unmated queen occasionally lays eggs, but these produce only drones.

2. Workers, under certain peculiar circumstances, lay eggs, but these develop only into drones. Worker bees have never been known to mate.

3. Old queens may exhaust their supply of spermatozoa received in mating, and thereafter produce only drones. As the supply diminishes they lay an ever increasing percentage of drone eggs.

While this theory is based on the work of Dzierzon, it must not be forgotten that its establishment is due in no small part to the researches of Professors Leuckart and von Siebold, of Germany.

The facts brought out in an examination of this work have an important bearing on the practical work of the apiary, and it is necessary for the queen-breeder, at least, to know the application. If, for example, a Cyprian queen is mated to an Italian drone, the resulting workers are a cross between the two races, or Cyprio-Italians. Any queens reared from this colony are also Cyprio-Italians; but the drones of this cross-mated queen are pure Cyprians, the Italian drone in the cross having no influence on the male offspring of the Cyprian mother. If, therefore, but one purely mated queen is obtained, her daughters produce pure drones, regardless of mismating, and the race may be established in an apiary.

The conclusion frequently drawn from this theory is that the queen can voluntarily control the sex of an egg by withholding or allowing its fertilization. It is sometimes further held that all eggs in the ovary are male, and the sex changed by fertilization. These conclusions are not based on observation, and proof is entirely lacking. In a statement of the theory, therefore, it is necessary to stick to known facts.

The Dzierzon theory has been combated by many different scientists, most recently by Dickel, a German bee-keeper with scientific aspirations. While the theory has been somewhat modified by recent work, it remains the prevalent view to-day, and Dickel generally receives the condemnation so richly deserved.

Parthenogenesis occurs in many other orders of both plants and animals, and a comparison of the various results is most interesting. Merely to cite some cases for comparison: In the bee, only males are produced parthenogenetically; in certain lepidoptera, only females are so produced; while in plant-lice and certain small crustacea, both males and females are produced from unfertilized eggs. Ants were formerly supposed to have a parthenogenetic development identical with that seen in the honey-bee; but more recent work makes this doubtful as a general statement. The silkworm is occasionally parthenogenetic.

PEDDLING HONEY. See HONEY-PEDDLING; also EXTRACTED HONEY.

PEPPER-TREE (*Schinus molle*). From Peru. This is really not a pepper-tree at all; its flowers and the honey have a peppery flavor, and the seeds resemble pepper. It is a magnificent shade-tree, and in California has been very largely planted. The honey is thick and dark, but it serves a very useful purpose in helping the bees to tide over bad times without feeding. It is under a ban now, as it is supposed to harbor injurious insects; but it seems probable these pests would still exist even if all pepper-trees were destroyed.

PERFORATED ZINC. See DRONES.

PHACELIA (*P. tanacetifolia*) has been boomed as a honey and forage plant in Europe, introduced there from California. Some, however, deny its value as a forage-plant, and not till 1904 did any Californian even mention it as such. There is no question, however, that it is a honey-plant of the first rank, having a blue flower much resembling heliotrope, the beauty of

which makes it worthy of a place in the flower-garden, where the bees may be found on it in great numbers.

PICKLED BROOD. See DISEASES OF BEES.

POISONED BROOD. See FRUIT-BLOSSOMS.

POISONOUS HONEY. There are cases on record, apparently authenticated, which seem to show that honey gathered from flowers of plants that are in themselves poisonous is also poisonous either to human beings or to the bees themselves, or both. Xenophon tells how, in the memorable march of the ten thousand Greek soldiers to the sea, some of them were taken seriously ill after eating poisonous honey. The facts are so carefully and minutely recorded as to leave no doubt of the honey-poisoning.

The wild honey in one or two of the Southern States, in a very few isolated localities, is reported to produce sickness, and in some instances this is so sudden and violent that it has given occasion for alarm. In certain regions of Virginia, especially near Halifax Court-house, there is grown in the mountains, quite extensively, mountain laurel. The bees are very fond of it; and while it does not seem to affect them particularly, it is dangerous to human beings, or at least so reported. The plant itself is an extremely distressing narcotic, varying in effects according to the quantity taken into the stomach. Dr. Grammer, of Halifax Court-house, reports that, during the late civil war, himself and quite a number of comrades were poisoned by eating honey from this plant. There was, he says, a queer sensation of tingling all over, indistinct vision, with an empty, dizzy feeling about the head, and a horrible nausea that could not be relieved by vomiting. This lasted for an hour or so, while the effects did not wear off for several days.

Another honey-plant yielding honey said to be poisonous is the yellow jasmine found in certain localities of Georgia, especially in the vicinity of Augusta. The roots, leaves, and flowers are all highly poisonous; and Dr. J. P. H. Brown, a bee-keeper, says the honey from it is also of like character, as he knows of several persons who came very near losing their lives by eating it. In his opinion bees do not work on it from choice; for when other bloom is yielding honey at the same time, the jasmine flowers are seldom visited. Notwithstanding these reported cases,

Prof. A. J. Cook, of Pomona College, Claremont, Cal., very much doubts whether the honey from any plant is poisonous. Some years ago instances were related of bee-keepers who had not only eaten of the honey from poisonous plants but ate of it quite

YELLOW JASMINE (*Jasimum odoratissimum*).

freely without any ill effects. But the question might arise as to whether they actually ate any honey from the plants in question, *or from some harmless plants* that were in bloom at the same time. In a matter involving severe sickness or possible loss of life it would seem to be policy to err on the safe side—that is, to let the honey from mountain laurel, yellow jasmine, and other poisonous plants, entirely alone. If it does not kill the bees, let them have it for brood-rearing, but make no other use of it.

POLLEN. Doubtless you have all heard bees humming about hollyhock blossoms, and perhaps most of you have passed on thinking that it was nothing strange, for bees are always humming about flowers. Suppose we stop just a minute, and look into the matter a little. The bee, although on the wing, is almost motionless as it hovers about the dust in the center of the flower, and, by careful watching, we may see that its tongue is extended to a considerable length. This tongue looks much like a delicate pencil-brush as it sweeps about among the grains of pollen; and as the

pollen adheres to it and is from time to time put away somehow, we are led to infer that there must be something adhesive on it. We believe the bee, when it starts out to gather pollen, carries some honey if it finds any in the blossom. Well, we will suppose it has moistened its long, flexible, brush-like tongue with honey, has spread it out and brushed it among the pollen-grains and then —right here we shall have to give you some pictures to explain what happens next.

The illustrations shown on the next page, taken from Cheshire's Bees and Bee-keeping, show the leg of the bee.

In a general way it will be noted that the legs are covered with rough hairs, fringes of coarser hairs, and short spines or combs. These are located on the different parts of the legs of the bees, and each set is designed for a different purpose; *ti*. at A, in the reproduction from Chesh-

ire, shows a pollen basket on one of the hind legs. Notice that the joint at this point is hollow and fringed on either side with coarse hairs or spurs. The pollen, as fast as it is gathered and made up into little pellets, is deposited one at a time, forming one large loaf or pellet in the pollen-basket —*ti* at A, but reference to this will be made a little later. Just below the pollen-basket at *wp*, in B, is shown a sort of jaw, or pincers. This is said to be used to gather the thin plates of wax that are secreted on

End of Tongue of Worker, Magnified 70 Times.

the under side of the body of the bee, and that the pincers form them so that they can be handled by the fore legs and deposited in the comb.

Below these jaws, or pincers, at B, will be found a series of combs, or spines, on the inner side of the legs. On the same joints of the other legs these seem to be absent, the fore legs to the middle ones, and from the latter to the pollen-pockets on the rear legs. By watching closely one can see the middle legs patting the pollen on the back ones, making quite a loaf of bee-bread for each leg.

It is probable, also, that the tongue is an important organ for gathering pollen-grains

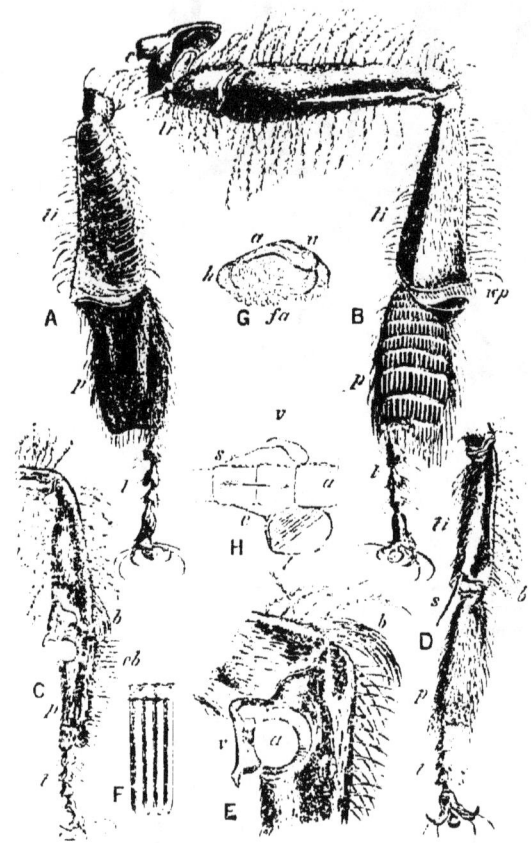

THE LEGS OF A BEE. FROM CHESHIRE.

and in their place long stiff hairs appear more to serve the purpose of a brush. When the bee goes into a flower, especially one with a narrow opening, the hair on the thorax and on the head, as well as on the legs, seems to become coated with pollen. This is removed by the brushes and combs on the legs of the bees. In some manner the combings of pollen dust are gathered into very small pellets which are then transferred from as well as nectar, for it seems to be fringed with fine hair on which pollen dust might readily lodge. Just how the bee cleans its tongue it is difficult to see; but the brushes on the fore legs are evidently designed for the purpose of rolling off these grains which possibly contain a little honey or nectar. In any event, they are transferred to the middle legs from the fore legs, and from the middle legs to the pollen-basket in a way that leaves

BEES WITH MASSES OF POLLEN ON THEIR LEGS.
Note the bee in the lower right-hand corner, with two masses of pollen almost as large as its body.

sleight-of-hand clear in the shade unless one watches the whole operation with a powerful glass. This transfer seems to go on in the the blossom and even after the bee is on the wing. Dust the bee all over with flour and it immediately begins the process of "brushing its hair." It will rub the palms of its legs and then begin the work of combing itself, reaching with its middle and fore legs over brushed and groomed, until every particle of pollen has been removed.

If one desires to witness some of these comical sleight-of-hand performances, for, indeed, they are little short of real legerdemain, he needs to dust only a few bees with common flour and then note what happens.

Reference was made to the fact that the bee cleans its antennæ with its fore legs. If

MASSES OF POLLEN TAKEN FROM LEGS OF BEES.
These were photographed with a thimble to show the relative size.

its back and cleaning its antennæ with its fore legs. All these maneuvers may take place while it rests on some object or while on the wing, but the bee is unable to reach over its entire body, especially the top of the head. On entering the hive it is cleaned by other bees, when after a little it will be these delicate organs of sense and hearing be in any way impeded by a smearing of pollen the bee is unable to communicate with its fellows or perform satisfactorily the functions of the hive. See SCENT OF BEES. By referring to the engraving, page 328 at E, there will be found a notch at a. Just over

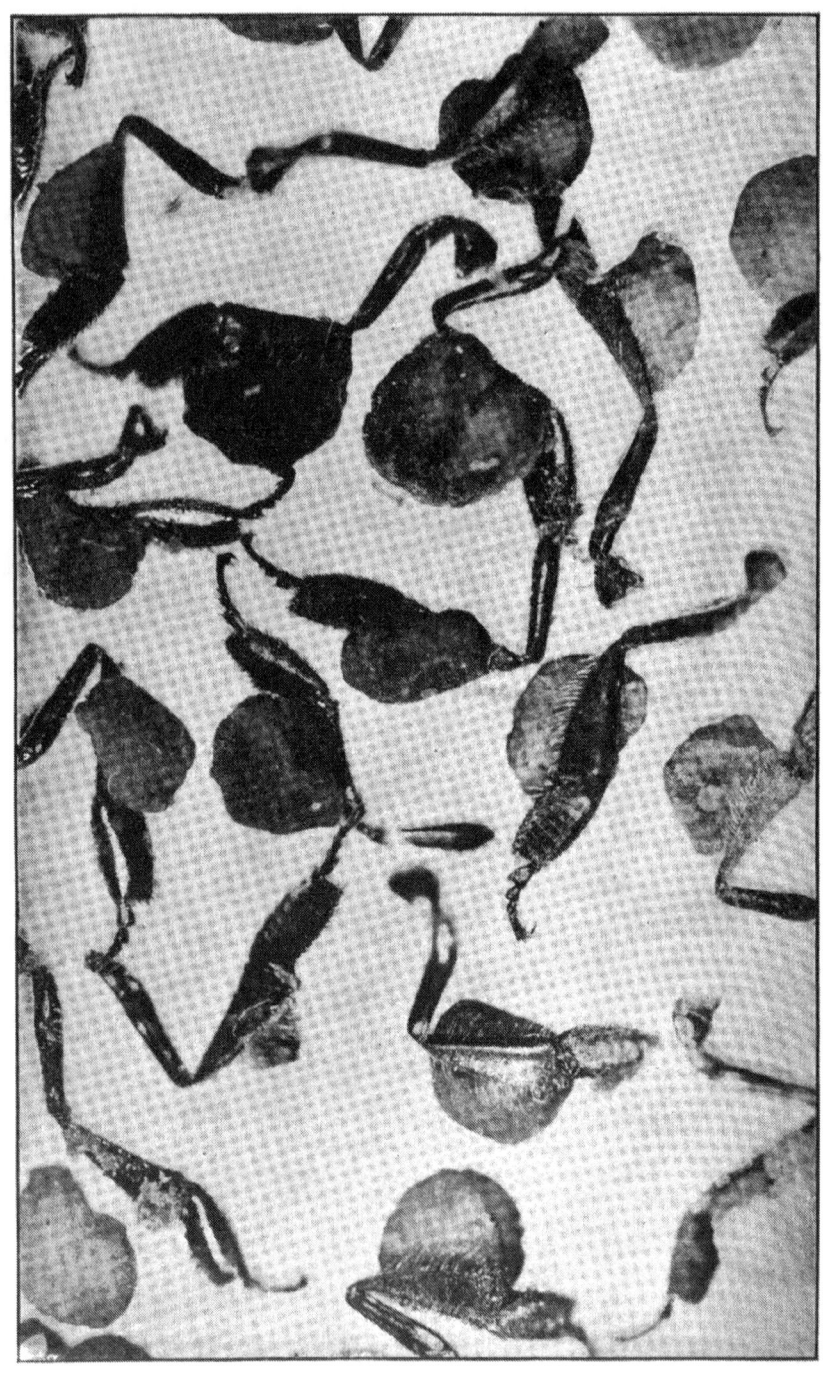

POLLEN MASSES ON LEGS OF BEES.—*Photo by E. F. Bigelow.*
Several show side hairs (like stakes on a hay-wagon), to hold the load.

this notch is a spur, or cap, *v*. The same thing on a smaller scale can be seen at C. This opening is fringed on the inside with a row of hairs, an enlarged view showing at F. It will be noted that this cleaner is located, we might say, in the "elbow" of the fore legs, and within easy reach of the antennæ. If flour is dusted upon these organs the bee will immediately slip this notch over the antennæ, push *v* over to place, cleaning every portion of the antennæ at two or three sweeps. Some have thought that the same device is used for cleaning the tongue in a similar manner, but this is hardly probable. The tongue, unless at the extreme end, is too large to go in this opening. If it could

A DIAGRAM of a SIMPLE HERMAPHRODITE FLOWER.

—After Fletcher.

be used for cleaning the tongue the delicate cleaner would become smeared with honey, and thus what would appear to be its primary function as an antennæ-cleaner would be destroyed.

When a bee gets into the hive (if a young bee), it has to go through with a series of rejoicings—see BEES; but if a regular laborer, it proceeds at once, or at least as soon as it has had a breathing-spell (for carrying large loads of pollen is like carrying a hod of brick to the top of a three-story brick building), to deposit the pollen in the cells. This is done very quickly by crossing its pollen-legs while they are thrust to the bottom of the cell, and then kicking the loads off, much like the way in which our blue-eyed baby kicks off her shoes when she takes a notion to go barefooted. After unloading, it

starts out again without paying any further attention to the matter.

After the pollen is dropped in the cells, it will fall out if the comb is turned over; and when the maples are first out in the spring, we have heard and seen pollen rattle out like shot, in turning the combs horizontally to look at the queen. Very soon after pollen is thus deposited, nursing-bees come and mash it down into a hard cake. We have not been able to discover how.

THE AGENCY OF BEES IN FERTILIZING PLANTS BY MINGLING THE POLLEN.

Before we consider the wonderful little schemes of nature to bring about the work of cross-fertilization, it will be necessary at this point to give a few of the common terms employed in botany to designate the different parts of the flower. In the accompanying illustration we have a case of what is known as the hermaphrodite flower, that is to say, a perfect flower that is capable of self-fertilization. In most of the specimens that we show, we shall present deviations from the perfect flower. In most flowers we have the male and female organs, the latter represented by what is known as the pistil at the top of which is a receptive surface called the stigma. Sometimes there is a tube connecting the stigma with the ovary. This is called the style. The male organs are designated by the name of anthers. These contain little granules of powder known as pollen. Around the male and female organs are what is known as the corolla consisting of leaves of various colors, and outside of these is the calyx, usually green. The stem that supports the anther is called the filament. The nectaries are usually located at the base of the pistil or the bottom of the flower as at B. The main portion of the pistil called the ovary is what constitutes the embryo fruit. In order that this may develop, the pollen from A must be conveyed in some manner to the surface of the stigma as at C. The fertilizing fluid passes downward, causing the fruit to develop. It would be well to bear in mind these botanical terms in the description which follows in order to understand how beautiful and perfect is the design of nature in bringing about cross-pollination.

Before we proceed to the general subject under this head, something should be said regarding the evident intent of nature to bring about crossing between the species both in the animal and the vegetable kingdom. For instance, among animals inbreeding has a strong tendency to weaken off-spring. The same principle holds true to a certain extent among plants. "A study of the devices provided by nature to in-sure cross-fertilization," says Dr. Fletcher, "forms one of the most charming branches of the whole study of botany." The great naturalist Charles Darwin is recorded as

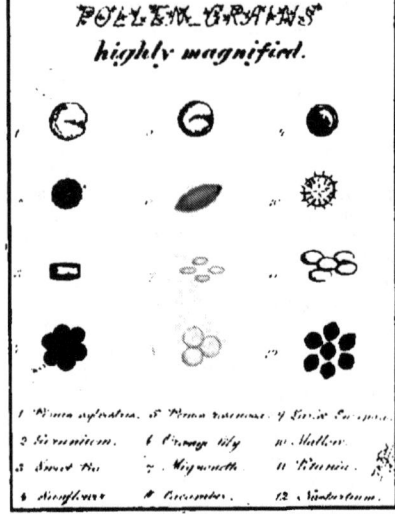

—After Fletcher.

saying that the general principle can be seen running through all branches of the animal and the vegetable kingdom. Although some plants, he says, can be and are fertilized by their own pollen, it is always of greater ben-efit to their descendants if the flowers be fer-tilized by pollen from other flowers of the same kind growing upon other plants. Dar-win summed up his observations with the statement that "Nature abhors perpetual self-fertilization." Since then, says Dr. Fletcher, "endless observations have con-firmed the accuracy of Darwin's law, and it has been found that in the vast majority of plants special appliances exist which will secure a more or less frequent inter-cross." And then he goes on to say that these ap-pliances completely exclude the possibility of self-fecundation.

Coming now to the special agencies for the fertilization of plants, we may say in a gen-eral way that there are two, the animate and the inanimate. Among the first mentioned may be included wind, rain, and the force of gravity. There can be no question but that

pollen from some plants is blown not only from flower to flower, but, in some cases, clear out to sea. Cases are on record where pollen from certain species of pines has been found hundreds and hundreds of miles floating in the air and lodging in the rig-ging of ships. Rain doubtless has a large influence, because it spatters the fertilizing element from one flower to another. Grav-ity must necessarily convey the pollen lo-cated on the tops of the trees or plants to the blossoms situated further down, whether on the same or other plant of the same species.

Among the animate agencies for the dis-tribution of pollen, insects (and especially bees) are by far the most important. To a very limited extent animals and birds may assist. While insects other than bees un-doubtedly perform a very valuable service, the honey-bee, from the very fact that it is out earlier in the spring than all other in-sects, must necessarily be regarded as by far

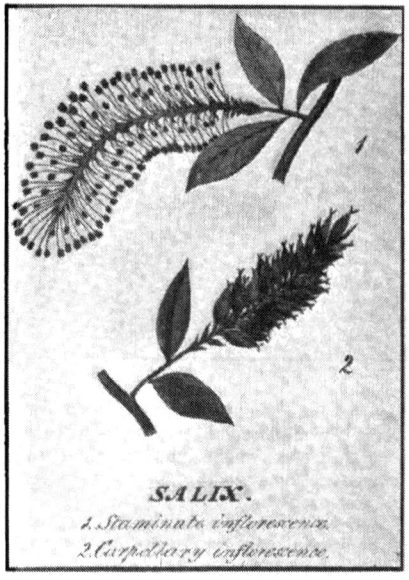

SALIX.
1. Staminate inflorescence.
2. Carpellary inflorescence.

—After Fletcher.

the most important means of bringing about cross-pollination among our fruit-trees; and even when other insects are in the air, it out-numbers any other species, and possibly, in some cases, all other species combined, a thousand to one. Its general shape and size, the special construction of its tongue and its legs, all together make it especially adapt-able for receiving and carrying pollen.

Cross-fertilization among some plants is brought about by the male and female organs, the stamens and pistils being located in different flowers, sometimes on the same plant or tree, and again on separate trees. In the willows, for example, the male catkins, that is, the portion of the flower bearing the stamens, appear on one tree while the pistils appear on another. This technically is called staminate and pistillate inflorescence. As the willows are a source of honey as well as pollen, and as they come to bloom very early in the season, it is apparent that bees must play a large part in their cross-pollination. Common cases of male and female flowers on the same plant are found in the butternut, hickory, birches, oaks, and hazels. In some instances the male portion of the flower comes to maturity before the female and *vice versa*. In others there seems to be an effort on the part of nature, through a special form and arrangement of the parts of the flower, to prevent self-fertilization. In this case it appears that the bee, or some insect, must carry the pollen from one plant to the other.

Common corn is an illustration of a class of plants that bear both kinds of blossoms on the same plant. The blossom that bears the seed is low down, and is

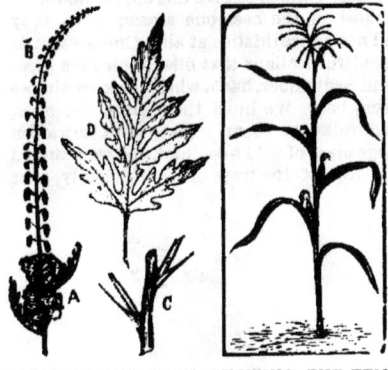

RAGWEED AND CORN, SHOWING THE TWO KINDS OF BLOSSOMS ON ONE STALK.

what we commonly term the silk of the ear. The one that bears the pollen is at the very summit of the stalk, and the pollen, when ripe, is shaken off and falls on the silk below; or, what is still better, it is wafted by the wind to the silk of the neighboring stalks, thus preventing in-and-in breeding, in a manner strikingly analogous to the way in which the drones fly out in the air, that the chances may be greatly in favor of their

meeting queens other than those from their own hives. You may object, that the silk from the ear of corn is not properly a flower, so we will give you a more striking instance.

The common ragweed, *Ambrosia artemisiœfolia*, also sometimes called bitterweed, or hogweed, bears two distinct and entirely unlike flowers. On the ends of the tall racemes, as at B, the pollen-bearing blossoms are seen very conspicuously; and many of you who are familiar with the weed, perhaps never imagined that it had any other blossom at all. If so, will you please go outdoors and take a look at them again? Right close to the main stem, where the branches all start out, you will find a very pretty little flower; however it possesses no color except green, and it is here where all the seeds are borne, as you will see on some of the branches where they are matured. Now, if you will get up early in the morning you will find that these plants, when shaken, give off a little cloud of fine green dust, and this is the pollen of the plant of which we have been speaking. As these plants are in no way dependent on bees for the fertilization of their blossoms, they contain no honey, or at least we never were able to detect any; although we have, during two seasons, seen the bees quite busily engaged gathering the pollen. It is said that corn sometimes bears honey as well as pollen, although we have never been able to get proof of it. These two plants, as we have before remarked, seem to insure crossing the seed with other plants of the same variety, by bearing the pollen-bearing flowers aloft, on slender stalks; also by furnishing a great preponderance in numbers of these blossoms, for precisely the same reason that a thousand or more drones are reared to one queen. A stalk that succeeds in pushing itself above the others, and bearing a profusion of pollen-flowers, will probably be the father, so to speak, of a multitude of the rising generation; and this process, repeated for generations, would develop just the tendency of corn and ragweed, to shoot up tall spires, clothed with an exuberance of the pollen-bearing blossoms. As the plants that give the greatest distance on the stalk between the lower (or seed) blossoms, and the upper ones, are most likely to shed the pollen on neighboring plants, this, too, fosters the tendency mentioned.

But what shall the great multitude of plants do that have no tall spires with which to shake their pollen to the breezes? Here is where the bees come in and fulfill their allotted task in the work of animal and vegetable life. They would, it is true, visit many plants for the pollen alone ; but with by far the greater part of them the pollen is only a secondary consideration, or not sought for at all. In vieing with one another, or in the strife to perpetuate their species, what will the plant do to offer the greatest attraction to the bees to visit them, and carry the precious pollen to the neighboring blossoms, for the purpose we have mentioned? Suppose we wish to gather a group of school-children about us, what will be the surest and most effectual method of doing it? Coax them with candy, maple sugar, and the like, of course; and that is just what the plant does ; or it does still more, for it ransacks its storehouse, and, we dare say, sends its roots abroad through the soil, with untiring efforts, to steal a more delicious and enticing nectar, more wonderfully exquisite than even the purest and most transparent maple-sugar syrup ever distilled or " boiled bown" by the skill of man, for the sole purpose of coaxing the bees to come and dust themselves in their precious pollen, or to bring from some other blossom the pollen they have previously been dusted with. Now, this honey is precious, and it must tax the plant to its utmost to produce it. Nature, therefore, who is a most careful economist, not only deals it out in small doses, but she places it in the most cunning nooks and corners, that the bee may be obliged to twist itself into all possible shapes, around and among the stamens, until the pollen is most surely dusted all over it. Observe that the flower secretes no honey until the pollen is ripe and ready to do its work; that the honey slowly exudes into the nectaries, that the bees may be kept coming and licking it out every hour in the day ; and that the flow of honey ceases just as soon as the pollen is ripened and gone. A lady has suggested a beautiful experiment to determine the amount of honey yielded by the spider-flower, *Cleome*. She tied lace over the stalk, to keep away the bees that were constantly visiting it. The honey collected in quite a large drop. We could measure the amount in many other plants by a similar method. The little cups on the flower of the FIG-WORT we have seen full to the brim with honey, when found standing alone out in the woods. Truly:

Full many a flower is born to blush unseen,
And waste its sweetness on the desert air.

Did you ever notice the spot of fur, or down, on the back of the bee, just between

the wings? Well, bee-hunters sometimes put a small drop of white paint on this spot, that they may know a bee when it comes back. Several years ago bees were going into many of the hives, with a spot of white on this fur that looked, at first sight, almost like white paint. For several seasons

Honey-bee enlarged four times; bee louse on its back. See ENEMIES OF BEES.

in succession we hunted in vain to see where they got this white spot. At one time it seemed to come from working on thistles; but we were obliged to give this up, for we found it most on the bees one season when they did not notice thistles at all. One swarm of beautiful Italians that filled their hive nicely in September, had a white back on almost every bee. We lined them from the hive, and followed them. They went toward a large piece of wild woodland, and we scanned the tops of the trees in vain ; finally, over

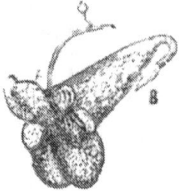

Flower of the Wild Touch-me-not, showing the manner in which the bee gets the pollen on its back.

between the hills, beside a brook, we found acres of the wild touch-me-not (*Impatiens*), the same plant that we have often played with in childhood, because the queer little seed-pods will snap all to pieces when ripe, if they are touched ever so carefully. The honey is secreted in the spur of the flower, shown at B.

The bee can reach this only by diving down into it almost out of sight; and when the coveted treasure is obtained it backs out with a ludicrous kicking and sprawling of its legs, and in so doing the down on its

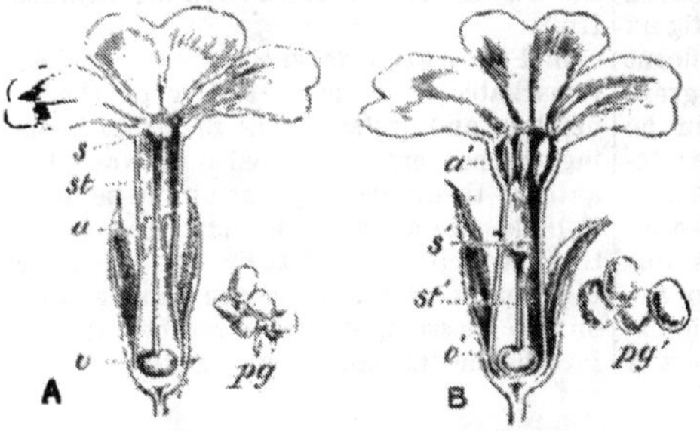

FIG. 3.—CROSS SECTIONS OF DIMORPHIC FLOWER (PRIMULA VULGARIS, COMMON PRIMROSE), Order *Primulaceæ.*

A, Long-styled Flower—*s*, Stigma; *st*, Style; *a*, Anther; *o*, Ovary; *pg.* Pollen Grains, more Magnified. B, Short-styled Form—*a'*, Anther; *s'*, Stigma; *st'*, Style; *o'*, Ovary, *pg'*, Pollen Grains, more Magnified.—*From Cheshire.*

back is ruffled up the wrong way. Now, this would be pretty certain to get the pollen dusted all over it; but nature, to make sure, has planted a little tuft that bears the pollen just on the upper side of the entrance to the flower, at A, and as the bee struggles to get out, white pollen is brushed all over its back most effectually, to be carried to the next flower, and so on.

But the wild touch-me-not is only one of hundreds of other cases that are even more remarkable. Mr. Cheshire in his magnificent work, "Bees and Bee-keeping," Vol. I., gives a number of very interesting examples. While he appears to have drawn from Charles Darwin and Prof. Asa Gray, his illustrations showing how Nature has sought to prevent self-pollination are so interesting and valuable, especially as they show the service performed by the bee, that we reproduce them here:

In Fig. 3 we have a cross-section of what is known as the common primrose (*Primula vulgaris*), that furnishes an example of one of the most remarkable cases of how Nature has schemed to bring about cross-fertilization. This is what is known as a dimorphic flower, that is to say, there are two forms of flowers on the same plant. At A the stigma of the female portion reaches up to the mouth of the flower tube. The anthers, or male portion, appear about half way down the flower tube as at *a*. At B we have just the reverse: the stigma stands about half way down the flower-tube while the anthers are clear at the top. The flower-tube itself is supposed to be about the depth of the reach of a bee's tongue. A bee comes to A, reaches down at the

FIG. 4.—EPILOBIUM ANGUSTIFOLIUM (ROSEBAY WILLOW HERB), Order *Onagraceæ.*

A, Young Flower—*s*, Stigma turned back; *a*, Anthers; *l*, Lobe, or Pod. B, Older Flower—*s*, Stigma, turned forward; *a*, Anthers; *l*, Lobe. C, Spike of Flowers. D, Section of Pollen Grain—*e*. Extine; *i*, Intine; *ti*, Thick Intine; *f*, Fovilla. E, Growing Point of Pollen Grain—*e*, *e*, Extine; *i*, *i*, Intine; *f*, Fovilla; *pt*, Pollen Tube.—*Cheshire.*

point *o* for its nectar. The anthers half way up dust the tongue at a point about half way up its length. After the bee has secured its coveted sweet, it passes to the next flower, B, where the upper portion of the tongue and mouth becomes dusted with the pollen from the anthers, and the pollen dust that was secured from the other flower A will just reach the stigma in the flower B. The pollen dust that was received from the flower B will just reach the stigma in the flower A. There is another significant and interesting fact, that the pollen granules of B are too large to be received in the stigma of B, but just right to go in the stigma of A. Thus we see how nature has cunningly devised a scheme of what is called dimorphic cross-fertilization. In other words, she has so planned it that the pollen of the same flower can not fertilize its own stigma, hence we see the necessity of some insect of brings to it from the anthers of A of the other blossom of the same plant. It will be apparent in this particular case, unless insects, particularly the bee, carry the pollen from A to B, there will be no fertilization of the plant, and the bloom will die without fruit.

In Fig. 5 we have another case no less remarkable of a near relative of rhododendron and azaleas. The filaments bearing the anthers are curved downward, the anthers themselves appearing to be held in little pockets of the flower. Apparently they have no power of their own to release themselves. But a bee comes along, alights on the blossom, and as it reaches around for the nectar jars these filaments loose,

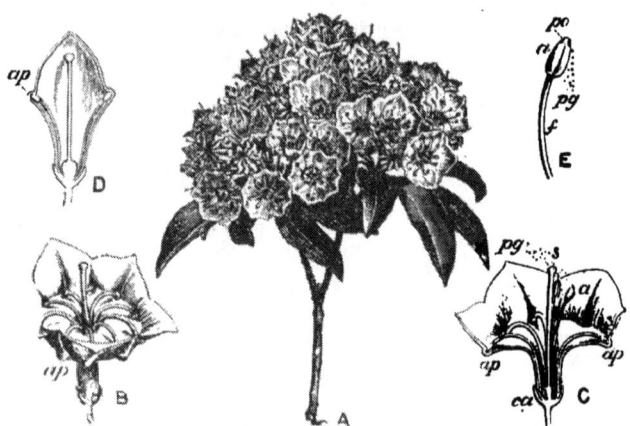

FIG. 5.—KALMIA LATIFOLIA, Order *Ericaceæ*.
A, Flowering Branch. B, Expanded Flower—*ap*, Anther Pocket. C, Section of Expanded Flower—*ap, ap*, Anther Pockets; *s*, Stigma; *a*, Anther (free): *pg*, Pollen Grains in Shower; *ca*, Calyx. D, Section of Flower Bud—*ap*, Anther Pocket. E, Stamens, more Enlarged—*a*, Anther; *po*, Pores; *pg*, Pollen Grains; *f*, Filament. —*After Cheshire.*

just about the right size, as the bee, of exactly the same tongue length that the bee has. Let us take another example.

In Fig. 4 we have a very pretty example of the fine honey-plant willow-herb; here the pollen of the anthers is sterile to the pistil or stigma of the same flower. At A, Fig. 4, we notice that the stigma, or the style, rather, as at *s*, is turned backward away from the anthers at *a*. At this stage the pollen at the anthers is ripe. A bee comes along, dusts itself over the pollen in the act of securing nectar, and then passes over to B of a flower of the same species. Here the pollen is gone from the anthers, but the pistil has straightened out and the stigma is ripe to receive the pollen that the bee when they immediately fly upward, dusting the bees with pollen. This pollen now on the bee may fertilize the stigma or pistil of B; but as the bee goes from flower to flower the pollen is mixed for it releases all the anthers, so that other insect visitation will continue on the process of cross-pollination. We have familiar cases of these anchored-down anthers in the rhododendrons, azaleas and some of the swamp laurels. They are all honey-plants, but the honey is said to be poisonous.

In Fig. 6 we have a familiar blossom of the pea and bean, or technically known as papilionaceous flowers. At C we notice embryo bean or pea pod. At *a* we see the anthers and *s* the stigma. This whole thing is covered by a sort of wings. The bee comes along, pries them apart, and reaches for the nectar as shown in cross-sectional drawing of B. The anthers and the stigma both touch the bee on the under side of the waist where there is a good deal of hair. The result is that powder is dusted on the waist of the bee; and as it goes from one flower to another, it mingles the pollen and dusts it over the stigma. The general shape of the flower is such that the wind could hardly accom-

lack of fruit during some particular season is ascribed to the fact that frosts kill the blossoms, when, as a matter of fact, the weather has been such that the honey-bees were unable to get out, and thus carry on the work of cross-fertilization.

In Fig. 8, we have the case of an apple that was imperfectly fertilized. There is perfect seed and perfect fruit formation except on the side that has an indention. The statement has been made by some prominent growers of apples that it is such fruit as this that rarely hangs long enough to ripen. The first severe storm that comes along causes it to drop prematurely. One fruit-grower told us there were thousands and thousands of bushels of apples every year that are nothing more nor less than windfalls because of

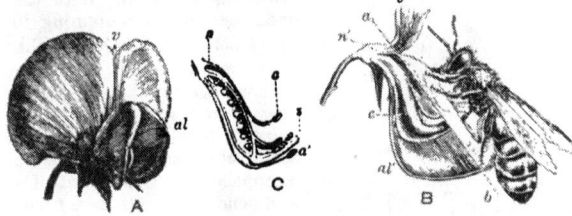

FIG. 6.—PAPILIONACEOUS BLOSSOMS, AND THEIR METHOD OF FERTILIZATION. A, Expanded Pea Blossom, Order *Leguminosæ*—*v*, Vexilium; *al*, Alæ, with Carina between. B, Partial Section of Flower of Vetch being Fertilized by Cyprian Bee (Magnified Twice), Right Ala removed below line *a*, *b*—*v'*, Vexilium; *n'*, Nectar Gland; *al'*, Ala; *c*, Carina containing the Pistil, the Stigma of which is striking the bee's breast. C, Section of Pistil, showing Ovules (Peas) in Ovary—*n*, Nectary; *a*, *a*, Anthers; *s*, Stigma.—*Cheshire*.

plish much in the way of cross-fertilization, and apparently the bee has to exert some strength in forcing apart the wings of the corolla in order to get its coveted nectar.

In Fig. 7 we have the familiar raspberry blossom. This is a case of where there is very little color but considerable pollen and nectar to attract the bees. The anthers and pistils separated from each other appear in large numbers on each blossom. The bee alights on the head and reaches down for the nectar. As it does so, it brushes against the large number of anthers and pistils. In doing so it mingles the pollen, fertilizing the flower with its own pollen and with the pollen from other plants.

In Fig. 8 we have the familiar example of the apple blossom. Note there are five stigmas and and ten anthers. In many varieties of the apple, pear, and plum, the flowers are sterile to their own pollen; but, as Fletcher points out, they can be fecundated readily with pollen from flowers growing on another tree of the same species. We therefore see how very important it is to have insects, especially bees, to carry on this most important work of cross-pollination, without which there will be imperfect or no fruit at all. Many and many a time a

imperfect fertilization. This same fruit-grower went on to say that if the bees could get in their work properly, and the trees were sprayed before and after blossoming, the number of windfalls would be very considerably reduced.

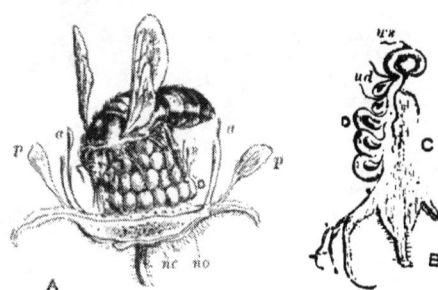

FIG. 7.—RASPBERRY (RUBUS IDAEUS, Order, *Rosaceæ*) BEING FERTILIZED, AND SECTION OF SAME. A, Flower (Magnified Twice)—*p*, *p*, Petals; *a*, *a*, Anthers; *s*, Stigma; *no*, Nectary Openings; *nc*, Nectar Cells; D, Drupels. B, Section through Core, or Torus (C) and Drupels (D)—*ud*, Unfertilized Drupel; *ws*, withered Stigma; *wa*, withered Anther.—*From Cheshire*.

In connection with this matter, the reader will be interested in referring to the subject of FRUIT-BLOSSOMS, elsewhere in this work, where limbs of trees and whole trees have been covered with netting while they were in bloom. The fact that almost no fruit develops under these nets shows that fertilization brought about by the agency of the wind is insignificent as compared with that accomplished by insects, and that, of course, means the bees, for almost no other insects are flying in the early spring when fruit trees come into bloom.

In Fig. 9 we have a remarkable example of the flower of the salvias, among which we

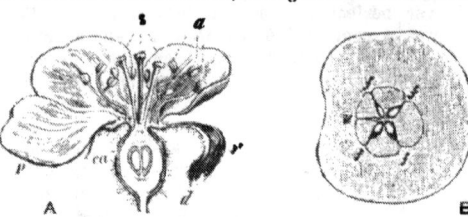

FIG. 8.—APPLE (PYRUS MALUS, Order *Rosaceæ*) BLOSSOM, AND SECTION OF FRUIT.

A, Blossom (Natural Size)—*s*, Stigmas: *a*, Anthers; *p*, Petal; *ca*, Calyx: *s'*, Sepal; *d*, Dissepiment. B, Section through partly developed Fruit—*f*, *f*, Fertilized Carpels; *u*, Unfertilized ditto. - *From Cheshire.*

may mention the celebrated white mountain sage of California Notice how Nature has made a convenient doorstep on which the bee may alight. But the more remarkable part of it all is, how the filament for the anthers is jointed. Turn to C, and it will be observed there is a spur or projection; namely, *ac*. The bee steps on the doorstep at *l*. Its head bunts against the projection, *ac*, causing the hinge-like movement to bend the anther, *a*, down upon its back, dusting it all over with pollen. The act can be seen a little more perfectly at D. Notice how the jointed anther is painting the back of the bee all over with pollen dust. In this particular flower, as at D, the stigma, for the time being, is sterile to the pollen of that flower, but the bee goes over to another specimen of the same species, as at B. It alights upon the doorstep, and, with its back all covered with dust, the stigma projecting out from its little canopy above brushes over the back of the bee, picking up the pollen, thus securing the fertilizing element from some other flower of the same species. When we remember that large quantities of beautiful honey are secured from what is known as the white mountain

sage, of California, we can realize the importance of this particular plant to the bee-keeper. Without this cross-fertilization the plant would undoubtedly "run out" as we say.

In Fig. 10 we have a still more remarkable case, as shown in the orchid. This flower is a little different in that the anther-sac has a sticky substance on the end, as shown at *r* in A. This pod adheres to the bee's forehead as shown at E and G. With this queer appendage containing its sac of pollen, the bee visits other blossoms, and, as seen at B, butts its head against the stigma and dusts it over with pollen. Chas. Darwin points out that this beautiful experiment can be accomplished with the point of a lead-pencil, but as it is not presumed that any foreign object should come in contact with the blossom except the insects, we can see how insect cross-fertilization is accomplished in this most remarkable manner.

Throughout the animal and vegetable kingdoms there seems to be a constant struggle for the perpetuation of their species, which is secured only by ripening perfect

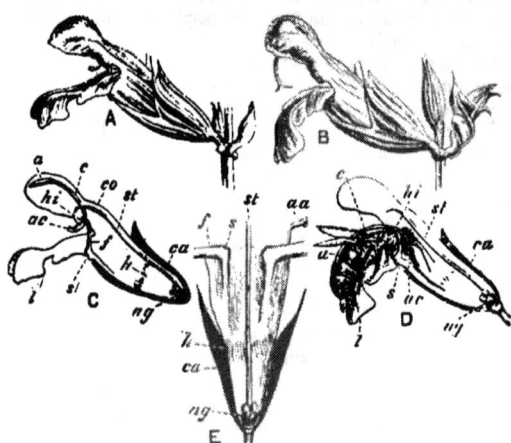

FIG. 9.—BLOSSOM OF SALVIA OFFICINALIS, Order *Labiatæ.* (Natural Size).

A, Young Flower, showing aborted Anther Cell. B, Older Flower, showing Stigma. C, Section of Young Flower; *a*. Anther Cell: *ac*, Aborted Cell; *c*, Connective; *f*, Filament; *ht*, hinge of Filament; *co*, Corolla; *ca*, Calyx; *st*, Style; *s*, Stiff Attachment of Filament; *l*, Labium; *h*, Interior Hairs; *ng*, Nectar Gland D, Section of Young Flower with Bee entering; Lettering as before. E, Section of Base of Flower flattened out, Lower Part shown—*st*, style; *s* and *f*. Stiff Attachment of Filament of Pollen-bearing Anther: *aa*, Aborted Anther; *h*, Interior Hairs; *ca*, calyx; *ng*, Nectar Gland.—*From Cheshire.*

seeds. Notice how the weeds in our garden will struggle and fight, as it were, to get a foot-hold until they can get a crop of seeds ripened, and then notice the numerous ways they adopt to scatter this seed as widely as possible. If the plants were animated beings, we might almost call it tricks and sharp practice; some of the seeds have wings, and fly like grasshoppers; others have hooks, and catch on our clothing, and on the fur of different animals, in the hope of being carried to some spot where they may have a more favorable place to germinate. Fruits and berries (when the

cased in a horny shell that is proof against the digestive organs of the bird, and these seeds and stones are, therefore, voided frequently, if not invariably, while on the wing, in just the condition to take root in the soil wherever they may be cast. Bear this in mind while we go back a little to the bees and flowers.

We have suggested that the honey is placed in flowers to attract the bees. After a bee has found honey in one flower it will be very likely to examine others of a similar kind or appearance. If the flowers were all green, like the leaves of the plant, the insects would have much more trouble in hunting them up than they now do, because contrasting colors, such as the white and red of the clovers, make them conspicuous. If you look back to what we said about corn and ragweed you will see that the flowers of both are a plain green, for they have no need of bees to insure fertilization.

It is easily proven that bees have a sort of telescopic vision that enables them to perceive objects at long distances. When a bee starts out in the morning it circles up aloft, then takes a view, and starts out for business. If one field of clover should be more conspicuous than the rest, it would probably give it the preference—at least, so far as to make an examination. If it has been at work on a profitable field the day before, it will, doubtless, strike for it again without any preamble. That bees look for honey, and hunt it out, we have proven to our full satisfaction; and we are well convinced that what is often called instinct, and allowed to drop there, is only profiting by experience and an excellent memory of past events, as human beings do. We say that bees instinctively go to the flowers for honey. We have watched them in the spring when the blossoms first open, and many a bee, very likely a young one that has never before seen a blossom, will examine the

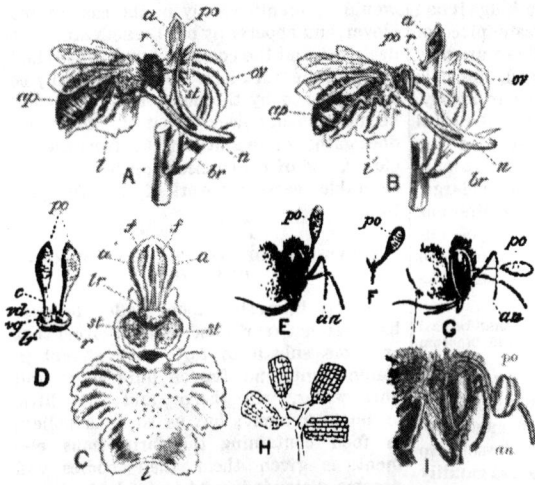

FIG. 10.—ORCHID (Order *Orchidaceæ*) BLOSSOMS AND DETAILS.

A, Flower of *Orchis Morio*, Sepals, two Petals, and side of Spur removed, with *Apis Mellifica* (*ap*), Hive Bee, sucking Nectar—*a*, Anther; *po*, Pollinium or Pollen Mass; *r*, Ro-tellum; *st*, Stigma (side view); *l*, Labellum; *ov*, Ovary; *n*, Nectary; *br*, Bract. B, Bee fertilizing *Orchis Morio*—*a*, Anther with Pollinium removed; *po*, Pollinium attached to Bee's Head and applied to Stigma; other Letterings as before. C, Front View of *Orchis Morio*, magnified three times, Sepals and two Petals Removed—*tr*, Lip of Rostellum; *f, f*, Fissures in Front of Anther Cells (*a', a'*); other Letterings as before. D, Pollen Masses, etc.—*po*, Pollinia; *c*, Caudicle; *vd*, Viscid Disc; *vg*, Viscid Globe; *tr*, Lip of (*r*) Rostellum; E, Head of Bee, carrying (*po*) Pollinium—*an*, Antennæ. F, Position of (*po*) Pollinia (thirty seconds later), partially depressed. C, Head of Bee—*an*, Antennæ; *po*, Pollinia (sixty seconds later) fully depressed. H, Pollen Granules (much magnified), held in packets by thin elastic threads. I, Head of Bee, carrying (*po*) Pollinia of one of the *Vandeæ*—*an*, Antennæ. —*From Cheshire.*

seeds are fully ripened), instead of clothing themselves in the sober green of the foliage surrounding them, affect scarlet red and other bright colors, and, sometimes, fancy stripes, just to induce the birds to take them in preference to the fruit of other trees. Why do they want their fruits to be eaten by the birds, if it is their purpose to secure a place for their seed? Well, if you examine you will find that the seed is en-

leaves, branches, and even rough wood, of the trunk of the tree, intently smelling and sniffing at every part, until it finds just where the coveted treasure is located. After it has dived deep into one blossom, and tasted the nectar, it knows pretty well where to look next time.

The touch-me-not has learned, by ages of experiment, to produce a bright orange flower, to secrete honey in the spur, to place the pollen-bearing stamens at the point where the bee must rub against them in getting the honey, to construct those wonderful seed-pods, which explode and scatter the seed far and wide, just that it may reproduce and multiply its species. We should judge it had succeeded pretty well in a waste piece of woodland near our home, for there are now acres of it as high as one's head, and it is quite a valuable acquisition to our apiary. As nearly as we can make out, the plant has much increased since the advent of the Italians, as might be expected. This is true of dandelions as well:* and the large, brilliant, showy blossoms that now line our roadsides and waste places, instead of unsightly weeds, should remind one how much an apiary of bees contributes to fulfill the words of sacred prophecy:

The wilderness and the solitary place shall be glad for them ; and the desert shall rejoice, and blossom as the rose.—*Isaiah* 35 : 1.

Now, we can not positively affirm that flowers were given their gaudy colors through bees selecting the brightest and most conspicuous, thereby inducing such blossoms to bear seed in preference to those less gaudily attired, neither do we know that cherries became red because the birds selected those that showed a disposition to that color, year after year, for many centuries; nor can we prove that the bright plumage of male birds came about in the course of time, simply because the females encouraged the attentions of and showed a preference for those most handsome. We can only suggest that the actions of birds, bees, flowers, and fruits, seem to point that way. You all know how quickly we can get fancy-colored flowers, yellow queen-bees, or birds of almost any shade or color, by careful selection for several generations. Have not the bees so colored the flowers, and birds the berries, etc., although they did it all unconsciously ?

It is significant that so many of the flowers have a form of construction and depth of flower tube that would indicate that it had adapted itself to the bee. While, of course,

* See DANDELION.

there are many exceptions, it appears that nature caters more to the bee than to any other insect. Just see how she makes a convenient doorstep or a flower tube of just the right size and shape, so that the bee can get the nectar which it has to offer. Cheshire has pointed out that so intimate and so perfect is the relation between the flowers and the honey-bees that there would be no advantage in breeding larger bees or of changing their general structure, because to do so would necessitate changing practically the whole of the floral kingdom. While it undoubtedly would be an advantage to breed bees with longer tongues, that advantage would be manifest only in the case of red clover, and apparently old Dame Nature has designed that the common bumble-bee shall perform the work here that can not fully be accomplished by the honey-bee. It should be mentioned, however, that the honey-bee does gather quite a little nectar from the red clover, and of course accomplishes to a considerable degree the work of cross-fertilization.

NECESSITY OF POLLEN FOR BROOD-REARING.

We are interested about pollen, because bees can not rear brood without either that or some substitute for it. Bees kept in confinement, and fed on pure sugar and pure water, will thrive and void little or no excrement; but as soon as pollen, or food containing the farinaceous element, is given them, their bodies will become distended; and instead of a transparent fluid they will void a liquid of a darkish tint which will soil their hives and emit quite an unpleasant smell. We once kept about 300 bees in a cage with a queen, and gave them only pure sugar and water. They built comb, and seemed quite contented, the cage emitting no smell whatever. In order to start brood-rearing we gave them some sugar candy containing flour, and they soon became uneasy and tried in vain to get out. At this time the cage gave off quite an unpleasant smell, and so they were allowed to fly. Had the pollen element not been given them, it is probable they could have endured the confinement a month or more. We once wintered a fair colony of bees on stores of pure sugar syrup, and when they flew in the spring there was no perceptible spot on the white snow about their hives. They had no pollen, and so, of course, no brood-rearing could go on without it. A few years ago we made some experiments with bees confined in a large room under glass. As it was late in the fall, after brood-rearing had ceased, we did not know whether we should succeed in starting them again. After feeding them for about a week, eggs were found in the cells, but none of them hatched into larvæ. A heap of rye meal was placed in the center of the room near the feed, and anxiously we waited to see them take notice of it. After several days a bee was seen hovering curiously about it. In breathless suspense we watched it until it finally began to dip its tongue into the heap, and then to pad it on its legs. It carried home a small load. we had the hive open, and the frame out, as soon as it was among its comrades, and watched the behavior of the rest while it shook itself among them, until it deposited its treasure in a cell, and hurried away for another load. Very shortly some of the rest followed it, and buzzed about the room until they found where it was loading up, and soon they were at work on the meal, as merrily as in spring. Of course, the eggs were very soon, now, transformed into unsealed larvæ, then into capped brood, and, in due time, we had young bees hatched out in the month of December.

By warming the room with a stove for several days in succession, we found we could start brood-rearing and pollen-gathering even in the month of January. It may be well to state here, that although we succeeded in rearing bees in midwinter, as strong and healthy, apparently, as those raised in summer time, the experiment was hardly a success after all ; for about as many bees died from what we suppose was the effect of confinement as were hatched out. It was a decided success, in determining many unknown points in regard to bees, aside from the office of pollen; and we presume, if it ever should be necessary, we could overcome the difficulties of flying bees under glass. Under the head of FRUIT-BLOSSOMS will be found further facts on this matter. See page 229.

ARTIFICIAL SUBSTITUTES FOR POLLEN.

It has been known for many years, that in the spring time bees will make use of the flour or meal of many kinds of grain, and many bee-keepers feed bushels of it every season. The favorite seems to be rye; and as the bees are apt to fall into it and sometimes get so covered as to perish, we have been in the habit of having the rye ground up with an equal quantity of oats. A great many plans have been devised for feeding it

without waste ; but, after all our experiments, a heap of meal on the ground is about as satisfactory as any way. Of course, it should be protected from rain; and as there is usually much high wind in the spring, which is, to say the least, very annoying to the bees, it is well to have it in a spot sheltered as much as possible, always aiming to give them as much sunshine as may be. By way of experiment, we have concentrated the rays of the sun on the meal heap by mirrors, that the bees might work on days otherwise too cold; we have also made glass-covered structures for the purpose, and have even kept their meals hot by means of a lamp ; all these plans have succeeded, but we are inclined to doubt whether stocks pushed along in brood-rearing, by such means, were really in advance of some that were left to take their chances. It is amusing to see the little fellows start from their hives on days so cold that they would not otherwise stir out, hie to the warm meal and load up, and then go home so quickly that they do not have time to get chilled.

Is there any danger of feeding them too much meal? There is. Reports and our own experience have shown that bees will sometimes get their combs packed with this inferior substitute for the real article; and we would advise giving it only during those seasons when there seems to be a lack of natural pollen. As a general thing, nature supplies bees with all the nitrogenous food they require, and quite early enough. If rye meal be given on a warm day when the bees can fly in mid-winter they will store some of this meal and start brood-rearing; then when cold weather comes on again, the brood is deserted and dies. Nature, on the other hand, will not supply this food before the proper time for brood-rearing to come on. But the question may arise, " How is the owner of the bees to know when nature is not supplying them a farinaceous diet? " If the bees seem to be hovering around chicken-houses, barns, and stables, then it is apparent that they are not getting sufficient pollen to feed, and they should be supplied artificially as already explained.

Not a few of our readers have been perplexed and astonished, doubtless, by seeing the bees, in early spring, greedily appropriating sawdust, just as they do rye meal. We have seen them at the sawmills, so thick on a large heap of fresh sawdust as to attract a large crowd of people; and when we caught them, and tasted of the pollen from their legs, we were somewhat amazed to find it sweet and very much like pollen from the flowers. They doubtless had plenty of honey but no pollen, and these fine particles of wood contained enough of the nitrogenous element to answer very well, mixed with honey, as they have it when packed in their pollen-baskets. The pollen from common sawdust contains an essential oil, besides some gummy matter, that gives an odor doubtless reminding the bees of the aroma of opening buds. Not only do they thus collect (to us) tasteless sawdust, but they have been found at different times on a great variety of substances. A friend in Michigan at one time found them loading up with the fine black earth of the swamps, and they have been known to use even coal-dust; but the strangest thing of all was told us by the owner of a cheese-factory, near by. He said the bees were one day observed hovering over the shelves in the cheese-room, and, as their numbers increased, they were found to be packing on their legs the fine dust that had accumulated from handling so much cheese. Microscopic investigation showed this dust to be embryo cheese-mites, so that the bees had really been using animal food as pollen, and living animals at that. If one might be allowed to theorize in the matter, it would seem this should be a rare substance to crowd brood-rearing to its uttermost limit.

HOW TO START BEES AT WORK ON RYE MEAL.

A beginner hears the feeding of oatmeal highly recommended as a substitute for pollen. He places some near the entrances of the hives, but not a bee touches it. He is told again to wait until early spring, before the bees have access to natural pollen, and then they will take it. He does so, but, as before, not a bee notices it. He is next told to put a heap of it in the sun, a few rods distant from the hives. This time he may succeed; but it would not be strange if he should once more report that his bees would have nothing to do with it. Finally he is directed to take a piece of honey and get some bees to feeding on it, then to set it on the heap of meal. The bees soon gather over it in great numbers; those who go home loaded start out many more searching all about the vicinity, to see where the treasure comes from. The hum of the busy ones on the honey soon attracts them, and, in snuffing about the pile of meal, some bee discovers that it can be used as a substitute for pollen; the others soon follow suit, and, in

a little time, both the bees and their owner are happy, and the pile of meal quickly disappears. After this he never has any more trouble in getting the bees to work on meal, for he *knows how*. The bees and their owner have both learned a valuable lesson about pollen. Is there any very great difference in the way they have been taught? Did they not both learn by practical experiment?

BEES ROBBING ARTIFICIAL POLLEN FROM BARNS AND STABLES.

There are times when bees will not only find sawdust but delve down into chop feed for cattle. On such occasions they will raid barns, stables, and chicken-houses in a way that seems almost like a regular case of robbing. In the spring of 1909 numerous reports from all over the country told how bees had invaded premises of farmers, driving cattle out of the stables, and causing annoyance generally. One of our own neighbors telephoned us one day, saying that a swarm of bees had taken possession of his chicken-house, and that he would like to have us come and take the bees out. Investigation showed there was no swarm, but the inside of the building was filled with bees. At first we were inclined to think that syrup of some kind had been stored there, as it looked like a genuine case of robbing; but a careful examination of the floor where the chickens had been fed showed the desire of the bees for nitrogenous food was so great that they had invaded this chicken-house and helped themselves to the bran and screenings.

A few days later a farmer located near one of our outyards complained that our bees had taken possession of his cow-stables, saying that the cows were stung, and that it was impossible for man or beast to enter the barn. We sent a man down to investigate, and he found, as in the former case, that the bees were after chopped feed.

The spring had been peculiar—so peculiar, in fact, that warm weather came on without any natural supply of pollen. The time for rearing brood had come; and the poor bees, through dire necessity, were compelled to help themselves to any thing they could find. When a few of their number found a substitute for pollen they were wild with excitement, and rushed pellmell into every stable and barn where there was any trace of meal of any sort. It is in seasons like this that the apiarist shou'd be forehanded enough to supply them with all the rye meal they can use. But this supply should be cut off just about as pollen from natural sour es begin s to come in.

During that spring a great deal of dead brood was reported, and it was believed at the time to be due to a lack of nitrogenous food.

POLLEN IN SECTION BOXES AND COMB HONEY.

We do not mean to convey the idea that we should be satisfied with pollen in our honey, for a very good and useful thing is sometimes a very bad one, if out of place. When pollen or meal is brought into the hive, it is taken, at once, very near the brood; in fact, it is placed in the comb opposite, if possible. When opening hives in the spring, we find pollen scattered all through the brood-combs to some extent; but the two combs next the two outside brood-combs are often a solid mass of pollen. Should a few stormy days intervene, however, this will disappear so quickly that one who has not witnessed the rapidity with which it is used in brood-rearing would not know how to account for it. When it is gone, of course the brood rearing must cease, although the queen may continue to lay. The amount of brood that can be reared by keeping a stock supplied with pollen artificially, during such unfavorable weather, is a very important item where rapid increase of stock is desired.

Some of those who use shallow hives have complained that pollen would go up into the sections. This can usually be obviated by putting a comb of pollen in the brood-nest. The presence of this below will usually induce the storage of more pollen in the same place, leaving the sections clear for the storage of honey only. The same principle will apply of course to deeper hives; but it is very seldom that pollen will be found in the sections where the brood-nest is as deep as the Langstroth. It is where there is less depth that there is danger.

QUEEN-EXCLUDING HONEY-BOARDS NOT NECESSARILY AN EXCLUDER OF POLLEN.

It is said that the strips of perforated zinc in the slatted honey-board will largely prevent the storage of pollen above. From what experience we have had, we are inclined to think the zinc will discourage it to some extent; but from the incident above related it will be observed that, if contraction be carried too far, the bees will put the pollen where they please, zinc or no zinc.

For a further consideration of this subject see FRUIT-BLOSSOMS.

PRIORITY RIGHTS. See OVERSTOCKING.

PROFITS IN BEES. This question is a hard one to answer, as so much depends on the locality and the man, and the number of bees to the area.

On the average, perhaps, in the Northern States, in what is known as the rain-belt, one might expect to get anywhere from 25 to 50 lbs. of comb honey, and perhaps from 25 to 50 per cent more of extracted. There will be some seasons when he might secure as much as 100 lbs. on an average, and occasional seasons when there would be neither comb nor extracted and the bees would require to be fed. Taking one year with another, a small bee-keeper ought to average about 35 lbs. of comb honey, on a conservative estimate, providing he has reasonable skill and love for the business. The comb honey might net him, deducting the expense of selling, from 10 to 15 cents; the extracted, from 7 to 10. These figures do not include the labor of producing the honey nor the cost of the fixtures. The cost of the supplies, exclusive of sections and foundation, ought to be sufficient to cover 10 to 20 years if no increase is made. Suppose we put the comb honey at 35 lbs. as the average, and the price secured 14 cents net. The actual money he would get from the commission merchant or grocer might be about $5 00 per colony; but out of this he must deduct a certain amount for labor, and 10 per cent on the cost of supplies, to be on the safe side.

With only a few bees the labor would count for nothing, as the work could be performed by some member of the family or by the man of the house, who should, during his spare hours, do a little with bees and work in his garden. In case of one, two, or three hundred the labor item must be figured. The larger the number crowding the available territory the smaller the profit per hive. A rough estimate for an apiary in a locality not overstocked, not including the labor on the $5.00 actually received for honey sold, ought to leave a net profit somewhere about $4.50. This would be on the basis that the locality did not require much feeding in the fall. If feeding was found to be necessary, 50 cents more would have to be deducted, making a net profit of $4.00. On this basis it will be seen that the profit in one season ought to pay for the hives and supers in one year, or come very close to it, leaving the investment good for ten or more years. If we figure it that way the ten per cent need not be added. For a professional man, or one who has other business, even these returns are not bad; for if he secured only enough for family use, the diversion or change to relieve the tired brain is worth something.

The question as to whether one should keep few or many bees will depend upon many conditions; but the principal one is the ability of the man. Many a person can handle a few chickens, and get good results; but when he runs the number up into the hundreds he meets with failure and disaster. Some of our friends have done remarkably well with a few colonies; but when they have attempted to double or treble the number they entered into a business proposition that proved to be too much for them.

Many years ago a neighbor of ours cleared a thousand dollars from one acre of onions. It made him wild. He bought ten more acres of the same kind of onion land, going into debt for it, and expected to clear the following year $10,000. When he managed the one acre he did all the work himself; but when he worked the ten acres he had to hire help. The help was incompetent, or did not understand. Onions fell in price; and at the final roundup that year he had a great stock of poor onions without a buyer. They rotted. He became discouraged, and lost all he had.

A good many, on account of a lack of experience or perhaps business ability, not understanding their own limitations and those of their localities, will plunge into bee-keeping too deeply and meet with disaster. There are, undoubtedly, some people who can keep more bees by scattering them in outyards; and if they have the requisite training and business ability they can make more money. But where we find one person who can manage 500 colonies or more successfully, there will be dozens who can not go beyond the 200 or 300 mark. The same rule applies to any business.

Now let us look at the other side of the question — the side of expansion. Perhaps here is a bee-keeper who has 300 colonies. During the busy season he is comfortably busy. But during six months in the year his time is not very profitably employed — a distinct loss; for it will take him only a short time, comparatively, to get his supers ready for the next season, nail his hives, repaint them, or do other preliminary work 'that can easily be done indoors, and yet his interest, or his rent and his living expenses are going right on. Suppose, for example, that this bee-keeper has 600 colonies, or 1000; that he has good business ability; that

he has plenty of bee-range. Suppose he scatters this number in 15 different yards, none further than 15 miles from his home, and a good part of them not over four or five miles away. In the busy season he will, or course, have to employ help. If he has the right kind of executive ability he will see that that help is profitably employed. When the rush of work is over he will look after the marketing of the crop, put the bees into winter quarters, perhaps doing the work himself with the occasional help of one man and a team. In cold weather he can devote *all* of his time profitably in preparing for the next season. Now, while he is operating 1000 colonies it costs him no more to live; the same horse and wagon that will carry him to two or three hundred will carry him to the other seven or eight hundred. If he is running for extracted honey, the same extractor, uncapping-knives, and smokers can be used at each yard. He is thus enabled to put his invested capital where it will be earning money for him *all the time* in the busy season instead of eating up interest part of the time. We will suppose that some of his swarms get away from him; we will also suppose that some of the work is not done as well as when he had only 300 colonies; but he has increased his honey crop by three times, possibly, and has increased his actual operating expenses only to the extent of the help that he has to pay for, extra hives, and sugar to feed. A couple of men and a boy three months in the year—the man at $2.00 and a boy at $1.00 per day—would make his expense $450. To this we will add $50 for extra team hire. The cost of the extra 700 colonies with hives and supers divided by ten (assuming that they would last ten years) would be $250 more, or $750. But we must add $250 more for sugar for feeding, and $250 for sections, foundation, and shipping-cases, making $1250 as the total added expense for the 700 extra colonies. Say he is producing comb honey, and that he can average 35 lbs. per colony. If this nets him 14 cts. he would get from 300 colonies $1500. If he has 1000 colonies his gross income will be $5000 by adding only $1250 to his general expenses.

This is a supposable and a possible case. The most that we would show is that the operating and overhead expenses will not be proportionately increased if the number of colonies be doubled or trebled — all on the assumption, of course, that our bee keeping friend has the necessary skill and business ability.

In deciding the question whether we ourselves should keep more bees, we must go very cautiously, not increasing the number all at once, but a little at a time, *making the bees pay their way*. Generally speaking, it would be the biggest piece of folly for one to borrow the money to treble his equipment of bees and hives in one season.

PROPOLIS. This is the gum or varnish that bees collect for coating over the inside of their hives, filling cracks and crevices, cementing loose pieces of the hive together, and for making things fast and close generally. It collects, in time, on old hives and combs, so as to add very materially to their weight. It is not generally gathered in any great quantity until at the close of the season, when it seems to be collected in response to a kind of instinct that bids them prepare for cold weather. We see them almost every day, during a dearth of honey, collecting propolis from old hives, old quilts, and pieces of refuse wax, when we are so wasteful and untidy as to leave any such scattered about. That the principal part of it comes from some particular plant or class of plants, or tree, we are pretty well satisfied, for almost the same aromatic resinous flavor is noticeable, no matter what the locality or season of the year. Bees gather propolis with their mandibles, and pack and carry it precisely as they do pollen. It is never packed in the cells, however, but applied at once to the place wanted. It is often mixed with wax to strengthen their combs, and is applied to the cells as a varnish, for the same purpose. In the absence of a natural supply, the bees frequently resort to various substances, such as paints, varnishes, resins, pitch, and the like; and the superstition, popular in some sections, that bees follow their owner to the grave, after his death, probably obtained credence from seeing the bees at work on the varnish of the coffin. To save the bees the trouble of waxing up the crevices in their hives, it has been suggested that a mixture of melted wax and resin be poured into the hive and made to flow along the cracks and corners. This may do very well, although we fancy the bees can do this better and cheaper than we can. Our principal trouble has been to get rid of the surplus propolis, and we would much rather hear of some invention to keep it out of the way than to add more.

HOW TO KEEP PROPOLIS FROM SURPLUS HONEY.

Of course, the readiest means is to remove all sections just as soon as a single one is capped over; and, as but little propolis is gathered during a strong yield of honey, but little will be found on the honey unless it is left until the yield has ceased. The bees not only cover all the wood-work of the sections if left on too long, but they also varnish over the whole surface of the white capping, almost spoiling the looks and sale of the honey.

It is next to impossible to keep propolis from the sections entirely. Bees will deposit at least some in the interstices between the sections. As Nature abhors a vacuum, so do the bees dislike a crack or crevice. The nearer we can get surplus arrangements so as to leave but few crevices or places of contact accessible to bees, the less propolis will be deposited. Some surplus arrangements are made so as to produce compression upon the sections, thus reducing the space formed by contact with sections to a minimum. Some prefer to have the outside of the sections covered entire. This can be accomplished either with the wide frames or with surplus arrangements having the top and bottom to correspond with the outsides of the sections. For removing propolis from sections, see COMB HONEY.

HOW TO KEEP PROPOLIS FROM STICKING TO THE FINGERS.

At certain times of the year, notably in the fall when propolis is very abundant and sticky, after the honey-flow is over and the bees have nothing else to do. they will sometimes gather a great deal of resinous matter which they chink into every available place, sometimes smearing over the brood-frames. When these latter are handled the fingers gather up a great deal of the sticky stuff, making the work unpleasant, not to say annoying. At such times one may wear gloves; but as many do not like them, the trouble can be overcome to a great extent by dipping the fingers in vaseline.

HOW TO REMOVE PROPOLIS FROM THE FINGERS.

A variety of substances have been suggested. Alcohol is perhaps the neatest, but is rather expensive; benzine or gasoline or common lye for soap-making answers nearly as well, and is cheap; soap will answer if a little lard be rubbed on the hands first but will have little effect on it otherwise. A friend down south says he has a pair of light cotton gloves which he slips on when handling his waxy frames, and his hands are left clean whenever he is obliged to stop work. For removing it from glass, etc., alcohol is perhaps best. When we have much glass soiled, it can often be cleaned most expeditiously by boiling it in a kettle of water with a quantity of wood ashes, or, better, lye. Right here we can not do better than to reprint an article by Miss Wilson, Dr. Miller's assistant, from *Gleanings in Bee Culture.*

When I cleaned the T tins with concentrated lye, I felt pretty sure that hives, supers, separators, etc., could be cleaned in the same way, but was so busy I could not take time just then to experiment, hence concluded to say nothing about it till I could find time to test the matter. This morning, May 5th, being the first opportunity I have had, I concluded to experiment a little.

I put on my wash-boiler with water and lye, then went to the shop and selected the most badly propolized supers and separators that I could find as fit subjects on which to experiment. I dropped a few separators into the boiler while the water was yet cold, to see what effect it would have on them. I couldn't see that it affected them in the least until the water almost reached the boiling-point, when the propolis disappeared.

What I was most afraid of was that the separators while wet would cling so closely together that the lye would not reach every part, and hence they would not all be perfectly clean. I was glad to find these few did not bother at all, but came out perfectly clean. I stirred them with the poker while boiling, although I don't know that it was necessary, as I tried another lot without stirring, and they came out just as clean. I next tied up a bundle of 59 separators, that being the number I had handy. Of course, they were tied loosely. I dropped them in, having a strong cord tied around the middle of the bundle to lift them out by. I let them boil two or three minutes, and took them out; 32 of them were perfectly clean. The rest, the center of the bundle, still had some propolis left on, and were treated to a second dose.

Taking a very large quantity of the separators at one time, there might be more trouble than I think, about getting them clean, but I don't believe there would be if the water were kept hot enough, and enough of the lye used. I don't think any harm would come from having it unnecessarily strong.

I next tried dipping the T supers. My boiler was large enough to clean only half a super at a time, so I had to dip in one half, reverse it, and dip the other half. Had I been able to dip one all at once, I think I could have cleaned one a minute. And they are beautifully cleaned. I don't know of any other way they could be cleaned so nicely—quite as clean, I think, as when new. We scraped all our supers before the lye was thought of; and while they are much improved by the scraping, they are not nearly as nice as when cleaned with lye, while the scraping is harder work.

I did not have any thing large enough to dip a hive into, but of course a hive would clean as readily as a super. With convenient apparatus to work with, a large number of such articles as separators could be cleaned at a time with no very great amount of labor. It is such a comfort to have every thing clean! Wood separators are so cheap that we have always thought it did not pay to clean them. I rather think we shall conclude that it does pay, after this, providing we can get them satisfactorily dried in good shape.

DO THE BEES NEED PROPOLIS?

Much discussion has arisen in regard to the habit bees have of making all openings tight with propolis. Theory says, if allowed to follow their bent, or instinct, they will smother themselves to death. Practice says they do, at least at times, so prevent the escape of moisture that their home gets damp and wet, filled with icicles, etc., so that they suffer; or, at least, such is the case in the hives we have provided for them. Who is right—the bees or the enlightened beekeeper? The greater part of the fault lies in the hive we have given them. The enameled cloth which we formerly used for covering bees is as impervious to air and moisture as the propolis they collect with so much pains and trouble. If the outside of this is allowed to get frosty, it will, most assuredly, condense the breath of the bees on the inside; and if the outside is but thinly protected from the weather, icicles will certainly form on the inside, and freeze the bees all fast in a lump. Now we would have no fear at all in having the bees wax up every thing as tight as they wished, if we could have their winter apartment made so small that they completely filled it—filled it so full, indeed, as to be crowded out at the entrance, unless in very cold weather—and have the entire outside protected with some non-conductor that would enable the bees to keep the inner walls warm at all times. We think then we should have no dampness. With chaff packing and chaff cushions, we have succeeded so well that we are perfectly willing the little fellows shall fix up just as snug for winter as their instinct prompts them to do.

VALUE OF PROPOLIS.

The gum has been used to some extent in medicine; also in the preparation of certain leather polishes. It is claimed that propolis for this purpose possesses a property that renders it superior to any of the pitches or resins.

Q.

QUEEN-REARING. Every honey-producer should know how to raise his own queens. There are times when it is better to buy them, and other times when it is certainly cheaper to rear them. Other things being equal, a queen that has never been compelled to go through the mails, shut up in a mail-sack, to be bumped about in this way and that for a period of two or three days or perhaps that many weeks, ought to live longer and give better results than one that is compelled to undergo such treatment. It very often happens that a queen which has been doing excellent service for a year or so, when introduced after being sent through the mails, dies within a few days, for the very probable reason that the journey was too much for her. It would seem, then, that every bee-keeper should himself rear the majority of the queens that he uses, buying only just enough to renew his stock or to introduce new strains. But before proceeding further with this subject, the reader would do well to read QUEENS (found in its alphabetical order), as this furnishes the groundwork of the subject we shall now discuss.

CONDITIONS FAVORABLE AND UNFAVORABLE FOR REARING QUEENS.

When a colony from some cause or other becomes queenless, the bees will set about rearing another.

In nature, the best queens are those that are reared either during the swarming-time or when the bees are about to supersede an old queen soon to fail. At such times we see large beautiful queen-cells, reminding one of big peanuts, projecting from the side of the comb. The larvæ in such cells are lavishly fed with royal jelly; and when the queens finally hatch they are usually large and vigorous.

We said there is one class of cells that bees rear when they are about to supersede an old queen. When a queen is two or three years old she begins to show signs of failing. The bees recognize the fact that their own mother will soon die, or at least need help from a daughter, and very leisurely proceed to construct a number of cells, all of which are supplied with larvæ, and fed in the same lavish way as those reared under the swarming impulse.

But we can never determine in advance when the bees will rear supersedure cells, and it may be true that the queen about to be superseded is not desirable stock from which to rear. In this case such cells should not be utilized. For a like reason, also, cells reared under the swarming impulse should be rejected; because it is certainly penny wise and pound foolish to rear queens from any thing but the very best select stock. But all swarming-cells from good queens should be reserved by placing them in West queen-cell protectors; then hunt up queens two or three years old, pinch their heads off, and replace them with one of these cells in each colony. But perhaps you have good queens even two or three years old. Perhaps; but the majority of our honey-producers think it profitable to replace all queens three years old, while a good many make it a practice to requeen all colonies having queens two years and over, and of late years there is a slight tendency on the part of a few to graft every year.

While these swarming-cells produce the very best queens, yet it may not be convenient to requeen during the swarming season, which in some localities may be a very bad season to do so, owing to the interruption that it makes in the regular production of honey; for it is well known that a good many colonies will not do as well in honey-gathering when they are queenless as when they have a good queen in the hive. But such cells can then be given to nuclei, for they ought not to be wasted.

Among the several systems of rearing queens, the one first put out by Mr. Doolittle many years ago forms the basis of some of the best now in vogue, is very simple, requiring no special tools more than one can improvise for himself. Thoroughly understanding this, the reader will be in position to carry out the more advanced ideas put forth by Samuel Simmins, E. L. Pratt, Henry Alley, and others.

THE DOOLITTLE METHOD OF REARING QUEENS.

While Mr. Doolittle's system is slightly artificial yet he endeavors to make his methods conform as nearly as possible to

Nature's ways. The first thing of prime importance in the rearing of queens is to bring about conditions that will approach, as nearly as possible, those that are present during the swarming season at a time when the bees supply the cell-cups lavishly with royal food. One of the first requisites, then, for cell-building is strong powerful colonies; second, a light honey-flow, or a condition almost analogous, viz., stimulative feeding if the honey is not then coming in. Queens reared during a dearth of honey, or in nuclei, are apt to be small, and the cells from which they come look small and inferior. The mothers that do the best work are those that are large, and capable of laying anywhere from 2000 to 3000 eggs per day. A queen that is incapable of this should not be retained. For instance, a colony with a good queen might earn for its owner in a good season $5.00 in clean cash. In the same season the same colony (or, perhaps, to speak more exactly, the same hive of bees), with a poorer queen, would bring in less than half that amount. A queen that can lay 2000 or 3000 eggs a day at the *right time of the year*, so that there will be a large force of bees ready to begin on the honey when it does come, is the kind of queen that we need to rear.

The old way of raising queens was to make a colony or a nucleus queenless: wait for the bees to build their own cells, then distribute them to colonies made queenless beforehand. This plan is very slow and wasteful, and, worst of all, results in the rearing of inferior queens. Mr. Doolittle takes advantage of Nature's ways to such an extent that he is enabled to rear a large number of queens from some selected breeder, in that he makes it possible to increase the number of cells ordinarily built; for the prime requisite in queen-rearing is cells—plenty of them—that will rear good strong healthy queens.

HOW TO MAKE DOOLITTLE CELL-CUPS.

Many times, when an apiarist is going through his yard he can cut out embryo cell-cups, such as the bees make. These can be utilized at some future time for the purpose of grafting. But such cells, after they are gathered, are exceedingly frail, irregular in shape, will not bear much handling; and most of the time one can not find enough.

Mr. Doolittle was among the first who conceived the idea of making artificial cell-cups that should not only be regular in form but of such construction as to stand any reasonable amount of handling. Contrary to what one might expect, such cells are just as readily accepted by the bees as those they make in the good old-fashioned way; and, what is of considerable importance, they can be made in any quantity by one of ordinary intelligence.

Mr. Doolittle takes a wooden rake-tooth, and whittles and sandpapers the point so that it is the size and shape of the bottom of

the queen-cell (see illustration). Two or three other sticks are then fashioned of the same shape and pattern. Preparatory to forming the cells Mr. Doolittle has a little pan of beeswax, kept hot by means of a lamp; also a cup of water. Seating himself before a table he is now ready for work. Taking one of these cell-forming sticks he dips it into water, after which he plunges it about $\frac{3}{8}$ of an inch into the melted wax. He then lifts it up and twirls it at an angle (waxed end lower) in his fingers. When cool he dips it again, but not quite so deep, and twirls it as before. He proceeds thus until the cup is dipped seven or eight times, but each time dipping it less deep, within $\frac{1}{8}$ inch of the previous dipping. The main thing is to secure a cup having a *thick heavy bottom*, but which will have a thin and delicate knife edge at the open top, or at that point where the bees are supposed to assume work. After the last dipping is cooled, a slight pressure of the thumb loosens the cell-cup slightly. It is then dipped once more, and before cooling it is attached to a comb or stick designed to receive it.

GRAFTING CELLS.

The next operation is to insert a small particle of royal jelly in every queen-cell so made. The amount in each should be about equivalent in bulk to a double-B shot, says Mr. Doolittle. But we have found that a much less quantity will answer. Out of an ordinary queen-cell well supplied with royal jelly we get enough to supply 20 cups. If we took a quantity equal in bulk to a BB shot we would have to rob two or three cells to supply that many. This royal jelly should come from some queen-cell nearly ready to seal, as that will contain the most. It should be stirred to bring all to about the same consistency, after which it may be dipped out of the cells by means of a stick whittled like an ordinary ear-spoon, or a toothpick bent to that shape.

The next operation is to take a frame of young larvæ just hatched from the eggs of our best breeding queen. Each little grub should be picked up with the aforesaid ear-spoon, and gently laid on the royal food previously prepared in one of the cell-cups. A larva should be given to every one of the cell-cups in this manner, and when all are supplied they are to be put into the cell-building colony.

Before grafting, however, it is advisable to stick a row of about a dozen of these cups on a flat stick with hot wax. When they are all mounted one may then graft as explained.

After this stick of grafted cups has been mounted in a brood-frame we are all ready for the bees to begin where man left off. If it is during the swarming season I would select some *very strong* colony having a queen, place on it a queen-excluding honey-board, and over this an upper story with a few frames of brood. If the colony is already a two-story one, the perforated zinc-board should be inserted between the two sections of the hive. When honey is not coming in freely it should be fed liberally for several days before giving the prepared cups, and until the cells are all capped over. This is important. Into the upper story of such a colony we place our frame with prepared cells between two frames of brood and bees. If the colony is *strong* enough the bees will go to work immediately, drawing out the queen-cells, giving them an added supply of royal jelly, and finally completing them. But if it is not very strong or has not been fed before and while the cells are being built, it may and probably will clean out and leave every cell.

But the average beginner would find it more satisfactory to use for cell-building a strong *queenless* colony that has been made queenless, broodless, and eggless four or five days previous to the giving of the cups. But it is important at the time of making this cell-building colony queenless to begin stimulative feeding, giving them half a pint of syrup daily. After the lapse of four or five days a frame of prepared cell-cups as before directed should be given, when the bees are almost crying for a queen or for something from which they may start cells. Under such circumstances they will immediately accept the cups and draw them out, feeding them lavishly with royal food, and the cells will be equal to any swarming cells, if liberal feeding has been continued until all the cells are capped over.

Another excellent cell-building colony outside of the swarming season is one having a queen which it is trying to supersede. One or more such colonies will be found in a large apiary, but as a general rule the queen is hardly good enough to use as a breeder. Having found our colony, we begin giving it daily feeds at once, being a prime requisite for the best results in cell-building with any colony, either with a queen or without one. This supersedure cell-building colony will not only draw out and complete one set of cups but several sets in succession; but it is best not to give any one such colony more than a dozen or a dozen and a half prepared cups at a time. Allow it to finish up one batch, and then, if necessary, give it another.

To one of our supersedure colonies, as we call them, we gave one batch of Doolittle cups after another until they had completed over 300 fine cells; but we were careful to take away each lot before any could hatch, of course, for a young virgin would very soon make havoc of the other cells unhatched, and besides would get the colony out of the notion of trying to supersede the old queen.

Just how far supersedure bees will continue to build out batches of cell cups one after another, we are not able to say; but if they are fed half a pint of syrup daily they appear to be willing to keep up the work indefinitely, in the hope that they will some day be able to rear a virgin that will supplant the old queen that appears to be failing.

REARING QUEENS IN LARGE NUMBERS.

Thus far we have considered the old original Doolittle system of rearing queens; and where one desires only a few for his own use he may find this method more conven-

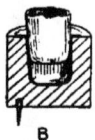

CROSS-SECTION OF WOODEN CELL HOLDER; CELL CUP PARTIALLY PUSHED INTO PLACE.

ient than the one we will now describe. But if he has any number to rear he should by all means carry out the following plan. The method of preparing the colonies for cell-building will be the same.

Instead of dipping the cells one by one with a stick, or dipping several sticks at once, compressed cell cups are made on a plan originally devised by E. L. Pratt. With a suitable die, cells more nearly perfect than can possibly be dipped by the slow process already described are punched out at the rate of 2000 an hour. These are furnished by dealers, and, generally speaking, it would

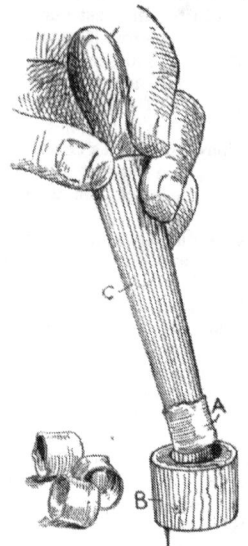

MANNER OF INSERTING CELL CUPS IN CELL-HOLDERS.

be better for readers of this work to buy cell cups than to attempt to make them by the dipping process.

To facilitate general handling, the modified Doolittle system calls for wooden cell-holders, which may, under certain circumstances, be used as direct cell cups.

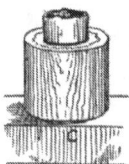

CELL-HOLDER WITH CELL IN PLACE.

These are nothing more nor less than cylindrical pieces of wood, ¾ inch in diameter, ⅜ inch long. A suitable drill bores out one end of the right size to receive one of the compressed cell cups. These wooden cell-holders can likewise be purchased by the thousand.

The compressed cups are forced into the hole in the cell-holders by means of a little plunger-stick. When enough of them have been prepared, and secured to a cell bar by means of nail-points forced into the soft

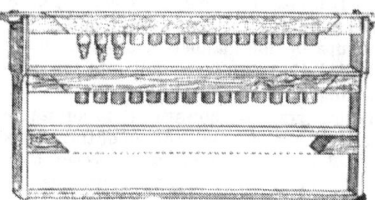

HOFFMAN FRAME WITH REMOVABLE BARS FOR CELL-HOLDERS.

wood, we are ready for the grafting, which process is much the same as that already described in the Doolittle method, except that a much smaller quantity of royal jelly is

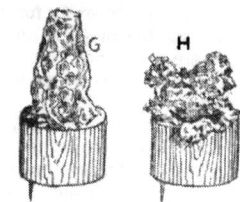

G, FULLY COMPLETED CELL FROM HOLDER; H, PARTIALLY BUILT CELL TORN AWAY TO GET AT THE ROYAL JELLY.

used, that special tools are provided for the purpose, these latter being obtained of the dealers. Sufficient royal jelly is gathered

SUPPLYING CELLS WITH ROYAL JELLY.

up from a series of cells, and the same is stirred with a special jelly-spoon. A spoon full is then held in the left hand, while the right hand uses the grafting tool to take a speck of the royal jelly, about the size of the head of a pin. This is then placed in the bottom of one of the compressed cups. Other cups are treated in the same way until the whole series of cells is provisioned.

If one should run short of compressed cups he can, with a keen-edged knife, cut off the old cell, from which the queen has hatched, even with the wood, and then with the plunger-stick ream out the hole in the cell-

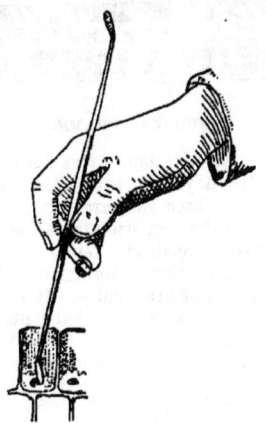

LIFTING A LARVA OUT OF A WORKER-CELL.

holder. This hole can be grafted in the manner already explained; but it will be found preferable to use the compressed cups, as better results will thus be secured.

The next operation is to take a comb of very young larvæ, just hatched, from a breed-

ing queen. In an atmosphere not cooler than 75 or 80 degrees (the warmer the better) a young larva is scooped or lifted up out of a worker-cell with the flattened end of the grafting tool, and deposited in the royal jelly of one of the compressed cups, and so on until all the cups are grafted. And just here it is proper to remark that this royal jelly serves a double purpose. It affords a downy bed, so to speak, in which to lay the larva, and at the same time provides food until the bees can give it a fresh supply. Despite the claim that royal jelly is not necessary we get more cells accepted with it.

Some queen-breeders say that a frame of these cells may now be put in the upper story of a strong colony, the two stories being separated by a perforated zinc honey-board. (See EXTRACTORS.) While such upper stories can be used with advantage to *complete* cells that the bees of a queenless colony have *already accepted*, we find them practically worthless for starting them. While an ordinary queenless colony supplied with brood will sometimes accept all the cells, we find it better to make such colony queenless and broodless, by giving the brood temporarily to other hives, and caging the queen over another colony. The deprived colony is then given a couple of frames of honey and a feeder of syrup with the frame of prepared cells placed down between frames of honey, one hour after being made queenless and broodless. We find it still better to shake all the bees at the time of doing this in front of the entrance, and make them crawl in. It is *absolutely essential* that they be fed several days prior to the giving of the cells, and also during the time

FULLY COMPLETED QUEEN-CELLS BUILT ON WOODEN CELL-HOLDERS.

they are working on them. After the cells are once accepted and started they may be changed to the upper story of a strong colony, where they will be completed and capped over.

The cells are now ready to be placed in nursery cages, one of which is shown herewith. This, it will be seen, is practically a

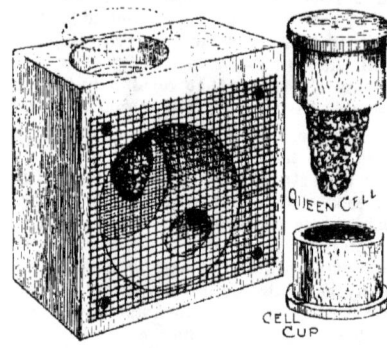

NURSERY CAGE FOR CELLS AND VIRGINS.

modified Alley cage. A surplus of cells often occurs in queen-rearing—that is to say, a lack of queenless nuclei or colonies to take them. One should arrange to have more than he will probably be able to use, to provide for bad weather, when cells will be destroyed or young hatched virgins be missing. At such a time, if one has extra cells or virgins that he can take out of a nursery, he can quickly make good the loss.

The nursery cage here shown has a large opening at the top to receive the wooden cell cup: the small hole in the lower right-hand corner is filled with queen-cage candy to supply the young miss after she hatches. Twenty-four of these cages, supplied with cells that are capped over, can be put in a nursery-frame having holders which may be tilted on an angle so that any one cage can be easily removed from a holder without disturbing the rest. There are three of these holders in each frame, pivoted at both ends as shown. When the nursery-frame has been filled with cages, each containing a capped cell, it should be put down in the center of a strong colony.

While various artificial-heat incubators using kerosene-lamps have been devised, experience has shown a majority of breeders that nothing is quite so good as a strong cluster of bees. What is still more, when the young virgins hatch, some of the bees will be inclined to feed them through the

wire cloth, providing a stimulus that they can not receive from the queen candy in the cage. After the virgins have hatched they should be transferred to Miller cages, and introduced *as soon after hatching as possible.* The younger the virgin, the more successful

will be her introduction. After she becomes four or five days old, even if she be accepted by the bees they are likely to mistreat her so that her usefulness thereafter will be greatly impaired. While it is possible to introduce these virgins to full-sized colonies it is not practicable. It is practicable to introduce them to baby nuclei, if not too old. See INTRODUCING VIRGIN QUEENS, under head of INTRODUCING.

DUAL PLAN OF INTRODUCING VIRGIN QUEENS.

It sometimes happens that a breeder will have a great surplus of cells, or more virgins than he has queenless nuclei or colonies. In such cases we have found it practicable to introduce two queens at a time. First a virgin, the younger the better, is introduced in a Miller cage to a baby nucleus. After two or three days she should be released; in about four days more, being seven days from the time of caging the first queen, another virgin may be caged among the same bees; but the candy of the second cage through which the bees liberate the queen must be covered with a little strip of tin or the bees will liberate her prematurely. In two days more the first virgin will be mated, and within two or three days will begin to lay if the weather is favorable. Then she is removed and sent out to fill an order; the strip of tin covering the candy of the second cage is opened to let the bees release virgin No. 2, and, having already acquired the colony odor, she will usually be accepted in less than a day's time. In about seven days from the time she was caged, if there is still a surplus of virgins, may be put into the nucleus while No. 2 is taking her mating-flight, and so the progress may continue so long as there is a surplus of virgins.

This is really high-pressure queen-rearing, and should be practiced only when there is a surplus of virgins, or when there are rush orders for cheap queens. We say cheap queens, because the queens introduced on the dual plan may or may not be the equal of those introduced in the regular way where a single queen is introduced at a time and is confined in a cage not more than a couple of days. If the virgin is very young, just hatched, and the nucleus has been queenless a couple of days, she can be let loose into the entrance of the hive without any caging; but care should be taken not to allow her to touch the hands, for the scent of the human body sometimes causes the bees to attack and kill her.

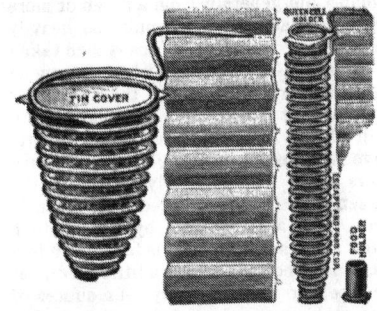

WEST QUEEN-CELL PROTECTOR.

Some queen-breeders prefer to give ripe queen-cells to their nuclei direct, claiming that too many of the virgins that they introduce anywhere from one to four and five days old are lost. It is doubtless true, the average beginner will succeed better with cells than with virgins; but if cells be given make sure that the nuclei are strong in bees. In some cases it will be necessary to use West queen-cell protectors to keep the bees from gnawing holes into them.

The long spiral cage shown at the right is designed to slip under the queen-cell protector, and when the young queen hatches out she will pass into the long cage, where she can be held secure from bees or other virgins in the colony that might kill her.

BABY NUCLEI, AND HOW TO MATE QUEENS IN LARGE NUMBERS.

After securing a large lot of nice cells in the cages already shown and described, it is next in order for us to consider the mating box or hive. As already explained, one can

use one or two full-sized Langstroth frames and put them in a three-frame box or hive, or in a full-sized hive, by using a division-board to reduce the space; or, better still, take an eight-frame hive-body and divide it off into three equal compartments by inserting two tight-fitting division-boards length-wise that will reach clear up to the cover. Each compartment will then be just wide enough to take two full-sized Langstroth frames. The under side of this hive should have a wire-cloth bottom, for reasons to be given later. The two outside compartments should each have an entrance, one on each side of the hive along the center. The center compartment should have one at the rear of the hive-body. These entrances should be made with a half-inch bit, and have a cleat nailed just below, forming a narrow doorstep.

When complete we shall have an ordinary eight-frame hive-body with wire-cloth bottom, having three two-frame divisions with an entrance on each side and one in the rear. Each of these compartments is to receive two frames of brood and bees, after which it is set over a strong colony of bees. The heat passing from the bees beneath will keep the three clusters above perfectly warm, no mat-

TWIN-NUCLEI FRAME.

ter if the weather should be a little cool. Queens or cells may be given to each one of these nuclei, as already explained, and queens will be mated from the upper story in the regular way. Where the climate is a little uncertain and the season short, there is nothing better than this divided-off upper story.

But where one desires to secure the largest number of queens possible from a given force of bees, a twin-mating nucleus on a much smaller scale is to be preferred.

The illustration shows one the authors use. It is just right so that one of its compart-

12

ments on either side will take two frames of such size that three of them will just fit the inside of a regular Langstroth frame, the division being made on vertical lines. The baby hive itself is on the same general principle as a full-sized one, having rabbets at the ends to support the frame projections. A division-board through the center lengthwise, ½ inch thick, divides the hive off into two bee-tight compartments. Tacked to this board is a square of enamel cloth which,

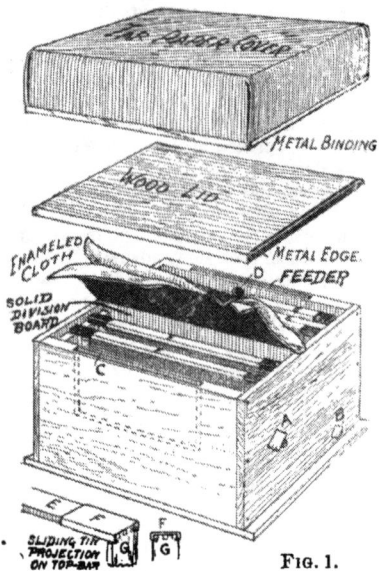

METAL BINDING

WOOD LID

ENAMELED CLOTH

METAL EDGE

FEEDER

SOLID DIVISION BOARD

C

A   B

E   F

SLIDING TIN PROJECTION ON TOP-BAR

G

FIG. 1.

when folded, covers both sides. In order that the little frames may hang in the rabbets and yet at the same time be fitted inside the full-sized Langstroth frame, projections or supports are made of metal, and so constructed that they can slide forward to form a projection, or be shoved back out of the way.

Early in the season these little frames are filled with full sheets of foundation; or, better, from a lot of old defective combs can be cut the good portions and fitted in these ½-sized nucleus-frames. When filled with comb or foundation three of them are inserted in a common Langstroth frame, which may be put down in the center of a good colony. Where preferred a colony may be supplied exclusively with these three-in-one frames. When filled they can be given bees and all to the baby hives by being taken out of the large frame, and the metal projections

shoved forward or outward, as shown at F and A. They are now ready to hang in the nucleus-box; but before this is done each division of the twin box should be supplied with about half a pint of bees. While the bees may be taken from the same yard in which the mating-boxes are to be stationed, it is strongly advised to procure them from an outyard; or, if one does not have one, to purchase three or four colonies of black or hybrid bees from some farmer.

FORMING BABY NUCLEI.

We take a regular eight-frame hive-body that has a wire-cloth screen bottom and a removable wire-cloth screen top. We then go to some one of the other yards and shake into this box some ten or twelve pounds of bees. These may come from four or five colonies, but generally from a dozen or more hives, so that we do not pull too heavily upon a few. This box of bees is then taken to the queen-rearing yard, where the nuclei are to be formed. Four of the twin baby hives are first placed upon a little light stand, each filled with empty combs ready to receive the bees, entrances closed, and ventilators open. The hive-body containing the shaken bees is then placed conveniently near. They are wet down by a spray, then given a jar so as to get the bees down in a mass in the bottom. With a little tin dipper we scoop up approximately four ounces of bees, making anywhere from a thousand to twelve hundred individuals. As the bees have been previously wet down they can not fly very readily, and can therefore be scooped up a la Pratt and dumped in one of the compartments as shown in Fig. 2. An attendant stands ready with a number of virgin queens. He removes one of the frames of one compartment, and, while the apiarist is scooping up a dipperful or two of bees and dumping them in the space made vacant by the removal of the frame, he drops in a virgin queen that had previously been dipped in honey or syrup. He now puts in the removed frame and folds back the enamel cloth. The operation is repeated in the other compartment of the box, and so on the process is continued until all of the twin mating-boxes are filled with bees and virgin queens. The baby hives are then set to one side for about 48 hours, when they are placed on their permanent stands for the summer. Their entrances are opened at night. The next morning, as the bees come out they will mark their location and begin housekeeping with their baby queen.

FIG. 2.—SCOOPING BEES WITH A SMALL DIPPER INTO BABY NUCLEI.

After the baby nuclei are in full operation we give ripe queen-cells, as shown in Fig. 3, in place of virgins given at first. The two frames are spread a little apart when the cell is placed in position and secured.

At the time of forming these baby nuclei, a thick syrup of about 2½ parts of sugar to one of water is poured into the feeder compartment at one side. At other times, if it is a little cool it is given at night, hot, when it will all be taken up before morning. This feeding may be required off and on during the season. In some years the baby nuclei will gather enough to supply their own needs. At other times they will require a little help.

These little twin nuclei serve only the purpose of mating. No cells are reared in them, and the comparatively small number of bees in each compartment makes it easy to find a laying queen or a virgin if present. If in doubt as to whether the nucleus has a virgin, another cell is given; and even should the virgin come back from her flight she will take care of that cell by gnawing a hole in its side and killing its occupant. Should she be lost in one of those flights the cell will provide another virgin, which will come on

in due course of time. It is better to have a surplus of cells than to lose time.

These baby nuclei have been carefully tested in one of our yards, and have given us good results; but one needs to remember a few things in handling them or he may become disgusted with the whole plan.

1. If the force becomes a little weak. give a frame of hatching brood; or if this can not be had, after the last queen is taken out dump in a few more bees from a strong colony of the main yard. While some of these will go back, many will remain.

2. After the young queens begin to lay they should be taken out almost immediately, otherwise they will fill the two small combs with eggs and lead off a little swarm. If not convenient to take the queen out at once, the perforated zinc slide should be shoved around to shut her in.

3. Always make up these little nuclei with bees from some outyard.

4. Do not allow one side of the nucleus box to become empty of bees. The combined heat of the two clusters brings about a better state of contentment. Where there is only one compartment of bees in a mat-

FIG. 3.—SUPPLYING BABY NUCLEI WITH RIPE CELLS AND SUGAR SYRUP.

ing-box we find they can not do as well as when there are two.

5. One should understand that these small mating nuclei are much more difficult to handle than larger ones on full-sized Langstroth frames; but the fact is, queens in them are more economically mated with one-third the bees and brood of the ordinary two-frame full-sized Langstroth nucleus.

6. Last but not least, give *cells* rather than virgins to these twin nuclei. While just-hatched virgins can be run into colonies and nucleus hives with a *single* compartment they can not be let loose in one of the compartments of a double or twin nucleus without incurring too great a percentage of loss. However, when forming both sides at once a young virgin can be dropped into each side.

QUEENS, HOW TO FIND. See FRAMES, TO MANIPULATE.

QUEENS. The most important personage in the hive is the queen, or mother-bee. She is called the mother-bee because she is, in reality, the mother of all the bees in the hive. So much has already been said of queens, in DRONES, and QUEEN-REARING, that we presume our A B C class is already pretty well acquainted with "her majesty," as she is frequently designated.

When we deprive a colony of their queen, the bees set to work and raise another so

THE QUEEN AND HER RETINUE.

long as they have any worker-larvæ in the hive from which to do it. This is the rule, but there are some exceptions—so few, however, that it is safe to assume that a queen of some kind is present in the hive whenever they refuse to start queen-cells on larvæ of a proper age.

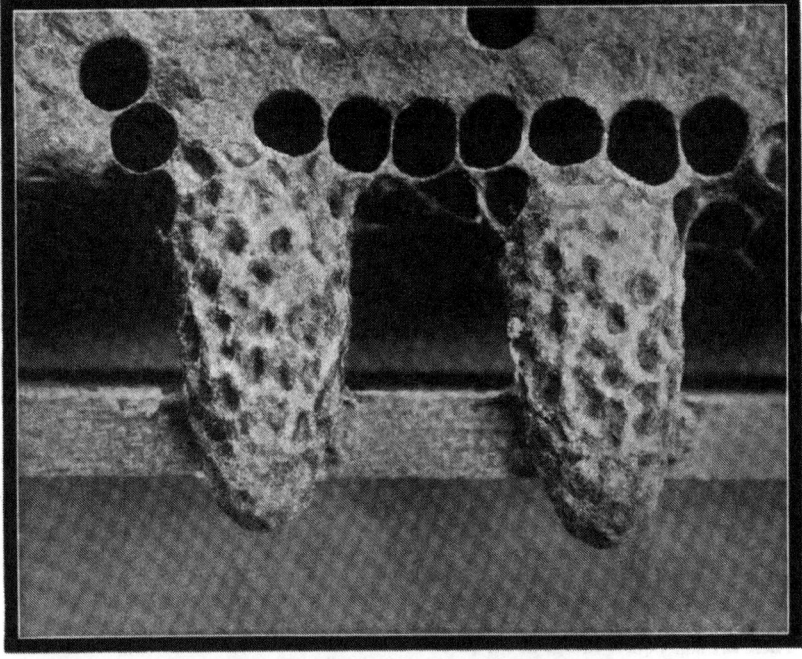

NATURAL QUEEN-CELLS GREATLY ENLARGED.

IMPERFECTLY DEVELOPED QUEENS.

Some queens are small, unusually dark in color, and sometimes become fertilized, which lay eggs for a little while (from a week to several months), but never prove profitable. Sometimes they will not lay at all, but remain in a colony all through the season, neither doing any good nor permitting any other queen to be either introduced or reared. A wingless queen, or one with bad wings, will produce the same result. The remedy is to hunt them out and remove them. Where they are so nearly like a worker-bee as to make it hard to distinguish them, they can often be detected by the peculiar behavior of the bees toward them. See INTRODUCING QUEENS, also cut on the previous page. In the fall, after the queen has ceased laying, she will usually look small and insignificant even though she be an extra good one. But if it is during the laying season, when all fertile queens are laying, and the queen looks small, she should be removed, and another put in her place. It doesn't pay to keep any thing but the very best stock. The loss in honey would pay for several good queens.

HOW A WORKER-EGG IS MADE TO PRODUCE A QUEEN.

This is a question often asked, and it is one that puzzles us about as much to answer as any question a visitor can ask. We can not promise to tell you all about it, but we will tell you all we know about it. First get a frame of eggs, as we did in studying BEES, but we will vary the experiment by putting it into a colony having no queen. The tiny eggs will hatch into larvæ as before; but about as soon as they begin to hatch, if we look carefully we shall find some of the cells supplied with a greater profusion of milky food than others. Later, these cells will begin to be enlarged, and soon at the expense of the adjoining ones. These are queen-cells, and they are something like the cup of an acorn in shape, and usually occupy the space of three ordinary cells. In the drawing given, you will see cells in different stages of growth.

At A (see next page) is a cell being converted into a queen-cell; at B, one where the thin walls are extended so as to form a queen-cell proper, almost ready to seal up. This occurs just about nine days from the time the egg was laid. In seven days more, fifteen or sixteen days in all from the time the egg was laid, the queen will hatch out, a perfect insect. C is a cell just vacated. Now bear in mind exactly what we say, or you will get confused. When larvæ three days old are given the bees instead of eggs, they will rear a queen, and, in this case, she will hatch in only ten days after the larvæ

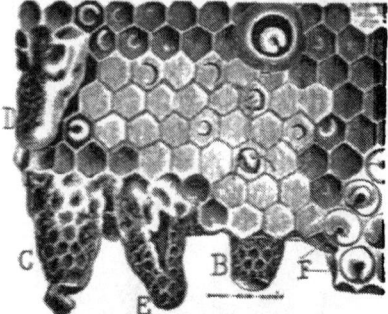

QUEEN-CELLS, AFTER CHESHIRE.

were given the bees. These ten-day queens probably are not as good as those reared from younger larvæ; and we think it well to supersede them as a rule.

There are some queer things about queen-cells, as you will notice. After the cell is sealed, the bees put a great excess of wax on it, make a long tapering point, and corrugate the sides something like a thimble, as shown at C, and in the enlarged view on the previous page. This corrugation, or roughness, when closely examined, will be seen to be honey-comb on a very small scale. Now right here is a point that you will not fail to observe: Bees, like other folks, sometimes make mistakes; for they do not seem to know any better than to use a drone-larva for rearing a queen, if such happens to be present.

Now, it is very handy to be able to tell nearly when any queen-cells you may happen to find unexpectedly will be likely to hatch; and the bees are very accommodating in this respect also; for, about the day before the queen hatches, or may be two days, they go and tear down this long peak of wax on the tip of the cell, leaving only a very thin covering, similar to the bottom cell here shown. We don't know why unless they are anxious to get a peep at their new mother. It has been said, they do it that she may be better able to pierce the capping; but sometimes they omit the proceeding entirely, and we have not been able to see

that she has any difficulty in cutting the cap off. If the cell is built on new comb, or on a sheet of foundation, and be held up before a strong light at about the fifteenth day, or a little later, you will see the queen moving about in the cell. Afterward, by listening carefully, you can hear her gnawing her way out. Pretty soon the points of her sharp and powerful mandibles will be seen protruding, as she bites out a narrow line. Since she turns her body in a circle while doing this, she cuts out a circle so true that it often looks as if marked by a pair of compasses. Now observe that the substance of which the cell is made is tough and leathery, and, therefore, before she gets clear around her circle, the piece springs out in response to her pushing, and opens just about as the lid of a coffee-pot would if a kitten should happen to be inside crowding against the lid. We have often seen them push the door open and look out, with as much apparent curiosity as a child exhibits when it first creeps to the door on a summer morning; often, after taking this look, they will back down into their cradle, and stay some time. This is especially the case when other queens are hatching, and there is a strife as to who shall be sovereign.

We will now consider the strange substance royal jelly.

The milky food before described, which is given to the young larvæ, and which is supposed to be a mixture of pollen and honey partially digested, is very similar, if not identical, in composition with the royal jelly. Bees are not the only examples in the animal kingdom where the food is taken into the stomach by the parent, and, after partial digestion regurgitated for the use of the offspring. Pigeons feed their young precisely in this way until they are able to digest their food for themselves. It has been stated that bees use a coarser food for the worker larvæ, after they are a few days old, and also for the drone larvæ during the whole of their larval state. What we mean by "coarser food" is, a food not so perfectly digested; in fact, drones are said to be fed on a mixture of pollen and honey, in a state nearly natural. This may be so, but we have no means of proving it to our satisfaction. It has also been said, that queens receive the very finest, most perfectly digested, and concentrated food that they can prepare. This we can readily believe, for the royal jelly has a very rich taste—something between cream, quince jelly, and honey—with

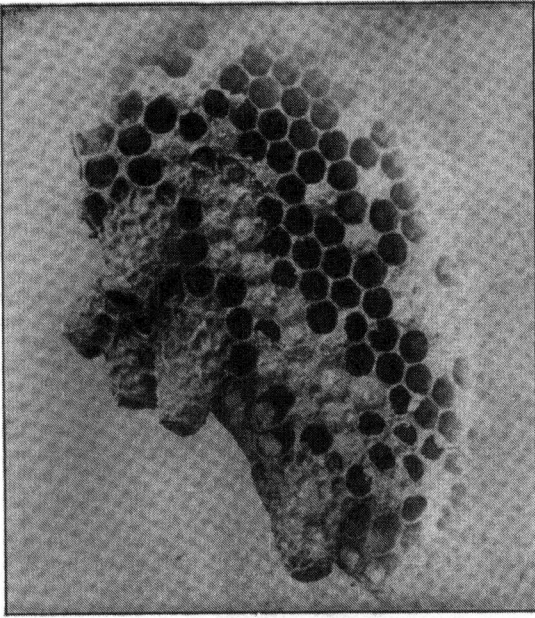

NATURAL-BUILT QUEEN-CELLS—LIFE SIZE.
Photographed by W. Z. Hutchinson.

a slightly tart and a rank, strong, milky flavor that is quite sickening if much be taken. See ROYAL JELLY, under the heading ANATOMY OF BEES.

WHAT DOES THE QUEEN DO WHILE SEALED UP?

Candidly, we do not know very much about it, although we have opened cells at every stage after they were sealed until they were ready to hatch. One day after being sealed they are simply ordinary larvæ, although rather larger than worker larvæ of the same age; after two or three days, a head begins gradually to be "mapped out," if that is the proper expression, and, later, some legs are seen folded up; last of all, a pair of delicate wings come from somewhere, we hardly know wh re. Two days before hatching we have taken them out of the cell, and had them mature into perfect queens, by simply keeping them in a warm place. We have also taken them out of the cell before they were mature, held the white, still, corpse-like form in the hand while we admired it as long as we chose, then put it back, waxed up the cell by warming a bit of wax in the fingers, and had it hatch out three days after, as nice a queen as any. Mr. Langstroth mentions

having seen the whole operation by placing a thin glass tube, open at both ends, into the cell, so as to have it inclose the queen, the bees being allowed to cap it as usual. This experiment was first made by Huber. With several such glass queen-cells, we presume the whole operation could be watched from beginning to end.

DAVIS' TRANSPOSITION PROCESS.

In the month of August, 1874, after I had discovered how to send larvæ for queen-rearing safely by mail short distances, our friend, Mr. J. L. Davis, of Delhi, Ingham Co., Mich., wrote that he would get a large number of queens from the piece we sent him, for he was going to remove the larvæ from the combs and place them in queen-cells already started in his hives—of course, removing the original larvæ first. We caught at the idea at once, and went to some hives of hybrids that had persisted in tearing down all the cells given them, and building others from their own brood, and removed the larvæ from all the cells, substituting larvæ from the imported queen in its stead. We used a quill toothpick for making the transposition. Almost every cell was built out and capped, just as well as if they had kept their own black stock. In due time we had as nice a lot of fine yellow queens as we ever reared. We have practiced this method almost every year

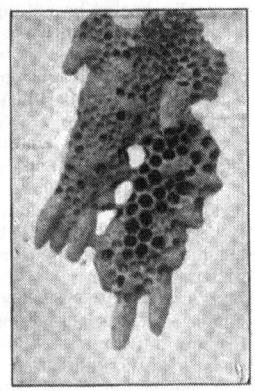

A small piece of comb containing an unusual number of queen-cells.

since, and now call it "grafting." See QUEEN-REARING.

WHAT BECOMES OF THE QUEEN AFTER SHE LEAVES THE CELL?

We can tell you, by personal observation, pretty nearly what a queen does after she pushes open that hinged door. which you

A FRAME FROM A COLONY THAT WAS PREPARING TO SWARM.
The combs had been spaced a little too far apart, and this gave the bees an excellent opportunity to build queen-cells.

where queens are wanted for other purposes, she has nothing to do but to promenade over the premises, monarch of all she surveys. If she ever sits down to take a rest, or takes a rest in any other position, during the first week of her life, we have never been able to discover it.

But suppose she does find another cell—what then? Well, she sometimes runs around it a while; sometimes the bees tear it down, and sometimes she tears it down herself, with the same strong mandibles that she used to cut her way out of the cell at first. She usually makes the opening in the side of the cell, as shown at E in cut on page 35s. Now, it is said that the queen immediately stings her helpless immature sister to make a sure thing of her destruction; but of this we are not certain, for we never have caught her in the act. We have seen spots in the side of the queen that

will find illustrated under the head of QUEEN-REARING. She generally begins by poking her head into the cells until she finds one containing unsealed honey, from which she takes a sup that, at least, indicates she likes that kind of provision.

After she has had her supper she begins to crawl about, partly to enjoy using the long strong legs God has given her, and partly because she knows that it is her allotted task to tear down the remaining queen-cells, if such there are. If other queens have hatched before her, it is one of her first and foremost duties to look them up, and either reign supreme or die in the attempt. When all other cells have been removed, as they usually are

NATURAL QUEEN-CELLS AT DIFFERENT STAGES.

[The capped cell on the left has been detached from the comb, and is ready to give to a colony; cell in the center, five or six days old, has been shaved down to show the queen larva just before it is ready to stretch out lengthwise of the cell; cell on the right shows the mouth of a cell just before capping.]

looked much as if she had been stung, but we have also rescued cells and put them into a wire-cage nursery after they had been torn open, and had them mature into nice queens. As these immature queens are very soft, the workers will soon pick them out of the cell, piece by piece, and we have sometimes placed them in the nursery and had them mature, minus a wing or leg, or whatever portion the mischievous worker had pulled away. We judge from many such observations that the queen generally tears a hole in the cell, or bites into it in such a way that the workers take hold of it, and tear it all down, much in the way they do any mutilated or broken piece of comb. When queen-cells have been cut out, all the larvæ that are in any way injured are at once thrown out, and none but the perfect cells preserved. Bees never fuss with cripples, or try to nurse up a bee that is wounded or maimed. They have just the same feeling for their fellows that a locomotive might be expected to have for a man whom it had run over. They battle against any thing that threatens the extinction of the colony, it is true; but we have never been able to discover any signs of their caring for one of their number, or even having compassion on their helpless brood when it is wounded and suffering. If a hole is made in a queen-cell by the queen or by anybody, they are almost sure to tear it down and throw it away. When a queen hatches the remaining cells are very soon torn down, as a general thing, but there are many exceptions. Where two queens hatch out at about the same time they also generally attempt to kill each other; but we have never heard of both being killed. This probably results from the fact that they can sting their rivals only in one certain way; and the one that, by strength or accident, gets the lucky position in the combat is sure to come off victor. This explains how a very inferior virgin queen, that has entered the hive by accident, may sometimes supplant an old laying queen. Two queens, when thus thrown together, generally fight very soon, but this does not always happen. Several cases are on record where they have lived in peace and harmony for months, even when hatched at about the same time, and it is quite common to find a young queen helping her mother in the egg-laying duties of the hive, especially when the mother is two or three years old. If the season is good, and the hive populous, they may divide up their forces, and we have AFTER-SWARMING, which see.

Sometimes the queen will pay no attention to the remaining cells, but will let them hatch out, and then their "little differences" are adjusted afterward, either by swarming or by the usual "hand-to-hand" conflict "until death." We once looked for a queen, and, not finding her, concluded she was lost. Another cell was inserted, and in due time hatched out. We were much surprised to find this new queen laying when only one day old; but a little further looking revealed two, both on the same comb. Many losses in introducing queens have resulted from two queens being in the hive, the owner being sure his hive was queenless—because he had removed one.

QUEENS' VOICES.

Queens have two kinds of voices, or calls, either one of which they may emit on certain occasions. It is almost impossible, on the printed page, to describe these sounds. One of them is a sort of z-e-e-p, z-e-e-p, zeep, zeep. Some call it piping, others teeting. Whatever it is, it consists of a prolonged tone, or, as we might say, a long zeep followed by several much shorter, each tone shorter than the preceding one. This piping is made when the queen is out of the cell, either virgin or laying, but usually by a young one. The older ones are generally too dignified, or too something, to give forth any such loud squealing; but they will squeal, and lustily, too, sometimes, when the bees ball them and grab them by the legs and wings. They shout just as we would when surrounded by enemies on every side, and in mere fright give a yell of alarm.

The other note that queen-bees are known to give forth is what is called *quahking*, for that more nearly describes the actual sound than any other combination of letters we can put together. If we mistake not, it is emitted only by a young queen in the cell, before she is hatched, and is made in answer to the piping or zeep, zeep, of one of the virgins that has already hatched, and is trying perhaps to proclaim aloud her sovereignty. The quahk will be heard, then, only when there are queen-cells in the hive. At other times the note will be a series of long z-e-ep, z-e-e-p, zeep, followed by shorter tones, as explained.

While a young queen is being introduced she frequently utters a note of alarm, a zeep, zeep, etc. The bees are almost always stirred by these notes of the queen, and they will often turn and run after her and cling around her like a ball, when they would have paid no attention to her had she not uttered this well-known note. When you have once heard it you will recognize it ever afterward. Queens, when placed near together in cages, will often call and answer each other, in tones that we have supposed might be challenges to mortal combat.

Some queens received one summer from W. P. Henderson, of Murfreesboro, Tenn., called so loudly when placed on our table, that they could be heard clear across a long room. One voice would be on a high, shrill key and another a deep bass, while others were intermediate. On watching closely a tremulous movement of the wings was noticed while the queen was uttering the note, and one might infer from this that the sound is produced by the wings, but this is probably not the case. Some one, we think, reported having heard a queen squeal, both of whose wings had been entirely clipped off. That these sounds from the queen have the power of controlling certain movements of the bees we are well aware, but we do not know just how nor to what extent this influence works.

VIRGIN QUEENS.

The newly hatched queen is termed a virgin simply to distinguish her from queens that have been fertilized by the drone and are laying. Virgin queens, when first hatched, are sometimes nearly as large as a fertile queen, but they gradually decrease in size, until when three or four days old they often look so small and insignificant that a novice is disgusted with their appearance, and if he is hasty pronounces them good for nothing. For the first week of their lives they crawl about much as an ordinary young worker does, and it is often very difficult, if not almost impossible, to find them, unless an amount of time is taken that is more than a busy apiarist can well afford to spare. We advise not to look for them, but to insert a frame having some unsealed larvæ just hatched from the egg; then if no cells are started, you can decide the queen is there without looking further. This plan answers a threefold purpose: It tells at a glance whether the queen is in the hive all right or not; for the very moment she is lost they will start more queen-cells on it; it enables the bees to start another queen, in case the queen is lost by any accident on her wedding-flight, which is frequently the case; and, lastly, it serves as a sort of nucleus to hold the bees together and to keep them from going out with the queen on her wed-

ding-trip, which they are much disposed to do, if in a small nucleus containing no brood. Unsealed brood in a hive is a great safeguard against accidents of all sorts, and we have often started a young queen to laying by simply giving the bees some eggs and unsealed brood. Whether it caused her to rouse up and take her wedding-flight, or whether she had taken it, but was for some reason idle, we can not say; but this we know, that young queens that do not lay at two weeks of age will often commence, when eggs and larvæ are given to their colonies. It may be that the sight of eggs and larvæ suggests to them the next step in affairs, or it may induce the workers to feed them, as they do a laying queen, an unusual quantity of food.

AGE AT WHICH VIRGIN QUEENS TAKE THEIR WEDDING-FLIGHT.

Our books seem to disagree considerably on this point, and we are afraid many of the book-makers find it easier to copy from the sayings of others than to try practical experiments. Some go so far as to say that the queen goes out to meet the drones the day after leaving the cell. Others fix the wedding-flight from two to ten days after birth. It is quite likely that some difference arises from the fact that queens often stay in the cell a day or two after they are strong enough to leave it.* Sometimes a queen will be found walking about the combs when she is so young as to be almost white; we have often seen beginners rejoice at their beautiful yellow queens, saying that they were yellow all over, without a bit of black on them; but when looked at again, they would be found to be as dark as the generality of queens. At other times when they come out of the cell they will look, both in color and size, as if they might be three or four days old. The queens in our apiary generally begin to crawl about the entrance of the hive, possibly looking out now and then, when 5 or 6 days old. The next day, supposing of course we have fine weather, they will generally go out and try their wings a little. These flights are usually taken in the warmest part of the afternoon. We know of no prettier or more interesting sight to the apiarist than the first flight of a queen. Perhaps a few hours before he had looked at her, and been disappointed at her small and insignificant appearance; but now, as she ventures out cautiously on the alighting-board, with her wings slightly raised, her tapering body

* Recent reports state that queens were confined in cells 4 or 5 days after they should have hatched.

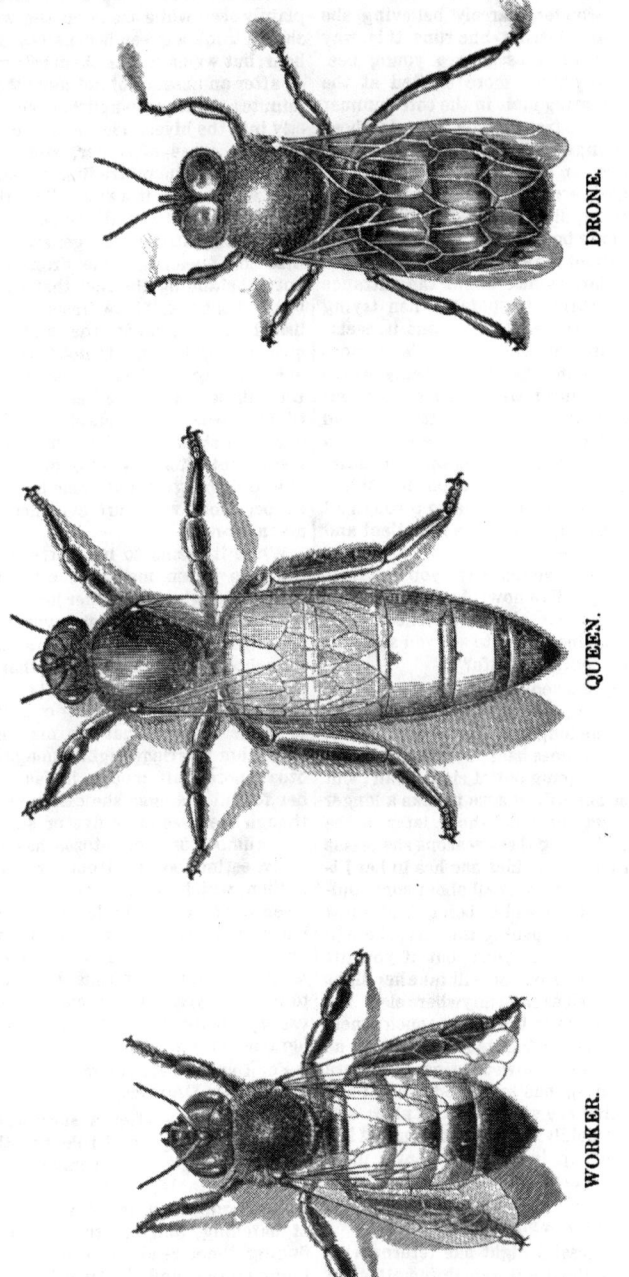

DRONE.

QUEEN.

WORKER.

elongated and amazingly increased in size, he looks in wonder, scarcely believing she can be the same insect. She runs this way and that, something as does a young bee, only apparently much more excited at the prospect of soaring aloft in the soft summer air. Finally she tremblingly spreads those long silky wings, and with a graceful movement that we can not remember to have seen equaled anywhere in the whole scope of animated nature, she swings from her feet, while her long body sways pendulously as she hovers about the entrance of the hive. A worker-bee hovers also about the entrance and carefully takes its points when trying its wings for the first time; but it, seeming to feel instinctively that it is of more value to the colony than many, many workers, the young queen with the most scrupulous exactness notes every minute point and feature of the exterior of her abode, often alighting and taking wing again and again, to make sure she knows all about it. When we saw one for the first time go through all these manœuvres, we became impatient and felt like saying,—

"There! there! young lady; you certainly know where you live now; do you suppose a fellow can stay here all the afternoon, neglecting his business, just to see you start off on your first journey in life?"

By and by she ventures to circle a little way from home, always verging back soon, but being gone longer and longer each time. She sometimes goes back into the hive satisfied, without going out of sight at all; but in this case she will be sure to take a longer flight next day or a half-hour later in the same day. During these seasons she seems to be so intent on the idea she has in her little head that she forgets all about surrounding things, and, instead of being frightened as usual at your opening the hive, she will pay no attention to you; but if you lift up the comb she is on she will take her flight from that as well as from anywhere else. We have caught them in the hand at such times, without their being frightened at all; but as soon as they were allowed to go, they were off as if nothing had happened. After she is satisfied that she will know the place, she ventures out boldly; and from the fact of her circling right up in the air, we have, until lately, supposed that fertilization took place above the ken of human eyesight. This has been shown to be a mistake.

After a successful flight she returns with the organs of the drone remaining attached to her body. See DRONES. This is a white

substance, and is frequently so large as to be plainly seen while she is on the wing. We should think a queen is usually gone half an hour, but we have seen them return fertilized after an absence of not more than 10 or 15 minutes. This accomplished, she goes quietly into the hive. The bees are much inclined to chase after her, and they sometimes pull at the protruding substance as if they would drag it away. That they do so, we think is pretty well proven.

Until recently it was generally believed that the queen met the drone only once, notwithstanding the fact that Francis Huber, in his book, "New Observations," published in 1814, made the statement that queens might or might not take more than one wedding-flight before beginning to lay. But this seems to have been overlooked until 1904, when considerable proof was adduced to show that the same queen *before* laying (not after) might not only take several wedding-flights, but come back on different occasions with sure evidence of having met a drone.

While it seems to be pretty well proven that the queen may take more than one marriage-flight *prior* to her laying, it is very much doubted whether she ever takes a second flight to meet the drone *after* laying, although there are some facts that seem to point that way. Against the belief that the queen meets the drone after once beginning to lay is the fact that she may receive on one of her marriage-flights enough spermatozoa—more than enough, in fact—to supply her for all the eggs she can ever lay, even though she lives to be five or six years old. The number of spermatozoa has been variously estimated at from two to twenty million, which she receives at one mating. Even if we accept the lesser figure, a good queen can scarcely lay more than two hundred thousand eggs in a season, even in a southern climate; and she then would have to live ten years, which she never does, to use up all the spermatozoa she receives at her one mating.

For further particulars on this subject of mating, see DRONES.

The next day after a succesful mating you will, as a general rule, find the queen depositing eggs. The average age at which queens begin laying is about nine days; we generally wait ten days from the date of hatching, and are then pretty sure of finding them ready to send off. Between impregnation and the time the first egg is laid a remarkable change takes place. After the queen has been out and fertilized, her appearance is much the same as before. She runs and hides when the hive is opened, and looks so small and insignificant that one would not think of calling her a fertile queen. A few hours before the first egg is laid, however, her body increases remarkably in size, and, if an Italian, becomes lighter in color; and, instead of running about as before, she walks slowly and sedately, and seems to have given up all her youthful freaks, and come down to the sober business of life in supplying the cells with eggs.

HOW OLD A QUEEN MAY BE AND STILL BECOME FERTILIZED.

As we have said before, our queens usually begin to lay when 8 or 10 days old, on the average; but during a dearth of pasturage, or when drones are scarce, they may fail to lay until three weeks old. The longest period we have ever known to elapse between the birth of a queen and her laying worker-eggs, was 25 days. We would destroy all queens that do not lay at the age of 20 days, when the season, flow of honey, flight of drones, etc., are all right. There is one important exception to this. Many times queens will not lay in the fall at all, unless a flow of honey is produced either by natural or artificial means. Queens introduced in the fall often will not lay at all until the ensuing spring, unless the colony is fed regularly every day for a week or ten days. Also young queens that are fertilized late in the season will often show no indications of being fertilized until the colony is fed as we have indicated. A lot of young queens that we thought might be fertilized but did not lay, were once wintered over, just to try the experiment; and although they went into winter quarters looking very small, like virgin queens, they nearly all proved fine layers in the spring.

DRONE-LAYING QUEENS.

If a queen is not fertilized in two weeks from the time she hatches, she will often commence laying without being fertilized at all. She is then what we call a drone-laying queen. Usually her eggs are not deposited in the regular order of a fertile queen, neither are there as many of them; but by these marks we are able only to guess that she may not be all right, and so keep her until some of the brood is capped, when the extra height of the cappings, as we have explained under DRONES, will tell the story. At times, however, the eggs are deposited so

regularly that we are deceived, and the queen may be sold for a fertile queen, when she is only a worthless drone-layer; but this we always discover after the brood is capped, and send our customer another queen. Such a case occurs, perhaps, once in a thousand. Whether these drone-layers are just as good to furnish supplies of drones for the apiary as the drones reared from a fertile queen, is a point, we believe, not fully decided; but if you care for an opinion, we should say if the queen lays the eggs in drone comb, and the drones are large, fine, and healthy, we believe them to be just as good. We should not want to use drones reared from fertile workers, nor drones reared in worker-cells, as those from drone-laying queens sometimes are.

SHALL WE CLIP QUEENS' WINGS?

The majority of honey-producers practice what is known as clipping; that is, two wings on one side are cropped off, leaving merely the stumps of what were once wings. The object, of course, is to prevent swarms from going off by making it impossible for the queen to follow.

As soon as a swarm issues, it will generally circle about in the air for a few minutes, until, discovering the absence of the queen, it will return to the old hive, where it will find her, probably, hopping about near the entrance. If the apiarist happens to be on hand he changes hives while the bees are in the air, and when they return they enter their new quarters with the queen. See SWARMING. Where he is not present, nor any one else to take care of them, no harm is done, for the bees with the queen simply go back.

If one does not practice clipping he is quite sure to be bothered with swarms clustering in difficult and inaccessible places, and going off, to say nothing of the general annoyance to neighbors and to himself in recovering and finally bringing back the absconders.

Some, instead of clipping, prefer to use entrance-guards or Alley traps (see DRONES), which prevent all possibility of any valuable queens getting lost in the grass, and save the marring of her symmetrical appearance. But outside of any sentimental reason, if we may call it such, the use of entrance-guards often saves an hour or two of hunting for the queen (for the purpose of clipping), especially if the bees are black or hybrid, or the colony is very populous. It takes but a moment to put on the entrance-guards, while it may, perhaps, on an average take five or ten minutes to find a queen and clip her wings, taking colonies as they run.

But entrance-guards are objected to because they obstruct more or less the passage of bees to and from the hive; and this, in the height of the season, it is argued, cuts down somewhat the actual amount of honey secured. We hardly think there is much in this; still we are willing to admit it may possibly make an appreciable difference.

There are very few who believe or profess to believe that clipping is injurious to the queen. The fact that queens after being clipped seem to do good service for two or

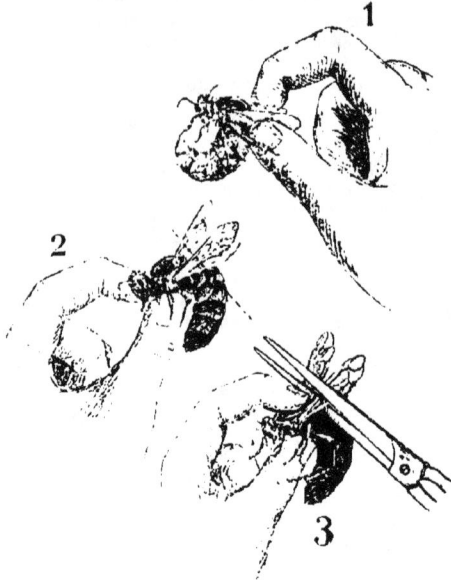

MANNER OF HOLDING A QUEEN DURING THE ACT
OF CLIPPING.

three years, and sometimes four, and the further fact that such queens do as well as those not clipped, would seem to show that no detrimental results follow.

HOW TO CLIP QUEENS' WINGS.

There are several ways of accomplishing this. One plan is to grasp the queen by the wings with the right hand, in the usual manner, as shown in No. 1 on this page. With the thumb and fore finger of left hand, take hold of her waist, or thorax, as at 3. In this way she can be held very securely and safely, leaving her legs as well as her wings entirely free. With a pair of slender-pointed embroidery scissors (or any

kind of scissors if these are not obtainable) clip off the *two wings* on one side, leaving anywhere from ⅛ to 1/16 of an inch, and being careful not to cut too close. This accomplished, drop her gently between two frames of brood; but in no case let her fall more than an inch; for a queen during the height of the egg-laying season is liable to be injured if handled roughly. Some prefer, after picking up the queen, to grasp her by the legs as shown at 2; but this is liable to pull one or more legs off unless done just right, and we therefore recommend plan 3.

Now, before you attempt any one of these plans, if you have had no experience you should first practice on drones. If these are not to be found, try picking up worker bees by the wings until you become reasonably expert; but don't attempt to put a worker between the thumb and finger of the other hand, as you will run a good chance of being stung. For this part of the work get drones if possible. Then, when you can do both operations well, try a queen. Even then we advise the attempt on one of not much value, as it is a nice piece of work to do it well.

Sometimes in an outyard, when a pair of scissors is not to be had, we use the sharp blade of a penknife. This is passed under the two wings in such a way as to cause them to bear directly upon the edge of the blade. The thumb is now pressed down upon the wings over the blade, and then drawn back and forth see saw fashion, perhaps two or three times. If the knife is sharp, the wings will be severed with two or three strokes. If it is dull, the queen should be laid on her back, still holding her between the thumb and finger of the left hand so that her wings will bear directly upon a hive-cover or any other piece of board or wood. The edge of the knife should be brought to bear upon the wings, when a slight pressure will cause the blade to pass through the wings into the cover.

During these operations be careful to handle a queen only by the wings or the thorax. This way avoids all danger of hurting her in the least, providing you are not *too* clumsy. But always be careful not to press the abdomen of any queen.

A very simple device, and something any one can make, is shown in the illustration on page 367. It consists of a piece of section stuff ¼ inch thick, whittled out as shown.

The two ends of the prong are split, and a light rubber band secured in the manner indicated.

This band must be stretched just tight enough so that, when the implement straddles a bee, the rubber band will hold it securely. For the purpose of determining just when the right amount of tension is secured, try it on common bees as they walk across on the combs. If it fails to hold one of them the band should be stretched a little tighter; and if not then sufficient, a heavier band should be used. After having perfected it on ordinary bees, use it on a queen-bee, and clip her wings in the manner shown.

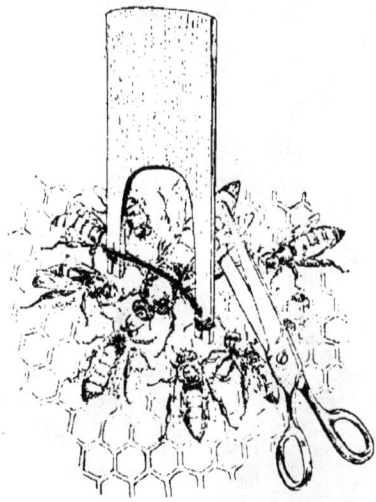

WILLIS QUEEN - CLIPPING DEVICE, AND HOW USED.

This is the invention of Mr. R. D. Willis, of Montrose, Col.; and after having tested the same we find that the implement works very satisfactorily.

In handling, the fingers sometimes taint the queens and cause bees to ball them after they have been clipped. This little device would obviate any trouble of that kind.

There are some bee-keepers, among whom may be mentioned Friedman Greiner, of New York, who prefer to clip the queen without picking her up off the comb. One edge of the frame is rested on the hive, as shown on the preceding page, while the free hand with a pair of fine-pointed scissors quickly clips the wings of her majesty as she stops for a moment on the comb.

Practice first on drones or workers before essaying the act on a queen. It is needful to work quickly and with considerable precision. Clumsy movements will be liable to cripple a queen seriously. It would be better to pick her up and follow any other method described.

HOW QUEENS LAY TWO KINDS OF EGGS.

That queens lay two kinds of eggs we think few are inclined to dispute, since the experiments with the microscope have decided the matter so clearly, as given under DRONES. Suppose a young queen goes out to meet the drones so late in the fall or so early in the spring that there are none; what is the consequence? Well, sometimes she will never lay at all; but frequently she commences to lay when 3 or 4 weeks old, and her eggs produce only drones. In fact, she can produce no other eggs, having never been fertilized. How shall we distinguish such queens from fertile ones? We can not decide positively concerning them, by any means we know now, until their brood is ready to seal up; then we will know by the round, raised capping of the brood, like bullets laid on a board, as we explained under DRONES. We can give a pretty good guess by noticing the way in which she lays the eggs; if they are few and scattering, and sometimes, or often, in drone-cells, coupled with the fact that she did not commence laying until two weeks or more old, we had better not send her off as an untested queen until some of her brood is sealed over. A young queen, if properly fertilized, never, or very rarely, lays an egg in a drone-cell; and when she commences to lay, she fills cell after cell in regular order, as men hoe a field of corn; her work also has a neat and finished appearance that says at once to the expert, "I am all right."

Now, friends, do not think us contradictory when we tell you that a young queen in rare cases does begin with all, or nearly all, drone-eggs, but, after a while, lays entirely worker-eggs as regularly as one could wish.* We do not know why this is: perhaps she has not yet got used to the "machinery." Once more, you must bear with us in telling you that any queen, the best one you ever saw, is liable, any day of her life, to begin laying drone eggs altogether, or in

* It has been suggested that this phenomenon may be accounted for by the fact that fertile workers were in the hive before the young queen began to lay; and the drone eggs are not from the queen but the fertile workers, and that, when the queen begins, she lays worker eggs at the very start, while the fertile workers are destroyed, and hence the drone eggs disappear. We are free to admit this is possible.

part. We wish you to remember this, that you may be more charitable toward each other in your dealings. A nice laying young queen, taken from a hive, and shipped to a distance, may prove to be a drone-layer shortly after or immediately after she is received. Such things are not very common, but they do occur. In an a virgin queen. Microscopic examination has shown an entire absence of spermatozoa in at least one or two instances where queens of this kind were killed and dissected. Similar experiments given by Dzierzon, show that the spermatozoa may be injured beyond recovery by chilling the queen, and yet the queen herself be resus-

GREINER'S METHOD OF CLIPPING QUEENS.

apiary of 50 or 100 hives we should expect to find one drone-layer, on an average, each spring. During the summer, perhaps one more will be found. It may be that the queen was not fertilized sufficiently, if we may use the term, and that the supply of spermatozoa gave out while she was in full vigor, thus reducing her to the condition of citated. We think it likely that hardship and being shipped long distances may produce the same results. Do not think we are going to excuse those who sell queens, and let the blame for unprofitable queens slip off their shoulders; on the contrary, we think they had better make up their minds to render a full equivalent for all the money they get. When a queen proves a drone-layer before the purchaser can receive any benefit from her, we think another should be sent. Of course, we can not give a rule for settling all such matters, but we would most earnestly advise that all try to do as we would be done by, and every one be *ready* to bear a little more than due share of such losses as may come up.

Well, queens not only turn suddenly to drone-layers, but they sometimes produce about an equal number of each kind of eggs. In all these cases, where the queen lays drone-eggs when she evidently intended to lay worker-eggs, they are in worker-cells; also the number of eggs laid usually rapidly decreases. The bees, as well as queen, evidently begin to think that something is wrong; queen-cells are soon started, and after the young queen is hatched she becomes fertile, and begins to help her mother. All hands evidently think that any kind of queen is better than none, hence a queen is seldom dragged out of the hive, as a worker-bee is, because she is ailing.

Very early in the spring, late in the fall, or at any time when forage is not abundant, a queen will pass right by drone-cells, taking no notice of them. We have often tried to get eggs in drone-cells by feeding, and can not but conclude that the queen knows what an egg will produce, and just what "wires to pull" to have every egg laid in a drone-cell produce a drone. We think it very likely the workers have something to do with this matter, but we have never been able to make out by what means they signify to the queen that some eggs in drone-cells, or even queen - cells, would be desirable. There seems to be a constant understanding in the hive as to what is going to be done next, and consequently there is no clashing. We wish, friends, the human family could understand each other as well. In our apiary there seems to be, in strong stocks, a kind of understanding that eggs shall be laid in drone-cells about the last of March, and we have drones, therefore, some time in April, ready for the first queens that may, by any accident, make their appearance. Those who insist that there is only one kind of eggs can satisfy themselves very easily by taking an egg from either a drone or worker cell and placing it in the bottom of a cell of the other kind. They will get a drone in a worker-cell, or a worker in a drone-cell. Again: If you give a young laying queen a hive supplied only with drone combs, she will rear worker brood in these

drone-cells, and the mouth of the cells will be contracted with wax, as mentioned under HONEY-COMB.

When they get ready to swarm they build shallow queen-cells, in which the queen then lays a worker-egg. Although we never saw her lay an egg in a queen-cell, we are satisfied that she does it, from the way in which it is put in. Like the rest of the eggs, it is fastened to the center of the bottom of the cell by one of its ends, and we suppose, when first deposited, it is covered with a sort of glutinous matter that makes it stick firmly where it first touches. We know that bees have the skill to remove both eggs and larvæ, for we have several times known them to take eggs and brood to an old dry comb when no queen was present in the hive.

Occasionally a queen is found that will never lay at all; again, queens that laid eggs which never hatched into larvæ have been several times reported. We have had several such, and they were in appearance fine nice-looking queens.

After having told you thus much of the faults and imperfections of queens, we would add, for their credit, that when once properly installed in a strong colony they are about as safe property as any thing, because, in the great majority of cases, they live and thrive for years. We have never heard of any disease among queens, and, while a worker lives only a few months, they often live 3 or 4 years. One that was imported from Italy by Dadant furnished us brood and eggs for queen-rearing for four summers. We then sold her for $2.00, and she died in being sent less than 50 miles. She was very large and heavy, and, probably, being so old could not cling to the sides of the cage like a younger one. We have never heard of queens being troubled with any thing but a European parasite, which quickly disappeared when introduced into American apiaries. See ENEMIES OF BEES.

LOSS OF QUEEN.

It is a very important matter to be able to know at once when a queen is lost. During the months of May and June the loss of a queen from the hive a single day will make quite a marked difference in the honey crop. If we assume the number of eggs a queen may lay in a day to be 3000, by taking her away a single day we should, in the course of events, be just that number of bees short right during a yield of honey. To put it very moderately, a quart of bees might be taken out of the hive by simply caging the queen for a single day. Beginners should remember this, for their untimely, or, rather, inconsiderate tinkering, just before the flow of honey comes, often cuts short their income to a very considerable degree. Whatever you do, be very careful not to drop the queens off the combs when you handle them at this time of the year, and do not needlessly interrupt the queen in her work by changing the combs about so as to expose the brood or upset their little household matters in the hive. With a little practice you will be able to detect a queenless hive simply by the way the bees behave themselves on the outside. Where they stand around on the alighting-board in a listless sort of way, with no bees going in with pollen, when other colonies are thus engaged, it is well to open the hive and take a look at them. If you find eggs and worker-brood you may be sure a queen is there; but if you do not, proceed at once to see if there is not a queen of some kind in the hive, that does not lay. If you do not find one, proceed at once to give them a frame containing brood and eggs, and see if they start queen-cells. You ought to be able to find incipient ones in about twelve hours, if the bees have been some little time queenless. As soon as you see these, give them a queen if possible. If no queen is to be had, they may be allowed to raise one, if the colony has bees enough. If it has not, they had better be united with some other stock.

ODOR OF A LAYING QUEEN.

After bees have been some time queenless they usually become, if no fertile or laying workers make their appearance (see LAYING WORKERS), very eager for the presence of a queen; and we can in no way describe this eager behavior, if we may so term it, so well as to describe another way of testing a colony you have reason to think is queenless. Take a cage or box containing a laying queen and hold either the cage or simply the cover of it over the bees, or hold it in such a way as to let one corner touch the frames. If queenless, the first that catch the scent of the piece of wood on which the queen has clustered will begin to move their wings in token of rejoicing, and soon you will have nearly the whole swarm hanging to the cage or cover. When they behave in this manner we have never had any trouble in letting the queen right out at once. Such cases are generally where a colony is found without brood in the spring.

There is something very peculiar about the scent of a laying queen. After having had a queen on the fingers, we have had bees follow and gather about the hand, even when we had gone some distance from the apiary. By this strange instinct they will often hover for hours about the spot where the queen has alighted for even an instant, and, sometimes, for a day or two afterward. Where clipped queens get down into the grass or weeds or crawl sometimes a considerable distance from the hive, we have often found them, by watching the bees that were crawling about along the path she had taken. When cages containing queens are being carried away bees will often come and alight on the cage making that peculiar shaking of the wings which indicates their joy at finding the queen. See SCENT OF BEES.

QUEENS' STINGS.

There is something rather strange in the fact that a queen very rarely uses her sting, even under the greatest provocation possible, unless it is toward a rival queen. In fact, they may be pinched or pulled limb from limb, without even showing any symptoms of protruding the sting at all; yet as soon as you put them in a cage or under a tumbler with another queen, the fatal sting is almost sure to be used at once. There seems to be a most wise provision in this; for if the queen used her sting on every provocation as does the worker, the prosperity of the colony would be almost constantly endangered. It is true, that instances are on record where queens have stung the fingers of those handling them; but these cases are so very rare it is quite safe to say queens never sting. We are inclined to think the cases mentioned were of queens that were not fully developed; for we have often seen the dark half-queen and half-worker, mentioned a few pages back, show its sting when handled.

CAUTION IN REGARD TO DECIDING A STOCK TO BE QUEENLESS.

As a rule, we may say that absence of brood or eggs is a pretty sure indication of queenlessness; but it should be borne in mind that all hives, as a rule, are without eggs and brood in the fall and early winter months, or, in fact, at any time when there is a considerable dearth of pasturage. At such seasons, beginners are more apt to think their hives are queenless, because the queens are much smaller than when they are laying profusely. In weak colonies queens often cease laying during the whole of the winter months. See INTRODUCING.

For particulars on how to find queens, see FRAMES, TO MANIPULATE.

R.

RASPBERRY (*Rubus strigosus* and *Rubus ideus*). Where this fruit is raised largely for the market it is quite an important honey-plant; but it would hardly be advisable to think of raising it for honey alone. Bees work on it closely in our locality, and its honey is of the very finest. If bee-keepers and growers of small fruits could locate near each other it would probably be a benefit to both. Langstroth says of the raspberry honey: "In flavor it is superior to that from white clover, while its delicate comb almost melts in the mouth. When it is in blossom, bees hold even white clover in light esteem. Its drooping blossoms protect the honey from moisture, and bees work upon it when the weather is so wet they can obtain nothing from the upright blossoms of the white clover."

In our locality it comes in bloom just after fruit blossoms and just before clover, so that large fields of it are a great acquisition indeed. The red varieties (especially the Cuthbert) are said to furnish most honey.

WILD RASPBERRY OF NORTHERN MICHIGAN.

This deserves special mention here for the reason that large quantities of raspberry honey are produced in Northern Michigan where forests of pine timber formerly grew. The fact that such land is very cheap, and almost useless for any thing but timber-growing, which, under present conditions, can not get a start, makes the business of honey-producing profitable and reasonably sure, for it is probable that the plant will continue to flourish, as there is nothing else that is adapted to take its place. The blossoms commence yielding honey in June, and continue to bloom more or less from then till frost.

As Langstroth says of it above, the honey is of the finest quality, and will rank in almost any market with the best clover. Indeed, connoisseurs pronounce it superior to any other table honey in the world, for it partakes somewhat of the beautiful flavor of the berry itself, with all the added qualities that are so much prized in clover.

The Michigan fruit ripens in July, and continues available for picking till frost.

The drawback about this wild raspberry is that the fruit will not keep for shipping, and it must, therefore, be used almost the same day it is picked.

WILD RASPBERRY OF NORTHERN MICHIGAN.

RATS. Rats may and can do a great deal of damage in a honey-house. There are some old fellows that are cute enough to avoid traps and poison. The only thing to do with such is to shoot them by watching when they congregate about five o'clock in the afternoon in and about the out-buildings. A 32-caliber Flobert rifle with shot cartridges, or, better, a taxidermist's 44-caliber shotgun, will do very good execution.

One of the best traps that was ever made is the old-fashioned rabbit-trap with grain spread on the bottom of the box. The trigger to close the trap should extend down to the grain. The rats in eating will bump against the trigger and set it off, when they are imprisoned alive, after which they may be drowned.

Poison can be given in the form of dough made of one-fifth part of barium carbonate, or barytes, and four-fifths meal. This poison has no odor nor taste; and it is better than strychnine because its action is slower, giving the rats a chance to get off the premises before they die.

RECORD-KEEPING OF HIVES. Almost every apiarist has a plan of his own, whereby he can record the condition of the hive at the time of its examination, so that, in future, without depending on memory, he may tell at a glance what its condition was when last examined.

Many of the large honey-producers, Dr. Miller among them, have what they call a "record-book." This book has a page for each colony, the number of the page corresponding with the number of the colony. The book should be small and compact, just about right to carry in the hip-pocket, and securely bound. It should always be carried when at work among the bees. On each page is supposed to be a record of each colony's doings within a year—when it became queenless, when it had cells or brood, when it swarmed, and, toward winter, the strength and quantity of stores it had when last examined.

There is an advantage in the book method—and that is, the book can be consulted in the house, and the work mapped out beforehand for the day. If the record-book be for an out-apiary, the work can be planned while riding to the yard; and, upon arrival, the plans formulated can be executed. We will know in advance just where we are going to get cells to give to queenless colonies; just which colonies will be likely to have laying queens; which ones may cast swarms, and which ones will be likely to need more room in the way of sections or surplus combs. There is one objection to the record-book, however. It is liable to be lost, or to be left out in the rain; and if the book is lost, the whole knowledge of the apiary, except so far as the apiarist can remember, is gone. Another thing, only one can use the book at a time.

RECORD-KEEPING WITH SLATE TABLETS. The plan we prefer is to attach the record right on the hive itself, or, what is better, on a slate* belonging to the hive. These are made expressly for the purpose, and cost only $1.25 per 100. They are large enough, if the records are abbreviated, to give the history of the colony for a year. Still further, the position that these slates occupy on the cover or on the side of the hive indicates at a distance the general condition of the colony, without so much as even reading the record on the slate. These slates are 2¼ by 1¼ inches, and they have a hole punched near one end, so as to admit of their being hung on the side of the hive. The accompanying cut shows one of these little slates. For making the records, a slate-pencil, a common lead-pencil, or a red lead-pencil, may be used. The slate-pencil marks wash out a little too easily in the rain, so we prefer, as a general thing, a lead-pencil, which does not erase except when the slate is rub-

bed with moistened fingers. By tilting it a little to the light, the marks show quite plainly. In the slate above we have given an example of the records we put on. Perhaps it may not appear very intelligible to the reader. Cell 6/19 means that, on the 19th of June, a cell from the best imported was given. Ht 22 means that the queen hatched on the 22d of that month. July 2d she was laying, and August 15th she was found to be a pure tested Italian queen. A large 9 inscribed over the whole will be noticed. This means that, on the 9th of September, the queen was sold. The accompanying cut illustrates still another record, which, interpreted, means that, on the 18th of June, a best imported queen was caged. On the 20th she was out and laying; and on the 10th of the following month she was sold.

Every apiarist can formulate a system of short longhand that will be intelligible to himself and workmen. It takes too much time to write the whole history of the affair, so it is better to use a system of abbreviations; and, besides, it saves room.

In order to economize time in running up to a slate to see what it says, it is desirable to indicate, so far as possible, the last record on the slate by its position on the cover.

The accompanying diagram shows a few of the positions that may be used ; and this number may be extended indefinitely by putting the slate cornerwise, endwise, etc., in the different positions shown. But it is desirable not to have too many, else you or your help will be confused.

The code below is one we have used in our apiary, and it is one that can be used in most yards. To make it really valuable, it will be necessary to memorize the meaning of each position. In the diagram given, 10 positions are shown ; and these have been proven by actual practice to answer our requirements. To aid the memory we will make use of a simple analogy. We have

then we turn the slate *parallel* with the grain, as shown at 4. If the virgin queen should be lost, the slate is put back as shown in No. 1—across the grain. Let us suppose that our queen is laying, and in a month's time she proves a purely mated Italian. The condition of the colony has much improved, as regards the value of the queen, so the slate is moved to the center of the hive, parallel with the grain.

So far the first five positions would cover the time of queen-rearing. But suppose we wish to introduce a queen—how shall we indicate it ? The colony with a caged queen is neither queenless nor is it possessed of a queen, because they may take a notion to kill her as soon as she is released. To carry out the figure, the colony is about half way between the normal and abnormal condition. So we turn the slate to a diagonal. Position 6 means that the colony has just received a caged queen. No. 7 means that, a day or two afterward, she was found to be out. A few days later, if she is laying, the slate is put in position 4. But, suppose she is missing. Then the slate is turned in the position of 8. In general, position 8 signifies that there is something radically wrong

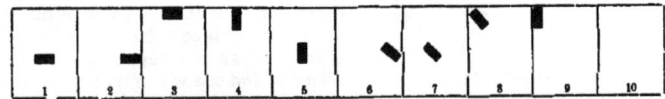

. :.. POSITION OF THE SLATE TO INDICATE THE CONDITION OF A COLONY.

1. Queenless; 2. Cell; 3. Hatched virgin; 4. Laying queen; 5. Tested queen; 6. Caged queen to be introduced; 7. Caged queen out; 8. Something wrong; 9. Hive needs supers and more room; 10. No slate—hive with empty combs, ready for a swarm.

heard about cross-grained people—people who are always out of sorts, and with whom something is always wrong. For convenience we will call a colony not in its normal condition, " cross-grained." A colony that is queenless is apt to be crosser than one having a queen. Such a colony, as a rule, never does as well as one that has a queen. It is true, also, but to a lesser extent, that a colony with a virgin queen is not doing as well as one having a laying queen. Well, now we start with No. 1, in the diagram as above. The slate is put *across* the *grain* in the center of the hive. This means that it is queenless. No. 2, the slate is still across the grain, but near the *edge* of the hive ; but this one has a cell. No. 3, the cell has hatched, and has a virgin queen ; but as the colony has not yet reached its normal condition, the slate is still laid across the grain at the *end* of the cover. In eight or ten days, if all goes well the virgin will be laying, and

with the colony. It may mean that it has a fertile worker, or that it is very short of stores and requires to be fed at once.

We have so far covered the history of a colony as touching the rearing and introducing of queens. When honey is coming in, it is desirable to know by the slates which ones will be likely to need supers soon. In 9, again, the slate is parallel with the cover. This means that it is overflowing with bees and honey, and will need, in a day or two, if not immediately, more room in the shape of sections or surplus combs. No. 10, without any slate on the hive, means that the hive in question is empty, having only frames of foundation or empty comb, and is, therefore, ready to receive a swarm. No. 1 might mean that the hive needs attention or is about to cast a swarm; No. 2 might stand for a parent hive, and No. 3 might indicate a second swarm, and so on we could vary the system.

Some bee-keepers, instead of using slate tablets, write with a lead-pencil on pieces of section as shown.

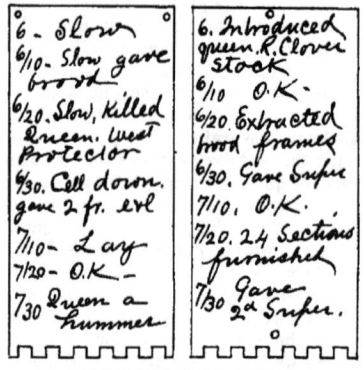

QUEEN-REGISTER CARDS.

Another system of record-keeping that is popular with some is what are called register-cards. The accompanying plan shows

Queen Register.

how they are used. To indicate the date, the pin heads are revolved so as to point to the proper place. There is no writing, and nothing to do except to turn the pointers to the right place. This is preferred by W. Z. Hutchinson and others.

REVERSING. This, as the term signifies, is the process of inverting, or turning over, the combs; and this may be accomplished by inverting the several frames individually or the whole hive at one operation. The subject began to be discussed in 1884; and for three or four years following there was much said on the subject. Reversible frames and reversible hives were invented by the dozen. Some of them were quite ingenious, while others were clumsy and impractical.

Taking into consideration the fact that the bees store their honey just immediately

over the brood, and, as a consequence, their combs at this point would be much better filled out. certain bee-keepers conceived the idea of turning the combs upside down at frequent intervals. "Why," said they, "when the combs are reversed, bringing the bottom-bars uppermost, the combs will be built clear out to the bottom-bars, and the honey now in the bottom of the combs will be carried up into the supers, just where it is wanted." This seemed very nice in theory, and even in practice it seemed to be partially carried out; for a good many bee-keepers reported that, when the combs were reversed, the bees, rather than have the honey in the bottom of the combs, near the entrance, and accessible to robbers, would uncap it and take it up into the sections. But the result was, that often poor and dark honey went up above; more often, we believe, the bees allowed the honey to stay at the bottom of the hive. and the only real advantage secured was getting the combs filled actually to the bottom-bars, being now at the top.

A very few claimed that reversing, when done at the proper time, would destroy queen-cells, and so control swarming. But it did not—at least in *our* case.

After all, the real and direct advantage of reversing is in the matter of getting combs filled out in brood-frames as solid as a board. When hunting queens it is much easier to find one where there is no horizontal space between the edge of the comb and the bottom-bar, and no holes to furnish her hiding-places. Then, of course, having combs filled out solid gives better fastening to the frame and increases the capacity of the hive just in proportion to the new comb built after reversing. Nearly every frame that is not reversed is liable to have a space of ¼ inch or ⅜; and this is certainly a waste that ought to be utilized if possible. To a certain extent this space can be filled in non reversing frames by having sheets of foundation reach from frame-bottom to top-bar, wired in with perpendicular wires; but even such combs are never as well filled as those reversed.

Several good reversible frames have been proposed; but we would never think of adopting any of them unless it had some points of merit outside the one exclusive feature of reversing. A reversible frame that is not good for all-around use would be very unprofitable.

One of the first practical reversing frames was the Van Deusen, having metal corners or ears. This is essentially a standing frame, and can be used just as well one side up as the other. The frames are spaced apart by "spacing-ears," and these very ears offer some distinctive advantages in the way of handling the frame. This frame was used

THE VAN DEUSEN REVERSIBLE FRAME.

very largely by the one-time most extensive bee-keeper in the world, the late Capt. J. E. Hetherington; also by his brother in Michigan. Outside of its reversing feature it offers one very decided advantage; namely, the facility with which it can be handled like the leaves of a book. By taking out one or two frames the rest can be thumbed over without lifting them out of the hive.

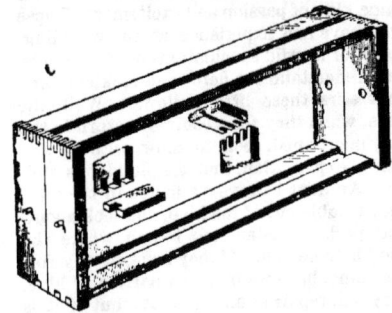

DANZENBAKER'S REVERSIBLE FRAME.

Two other very excellent reversible frames are the Danzenbaker and the Heddon (see HIVES; also FRAMES, SELF-SPACING, and FRAMES, TO MANIPULATE), either one of which can be used as well one side up as the other; in fact, any closed-end standing frame can be used as a reversible frame. Where one can get the advantage of reversing without cost it is certainly advisable to reverse the frames at least once in order to get the combs completely filled out. For further consideration of this subject see booklet, "Facts about Bees," by E. R. Root, published by The A. I. Root Co.

ROBBING. Paul says, "The *love* of money is the root of all evil." We should be inclined to state it in this way: The disposition to get money without rendering an equivalent is the root of all evil. Well, the root of a great many evils in bee-keeping is the disposition of the bees to gain honey without rendering any equivalent. Some one of our A B C class has said that he found bees making visits to over 100 clover-heads before they obtained a load sufficient to carry to their hives. We think it very likely that during a great part of the season a bee will be absent a full hour, or, it may be, during unfavorable spells, as much as two hours, in obtaining a single load. Is it at all strange that a bee, after having labored thus hard during the fore part of the day, should, in the afternoon, take a notion to see if it could not make a living in some easier way? Would it be very much worse than many types of humanity? Well, as it passes around to other hives it catches the perfume of the clover honey they have gathered in a like manner, and, by some sort of an operation in its little head, it figures out that, if it could abstract some of this, unperceived, and get it safely into its own hive, it would be so much the richer. We presume it has no sort of care whether these other folks die of starvation or not. That is none of its concern.

With all their wonderful instincts, we have never been able to gather that the bees of one hive ever have any spark of solicitude as to the welfare of their neighbors. If, by loss of a queen, the population of any hive becomes weak, and the bees too old to defend their stores, the very moment the fact is discovered by other colonies they rush in and knock down the sentinels, with the most perfect indifference, plunder the ruined home of its last bit of provision, and then rejoice in their own home, it may be but a yard away, while their defrauded neighbors are so weak from starvation as to have fallen to the bottom of the hive, being only just able to attempt feebly to crawl out at the entrance. Had it been some of their own flock, the case would have been very different indeed; for the first bee of a starving colony will carry food around to its comrades, as soon as it has imbibed enough of the food furnished to have the strength to stagger to them.

Well, suppose the bee mentioned above, in prowling around in the afternoon or some other time, should find a colony so weak or so careless that it could slip in unobserved, and get a load from some of the unsealed cells, and get out again. After it has passed the sentinels outside it usually runs little danger from the inmates, for they seem to take it for granted that every bee inside is one of their number. There is danger, though; for should it betray too great haste in repairing to the combs of honey they often suspect something; so it assumes an indifference it is far from feeling, and loiters about very much as if it were at home, and finally, with a very well-assumed air of one who thinks he will take a lunch, it goes to the cells and commences to fill up. Very often, when it gets pretty well "podded out" with its load, some bee approaches, apparently to see if all is right. When the robber once gets its head into a cell, however, it seems to have lost all sense or reason; and if it is discovered at this stage to be a stranger and a thief, it is often pounced upon and stung with very little ceremony. How do they know a stranger from one of their own number, where there are so many? It is said they tell by the sense of smell; this may be the principal means, perhaps, but apparently they depend greatly on the actions and behavior of a bee, much as we do when judging of the responsibility of a man who asks to be trusted. We can give a very good guess, simply by his air or manner, or even by the sort of letter he writes. If a robber is suspected, and a bee approaches for the purpose of satisfying itself, it is a very critical moment, and one becomes intensely interested in watching the performance. The robber will stand its ground, if it is an old hand, and permit itself to be looked over with wonderful indifference; but one who has watched such scenes closely will detect a certain uneasiness, and a disposition to move slowly toward the entrance, that it may be the better able to get out quickly, when it discovers things to be too hot for it inside. If the bee that first suspects it concludes it is an interloper, it begins to bite it, and grab hold of its wings to hold on until others can come to help. The thief has now two chances to escape, and sometimes it seems meditating which to adopt; one is, to brave it out until they shall perhaps let it alone, and then slip out unobserved. The other is, to break away and trust to its heels and wings. The latter plan is the one generally adopted, unless it is a very old and "hardened sinner" in the business. One that has been many times in such scrapes will usually get away, by the latter plan, by an adroit series of twists, turns, and tumbles, even though three or four bees have hold of it at once. Some of these fellows, by a sudden and unexpected dash, will liberate themselves in a manner that is also wonderful, and then, as if to show their audacity, will wheel about and come back close to the noses of their retainers of a minute before.

In case the bee secures its load and makes its way out unobserved, it gets home very quickly, you may be sure, and, under the influence of this new passion for easily replenishing its hive with the coveted sweets, it rushes out with a vehemence never known under any other circumstances. Back it goes and repeats the operation, with several of its comrades at its heels. Does it tell them where to go? We wish to digress enough here to say that we do not believe in a so-called language among bees, or animals in general, further than certain simple sounds which they utter, and which we may learn to interpret almost if not quite as well as they do. When a bee comes into the hive in such unusual haste, podded out with its load in a way also rather unusual when obtained from ordinary stores, its comrades at once notice it, and, either from memory or instinct, they are suddenly seized with the same kind of passion and excitement. Those who have had experience at the gambling-table, or in wild speculations of other kinds, can understand the fierce and reckless spirit that stirs these little fellows. Well, the bees, when they see a comrade return in the way mentioned, seem to know, without any verbal explanation, that the plunder is stolen. Anxious to have " a finger in the pie," they tumble out of the hive, and look about, and perhaps listen, too, to find where the spoil is to be had. If they have, at any former time, been robbing any particular hive, they will repair at once to that; but if it is found well guarded, those used to the business will proceed to examine every hive in the apiary.

INTELLIGENCE OF THE HONEY-BEE.

One afternoon the door of the honey-house being left open, the bees were soon doing a "land-office" business before the mischief was stopped by closing the door until they had clustered on the windows in the room, which were then opened, and the process repeated until all were out. All the rest of the afternoon they were hovering about the door. Toward night they gradually disappeared; and when we went down, about sundown, to try a new feeder, not a bee was near the door. We put the feeder in front of a hive where the bees were clustered out; and as soon as a few bees had got a taste, and filled themselves, they of course went into the hive to unload. We expected a lot to come out, as soon as these entered with their precious loads, but were much astonished to see an eager crowd come tumbling out as if they were going to swarm, still more when they rushed right past the feeder and took wing for—where do you suppose? the honey-house door, of course. How should they reason otherwise, than that it had again been left open, and that was where these incomers had found their rich loads? On finding it closed, back to the hive they came, to repeat the manœuvre over and over.

As another evidence of the wonderful intelligence and almost reasoning power of the honey-bee, we will make an extract from *Gleanings in Bee Culture*. This item was written by A. I. Root.

On the 12th of September a shipment of honey came in, with two 60-pound cans so badly damaged that the contents had leaked out and run through the floor of the box car. The railroad company had agreed to take the car away at half-past ten; and as the weather was cool the bees had not discovered it at that time. Unfortunately the company failed to move the car as agreed, and I knew nothing of it till I was apprised something was wrong by the unusual number of bees swarming around the windows and doors of the factory. Then I made a little row in the camp. We carried a hose over to the leaky car and washed away the honey, cleaning it from the gearing, ironwork, and under side of the car until the bees were pretty well satisfied there was nothing more to get, although they were hanging around in great numbers. To prevent the bees from getting the honey inside the car, our boys covered the floor pretty well with sawdust. About three o'clock the engine came around and pulled the car away. A little after four, some men who were loading wheat informed us our bees were making them a great deal of trouble. I at once jumped to the conclusion that the company, instead of taking the car entirely away, as agreed, had only removed it to another location in the yard, and that the sticky car was still enticing our bees. I went over, saw the sawdust on the floor on which they were dumping bags of wheat, and concluded it was the honey-car; but while I was puzzling my head to account for the fact that the ironwork under this car showed no trace of honey or water either, a man called to me and pointed to *another* car in still another location, just swarming with bees around its door, inside and out. Then I "caught on." Do you see the point, friends? There was not a particle of honey in or around either of the two cars I was looking at. After the honey-car had been pulled clear out of town, the bees, not willing to give up, proceeded to "leave no stone unturned," and were investigating every car having an open door that, in their judgment, *might* be the one that had been pulled away. When they found one with sawdust spread over the floor they naturally concluded *that* was the car, and got down on their hands and knees (figuratively) searching in the sawdust for the honey. The other bees, seeing them thus employed, naturally concluded this was the place. Others, having learned that one box car contained so rich a find, concluded that a search through all the cars in the yard might possibly reward them for their investigation; and it was only in the cool of the evening that they were willing to stop digging in that sawdust, and be convinced there were no more honey-cars about.

Now, friends, it may not be true that bees recognize colors, but they certainly do take in the general makeup of objects. They are not only able to recognize a hive, but they know a box car at sight; and even if you move it to a different location they take in its general appearance so that they know pretty well how to find it in case of removal. I am not prepared to prove that they read the letters "Big Four" on the side of that car, nor that they remembered there was an enormous figure 4 printed in white on the red door of the car they wanted; but I tell you they came pretty close to it.

Of course, bees have particular notes, as for joy, sorrow, anger, despair, etc., which are produced by the wings, usually when flying; but we are quite sure they are unable to communicate to each other more than a single idea. In other words, they have no faculty of telling their fellows that a lot of honey is to be had in a feeder at the entrance, and that it would better be brought in quickly, or other bees may find it. A bee goes out in the spring, and, by smelling around the buds, discovers honey and pollen; when it comes into the hive the others see it and start out to hunt up the source of supply in a similar way. For further information on this subject, see SWARMING.

If you will turn back and read ANGER OF BEES, you will get a very good idea of the causes that start bees to robbing. Read, also, BEE-HUNTING, FEEDING, etc. As a general thing, bees will never rob so long as plenty of honey is to be had in the fields. During a bountiful flow we have tried in vain to get bees to take any notice of honey left around the apiary. At such times we can use the extractor right in the open air, close to the sides of the hives, if need be. On one occasion we remember leaving a comb of unsealed honey on the top of a hive from morning until noon, and not a bee touched it. It seems they preferred to go to the cloverfields in the regular way rather than to take several pounds from the top of a neighboring hive. We can readily suppose that they did not have to visit anything like a hundred blossoms at this time, and perhaps they secured a load in going to not more than a half-dozen. Such a state of affairs is not very usual in our locality. We have very few days during the season when it would be safe to use the extractor for a whole day in the open air, the bees generally learning to follow the freshly uncapped combs about, and that it is easier than going to the fields. The first indication of robbing which you will probably have will be the cool and wicked way of stinging that we have described in ANGER OF BEES.

After the season begins to fail, you may expect that every colony in your apiary will be tried. As a rule, any fair colony will have sentinels posted to guard the entrance as soon as there is any need of such precaution. The bee that presumes to think it may enter for plunder will be led off by " the ear," if we may so express it, and this will be repeated until it learns that there is no chance for peculation at that house. At the close of the honey harvest we should be sure that there are no feeble hives that may be overpowered, for one such may start the fashion of robbing, and make it a much harder matter to control the propensity. An apiary, like a community, may get so demoralized that thieving becomes a universal mania. "A stitch in time will save" a great many more than nine in this case. Be sure that each colony has the entrance contracted, and, in fact, the space occupied by the bees also, in proportion to their numbers. Give them only so many combs as they can cover, if you wish them defended properly from either moths or robbers. Colonies without either queen or brood are not apt to fight for their stores very vigorously, so it will be well to see that they have either one or both, should there be an attack made on them. It is hardly necessary to repeat what has been said about Italians being better to defend themselves than the common bees. A few Italians will often protect the hive better than a whole swarm of black bees.

HOW TO KNOW ROBBER-BEES.

It sometimes puzzles beginners exceedingly to know whether the bees that come out are robbers, or ordinary inmates of the hive.

When the robber-bee approaches a hive, it has a sly, guilty look, and flies with its legs spread in a rather unusual way, as if it wanted to be ready to use its heels as well as wings if required. It will move cautiously up to the entrance, and quickly dodge back as soon as it sees a bee coming toward it. If it is promptly grabbed on attempting to go in, you need have but little fear. When a bee goes in and you can not definitely determine whether it is a robber or not, keep a close watch on all the bees coming out. This is a very sure way of telling when robbers have got a start, even at its very commencement. A bee, in going to the fields, comes out leisurely, and takes wing with but little trouble, because it has no load. Its body is also slim, for it has no honey with it.

A bee that has stolen a load is generally very plump and full; and as it comes out it has a hurried and "guilty look;" besides, it is almost always wiping its mouth, like a man who has just come out of a beer-shop. Most of all, it finds it a little difficult to take wing, as bees ordinarily do, because of the weight. In BEE-HUNTING we related how a bee, laden with thick undiluted honey, would stagger under its load before it could take wing for the final trip home. Well, the bee, when coming out of the hive with honey it has very likely just uncapped, feels instinctively that it will be quite apt to tumble unless able to take wing from some elevated position, and therefore crawls up the side of the hive before launching out. When first taking wing it falls a little by the weight of its load, before its wings are fully under control, and therefore, instead of starting out as a bee ordinarily does, it takes a downward curve, coming quite near the ground before rising safely and surely. With a little practice you can tell a robber at first glance by its way of coming out of the hive, particularly by that fashion of running up the side of the hive before taking wing.

HOW TO TELL WHERE THE ROBBERS BELONG.

If you are a bee-hunter you will probably line them to their hive without any trouble; but if you are not, you can easily find from which hive they come by sprinkling them with flour as they come out of the hive being robbed. Now watch the other hives, and see where you find the floured bees going in. We can generally tell in a very few minutes, by the excited actions of the robbers, already mentioned. If you find that the robbing is confined to one or two colonies, as is often the case, put them down cellar and keep them there for several days where they can not incite other colonies. Reference will be made to this further on.

HOW TO STOP ROBBING.

As to the best mode of procedure, a good deal will depend on circumstances. When bees in the whole apiary are robbing in a wholesale way from the honey-house, or from any place where a supply of honey or syrup is kept, the obvious remedy is to shut the door of the dwelling to cut off the supply. If the bees have entered a barrel through the bunghole, the chances are we shall find, after the head of the barrel is taken out, that there is a peck or more of bees swimming around in the honey. If robbing became very bad we would drive the bung into the barrel, and then, after the uproar has quieted down, remove it and run the honey through a strainer from the bung-hole.

Bees soon stop robbing when all sweets within their reach are removed or so protected that they can not get at them; but even then the apiary will be out of balance for the rest of the day, and more or less for two or three days following, because the bees will be trying to find where they can find more sweets.

Sometimes robbing is started by some one in the neighborhood making sweet pickles, canning fruit, or doing any thing that causes a strong odor of sweet or sour during its preparation; then the only thing the bee-keeper can do is to have the house screened; or if the case is very bad, and the bees keep on "sticking their noses into other people's business," we would recommend smoking the entrances of all the hives with tobacco smoke. Half a dozen whiffs of smoke should be blown into each entrance, one after the

PREVENTING ROBBING BY COVERING THE ENTRANCE WITH WET HAY.

other. In half an hour the dose should be repeated. This will cause the bees to quiet down until such time as the canning-work or the pickle-making is over at the house where bees are "making themselves too familiar."

The best treatment for a general robbing throughout the apiary is prevention. The screen doors and other openings into the honey-house should be self-closing. Unless they are, some one will be almost sure to forget and leave one of them open. If the doors are not self-closing, then all the honey that is stored in the building should be put into hives, shipping-cases, cans, barrels, or any receptacle where bees can be kept from helping themselves; then if perchance the door is left open no harm will be done.

ROBBING OF NUCLEI OR WEAK COLONIES.

There is another kind of robbing that is much more common, and which is apt to perplex the beginner more than any thing

else, and that is the onslaughts that are often made on weak colonies or those that are disinclined to make a defense. Nuclei with large entrances are especially subject to the attacks of bees from strong stocks, and will very often be cleaned out entirely before the apiarist discovers the mischief. By that time the whole apiary will be in a perfect uproar; and as soon as the supply of honey has been exhausted in the one nucleus the robbers will hover around all other entrances, and on finding one poorly defended they will get in more bad work later. During a dearth of honey there are always some bees that make a business of smelling around, and it is a wise precaution always to have the entrances of nuclei contracted down to a width where only one or two bees can pass at a time. We will suppose that a hive has been overpowered, and that its own bees are making no defense, realizing, probably, that resistance is useless. If any thing is to be done to save the colony it must be done quickly. One way is to grasp up a handful of long grass, strew it closely around the entrance, and then spray or sprinkle a dipper-ful of water on it, and scatter more wet grass over the entrance. A very little carbolic acid added to the water makes the spray more offensive to robbers. The invaders will not, as a rule, crawl through wet grass to get into the hive, while on the other hand those that have already entered the hive will get out and return to their homes. In the mean time the regular inmates of the hive, as soon as they are given a little assistance, will begin to set up a defense. The grass should be kept wet for at least an hour or two, and possibly till sundown; but before strewing the grass on the entrance we would advise contracting it down so that only one or two bees can pass at a time. *Never close the entrance up entirely*, no matter how bad the bees are robbing. On a hot day the large number of robbers in the hive, together with the regular inmates, would be almost sure to smother to death.

Another and better way to treat colonies that are nearly robbed out is to take them down cellar and put robber-traps in their place. This will be more fully explained further on.

When robbers get to be very bad in the yard, a pailful of water and a small dipper can be used to good advantage. We will say that here is a hive where the cover does

as fast as they come out of the hive, will escape into the tent. In the mean time no more can get in, because the hive is closed to all outside bees. In half an hour or so the tent should be lifted for a moment, turned upside down, when the robbers will immediately fly toward home. Or, better, make a hole in the peak of the tent—one or two holes will do no harm. The robbers will gradually work up toward the peak, and, traveling along, will discover the opening and return home; on the principle of the bee-escape, not one of them will think of going back to the hole whence it came, but will make a dive for the front of the entrance, which is barred by the mosquito-netting. In lieu of the tent a large piece of mosquito-netting could be thrown over the hive, and held down by means of a few bricks or stones around its edges.

Sometimes where a colony has been almost completely robbed out it is better to let the robbers finish up the job; for it is a fact that when the entrance is closed or further ingress to the hive has been shut off by means of a tent or otherwise, those same robbers will then pounce on other nuclei in the immediate vicinity, because the use of the tent or the wet grass does to a certain extent change the appearance of the hive, causing the robbers to conclude they have made a mistake, and that, therefore, the

CONVENIENT CAGE TO SET OVER HIVE THAT IS BEING ROBBED.

not fit closely. Around the crack the robbers are clustering in large festoons. To blow smoke on them drives them away for only a moment; but to wet them down with a dipperful of water has a very much better effect, especially if you succeed in wetting the crack. Covering the hive that has been attacked, with a wet blanket, also works well. Use water and plenty of it, but smoke sparingly around the colony that is being attacked.

Another way to protect a robbed hive is to put a bee-tent or screen over it, as described further on. This should be anchored to the ground, and then the robbers,

hive they have been robbing is one next to or near it. Dr. C. C. Miller and a number of other prominent bee-keepers believe that, when a colony has been almost completely robbed, it should be left alone. As soon as all the honey is gone, and there is nothing more for the robbers to get, they will quietly withdraw, go back home satisfied, and conclude they have taken all the honey; but when the supply is shut off *suddenly* those same bees *know* there should be more, and conclude there must be a way to get it, and so they keep up the search for some other colony that may have a supply equally available.

Well, we will say the colony has been almost cleaned out, night has come on, and things in the apiary have assumed their natural order. If there are not enough bees left to make up a colony or even a fair nucleus, take away all the old combs, sweep out all the dead bees, and give them a frame containing a very little honey; contract the entrance down to one bee-passage, and then watch them the next morning to see whether they will put up a defense. As a further precaution it might be well to throw a little wet grass in front of the entrance. In general, bees that are given a little rest, and a chance to recover from their demoralization, will fight very hard; and probably the second time after they have been helped a little they will be able to maintain their rights. But the robber - trap scheme described on next page is much better than the tent.

Trying to people our house - apiary in the fall, when it was first built, we had trouble with one certain colony. In fact, when robbing was going on anywhere it was sure to be these hybrids that were at the bottom of the mischief. After we had tried every plan recommended, and still finding these fellows would persist in pushing into every new colony we started, the idea occurred to us that, on the principle that it takes a rogue to catch a rogue, it would be well to try to see how these would repel other robbers. We simply took the greater part of the combs from the robbers, bees and all, carried them into the house-apiary, and put them in place of the colony which they had been robbing. The effect was instantaneous. Every laden robber-bee that went home with its load, on finding the queen and brood gone from the old stand at once showed the utmost consternation, while the passion for robbing was instantly changed to grief and moaning for the lost home. The weak colony which they had been robbing, and which had only a queen-cell, was carried to them, and they soon took up with it and went to work. The robbers newly domiciled in the house-apiary repelled

all invaders with such energy and determination that the rest seemed to abandon the idea which they, doubtless, had previously formed; viz., that the house-apiary was a monster hive but ill garrisoned, so we had very little trouble afterward. Before we transposed them, as mentioned, we had serious thoughts of destroying their queen, simply because they were such pests; but the year afterward, this colony in the house-apiary gave in the house-apiary over 100 lbs. of comb honey.

HOW TO KNOW WHEN A HIVE IS PUTTING UP A GOOD DEFENSE.

The accompanying half-tone is a good illustration of how a powerful colony will de-

FIG. 4.—A COLONY THAT IS READY TO MEET ANY KIND OF ONSLAUGHT FROM ROBBERS.

Robbers had hovered around the entrance. The result was, the guards were out in good force to repel the attack.

ploy its sentinels or guards during the time when other colonies near by are being robbed. This colony is prepared for any kind of an onslaught; for the minute that a robber hovers over the entrance it is promptly met in mid air by one of the sentinels. They immediately clutch in a rough-and-tumble fight, drop to the ground, roll over and over, and lucky is the robber if it gets away without having its hair or legs pretty vigorously pulled. Such "a warm reception" will discourage any would-be robber from tackling that colony again. The entrance is rather wide open and the colony is strong enough to put up a defense and a vigorous one at that. If the colony were not so strong it would be proper to contract the entrance as shown under ENTRANCES and WINTERING elsewhere.

ROBBER-TRAPS.

We have been using in our yards, for some years back, various forms of robber-traps. Their purpose is to catch the hardened " old sinners"—bees that are professionals in the art of robbing, and which are of but little practical value for the purpose of getting

er they are out of the way the better for all concerned. As long as they are allowed to prey on their honest neighbors they will *continue* to make work in the yard disagreeable by keeping every colony stirred up and more or less cross, despoil baby nuclei, and make trouble generally. But this is not all. They incite other bees to rob. The force of example is very potent among bees as well as human beings.

While one does not need to use traps continuously, they are required on occasions; for if a few bees once get started to robbing they will day after day pounce on the combs every time a hive is opened, and render life miserable for their owner and for the baby nuclei. Time and time again in our yards we have restored every thing to absolute order and quiet by the use of the trap. It works like magic; and after the rascals are caught, one will be surprised to note how *few* bees can make such an uproar as is evidenced by the number in the trap. Their intrinsic value is practically nothing, even if they were good honest bees. To let them loose would only invite more trouble. The amount of honey that they might gather if they could be "reformed" would be a very insignificant item. But the amount of damage that they can do in interfering with our queen-rearing operations is no small item.

It has been suggested that, if a robber-trap will catch robbers, it will also catch *honest* bees, and why destroy good property? There is no need for catching any thing but the hardened old sinners—those that we consider hopeless beyond redemption. As explained, we do not run the trap continuously throughout the season—perhaps one or two days in a week, and not even then if no robbers show up. During the entire season at our home yard of 400 colonies and nuclei the total number of robbers that we catch would hardly fill a two-gallon measure; and we venture to say there was not one honest bee out of five hundred in the whole number. It is penny wise and pound foolish to try to save such bees.

FIG. 1.—Wire-cloth-cone bee-escape on the inside of robber-traps. Note that the large end of the cone communicates with the regular entrance of the hive. Robbers pass in at the entrance up through the cone into the hive and are caught.

honey honestly from the fields. We catch these shiny-backed bees and kill them. While some protest has been raised on the ground that they might be made over into a colony, yet the kind of "old sinners" to which we have referred are useless for *any* purpose. In a queen-rearing yard the soon-

How do we avoid catching honest bees? Easy enough. The traps are put in operation only when the prowling thieves are around. They are constantly on the alert, skilled as they are in the art of stealing and in finding any exposed sweets; that is to say, they are ever following one about, while the honest bees are either in the field or hive.

Let us assume a case. After we have been working in the yard a few days there are a few robbers that accumulate. But we do not let them continue on with their nosing into other people's business till they make work in the yard exceedingly disagreeable, and the colonies that are being worked cross. Before they become very numerous, two or three robber-traps are put into operation; and in an hour absolute peace is restored and not a prowler is in sight.

cloth cones.) We open up the robber-trap hive, and just over the entrance of it we find a wire-cloth cone tacked up against the inside hive-front. This is made by cutting and folding a piece of wire cloth in the form of a triangle. The large end fits over the entrance, while the other end, gradually tapering to a small orifice (about ⅜ inch square), reaches nearly to the top of the hive, or within an inch of the rabbet on which the frames rest; it is then secured by double-pointed tacks as shown at the top of Fig. 1. As an additional precaution we find it desirable to have a smaller wire cone of the same construction under the larger one. Where there is only one cone the bees are liable to go back out through the entrance. Other forms of cones are shown in the two lower views of Fig. 1 on previous page.

Fig. 2.—Outside detail of the robber-trap. A double screen is used, and honey is painted on the inner screen. Robbers are attracted by the odor of the honey. As they can not reach it from the outer screen they enter the hive and are trapped.

The value of the trap depends on the fact that it stops a would-be bad case of robbing *before* it has progressed to any extent. A little syrup (and a very little) is put into one or two traps. The robbers, because hunting for sweets, are caught *long before* any honest bees think of looking for them.

CONSTRUCTION OF ROBBER-TRAPS.

Let us now look over one of these traps at the Root apiaries and see how they are constructed. An ordinary hive, such as is used in the yard, two wire screens such as are employed for moving bees, a super-cover, and a wire-cloth-cone bee-escape, make up the complete outfit. (The ordinary Porter spring escapes for this purpose have not been found to be as satisfactory as the wire-

One of these traps is placed at a convenient location in the yard, when one of the wire screens for moving bees is laid on top. With a brush we smear a little diluted honey (honey is better than syrup) over the wire cloth at one end—the back one. This film of honey is spread over an area of about two inches wide by the width of the screen. Another screen is placed on top of this, and over the whole is placed a super-cover, as at the left in Fig. 2. Notice that this super-cover is set back about two inches, leaving a portion of the wire cloth—the part smeared with honey—exposed where the bees can get a *smell* of it, but not touch it, because the upper screen keeps them from it. Now, a robber-bee, if a hardened "old sinner" or a professional, when it smells honey in this way will immediately begin to "investigate." It will hover around the wire cloth (not covered by the super cover) for a minute or so, and then, like a duck to water, it will make a dart for the entrance. There are no guards there to stop it; it rushes in pellmell, crawls up through the two wire-cloth cones shown in the previous illustration, and out through the apex, when it is a prisoner. It may take a sip of the honey, and when it gets its fill it will go toward the light at the point where the super cover is slid backward. The chances are only one in a thousand that it will get back through the wire-cloth cones as mentioned, and it soon worries itself to death. Thus the trap works after it catches all the criminally inclined bees. The small amount of diluted honey on the inner wire cloth is used up, and automatically the robber-trap goes out of commission. The old sinners are all caught; and as there is no more honey to attract honest bees, none will be caught.

The question may arise right here, "Is the robber-trap of any use to the honey-producer?" Certainly not to the same extent that it is useful in a queen-rearing yard; but during a period of extracting, there are times when it appears to us it might be used to good advantage, especially if some careless employee should happen to leave the door of the honey-house open or allow a colony to be robbed to death.

As we have before pointed out, if robbers can be caught at the very start they will be found to be mainly from one hive, and a little later from two or three. If they get well agoing they will attract other bees by their uproar; but if robber-bees be floured, and followed back to their hives, it will be seen that the great bulk of them go to only two or three hives. A yard-man has to be extremely careless to allow robbing to get started throughout the entire yard.

HOW THE ROBBER-TRAP CAN BE MADE TO CURE THE ROBBING NUISANCE.

It often happens that a colony will be nearly conquered by robbers, and it may be a fairly good-sized one too. The thing to do then is to take it off its stand and put a robber-trap on its stand, when, presto! the thieves will be imprisoned. In the meantime the attacked colony is taken down cellar where a window has been left open. The marauders that don't belong there will pass outward through the window, which then should be closed. In very short order the robber-trap on the stand of the hive that was being robbed will have collected all the robbers. When every thing becomes quiet in the yard, put the trapped bees down cellar and keep them there for some days as already directed. If confined more than two days they will, of course, have to be fed.

The robbed colony, after its despoilers are caught, may now be put back on its stand, when the entrance should be contracted to about the space that one bee can pass at a time. The bees in the trap down cellar can not of course molest it; and, during the time that they are held in confinement, it will have recovered itself, and with its contracted entrance will be able to put up a very stiff defense in case another onslaught is made.

It often happens that one or two colonies will do the greater part of the robbing in an apiary. If that is the case, trap them all and then carry them to an outyard or location a mile or more from their own yard or the scenes of their recent pow-wows, where they would be only a constant menace and annoyance unless removed. If they give trouble at the outyard, trap them again, and then fumigate them to death by putting sulphur in the smoker. Better by far that they be put out of the way; for having learned bad tricks they are of no further use in the yard.

FOLDING BEE-TENT.

One of the great conveniences in a well-regulated apiary is some sort of bee-tent or large cage covered with mosquito-netting which one can put over himself and hive too while he is making the necessary examination. It should be quite light so that it may be easily handled; should be at least six feet high inside, and long enough and wide enough to take in the hive and the bee-keeper comfortably while he is working. In our apiary we use two forms of tent—one a regular square house made of wire cloth, and another one which can be folded as shown in the illustration, when not in use. With either one of these, preferably the former, one can, during the robbing season, even when bees are acting their very meanest, perform all the necessary work about the hive, such as cutting out queen-cells, introducing, etc., without a robber being able to get at the combs. Of course, the bees in the hive will fly out, bump their heads against the mosquito-netting, and finally reach the roof of the tent; but as soon as they find themselves caged they immediately try to get out through a hole in the top, where they can very soon make their escape.

HOW TO MAKE.

Take four basswood sticks, about 8½ feet long, and fasten them together like letter X's, with a good strong screw where they cross. A piece of good strong tarred twine, or small rope, makes the ridgepole, as seen in the engraving, and this same twine unites the sticks at their tops. The mosquito-bar is sewed into a sort of bag, having the same strong twine all round its lower edges, and down each of the four corners. At these corners are also sewed metal rings, and these rings, when pulled down strongly, will loop over screw-

Queens having been already hatched in the lamp nursery, would all be lost unless the colonies were divided at once, so as to make use of them. The surplus combs for making these late swarms were in the upper stories, and the robbers knew it; for no sooner was a cap raised than they were on hand; and before we could get the brood-combs to go with them (required because the bees would not adhere even to their own combs, unless some of them contained unsealed brood), a smart traffic would be under way. It came night, and hives and queens were in all sorts of bad shapes. We were glad to have night come,

TENT FOLDED. FOLDING BEE-TENT, READY FOR USE.*

heads, near the lower ends of the four sticks. When thus looped over, the sticks are bent, or bowed, so as to give room in the top of the tent. The whole structure weighs less than five pounds, and yet it gives room inside for a hive, and to do all necessary work. The basswood sticks are 1, x ⅞ at the lower end, and tapered to 1 x ⅝ at their upper end, with the corners taken off, to make them as light as possible.

In the small cut above at A is shown the way the ring is looped over the screw-heads, and just below is seen the end of a 2¼-inch wire nail, bent so when turned with the point downward it can be used as an anchor to keep the tent from blowing over. If the sticks are spread a little when the anchors are pushed into the ground, the tent stands very securely.

WORKING WITH BEES BY LAMPLIGHT WHEN ROBBERS ARE TROUBLESOME DURING THE DAY.

We have before mentioned our troubles in trying to people the house-apiary in the fall.

we assure you, for we longed for the time when the robbers would be compelled, by the gathering darkness, to go home. Many of you have doubtless had cause to repent trying to work with bees when it began to grow dark, but we somehow got the idea that, with some good lamps having nice shades on them, we could do work in the evening. We went at once, took a lamp, and walked around the apiary viewing the inmates of different hives clustered out at the entrances, humming merrily, we presume in remembrance of the rich loads they had but an hour before snatched from us. Scarcely a bee took wing, and we then ventured to open a hive. With the lamp on one of the posts of the trellis, we found we could handle the bees almost as well as in daylight, and, to our intense relief, not a bee would leave its hive, no matter how many combs were held temptingly under their very noses. We went to

*Our artist has shown the bottom fringe of the tent as common cloth; it is nothing but a continuation of mosquito-bar.

13

work, divided colonies, caught queens, and even handled vicious hybrids with fewer stings than we could possibly have avoided in the daytime.*

This experience of working by lamplight was at a time when an A B C scholar did not know how to control, or, better, prevent, robbing in the *day time*. But prevention is better than cure. Keep the entrances of weak colonies and nuclei contracted, and keep all sweets in a closed room or sealed cans where the bees can't get a taste, and you will have no trouble. But if you *must*

Convenient Wire Cage for Use duringRobbing and Swarming Seasons.

open your hives much during the dearth of honey, as in the case of queen-rearing, then follow the plan now to be described.

HOW TO REMOVE THE ROBBING TENDENCY BY OUTDOOR FEEDING.

When honey is coming in fast or even slowly, of course there is no robbing; but as the nectar supply stops, bees begin to pry around to find what they can steal. At such times, when hives are opened for examination robbers will be about; and if the combs are exposed very much by such handling they will pounce upon the hive and combs in great numbers, and then attack the entrance after the hive is closed up. If one is

---

* Since the above was written we have found that a good lantern is preferable to a lamp. The latter is apt to be affected by light breezes, and is often blown out. The former, while not open to this objection, will receive rougher handling. During the season of 1886 we used the lantern in the apiary with entire success.

trying to rear queens the results will be discouraging. Bees get cross, refuse to start cells, or, if built out, tear them down, and kill off drones, and destroy drone brood.

The fact that there is no robbing when honey is coming in suggests the remedy; viz., feed *outdoors* a thin syrup of the consistency of raw nectar, half granulated sugar and half water, made as directed under FEEDING, which see. This should be put into a 60-pound square honey-can with holes punched in the top, as described under subtitle of OUTDOOR FEEDING, in FEEDING AND FEEDERS, which see. This feeder should be stationed about a hundred yards from the apiary, and filled as often as emptied. While this feeding is going on the conditions are much like those of a natural honey-flow. The robbers are all busy around the outdoor feeder. Brood-rearing commences, cells are started and built out, drones even permitted to remain, and queen-rearing operations can continue just about as in a honey-flow.

Where other bees are near, usually some arrangement can be made with their owner whereby he will pay his part of the expense. If no satisfactory agreement can be arrived at, of course the colonies will have to be fed individually, as directed under FEEDING.

CAUTION ABOUT OUTDOOR FEEDING.

Don't use honey for this purpose unless it is diluted with water to about the consistency of nectar from the flowers; and even then it is safer to use sugar, as it is not so apt to excite the bees. Once feeding is begun it should be kept up either till the colonies are supplied with needed stores or work about the colonies is finished. To feed a little one day, then skip the next, is apt to make the bees on the off days prowl around among your neighbors and into their kitchens, greatly to the annoyance of the occupants.

HOW TO FEED OUT UNFINISHED SECTIONS OR WET EXTRACTING-COMBS.

While these *can* be scattered out in the open, it is quite sure to result in fearful robbing and stinging after the supply is exhausted. To forestall this, put the combs and sections in hives or supers, one tiered above another on a regular bottom-board, and then contract the entrance so that *not more than one or two bees can pass at a time.* To make it wider results in a scramble, and robbing of weak colonies in the yard. The top of the tier of hives or supers should, of course, be covered. While a regular hivecover *can* be used, a wire-cloth screen is much to be preferred, to prevent suffocation. But it must be provided with a bee-escape; otherwise nearly all the visiting bees will perish, vainly trying to force an exit through the wire screen.

These tiered-up hives with small entrances are much used to clean up scraps of honey, extracting-combs, and to empty out partly finished sections — see COMB HONEY. This slow robbing also has a tendency to draw off robbers from the nuclei and weak colonies and therefore serves a double purpose.

WHAT HAPPENS IF ROBBING IS NOT STOPPED.

When robbing is under genuine headway, the honey of a strong colony will disappear in from 2 to 12 hours; the bees will then starve in the hive, or go home with the pillagers, or scatter about and die. This is not all: when the passion is fully aroused they will not hesitate to attack the strongest stocks, and you will find your bees stung to death in heaps before the entrances. This may put a stop to it, in time, but we have seen them push ahead until every hive of the apiary was in an uproar, and it seemed as if every bee had certainly gone crazy. At such times the robbers will attack passers-by in the streets, and even venture an attack on cats, dogs, aye, and hens and turkeys too. Like the American Indians when infuriated at the sight of blood, every bee seems to have a demoniacal delight in selling its life while inflicting all the torments it possibly can, feeling sad only because it can not do any more mischief.

The worst robbing time seems to be after basswood is over, when bees become especially crazy, if they get even a smell of this aromatic honey left carelessly about the hives. One who has never seen such a state of affairs can have but little idea of the furious way they sting every thing and everybody. The remedy is to get a good smoker and put in enough chips or planer shavings to insure dense smoke; then, using one hand to work the smoker bellows; with the other, proceed to close every hive that shows any symptoms of being robbed. Shut up every

bit of honey where not a bee can get at it, and do your work well; for at such times they will wedge into and get through cracks that would make one think *inch boards* were hardly protection enough. Just before dark let all the robbers go home, and be up betimes next morning to see that all entrances are close and small, and that all the hives are bee-tight. An experienced hand will restore peace and quietness in a very short time, to such a demoralized apiary. Black bees are much worse than Italians, for the latter will usually hold their stores against any number of assailants; good, strong, well-made hives, filled with Italians, with plenty of brood in each, will be in little danger of any such "raids," although we have seen the wounded and slain piled up in heaps before robbers would desist and give up trying to force an entrance. See ANGER OF BEES.

BORROWING.

Before closing this subject of robbing there are a few more points to be mentioned. There is a kind of pillaging called borrowing, where the bees from one hive will go quietly into another, and carry away its stores as fast as gathered; but this usually happens where the robbed stock is queenless, or has an unfertile queen. As soon as they have eggs and brood, they begin to realize what the end of such work will be. This state of affairs seldom goes on long; for it either results in downright robbing, or the bees themselves put a stop to it.

Caution to Beginners.—The first year we kept bees there was constant fear that they would get to robbing, as we had read so much about in the books. One afternoon in May we saw a large number of bees passing rapidly out and in a particular hive, and the more they were examined the more we were persuaded that they were being robbed. We contracted the entrance, but it seemed to make little difference. We finally closed it almost entirely, compelling the bees to squeeze out and in, in a way that must have been quite uncomfortable, at least. After awhile they calmed down, and we had only the ordinary number of bees going out and in. "There," thought we, "had we not read the books and known how, we might have lost our bees," and we undoubtedly felt very wise if we did not look so. On turning our head, behold, the robbers were at another colony, and they had to be put through the same program; then another and another; until we concluded a host of robbers had come from somewhere, and made a raid on the apiary, and that, had we not been on hand, the whole of them would have been ruined. We had got very nervous and fidgety, and, when we found the whole performance repeated the next day, we began to think bee culture a very trying pursuit. Well, in due course of time we figured out that there was no robbing at all, but that it was just the young bees taking their afternoon playspell.

ROCKY - MOUNTAIN BEE - PLANT (*Cleome integrifolia*). This is a beautiful plant for the flower - garden, to say nothing of the honey it produces. It grows from two to three feet in height, and bears large clusters of bright pink flowers, as shown in the cut.

A near relative of the SPIDER-PLANT, it grows naturally on the Rocky Mountains and in Colorado, where it is said to furnish large quantities of honey. Although it succeeds easily under cultivation we can not learn that it has ever been a pecuniary success in our locality. With this, as well as all other plants, it must be borne in mind that a fair test would require acres instead of little patches in the garden.

The engraving was copied from a larger-sized picture, in Prof. Cook's "Manual of the Apiary." During the season of 1879 we had a number of the plants growing in our honey-garden. It was, however, so much inferior in looks, as well as in the amount of honey produced, to the spider-plant, that we did not take the pains to save any of the seed. The two plants very much resemble each other, but the latter is a much stronger and finer-looking plant, and has a rank luxuriance of growth that the Rocky-Mountain bee-plant lacks.

The Michigan Agricultural College experimented, in 1891, with several acres of the plant, for the sole purpose of testing its honey-producing qualities. They found it exceedingly difficult, however, to get a good stand of plants. In fact, we do not know how

ROCKY-MOUNTAIN BEE-PLANT.

a perfect stand can be obtained without transplanting; and as this makes the expense equivalent to a field of cabbages or strawberries, of course the honey produced did not come anywhere near paying expenses.

ROYAL JELLY. See ANATOMY OF THE BEE; also QUEENS.

S.

SAGE (*Salvia*)—a geneial name for white sage, black sage, and button sage, in California. These honey-bearing plants also belong to the *Labiatæ*, or mint family. The word "labiate" means lip-shaped; and on looking closely you will see that plants belonging to this family have blossoms with a sort of lip on one side, something like the nose to a pitcher. Many of this family, such as CATNIP, MOTHERWORT, FIGWORT, GILL-OVER-THE-GROUND, have already been mentioned as honey-plants, and the number might be extended almost indefinitely. The sage we have particularly to do with is the white mountain sage of California; and we do not know that it would be far out of the way to call this one of the most important honey-plants in the world. The crops of honey secured from it within the past 25 years have been so immense that fine sage honey is now offered for sale in almost all the principal cities of the world, and a nice sample of well-ripened California honey, whether comb or extracted, is enough to call forth exclamations of surprise and deligh from any one who thinks enough of son thing good to eat, and pleasant to the taste, to commit himself so far. We well remem ber the first taste we had of the mountain-

A BUSH OF CALIFORNIA BUTTON SAGE.

sage honey. Mr. Langstroth was visiting us at the time, and his exclamations were much like our own, only that he declared it was almost identical in flavor with the famed honey of Hymettus, of which he had received a sample some years before. Well, this honey of Hymettus, which has been celebrated both in poetry and prose for ages past, is gathered from mountain thyme, and the botany tells us that thyme and sage not only belong to the same family, but are closely related. Therefore it is nothing strange if Mr. Langstroth was right in declaring our California honey to be almost if not quite identical in flavor with the honey of Hymettus. The California sages grow along the sides of the mountains, and blossom successively as the season advances; that is, the bees first commence work on them in the valleys, and then gradually fly higher up, as the blossoms open on the mountain-side, giving them a much longer season than we have in regions not mountainous.

The late John H. Martin, who was then traveling in California, had this to say of the mountain sages. The manner in which the bee has learned how to open the trap-door is particularly interesting.

The first sage to come into blossom is that variously called black sage, button sage, and bolled sage. Upon these buttons, or bolls, the little flower-tube appears, and is much like the flower-tube in the red-clover blossom. Flowers develop from the outer edge of the button for several weeks. The bush is about five feet in height, bearing a large number of stalks, with several buttons to the stalk, the largest one being a little over an inch in diameter, and diminishing in size toward the tip of the stalk. A tiny drop of nectar can be squeezed from the little tube, just as we can squeeze it from the tube of red clover. When the flowering season is past, the buttons turn nearly black in hue, and cling to the bush until the next season.

In habit and appearance the white sage is entirely different. The woody portion and the leaves are nearly white, which gives it its name. The flowering stalk makes a rapid growth of several feet in one season, and the plant throws out a dozen or more of these stalks, all the way from three to eight feet in height. Each stalk is loaded with racemes of buds, which continue to produce flowers for several weeks.

The description of the white sage is not complete without giving the way in which the bee sips the nectar from the white-sage blossom. The opening in the corolla is nearly large enough for the bee to thrust its head into; but, as if jealous of its treasured sweets, the flower is provided with a long projecting lip that curls up not unlike a letter S, and in such a manner as to close effectually the entrance. When I first saw a white-sage blossom, it was with much interest I speculated upon how the bee gained access to the nectar. Soon a busy worker darted in among the flowers, and alighted upon the projecting portion of the S-shaped lip, which bent down under the weight of the bee, opening the door to its treasure-house, which the bee soon relieved of its contents. Upon the departure of the bee the door immediately closed again, to be opened and reopened by the successive foragers. When the rainfall has been light, white sage does not bloom so profusely; and, furthermore, the lip of the flower is stunted and so short that the bee can not find standing-room upon it; hence, after vainly striv-

A STEM OF CALIFORNIA BUTTON SAGE WITH BLOSSOMS.

ing to gain an entrance, it reluctantly seeks another flower with well-developed lips which readily yields to the bee, and a load is secured as quickly from this flower as from the simple tube of the button sage. It is when the sages are in blossom, in May and June, that the bee-keeper has to hustle in order to keep his dish right side up.

A peculiarity of this honey is that it is not inclined to candy, but remains limpid during the severest winter weather. We have taken a sample so thick that the tumbler containing it might be turned bottom upward without its running at all, and placed it out in the snow, in the dead of winter, and

STEMS AND BLOSSOMS OF CALIFORNIA WHITE SAGE.

failed to crystallize it. This is a very valuable quality, although it does not invariably remain clear.

Most of the white-sage honey, so called, comes from the black and button sages. The honey from these two is fully the equal of that from the white sage in body and color; hence the yield of all three varieties is known as white "sage honey" in the great markets.

SAINFOIN. See CLOVER.

SELF-SPACING FRAMES. See head FRAMES, SELF-SPACING.

SCENT OF BEES.—Any one who has observed bees has seen that they are guided very largely in their movements by the sense of smell. They have been known to fly a mile or more over water to reach flowers on an opposite bank toward which they could be guided only by scent.

The celebrated naturalist Huber first discovered that the organs of smell in the bee are located in the antennæ. and he perform-ed some interesting experiments by cutting them off and thus depriving the bees of their power to detect odors. We have recently repeated some of his experiments on workers, drones. and queens, with some modifications, and all our results confirm his position.

Concerning the queen, Huber says, "When one of her antennæ is cut off, no change takes place in the behavior of the queen. If you cut off both antennæ near the head, th's mother, formerly held in such high consideration by her people, loses all her influence, and even the maternal instinct disappears. Instead of laying her eggs in the cells she drops them here and there." As is well known, a young virgin queen is normally accepted without difficulty by any colony which has been queenless long enough to know its queenless condition. In experimenting along this line we cut the antennæ :rom a virgin queen about three hours old and put her on the comb of an observatory hive, and she was at once balled. This was repeated in another hive. She was then rescued from the workers, and confined in the hive in an introducing-cage containing candy, but in a short time died, probably of starvation, for we are sure she was not stung by the bees in the ball, for she was taken out at once and we never lost sight of her. Although there was candy in her cage she evidently did not recognize it as food, since she was not attracted to it by smell, and on account of the loss of her antennæ she was not fed through the meshes of the wire cloth.

When the workers are deprived of their antennæ they remain inactive in the hive, and soon desert it since they are attracted only by light. We cut the antennæ from several workers, marked them on the thorax to make it more easy to follow their actions, and then put them in an observatory hive from which they had been taken. The other bees at once recognized that there was something wrong with them, and gathered around them much as they surround the queen, and repeatedly tried to feed them; but the injured workers could not guide their tongues, and consequently did not take food readily. One worker with its antennæ off was put on the alighting-board of its own hive, but was at once repelled and carried away by one of its own hive-mates.

Drones act in a very similar manner, but are frequently rejected by the workers as soon as they are put in the hive. Huber reports that, as soon as the light was excluded from his observatory hive, although it was late in the afternoon, and no drones were flying out, the drones from which the antennæ had been cut deserted the hive, since light was the only thing which attracted them.

From these observations it seems clear that bees recognize each other very largely by scent, but also by touch. The workers and drones operated on were returned to their own hive, and we might suppose that they would retain the odor of that hive; but since they were not able to extend their antennæ to the other bees they were at once recognized as differing in some way, and received different treatment. Langstroth says of these experiments, "The inference is obvious, that a bee deprived of her antennæ loses the use of her intellect;" yet this statement should be modified somewhat, for the intellect is in no way influenc ed by the operation. The bee continues to respond normally to all sensations which it has the organs to receive, for we see that light still attracts them as it did before;

but on account of the one sided reception of stimuli its actions become abnormal.

It remains to be seen which segments of the antennæ receive certain odors, for probably they are not all alike. It has been found in ants that the different segments of the antennæ perceive different kinds of odors, and the same is very probably true of the bees.

For a further consideration of this subject see INTRODUCING QUEENS.

SECTIONS See COMB HONEY.

SELF-SPACING FRAMES. See FIXED FRAMES and HIVES.

SEPARATORS. See COMB HONEY.

SHIPPING BEES. See MOVING BEES.

SIZE OF FRAMES. See HIVES.

SKEP. The term "skep" is often used by old-fashioned bee-keepers to refer to a colony of bees in any kind of hive; but more properly it applies to box hives and straw skeps—the last named rarely seen in this country. In England and even many of the countries on the continent of Europe, the old straw skep is still used quite largely, because lumber is expensive and straw cheap, but movable frames are never used in these hives. The bees are allowed to build the

combs just the same as mentioned under the head of BOX HIVES; also see HIVES, EVOLUTION OF. On top of these skeps modern supers containing sections are sometimes used. The making of straw skeps for cottagers is quite a little business of itself—requiring a certain degree of skill. We do not know what these skeps are sold for, but we are told at a much less price than modern movable-frame hives.

Straw skeps are never used in this country —at least at the present time; and if it were not for the familiar pictures of "ye olden times" we Americans would know but little about them.

SMARTWEED. See HEARTSEASE.

SMOKE AND SMOKERS. We can drive cattle and horses, and, to some extent, even pigs, with a whip; but one who undertakes to drive bees in any such way will find to his sorrow that all the rest of the animal kingdom are mild in comparison, especially as far as stubbornness and fearlessness of consequences are concerned. You may kill them by thousands; you may even burn them up with fire, but the death agonies of their comrades seem only to provoke them to new fury, and they push on to the combat with a relentlessness which we can compare to nothing better than a nest of yellow-jackets that have made up their minds to die, and to make all the mischief they possibly can before dying It is here that the power of smoke comes in; and to one who is not conversant with its use, it seems simply astonishing to see them turn about and retreat in the most perfect dismay and fright, from the effects of a puff or two of smoke from a mere fragment of rotten wood. What could we bee-keepers do with bees at

DUTCH SWARM SPECIALISTS INSPECTING BARGAINS AT THE BEE-MARKET IN HOLLAND.
THE BEE-MARKET IN BENNEKOM, HOLLAND.
Skeps with bees and honey sell for $2.00 each.

times, were no such potent power as smoke known?

There have been various devices for getting smoke on to the bees, such as, for instance, a common tin tube having a mouthpiece at one end, and a removable cap with a vent at the other end for the issue of smoke. By blowing on the mouth-piece, smoke can

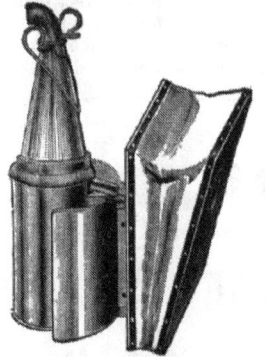

BINGHAM SMOKER.

be forced out. Others, again, have used a tin pan in which was some burning rotten wood. This is put on the windward side of the hive so as to blow smoke over the frames. All of these, however, were miserable makeshifts in comparison with the smokers of to-day.

It is to the credit of father Moses Quinby for first giving us a *bellows* bee-smoker. This was a most decided step in advance over the old methods of introducing smoke among the bees. In principle his original smoker did not differ essentially from the Bingham and the L. C. Root, which were introduced later. It had, however, one serious defect; and that was, it would go out, the fire-pot not being properly ventilated to insure a good draft. Some years after, Mr. T. F. Bingham, of Farwell, Mich., and Mr. L. C. Root, son-

in-law of Quinby, then of Mohawk, N. Y., but now of Stamford, Ct., introduced bee-smokers to the world on the principle of the original Quinby bellows smoker, but with several decided improvements. The fire-cups, at the same time, were made rather larger, and were ventilated in such a way that a continuous draft could be maintained, even when the smoker was not in use, thus preventing them from going out like the old original Quinby.

Of the two smokers the Bingham is the better—more reliable and more substantially made. While the L. C. Root smoker is not made any more, the Bingham has a very large sale. It has recently been improved by the addition of a detachable curved snout to prevent fire dropping, a safety device (a wire handle) by which the top can be removed for replenishing without burning the fingers, and an arrangement for burning the creosote.

Both smokers employ what is known as the hot-blast principle—that is, the blast of air from the bellows is blown *through* the fire. This makes a heavy volume of smoke—volume enough with the proper fuel to subdue the worst kind of hybrids.

The improved Root smoker on the same principle with its new snout is very neat and substantial. The old-style nozzles were somewhat top heavy, having a tendency to tip over or flop open at a most inconvenient time. The one here shown is not only compact in appearance, but will hold its position on top of the stove without danger of toppling over, no matter how roughly used. There is no reason why the nozzle or snout should be large and heavy, having a capacity rarely if ever needed. The hinge is a light skeleton stamping, yielding just enough to make it fit nicely on the smoker-barrel, and yet crowd the creosote out of the way. A very neat wire-coil handle, which will remain cool under all circumstances, is riveted securely in place on the back of the snout

THREE SIZES OF ROOT SMOKERS.

at a point that is most convenient for lifting and shutting the cap. It works so easily that it will not be necessary to bang or pound the nozzle to open the smoker. The legs are of skeleton sheet-metal stamping, with a projecting brace which is very strong and rigid. They are riveted to the stove and bolted to the bellows-board. No matter how rough

DETAILS OF THE ROOT SMOKER.

A.—Metal projection to aid the fingers in holding bellows.
B.—Coiled-wire handle.
C.—Hook on back of bellows.
D.—Locked nuts.
E.—Stamped metal legs.
F—Flexible hinge.

the usage, these bolts and rivets will not let go. The shield has been omitted, as it has been learned by experience that the cylinder comprising the stove burns out under the shield, destroying the actual life of the metal itself. An anti-spark tube is situated just below this grate, as shown, and of such construction as to prevent the suction of sparks into the bellows or out into the air, setting fire to clothing. The bellows itself is metal-bound (see A), a feature which is greatly appreciated for several reasons. It serves to increase the life of the bellows, protecting the leather edges from wear; prevents absolutely the warping of the bellows-boards themselves, and the binding is of such construction that it forms a very convenient hold to the bellows-boards while the smoker is being operated. This feature makes it possible to reduce the tension of the spring, permitting of a bellows that will respond instantly with a good strong blast, and yet the action is perfectly easy. The hook, C, is for hanging the smoker on a hive or carrying by the little

finger when the hands are full of other stuff. There are three sizes of these smokers, comprising stoves 4, 3½, and 2½ inches.

The object of the curved nozzle on all three of the leading hot-blast smokers is to prevent fire dropping. In the old-style smokers it was necessary in blowing smoke to tip the barrel almost upside down, or at such an angle that fire-embers would sometimes fall on the brood-frames and the bees. The new curved nozzle permits one to use the smoker almost right side up, and yet a stream of smoke can be poured on the combs.

COLD-BLAST SMOKERS.

All the foregoing are of the hot-blast type — that is, the blast is forced through the fuel. Cold-blast smokers are constructed somewhat on the principle of an ejector; that is, air is conducted directly from the bellows by means of a tube, to a point inside of the fire-box, *ahead* of the fire, not through it; the result is a blast of cold air charged with smoke. In other words, the blast of air that is forced through the nozzle sucks with it the smoke just back of it, from the burning fuel. This principle was invented almost simultaneously in 1879 by J. G. Corey, of Santa Paula, Cal., and Norman Clark, of Sterling, Ill., each without the knowledge of the other. Of the two smokers, the Clark has the better construction.

In later years Mr. F. Danzenbaker adopted a combination of both hot and cold blast

DANZENBAKER SMOKER.

in the form of a vertical grate; but, like the cold blasts, it does not give as dense and subduing smoke as the regular hot blast previously described.

RELATIVE MERITS OF THE HOT AND COLD BLAST SMOKERS.

For a large volume of dense smoke, the hot-blast smokers are far superior. There was a time when the cold-blast bid fair to

CLARK COLD-BLAST SMOKER.

run out the hot-blast. The former was thought to have the advantage of being cheaper, using the fuel more slowly, and sending a *cold* blast of air upon the bees.

COLD-BLAST PRINCIPLE ILLUSTRATED.

But we doubt if this last feature is an improvement after all. Cold-blasts are used principally by bee-keepers having few colonies, the more extensive ones finding the hot-blast preferable.

One must work the bellows of a cold-blast almost constantly in order to get a smoke dense enough to subdue bees. Even then the force is too strong; while a hot-blast furnishes a gentle whiff of strong smoke that will conquer.

FUEL FOR SMOKERS.

It will be unnecessary to give directions for using these hot or cold blast smokers, as printed directions accompany all smokers sent out by each manufacturer; yet it may be well to allude to the different kinds of fuel that have been used. Rotten wood is good, and accessible to all, but it burns out too rapidly. In the Clark we prefer a kind of stringy sawdust packed solid that comes from the hand-holes made in making hives. Mr. Bingham recommends sound hard wood for his smoker. Dr. Miller and some others prefer turning-lathe hard-wood shavings, or, if these are not available, planer shavings. In certain localities peat can be obtained very cheaply, and it makes an excellent fuel. Some use old rags; others old discarded hive-quilts that are covered with propolis. These last make a very pungent subduing smoke. In some parts of the South, dry pine needles are used. One's locality as well as notions will decide what fuel to use.

W. L. Coggshall, one of the most extensive bee-keepers in the world, uses a special fuel made out of old phosphate-sacks rolled around a half-inch stick, tied at regular intervals, and then chopped into convenient lengths with a sharp ax. The rolls should,

FIG. 2.—Chopping up rolls of burlap for smoker-fuel. An old sack is rolled up, tied at intervals, and then cut in pieces between the strings.

of course, be of the right diameter and length to fit inside the smoker used. The sacking must not be rolled too tightly nor made too snug a fit, or else it will choke the draft and put out the smoker. The reader is, therefore, recommended to make a few experimental rolls before he makes up a lot for a season's use.

To facilitate lighting with a match, one end of the roll is dipped half an inch into a solution of saltpeter, and allowed to dry. If a little red lead be sprinkled in the solution it will be very easy to tell which end of the roll is for lighting.

A quantity of old sacking, says Mr. Cogg-shall, will be sufficient for one season's use, and the fuel gives a lasting smoke without sparks. He further says that he can

FIG 3.—A smoker house for smokers, tools, veils, and fuel. The fuel is kept in the lower part under the shelf.

take a cold smoker, and in *ten seconds* have all the smoke he requires, as the saltpeter ignites instantly.

When old sacking can not be obtained, old carpets or old burlap can doubtless be used. Even new burlap would not be expensive, although Mr. Coggshall says the fabric should be partly rotted to give the best results. He lays his old phosphate-sacks out in the weather for about three months, and then rolls them up.

We have been using greasy waste in a smoker with great success. It requires no treatment with any chemical to make it light easily, and it is almost impossible to extinguish it after it is once lighted, even though it be stamped in the mud. There is no question but that this is perhaps the very best smoker fuel, although in some places it may be somewhat difficult to obtain. It can usually be had for the asking at any machine-shop or printing-shop, and it may be picked up along railroads, although as a rule it would take too much time to hunt up greasy waste in this way. A piece could be found here and there, but generally not enough to be of any great use. A supply can be obtained at a printing-establishment to last a whole season; and we always advise its use, therefore, when it can be obtained. It gives a strong, pungent smoke; does not make a hot fire; is easily lighted; will not go out, even though the smoker be left standing for four or five hours at a time.

If you use the fuel that suits you best you are using the best fuel in your locality. Like many another important question, "locality" has a bearing in the case.

ABUSES OF A SMOKER.

A good smoker should last a number of seasons, but it will very quickly cease to be a good implement if it is not well taken care of.

One of the most common abuses of a smoker is to leave it out in the rain. We have seen many smokers left out in all kinds of weather; and it is needless to say that the bellows leather soon becomes hard, and cracks, and the fire-box gets rusty. A good many bee-keepers keep their smokers in an empty hive and thus avoid the danger of a costly fire. If the whole hive should burn, the loss would not be so very great.

A better plan than this would be to build a small smoker-house similar to the one shown. This need not be over five or six feet high. There is a substantial shelf as shown, on which smokers, hive-tools, veils, etc., may be kept. It is a good plan to provide a piece of heavy sheet iron about half an inch above the shelf for the smokers to stand on, so that there will be no danger of setting fire to any thing. The fuel is kept below this shelf. There is room enough usually to hold a supply for a whole season; and when it is kept in this way it is always dry and ready for use. We have such small buildings at all our outyards, and consider them almost indispensable.

Another common abuse of the smoker is to allow creosote to collect at the top until the cap will not fit down over the fire-box. In a new smoker with the flexible hinge there is not apt to be so much trouble in this

Fig. 4.—It is very seldom that a grate becomes so filled up that it has to be cleaned; but when this does happen it is the work of only a moment to insert the point of a file in one of the holes and lift out the grate, as here shown. It pays to keep the grates clean. There are a larger number of holes near the outside of the grate than in the center, consequently the fuel burns evenly and does not throw sparks until it is all consumed.

way, but at the same time it is well to spend about ten seconds once a week or so with a screw-driver in cleaning off this accumulation. We have seen smokers with caps or nozzles so filled with creosote that they would not fit down over the fire-box at all, and of course leaked smoke very badly or else had to be pounded on the top with a stick. It takes but little time to remove the greater part of the creosote so that the parts will fit. Most smokers are made with the caps a trifle large; and while they leak

Fig. 5.—How to hold the smoker when raising the cup. Compress the bellows in order to give the fingers a firmer hold.

smoke at first the collection of creosote will stop this in a short time.

Sometimes beginners in their eagerness to test new smokers work the bellows so vigorously as to blow fire from the nozzle, and before they know it the fire-box is red-hot. This means, of course, that the tin is all burnt off, leaving the bare iron to rust through in a short time. There is usually no need of having a hot flame in the fire-box, for this implies perfect combustion; while the secret of getting lots of smoke is to have imperfect combustion. Sometimes this is a fault of the fuel. It is best to use fuels that burn slowly.

While it is impossible to avoid dropping a smoker once in a while, still we think as a

Fig. 6.—The convenience of a hook on the back of the bellows. The smoker is always at hand at a second's notice.

rule bee-smokers are handled pretty roughly. It does not take long to learn to use reasonable care in handling a smoker, whereby it will last enough longer to pay.

When a fuel is used in which there is a good deal of pitch it is sometimes difficult to raise the cap or nozzle after the fire is out and the metal has become cold. We have known of instances where the cap had been battered almost out of shape after being stuck down solid. It is always best where such fuel is used to raise the cap when putting the smoker away. If it is left open there will be no sticking.

The grate will usually keep clean; but in some cases it might get stopped up, then insert the point of a file into one of the holes and lift it out as shown in Fig. 4. It can then be very easily cleaned and replaced.

HOW TO USE A SMOKER.

Perhaps the majority of bee-keepers understand using a smoker without any special instructions, but we believe that, as a rule, too much smoke is used. It is best to use just as much smoke as is necessary and not any more. A beginner so often stupefies the bees that they become practically demoralized. It is needless to say that this is a

FIG. 8.—Holding a smoker between the knees while manipulating frames.

and carefully, the bee-keeper doing nothing to disturb or excite the bees.

Fig. 5 shows the most natural way of holding the smoker when the cap is opened. A better hold is secured with the left hand if the bellows is compressed as shown. Take hold of the coiled-wire handle with the right hand and it will be seen that the cap can be raised very easily without the least

FIG. 7.—Carrying a smoker with the little finger when the hands are full.

very bad plan. Very often colony after colony can be opened, especially when the bees are working, without the use of smoke; but at the same time it is well to have a smoker near at hand.

It is not considered good practice to smoke bees out of comb-honey supers, as they are frightened at the smell of smoke, and, in their desire to save honey, uncap some of the cells and thus spoil the appearance of what might otherwise be fancy honey.

In looking for a queen, use little or no smoke, as it is very easy to set the bees running all over the combs, making it next to impossible to locate the queen. At such times the frames should be handled slowly

FIG. 9.—Working the bellows of the smoker while holding between the knees manipulating frames.

danger of burning the fingers. A coiled-wire handle remains cool, no matter how hot the fire is.

SOCIETIES OF BEE-KEEPERS. See ORGANIZATION OF BEE-KEEPERS.

SOLAR WAX-EXTRACTOR. See WAX.

SOURWOOD (*Oxydendrum arboreum*). This is considered a great honey-bearing tree in some localities, especially in the South; but as we have had no personal experience with it, we submit a description from one of our friends who has furnished us with the specimen of the leaves and flowers from which our engraving was made.

The sourwood, sometimes called the sorrel, is a fine tree from 40 to 60 feet in height, and about a foot in diameter; although it sometimes reaches 70 feet in height and a foot and a half through. The popular name, sourwood, is derived from the odor and the peculiar sour taste of the leaves and small twigs.

It is entirely distinct from the black-gum and sour-gum, or pepperidge, with which it has been unwittingly classed by some writers on honey - plants, much to the injury of sourwood. The former are honey - producers to a small extent, but are not worthy to be compared with sourwood, which, we are convinced after living where basswood, poplar, clover, buckwheat, goldenrod, persimmon, and aster abound, has not its superior among the honey-producing plants of America, either in the amount of yield, or in its beautiful appearance. Basswood is more important, only because of its widely extended growth. We write this article, to call attention more directly to this tree as a honey-producer. Bee-masters are familiar with other flora which abound where those who have written our books on bee culture reside, yet few are aware of the merits of sourwood, outside of the regions where it is found.

We are not familiar with the extent of its growth, but know this much: It abounds in the native forests from Southern Pennsylvania into Georgia and Mississippi. It seems to be more abundant along the whole mountainous tract of country on both sides of the Alleghenies and the Blue Ridge, reaching, in places, even as far as the tide-water on one side, and to Central Tennessee on the other. In many sections where poplar abounds and much buckwheat is raised, sourwood is considered *the honey-plant*, and yields the largest amount of surplus honey. It seems to flourish best on high, dry soil, and often abounds on poor woodland ridges, which can be purchased at a nominal price: though the forests along the rivers, in rich cultivated soil, are often beautifully checkered with the white blossoms in July. Being a forest tree, it is tall and generally spare of branches along the trunk, except when it grows in the edges of fields, where it yields the greatest amount of honey. The trunk preserves its uniformity of size for some distance up from the ground. The wood is white, with straight grain, which splits nicely. It is brittle and quite fine-grained, and is used for posts by cabinet-makers.

The flowers (see engraving) are produced on spikes five or six inches long, which hang in clusters on the ends of branches. Many of these flower-bearing spikes are thrown out from one central spike, and are all strung with white, bell - shaped flowers, rich in honey. The flower is midway in size and appearance between the whortleberry blossom and the lily of the valley. Unless there is a failure of the blossom, the honey-yield is sure to be abundant; for, being in the woods with good roots, the flow is not checked by ordinary drouths, nor do the rains wash out the honey from the pendant, cup-shaped flowers. Often have we regaled ourselves, while riding along the road, by breaking a bunch of the blossoms, shaking out the honey in the hand, and licking up the delicious nectar. It bears no fruit; but each flower, as it dries up, produces a brown seed-pod about the size of a large grain of wheat, which separates, when ripe, into five parts, and permits the very fine seed to fall to the earth.

SOURWOOD LEAF, FLOWERS, AND SEED-PODS.

We omitted to state that the tree commences to bloom the latter part of June, and the harvest from this source lasts until the middle of July.

We are inclined to think that the tree would thrive in our more northern latitudes ; perhaps anywhere in our land. It is found abundantly in many parts of the Allegheny Mountains, where it is very cold, the thermometer often indicating several degrees below zero.   JAMES W. SHEARER.
Liberty Corner, N. J.

The following is from *Gleanings in Bee Culture :*

SOURWOOD HONEY, ETC.

I send you to-day a sample of sourwood honey. Examine it and let us know what you think of its quality. I get more of it than of any other kind. I took about 800 ℔s. last year from the poplar, and something more than 1200 from the sourwood, all extracted.

Now, Mr. Root, nearly all of you bee - men up North say that all pure honey will candy in cold weather; and I want you to keep the sample I send you through the winter, and report if cold weather candies it. I know you have colder weather than we have down here, but I don't believe it will get cold enough to candy sourwood honey.
Lincoln, Tenn.   J. F. MONTGOMERY.

SPACING FRAMES. In nature we find combs variously spaced from 1⅛, 1¼, 1½, and sometimes up to two inches from center to center. Dzierzon, one of the very first to conceive the idea of a movable comb, gave 1½ as the right distance until Wyprecht made accurate measurements on straw hives having straight combs built in them. Out of 49 measurements, the average distance was scant 1⅜ inches. Baron von Berlepsch, by 49 other measurements, verified this result. In the United States, prominent apiarists have found the distance of natural-built combs averaged 1½ inches from center to center. It has been observed, that, in the center of the brood-nest, the combs are spaced more closely than those on the outside, the latter ranging anywhere from 1½ to 2 inches to centers.

It has been urged that we follow nature in the spacing of brood-frames. But it seems a very poor guide, inasmuch as we find such a diversity of measurements. The bee-keeper should adopt that spacing which will give him the best results—the most brood and surplus honey. Quite a number of bee-keepers are using 1½ spacing for their frames. The reason for this is, principally, because they happened to *start* with this spacing. But those who have given special attention to the matter, trying *both* spacings, agree almost uniformly that the right distance is 1⅜, or, if any thing, a trifle scant, and some use quite successfully 1¼-inch spacing. Many, indeed, who had fixed-distance frames adapted for 1½ inches, have gone to the enormous expense of changing over to 1⅜. The advantages of this latter spacing are so evident that very few deny that better results can be obtained with it. Brood comb is found to be, on an average, ⅞ inch thick; capped brood, one inch thick. On 1⅜ spacing, this will allow ½ inch between uncapped comb and ⅜ between capped brood combs.

The following paragraph is taken from an article published in *Gleanings in Bee Culture*, page 673, Vol. XVIII., written by Mr. Julius Hoffman, and it applies right here exactly:

> If, for instance, we space the combs from center to center so as to measure 1½ instead of 1⅜ inches, then we have an empty space of ⅝ inch between two combs of brood instead of ½, as it ought to be; and it will certainly require more bees to fill and keep warm a ⅝ than a ½ space. In a ½-inch space, the breeding bees from two combs facing each other will join with their backs, and so close up the space between the two brood-combs; if this space is widened, however, to ⅝, the bees can not do this, and more bees will be required to keep up the needed brooding temperature. What a drawback this would be in cool spring weather, when our colonies are still weak in numbers yet breeding most desirable, can readily be understood.

Where wider spacing is adopted, there is apt to be more honey stored in the combs, and less of worker (but more drone brood). Close spacing, on the contrary (1⅜), tends to encourage the rearing of more worker brood, the exclusion of drone brood, and the storage of less honey below. This is exactly as we wish. We said there is ½ inch between the uncapped brood. The bees need a little more room in backing in and out of the cells for the purpose of feeding the larvæ than they do after these cells are capped over into sealed brood. Sealed brood, requiring less attention from the bees, and less heat from the cluster, is spaced ⅜ apart, and this is ample. For further hints on this subject, see FRAMES, SELF-SPACING; HIVE-MAKING, also HIVES.

SPANISH NEEDLE. This plant yields immense quantities of honey along the low bottom-grounds of the Mississippi and Illinois Rivers. The following from GLEANINGS, p. 162, Vol. XVI., is from the Hon. J. M. Hambaugh, and tells all about the plant, and the immense quantities of honey that are often produced by it.

> Something over a year ago I wrote a letter for GLEANINGS, claiming that the honey gathered from this plant is superior to that produced from other fall flowers, and that it should rank among the very best grades, and command the same price in the markets as clover and linden honey. My peculiar location has, fortunately, placed me in a position to understand pretty thoroughly the nature of this plant, and the quality of the honey it produces. Located at the foot of the bluffs of the Illinois River, there is a broad expanse of low marshy lands to the east and south, from three to five miles in width. These lands are subject to overflows from the river once a year, which usually take place in early spring. This renders a large portion of the soil unfit for tilling purposes; and the consequence is, the Spanish needle has secured a permanent foothold, almost to the exclusion of nearly all other plants. Early in September they begin to open their beautiful petals, and in a short time whole districts are aglow, and their dazzling brilliancy reminds one of burnished sheets of gold. It is now, should the weather prove favorable, that the bees revel in their glory, and the honey comes *piling in;* and the beauty about this kind of honey is, it needs but little "boiling down," and the bees no sooner fill their cells than it is cured and ready to seal. This is one great advantage, and saves the bees lots of labor, making the storage of honey more rapid. I had one colony of bees that stored 63½ lbs. of honey in six days; another one, 86 lbs. in nine days, while 43 producing colonies netted me 2,21 lbs. in ten days—an average of 47 lbs. to the colony. Though not quite as clear as clover or linden, the honey has a golden hue, an exquisite flavor, and a very fine body, weighing fully 12 lbs. to the gallon, and, as previously stated, I can not see why it should not rank on the market in grade and price with clover and linden honey.
>
> So far as my market is concerned, there is no honey so universally liked by the consumers as my "golden coreopsis;" in fact, not one word of complaint has ever come back to me from this honey, save one. A neighbor ceased buying it; and when

asked for a reason, he stated, "My children eat it up too fast." I am now running a peddling-wagon, and my salesman states he can sell more honey going over territory he has previously canvassed than to hunt up new routes. This certainly speaks well for this kind of honey. I have sold over 4000 lbs. in my home market this season, and the demand seems to be on the increase; and I believe if apiarists will locate their bees so as to get the benefit of these large areas of coreopsis they will not only confer a boon on their fellow-man but reap a financial reward for themselves. Another word in favor of coreopsis honey: It is less inclined to granulate; and at this date there is but little sign of granulation, while my two barrels of linden honey is as hard as New Orleans sugar.

J. M. HAMBAUGH.

Spring, Brown Co., Ill., Jan. 21, 1889.

In 1891 Mr. Hambaugh wrote another article on the subject, from which we make the following extract:

The "golden coreopsis," or Spanish needle, stands at the head of all the honey-producing plants with which I have had any experience. It is not only the richest in nectar, but the quality is *par excellence*, and sells in my home market equal to, if not better than, clover honey. Its weight is fully 12 lbs. to the gallon, and it seems to need little if any curing by the bees when gathered. I have never yet seen any crude or unripe Spanish-needle honey, notwithstanding I have extracted it from the same supers three times in two weeks, and on one occasion twice in five and six days. One colony netted 73 lbs. in 5 days, and the apiary of 43 producing colonies in 8 days produced 2083 lbs., being upward of 47 lbs. per colony; and this is not true of that particular year only, but it has proven the surest honey-producing plant we have in this locality. Nothing short of cold rainy weather spoils the harvest from this plant.

SPRAYING FRUIT-TREES. See FRUIT-BLOSSOMS.

SPRAYING DESTRUCTIVE TO THE BROOD. See FRUIT-BLOSSOMS.

SPREADING BROOD. As is very well known, queens are inclined to lay their eggs in circles in the comb, the circle being larger in the center combs and smaller in the outside ones. The whole bulk of eggs and brood in several combs thus forms practically a sphere which the bees are able to cover and keep warm. When the queen has formed this sphere of brood and eggs she curtails her egg-laying for the time being until enough brood is hatched out to increase the size of the cluster; and then she will gradually enlarge the circles of brood to keep pace with the enlarged ball of bees. Yet the queen very often is overcareful—that is, she errs on the safe side, so that when warm weather has fully set in she sometimes lays fewer eggs than she should in the judgment of the apiarist, and accordingly he inserts a frame of empty comb in the center of the brood-nest. In this comb the queen will commence laying at once to unite, as it were, the two halves of brood; and when she has filled this with eggs the apiarist may insert another empty comb. If the queen has filled the first one given she will be likely, if the weather is not cold, to go into the second comb and fill it with eggs on both sides; for nice clean empty cells are very tempting to her. In a word, this operation of inserting empty combs in the center of the brood-nest is called "spreading brood," its object being to increase the amount of brood, and thus insure a larger force of workers for the prospective harvest. While this spreading of the brood *may* be done by practical and experienced beekeepers, because it stimulates the queen to greater egg-laying capacity, yet when practiced by beginners and the inexperienced it generally results in much more harm than good. An A B C scholar without previous experience might, on a warm day in early spring, think it high time to put empty comb in the center of the bood-nest. The queen, we shall say, immediately occupies it, filling it with eggs. This, of course, requires a large force of nurse-bees to take care of the young bees and hatching larvæ. A cool spell of weather is almost sure to come on, with the result that the cluster of bees is contracted, leaving the brood that was forced outside by inserting the empty comb, out in the cold, where it chills and dies. The outside edge of the cluster, in its effort to take care of this brood, is likewise chilled, with the result that the colony suffers a check and setback far worse than had it been left to its own devices.

Ordinarily we may say that the spreading of brood can be practiced safely only after settled warm weather has arrived. The beginner, who desires to give extra combs for egg-laying, especially in early spring, would do well to put those extra combs at the *outside;* but after settled warm weather has come, when the temperature does not go below 40 degrees Fahrenheit at night at any time, he may insert a frame of empty comb at the center of the brood-nest.

It should be borne in mind that the practice of spreading brood has been largely abandoned, even by experienced bee-keepers. Where the queen has plenty of room somewhere in the brood-nest (and that "somewhere" should be outside the brood-cluster), both bees and queen will ordinarily rear as much brood as they can safely and profitably care for.

SPRING DWINDLING. See WINTER-ING.

SPRING MANAGEMENT. All colonies should be gone over very carefully the first warm day the bees can fly in the spring. Unless they have two or three combs of honey, stores should be taken from some other colonies that can spare them. If no hive has a surplus, then the needy should be fed a thick syrup consisting of two parts of sugar to one of water. See FEEDING, especially those instructions urging fall rather than spring feeding.

Feeders should be placed on top of the frames, and covered with packing. It may turn cold shortly after; and even if the syrup is left in the feeder, starvation will be averted, for the bees will cluster around it and help themselves as they have need.

If colonies have been well housed and fed in the fall, there will usually be no occasion for feeding or equalizing of stores. Of course, there is liable to be here and there

DOVETAILED WINTER-CASE.

a colony which, by reason of bad stores, may have dysentery. In that case the front of the hive will be soiled with dark brown spots, and there will be a quantity of dead bees in front of the entrance and on the bottom of the hive. Such a colony, even with the best of nursing, may die before settled warm weather comes on. If considerable honey-dew has been gathered during the previous summer, one is likely to find some spring dwindling and dysentery in some of the hives. Some honey-dews will make a very fair winter food; but the majority of them, especially those gathered from hickory and oak, are bad. Where this is gathered, we would endeavor to use as much of it as possible in brood-rearing in the summer, and then feed sugar syrup on top of it.

Some springs the weather will open up warm very suddenly with no natural pollen available. The warm weather may last several days. During this time brood-rearing will start up rapidly; and if there is no pollen in the hives the bees will be hunting around in the barns and stables and chicken-coops for bran or chopped feed. It is

RIGHT WAY OF PUTTING ON THE PAPER.

necessary at such times to give artificial pollen. Trays should be set out in sunny places, under cover if possible, containing a few quarts of rye or pea flour.

Unless bees can have natural or artificial pollen when brood-rearing starts, considerable brood will be found dead. On seeing this the beginner is apt to conclude he has some form of bee disease — possibly foul brood. If the brood dies shortly after a sudden warming-up spell, during which there is very little natural pollen in or out of the hives, the owner of the bees should await further developments. See the last paragraph of the general subject of POLLEN and BEE DISEASES for further particulars.

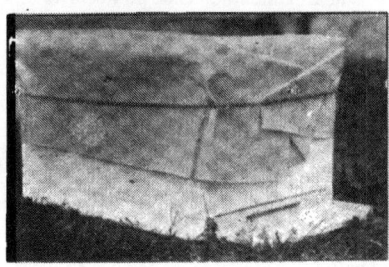

WRONG WAY OF PUTTING ON THE PAPER.

It may be necessary in some climates, after the bees are set out of the cellar on their summer stands, to provide some sort of protection. Some use wooden winter cases, and others use paper folded over the hives as shown in the accompanying illustration.

Where colonies are very weak it may be advisable to unite; but this uniting, if the bees are in the cellar, should take place before they are set out. See UNITING.

One difficulty in uniting outdoor bees is that those moved to a new stand are quite inclined to go back to the old hive. This can be overcome to a certain extent. See UNITING. Uniting in the spring is often unsatisfactory. Unless the colony is very weak we advise taking out the surplus of combs that they do not occupy or use, and crowd the little cluster on as few frames as they can occupy. In that case, division-boards should be moved over, and the frames set over on the other side. The hive should be warmly packed, and the entrance contracted down to one inch wide to prevent robbing and to conserve the heat.

In going over the yard in early spring one is likely to find, if the bees are wintered outdoors, one or more dead colonies. Their entrances should be shut up bee-tight, for on the first warm fly day they will be robbed out by the other bees, resulting in a general disturbance of the whole yard. See ROBBING. Combs on which bees have died may be used later on by putting fresh bees on them. Unless they are very badly soiled with dysentery so they are fairly smeared over with a brown excrement, or the stores are very bad, they can be used again. But badly soiled combs, or otherwise undesirable, should be put through the wax-extractor. See WAX; also DYSENTERY.

In early spring it may be necessary to rake out the dead bees in the entrances of some colonies. If a colony is strong it will usually do its own house-cleaning; but sometimes the dead accumulate in such numbers as actually to block the entrance. In all such cases there is danger that the few survivors may die outright.

Some very weak colonies will be found with queens, while there will be some other colonies fairly strong without any queen. In that case it is best to unite these two, moving the weak colony over to the strong one. See UNITING; also INTRODUCING.

Some experienced bee-keepers can "spread brood" in early spring; but the beginner had better not practice it. See SPREADING BROOD.

STINGLESS BEES. See BEES, STINGLESS.

STINGS. It is true, that bees can not bite and kick like horses, nor can they hook like cattle; yet most people, after having had an experience with bee-stings for the first time, are inclined to think they would rather be bitten, kicked, and hooked, all together, than to take the risk of a repetition of that keen and exquisite anguish which one feels as he receives the full contents of the poison-bag from a vigorous hybrid during the height of the honey-season. Stings are not all alike, by any means; and while we can stand the greater part of them without even wincing, or stopping our work, we *occasionally* get one that seems as if it could not possibly be borne. Always obliged to bear it, however, we do so as best we can.

The pain is much harder to bear if we stop to allow our minds to dwell on it; or after being stung, if we just think of former times when we received painful stings, at the mere thought a sudden pang darts along the wounded part. We do not know why this is, unless it is the effect of the imagination; if so, then it is clear that even imaginary pains are very hard to bear. We have sometimes purposely, by way of experiment, allowed the mind to dwell on the pain of the sting the moment it was inflicted, and the increase would be such that it would almost make one scream with pain. If you doubt this, the next time your feet get very cold, just think of wading barefooted in the frozen snow, at a zero temperature.

Of course, where stings swell on one so badly as to shut an eye, or the like of that, one possibly might be obliged to stop work awhile; but even then, it would be advisable to pay as little attention to the matter as possible, and by all means avoid rubbing or irritating the affected part. We have known stings to be made very painful by rubbing and fussing with them which we have good reason to think would have given little if any trouble otherwise. You all know that, when you get warmed up with hard work, a bruise, a bump, or a slight flesh wound, gives little if any pain; but to sit down calmly and cut into one's flesh gives the most excruciating pain. When young we repeatedly cut great gashes on the fingers with a jack-knife, and felt but little pain at the time; but when it became necessary to lance the flesh to get a sliver out of the foot, or to cut open a stone-bruise, the pain was most intense.

To pare away with the razor until you get through the skin, and see the blood start—why, it makes the flesh creep to think of it now; but the clips that came unawares with the dull jack-knife were scarcely heeded at all, more than to tie up the wound to keep the blood from soiling the work. Well, the point is, we are to take stings just as we used to take the cuts with those jack-knives in our boyhood days. Of course, we are not to rush needlessly into danger; but when it comes, take it philosophically. Pull the sting out as quickly as possible, and do it in

EFFECT OF ONE BEE-STING ON THE LIP.

such a way as to avoid, as much as possible, squeezing the contents of the poison-bag into the wound. If you pick the sting out with the thumb and finger in the way that comes natural, you will probably get a fresh dose of poison in the act, and this will sometimes prove the most painful of the whole opera tion, causing the sting to swell when it otherwise would not have done so.

Too much emphasis can not be placed on the fact that the sting should be removed at once, for the reason that not only the pain but the swelling will be very much reduced Of course if the poison-bag is squeezed, thus forcing the poison into the wound, in the act of removing, the effect will be as bad as if the sting were left in. We once received a sting on the upper eye-lid; and as we were wearing glasses it was impossible to scratch it out immediately. The eye was suffused with tears, and it was impossible to locate the sting. Not being able to find any one to pull it out, the sting remained in the wound. This was certainly the worst "knock-out blow" that we ever received from a bee. Had we not been wearing glasses, the sting could easily have been brushed away with very little inconvenience.

THE PROPER WAY TO REMOVE A STING.

The blade of a knife, if one is handy, may be slid under the poison-bag, and the sting

lifted out without pressing a particle more of the poison into the wound. When a knife-blade is not handy, push the sting out with the thumb or finger nail in much the same way. It is quite desirable that the sting be taken out as quickly as possible, for if the barbs (to be described further along) once get hold of the flesh, muscular contractions will rapidly work the sting deeper and deeper. Sometimes the sting separates, leaving part (one of the splinters, so to speak) in the wound. It has been suggested that we should be very careful to remove every one of these tiny points; but after trying many times to see what the effect would be, we have concluded that they do but little harm, and that the main thing is, to remove the part containing the poison-bag before it has emptied itself completely into the wound. When very busy, or having something in the other hand to make it inconvenient to remove the sting with a knife or finger-nail, we have been in the habit of rubbing the sting out against the clothing, in such a way as to push the poison-bag off sidewise; and although this plan often breaks off the sting so as to leave splinters in the wound, we have found little if any more trouble from them than usual.

REMEDIES FOR BEE-STINGS.

For years past we have taken the ground that medicines of all kinds are of so little

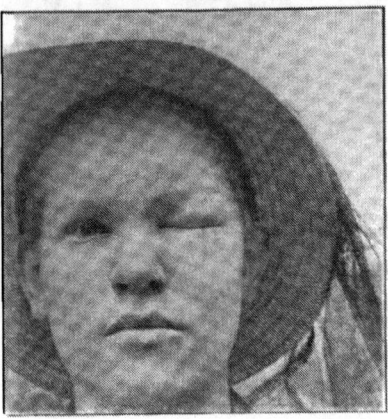

EFFECT OF A STING NEAR THE EYE.

avail, if of any use at all, that the best way is to pay no attention to any of them. This has awakened a great deal of arguing, and the remedies that have been sent, which the writers knew were good, because they had tried them, have been enough to fill this whole chapter. We have tried a great many of them, and, for a time, we imagined they "did good;" but after giving them a more extended trial, we have been forced to conclude that they were entirely futile. Nay, further: they not only did no good; but if the directions with the remedy were to rub it in the wound, they did positive harm; for the friction diffused the poison more rapidly into the circulation, and made a painful swelling of what would have been very trifling, if let alone. Please bear in mind that the poison is introduced into the flesh through a puncture so minute that the finest

IT PAYS TO GRIN AND BEAR IT.

Mr. Chalon Fowls, of Oberlin, Ohio, numbers among his customers an amateur bee-keeper who has the faculty of seeing the bright side of life under adverse circumstances. This picture, sent to Mr. Fowls as a postcard, shows that it pays to "grin and bear it."

cambric needle could by no manner of means enter where the sting did, and that the flesh closes over so completely after it as to be practically impossible for the remedy to penetrate this opening; now, even if you have a remedy that will neutralize the poison, in something the same way that an alkali neutralizes any other acid, how are you to get it in contact with the poison? We know of no way of doing it unless we resort to a surgical operation; and if you will try that kind of "tinkering" with one bee-sting you will probably never want to try another. There is no remedy in the world like letting an ordinary sting alone, and going on with the work without even thinking about it. But, suppose we get a sting under the eye—one that closes up that very important organ; shall we go on with our work? That depends. If it brings on headache or causes great discomfort we would rest a while, and in the meantime apply a cold wet cloth until the local fever is allayed. Sometimes applying a hot and cold wet cloth alternately brings relief.

A year or two ago kerosene oil was suggested as a remedy, and two of our friends regarded it of such importance that they almost got into a controversy about who was entitled to the honor of the discovery. Well, having received a very bad sting on the hand, we went for the oil-can and dropped oil on the spot for some time. As kerosene will remove a rusty bolt or screw when nothing else will avail, and as it seems to have a wonderful power of penetrating all cracks and crevices, we began to have faith that it might follow the sting of the bee, and in some way neutralize the poison. But the only result was one of the most painful and lasting stings we ever had.

WHAT TO DO WHEN STUNG A GREAT NUMBER OF TIMES AT ONCE.

Severe cases of stinging are usually the result of carelessness, either from allowing combs to be scattered, causing robbing, or because a hive has been bumped over by careless driving, or by some animal allowed the range of the apiary. There are a number of cases on record where horses have been stung to death; and it is hardly safe to hitch such animals within a few feet of a hive, nor yet to let them run loose in a bee-yard, although a few sheep may be let in to keep the grass down to advantage.

Mr. Chalon Fowls, of Oberlin, Ohio, left a horse hitched near some hives of what he thought were gentle Italians; but by some means or other the animal bumped one of the hives, irritating the bees, causing them to rush out and sting. The horse, of course, began to plunge and kick, with the result that he demolished completely all the hives within reach. Mr. Fowls said the horse, when he could get to him, was almost literally covered with stings. He unhitched and led him away, and immediately called for a boiler of hot water. This was brought out as soon as it could be heated. Cloths and blankets were immersed in it. almost boiling hot, wrung nearly dry, and laid over the animal, now writhing in the severest agony. The moment Mr. Fowls

Be proud of your swollen eye!
It isn't the fact that you're licked that counts;
It's how did you fight—and why?
EDMUND VANCE COOKE.

applied the hot blankets he says the horse quieted down. During the escapade he himself was terribly stung in the face and on the hands; and he says that, as soon as the hot cloths were applied to his face, he felt almost instant relief. The hot cloths were applied to the horse on every portion that was stung, and Mr. Fowls had the satisfaction of knowing that he could save his horse, which was soon as well as ever.

Cases are on record of severe stinging of human beings where cold applications were used instead of hot, with almost as good results, apparently. In such cases the patients are wrapped in a bed sheet, wrung from cold water, and put to bed, and applications renewed until relief followed.

During the summer of 1902 at one of our outyards we had an experience which we thought at the time would be fatal to both man and beast. It came about somewhat in this way. A neighbor of ours who had a field of timothy near our yard had allowed

his horse to eat grass within a few feet of the yard while he went to the further end of the field to look after some work. In the mean time the horse had managed to get over among the bees. The result was, she knocked over five hives, and was literally covered with stings when our neighbor came up. Being a practical bee-man as well as a horseman himself, he rushed into the fray, freed the horse, and started her for the barn. The animal was beginning to swell badly, and it was evident to him that she would die before relief could be given by a veterinary, even if called. He accordingly rolled up about a pound of common table salt in a paper, opened the animal's mouth, and with the left hand grasped her tongue, pulling it out as far as he could. He then with his right hand shoved the salt clear down her throat, reaching to his elbow. This done, he quickly closed her mouth and elevated her head until he saw the wad of salt go down the gullet. In a short time the horse showed relief, for the salt probably neutralized, to some extent, the effect of the acid poison. It also acted as a physic; for when a horse is sick at the stomach he can not vomit, and it is necessary to give him something at once to keep the bowels free. In three or four hours the horse was as well as ever.

Our neighbor did not apply wet blankets wrung out of hot water; but the veterinary, whom we consulted afterward, said that the giving of the salt was one of the best things that could have been done, and added that he would have wrapped the animal up in a

"GO' VAY, YOU BEE!"

blanket wrung out of hot water. If to this water was added a small quantity of ammonia, all the better. We suggest, then, if a horse is badly stung, it be given a dose of common salt, and treated to applications of hot blankets, and that the blankets be renewed often. Where hot water can not be obtained, use cold.

GETTING HARDENED TO STINGS.

When we first commenced bee-keeping, stings swelled so badly, and were so painful, that we had either hands or eyes swelled up most of the time, until we seriously contemplated giving up the business, just on this

" OU-OO-OW-OO-O-U-C-II ! ! "

account alone. After we had had a little more practice, we discovered that there was very little need of being stung at all, if one was careful not to provoke the ire of the little insects. Still further, we found the swelling to be gradually less and less; and before the first

summer was over, we very seldom felt the effects of any sting, the day afterward. When first commencing, if the eye was swelled so as to be closed by a sting, it often took until the third day to have it go down entirely. The A B C class, almost without exception, corroborate this experience.

HOW ONE WHO IS SERIOUSLY AFFECTED BY A SINGLE STING MAY BECOME COMPARATIVELY IMMUNE TO THE POISON.

There are some who are so seriously affected by the bee-sting poison that even a single sting will cause the body to break out all over in red blotches. This may or may not be accompanied by a difficulty of breathing, and heavy pulsations of the heart—so heavy, indeed, that they seem like blows of a hammer. At such times there is danger, and a physician should be called at once. There is, perhaps, only one person in ten thousand who is thus affected. So rare are the reported cases that the editors of *Gleanings in Bee Culture*, a journal with a circulation of over 30,000, do not hear of them once in ten years. But there are quite a number of others who are less affected but who inform us that a single sting produces great discomfort. While there is no danger of loss of life, the results of a sting are such that they have been obliged to give up the delightful pastime of keeping bees, very much to their regret. We have formerly advised all such persons when going among bees to be veiled and to wear gloves. But in late years, we have found a better remedy. It was suggested by the fact that the average person becomes less and less affected by the bee-sting poison; and it occurred to me that, inasmuch as the human system has the power to withstand increasing doses of many poisons, after the first one, why should it not be able to immunize itself to a certain extent against the virus of bee-stings ? It is a well-known fact. opium and morphine fiends are able to take doses of those drugs in amounts that would kill ten people who are not in the habit of taking them. The same thing is true of alcohol. Returning to the subject under consideration, we reasoned that, if one who is very seriously affected by bee-sting poison would just merely prick himself with a sting and then brush it off before it has had time to throw much of its virus into the wound, the after-effects would not be very serious; and that if the dose were repeated some four or five days afterward, or about the time the effect of the previous sting had passed away, one could, by continuing this process, ultimately apply the dose at more frequent intervals until in time his system would be no more affected than that of an ordinary person.

An interesting case came under observation, and we will relate the circumstances which may help others. A boy in our neighborhood, when stung, became so affected that his body would break out in great red blotches; his breathing grow difficult, and his heart begin to pound like a sledge hammer. It was really a question whether there was not danger of losing his life. Nevertheless he was very desirous of engaging in bee-keeping, and determined to work with them. We finally suggested taking a live bee and pressing it on the back of his hand until it merely pierced his skin with the sting, then immediately brush off both bee and sting. This was done; and since no serious effect followed it was repeated inside of four or five days. This was continued for some three or four weeks, when the patient began to have a sort of itching sensation all over his body. The hypodermic injections of bee-sting poison were then discontinued. At the end of a month they were repeated at intervals of four or five days. Again after two or three weeks the itching sensation came on, but it was less pronounced. The patient was given a rest of about a month, when the doses were repeated as before. He then went to school and was not back for eight or nine months. On his return the applications were given again, when it was plainly noticeable that the after effects were becoming markedly less. He then went out into the bee-yard and was stung occasionally, but, beyond a small swelling locally, there was no unpleasant effect However, as a matter of precaution when he went among the bees he always wore a veil and heavy gloves; for the stings, after passing through these goods would retain only slight effect.

Some months afterward he was assisting one of our men at one of our yards, when, without warning, a colony of bees that was being dissected made a most furious attack on both the men. The young man who had been taking the immunizing doses of bee-virus received, he estimates, ten or a dozen stings all over his body. He had no veil nor gloves, for the other man was doing the work with the bees. He expected serious consequences; but, greatly to his surprise and gratification, no unpleasant effects followed. What was more, there was no swelling. Now, remember that this person used to be so seriously affected that a single sting would cause his parents to worry, as they feared he would not be able to survive the attack. He now handles bees with the same freedom that any experienced bee-keeper does.

HOW TO AVOID BEING STUNG.

Some may imagine that it is necessary for one who keeps bees to endure the pain of being stung several times every day. A lady once said that she could never stand it to have her husband keep 100 colonies, for she got stung four or five times a day from only a dozen, while 30 or 40 stings a day would be more than she could possibly bear. We could take any one of you into an apiary of 100 colonies, and have you assist us all day long, without your getting a single sting. Nay, further: if you are very timid, and can not bear a single sting, by taking some pains you may be able to work day after day, without being stung at all. The apiary must be properly cared for, no robbing allowed, and you must do exactly as we tell you. See ANGER OF BEES. In the first place, avoid standing right in front of any hive. We are often very much tried by visitors (some of them bee-keepers, too, who ought to know better), because they will stand right before the entrance until they have a small swarm scolding them because they can not get out and in the hive, and then wonder why so many bees are buzzing about in that particular spot. If you should go into a factory, and stand in the way of the workmen until a dozen of them were blocked up with their arms full of boards and finished work, you would be pretty apt to be told to get out of the way. Now, you are to exercise the same common sense in an apiary. By watching flying bees you can tell at once their path through the air, and then keep out of their way. Right back of any hive is a pretty safe place to stand.

One of the first things to learn is to know whether a bee is angry or not, by the sounds it makes. You should all know by the hum of a bee, when it is gathering honey from the heads of clover in the fields, that it has no malice toward any living thing; it is the happy hum of honest industry and contentment. People sometimes jump when a bee sings harmlessly, whereas they should know better; but it is because bees are not in their line of business, and they don't know "bee-talk."

Well, when you go in front of a hive, or approach colonies that are not accustomed to being worked with, one of the sentinels will frequently take wing, and, by an angry and loud buzz, bid you begone. This note is quite unlike that of a bee upon the flowers, or of the ordinary laborer upon the wing; it is in a high key, and the tone, to us, sounds much like that of a scolding woman, and one who will be pretty sure to make her threats good if you do not heed the warning. When one of these bees approaches, you are first to lower your head, or, better still, tip down your hat-brim; for these fellows almost always instinctively aim for the eyes. It will often be satisfied, and go back into its hive if you move away a little; but one should be sure not to give it to understand that you admit yourself a thief, and that it has frightened you. If it grows very threatening, and you are timid, you had better enter some building. We are in the habit of opening the door of the honey-house, and asking visitors to go in there, when an angry bee persists in following them. Very many times we can hardly get them to go in as we direct, because they can not see why the bee will not follow them, and thus corner them up a sure prey. We do not know why it is, but a bee very seldom ventures to follow one indoors. A single bee seldom does, but a very vicious colony of hybrids, when fully aroused, may do so

WHAT TO DO WHEN A SINGLE BEE FOLLOWS YOU ABOUT BY THE HOUR.

It not unfrequently happens, especially in an apiary where there are many hybrids, that a single bee (of this "cross") will follow you about the apiary for hours, poising itself just before your eyes, making believe to sting. It does not pay to be humane toward such bees. While this offender is holding itself aloft before your face in a menacing manner, smash it between your hands, or, with a stick, give it a smart rap; but take care that you don't miss it, or it will stop its dallying and deliver its sting. In the use of the stick it is quite useless to strike at individual bees on the wing. It is our plan to take up two sticks, or any thing that is handy, say an inch or so wide and a foot or two long. With a couple of these, one in each hand, we make rapid back-and-forth motions like an inverted pendulum in front of the face, working the sticks for a full minute or more. This excites the ire of cross bees, causing them to rush right out at the rapidly moving objects, with the result that they get their heads rapped right and left. We have had at various times perhaps a hundred bees buzzing about the head, and killed them all, by the method explained, in less time than it takes to tell it. Such bees, unless killed, will harrass one for perhaps an hour. If there be only a single bee you can kill it by slapping the palms of the hands together; but since you may receive a sting in so doing it is perhaps better to use a paddle having wire cloth through the center to avoid fanning the bees away.

HOW TO SAVE YOURSELF FROM A STING.

Sometimes a bee is noticed in the act of inserting its sting in your hand. When the other hand is not holding a frame, nor otherwise engaged, bring it to the rescue by smashing the bee before it succeeds. But where, as is sometimes the case, the other hand is holding a frame, slap against your person the hand which is being attacked. Should you do it aright you both smash the bee and also rub out the sting its owner has succeeded in plunging into the flesh. Never slap the hand directly against yourself, but give it a sort of sliding motion. You will thus accomplish the double purpose. If a bee strikes you in the back of the neck (when you have no veil), and lodges in your hair, smash it by that half-slap and half-rubbing motion. We recommend killing bees as above, when they have actually begun to insert their sting, because they are then, so far as we have been able to observe, determined to accomplish their purpose or die. Whenever possible we prefer to have them do the latter; for a bee if foiled after it has gone so far will carry out the principle most persistently of the little adage, "If at first you don't succeed," etc. See ANGER OF BEES.

Where no robbing has been going on, one usually gets warning enough, in ample time to take precautions. When colonies are quietly busy during the working season there is but little danger from bees in the air. While working with a hive, bending right over uncovered frames, you are comparatively secure from the bees of other stocks; for unless robbing, bees seem to have no disposition to meddle or hang around their neighbors' homes. This is one reason why bystanders at a little distance are so much more apt to be stung than the apiarist who is right among them.

JERKING THE HANDS BACK.

A good many times, especially where bees seem maliciously inclined, as you proceed to lift the frame three or four will strike against the hands, feinting to sting. The natural tendency, of course, is to jerk back the hand. This is the worst thing that you can do, ensuring a sting; whereas by holding your hands motionless to let the bees see that the new objects are not afraid they will rarely if ever go beyond a pretense of using their weapon. It is certain a large number of stings received by beginners on the hands are attributable to this jerking-back of the hands. The same is true in reference to the face, when unprotected by a veil. Nine-tenths of the bees which make such demonstration will not sting if you control your nerves, letting your tormentors know that you can not be frightened.

TO OPEN A HIVE WITHOUT BEING STUNG.

Have your smoker lighted and in good trim, then set it down near the hive you intend to examine. Now, we never use smoke on bees unless needful to subdue them; for why should we annoy the little fellows quietly going about their household duties unless obliged to? We frequently open hive after hive with no kind of use for smoke at all, and yet we often see bee-keepers drive the poor little chaps down to the bottom of the hive with great volumes of smoke, when they have not shown the least symptom of any disposition but the most friendly. It is true, where the colony is very large, the bees sometimes pile up in the way, on the rabbets and ends of the frames, so that it becomes desirable to drive them off for their own safety. This requires very little smoke; and if you are in no great hurry they will clear out of the way if you just pat them on the backs gently with a weed or bit of grass. When bees are disposed to be cross, and show fight, you will readily discover it the minute you turn up the first corner of the cloth covering; and if it takes smoke to make them beg pardon, give it to them only in small quantities until you are sure more is needed. See FRAMES, HOW TO MANIPULATE.

WHAT KIND OF BEES STING WORST.

The general decision now is, that pure Italians, Caucasians, and Carniolans are the most easily handled See BEES. Not only do they sting less, but as they keep their places on the combs without getting excited* when the hives are opened properly, they are far less likely to get under one's clothing than common bees. A great many stings are received from bees that are in no way badly disposed at all, simply from getting pinched accidentally, while on the person of the bee-keeper. The pure races may be handled all day, with no such mishap; but after working among the old-fashioned blacks or hybrids we often find a dozen or more under the coat, in the sleeves, if they can get up, and, worst of all, up the trousers, unless the precaution has been taken to tuck them into the boots or stockings when wearing low shoes. See VEILS. This one thing alone would decide one in favor of the Italians, if they were simply equal to the blacks in other respects. Hybrids, as before stated, are worse to sting than either of the races when pure; while Cyprian and Holy-Land bees are so much worse still, that sometimes smoke has no effect on them. See CYPRIANS, under ITALIANS; also BEES.

It may be well to add, that we find many exceptions to these rules; a colony of blacks will sometimes be much easier to handle than one of Italians in the same yard; and the progeny of a queen that we may have every other reason to call pure may be as cross as the worst hybrids. Still further: A very cross colony of bees may be so educated, by careful treatment, as to become very gentle, and vice versa. The colony in front of the door of the honey-house was always a gentle one, season after season; the explanation being that they became accustomed to the continual passing and repassing of the bee-keeper in front of their hive, and learned to be dodging past some one almost all the time. On the contrary, those located in the remote corners of the apiary are very apt to sting, if you just come round to take a view of their entrance. Egyptian bees are said to be much worse than any of the other races; and as they do not yield to smoke, as do others, they have been discarded principally on account of this unpleasant feature.†

BEE-STING POISON.

When bees are very angry and elevate that portion of their bodies containing the sting,

---

* Queenless bees are not as quiet. It may be because they seldom work with energy, and have therefore no fresh accumulation of stores, which tend so much to put bees on their good behavior. All bees are much worse after a sudden stoppage of nectar secretion, especially after a basswood or buckwheat flow.

† Carniolans have the reputation of being very gentle, but we think no more so than Italians.

you will often see a tiny drop of some transparent liquid on its point. This liquid is the poison of the bee's sting. It has a sharp, pungent taste; and when thrown in the eyes, as sometimes happens, it has a stinging, acrid feeling, as if it might be a compound of cayenne pepper, onion-juice, and horseradish combined; and one who tastes it or gets it in his eyes concludes it is not so strange that such a substance, introduced into the circulation, should produce severe pain. The poison of the bee's sting has been thought to be similar in composition to that of the viper and scorpion; but at the present writing we can not learn that any chemist has ever given us an analysis that would tell us just what the poison is. The virus obtained from ants is called formic acid, and we have wondered whether that from bee-stings is not similar, or the same. The odor from a disturbed ant-hill very much resembles that from a colony of bees when opened up on a cool morning. It seems probably a vegetable acid, derived from the honey and pollen that constitute the food of the bee, since the poison is much more pungent while the bees are working in the fields, accumulating stores largely, than when they are at rest during the winter months. It is generally during basswood-bloom that we get those severe stings which draw the blood and show a large white spot around the wound.

HOW IT IS DONE.

It is quite an interesting experiment to let a bee sting you on the hand, and then coolly observe the whole performance without disturbing it. We have sometimes, in trying to see how far we could go with an angry colony of bees without the use of smoke, had a lot of them strike the face with a sud len dash; but as we kept perfectly still they would alight without stinging. Now, the slightest movement, even an incautious breath, might result in some pretty severe stinging; but by keeping cool and quiet, carefully walking away, escape becomes possible without any stings at all. Very often a single bee works itself up in a sufficient passion to try to sting; but to commence while standing still, we have always found to be rather difficult work for them; although they sometimes prick slightly, giving one a touch of poison, they seldom sting very severely without taking wing again. To go back: After the bee has penetrated the flesh of your hand, and worked the sting so deeply as to be satisfied, it begins to find itself a prisoner, and to consider means of escape. It usually gets smashed at about this stage of proceedings,

unless succeessful in tearing the sting—poison-bag and all—from the body; however, if allowed to work quietly it seldom does this, knowing that such a proceeding seriously maims for life, often even kills the bee. After pulling at the sting to see that it will not come out, it seems to consider the matter a little, and then commences to walk around the sting, in a circle, just as if trying to twist a screw out of a board. If you can be patient and let the bee alone, it may work it out, but in most cases the sting either tears out from the body of the bee or breaks off. We need not tell you that it takes some heroism to submit patiently to all this manœuvring. The temptation is almost ungovernable, while experiencing the intense pain, to say, while you give it a clip, "There, you little beggar, take that, if you can not learn better manners in future."

ODOR OF BEE-STING POISON.

After one bee has stung you on the hand, its use among the bees in the hive will be pretty sure to get you more stings, perhaps due to the odor of virus, unless you are very careful. After one sting has been inflicted, there seems a much greater chance, when about in the apiary, of getting more stings. Mr. Quinby has suggested that this is owing to the smell of the poison, and that the use of smoke will neutralize this scent. We very often blow smoke on the wound. The heat relieves the pain somewhat, and the smoke obscures the bee-sting odor. There is no doubt about that.

THE POISON OF THE BEE'S STING AS A REMEDIAL AGENT.

For some years past there have been running in our bee-journals many reports in regard to the agency of bee-stings in the cure of certain forms of diseases, especially rheumatism. From the facts put forth, any candid reasoner will have to admit that being stung frequently does have the effect of relieving certain forms of rheumatism, paralysis, and perhaps dropsy.

Numerous accounts have also appeared in the daily papers of various persons affected with rheumatism being greatly relieved by stings, especially on the affected parts. Some others have reported that they could discover no appreciable effect one way or the other.

It has happened at various field day gatherings of bee-keepers that certain parties who read these reports, having suffered severely because of rheumatic pains, presented themselves and asked to have experts cause the bees to sting them on the affected parts. The operator picks a bee off a comb by the wings and presses it against the flesh until the sting is driven into the skin. This has been done on several occasions, and in each case the parties who came forward for this kind of treatment have said they experienced relief. At the Jenkintown field-day meeting, June 26, 1906, an old gentleman got up on the platform, and, before something like a thousand people, stings were applied to his arm until something like a hundred were imbedded deeply in the flesh. Did it hurt? Oh, yes! But the induced fever of the stings, he said, seemed to bring a warmth and toning of the muscles that was after all a relief; for, strangely enough, this large number of stings did not seem to affect a rheumatic leg or arm as it does a healthy member.

It is a well-known fact that the homeopathic school has for many years used bee-sting poison in a remedy called "apis mellifica." There are large wholesale drug-houses that have made a business of buying stings taken from live bees, being dropped, as they are extracted, into small vials containing sugar of milk. We have filled orders from our apiaries for bee-stings to the extent of 10,000 in one lot. From a frame of live bees placed in a convenient position a bee is picked up with a pair of broad-nosed tweezers and immediately crushed. This act forces out the sting, when it is immediately grasped by another pair of fine-pointed tweezers. These are then given a sharp rap over a wide-mouthed bottle containing sugar of milk. In this way the stings are extracted one by one until the whole number has been pulled. But the operator, after having extracted four or five thousand, experiences a sort of tingling and itching sensation in the face, and finds he has to take a rest of some days before he can renew the work. At other times it happens that he can extract only a few hundred a day when that itching sensation will reappear. This is probably due to the fact that he inhales some of the fumes of the poison, which, entering the lungs, is absorbed by the blood and carried through the system.

At other times a pound or so of bees is put into a large wide-mouthed bottle or jar of alcohol. But the poison of the stings extracted in this way must necessarily be mixed with the other juices of the bees. Homeopathic physicians have "apis mellifica," thus made from bee stings, supplied to them in the form of a liquid. It smells not unlike bee-sting poison, and is often given internally to relieve the pain of rheumatism or swellings in general. But it is evident that a hypodermic injection of the bees, given directly on the affected part, would be a hundred times more productive of good results, assuming, of course, that the poison does have a remedial effect.

DOES A BEE DIE AFTER LOSING ITS STING?

It has been stated that the loss of the sting results in the death of the bee within a very few hours; but this can hardly be true. Colonies have at times become so enraged as to sting every thing within reach, even plunging their little javelins into fence-posts and other inanimate objects, the result being that nearly every bee of the hives in the fracas would lose its sting, and yet these same colonies live and prosper. One correspondent in particular relates the following incident:

Through carelessness he allowed a certain one of his colonies to become so infuriated as to sting everybody and every thing within reach. He declared, upon a subsequent examination, that there was scarcely a bee in that whole colony which did not show unmistakable evidence of having lost its sting in the uproar just mentioned. Now, the singular fact was that these bees actually lived, gathered honey, and prospered.

That *some* bees die after losing their sting, may be true; but that they invariably do so is a claim now thoroughly discredited.

SMOKE NOT ALWAYS A PREVENTIVE OF BEE-STINGS.

There are some colonies that, under some conditions, can not be conquered, even with smoke. If the atmosphere is a little chilly, or immediately after a rain, or if the supply of nectar has suddenly stopped short off, a few colonies may be very hard to handle. While most bees under these conditions will yield to smoke, it seems to infuriate others. The only thing to do is to let them alone for the time being; then the next day or two, when the weather is favorable, blow a little smoke in at the entrance, raise the cover very gently, blow in a few whiffs more, when, presto! the fiends of the day before are as gentle as kittens.

MECHANICAL CONSTRUCTION AND OPERATION OF THE STING.

After a bee has stung you, and torn itself away from the sting, you will notice, if you look closely, a bundle of muscles near by and partly enveloping the poison-bag. Well, the curious part of it is that for some considerable time after the sting has been detached from the body of the bee, these muscles will work with a kind of pump-like motion forcing the sting further into the wound, as if they had a conscious existence and burned with desire to wreak vengeance on the party attacked. Nay, further, after the sting has been pulled from the flesh, and thrown away, if it should stick in your clothing so your flesh will come in contact with it, it will commence working again, pull itself into the flesh, and empty the poison into the wound, precisely as if the living bee were itself working it. We have suffered many times from a sting unconnected with any bee. Without precise figures, we should say a sting would hold life enough to give a very painful wound, for fully five minutes, and it may be in some cases even ten minutes.* This phenomenon is wonderful, and we have often, while watching the sting sink into the rim of a felt hat, pondered on that wonderful thing, animal life. Why should that isolated sting behave in this manner, when the bee to which it belonged was perhaps far away, buzzing through the air? Why should this bundle of fibers and muscles behave as if it had a life to throw away? We do not know. This, however, we do know; when you pull a sting from the wound, you should throw it far enough away so that it will not get back on your face or hands, or into your hair, to sting you again.

In giving the following description of a bee-sting, we are indebted to the drawings and description given by J. R. Bledsoe, of Natchez, Mississippi, in the *American Bee Journal* for August, 1870. We are also indebted to Prof. Cook's excellent Manual.

Under the microscope the sting is found to be a beautifully fashioned and polished instrument, whose delicate taper and finish make a most surprising contrast with any instrument man has been able to produce. In shape it appears to be round ; but it is, in reality, egg - shaped, and is of a dark-red color, but transparent enough to show the hollow running through the center of each of its parts. These probably secure lightness as well as strength.

We give you three views, like letters representing like parts in all. Bear in mind that the sting proper is composed of three parts—the outer shell, or husk, D, and two barbed spears that slide partly inside of it. In Fig. 2 we show you the spears. The barbs are much like those on a common fish-hook;

* Muscular contraction of the sting has taken place under the field of the microscope 20 minutes after being detached from the bee.

and when the point of one spear, A, penetrates far enough to get one barb under the skin, the bee has made a hold, and has no difficulty in sinking the sting its whole length into the wound; for the pumping motion at once commences, and the other spear, B, slides down a little beyond A, then A beyond B, and so on. The manner in which these

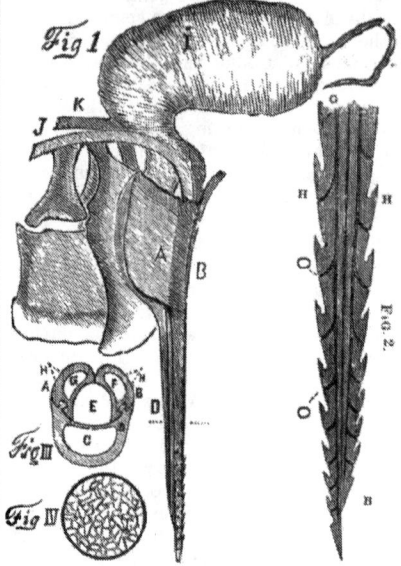

BEE-STING MAGNIFIED.

spears are worked is, as nearly as we can make out, with a pair of something like pump-handles, operated by small but powerful muscles. We have shown you the arrangement of these handles at J and K, Fig. 1, as nearly as we could conjecture what it must be, from watching its workings under the microscope. These muscles will work, at intervals, for some time after the sting has been torn from the bee, as we have explained. They work with sufficient power to send the sting through a felt hat or into a tough buckskin glove. We have often watched the bee while attempting to get its sting started into the hard cuticle on the inside of hand. The spears often run along the surface diagonally, so that you can see how they work down by successive pumps. The hollow in these spears is indicated at G and F, in Figs. 2 and 3; O, O, ducts leading from G and F.

We are not certain as to the real office of these ducts, O, O, but have sometimes thought that they were for the purpose of conducting the poison to the wound from the canals G and F, the latter communicating directly with the poison-bag itself. Indeed, Frank Cheshire says they afford the only means of exit for the poison, but Entomologist Snodgrass, of the Bureau of Entomology, says this is a mistake.

Fig. 3 is a transverse section, sliced across the three parts, at about the dotted line D. A and B are the barbed spears; F and G, the hollows to give them lightness and strength; H, H, the barbs. It will be observed that the husk, D, incloses but little more than ⅓ of them. Now, the purpose of this husk is to hold the barbs in place, and to allow them to slide easily up and down, also to direct them while doing this work. To hold all together, there is a groove like a chopping-knife in both spears, with a corresponding projection in the husk, which fit each other as shown. This allows the barbs to project to do their work, and yet holds all together tolerably firm. We say tolerably firm, for these spears are very easily torn out of the husk; and after a sting is extracted they are often left in the wound, like the tiny splinters we have before mentioned. When torn out and laid on a slip of glass they are scarcely visible to the naked eye; but under the microscope they appear as in Fig. 2.

Stings do not all have the same number of barbs. We have seen as few as seven and as many as nine. The two spears are held against each other as shown in Fig. 3, and you will observe that the shape and the arrangement of the three parts leaves the hollow, E, in their center. The working of the spears also pumps down poison, and quite a good-sized drop collected on their points while we saw them working under the microscope. Friend Bledsoe found a valve that lets it out of the poison-bag into this wonderful little pump, but prevents it returning. We have not been able to see this, but have no doubt that it is there. The drop of poison, after lying on the glass a few minutes, dries down and seems to leave a gummy substance that crystallizes, as it were, into strange and beautiful forms. We have tried to show it to you in Fig. 4.

SUCROSE. See CANE SUGAR.

SUGAR. The term sugar is applied, by common consent, to the pure sugar commercially prepared from the sugar-cane and the sugar beet, or sucrose. There are, however, many more sugars of varying character.

Common sugar is composed of the elements —carbon, 12 parts; hydrogen, 22 parts; oxygen, 11 parts. A white sugar or granulated sugar is a pure sucrose, while the varying-off colors ranging from light yellow to brown, are mostly mixtures of sucrose and varying quantities of molasses. These are prepared first in the process of manufacture, and are known as coffee, yellow prime, yellow clarified, and brown sugar. By washing with water, and also refining, they are made into white sugar.

The yellow sugars have somewhat of a molasses taste which is particularly agreeable to some people. See CANE SUGAR.

SUMAC (*Rhus glabra*). This is a sort of shrub, or small tree, readily known by its bunches of bright-red fruit, having an intensely sour taste. The acid property, however, seems to be only on the surface of the fruit, in the red dust that may be brushed off. We have had no experience with the honey, which the bees sometimes get in large quantities from the small greenish flowers, but give the following from page 96, GLEANINGS for 1874:

June 22, 1874.—Contrary to expectations, we are now in the height of a wonderful flow of honey from sumac, which of late years has not yielded much. Every thing in the hives is filled full, and I am kept busy hiving swarms, as it has become too much of a job to keep them from swarming by removing frames of brood.   G. F. MERRIAM, Topeka, Kan.

SUNFLOWER (*Helianthus species*). This plant embraces an extensive genus; but the principal ones for honey are the common sunflower and the Jerusalem artichoke. Some seasons and in localities we find bees very busy indeed on these plants all day long. The mammoth Russian sunflower bears flowers of enormous dimensions; and from the way bees crowd one another about the nectaries, one would suppose they furnished much honey. The seed, which is yielded in large quantities, seems almost to pay the expense of cultivation. The following is taken from page 86, Vol. III., of GLEANINGS:

My boy had a small box of sunflower seeds which he kept as one of his playthings. Last spring he accidentally spilt them in the garden by the fence, and, old as they were, they came up profusely. They looked so thrifty I took it into my head to transplant them. I set them all around in the fence, out of the way, where nothing else would grow to advantage, and, if you will believe me, I had an enormous crop. When they blossomed the bees went at them in earnest; and after the bees got through with them there were several quarts of seed. I sold a dollar's worth to my druggist; the remainder I fed out to my hens, and, as a writer of old has said, I found nothing so good and nourishing for laying hens as sunflower seeds. Then I cut off the empty heads, place them near the bee-hive, fill them with sugar and water, and that suits the bees to a T. So you see I was at no expense, and they paid well. I write this that others may be benefited as well as myself.

DR. R. HITCHCOCK.

South Norwalk, Conn., Feb. 2, 1875.

SWARMING. All animated nature seems to have some means of reproducing its kind, that the species may not become extinct; and, especially among the insect tribes, we find a great diversity of ways and means for accomplishing this object. In the microscopic world we find simple forms of animal life contracting themselves in the middle until they break in two, and then each separate part, after a time, breaks in two, and so on. With bees we have a somewhat similar phenomenon. Where a colony gets excessively strong, the inmates of the hive, by a sort of preconcerted mutual agreement divide themselves off into two parties, one remaining in the old hive, and the other starting out to seek their fortunes elsewhere.

We have carefully watched this proceeding, with a view of determining how the matter comes about, that is, whether it is because a part of the bees become dissatisfied with their old home and seek to better their condition, or because the queen leaves, for some reason of her own (because she has not room to lay her eggs, for instance), and the bees simply follow from a sort of natural instinct, since she is the mother of the colony and an absolute necessity to their prosperity. After seeing a number of swarms issue, and finding that the queen was among the last to leave the hive, we concluded that the bees take the lead, and that the queen simply followed as a matter of course in the general melee. Suppose, however, that the queen should not take a notion to join the new adventure. Swarms do sometimes start out without a queen accompanying them, but they usually go back to the hive after a time, to try it again next day. If she does not go then, nor at the next attempt, they often wait until they can rear a new queen, and then go off with her. After we were pretty well satisfied that this is the correct idea of their plan, a little circumstance seemed to upset it all. A neighbor, wanting to make an observatory hive, drummed perhaps a quart of bees from one of his old hives. As he had no queen, we gave him a black one taken from a colony purchased several miles away. We mention this to show that the queen had never been out of the hive, in the location which it then occupied. After a day or two, this neighbor informed us that

we had played a fine trick on him, for our queen had gone home, and taken his quart of bees with her. We told him it was impossible, for she had never been out of the hive, except when we carried her over in the cage.

We went and looked in the hive she came from, and there she was, true enough; with the bees she had brought with her stung to death in front and on the bottom-board. It is possible that the bees swarmed out first; but even if they did, they certainly followed the queen in going back to her old home. We also know that bees sometimes follow a young queen when she goes out to take her wedding-flight.

It is our opinion that neither queen nor workers alone make the first start, but all hands join together and act in concert.

WHY BEES SWARM.

If we attempt to contract the size of the hive when honey is coming in bountifully, the bees will be very apt to take measures toward swarming about as soon as the combs are full of brood, eggs, pollen, and honey. They will often wait several days after the hive is seemingly full; and while this course may not cause them to swarm at all, it is very likely to. As soon as it has been decided that the hive is too small, and that there is no feasible place for storing extra supplies of honey where it can be procured in the winter, as needed, they generally commence queen-cells. Before doing this we have known them to go so far as to store their honey outside on the portico, or even underneath the hive, thus indicating most clearly their want of extra space for stores where they could protect them.

Want of room is probably the most general cause of swarming, although it is not the only one; for bees often swarm incessantly when they have a hive only partly filled with comb. First swarms usually come about from the cause we have mentioned; but AFTER-SWARMING (which see) often gets to be a sort of mania with the bees, and they swarm, apparently, *without* a reason.

AT WHAT SEASON BEES USUALLY SWARM.

The old adage runs,—

A swarm of bees in May
Is worth a load of hay;
A swarm of bees in June
Is worth a silver spoon;
A swarm of bees in July
Is not worth a fly.

There is much truth in this, especially if managed on the old plan; but with modern improvements a swarm in July may be worth a silver spoon, or even a load of hay; possibly both together. See AFTER-SWARM-ING. A colony that was very populous in the fall, and has wintered finely, may cast the first swarm in May, in this latitude; but such events were very unusual before the advent of Italians. The latter often swarm during fruit-bloom, and in some cases even earlier. In our locality swarms do not usually issue until the middle or last of June. If the season is a little late, sometimes the greater part of them will come in July, and we almost always have more or less swarming going on during our national holiday. At this time basswood is generally at its height, and we frequently have quite a yield from clover after basswood is gone. On this account, swarms that come out during the first week in July usually get enough to winter, and are therefore worth the price of a swarm of bees any way. The old adage doubtless referred principally to the amount of honey they would store; if the July swarms did not secure enough to winter over, and were allowed to starve, they would not be worth the trouble of hiving them, and so they might be rated as of less value than a fly. Swarms that come out in June would fill their hives, and perhaps make a surplus that, on an average, would bring at least a dollar, the old price of a silver spoon; while those that were so thrifty as to be able to start in May would have the whole season before them; and if they did not get set back before white clover came out, would very likely make a surplus worth $5.00, the market price of a load of hay. In some localities bees seem to swarm in the latter part of July and August, and reports seem to show that they do so when little or no honey is to be had, and when the bees are disposed to rob; but such is certainly not the case here, for our bees give up all preparations for swarming some little time before the honey flow has ceased. In some localities buckwheat swarms are a very common thing. Where the apiarist has plenty of extra combs filled with stores, it is an easy matter to care for and make valuable stocks of swarms that issue at any time.

SYMPTOMS OF SWARMING.

Although we can sometimes tell when bees are going to swarm, we do not think it will be safe, by any means, to assume we can always do so. It has been said that all the bees which have been clustering on the outside will, the morning of the day they are intending to swarm, go inside the hive; but this can not always be so, for we have seen a swarm issue while the loafers were hanging on the outside as usual; and at the sound of the swarming-note they took wing and joined in. Where a colony is intending to swarm, they will not be working like the rest, as a general thing; and, quite likely, on the day they are intending to swarm, very few bees comparatively will be seen going out and in at the hive. With movable combs we can generally give a very good guess of the disposition to swarm by opening the hive. Bees do not, as a rule, swarm until they have their hive pretty well filled up, and have multitudes of young bees hatching out daily. The presence of queen-cells is generally considered an indication of the swarming fever.

Many think that the clustering of the bees on the outside of the hives is an indication that they are going to swarm. To a certain extent this may be the case, but it is by no means an indication that they are going to swarm very soon. We knew a colony, belonging to a neighbor, that hung out in great masses nearly a month before the bees came out. His new hive was in readiness, and he stayed at home and watched day after day, until clover and basswood both were almost gone, when finally they cast a large fine swarm.

DO BEES CHOOSE A LOCATION BEFORE SWARMING?

While it is true that a swarm will issue without any previous preparation when a swarming craze is on in the yard, the great majority of colonies, preparing to swarm, send out scouts, or prospectors. These bees hunt up cavities in hollow trees, or even seek out empty hives, and commence cleaning house. The number of scouts having located a home will increase until there appears to be quite a little swarm, and sometimes one is led to believe there is a case of robbing going on, especially if the scouts have entered an empty hive containing combs. They will continue to make their visitations day by day, and in the mean time they busy themselves by "cleaning house." When the day comes for the swarm to issue, the scouts appear to make it their business to lead the flying bees to this new location. Just how they do this can not be definitely shown; but that they do lead these swarms to particular abodes has been so clearly proven that there is no further question about it. This shows why a swarm will sometimes "light out" without even clustering. Following the lead of their scouts they will go directly to their new home which has been already prepared.

14

As a general rule a swarm clusters first. Whether this is for the purpose of getting the scouting party "organized" and into action, no one knows. If the scouts have not already found a location it is possible that the clustered swarm is sending out some scouts to prospect; and having found a hollow tree they will go back to the cluster, when all will "hike" for the new home.

While these may be fanciful suggestions it may account for the reason why a swarm will sometimes hang on a tree for several days, the inference being that the scouts have failed to locate any suitable home.

HOW A SWARM WILL SOMETIMES OCCUPY A SMALL TREE AND BEND IT OVER BY ITS WEIGHT.

NEVER ALLOW BEES TO HANG OUTSIDE THE HIVE.

One of our swarms hung outside the hive during a great honey-harvest; and as it is no unusual thing for a colony to store 10 lbs. a day during the height of the season, they may have lost 100 lbs. of honey, for the swarm was an unusually fine and strong one. They might easily have secured this amount if they had worked, but it is by no means certain that they could have been made to go to work as they did after they swarmed and were put into a new hive. Within two or three weeks after they swarmed, if we remember, they filled their hive and gave about 25 lbs. of surplus. How shall we deal with such bees?

This clustering-out may be caused by the fact that the bees need room. In that case,

A FINE SYMMETRICAL SWARM WITHIN EASY REACH.

obviously, an extracting or comb-honey super should be placed on top; for where bees get into the habit of loafing it becomes a little hard to get them to go up into the supers. In such case we advise giving the bees a section or two of foundation partly drawn out, as previously explained under COMB HONEY. We would at the same time also enlarge the entrance. Set the hive up on four blocks ⅜ inch thick, as shown under ENTRANCES, and further on under this head, sub-head CONTROL OF SWARMING BY

MEANS OF LARGE OR PLURAL ENTRANCES. This will leave an open space all around the hive, but that will do no harm. If the primary cause of the bees clustering out in the first place is lack of ventilation, or too great heat, this raising-up of the hive will cause the bees to go in, and possibly prevent swarming.

SWARMING MODIFIED BY LOCALITY.

The commencement of the swarming season varies, of course, according to the locality, and it may be said that the swarming propensity itself is modified very materially also by the same cause. In places where the honey-flow is very heavy and continues so for some time, swarming seems to be checked, for the bees are all intent on gathering honey. Indeed, they have no time to waste on such foolishness. In such localities the swarming season comes on when the first or light honey-flow begins, and continues so long as it is light; but just as soon as the secretion of nectar gets heavy then just that soon swarming stops.

It sometimes happens that a bee-keeper residing in one of these localities wonders why his brethren in the craft make so much fuss in the bee-journals about swarm control when he has no trouble from that source at all. The other fellow, on the other hand, can not understand how the first-mentioned bee-keeper can perform certain manipulations with his bees, and not have excessive swarming. In reading the following pages treating on this general subject one must bear in mind this question of locality. It should, therefore, be said that much of the matter that follows relates to conditions as we generally find them in the Northern States, and not as they are found in parts of Texas, California, and some portions of the tropics. In these localities there may or may not be swarming. On the other hand, the bee-keeper encourages it to a certain extent; and when he wishes it to cease by reason of the heavy honey-flow it stops naturally.

PREPARATIONS FOR SWARMING, TO BE MADE BY THE BEE-KEEPER.

Every apiarist, even if he have but a couple of hives, should make preparations for swarming, to some extent; for, even though dividing (see NUCLEUS, also INCREASE) is practiced, and utmost care used to prevent swarms, there will always be a chance that one may come out unexpectedly. First of all before the swarming season the wings of

A LIVE BEE-HAT.

all queens should be clipped, and hives made ready, extra combs placed in the honey-house where you can put your hand on them at any minute. We would also have some colonies marked where we could get a comb of unsealed larvæ without very much trouble; that is, make up your mind what hive you are to go to, in case you should want such a comb in a hurry. Bees will often swarm on Sunday; and as we do not wish to work with our bees on the Sabbath more than is absolutely necessary, it behooves us to be at all times prepared to take care of a swarm with very little trouble. We can remember

having swarms on Sunday, when it became necessary to hunt up a hive, decide on its location, hunt up some empty combs, and then look over colonies to find one with no surplus boxes on, that we might get at a brood-comb with as little trouble as possible to put in the new hive, to prevent them decamping. All these things take time, and more than one swarm has departed while a hive was being made ready to receive them. If you keep the wings of your queens clipped as we have advised, you will need some queen-cages where you can lay your hands on them at a minute's notice, for there are times when you need to step about as lively as you would at a house on fire, so you do not want to be bothered by hunting for things.

MILLER QUEEN-CATCHER.

The best queen-catcher, or, rather, cage for confining the queen during the swarming season, is the Miller introducing-cage, a cut of which will be found under INTRODUCING. We will suppose that a swarm has just issued, and that your clipped queen is hopping around the entrance of the hive. Your wife or attendant, feeling some hesitancy about picking up so delicate an object by her silken wings, can take a cage of this kind and place the mouth directly over her. In a moment, finding herself confined, she will ascend into the cage. The little wooden plug is now inserted, when your captive queen can be placed among the flying bees, and the swarm hived as next described. The cage is also used for introducing. See INTRODUCING.

HOW TO HIVE A SWARM WITH CLIPPED QUEEN; THE PLAN WE PREFER.

Under the general head of QUEENS, sub-head CLIPPING, we have already given intimation how swarming can be controlled to a certain extent by clipping. Where the plan of forcing the swarm ahead of time by brushing or shaking* is not practiced, clipping has come to be almost universal among comb-honey producers; for where queens' wings are clipped, or they are prevented from leaving the hive by the use of Alley traps or entrance-guards (see DRONES), a great amount of labor will be saved.

We shall assume that all queens in the apiary have their wings clipped. A swarm comes forth. Go to the hive from which it is issuing; and, while they are coming out, find the queen, which will be found, in all probability, hopping around in the grass

---

* This plan is described under PREVENTION OF SWARMING a few pages further on.

A COLONY CAUGHT IN THE ACT OF SWARMING.

A SWARM ENTERING A HIVE.

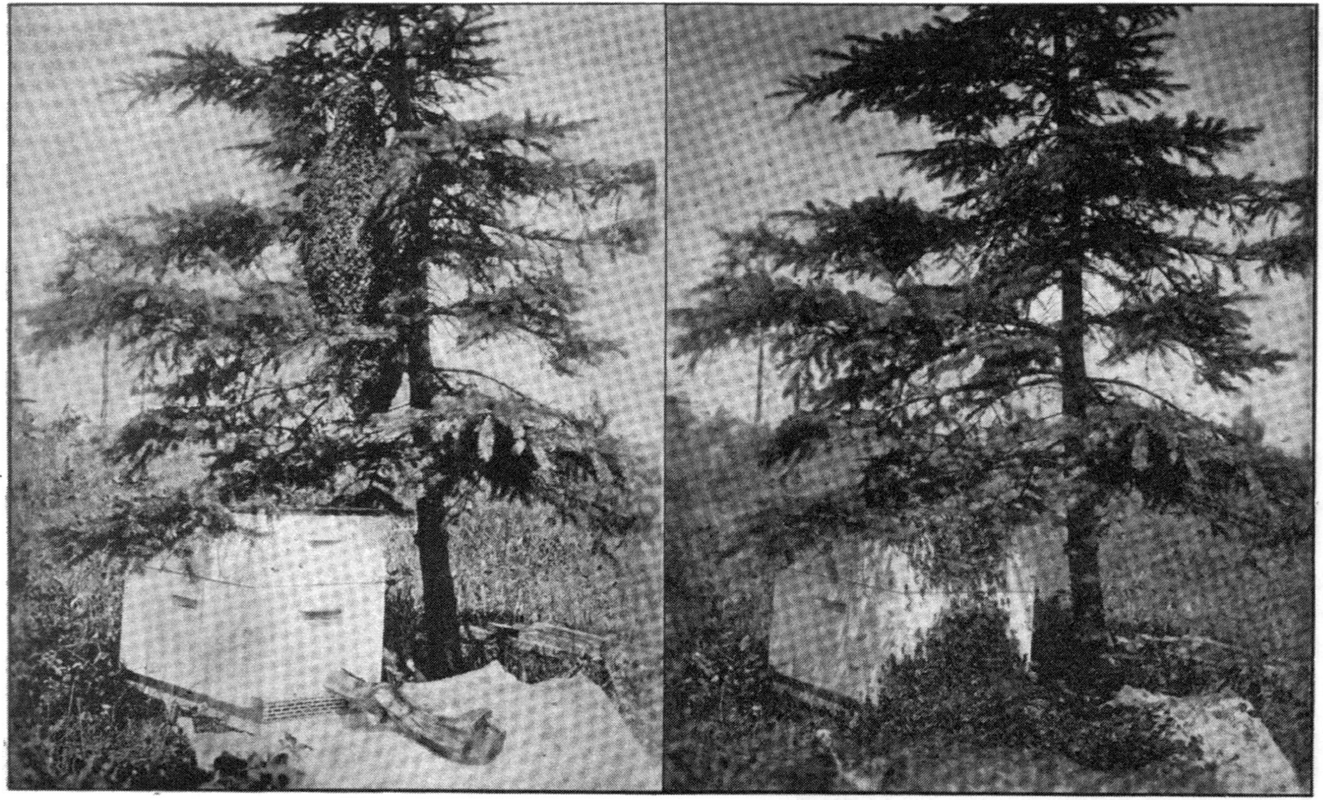

A SWARM CONVENIENTLY CLUSTERED FOR EASY HIVING.

near the entrance, vainly endeavoring to fly with the rest of the bees. Cage her, and then slip the cage into a pocket or some cool place, temporarily. Remove the super or supers in which the bees have already started work, and set them on the ground near the hive. The brood-chamber should now be removed just as it is, to an entirely new location. Put in its place on the old stand a hive containing frames of founda-tion or empty comb, and on top of this a queen-excluding honey-board. Some prefer having only starters of foundation. Next put the supers, placed on the ground tem porarily, on the new hive containing these frames of foundation or comb. Now lay the caged queen in front of the entrance.

All this may be done while the bees are in the air, and it will not be long before they discover that the queen is not with them, and return pellmell to their old location, and rush into the new hive. After they are well started going in, the queen may be releas-ed, when she will go with them.

The work already begun in the supers will be pushed on and completed with more vim and energy than before, because a new swarm always works with new energy. If only frames containing starters have been given them, what honey does come in is forced right into the supers, for the bees have absolutely no place to store it, at least until foundation below has been drawn out; but as soon as this takes place it is occupied immediately by the queen.

The old hive containing frames of brood and queen-cells now in another location may cast a second or third swarm; but if queen-cells are cut out, even second swarming may, to a very great extent, be checked.

This method of handling swarms where natural swarming is allowed commends it-self especially to the women-folks, who are generally at home. All they have to do is to hunt up the clipped queen, cage her, and then put an empty hive containing frames of foundation in place of the old one. As it might not be practical for the women to carry the old hive to another location, they can simply drag it over to one side, and change the entrance so that it will face to the rear. When the "man of the house" returns, he can lift the supers off from the old stand on to the new one, then take the old brood-nest over to another location. This may be done any time within a day; or, when preferred, the old stand can be left alongside the new one, providing the en-trance is reversed.

If two or more swarms come out at the same time, and one of them has a virgin queen, all the bees will be likely to unite with the one having the queen; then, of course, this plan of bees returning will come to naught. But in a well-regulated apiary there will be few such occurrences, and

A SELF-HIVED SWARM.

ninety-nine out of a hundred swarms may be hived as easily as this, without any trouble.

PERFORATED ZINC TO RESTRAIN QUEENS.

Under Drones, an incident is given in regard to the matter of entrapping the queen when she issues with the swarm. The employment of perforated zinc will not pre-vent swarming—it only hinders the bees from accomplishing their purpose; that is, absconding and taking their queen with them. In other words, the perforated zinc simply takes the place of clipping the queen's wings. In some cases it may be desirable to use the zinc instead of clipping. Usually, from our experience we should deem it preferable to clip the queen's wings rather than to cause the bees the inconvenience of crawling, during the continuance of the honey-flow, through narrow perforations of zinc, simply to hold back the queen should a swarm issue.

While we recommend clipping in place of using perforated zinc, yet in the case of very strong colonies in the height of the honey-

THE ALLEY TRAP IN HIVING SWARMS.

When a swarm issues (see cut under DRONES), the bees pass the metal guard readily; but the queen, finding herself shut in, mounts "upstairs" in the same way as the drones. Sometimes, however, instead of going above she will return into the hive. In five or ten minutes, the bees, discovering the absence of their queen, will go back to the hive. They should not be allowed to make

LIMB OF A TREE CUT OFF WITH THE SWARM READY TO HIVE.

flow, especially when such colonies are in two-story hives, it is more practical to put on entrance-guards or Alley traps. In the first place, attaching the traps can be done in a tenth of the time it takes to find the queen ; and in the second place, pulling the hive all apart to find her majesty causes more or less interruption ; but, of course, the queens should be clipped early in the season when it is easy to find them.

more than one attempt to swarm in this manner, because, after a second failure of the queen to follow she will likely be killed. The bees may, however, cluster without the queen, and remain clustered a short time.

When the queen enters the upper apartment, the entire trap can be detached, fastened to a rake or some other object, and placed among the flying bees. Of course, they will readily cluster about the cage, when they can be hived; but to keep an Alley trap attached to all hives that are likely to send out a swarm during the ensuing ten or twenty days would be rather expensive, both because of the cost of the trap itself, and because of the inconvenience to the laden workers coming home. The same or very nearly equal results can be attained by clipping the queen's wing, at no expense whatever; and at the same time let the bees retain, up to the time of swarming, a free and unobstructed entrance. See DRONES.

SWARMING - DEVICES VARIOUSLY CONSTRUCTED.

Every apiarist engaged in the production of honey should certainly have the wings of *all* his queens clipped. He *can not afford not to*, unless he uses perforated zinc (see DRONES). It is much more difficult to take care of swarms when queens are allowed to go with the swarm. But as there are people who dislike to "disfigure" or "mutilate" their queens, and as some swarms in any case will get out with a virgin queen, we

TWO SWARMS UNITED IN ONE.

have thought best to describe the various devices for capturing swarms with unclipped queens. See QUEENS, subhead CLIPPING.

Almost every apiarist has his own peculiar notion as to how a swarming-device should be constructed. Some of these implements are very ingenious, and of valuable assistance during the swarming season. Their partic-

the bees turn it inside out. The bag has the same diameter as the hoop, and is about four feet long.

A. E. MANUM'S SWARMING-DEVICE.

This consists of a wire-cloth basket made in the shape of an inverted pyramid, and pivoted at the two opposite corners so as to hang always in an upright position. When a swarm is captured the basket may be

This swarm of bees issued June 7 from a colony of bees that produced 180 pounds of comb honey this season.

ular use is to remove a swarm after it has clustered, and place it in the hive where it is desired that it take up a new abode. The first one to which we call attention, not because it is the best, but because it is the simplest, is a sort of butterfly-catcher.

The hoop is made of band iron, and is about 20 inches in diameter. The ends are secured, as shown, to a suitable pole. The bag is to be put up under the swarm, and the hoop is then made to cut off gently the cluster so that the bees will fall into the bag. It is then turned edgewise, so as to confine them while being taken down and carried to the hive. As the bag is made of cheese-cloth, the bees have plenty of air. To empty

MANUM'S SWARM-CATCHING DEVICE.

grasped by the ring at the small end, and inverted, dumping the bees into the hive prepared for them.

Fig. 1 represents the wire-cloth cage or basket; Fig. 2, the device in position, receiving the bees as they cluster on the outside of the cage. Fig. 3 shows the cage open. As soon as the cluster beginning to form is half or wholly completed, run the basket up to and around the cone of bees. An assistant, if present, gives the limb a jar, so as to disengage the bees into the basket. In case no one is ready to assist, a sliding movement will precipitate the cluster into the wire-cloth cage, when it is quickly lowered. This operation, in passing down through the limbs, will usually catch the wire-cloth lid, and close it with a slam. In case it is not closed, the apiarist steps forward and does it himself. Half or two-thirds of the bees are generally confined. In all probability the queen is there also. As the bees can not get out, those still flying in the air will very readily cluster on the wire cloth, surrounding the majority of their companions inside. To make this more expeditious the tripod is adjusted and the cage suspended in the air, as shown in Fig. 2, right where the bees are flying thickest. In two or three minutes the remainder of the bees will be clustered on the outside. At this stage of the proceeding the apiarist comes forward, folds the two short legs against the pole, grasps it at its center of gravity (see Fig. 1), and walks off to the hive, which he has previously prepared. The wire fork is made of steel, and is light and springy. The walking of the apiarist has no tendency to jar the bees off the basket.

One of the special features of the Manum arrangement is that the basket can be adjusted to almost any position, all the way from two to ten feet off the ground. All that is necessary is to spread the tripod legs, catch them into the ground, and leave them standing. In the mean time, unless the hive is already prepared, the apiarist has ample time to get it ready. After this he can return to the swarm just now clustered. Most of the devices require to be held until the cluster has settled. It is a tedious job to hold a pole at arms' length, with face upturned. If the swarm clusters very high, some other arrangement, perhaps, would be better than the Manum; but for low shrubbery it is just the thing. The other special feature of the device is, that, after you have gotten about half or two-thirds of the bees into the basket, they can not escape and seek their original point of attachment.

THE SWARM-HIVING HOOK.

With most of the hiving-devices we have illustrated, what might be called a hiving-hook can be used to considerable advantage at times. It is simply an iron hook large enough to compass an ordinary limb on which swarms cluster, mounted on the

end of a long pole, and resembling, somewhat, a shepherd's crook. One of the hiving-devices is passed beneath the swarm. This hook can be used to reach over, grasp the limb on which the swarm is clustered, and by one or two smart jerks jar the bees into the basket, bag, or box, as the case may be.

STRIMPL'S SWARMING-LADDER.

Swarms usually alight low, so the ordinary hiving-apparatus and tools previously described can reach them from the ground. But there are times when they will settle on pretty high limbs. It is then that a ladder is called into requisition. If it will not reach the swarm it can at least land the climber among the upper limbs, so that he can step from one limb to another, and finally reach the bees. But it is difficult to stand an ordinary ladder against a limb of a tree so that it will be secure for climbing, on account of the unevenness of the branches. A foreigner by the name of R. Strimpl, of Seltzschau, Bohemia, sent us a drawing of a ladder that can be lodged—that is, the upper part of it—securely on some limb above. The engraving illustrates its principle of application.

The two side feet, or forks, prevent the ladder from revolving, while it will be observed that the ladder terminates in a single pole, which may be very easily lodged in the fork of a limb, where a two-pronged ladder can not. The three prongs below the ladder are sharpened at the end, and securely pushed into the ground. The perfect lodgment of the other end in the crotch of the limb makes the ladder a safe means of as-

GUMBERT'S APPARATUS FOR HIVING SWARMS.

cent. Aside from this it will be lighter. But it is more desirable to prevent swarms from going beyond our reach—at least clustering on elevated limbs.

HOW TO GET A SWARM FROM AN INACCESSIBLE LIMB.

Sometimes a swarm will alight upon a limb beyond the reach of any ladder. Possibly, also, the limb upon which the bees are clustered is so far out from the body of the tree that it would not sustain the weight of any one climbing after them. Such a swarm can usually be reached in the following manner: Secure a ball of good strong twine, and tie on the end of it a stone about as large as the single fist. If you are not a good thrower yourself, get some boy who is a good ball-player to perform the throwing act. Uncoil a considerable quantity of the line, then throw the stone into a crotch if one is near the swarm. If you are lucky enough to land the stone in the right place, right in the crotch, draw gently on the line until the stone catches in the fork of the crotch. Give one quick jerk to dislodge the bees and after that keep the limb in a tremble until the bees cluster on some other spot which they will do presently if the limb is kept agitated for five or ten minutes. They may cluster higher up, but the probabilities are they will seek some other spot more ccessible.

If there is no convenient crotch at the right point, throw the stone so it will pass over the limb, taking about one foot of line; then give the string a good jerk, causing the stone with the line to whirl around the limb a couple of times. If you do not succeed in doing this the first time or two, a second or third attempt may be successful. It is not a very difficult trick; but the main thing is to get the line attached to the limb at some point near the swarm. Then the rest is easy.

SPRAY-PUMP FOR CONTROLLING SWARMS WHILE IN THE AIR.

One of the most useful implements in the apiary during the swarming-time is a good hand force-pump. A swarm of bees in the air with a queen that might otherwise circle about for fifteen or twenty minutes, can usually be made to cluster in from two to five minutes by its use. Whether the fine particles of water dampen the wings, and so impede their flight, or cause the bees to think it is raining, and that therefore they had better cluster at once, or both, we can not say; but certainly the spray has a very decided effect. One who becomes moderately expert will be able not only to make the bees settle but to *compel* them to cluster on some point easily accessible to any of the ordinary hiving-devices just described. Occasionally a swarm will make for the top of a tall tree. With the pump we head them off, causing them to settle on a lower branch. Even when a swarm is clustered twenty or thirty feet from the ground, by adjusting the stream nozzle and letting it play directly on the swarm itself, we can, many times, dislodge them, causing them to take wing and finally settle again upon a lower point of attachment. Again, several swarms will come out simultaneously, and two or more attempt to cluster together. By the timely use of the spray, each swarm can be kept separate by dampening the wings of the stragglers of the two swarms about to come together. A good many times a swarm that is about to abscond can be headed off and made to cluster; in fact, our boys, during the summer of 1889, would drive a swarm about like a flock of sheep. It is very annoying and inconvenient to have a swarm pass from our premises over to those of a neighbor. During the summer of 1889 we had something like eight or ten swarms come out every day for nearly a week, and yet in only one or two cases did they leave the immediate vicinity of the apiary; and had it not been for the pump, we should, in all probability, have had to chase all over the neighborhood, to say nothing about climbing tall trees.*

After a swarm begins to cluster on a desirable spot, stop spraying in that direction. Retreat, and drive the stragglers toward it, but be careful not to spray the place where they are clustering. As a general rule, two or three small clusters will be forming at once. Spray the undesirable ones, and keep them sprayed until these points of attachment are abandoned.

During the swarming-season it is a good idea to keep several barrels of water in and around the immediate vicinity of the apiary, so as to have the same handy. If you must run to the pump every time you need a pail of water, the swarm may get away from you, or cluster in the top of a tall tree.

SWARM-CATCHER.

This is simply a large wire-cloth cage, in the shape of an oblong box, about three or four feet high, by 12 or 15 inches square, one end being open, and made to fit against an ordinary hive-front.

It very often happens that the apiarist is on hand just at the time the swarm pours out the entrance like hot shot. Well, with

one of these swarm-catchers handy he simply attaches the mouth to the entrance, and the outpouring bees fly pell-mell into the top of the cage, and are there confined. When the apiarist succeeds in catching two-thirds of the bees, the rest will cluster on the outside. Then the cage is set very near where the bees come forth, mouth end down. Meanwhile he prepares his hive, if he has not already done so, and then brings the cage of bees and dumps them right into the hive, replaces the cover, and the swarm is hived without having had any swarm in the air—no, not even giving them a ghost of a chance to fly all over the neighborhood,

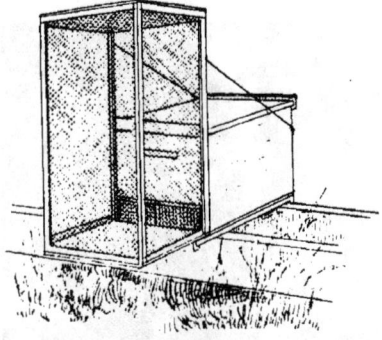

SWARM-CATCHER.

and possibly finally alight upon the limb of a tree 40 feet from the ground. But it should be borne in mind that the swarm-catcher is serviceable only when the apiarist happens to be on the ground just as the bees are beginning to pour forth.

We consider a large cage that comes down over the whole hive much better than something adjusted to the entrance, as shown above. The one shown in the half-tone, page 386, is more quickly applied, because it can be clapped down over the hive and stop proceedings instanter. As soon as the bees are all out, lift up the cage gently, and carry it to the hive where you propose to dump the swarm. Hold the cage squarely over the prepared hive with its cover off, and give it one quick jounce. This will dislodge the bees so that most of them will land in and around the hive. As soon as they have settled, remove the cage and put on the cover.

THE AUTOMATIC HIVING OF SWARMS.

For many years back there has been an effort on the part of bee-keepers of an inventive turn of mind to get up an arrangement that would automatically hive swarms

---

* We didn't then clip the wings of our queens as we now do, hence that chasing is dispensed with.

in the absence of an apiarist or attendant; and since out-apiaries have begun to assume such importance where the production of honey is carried on extensively, some sort of device that will hive automatically the swarms—yes, do the work just as well as if the apiarist were present himself is some thing greatly to be desired. A great many devices have been introduced; but most of them have been proven to be more or less a failure.

The general plan contemplates some scheme having an empty hive placed near the colony expected to swarm. This empty hive may be alongside, in front, or below the other one. In the case of the first-men-

CARRYING A CAPTURED SWARM ON BICYCLE.

tioned plan, an entrance-guard is placed in front of each hive; and connecting the two is a tube of wire cloth or perforated zinc. When the swarm comes forth, the queen, finding herself barred by the perforated metal, runs along until she finds the tube communicating with the entrance-guard of the other hive. In this tube she runs up against a bee-escape or wire cloth cone. She

passes this; but, being unable to return, is compelled to enter the entrance-guard of the new hive. Upon discovering that the queen is not with them, the bees rush back to the old stand; a part of them find the queen in front of the new hive, enter with the queen and "set up house-keeping." But the plan fails, because the majority fail to find her, and re-enter the parent colony. See page 423.

We have tried these plans to some extent, but, taking every thing into due consideration, consider it cheaper and more practicable to hive the swarm on the clipped-wing plan, or, better, practice brushed-swarming, as described further on.

HOW TO HIVE SWARMS WITHOUT SPECIAL DEVICES.

If the apiary is located in a locality where there are no tall trees, but only low-growing shrubbery, or, at most, dwarf fruit-trees, or, better still, if the wings of all queens are clipped, the special tools we have already described will not be found absolutely necessary, and perhaps not even a convenience, if we except Manum's arrangement. Our own apiary, illustrated in connection with some of the factory engravings shown in the picture-gallery at the close of this work, you will notice contained no trees. Outskirting it are rows of bushy evergreens furnishing absolutely the only place for the bees to cluster in the immediate vicinity of the apiary besides grapevines in the apiary itself. Rarely do we have swarms clustering elsewhere. When a swarm alights on one of the two places just mentioned we select a frame of unsealed larvæ, the use of which has been previously anticipated. As the swarm is but rarely more than four or five feet from the ground, this frame is gently thrust among the bees. A large majority of them will very soon lodge upon the frame. This together with the adhering bees is placed in a hive on the shady side of the evergreen or grapevine, in company with three or four more frames. Those bees which have already clustered on the frames will begin to call their companions; and as soon as a few bees find the entrance, they announce their discovery by the usual humming of the wings. Put an enamel sheet over the hive, and brush the bees out of the way with a bunch of grass so the cover can be shut down without killing any. The hive is then left until the bees have all entered, then they are removed to their permanent location in the apiary before they have had time to fix a location.

You will scarcely appreciate the absence of large trees and the presence of small undergrowth until you have had an apiary so circumstanced whereby swarming has not half the terrors to the bee-keeper as where the clusters are just as likely as not to attach themselves to high positions.

The method we have just described applies when the queen's wings are not clipped, either because we do not wish to mutilate her fair proportions or because she happens to be young. Wisely, a great many apiarists prefer to clip their queens' wings. Perhaps we might say a majority do so, because it saves the use of expensive tools, tree-climbing, and, to a great extent, prevents swarms uniting.

HOW TO BRING HOME A SWARM A MILE OR SO FROM THE APIARY.

A swarm will sometimes escape and be traced a mile or so from the bee-yard. At other times a farmer will report that a swarm of bees is hanging to one of his trees, and that, if the bee-man will come and hive them, he can have them. A good swarm is always worth going after; but how shall it be brought back with the least expenditure of time when bees are swarming at home? At our apiary we have been in the habit of sending one of our yard-men on a bicycle, equipped with a burlap sack, a pair of pruning-shears and a smoker, these latter fastened to the rider. The bicycle enables him to make a quick trip, and on arrival the bag is quietly slipped around the cluster of bees, if attached to a limb of a tree, and tied. The pruning-shears cut the limb, when bag and all is slung over the handle-bars, or carried in one hand while the other guides the machine home.

PLURAL SWARMS UNITING.

When the swarming-note is heard in the apiary it seems to carry with it an infec-

tion; this may be a mistake, but in no other way can we account for swarms issuing one after another while the first is in the air, unless they hear the sound and hasten to go and do likewise. Of course, they will all unite in one, and as many as a dozen have been known to come out in this way and go off to the woods in a great army of bees before any thing could be done to stop them. If your queens are clipped, and you " hustle

NOT CROSS BEES, BUT A CROSS OF BEES.

around" and get them all in cages deposited in front of the hives, they usually separate and each bee goes where it belongs. Unless employing plenty of help you will be unable to get the hives all moved away and a new hive fixed for each one before they come back. In this case they will return to their old hive, and, if the queen is released, will sometimes go to work; but more often swarm out again within a few hours, or the next day. If you keep putting them back they will soon attack and kill their queen, then loaf about until they can rear a new one and swarm again. This is very poor policy, and we can by no means afford to have such work. If they swarmed for want of room, they may go to work all right, after having room given them. If they come out the second time, we should give them a new location, divide them, or do something to satisfy their natural craving for starting a new colony, otherwise they may loaf, even if they do not try to swarm again.

To go back: Suppose they get a queen or queens having wings, and cluster in one large body. In this case you should scoop off bees from the cluster with the swarming-bag, a tin pan, or a dipper, as may be most convenient, and apportion parts, made about as nearly of the size of a swarm as may be, about in different hives. Give each hive a comb containing eggs and larvæ as before, and then get a queen for each one if you can. In dividing them up, should you get two or more queens in a hive they will be balled as we have before described, and you can thus easily find them. Where more than one queen is in a hive, you will find a ball of bees, perhaps the size of a walnut or hen's egg, about them, and this can be carried to the colony having none. When you can not tell at once which are queenless, you will be able to do so in a few hours by the queen-cells they have started. If you are more anxious for honey than bees, you may allow two swarms to work together; and if given sufficient room you will probably get a large crop of honey from them; but this plan does not pay, as a general thing, because the extra bees will soon die off by old age, and your colony remains no larger than where the queen retains only her ordinary number of bees.

PREVENTION OF SWARMING.

If we can entirely prevent swarming, and keep the bees at home storing honey all the season, we sometimes get large crops from a single hive. Whether we shall get more in that way than from the old stock and all the increase, where swarming and after-swarming is allowed, is a matter as yet hardly decided. Should a swarm come out in May, and the young queens get to laying in their hives by the first of June, their workers would be ready for the basswood-bloom in July, and it is very likely that the workers

from three queens would gather more honey than those from the old queen alone. But another point is to be considered. The two or three new colonies must have stores for winter; and as it takes nearly 25 lbs. to carry a colony through until honey comes again, this amount would be saved by the prevention of swarming. Where one has plenty of bees, and desires honey rather than increase, a non-swarming apiary becomes quite desirable.

This subject is a mooted one, and some of our best and most experienced bee-keepers confess they have been baffled in their efforts to confine swarming within reasonable limits. Usually it is not desirable to prevent first swarms. Second swarms or after-swarms are the ones we should *like* to control. Some prominent bee-keepers practice cutting out all queen-cells but one eight days after the issue of the first swarm ; that is, they allow all the unsealed larvæ to become capped over, leaving no opportunity for further building of cells. If only one cell is left in the hive, of course only one queen can be hatched and reared. If she is successfully fertilized the colony will generally settle down to business. Excessive swarming is often induced by a number of young queens being allowed to mature about the same time. These unfertile queens will be pretty apt to keep up swarming in the hive so long as there is a surplus of queens. See AFTER-SWARMS.

PREVENTION OF SWARMING BY CAGING OR REMOVING THE QUEEN.

Hetherington, Elwood, and some others, have practiced caging or removing the queen during the honey harvest. Of course, no swarm will issue regularly where no queen is in the hive; and if no cells are allowed to hatch, prevention is accomplished. When the harvest has commenced, before giving the bees a chance to swarm, the queen is caged in the hive, or, perhaps, preferably given to a nucleus. If queen-cells are not already started they certainly will be on removal of the queen; and if the queen is caged they will just as certainly be started in a short time. In any case they must be cut out before there is any danger of the queen hatching. If all the cells are destroyed at the time of removing the queen, then a second time, eight days later, and a third time eight days later still, there will be no possibility of any swarming. The advocates of this plan claim that the bees that could be raised from eggs laid during the time the queen is caged or removed would be too late for service in gathering the harvest, hence only consumers.

On the other hand, there are those who question whether the bees work just as industriously without a laying queen in the hive. One difficulty about the plan is, that it is almost impossible to be sure that no queen-cell has been missed to give rise to very undesirable complications.

GIVING PLENTY OF ROOM AND RUNNING FOR EXTRACTED HONEY.

Many times bees will swarm because the apartment for brood-rearing is limited. Contraction and the queen-excluding honey-board give the queen only a limited amount of room, with swarming as the consequence. For this reason it is desirable not to reduce the brood-chamber too much. But whether contraction is practiced or not, the fever may be greatly allayed, and perhaps prevented altogether, by giving an abundance of surplus room on the plan of tiering up. Do not let the colony at any time feel crowded for space. Judicious tiering up, as described under COMB HONEY, will not only secure more honey, but it will largely discourage natural increase when not desired. When running for extracted honey the problem is much easier. Mr. N. E. France, of Platteville, Wis., who produces enormous crops of honey, says he is troubled very little by excessive swarming. He does not practice contraction, but allows the queen and bees plenty of room. If the queen desires to go above, she is allowed that privilege. Charles Dadant & Son keep about 500 colonies in large Quinby hives. These hives being so large, the bees are but little inclined to swarm. In fact, Mr. Dadant says, in the *American Bee Journal*, page 311, Vol. XXV., "For more than fifteen years we have dispensed with watching the bees of our home apiary, numbering from 80 to 100 colonies. As the yearly number of natural swarms does not exceed two or three, the expense of such watching would be far above the profit." While large hives filled with combs or foundation tend to prevent if not discourage swarming altogether, for other reasons other bee-keepers seem to prefer smaller sizes, such as the Langstroth. See Dadant hive, under HIVES.

THE PREVENTION OF SWARMING BY THE SHAKE-OUT OR BRUSHED-SWARM PLAN.

The control of swarming when operating for extracted honey, especially if large hives are used (or small hives with one or more stories), is comparatively simple; but when one proposes to run for *comb* honey, and feels compelled to use small brood-chambers because of the shortness of the season in this locality, the problem has not been so easy of solution. But in Germany, and lately in America, a plan has come in vogue that looks now as if it *might* give us control. At all events, those who have tried it are very enthusiastic in its praise, and feel that for them, at least, the vexed question has been settled for all time. The plan is, in brief, this:

After the honey-flow has begun, and perhaps three or four days (not earlier) before the colony is expected to cast a swarm, the hive is moved to one side of the stand, and an empty one, just like it, is put in its place.[*] In this hive are placed frames having foundation starters or frames with full sheets —preferably the latter. But if neither is available, empty combs may be used. The bees of the parent colony are then shaken or brushed in front of the entrance of the *new* hive on the *old* stand. Some go so far as to brush *all* the bees out of the old hive; and this can be done if the weather is hot and the nights warm; for young hatching brood will soon be out to take care of the young brood. The supers from the parent hive are next put on the new one. The parent colony is then moved to a new location or left by the side of the new hive with its entrance facing in the same direction. In either case the entrance should be contracted.

If work is already partly begun in the super, the bees will continue work, and rush the honey above. In some cases it may be advisable to use perforated zinc between the super and brood-nest to keep the queen below.

The plan will meet favor, especially with those in localities where the season is short and the honey-flow rapid; and it will doubtless enable many usually getting no comb honey at all to secure a good crop.

The question may be asked, "What is done with the parent hive and all its brood?" If left beside the new colony, the brood, when hatched out, is shaken in front of the new hive, so that at the last drive all the bees that would have been hatched in the original colony are now given to the brushed

---

[*] Reports show that, if the colony is shaken or brushed, from a week to ten days before a swarm would otherwise issue, no good will be accomplished, and that the bees will be likely to swarm. The shaking should not take place *before the bees feel and show the desire to swarm.*

swarm, after which the hive is moved away. In this respect a brushed or "shook" swarm, as some call it, will secure more comb honey than a natural swarm because it has the additional strength of the young bees. The queen from the old hive (if one has been raised or introduced) should, of course, be

![A case of too small an entrance]

FIG. 1.—A CASE OF TOO SMALL AN ENTRANCE.

It was a warm day when this picture was taken. The bees, being unable to ventilate through the small entrance (8x⅜ in.) clustered out.

removed before the last drive, and given to some other colony.

While this plan of forcing the swarm ahead of time at the convenience of the apiarist generally gives satisfaction among beekeepers, some do not make it work; but so many have reported favorably through the bee-journals that we are satisfied that, if details are carefully followed, it will prove successful with most people.

Another plan has been suggested that is somewhat similar to that already described; but instead of shaking all the bees at once the operation is performed at two different times. For example, a colony in an eight-frame hive has four combs of brood taken out of the center of the brood-nest and in their place is put an equal number of frames of full sheets of foundation. The combs removed are now shaken one by one in front of the entrance. Two or three days afterward, when work gets nicely started on the first frames of foundation the remaining old combs with their brood and honey are removed and a second set of frames are put in their place. The

combs of brood are then shaken in front of the entrance as before. The beeless brood should, of course, be given to other colonies that can use them to advantage.

This involves the principle of the brushed or shaken swarm idea, and has the further advantage that the bees are not liable to swarm out as when they are shaken all at one drive on nothing but foundation.

CONTROL OF SWARMING BY MEANS OF LARGE OR PLURAL ENTRANCES.

When we see colonies clustered out at the beginning of a honey-flow, there is a lack of room, a too contracted entrance, or both. A colony that hangs out day after day when there is a light flow of honey is almost sure to start cell-building; for bees will swarm much worse during a light or moderate yield than when it is heavy.

If bees have been hanging out for perhaps a week, in all probability there will be queen-cells with eggs or larvæ in them. The thought of swarming seems to be in the mind of the colony. While the cells may be cut out and delay the swarm, it is better to enlarge the entrance and give room. Far better still is it to provide a very ample entrance *before* the bees cluster out at all in the first place; and before they feel cramped for room they should be given extra super capacity. We have often made colonies that were clustering out go into the

FIG. 2.—A HIVE WITH PROPER VENTILATION AT THE BOTTOM TO PREVENT CLUSTERING OUT AT THE ENTRANCE.

hives by simply enlarging the entrances and giving room. Other colonies that are given large entrances will often never start cells nor prepare to swarm. We are satisfied, from experiments that we have been conducting, that swarming can be brought very much under control, if not entirely prevented before the swarming idea gets into the mind of the colony, by enlarging the entrances or giving plural entrances and room.

The ordinary double-walled or chaff hive will not give that degree of entrance enlargment that is always desirable. While it has been made to provide a maximum of one inch by the inside width of the hive, yet

rear and sides for flight, as well as the front. We visited his yard a couple of times in the midst of the swarming season. Not on a single hive in the yard of something like 200 colonies was there a case where the bees were clustered out in front. They were flying merrily, and very much at work. Contrary to what Dr. Miller reports, we observed that they were utilizing the back and side entrances as well as the main entrance, although it was easy to be seen that the latter was used more frequently than any of the other three. In Fig. 3 the camera caught a

FIG. 3.—ONE OF VERNON BURT'S HIVES FOR THE PRODUCTION OF COMB HONEY.
Mr. Burt says this scheme of putting his brood-bodies upon four blocks so as to provide entrances for all four sides goes a long way toward eliminating swarming.

there come times when a much larger amount of ventilation should be provided.

Dr. Miller and other prominent bee-keepers have for years been raising their hives up on four blocks so that there are really four entrances, back and sides as well as in front. Our neighbor Vernon Burt, of Mallet Creek, has for some time practiced this plan, and he says it so nearly eliminates swarming that he has practically none at all.

Fig. 2 shows the front of one of his hives with its easy slanting approach to the main entrance in front, while the larger view, Fig. 3, shows how the bees are utilizing the

number of bees just ready to take wing at these side and end openings, for the bees were flying quite freely from all sides of the hive.

Of course, merely raising the hives up on four blocks alone will not prevent nor discourage swarming. The bees must be given plenty of room before swarming-cells are started. They should also be given a reasonable amount of shade. In Fig. 3 one will see that Mr. Burt has some old telescope covers that he formerly used on double-walled chaff hives. These are a good deal larger than the present hives, and, when placed over the supers, they project on the front and rear, and on the sides enough to give a reasonable amount of shade. In the middle of the day the hive is fairly well shaded.

Further particulars on the subject of entrances, and their relation to the prevention of swarming, will be found under the head of ENTRANCES.

DOOLITTLE MODIFIED SHOOK - SWARMING METHOD.

This is a plan that involves some of the principles of shook swarming; and in certain localities it can be employed to very good advantage. The method in brief is as follows: Sets of partly filled extracting-frames from weak colonies the year before, as will be explained later, are kept over winter in the honey-house, until the spring or early summer, when upper stories are filled with them, and placed on all strong colonies. The idea of this procedure is to make the colony below feel rich in stores so that there will be no curtailment of brood-rearing. If any honey should come in from fruit-bloom or other sources before the main flow it is promptly carried upstairs without crowding the queen below.

A week or two prior to the expected honey-flow or swarming season this upper story is lifted off and the old colony moved to one side. On the old stand is placed another empty hive. The set of combs, all save one, that were originally in the upper story, containing more or less honey, are now put down in the empty hive on the old stand. One comb is left out in the center, and replaced by a frame partly filled with brood from another hive. On this hive, at the parent stand thus prepared is placed a comb-honey super containing sections filled with full sheets of foundation, and having at the center ten or twelve other sections with partly drawn combs. On this super is placed another of sections with only full sheets of foundation. Last of all the cover is put on. The frames of brood put in the old hive removed to one side are now taken out and shaken in front of the entrance of this newly prepared hive at the old stand. The brood is then stacked up on the few weak colonies not run for comb honey. As the bees hatch the combs are more or less filled with honey during the season, thus furnishing the sets of extracting-frames to be used for the comb-honey colonies the next year. The queen in the comb-honey hive will have the one frame of brood partly filled where she can begin

laying. The large amount of honey in the brood-nest the bees will begin carrying upstairs to the supers in order to give the queen more room in which to lay. Thus work is started in filling the sections before the honey-flow actually begins; and when honey does come in, the bees continue to store it above without any swarming. In the meantime the queen occupies every available cell in the lower part of the hive.

Mr. G. M. Doolittle, the author of this system, has tested it most thoroughly several seasons; and one year in particular, when the season was only fair, secured an average of 114¼ pounds of comb honey per colony, *with no swarms* at any outyard.

While the first sections will contain a little old honey, yet if it be buckwheat or other good honey it does not impair the flavor, for there are many who like a little buckwheat flavor in comb honey; and such sections, Mr. Doolittle says, sell at the highest market price.

THE HAND SYSTEM OF SWARM CONTROL.

Mr. J. E. Hand, of Birmingham, O., has developed a system of comb-honey production and swarm control, in connection with a modified Heddon hive, for certain localities, that is quite unique. While we have not tested it ourselves, there are some features about it that look as if they might work.

It should be understood that this system of swarm control is adaptable only to divisible hives which will be found described and illustrated under HIVES elsewhere. Indeed, the reader would do well to peruse carefully what is said on the Heddon divisible hive and the Hand improvement before he considers its treatment here.

Early in the spring Mr. Hand divides his colonies into three groups, each colony being in two brood-chambers of his divisible hive. The very strong he puts in one group; the medium in another; and the light form the last group. As this system involves the use of only strong colonies for honey production he aims to force all except the very light ones into powerful stocks in time for the honey-flow. To that end the strong-colony group is left to itself, and the medium are to rob from the light. From the latter he takes one brood-section, with most of the bees and the queen, and gives it to one of the medium group, placing a perforated zinc honey-board between the added portion and the other colony. The light colony from which the brood-chamber was taken will be made, by the operation, a mere nucleus, although some returning bees will, of course, add to its force. So he strengthens up every medium group colony by drawing a brood-section from each of the light group; for it should be stated that the medium and light class are equal in number, or at least they are made so; and, contrary to what many would suppose, the queen in the upper brood-section that was given to the medium-group colony will go on with her egg-laying, and in a comparatively short time the two queens in the colony so treated will have a larger force of bees for the harvest than the strong colonies in the group first mentioned.

As soon as a little honey begins to come in he puts an extracting-super, with a perforated zinc honey-board underneath, on top of each of the strong colonies having one queen, and likewise he gives an extracting-super to each of the triple-deckers, as we shall call them, containing two queens. The object of this is to get the bees in the *habit* of going above, and to discourage any tendency on the part of the bees to store in the brood-sections; for it is a basic principle of the Hand system to have each brood-section jammed full of brood in various stages of development, so that, when the honey does come, it must go into the supers.

As soon as the honey-flow starts up briskly, he is ready to put on the comb-honey supers, containing sections partly drawn out during fruit-bloom. The extracting-super on each of the triple-decker two-queen colonies is changed to the bottom of the same stand—that is, placed between the bottom-board and the lower brood-section. The top brood-section with its queen is now given to one of the one-brood-section nuclei. The super of partly drawn sections being placed between the two remaining brood-sections; after, the queen is driven into the lower section and there confined by a perforated zinc honey-board. All the other two-queen triple-deckers are treated in precisely the same way.

Mr. Hand explains that the honey in the extracting-super next to the bottom-board will be removed by the bees and put into the comb-honey super, that being the only place for it. This starts work in the sections immediately—an important factor in swarm control. When work is nicely begun in this, another super of sections is put on top of the first one with the other brood section still on top of the whole. This manipulation breaks up all tendency to swarm, and the bees go on merrily storing honey.

The first-mentioned group, that consisted of strong colonies having one queen each, is now given another extracting-super, one to each hive, the same being placed under the first one given; and at the same time each of the nuclei to which was given a good brood-section from the two-queen hives is given a super of extracting-combs.

It will be observed that Mr. Hand runs for both comb and extracted honey. The hives being all in divisible sections it takes but a few moments to perform these manipulations, as there is no handling of frames.

The principle of swarm control comes in right here: The bees of all the colonies start going above into extracting-supers, which they enter without hesitation. When they get to work nicely in these they are given a comb-honey super, as explained under the general subject of COMB HONEY. See the Barber and Townsend methods. But Mr. Hand goes one step further. He *does not allow a single section in the comb-honey supers to be capped over*, as he says that would be likely to induce swarming. When the honey of such supers is about ready to cap they are removed and others given in their stead. After the honey-flow is over, the sections are completed by feeding back thinned-down extracted honey in a large feeder under the two brood-sections. The honey fed back is that secured in the extracting-supers already mentioned. The bees are fed two days in succession followed by an interim of two days alternately, during which they have time to thicken the honey and deposit it in the sections not quite completed. But in feeding back, there must be a *young* vigorous queen, and a large force of *young* bees in a colony reduced down to one brood-section of combs that are not old, for dark ones will soil the sections above. Instead of using colonies that produced most of this honey, Mr. Hand prepares a few special ones, reducing them down to the one brood-section. This work is all done after the honey-flow. The secret of Mr. Hand's success in the control of swarms rests on the frequent manipulation of the brood-sections and getting the bees started into extracting-supers (into which they go readily); then substituting for them sections of combs partly drawn out (we omitted to state that these were drawn out during fruit-bloom). Another factor in the problem is not allowing any comb-honey super to be capped over, but giving the bees fresh supers; and then, last of all, feeding back *after* the harvest is over, when there will be no tendency to swarm, and the bees can, at leisure, fill out to the wood and complete each section. And right here Mr. Hand claims to be able to produce all fancy honey, because, by his process of feeding back, he can have every section nicely completed, with no unfinished boxes at the close of the harvest, the honey being so nice because finished with a rush. There is no slow work and no travel-stain; and, what is more, he has a lot of extracted honey that is not all taken up by the feeding-back process. For the principles involved, see FEEDING and FEEDERS; sub-head, FEED-ING BACK.

THE ASPINWALL NON-SWARMING HIVE.

All systems thus far described relate to a method or methods of management of the colony to prevent swarming; but Mr. L. A. Aspinwall, of Jackson, Mich., has been directing his thought to the construction of a *hive* to accomplish the same purpose. He has devised one embodying some new principles which experts believe will effectually handle the swarming problem without any

ASPINWALL HIVE CLOSED.

shaking or brushing of bees—cutting-out of queen cells, caging of queens, clipping of queens' wings—in fact, without the employment of any methods formerly used for the purpose.

We are not prepared to pass an opinion yet, but believe Mr. Aspinwall has a *princi-ple* that is good, relating to a scheme for sep-arating the combs during the swarming sea-son about one inch apart by a series of bee-spaced slatted dummies inserted alternately with the frames. These dummies have per-pendicular slats ⅜ inch wide, a bee-space apart, held together in a suitable frame. The brood-frames proper have three perpen-dicular slats at each end, which some might

call a series of extra end-bars bee-spaced apart. This breaking-up of the brood-nest or brood-cluster so that the brood-frames are spaced an inch apart, it is thought, has the effect of keeping the bees quiet and al-laying excitement so that a whole apiary of hives of this kind will go through the sea-son without any swarming. Thus, it is ar-

ASPINWALL HIVE WITH COVER REMOVED.
Showing slatted dividers between frames, and bee-space strips over the ends of the frames.

gued, the energy wasted in getting ready to swarm, building queen-cells, and finally throwing off half the force of the bees into another hive, is all concentrated as *one force* in one hive, where the bees seem disposed to devote all their resources to the supers. While this hive has not been tested more than two or three seasons, yet results thus far have been very favorable; but, like a good many other things that have promised much, it may fall short of the anticipations of its friends.

Details of construction are shown in the illustrations herewith. Each comb, it will be noted, is surrounded on each side and each end by a series of bee-spaces made by perpendicular slats. If the bees would al-low combs an inch apart, and occupy this space without building comb, the same re-sults might be secured; but as they fill up any space larger than ⅜ inch with comb it becomes necessary to put in a scheme of bee-spaces which they will not fill. It therefore comes about that the hive is nearly twice the size for the same capacity of an ordinary hive.

It has no shell, or outer case, but employs the well-known principle of closed-end frames and panels to enclose the brood-nest the same as the Quinby hive (see HIVES); but

ASPINWALL HIVE DISSECTED, SHOWING BROOD-FRAMES AND SLATTED DIVIDERS.

instead of having the frames stand on the bottom-board or hang in rabbets on the end-boards they hang on a pair of cross-arms bolted to a frame. The outside panel is crowded tightly against the set of frames by means of a wedge between the panel and a rod passing through opposite holes as shown.

A bee-space between the frames and super is formed by laying strips of wood ¼ inch thick upon the top of the frames. The comb-honey super employs precisely the same principle of slatted dividers between the sections, and, in general, is constructed on the same general lines as the brood-chamber.

These dividers are used only during the swarming or honey-producing season. At the end of that time they are removed. In cool or cold weather they would be a positive detriment.

The remarkable claim is made that bees never cluster out in front of a hive having these slatted dividers, no matter how powerful the colony — at least that has been the experience of those who have tested it.

DECOY HIVES.

Many bee-keepers have followed out the idea given on page 417 (Do bees choose a location before swarming?), by locating hives in the forests, in the trees, and such hives have in many cases been quickly accepted and appropriated. We are indebted to the late Mr. John H. Martin for first suggesting to us the idea. Hives left standing on the ground in the apiary have many times been selected by swarms, and, if correct, the bees, in such cases, often come out of the parent colony, and go directly to these hives without clustering at all.

One of our bee-keepers in California, by trading and otherwise, had secured over a dozen empty hives. Having no immediate use for them he packed them up in a couple of tiers, about six high each. Each hive contained four or five combs, spaced so as to prevent the ravages of the moth-miller. One day, by accident he discovered some bees going into one of these empty hives. On examination he found that a swarm of bees had taken possession. His curiosity being now aroused, he examined some of the other empty hives. He kept on until he found six good swarms, each nicely housed, without any effort or expense on his part. In a few days more the remaining hives were filled with absconding swarms. When the swarming season closed he had 17 colonies secured. The point is this: By accident he had stacked up his empty hives in tiers, so that they resembled trees in the forest. Having combs in them, and entrances open, they were an inviting place for a passing swarm.

SWARMING, ARTIFICIAL. See INCREASE, also NUCLEUS.

SWEET CLOVER. See CLOVER.

SYRIANS. See HOLY-LAND BEES, under ITALIANS.

SYRUP. See FEEDING.

T.

TRANSFERRING. Make all arrangements several days before if possible, so the bees may grow accustomed to the surroundings, and be all at work; remember we wish to choose a time when as many bees as possible are in the fields and nicely out of the way. About 10 o'clock A. M. will probably be the best time, if it is a warm, still day. Get all your appliances in readiness, every thing you think you may need, and some other things too, perhaps. You will want a fine-toothed saw, a hammer, a chisel to cut nails in the old hive; tacks; string, such as the grocers use; a large board to lay the combs upon (the cover to a Dovetailed hive will do); a table-cloth or sheet folded up to lay under the combs to prevent bumping the heads of the unhatched brood too severely; a honey-knife or a couple of them (if you have none, get two long thin-bladed bread or butcher knives), and lastly a basin of water and a towel to keep every thing washed up

BOX HIVE TURNED UPSIDE DOWN PREPARATORY TO DRUMMING OUT THE BEES.

clean. A great part of this is really women's work; and unless you can persuade your wife or sister, or some good friend among the sex to help, you are not fit to be a bee-keeper. A good smoker will be very handy; but if you have none, make a smoke with some bits of rotten wood in a pan; blow a little in at the entrance of the hive, tip the old hive over backward, and blow in a little more smoke to drive the bees down among the combs; let it stand there, and place the new hive so the entrance is exactly in place of the old one; put a large newspaper in front of the new hive with one edge under the entrance. The bees returning laden with pollen and honey now alight and go into the hive, only to rush out again in dismay at finding it empty; we therefore want to get one comb in for them, to let them know it is their old home. Move back the old hive a little further, in order to get all round it, and give the bees a little more smoke whenever they seem disposed to be "obstreperous." Some bee-keepers pry off the hive-side and proceed to cut out the combs, with the bees running all over every thing. Of

FIG. 1.—DRUMMING BEES UP INTO THE EMPTY BOX.

course, this necessarily kills many, to say nothing of the nuisance of having bees crawling over the ground, up your trousers-legs, etc. A better way is to place a small box over the inverted hive, large enough to receive the whole cluster of bees. Now drum on the hive-sides with a couple of sticks or the palms of the hands, until the bees run up into the box above. Nearly all of them can be induced to leave their combs for the box, which should be removed as soon as a majority of the bees have gone up into it, and placed, to one side. You can now pry off a side of the box hive, having the bees practically out of the way. On a flat board lay each comb or sheet of brood, as rapidly as cut out, and over it the frame into which you are to transfer the comb. With a sharp, keen-edged knife mark out on the comb the size of the frame—that is, its inside dimensions. Remove the frame and cut along the mark, after which slip over the

frame. If the comb will not stay securely without any fastening, wind string a couple of times around, and tie. We recommend string in preference to transferring-clasps, transferring-wires, and every thing of that sort, for the reason that the bees will not forget to remove the strings, bit by bit, by the time the comb is fastened. Rubber bands are said to be applied more quickly than strings. Proceed thus until you have used up all the brood and *good* comb, as it does not pay, at present prices of foundation, to use small pieces. All such should be put into the solar wax-extractor. See WAX.

Pieces of comb containing brood *can* be fitted into the frames; but somehow we would manage to secure all the brood possible inside of the frame in one large piece; whereas little scraps that may be left had better be consigned to the solar wax-extractor. After all good combs are transferred, any remaining space in the hive should receive frames of foundation to fill up.

There remains to dump the box of bees you had laid at one side, over the top of the

FIG. 2. — REMOVING ONE OF THE SIDES OF THE BOX HIVES.

transferred combs, and in front of the entrance, and your work is done, after you have carried away all the refuse, and made sure there are no dripping pieces of honey lying around. Any chunks of good honey left after transferring are put into a pan, to be used up at the family table. All the rest should be consigned to the solar wax-extractor, as stated.

In transferring it makes no difference which side up the brood-combs are placed; turn them horizontally from their original position, or completely upside down, as you find most convenient.

WHEN TO TRANSFER.

Several inquire if we would advise them to transfer bees in the months of June, July, August, etc. We really do not see how to answer such a question without knowing the persons. Among our neighbors are those who would work so carefully as to be al-

most sure to succeed; and, again, others who would be almost sure to fail. We are inclined to think those who make these inquiries would be quite apt to fail, for careful people would go to work without asking questions, and do it at *any* season if they were sufficiently desirous Bees *can* be transferred any month in the year. When done in June or July, we need an extractor to throw out the honey from the heaviest combs, before fastening them into frames. Spring, or, more exactly, the time of fruit-bloom, is decidedly the best time, because there are then fewer bees and less honey, as a general thing, than at other times. Bees fix up the combs better when honey enough is being gathered to induce wax secretion to some extent, and the period of fruit-blossoming seems to secure all the above advantages more fully than any other season.

TRANSFERRING WHEN THE BEES ARE DISPOSED TO ROB; OUTDOOR FEEDING TO PREVENT ROBBING.

We recommend the time of fruit-bloom, because then the bees usually get honey enough to prevent robbing. Should it be necessary to do it a little later, say between fruit-bloom and clover, use the mosquito-bar folding tent described under ROBBING.

Bring the bee-tent and all other necessary tools for transferring, and stand them near

FIG. 4.—BOX OF BEES PLACED IN FRONT OF THE ENTRANCE OF THE HIVE.

the old box hive. Drum the bees into a box as previously described. With a cold-chisel cut the nails so that one side can be removed. After the side is taken off, arrange every thing as compactly as possible. This done, step inside the tent, grasp the intersections and "spread" yourself, as it were, over your work.

The operator inside has the old hive from which he is transferring, together with the new hive and all necessary fixtures for holding the combs in the frames. Besides these he has a saw, chisel, thin-bladed knife, smoker, bee-brush, a large shallow drip-pan to catch drippings of honey, and clean wired frames. To make his work as easy as possible.

hive over it, making all the joints bee-tight. Now hang frames filled with foundation in this new hive, and the bees will soon work up into it. After the queen gets to laying in these combs the bees will soon all move up into it, when you can lift it off and transfer, or do what you please with the old hive and combs. Where you are hurried, this plan gets your stock gradually into improved hives without very much trouble, and no mussing with dripping honey.

HEDDON SHORT WAY OF TRANSFERRING.

The prying off the hive-side, incurring the risk of robbers, cutting brood, and all other incidental difficulties of older methods in

MIKE WALL, TEMPE, ARIZ., AND PILE OF ODD-SIZED FRAMES FROM WHICH HE HAD CUT THE COMB AND FITTED THEM INTO LANGSTROTH FRAMES.

ble, he sits on a tool-box. In case he wants a frame or tool which by oversight he does not happen to have, an assistant, who may be engaged elsewhere in the apiary, at a call brings him whatever he desires. In the engraving the assistant is in the act of passing an empty comb under the mosquito-netting.

One may think that transferring in this tent is pretty close work, but we have transferred in this way a number of times easily and successfully, and the tent proved no real hindrance.

A SHORT WAY OF TRANSFERRING.

A little before swarming-time, pry the top from the box hive and set a single-story

transferring, suggested to Mr. James Heddon a new way that will commend itself especially to beginners who dread stings and the "awful sticky" job. Foundation is now so cheap, and combs built from it so much superior to those built naturally, while the combs in box hives are almost universally crooked, we believe our readers will, on the whole, do better to follow the Heddon short method. Indeed, whenever we have occasion to transfer we use it exclusively.

Let us assume that the hives, having been received in the flat, are put together and painted, and contain frames of wired foundation ready for the bees. Light the smoker and use a bee-veil. Move the old hive back four or five feet, and put the new hive in its place. Prepare a small box about eight inches deep having one side open, that will just cover (not slip over) the bottom of the box hive. Turn the old hive upside down; place the hiving-box over it, and then drum on the sides of the hive with a couple of sticks until about two-thirds of the bees pass up into the box. Gently lift off the box containing the bees, and dump them in front of the entrance of the new hive. Make sure the queen is among them, by watching for her as she passes with the rest toward the entrance. If you do not discover her, look inside the hive. When you still fail to find her, drum more bees from the old hive again until also those in the hiving-box, after which dump it in front of the entrance of the new hive, as before. The smoking is to prevent any fighting on the part of the bees at the second shake, and the entrance-guard will catch the queen or queens that have been raised meantime in the old hive. These one or two, if virgins, should be caught on the perforated metal and given to queenless stocks. Where the old queen in the new hive is valuable she should be caged at the time of making the second drive. If neither the one in the old hive nor that in the new is preferred, perforated zinc need not be used, nor the old queen caged.

The work of transferring is now complet-

A FRAME BONE-YARD.

you do get her, for, to make the plan a success, she must enter the *new* hive.

Replace the box hive right side up, two feet back of the new one, with its entrance turned at right angles. It still retains about one-third of the original colony, together with all the combs and brood. Allow the old hive to stand at least 21 days, by which time the brood will be hatched out, with the exception of a few drones of no value. Turn the hive upside down, and drum out the remaining bees into the hiving-box, as before. Next put an entrance-guard of perforated zinc (see DRONES) over the entrance of the new hive. Smoke the bees of the hive and ed, and all you have on hand is a box hive having a lot of old crooked combs, containing perhaps a little honey and drone brood. The honey can be extracted, or used as chunk honey on the table, where fit for use, the combs melted into wax, and the hive itself becomes first-class kindling-wood, because smeared on the inside with propolis and bits of wax.

The method above described is known as Heddon's short way. As it is neat, quick, cheap, and certainly more satisfactory in results, we recommend it above the old way.

There is one difficulty with the Heddon method: When transferring by that plan shortly after the honey season the combs are apt to be filled with honey. How shall we get it out? When the bees have all been driven out for the last time, we may cut the combs in pieces and extract the honey from them. But a better way is to stand the box hive 100 yards or so from the apiary, on a board, and contract the entrance so that only one bee can get through at a time, as explained at the close of the subject of ROBBING, which see. A little furore of bees may start up at first; but it soon quiets down, and in a few days the bees will have quietly removed all the honey from the combs. No unpleasant disturbance follows in the apiary, because the bees have taken the honey slowly, about as they do from natural sources. When the hive is emptied of honey the bees stop visiting it, of course, and then you may cut out the combs, put them in a solar wax-extractor, and consign the old hive to the kindling-pile.

TRAVEL-STAIN.—See COMB HONEY.

TULIP-TREE.—See WHITEWOOD.

TUPELO, a common southern tree, and a liberal producer of honey of fine quality. There are four species of tupelo or gum trees. The first and most common is the sourgum (*Nyssa multiflora*), or the common tupelo. This tree is very common in some sections of the South, but is rapidly being destroyed by the sawmills, as it is popular for making orange-boxes and for similar uses. *Nyssa aquatica* is common in Southern Georgia and Western Florida, where it is the standby for professional bee-keepers. The honey obtained is of high quality, but the copious flow is of short duration.

Further north there is the large tupelo *Nyssa uniflora*) growing largely in swampy places from Virginia and Kentucky southward. There is also another tupelo often termed the Ogeechee lime (*Nyssa capitata*) confined to swamps in the extreme south. Ordinary observers usually confuse all these trees under the common name of "gum" tree, or tupelo, so it is with difficulty we can sift our information in regard to them. It is clear, however, that all four are extra honey-yielders, probably producing as much as basswood. Tupelo honey has been sold in the North for orange honey, but there is quite a difference between the two. It is somewhat unfortunate that the tupelos are being ruthlessly cut down for lumber purposes all over the South. Tupelo should not be confused with SOURWOOD, which see.

U.

UNITING BEES. Uniting colonies is much like introducing queens, inasmuch as no fixed rule can be given for all cases. It is a very simple matter to lift the frames, bees and all, out of one hive and set them into another, where the two are situated side by side. Usually there will be no quarreling, if this is done when the weather is too cold for the bees to fly, but this is not always the case. If one colony is placed close to one side of the hive, and the other to the other side, and there is room enough for a vacant comb or two between them, they will very rarely fight. After two or three days the bees will be found to have united peaceably, when the brood and stores may be placed compactly together, and division-boards put in at each side. If there are frames containing some honey that can not be put in, they should be placed in an upper story, and the bees allowed to carry it down. You should always look to them 20 minutes or half an hour after they are put into one hive, to see if every thing is amicable on "both sides of the house." If you find any bees fighting, or doubled up on the bottom board, give them such a smoking that they can not tell "which from t'other," and after 15 or 20 minutes, if they are fighting again, give them another "dose," and repeat until they are good to each other. We have never failed in getting them peaceable after two or three smokings.

When you wish to unite two colonies so large that a single story will not easily contain them, which, by the way, we feel sure is always poor policy, or if their honey is scattered through the whole ten combs in each hive, proceed as before, only set one hive over the other. When done during cool weather, and the bees kept in for two or three days, few, if any, will go back to the old stand. If the hives stand within six feet of each other, they all get back without trouble any way, for they hear the call of their comrades who have discovered the new order of things. Sometimes you can take two colonies while flying, and put them together without trouble, by making their comrades call the lost bees. Only actual practice, and acquaintance with their habits, will enable you to do this; and if you lack that knowl edge, you must get it by experience. Practice on a couple of colonies that you do not value much. As we have said all along, beware of robbers, or you will speedily make two colonies into none at all, instead of into one.

In uniting bees it is excellent to change both colonies to be united from their own hives into a third empty one. This seems to take the spunk out of them.

WHAT TO DO WITH THE QUEENS.

If one of the colonies to be united has been several days queenless, all the better; for a queenless colony will often give up its locality and accept a new one, if simply shaken in front of a hive containing a laying queen. From a hive containing neither queen nor brood, we have induced the whole lot to desert and go over to a neighboring colony, by simply shaking some of the bees in front of it. They were so overjoyed at finding a laying queen as to call all their comrades to the new home, then all hands set to work and carried every drop of honey to the hive containing the fertile queen. By taking advantage of this disposition we can often make short work of uniting. If you are in a hurry, or do not care for the queens, you can unite without paying any attention to them, and one will be killed; but, as even a hybrid queen is now worth 15 cts., we do not think it pays to kill them. Remove the poorest one and keep her safely caged until you are sure the other is well received by the bees. If she is killed, as is sometimes the case, you have the other to replace her. Where stocks are several rods apart, they are often moved a couple of feet a day while the bees are flying briskly, until they are side by side, and then united as we have directed. This is so much trouble that we much prefer waiting for cold weather. If your bees are in box hives, we should say your first work on hand is to transfer them. If you have several kinds of hives in your apiary you are about as badly off, and the remedy is to throw away all but one.

In conclusion, we would advise deferring the uniting of your bees until we have several cold rainy days, in October, for instance, on which bees will not fly. Then proceed as directed. If you have followed the advice we have given, you will have little uniting to do, except with queen-rearing nuclei; and with these you have only to take their hives away and set the frames in the hive below, when you are done with them. If the hive below is a strong one, as it should of course be, just set the frames from the nucleus into the upper story, until all the brood has hatched. If you wish to make a colony of the various nuclei, collect them during a cold day, and put them all into one hive. If you have bees from three or four, they will unite better than if they came from only two hives, and you will seldom see a bee go back to its old home. A beginner should beware of having many weak colonies in the fall to unite. It is much safer to have them all strong and ready for winter, long before winter comes.

UNITING NEW SWARMS.

This is so easily done that we hardly need give directions; in fact, if two swarms come out at the same time, they are almost sure to unite, and we do not know of two such swarms quarreling. One of the queens will very soon be killed, but you may easily find the extra one by looking for the ball of bees that will be found clinging about her, very soon after the bees have been joined together. A swarm can almost always be given without trouble, to any swarm that has come out the day previous; and if you will take the trouble to watch them a little, you may unite any swarm with any other new swarm, even if it came out a week or more before. Smoke them when inclined to fight, as we told you before, and make them be good to the new comers.

UNITING BEES IN THE SPRING.

As we have pointed out elsewhere, uniting two weak colonies in the spring is usually unprofitable.* When there are two little weak colonies, or nuclei, one having a queen, it would seem the most natural thing in the world to put the two together for additional warmth and to provide a queen for all the bees; but, unfortunately, theory is not here borne out by facts. We have united nuclei in the spring; and while at the very time of uniting they would seem to make up a fairly good colony, yet in two or three days there would seem to be just about as few bees as there were before the uniting took place. The trouble is, that, if there is weather when they can fly, the bees that have

* Uniting a weak to a strong colony is quite a different thing, as will be presently explained.

been moved will go back to the old home to die, and, as a natural result, in three or four days there will be only a little cluster where there was the fair colony before. Uniting, when practiced to any advantage at all, is usually done late in the fall.

A nucleus from an out-apiary can be brought home and united with a nucleus at the home yard, or at any other yard. There would be no returning of bees then, and the two clusters will stay together, sharing each other's heat and enjoying the privilege of having a queen over all.

THE ALEXANDER PLAN OF UNITING WEAK COLONIES.

During the year 1905, and again in 1906 and '7, a good deal of interest was manifested through *Gleanings in Bee Culture* in the Alexander plan of uniting a weak colony to a strong one in the spring. Many of those who followed the method were very successful. A few, however, failed. To these latter we will refer later. The Alexander plan of uniting is given by Mr. Alexander himself as follows after he had carefully revised it:

ALEXANDER METHOD OF BUILDING UP WEAK COLONIES IN EARLY SPRING.

About six or seven days after taking your bees from their winter quarters, pick out and mark all weak colonies, also your strongest ones, marking an equal number of each; then all weak colonies that have a patch of brood in one comb about as large as your hand. Set all such on top of a strong colony with a queen-excluder between, closing up all entrance to the weak colony except through the excluder. Then there are those that are very weak that have only a queen, and perhaps not more than a handful of bees with no brood. Fix these last named in *this* way : Go to the strong colony you wish to set them over, and get a frame of brood with its adhering bees, being sure not to take their queen; then put the queen of the weak colony on this comb with the strange bees, and put it into the weak hive; leave them in this way about half a day; then set them on top of the strong colony where you got the brood with a queen-excluder between. Do all this with very little smoke, and avoid exciting the strong colony in any way. If a cool day, and the bees are not flying, I usually leave the strong colony uncovered, except with the excluder, for a few hours before setting on the weak colony. The whole thing should be done as quietly as possible, so that neither colony hardly realizes that it has been touched. When the weak colony has been given some brood, and put on top in this careful and still manner, hardly one queen in a hundred will be lost, and in about 30 days each hive will be crowded with bees and maturing brood. Then when you wish to separate them, set the strongest colony on a new stand and give it also some of the bees from the hive that is left on the old stand, as a few of the working force will return to the old location, especially if they are black bees or degenerate Italians.

In every case that has come to my notice where this method has been reported a failure it has been from one of two causes—either lack of brood in a weak colony to hold the queen and her few bees in the upper hive, or smoking the strong colony so that, as soon as the weak one was set on top, the bees from below would rush up and sting every one above. Therefore avoid using smoke or doing anything to excite the strong colony.

If done in a careful manner the bees in the lower hive never seem to realize that any strangers have been put above them, and they all work in harmony together.

At the outset we spoke of those who met with failure in following the method. As Mr. Alexander says, the difficulty doubtless arose from the fact that they failed to put brood along with the weak nucleus to hold the queen and her few bees, or else the uniting was so clumsily done that it stirred up both lots of bees, with the result that they came together before they had the same scent; and the queen, having a strange odor, was killed. (See INTRODUCING.) Mr. Alexander's injunction is to put the bees together soc arefully that the clusters do not really unite for some two days, at which time there is a peaceful union, and the two queens go on laying so as to make up one rousing colony, which can be divided, making two strong colonies where there would have been only one, since the nucleus left to itself would have died.

Where one desires to proceed with extreme caution he is advised to put a wire-cloth screen between the two lots of bees at the time of uniting, and keeping it there for two or three days, after which its place is taken by a perforated zinc honey-board. In this connection we would remark that the wire-cloth screen should be mounted in a wooden frame about $\frac{1}{2}$ inch thick, and of the same outside dimensions as the hive.

While this plan of uniting contemplates performing the act in early spring, something can be done at it in the fall. Mr. Josiah Johnston, in a communication sent to *Gleanings in Bee Culture* in 1907, tells how he unites on the Alexander plan in the fall.

Some have had trouble in following the Alexander plan of building up weak colonies. I think the trouble in many cases is due to rousing up the bees and getting them uneasy before the weak colony is put over the strong one. Then the two colonies have war for a while. I always use wire cloth between the two hives and never have any trouble from the lower colony going up and killing the bees in the upper hive. For some time I have wintered my weak colonies this way, on the summer stands. Last winter I had several weak colonies, and I put them all over strong colonies, making an entrance in the back with my knife through the hand-hole of the upper hive. This should be just large enough to allow two or three bees to pass out at a time. This is done on some cloudy day after very cold weather comes and the bees have quit flying.

Last year I had a weak swarm of bees. There was just one frame of bees and a young queen. I put this frame of bees in with nine frames of honey, and put the frames in a hive and set it on top of one of the strongest colonies I had, and in February they got pretty strong, and I left them on till April; and when I set them off I had two strong colonies.

Milan, Ill.   JOSIAH JOHNSTON.

V.

VEILS. The necessity of using face protectors will depend largely upon the race of bees to be handled. To deal with hybrids, Cyprians, or Holy-Lands, we would recommend one to wear a veil. With pure Italians it is not so necessary; still we always prefer to have one handy. Its use in any case gives the apiarist a sense of security to enable him to work to much better advantage than he would if continually in fear of every cross bee that chanced to buzz near his eyes.

The two great objections to the use of veils are that they necessarily obstruct the vision more or less, and obstruct the free circulation of air in hot weather, and thus tend to make the wearer sweaty and uncomfortable.

steel hoop; and when the veil is placed over the hat and properly drawn down it can not touch the face or neck, and hence leaves no possible chance for stings. During hot days when bees require the most attention in the apiary, a coat or vest is simply intolerable. In the absence of either one of these garments the corners of the veil may be drawn under the suspenders. The four plates herewith show successively this manner of drawing the veil under the suspenders, and its position when in use. The last view of the series shows how easily it can be drawn out from under the suspenders and raised above the hat while not in use. Many apiarists work a good part of the time with the veil raised. When the suspender method of

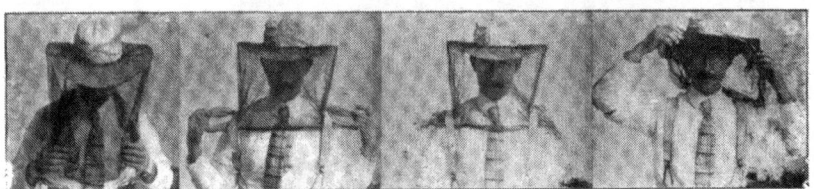

MANNER OF ADJUSTING A BEE-VEIL UNDER THE SUSPENDERS WHERE THERE IS NO ELASTIC CORD IN THE BOTTOM.

The very *nicest* veil is one made entirely of silk tulle, although somewhat expensive. The material is so fine that a whole veil of it can be folded to go in a small vest-pocket. We carry one of these constantly during the working season of the bees, and it is always ready for an emergency. It neither obstructs the vision nor prevents the free circulation of air on hot days. A cheaper one, though not so light nor cool, is made of grenadine with a facing of silk tulle net sewed in. The grenadine is strong, and the brussels-net facing obstructs the vision but little if any. The top of the veil is gathered with a rubber cord, so that it may be made to fit closely around the crown of the hat.

Our boys wear a broad-brimmed cloth hat, costing about 20 cents each. These hats are very light, will fit any head, and can be folded and put in a coat-pocket. The under side of the brim is green; the upper side of the crown is a drab color. This broad brim is supported and held out by means of a

holding is used one can raise or lower and fasten the veil in a moment's time. Where a rubber cord is used it can be stretched around the shoulders, and caught at the bottom of the waist or shirt front with a safety-pin, as shown in the next illustration.

But there are many who prefer a veil with a rubber cord inserted in the bottom, fastening the same by means of a large safety-pin to the clothing. Unlike the other veils shown with no elastic in the bottom of the fringe, this veil can be used by a man or woman, because the safety-pin can be secured to the clothing of either. But in putting this on, care should be taken to draw the elastic clear down near the bottom of the waist, securing it with a pin as shown in the first illustration. No. 2 looks very nice, but the movement of the arms will soon push the cord above the shoulders. leaving it so loose that bees can readily crawl up. No. 3 is better; and if the elastic is stiff enough very good results will be secured. But if not, the

15

veil must be drawn down as shown in the view at the extreme left, or No. 1.

The one to the extreme right shows a good method of fastening by means of a long string, inserted in the bottom edge of the veil. The ends are crossed in front of the waist, brought to the rear, pulled clear around to the front again, and tied. This holds the veil very securely as shown, and some seem to prefer it. An objection is that one can not very well push his hand up under the veil to get at his face to wipe off the perspiration as he can where rubber cord is used as shown, or where the edges of the veil are tucked under the suspenders. It is very important to have a protection that will secure freedom and ready access to the face. While a stray bee may get under without much danger of being stung, it is annoying to have it crawl around promiscuously. With the veil properly adjusted, one can easily reach his hand up under, pick up the bee, and at the same time be very little discommoded in his work.

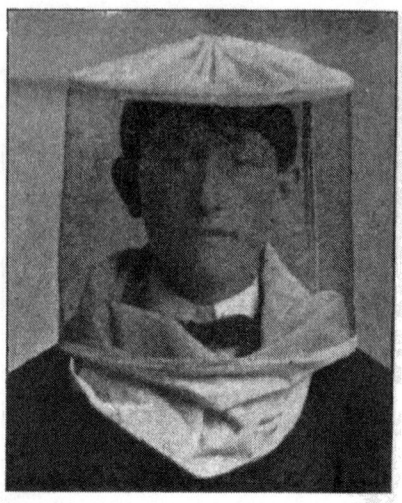

THE ALEXANDER BEE-VEIL.

The next illustration shows a wire-cloth-screen headgear that is used by some of on again. The muslin skirt fits loosely yet fairly snugly around the shoulders and neck.

RIGHT AND WRONG WAY TO FASTEN A BEE-VEIL HAVING A RUBBER CORD INSERTED IN BOTTOM.

the most extensive bee-keepers in the country. It is nothing more nor less than a plain wire-cloth cylinder having a circular gathering of muslin at the top, and a sort of skirt of the same material sewn to the bottom edge. With this outfit one will be required to go bareheaded or wear a small cap. Much of the work in the apiary is done during the hottest weather, and this veil is very cool because the wire cloth rides on top of the shoulders, leaving a free circulation of air over the top of the head. In passing among trees or shrubbery it does not get "hooked," nor torn like some of the veils of fabric. It has the further advantage that it can be removed in an instant without breaking any fastening, and is quickly put

There are many practical bee-men who prefer wire-cloth head-protectors to any thing else. When first used they seem a little awkward; but the extreme comfort that one enjoys more than compensates for its apparent outlandishness. The one shown in the cut uses a strip of wire cloth approximately a foot wide and a yard long. A yard of muslin completes the material required. Where one uses a coat, the skirt of this head protection can readily be tucked inside; but even without coat or vest, the loose folds of the cloth fit with a fair degree of snugness around the shoulders and neck.

One of our boys has used with much satisfaction a sort of chopping-bowl or basket inverted. It is a hat that is worn in India and other hot countries, and is slowly working its way into this country, particularly in the South. It is made of palm-leaf, and it is

HOPATCONG HAT AND VEIL.

supported above the head in the manner shown above. The cut will render further description unnecessary.

As light breezes can circulate above and around the head, it is perhaps the coolest sun-shade of any herein illustrated and described. If you can not secure one of these, and would like to get the ventilating feature, take an ordinary palm-leaf hat several sizes too large. On the inside of the hat-banb sew four or five ⅛-inch corks that have been cut in halves lengthwise. These, if spaced at regular distances, will keep the hat from the head, and permit ventilation.

CAPEHART'S GLASS-FRONT VEIL.

We have before remarked that one objection to bee-veils is the obstruction to the eyesight. To overcome this, Mr. John C. Capehart, of St. Albans, West Va., glued a piece of glass in front of the veil. The difficulty with this was, that the glass would hardly ever be in range with the eyes, on account of its weight, and then it would be covered with steam from the breath; and, worse than all, it would get broken. The brussels net is open to none of these objections, and is almost as transparent as glass itself.

Mr. Walter S. Pouder made an improvement on this by substituting celluloid film such as is used for photographic film negatives. While this overcomes the objection of weight it does not prevent the moisture of the breath from accumulating on it. So far we have found nothing better nor as good as silk tulle.

Mr. Martin and Mr. Coggshall both make use of sleeve-protectors. They will be found exceedingly useful for protecting the hands and wrists, and also prevent their getting daubed.

THE GLOBE BEE-VEIL.

This is a veil that has had a very large sale, and is preferred by a great number,

THE GLOBE BEE-VEIL.

because it is large enough to extend down over an ordinary hat or cap; and it is so constructed that it can not possibly get against one's face at any point. Sometimes an ordinary veil will touch one's nose or the back of his neck. At these points a bee can, if it

MRS. R. H. HOLMES' BEE-HAT.

will, insert its sting through the meshes of the veil. The globe veil is made so as to fold up compactly and can be carried in the pocket. With cross bees to handle, this is by all odds the best veil in the lot.

Mrs. R. H. Holmes, of Shoreham, Vt., uses a bee-hat like that shown in the above cut. It is simply a straw hat with a broad rim, the veil being made of mosquito-bar, and the facing of brussels net. A strip of cloth lines the lower edge of the veil, and is made just large enough to fit snugly around the shoulders. A couple of cloth straps hitched to buttons pass under the arm-pits, and button on behind. While this arrangement is good, the rubber cord and safety-pin is better.

HOW TO GET ALONG WITHOUT A VEIL.

It is a very great convenience to be *able* to dispense with a veil altogether, when circumstances permit it. The only obstacle is natural dread that a bee may possibly sting the face if it has a chance. This fear will

WOODMAN'S ADVANCED BEE-VEIL.

wear off as you become more and more accustomed to handling bees. When without a veil, if a bee comes up, and, by its hum, reveals anger, do not dodge nor strike at it, but control the muscles of the face as perfectly as though you were not at all aware of its presence. A little wince of the cheek or of the eye encourages its fighting qualities. A careless, indifferent behavior, on the other hand, shows you are not afraid, and it therefore very sensibly concludes that there is no use in wasting a sting for nothing. Sometimes we put our hand up to the face when one of these rascals persists in its annoyance. Should it actually begin to sting, smash it. In your community you will probably acquire the reputation of a bee-keeper, and, as such, when suddenly called upon to hive a swarm of bees without preparation for a neighbor, it would be a little unbecoming,

and perhaps a little humiliating, for you to show signs of fear. You should learn to "astonish the natives" barehanded and barefaced, and you need not incur risk, either, if you manage rightly.

BEE DRESS OR CLOTHING FOR BEE-KEEPERS.

Under the head of GLOVES, following in its alphabetical order, will be found some long-sleeved gloves or gauntlets that reach away up above the elbows. Many bee-keepers use these to keep bees from getting up the sleeve, and at the same time protect the wrists, especially the inside fleshy portions of them where they are very sensitive. Others carry this same principle further, combining the gloves and headgear all in one. The accompanying illustrations show

THE COGGSHALL BEE-VEIL AND SUIT.

the outfit worn by Mr. David Coggshall, of West Groton, N. Y. The lower part of the blouse is taken up by a string hemmed in at the lower edge, which is drawn and tied. When not desired to use the veil it is pulled down from the hat as shown in the second illustration.

As for pants, one can get a pair of overalls at any clothing-store, and it is suggested

THE COGGSHALL VEIL WHEN NOT IN USE, BUT READY FOR EMERGENCY.

that he get outfits such as are used by machinists and engineers. These have numerous handy pockets, large and small, in which various tools may be placed.

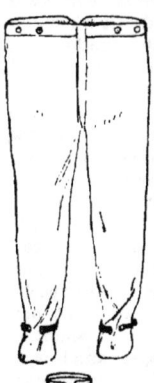

Bicycle pants-guards can be used to very good advantage during extracting and all other times, when one is shaking or brushing bees off combs The bottoms of the pants should be neatly folded around the ankles, and the guards slipped on to hold the folds in place.

A woman should ordinarily work in short skirts or walking costume. Such a dress, with high-topped shoes, makes a very neat and becoming outfit. Some women go so far as to dress in what are called "divided skirts," the lower parts of which are fastened below the knee; and a few go even a little further and wear regular man's attire, and one can scarcely blame them for so doing.

VENTILATION. Bees get it, ordinarily, through the entrance, and through the cracks and crevices which are generally found in even the best-made hives, providing the hive is properly constructed in other respects considered under the head of WINTERING. We do not believe in holes made in different portions of the hive, and covered with wire cloth, because the bees persistently wax it over, when they get strong enough. If we omit the wire cloth, they will, in time, build the holes up, by much labor, with walls of propolis, until they have effectually stopped the inconvenient drafts that the improved(?) ventilators would admit at all times through the hive. During extremely hot weather, a powerful colony may need more air than is afforded by an ordinary entrance, especially if the hive stands exposed to the sun. In such a case we much prefer giving the bees shade to cutting ventilation-holes, which the bees soon begin to use as entrances; for when the hot weather is over, and it is desirable to close these entrances, you confuse and annoy the bees by so doing. On this account we would give all the ventilation that a strong colony might need to keep them inside at work in the boxes, by simply enlarging the entrance. This can be done very readily with the Dovetailed or Danzenbaker hives, and in summer we make it a practice to give abundant entrance. See ENTRANCES. The chaff hive with its entrance 12 in. by 1 in. has always all the ventilation it seems to require, because the sun can never strike directly on the walls of the apartment containing the bees and honey. During winter this 12x1 inch should be cut down to about 2 x ⅝ inch, if the colony is a fairly average one. If weak, contract to one inch wide. In very cold zero weather put snow over the entrance, or, if none, then loose sawdust, as, in severe weather, bees do not need much air; but when it warms up, clear out the dead bees with a hooked wire. Too much ventilation of bees in winter is too much of a good thing. The chaff cushions placed over the bees in winter are kept over the surplus frames for the greater part of the time in summer, to confine the heat during cool nights; and from their porous nature they allow of the escape of more or less air that comes in slowly through the entrance, the honey-boxes having no other covering than the wide frames that hold the sections and these same chaff cushions. We have obtained more surplus honey with this arrangement than with any other, and are firmly persuaded that a great loss of honey often results from allowing so much draft of air through the hive that the bees can not work the wax, except during extremely warm weather. To test this matter we covered a large colony in the house-apiary with woolen blankets while they were gathering clover honey, to induce them to remain in the boxes, even after the weather had turned quite cool. So long as the blankets remained on, the bees did remain in the boxes working wax; but as soon as the blankets were removed, each time the experiment was tried they retreated to the body of the hive. The same thing was tried with thin-walled hives out of doors.

SMOTHERING BEES BY CLOSING THE ENTRANCE.

Although bees manage to get along with even a very small entrance, we should be very careful about closing the entrance entirely, in warm weather, even for only a few minutes. Many are the reports we get almost every season, of bees destroyed by simply closing their entrance while undertaking to stop swarming for a few minutes, until some other colony can be attended to. See SWARMING, ENTRANCES, and ROBBING, especially the last head, *How to Stop Robbing.*

When bees have the swarming fever, as a general thing they are gorged with honey and in a feverish state. They are like a man who has been taking violent exercise after a hearty meal, and require more than an ordinary amount of air. Their breathing-tubes are in different parts of the body, under the wings and on each side of the abdomen (see ANATOMY OF THE BEE); hence as soon as the entrance is closed, and they crowd about it the heat of so many becomes suffocating in a very few minutes; the honey is involuntarily discharged, wetting themselves and their companions, thus most effectually closing their breathing-tubes in a way that causes death to ensue very quickly. We have known of heavy swarms being killed in the short space of fifteen minutes, when the hive was thus closed on them. The heat generated by the smothering mass often becomes great enough to melt down the combs, enveloping bees, brood, honey, and all, in a mass almost scalding hot. Bees are some-times smothered in this way, in extremely hot weather, even when they have very large openings covered with wire cloth. In fact, we have once or twice had bees, shipped by railroad, in July and August, get hot and smother, when the whole top of the hive was covered with wire cloth. We took a lesson from this, and put wire cloth over both top and bottom of the hive, and then put inch strips across, so the hive could not be put in such a way as to cover the bottom. When thus prepared, we have sent the heaviest colonies, during the hottest of summer weather, in hives full of honey, and had no trouble. See MOVING BEES.

HOW BEES DO THEIR OWN VENTILATING.

If you watch a colony of bees during a warm day, you will see rows of bees standing around the entrance, and far inside of the hive, with their heads pointing one way, all making their wings go in a peculiar manner, much as they do in flying; but instead of propelling their bodies along, they propel the air behind them, and a pretty strong " blow " they get up too, as you may tell by holding your hand near them. Well, if the air is very hot and close inside the hive, so that there is danger of the combs melting down, they manage to send cooling currents clear to the furthest parts of the hive, and even up a small hole into honey-boxes, when made after old-fashioned patterns. This idea is not by any means new, and those who have invented patent ventilators will tell us, with a very fair show of reason, how many bees are thus employed blowing through the hive, that might just as well be out in the fields gathering honey. We once thought so, and that ventilators were needed; but after watching the matter longer, we concluded the harm done by excessive heat was far less than that from cold drafts when they were not needed, and that it is better to let a few of the bees waste some time in the middle of the day than to have comb-building stopped entirely at night, on account of drafts caused by these thoroughly ventilated hives. The most prosperous colony we ever owned was one that was so completely enveloped in chaff that they sent a stream of warm air out of their hive during frosty nights in March, strong enough to melt the frost about one side of the entrance. Of course, a stream of cold air went in at the opposite side as fast as the warm air went out. When we can get a hive into this condition of things they always prosper; and it is on this account that we would have no other arrangement for ventilation than that furnished by the entrance. See WINTERING.

VINEGAR. This is one of the legitimate products of honey ; and when properly made it has a quality quite superior to any other vinegar, especially for making pickles. It will not die, nor lose its strength like most other vinegars; and one can have light or dark vinegar by taking light or dark honey to make it from—at least so says R. R. Murphy, of Fulton, Ill., who has made and sold large quantities of honey vinegar. Speaking of pickles made of honey vinegar, Mr. G. W. Gates, of Bartlett, Tenn., says: " We have used no other for two years ; and nearly every one who tastes our pickles asks my wife for her recipe for making them. When told that we use nothing but honey vinegar, they are surprised." Mr. E. France, of Platteville, Wis., asked the wife of one of the merchants why she always bought his vinegar ; and her reply was, that the stuff from the store always ate up her pickles ; but that, when she uses honey vinegar, her pickles keep, and have a beautiful fine flavor.

Notwithstanding the fact that vinegar from honey is the finest in the world, the very low price of the ordinary product from cider makes it impossible to get a very high price for honey vinegar. The length of time it takes to make it, and the quantity of honey required, would make the vinegar too high-priced to compete with the other kinds on the market. But every bee-keeper always has some poorer grades, some from broken combs, washings from honey-barrels, honey-cans, etc., that will be practically wasted unless made into vinegar. Mr. E. France always uses the washings of his honey-barrels ; and this sweetened water he converts into vinegar. When we can utilize honey that would practically all go to waste, and convert it into cash, we are just that much ahead.

HONEY VINEGAR, HOW TO MAKE.

The honey - water and honey - washings should be put into a barrel with the top head taken out. To determine whether the water is sweet enough, drop in a fresh egg. If the egg will just float so as to leave a spot above the liquid, about as big as a ten-cent piece, then it is " all right," according to E. France. Another bee-keeper, Mr. G. D. Black, of Brandon, Ia., uses an ordinary hydrometer, which he says he bought for 35 cents. When this sinks into the liquid so the scale registers at 11, it is of the right consistency. Next cover the top of the barrel with cheese-cloth, and let it stand in a warm place where it can work and sour. In winter it should be put into the cellar. It will take anywhere from one to two years to make good vinegar. But the process can be greatly hurried by putting in "mother" from another barrel.

VIRGIN QUEENS. See QUEENS.

W.

WATER FOR BEES. That bees need water has been pretty well demonstrated; but the best means of supplying them is not very satisfactorily settled. The amount of water required depends largely on rearing brood in considerable quantities, and whether their food is old, thick (possibly candied) honey, or new honey right from the fields. The latter contains usually a large quantity of water that must be expelled before the honey can be ripened. See HONEY; also VENTILATION. While the bees are gathering this thin, raw nectar, as a matter of course they want less water, if any at all, besides what the honey affords them. This new honey is frequently so thin that it runs like sweetened water out of the combs when they are turned horizontally, and tastes like it. The excess of moisture is probably—for we do not have positive proof on the matter—expelled by the strong currents of air the bees keep circulating through the hive to take up watery particles and speedily reduce the honey to such a consistency that it will not sour. If you examine a hive very early in the morning during the height of the honey season you will find the blast of air that comes out, quite heavily charged with moisture; and when the weather is a little cool, this moisture often condenses and accumulates on the alighting-board until it forms a little pool of water. Where the alighting-board was of the right shape to retain water, we have seen it so deep as to drown bees passing out. These bees, it would seem, at least were in no need of water.

Admitting that bees need water at other times, how shall we give it? If there is a creek or a pond within a few rods of the apiary do not fuss to make any watering-place, as, nine times out of ten, bees will ignore what we prepare for them. But where there is no water-trough, creek, or pond within easy reach it may be well to give the bees two or three watering-places in or near the apiary. The best arrangement is a grooved board having an inverted glass or stone jar on it, as seen in the accompanying illustration. The water will run down and fill the grooves as fast as the bees remove it, on the atmospheric principle; but as it is difficult to make such a board, one can, in lieu of it, use a dinner or pie plate. Fill the jar full of water: lay across its mouth two strips of wood ¼ inch thick and ¼ inch wide. On top of this set the plate, upside down. Place the right hand on the bottom of the plate, then with the left hand grasp the jar. Now in-

WATERING-JAR AND BOARD, OR OPEN-AIR FEEDER.

vert the whole thing. The water will bubble out immediately till the plate has a depth of water of about ¼ inch, or whatever the thickness of the sticks is. Set the device in a convenient spot near the apiary; and to prevent the bees drowning lay little strips of wood in the water. If previously salted a little, this water serves as an additional attraction.

Let it be distinctly understood as entirely unnecessary to go to all this trouble, providing bees can get water in abundance from some pump, creek, or pond, as mentioned. If, however, there are neighbors who complain about the bees congregating about their pumps or troughs, it may be well to fix up counter-attractions such as jars of water slightly salted, to draw the bees away. In addition to this, take a pail of water and put into it a tablespoonful of commercial carbolic acid. Stir it well, then spray or spatter this water around the pump of your neighbor who complains of your bees. As explained under ROBBING, bees seem to have a great aversion to carbolic acid; and where a solution of it is sprinkled they keep entirely away.

WAX. This is a term that is applied to a large class of substances very much resembling one another in external characteristics, but quite unlike chemically. The wax of commerce may be divided into four general classes: Beeswax, familiar to us all; mineral wax, or by-products from petroleum; wax from plants, and wax from insects other than bees. But the first two are by far the most important commercially, in this country. Of the mineral waxes we have what is most common, viz., paraffine and ceresin. Beeswax is the most valuable, and has a specific gravity of between 960 and 972, and melting-point of between 143 and 145° F. The mineral waxes vary so much in hardness, melting-point, and specific gravity, that it would be useless to name exact figures. As a rule, however, it may be stated that the fusing-point of paraffine is much below that of beeswax, while that of ceresin may be either above or below, or practically the same. In general, we may say that the specific gravity of both commercial paraffine and ceresin is below that of beeswax; which fact renders it an easy matter to detect adulteration of beeswax with either paraffine or ceresin, by a method that will be explained further on, under the head of ADULTERATION OF BEESWAX.

There are also known to commerce Japanese wax and China wax, both of which may or may not be the product of insects or plants. As they are so much more expensive than either paraffine or ceresin, little fear need be entertained of their use as adulterants of beeswax.

BEESWAX.

For the bees and their keeper, no product has ever been discovered that can take the place of that which the bees themselves furnish. Real beeswax retains ductility and tenacity under greater ranges of temperature than any mineral, plant, or insect wax. Combs made from foundation containing 25 to 50 per cent of adulterations of paraffine or ceresin are very liable to melt down in the hive in hot weather. Paraffine is ductile enough to make beautiful foundation, but does not stand the heat of the hive. Ceresin, on the other hand, while more closely allied to genuine beeswax in point of specific gravity and fusibility, is too tough and brittle, under some conditions, for bees to work. Work it? Yes, they *will*, and construct combs; and in Germany we understand that considerable ceresin foundation has been and perhaps is being sold now; but our experience leads us to believe that it is

poor economy, and will lead the bee-keeper or the poor bees to grief sooner or later. Practically, then, we can say that genuine beeswax is the only product that ought to go into foundation; and we are glad to say that it is the only article that foundation-makers in this country use.

HOW BEES "MAKE" WAX.

If you watch the bees closely during the height of the honey-harvest, or, what is perhaps better, feed a colony heavily on sugar syrup for three days during warm weather, toward the end of the second or third day, on looking closely you will see little pearly disks of wax, somewhat resembling fish-scales, protruding from between rings on the under side of the body of the bee, which, examined with a magnifier, reveal little wax cakes of rare beauty. Sometimes, especially when the bees are being fed heavily, these wax scales fall on the bottom-board and may be scraped up in considerable quantities, seeming for some reason not to have been wanted. During the seasons for natural secretion of wax, where the colony has a hive affording plenty of room for surplus we believe wax scales are seldom wasted. At swarming-time there seems to be an unusual number of bees provided with them; for when bees remain clustered on a limb for only a few minutes, bits of wax are attached, as if they were going to start comb. When domiciled in their new hive, comes the time, should it please them, to show astonishing skill and dexterity in fabricating honey-comb.

BEESWAX IN THE ARTS.

Under the action of the United States pure-food law that went in effect Jan. 1, 1907, beeswax will have much larger use than ever. Indeed, there is already a notable increase in the price. Druggists (thousands and thousands of whom in the country formerly used paraffine, ceresin, and the like) will now be *compelled* under the new law to use nothing but pure beeswax, and the amount will run up into the hundreds of thousands of pounds. But what use have druggists for wax? They require it in making plasters, certain kinds of ointments, and for certain medicines known to the pharmacopoeia.

There has always been a large use for paraffine and ceresin in making candy; but now this must cease, while beeswax will be permitted as before. These two industries alone will increase the demand for the product of the hive to a great extent; and while we do not expect an immediate advance in the price of wax over and above what has already taken place, the time is not far distant when bee-keepers having dark honeys will do well to consider the possibility of making wax-production a business.

The new pure-food law will have no effect one way or the other on the use of paraffine, ceresin, and the like in any compound or mixtures that do not belong either to the food or drug classes. Electrotypers can use a substitute for taking impressions, although the great majority, we understand, prefer pure beeswax, even at a higher price. Natural-wood finishers can still use paraffine and ceresin; but most of them assert that there is nothing to compare for that purpose with pure beeswax. The first mentioned gives a greasy, smeary finish, while the product from the hive yields a highly polished surface—one that stands wear as nothing else will; a finish cheaper than hard oil—not by the gallon, but to apply.

The Roman Catholic Church uses large quantities of beeswax in the form of candles. She does not tolerate paraffine, ceresin, nor any of the mineral waxes, all of which give off a nasty greasy odor, while burning, whereas candles made of beeswax leave a delightful perfume. Then, too, the burning of mineral wax causes a deposit that injures pictures, while beeswax mellows and preserves them.

Certain grades of blacking, harness oils, and lubricants require pure beeswax in their manufacture. A blacking containing beeswax will withstand more dampness than that made of any other substance.

The electrical-supply business is a consumer of our product. The windings of the wire are soaked in paraffine or beeswax—preferably the latter, because it seems less affected by extremes of heat and by moisture. Pattern-makers also use beeswax. The profession of dentistry consumes large quantities of pure wax every year to take impressions of the mouth.

In all the arts, paraffine, ceresin, and certain other mineral waxes can be used ; but, if we are correctly informed, none of them have all the desirable qualities furnished by the product from the hive.

WAX-RENDERING.

SOLAR WAX-EXTRACTORS.

It is said the sun wax-extractor was originated in California about the year 1862. At that time it was used for extracting honey from the combs. The honey-extractor of to-day being then unknown, it is related that the early Californians extracted their honey largely by means of the sun's heat. They simply placed their cards of comb in large trays covered with glass, where old Sol, by the mere beaming of his countenance, did the work. As the combs melted, the honey and wax ran together into a receptacle. In the evening, the wax, by reason of its lighter weight, was hardening, and floated on the surface of the honey. The Californians thus practically accomplished two objects at one and the same operation—extracting both honey and wax—the latter already in marketable shape. As to the quality of the honey so separated from the combs, it is much better than one would suppose, but inferior to the ordinary extracted. Recently the use of the solar wax-extractor has been restricted to the melting of wax.

To a casual observer it seems almost incredible that wax can be melted by the aid of the sun. It is well known to the bee-keeper that little scraps of wax in summer weather will melt on a hive-cover exposed to the direct rays of the sun. If, therefore, we cover a shallow box with a sheet of glass, and place therein a piece of comb, it will utilize a much larger percentage of heat. Still further, by collecting more rays of the sun, and casting them into the box by means of a reflector (a sheet of tin, for example), a correspondingly greater increase of temperature may be expected. The reflector, however, is unnecessary, as sufficient heat is obtained without it.

THE DOOLITTLE SOLAR WAX-EXTRACTOR.

This machine has had a very large sale. Its general design is after a pattern made and used by the well-known bee-keeper G. M. Doolittle. The only objection to it is that it is rather small, but just the right size to take pieces of burr-comb and other bits of wax, etc., that accumulate in every-day working of the apiary. These accumulations can be thrown into the machine whenever one happens to pass by it; and instead of having a lot of little pieces scattered here and there through the apiary, to be melted up at some future time, they may be converted at once into a marketable product.

These small machines are not suitable for melting up combs. For that, something as large as the Boardman (described further on) should be used.

THE RAUCHFUSS SUN WAX-EXTRACTOR.

Mr. Frank Rauchfuss, of Denver, Colo., made an improvement. Instead of having the wax run into a single pan as in the case of the Doolittle, he arranged so the lip is turned to deliver the wax in the right pan, which catches the impurities, and is deeper. It overflows into pan No. 2. When No. 2 is full this overflows in turn into No. 3. There the wax cools into neat marketable shape, without further melting. Unless the wax is dirty in the first place, that in pan No. 1 will be fit for market; otherwise any dirt will be on the bottom of the cake, and may be scraped off, leaving the wax as clean, practically, as that in the other two. Bee-keepers of Denver and vicinity have tried this extractor, and much prefer it to the other form shown.

THE BOARDMAN SOLAR EXTRACTOR.

This is built very much on the same general plan as the one just described, but is larger. The rockers, or runners, afford facility for transportation, and also for tilting the machine at the proper angle to the sun. Common greenhouse sash may be used; but a large glass, say 30 x 60, is better, for the reason that the sash cut off a good deal of the sun's rays, making shade-lines along which the wax fails to melt.* The size of glass that one is able to buy will, of course, regulate the size of the extractor; the depth of the box, or tray, may be anywhere from 6 to 8 inches, the bottom being made of cheap lumber. This box or tray should be lined with common black sheet iron. Tin should not be used, because it reflects back too much of the sun's light. The whole tray, including the frame for the glass, should be painted black; and the glass, while the machine is in use, kept scrupulously clean.

SOLAR WAX-EXTRACTORS NOT SUITABLE FOR OLD COMBS.

Solar wax-extractors have their use to handle new combs, particles of fresh wax, pieces of burr-combs, and the like, and can be used to clarify and bleach to a certain extent wax already caked, but are not adapted to the handling of old black combs that have several generations of cocoons in them. Large sun extractors like the Boardman will get the bulk of the wax out of such combs, but they do not get all of it. If sun heat is used at all for melting, the slumgum (or refuse) should be further treated.

RENDERING WAX FROM OLD COMBS.

For new combs the problem of rendering wax is a comparatively simple one, since the operation consists simply in melting them in hot water and dipping the wax off the top. This is true also of cappings where the total amount of refuse or impurities is so small that there is practically no difficulty in getting all the wax. Here a solar wax-extractor is satisfactory, although not to be depended upon for speed nor great capacity unless very large, which would be expensive. However, one extensive bee-keeper, R. C. Aikin, of Loveland, Colorado, thinks that it pays him to have made a large enough solar extractor to handle all his cappings and comb. See Fig. 1. When old comb is to be rendered, on the other hand, the problem becomes much more difficult, as the many layers of cocoons found in the cells used for brood-rearing, confine the wax and make it hard to remove. It can be readily seen that,

*If the large glass can not be had, better purchase three sheets of 20x30, and put them in the frame crosswise—the glass butting tight up against each other.

if old comb is simply melted in hot water or steam, these cocoons will become saturated with wax, making the loss very great. The following discussion, therefore, will have to do especially with the difficulties encountered in rendering wax from old combs.

There are many different methods practiced by bee-keepers all over the world to obtain the wax from old brood-combs; and it is needless to say that, in many of them,

FIG. 1. — AIKIN'S MAMMOTH SOLAR WAX-EXTRACTOR; THIS WILL HANDLE THE COMBS AND CAPPINGS FROM A LARGE APIARY.

the loss is considerable. One of the crudest methods is to throw the combs into a large iron kettle of water and then build a fire and boil the contents for several hours, skimming the wax off the top of the water meanwhile. More comb is added from time to time, and

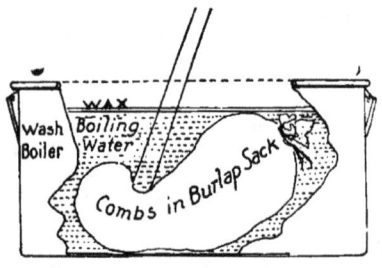

FIG. 2.—A VERY CRUDE AND WASTEFUL METHOD OF RENDERING.

the process is continued perhaps all day. Finally a piece of wire screen is weighted down on the refuse to keep it out of the way and facilitate dipping the wax. Careful experiments have shown that this method wastes from 25 to 40 per cent of the total amount of wax, while a great deal of time is required to clean and refine what little wax is secured.

Another plan which has been advocated to some extent is that shown in Fig. 2. A sack of comb is held under the surface of the water, and agitated or punched with a stick for a long time until much of the wax is released and floats to the surface, where it may be dipped off. This method results in somewhat cleaner wax; but there is apt to be nearly equal waste to the plan before mentioned.

There is another method that is used more, perhaps, than the two which have just been described. It is a somewhat better plan, for the amount of waste is not so great. It is shown in Fig. 3. In order to get the best

FIG. 3.—A POPULAR BUT WASTEFUL AND SLOW METHOD OF OBTAINING WAX.

results the weights should be arranged that they can be lifted up a few inches in order to give the refuse in the sack a chance to become saturated again with hot water. The weights should then be lowered, and this process kept up for several hours, the water meanwhile boiling vigorously. The wax should be dipped off almost as fast as it rises to the surface, in order to keep it from discoloring due to long continued heat.

In 1904 Mr. T. J. Pennick, of Williston, Tenn., suggested the use of centrifugal force applied to hot slumgum just taken out of boiling water. It was his opinion that the free wax, when hot, would by this means readily separate from the solid matter in a very short time. Extensive experiments have developed the fact that there would be a great deal of wax which would not escape from the refuse, no matter how fast it might be whirled in an extractor, showing that even great centrifugal force could not separate the wax from the refuse. Wax nearest the outside might be thrown out; but that nearest the center would be held back and not allowed to escape.

Mr. A. C. Miller, of Providence, R. I., some time ago devised an agitator and applied it to the rendering of wax. The old combs in such an agitator are thoroughly stirred and rubbed under hot water so that the wax is liberated and rises to the surface, where it is drawn off through a spout. As will be seen, this is somewhat similar to the plan shown in Fig. 2, before mentioned, although it would be, of course, a great improvement on that very crude method.

From our experiments, and from reports we have received from hundreds of beekeepers, it would seem as though the wax-press were by all means the most satisfactory wax-extractor yet devised. We doubt

FIG. 4.—AN UNHANDY AND UNSATISFACTORY PLAN.

whether any thing but pressure combined with heat can remove all of the wax. In saying this, we realize that there will probably never be a wax-extractor of any kind that will economically remove the last particle of wax; but if the amount of waste can be reduced to less than one per cent, the loss is an item that can be neglected.

Before entering the discussion of wax-presses it may be well to add a word of caution to bee-keepers who are sure that the particular method they are using enables them to obtain all the wax or practically all. If the refuse, when they are done, has not been put through a well-constructed press we believe that there will be no way of determining the amount of waste, for it might contain as much as 20 per cent of wax and still look perfectly clean and show no traces of it when examined. On a small scale it is possible to get some idea of the amount of wax left in refuse by the following very simple plan:

Thoroughly heat in boiling water the refuse to be tested, then allow it to cool slightly; seize a large handful, and squeeze it as much as possible in the fingers. If fine lines of wax appear in the creases between the fingers a good deal of wax is left—perhaps from five to ten per cent or more, depending upon the amount of wax shown. The hand will not be burned in the very short time

necessary to make this test. But, as before stated—the most conclusive method of determining the waste is to run the refuse through a well-constructed press.

HOT-WATER WAX-PRESSES.

In these the pressure may be continued without the least danger of chilling the combs. This method has also a decided advantage in that the screw can be raised after having been turned down, and the cheese allowed to become saturated again with boiling water. The screw may then be lowered, and this hot water forced out of the refuse, carrying with it more of the wax. This operation must be repeated as often as found necessary by experience. It is thus seen that there is no disagreeable handling of the refuse until all the wax is out. Furthermore, the work, if necessary, may be confined to the one tank.

Mr. Orel L. Hershiser, of Buffalo, N. Y., devised the hot-water press shown in Fig. 5. The capacity of this is large, so that it is possible to obtain as much as 75 pounds of wax in one day over a common stove. One great objection to hot-water presses heretofore has been their relatively small capacity of wax per day. Mr. Hershiser, by making the press very large, overcomes this difficulty.

The quality of wax from hot-water presses is usually not very good, because of the long-continued high temperature. In the Hershiser press more hot water is introduced at short intervals into the lower part, causing the melted wax to overflow through the outlet at the top. In this way the wax is not left for any great length of time on the boiling water, so that the color is not darkened.

Perhaps one objection to hot-water presses is the cost of the outfit; but for extensive bee-keepers we believe that they are the most practical, as somewhat cleaner work can be done, owing to the long-continued intermittent pressure on the refuse surrounded by hot water. In other words, old combs rendered in a hot-water press may be pressed as many as fifteen or twenty times, so that it is possible to reduce the final loss to only a fraction of one per cent.

If one wishes to try the hot-water method by using an outfit constructed at home he can follow the plan shown in Fig. 6. An ordinary kettle may be used, although it would be advisable to have one with a flat bottom. As it would be rather difficult to construct a cross-beam over the kettle rigid enough to stand the pressure exerted by a screw, a lever had better be used as shown, though some means will have to be employed to keep it from falling over sidewise, such as a loop around a tree or post. In using a lever it is important to have it so adjusted that the pressure will be uniform and directly downward. Any pressure exerted from a point not directly over the kettle will result in pressing the refuse to one

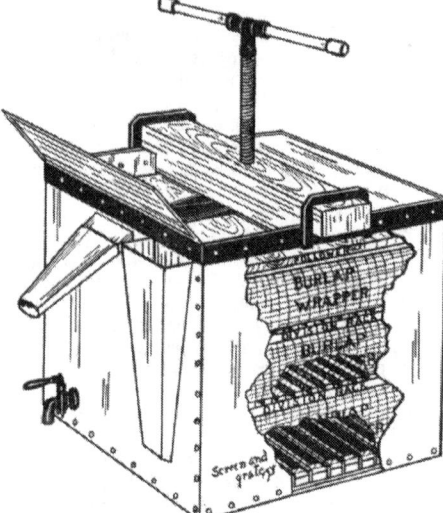

FIG. 5.—HERSHISER HOT-WATER WAX-PRESS.

side, so that the "cheese" will be very thin on one edge and very thick on the other. If this were the case there would, of course, be too much wax left in the thick portion. To get the best results the cheeses should not be over an inch or an inch and a half thick after pressing.

Cleaner work can be done by an intermittent than by continuous steady pressure; and so, whether using a lever or screw it is well to relieve the pressure about every ten minutes, allowing the cheese two or three minutes in which to become thoroughly saturated again with boiling water. Pressure should be applied slowly at first in order to avoid bursting the burlap.

With the outdoor-kettle plan the wax will be discolored on account of the long-continued heat unless it is dipped off the surface of the water almost as fast as it rises. About three hours of intermittent pressure for one batch of combs in a kettle will render out the wax.

STEAM-PRESSES.

Methods of rendering wax, embodying the principle of applying great pressure to combs surrounded by steam, are quite old, both in this country and in Germany, where they originated. In many ways steam-presses have advantages over other methods; but the quality of wax is usually not so good, because of the high temperature to which the comparatively thin surfaces of melted wax are subjected; although the wax, as it leaves the refuse, falls down out of the way so that the work can be much more conveniently carried on, since there is no great depth of water in the way.

A steam-press of popular design is shown in Fig. 7. Steam is generated under the false bottom G, of the compartment H, and, passing upward through an opening in the center of the false bottom, surrounds the combs beneath the plunger in the perforated metal

FIG. 6.— USE OF THE LEVER IN PRESSING WAX.

basket. As the wax, falling down from the refuse can not get into the water on account of the false bottom, it passes out of the tube shown.

Steam-presses are very convenient as uncapping-cans; for when the perforated metal basket is full of cappings the cross-arm can be placed in position, the screw run down, and practically all honey forced out. Then steam may be generated, and the wax melted into marketable shape without any second handling and with little extra trouble; or the "cheeses" of cappings, pressed nearly dry of honey, may be stored away to be rendered into wax at a more convenient time later.

These presses are also very useful in pressing honey from broken combs, unfinished sections, etc., and rendering the pressed comb into wax.

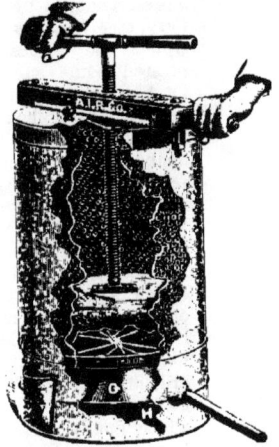

FIG. 7.—GERMAN STEAM WAX-PRESS.

Mr. Edward G. Brown, of Sergeant Bluff, Iowa, has described an excellent plan for rendering wax on a large scale, making use of an open press heated with a steam-jet. Where one has access to steam this is a very practical method. His plan in full is as follows:

The wax-rendering apparatus which I use is somewhat beyond the reach of many bee-keepers; but it gets the wax, and I think a little nearer all of it than most of the various outfits in use. I will give the figures of the wax rendered, and later describe the apparatus.

The best results which we have secured were from a lot of combs, many of which were 25 years old. There were 400 of these combs in the lot, and we obtained 164 lbs. of wax, or a little over 4 lbs. of wax to every 10 combs. There were two working at the job, and the total time for rendering, including firing up the boiler, etc., was a little less than five hours. We have made a few full-day runs on combs varying in age from one to twenty-five years, and the results average about 250 to 375 lbs. of wax to the thousand combs. In a day we can usually render from 800 to 1000 combs, the number depending, of course, upon the condition of the combs, etc. When I buy old combs I usually figure on about 2½ lbs. of wax to the hive of ten combs, Langstroth size.

In the last two years we have rendered something like 8000 or 9000 combs on account of foul brood, and

I believe that this is the only way to eradicate the disease completely from a yard when it once gets a start. There is just one other way; and that is, to build a bonfire and burn up all the supplies, etc., in connection with the yard. Incidentally the latter plan is somewhat expensive, for it leaves the apiarist at the foot of the ladder, ready for a new start.

The figures given above may seem a little large to some; but the apparatus is of fair size, and requires two to work it at full speed, and a part of the time there were three of us. Our work-shop is an old cheese-factory which I also use for storage room; and the heat for the wax-rendering is furnished by a big boiler from which I also get the power for running my buzz-saws, as I make all my own hives and heavier supplies.

The engraving shows the various parts of the tank, which is 2 ft. wide, 7 ft. long, 16 in. deep. It is divided into two parts, as shown, both parts being lined with galvanized iron, and fitted with a cover of the same material. Each part is about half filled with water; and steam for boiling the water is introduced by means of a ¾-inch pipe, on the under sides of which holes are drilled so that, when the steam is turned on, the contents of the tank are kept in motion. Each division of the tank has a separate pipe controlled by a valve so that heat can be applied when wanted, and as hard as desired. The press as shown in the second engraving is made from an old cheese-press. The construction is sufficiently clear, hence no detailed description is necessary. A pipe is arranged under the press in such a way that steam

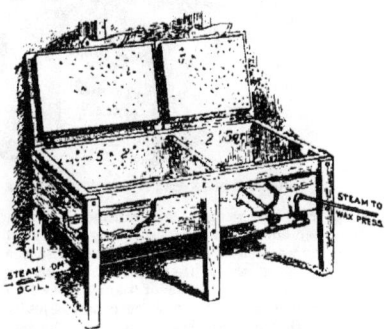

STEAM-HEATED VAT FOR MELTING OLD COMBS.

may be forced between the cleats of the bottom of the press, thus keeping the slumgum hot.

Two pieces of heavy burlap are used for holding the slumgum, the outer one being about 30 by 30 inches, and the inner one about 20 by 20. These are laid over a form 10 inches square and 4 inches deep, which will hold about two gallons of the melted combs. After the comb is dipped in the sides, the cloths are folded together, then the form is removed, the upper block placed in position, and the pressure applied. Unless these sacks are of extra good quality they do not last longer than eight or nine times, and even the best ones usually burst after fifteen or twenty pressings. A short-handled pitchfork, a wire strainer, and a number of 50-pound honey-cans with the top cut out, to be used as molds, complete the apparatus.

When rendering, the tanks are filled about half full of water brought to a boil by the steam. The larger compartment is then filled with combs still in the frames. About 30 frames of combs can be put in at once. The cover is then shut down and the steam turned on. From three to five minutes is required to do the work, and when the contents are

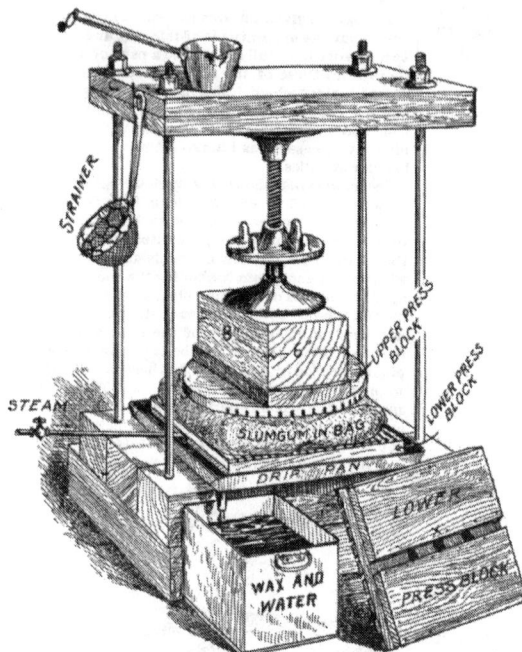

BROWN'S WAX-PRESS FOR WHOLESALE WORK.

boiling thoroughly the cover is raised and the steam partly turned off, so that the frames may be swished about in the water and finally picked out with the pitchfork. The steam is then turned off, and the slumgum skimmed by means of the strainer into the small division of the tank, when a new batch of frames containing combs may be put into the first or larger compartment.

While one man works at melting up the combs and tending the fire under the boiler, the other is kept busy working the press. The room is so hot and full of steam that the operators can wear but few clothes, and even then it is rather hot work.

The slumgum which is kept boiling is dipped from the small compartment of the tank into the burlap in the press, and the wax is run directly into square cans or molds. The frames as they come from the tank are washed cleaner than they could be scraped with a knife, and from experiments which I have made they are entirely free from any disease. We have not been able to make it pay to rerender the refuse from the press; but with what wax and propolis are left in the cheeses they make good fuel and furnish nearly enough fire to keep up steam. The cheeses are dumped directly into the boiler-room, and are burned as fast as pressed.

During the year 1907 we rendered about 1500 lbs. of wax, and in 1908 nearly 1100 lbs., so we think we have had quite an opportunity for testing the apparatus thoroughly.

UNHEATED PRESSES.

Mr. C. A. Hatch, of Wisconsin, was probably the first one to make extensive use of this method of wax-rendering. He had used for a short time a press designed by W. W. Cary, of Massachusetts, in which the combs were pressed while submerged in hot water; but he believed that he could improve on this plan by applying pressure in a different receptacle without the use of so much hot water. While there may be hundreds who used a similar plan before this, Mr. Hatch is probably the first one in this country to bring it to the notice of the public. Later Mr. F. A. Gemmil, of Ontario, Canada, also used such a press, which finally came to be known as the Hatch-Gemmil wax-press. This is shown in Fig. 9.

Wax-presses very similar to the Hatch-Gemmil have been constructed and used by various bee keepers all over the country. Since

Fig. 9.—The original Hatch-Gemmil wax-press.

the essential features of this method have been in use so long it is very evident that the unheated press has merit. The authors of this work have rendered large quantities of wax, and have made many experiments which all go to prove that the unheated press is a most desirable one for the average bee-keeper.

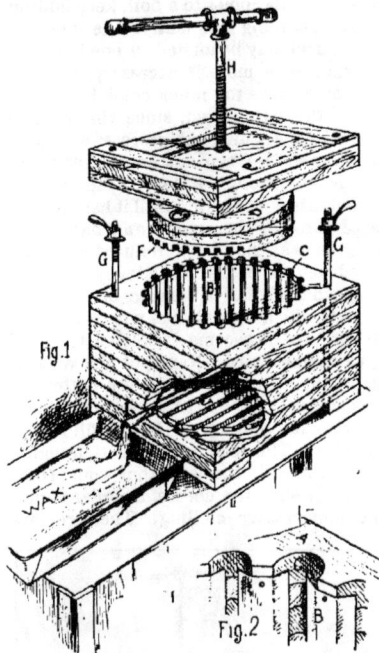

Fig. 10.—Salisbury's press, constructed almost entirely of wood.

Mr. F. A. Salisbury is an enthusiastic advocate of the unheated press. The form which he likes best is shown in Fig. 10. It will be seen that the loss of heat is prevented by having no circulation of air; hence, since wood is an excellent non-conductor, the combs remain hot for a considerable length of time. The construction is sufficiently clear from the illustration.

Another form is that shown in Fig. 11, representing a press constructed by Mr. John Rockwood, of Utah.

The particular form of unheated press preferred by the authors is shown in Fig. 13. It will be noticed that a round can, constructed of tin, is used instead of the square wooden box and tray shown in Fig. 9. The principal reason for this change is that it is easier to keep the cheese from bursting out

sidewise when a round box or can is used, for the square box tends to bulge out in the middle, thus allowing the burlap to burst. If a round can is used. the pressure sidewise is always in a direction directly away from the center, and the horizontal pressure is thus equalized. With the round can the cheeses do not chill so quickly as they do in the square box, for the reason that they are more compact, and there is always less chance for cold air to circulate around under the cheese. Mr. Hatch now uses two screws instead of one, for he believes that he can get more pressure with the two; but it is doubtful if two screws are necessary, since one screw will exert more pressure than is needed, and is, besides, more easily handled.

It will be noted in Fig. 13 that the screw extends down into a hole in the center of the cast-iron follower. If the screw simply rests on the top, the follower shows a great tendency to go down sidewise, especially if one is not exceedingly careful to place the melted comb evenly in the can. It is easy to see that, when the follower does not go down straight, one side of the cheese will be much thicker than the other, and contain

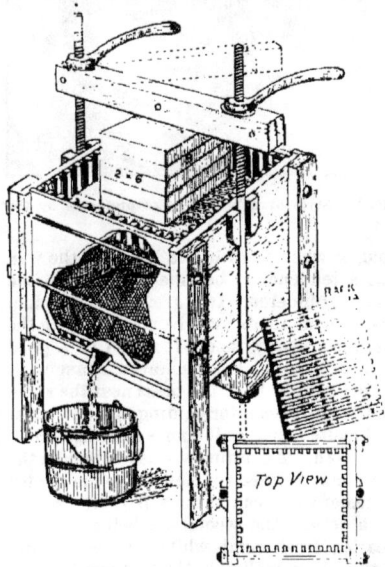

Fig. 11.—Rockwood's press with a double screw.

quite a good deal of wax after the work is done. With this arrangement the follower must go down straight unless the screw bends; but there has never been any trouble from that source. The circular follower above the cheese must be cleated, as shown on the under side, to aid the wax and water in running off.

With this press, since there is no heat applied to the combs during the pressing, it is well to do the work in warm weather, or in some room that can be kept warm by the heat of the stove used; for when the air is

Fig. 13.—Style of unheated press preferred by the authors.

cold, or when the wind is blowing, the wax has a tendency to become chilled, and the work is hindered. In warm weather or in a warm room there need be no chilling if the work is properly done. It would be a good plan to have all the apparatus arranged in order—that is, have the press near the stove and the large can for holding the hot water and melted wax, as it comes from the press, near both. An ordinary wash-boiler on the stove may be used for melting up the combs; or faster work can be done if there are two such boilers, the second one being used for heating fresh comb while that which has already been melted in the first one is being rendered. The press should stand as near the boiler as possible to avoid the drip when the melted comb is dipped from the boiler into it. Cleats should be nailed outside of the press platform, Fig. 16, to keep it from twisting when the screw is turned, and two

hinges should be screwed to the front edge, as shown, in order to allow it to be tipped up on edge when necessary, to let the wax and water drain out. It is best to have the back of the press a little higher than the front at all times.

To begin the work, pour about two pailfuls of water into the boiler and set it on the stove. As this comes to a boil, keep adding old comb, stirring frequently. As much as half a barrel may be melted in one boiler at a time, or even more if necessary; but it is best not to have too much comb in proportion to the water used, since this plan is essentially a washing-out process; and good results, therefore, can not be secured when there is not enough water. Keep stirring the contents of the boiler until it has all been heated through thoroughly and has boiled until the wax has been reduced and the melted comb is of the consistency of mush; then push the boiler to the edge of the stove, where it will keep hot, but where the wax will not burn or become discolored from too high a temperature. Next put the wooden plug in the spout or tube at the bottom of the wax-press can; and after putting folded-up burlap and follower in the can, fill it with hot water. This is done to heat thoroughly the press and all the parts that would come in contact with the cheese, in order to prevent unnecessary chilling. Then remove

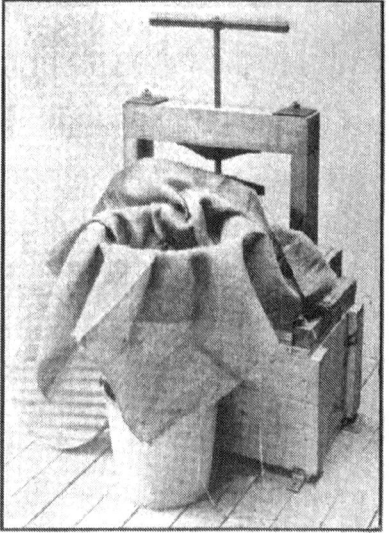

Fig. 14.—Showing can slid forward on the platform and the burlap spread out ready for the melted comb.

the wooden plug and draw off the water and pour it into the second boiler on the stove, which, as before explained, should be used for melting up the second lot of comb in case it is necessary to do rapid work. Now slide the can forward on the platform, as shown in Fig. 14, and spread the piece of burlap over it. Dip about one gallon of

Fig. 15.—All ready for pressure.

melted comb *and water* into the press and fold the burlap neatly over it. The wooden plug must be kept in the outlet tube in order that the water and wax may not run out. In dipping in the melted comb do not use a strainer or dipper with a wire-cloth bottom, for the idea is to transfer *plenty of water with the comb* in order to keep the wax from chilling, and also to aid in washing it out. Use an ordinary dipper, then, of pretty good size. The square piece of burlap should be of such size that there will be plenty of room on top to keep the slumgum from washing out; but, on the other hand, there should not be so much as to make a great roll of useless cloth that will only be in the way. A foot on each side to fold over is enough if this burlap be folded over neatly, as one would fold paper in tying up a package; there is no need of nails for keeping the edges together. Place the cleated

follower on top of the burlap package of comb with the cleats running toward the spout, then push the can back under the screw. Apply the pressure slowly, turning the screw down more and more as the wax and water are pressed out of the comb. Enough water should usually be transferred with the comb so that the cast-iron follower will be completely covered when the screw is turned down about half way. If not enough water has been dipped over, more hot water should be added; but, usually, enough water can be dipped in with the combs so that no further water need be put in. Next, place the wooden cover in position over the can. These will warp somewhat with the steam; but they can be reversed occasionally in order to make a good fit. These covers are used to keep away the cold air and thus prevent the wax from chilling. Keep turning the screw down slowly until it has reached the limit. This should take about two minutes. Then raise the screw about two inches, and with a piece of bent wire pull up on the rope handle of the wooden plunger until it floats to the top, so that the hot water may again saturate the contents of the burlap. In about one minute apply the pressure again

Fig. 16.—The press tipped up on edge to allow the last of the wax and water to run out.

slowly, until the limit has again been reached. Then release the pressure as before, and after this turn the screw down again for the last time. This whole process of pressing will take about ten minutes in all. While the pressure is still on the comb, remove the wooden covers from the can, and tip up the press as shown in Fig. 16, so that the water and wax may run out into a small tub or large pail on the floor under it. Leave the press turned over for a few moments until all of the water and wax drain out, and then tip it back to its regular position. An old sack or piece of carpet should be thrown across the top of the small tub to keep the wax from chilling until it is emptied into the large can, as explained later.

The screw should now be raised, the follower lifted out, and the burlap shaken into a box near by. If the piece of burlap is rub-

Fig. 17.—Hatch's outdoor furnace for melting comb.

bed quickly with the hands, most of the refuse can be shaken out. Now place this burlap over the press-can again, and repeat the process with another gallon of comb just as soon as possible. There should be no time wasted between the one pressing and another, for the can, follower, etc., are liable to become cold.

When the screw is turned down the first time on the next batch of melted combs, empty the hot water and wax in the shallow tub into the large can near by ready for it.

For convenience this can should have a faucet or gate at the bottom so that hot water may be drawn off when it gets too full, th s hot water to be used over again in the next boiler of comb. It does not matter even if it is quite black and thick, for experience has shown that this dark-colored water does not discolor the wax. A piece of carpet should be kept over the top of this large can in order that the wax may not become chilled. At the end of the day, or whenever the work is over, the hot water may be drawn out until just before the wax begins to come. The wax may then be run out into suitable molds, which, if made of metal, should be well moistened on the inside with soapsuds to prevent the wax from sticking.

The refuse from the press, which has been shaken out in a large box, *is not yet free from wax*, and this point should be plainly understood. We have found that one treatment as above described will remove only 90 per cent of the total amount of wax. The refuse will look perfectly clean and dry, and many will be deceived and throw it away, thinking it not worth a second melting; but from quite a good many samples that we have tested from different lots of refuse that have been sent in from other producers, we are very sure that there is a waste of from eight to ten per cent of the wax unless this refuse is run through the press again. For this reason, when a sufficient amount is accumulated it is well to put it back in one of the boilers and boil it again in water. The second treatment will take a little over half the time the first did, since rather more can be pressed at a time; but the average bee-keeper can well afford to do it. Wax from very old combs can be extracted in this unheated press, even though it is gone over twice, at the rate of about seven or eight pounds an hour, and the final waste need not be over three per cent.

An important fact that must not be overlooked is that the quality of wax from this press is the very best. The cakes need only a little scraping on the bottom, to be ready for market. The color is good, so that there is no need of refining the wax afterward. If the combs were melted up without water, however, the wax would very probably be discolored from too high a temperature.

The above plan sounds somewhat complicated, but it has been found to be no more so than most methods of rendering wax. Of course it is not possible to do work of this kind without making some muss, and it is always a good deal better if the work can be done in a basement or in a shed where it does not make so much difference if a little wax is spilled. If the work is done in a kitchen, the floor should be well covered with newspapers, which can afterward be taken up and burned. When boiling comb in a boiler, great care should be exercised to prevent the wax from boiling over on the stove and possibly causing a fire.

When diseased combs are rendered, every precaution should be taken to prevent bees from robbing. If the building can not be made bee-tight, the work should be done at night, and every tool and utensil used should be thoroughly scalded again before daylight. The refuse from diseased combs should be burned or buried immediately, and the water that was used should be poured where the bees can not possibly get access to it.

HOW TO RENDER WAX WITH HOME-MADE APPLIANCES.

The unheated press is not difficult to construct, as there are no materials used that could not be obtained easily. If one should have on hand an old lard-press he can make few changes and get along quite well by using it for rendering wax. See Fig. 18. Usually, however, the threads of the screw used in a lard-press are rather too coarse to give the pressure needed without making it necessary to exert a very great amount of strength in turning the screw. There are many erroneous ideas concerning the pressure which can be exerted by a screw. For instance, it is not the diameter of the screw that determines the pressure, but the pitch of the thread. Screws which can be lowered as much as half an inch in a single complete revolution will hardly be powerful enough for pressing out wax to the best advantage. It is better to have finer threads, so that less exertion is needed to do the work properly.

If one wishes to construct a good wax-press with as little trouble as possible he had better follow quite closely the design shown in Fig. 19. There are many things that must be taken into consideration in designing a wax-press; and we know that the one shown will be satisfactory, although, of course, it will not be quite so convenient as one made where the proper castings, etc, can be obtained.

A bench-vise screw will answer the purpose if the thread is not too coarse. Two half-inch rods threaded on each end 1 old

Fig. 18.—A lard-press modified for pressing wax.

the framework rigid; but it is advisable to use very large washers under the nuts, as the strain tends to sink small washers into the wood, even if oak is used. Thick iron plates with half-inch holes drilled in the centers would answer the purpose better than washers.

In making a press be very careful to see that every part is perfectly square and plumb; for if the screw is not absolutely vertical it is almost impossible to succeed. The secret of doing good work is to manage so that the cheese shall be the same thickness all the way through; and if the screw is not perpendicular to the platform it is impossible to do this.

In a home-made press, since it is hardly practicable to construct any thing without too much expense that will keep the follower always at right angles with the screw, it is necessary to place the old comb evenly in the box so that the follower shall go down

Fig. 19.—A good design for a home-made unheated press.

as straight as possible. In the illustration the screw rests on top of a thick iron plate on the follower to keep it from entering the wood.

Fig. 20 shows more clearly the construction of the pressing-box and the tin tray under it.

A solid wooden bottom might be made for the box, but the wax and hot water would leak through it too much, and so it is better to have nothing but cleats and allow both wax and hot water to run directly through them on to the tin tray and then out at the opening in front. The front piece of the box should be about half an inch narrower than the other sides, in order to give an opening for the wax to escape. The corners of the tin tray do not need to be soldered.

A press somewhat similar to this has been used with good satisfaction by Mr. E. D. Townsend, of Remus, Michigan. It will be noted that, in the old original Hatch-Gemmil press, Fig. 9, a tin tray is also used in connection with the wooden pressing-box;

in fact, this home-made press is very similar to that one, except that it is simpler, stronger, and easier to construct.

It must be borne in mind that, since there is no way to fill the pressing-box with boiling hot water and allow it to remain full until thoroughly heated, when starting work, boiling water must be poured over the box and contents until they are thoroughly heated; and then if the work is continuous the parts will not become cold enough to chill the wax.

A plain square box would burst if the corners were not strengthened, hence it is necessary to bind them by nailing on pieces of very heavy tin or galvanized iron as shown. Thus reinforced the box is amply strong.

SCREW PRESSURE VS. LEVER.

A long heavy lever may be preferred in place of a screw, and in some places it may be easier to construct and operate. The same plan can be followed as that shown in Fig. 6. It is very necessary to guide the lever in some way in order to keep the pressure always vertically above the center of the pressing-box. It is much more difficult to handle a lever than a screw, for there is so much weight to manage. The argument is often advanced that the lever is preferable for the reason that the operator can

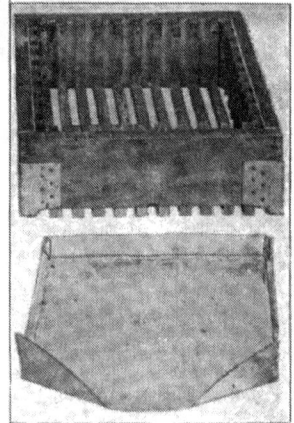

Fig. 20.—Pressing-box and tin tray of the home-made press.

leave it alone, knowing that the pressure will be applied constantly if heavy weights are hung on the end. While this point is valuable in connection with pressing combs submerged in boiling water, as shown in Fig. 6, it is of little advantage in the unheated press; for left for even a few minutes the wax would chill and the press become cold. Quite thorough work with the unheated press is possible if rapidly done; but if the combs are left they soon cool off, so that it is necessary to heat thoroughly everything with boiling water before going on.

If a lever is used, a very heavy construction is necessary unless one end is securely anchored to a stump. It is seldom that a wall or floor in a building can be found heavy enough to withstand the pressure of a 12-foot lever without giving away. In most places, therefore, a screw is much more convenient and easier to manage.

WHICH IS THE BEST METHOD TO RENDER WAX?

The answer to this question depends entirely upon circumstances. If cappings or new comb are to be rendered, and there is no particular need of doing rapid work, a solar extractor is the best by all means, as it works for nothing and boards itself. For rendering large quantities of cappings or new comb we think the unheated press is the best one to use, as the bulk of the wax can be simply dipped off the top of the hot water into molds to harden, leaving only a comparatively small amount of refuse to be run through the press.

For general rendering of old combs we believe the unheated press to be the most practical for the average bee-keeper. It is not possible to do quite as thorough work with this press, but the relatively small amount of loss of from two to three per cent of the total amount of wax would not warrant the average bee-keeper in going to the expense of purchasing or making a large hot-water press. It is our opinion that the producer who makes less than 300 pounds of wax per year can do no better than to follow the plan here described, using the unheated press. Some may want to know why a very small hot-water press would not be the best for the small bee-keeper; but we have never found such economical, if the time and fuel required are taken into consideration.

For the larger producer who makes more than 300 pounds of wax a year we believe a good-sized hot-water press is a real necessity. By having the capacity very large, a large amount of wax can be produced in a day, leaving less than one per cent of the wax in the refuse.

THE AMOUNT OF WAX IN COMBS.

We are often asked how much wax can be rendered from comb holding a given amount of honey; but it is quite difficult to answer such questions, as it makes considerable difference whether full sheets of foundation were used, and also whether such foundation was thick or thin. In general, however, we might say that it requires about 4 lbs. of wax in comb to hold 100 lbs. of honey; or, in other words, that a pound of new comb will hold about 25 lbs. of honey.

A sixteen-ounce section of honey consists approximately of 14½ ounces of honey—a little over one-half ounce of wax and about one ounce of wood. Fig. 21 shows the re-

Fig. 21.— Honey pressed from a section; result — over 14 ounces honey, ½ ounce wax, and 1 ounce of wood.

sults after separating the honey, wax, and wood, in a sixteen-ounce section. Of course, these results, as before mentioned, are not always the same, and the different amounts vary considerably.

On one occasion we melted over 600 lbs. of candied comb honey. Keeping careful account of the weights, we found that the percentages of honey, wax, and wood were approximately 88, 5, and 7, respectively.

HOW TO REFINE WAX WITH SULPHURIC ACID.

Wax cakes, as they are bought up, are usually of all grades and colors. The difference in color is due largely to the amount of impurities the wax contains. In all the years that we have been in the business we have found no practical or satisfactory way of bringing the wax to a yellow color—that is, to its original state of purity, except by treating it with acid.

The method, in brief, is as follows: Fill a wooden tank or barrel a quarter full of water, and add cakes of wax until nearly full. The water is then boiled until all the wax is melted, when a quantity of commercial sulphuric acid is poured in, and the boiling continued until all is thoroughly mixed. The heat is then removed and the impurities allowed to settle.

For a detailed account, it may be well to describe our own system of refining wax.

Our tank is a little over 3½ feet in diameter, and about 5 feet high. Water is run into it to a depth of 12 inches, and then 1500 lbs. of wax is thrown in, making it about full. The mass is then heated by means of a jet of steam from a pipe projecting down into the water from the top. When all the wax is melted, the acid is poured in. Dark wax to make brood foundation requires three pints of acid; but if light enough for surplus foundation, not more than 1½ pints is used. If the wax is already of good quality, so small an amount as one pint of acid will answer. On the average, therefore, we use one quart of acid in 80 gallons of water for 1500 lbs. of wax. Soon after this is poured in, the color of the boiling wax will be seen to grow lighter, and, after a minute or so, the boiling is stopped.

The steam-pipe is now drawn out, the tank covered with a cloth or carpet, and allowed to stand as long as the wax will remain liquid, or about 24 hours. At the expiration of this time the water and acid will have settled to the bottom by reason of their greater specific gravity; and the acid, in turn, having a greater specific gravity than that of water, will settle below the water; and the consequence is, that the wax itself, after being purified, is allowed to become thoroughly cleansed of any residue of acid, and the dirt accumulation, all have settled beneath the wax into the water. The melted wax is now drawn off from the top, and poured into any sort of receptacles with flaring sides. When the wax is nearly all removed or shows evidence of coming near the dirt, the rest is allowed to stand. As soon as it cakes in the tank it is lifted out, and the dirt clinging to the bottom scraped off.

We do not recommend the use of acid for refining wax on a small scale, for, without proper receptacles and facilities for heating, the wax is more often injured than benefited.

BLEACHING BEESWAX.

There are methods by which beeswax can be bleached by the use of chemicals; but after some experimenting we have not been successful with any of them, and finally discovered that, for the economic uses of the bee-keeper, foundation made of bleached wax was no better than if as good as that having the natural yellow color, refined by the use of sulphuric acid as explained elsewhere. Yellow wax is more ductile, and therefore more easily worked by the bees; and even when used for section honey-boxes, the combs from yellow wax are about as white

as those from the bleached; so that when capped over, no one can tell the difference. But very often dealers have a call for bleached beeswax; and the only practical way of getting it is to convert the product into thin sheets or small particles, and then subject them to the sun's rays for a suitable length of time. When sufficiently bleached it may be melted up and caked.

The illustration given on next page shows how it is done at a large wax-working establishment where wax-bleaching is made a specialty. We refer to the firm that was formerly Eckerman & Will, of Syracuse, N. Y., but now bearing the name of Will & Baumer. The wax is reduced to thin sheets or shreds, or, what is often done, is allowed to drop on a revolving cylinder, forming small chunks or drops, as it were, which immediately cool. These particles of wax, or thin sheets, are spread on canvas trays, and then exposed to the rays of the sun until they are bleached. When the wax is first put out it packs more or less and has to be frequently showered with water, or raked over, to keep it loose so that the air and sun can get at it. If the process has been properly carried on, the finished product, when caked, will be of a pearly whiteness.

At this factory of Will & Baumer, immense quantities of candles are made for sacramental purposes of the Roman Catholic Church, which prefers them of pure beeswax. Some are of immense size, but all are not made of pure beeswax. Paraffine is used very largely for the purpose, and the small candles for lawn-fetes and Christmas times, variously colored, are probably wholly paraffine, because that article costs less than half as much as beeswax.

HOW TO DETECT ADULTERATED WAX.

We have already mentioned the fact that beeswax is liable to adulteration with paraffine or ceresin, and sometimes with ordinary bee-keepers, after brimstoning their old grease or fat. Some unscrupulous box-hive "skeps," and melting up the wax,* add just enough tallow to increase the weight, because grease is cheap compared with the ordinary product of the hive. But such adulterations are very easily detected, both by smell and sight. The cakes have a greasy smell and feeling; and when subjected to the float test, presently described, they will immediately rise to the top of the liquid. Paraffine and ceresin adulterations are not so easily recognized; but nearly all pure bees-

*See BOX HIVES and STRAW SKEPS.

wax, when chewed for a few minutes, will crumble in fine particles, while wax containing a small percentage of paraffine or ceresin will chew like sealing-wax and ordinary chewing-gum.

The simplest and most reliable test is the float or specific-gravity test. We have already stated that the specific gravities of our ordinary commercial paraffines and ceresins are below that of beeswax. As an ordinary article of pure beeswax is lighter than water (wax standing 965 and water at 1000), of course it will float when put into that liquid. Into a jar partly filled with water pour alcohol until a small piece of beeswax of known

gradually settle to the bottom of the jar, perhaps standing upon a single point.

For all practical purposes we have found this float test to be entirely reliable; that is, it has so far shown us unerringly every adulterated sample. We remember particularly one instance where quite a large shipment of beeswax was sent us. It was very beautiful, and the cakes were all of a uniform size; but the price was very low. It was suspicious, and accordingly we subjected it to the float test. Sure enough, a small piece of the wax stayed nicely on top of the test liquid without the least effort. We then put it into a liquid that would let a 25-

FACTORY AND BLEACHING-YARD OF WILL & BAUMER, SYRACUSE, N. Y.

purity settles to the bottom, taking care not to pour in too much alcohol, for we want the wax to sink just to the bottom; that is, we desire the alcoholic liquid and the wax to be of the same specific gravity. Now, then, if we put in a piece of adulterated beeswax containing, say, 50 per cent of paraffine or ceresin, it will float on the surface of the liquid. Now take another piece of wax that contains only 10 per cent of adulteration. It still floats, but has a tendency to sink almost under the surface. If we take another piece containing only 5 per cent, it may float or

per cent ceresin adulteration sink. After hovering near the surface it gradually sank, and behaved like the piece of wax that we knew contained 25 per cent of ceresin. We wrote to the shipper that we did not want adulterated beeswax; that we *must* have the pure article; that he had got to take the stuff off our hands. He did it very promptly, without even trying to defend himself, any more than to say that he thought we were not very particular. He knew better, but thought he could unload the stuff on us without our being any the wiser.

CLEANING WAX FROM UTENSILS.

Perhaps the readiest means is to immerse them in boiling water until all the wax is thoroughly melted off, then drain, while kept hot, until the wax which adheres to them when being lifted from the water is thoroughly melted, and can be wiped off with soft newspaper. Where the article can not be easily immersed, benzine or a solution of sal-soda will readily dissolve the wax so it can be cleaned off with a cloth. Benzine dissolves wax almost as readily as water dissolves sugar.

Caution in handling wax.—We have spoken about order, care, and cleanliness, in handling honey, candy, etc.; now, friends, it is a much more serious thing to daub melted wax about the house, on the carpets and on your clothes, than it is to daub either honey or candy. You can very easily spoil a dollar's worth of clothing while fussing with 10 cents' worth of wax, as we know by experience. When you commence, bear this in mind, and resolve that you are going to have things clean and neat at every step, no matter what the cost. Newspapers are very cheap, and it takes but a minute to spread them all around the room where wax may be dropped.

WEIGHT OF BEES.

Some very interesting experiments were conducted by Prof. B. F. Koons, of the Agricultural College, Storrs, Ct., to determine the weight of bees and the amount of honey they can carry. The results of these experiments were given in *Gleanings in Bee Culture;* and the article is so valuable we have thought best to preserve it in permanent form :

Some two years ago, in a leisure hour I went to my apiary and captured one outgoing bee from every hive and subjected them to the fumes of cyanide of potassium for a few moments to render them inactive, and then weighed each bee upon our chemical balances—a pair of scales so delicately adjusted that it is an easy matter to weigh the one-millionth part of a pound or the one-thousandth part of a bee. From the weight of each separate bee it was a very simple problem in arithmetic to compute the number of bees in a pound. The results showed that mine, which perhaps are a fair average in size and weight, ran from 4141 to 5669 in a pound. These results you published in *Gleanings,* and there expressed a wish that I would also determine the amount of honey carried by a homing bee. In my research for the weight of bees I took those just leaving the hive, which naturally would represent the normal weight, without extra honey or pollen.

During the present summer, when the bees were very active, I have undertaken to carry out your request as to the amount of honey carried by a bee.

My method was this : From the chemical laboratory I secured a couple of delicate glass flasks with corks, marking them A and B. Each was very carefully weighed, and the weight recorded. I then went to a hive, and, with the aid of a pair of delicate pliers, or pincers, I captured a number of incoming bees and dropped them into flask A. I then secured about an equal number of outgoing bees in flask B. These were then taken to the laboratory immediately, and each flask again weighed, after which the bees were carefully counted and released. This operation was repeated quite a number of times, not on the same day, but as opportunity offered, and when the bees were bringing in an abundance of honey. I captured from 20 to 45 bees for each flask at each trip, aiming to have, as n early as might be, the same number in each flask on any particular trip. I always weighed the flasks before starting out, lest some little bit of soil or stain, or even moisture on the glass, would render the results less accurate; I also always allowed any moisture condensed upon the inside of the flasks, while the bees were confined, to evaporate before weighing for another trip. I then treated my results as follows : From the weight of flask and bees I deducted the weight of the flask; the remainder I divided by the number of bees confined on that trip. This gave me the average weight of the bees captured at that time. The average weight of the bees in flask A, or loaded bees, was always greater, as it should be, than the average weight of the bees in flask B, or unloaded bees. The difference between these two weights gave me the average amount of honey carried by that lot of bees.

Mine are Italian and hybrid bees, but I made no attempt to determine the difference in the amount carried by the different swarms or breeds. I kept no record of the swarms except that I guarded against going to the same hive for a second lot of bees. A considerable difference does appear, but probably that arises in part from the abundance or scarcity of honey on any particular day when the colony was visited. My aim was to secure reliable results, as nearly as possible representing the average amount of honey carried by bees.

The following is the result of weighing several hundred each, of returning and outgoing bees. The smallest number of bees necessary to carry one pound of honey, as shown by my results, is 10,154 ; or, in other words, one bee can carry the $\frac{1}{10154}$ (one ten thousand one hundred and fifty-fourth) part of a pound of honey; and the largest number, as shown by the results, required to carry a pound is 45,642; and the average of all the sets weighed is 20,167. Perhaps, then, it is approximately correct to say that the average load of a bee is $\frac{1}{20000}$ (one twenty thousandth) of a pound; or, in other words, if a colony has 20,000 bees in it, and each one makes one trip a day, they will add the pound to their stores. Of course, not all the bees in a colony leave the hive, the nurses remaining at home, hence necessitating more trips of those which do "go a-field."

I also repeated my observations of two years ago on the weight of bees, and found that my numbers ran from 3690 to 5495 in a pound, and the average about 4800, the same as in my former test. I likewise secured the following on the weight of drones: Of a dozen or more weighed, the largest would require 1808 to make a pound, and the smallest 2122, or an average of about 2000 drones in a pound, over against nearly 5000 workers.   B. F. Koons.

Agricultural College, Storrs, Ct., Sept. 3, 1895.

In a nutshell, and speaking in round numbers, we may say that it takes 4800 bees to make a pound; and that, while 10,000 bees may carry a pound of nectar, twice that number, or 20,000, is probably more nearly the average. During basswood bloom, the first figure should be considered as the nearer correct one because the bees drop down at the entrance; but from almost all other sources of nectar the twenty-thousand mark is the one to accept.

Let us now look at these interesting figures in another way: A bee *can* carry half its weight in nectar; and perhaps, under certain circumstances, a trifle more; but, generally speaking, one-fourth its weight is the amount. A single strong colony has been known to bring in a trifle over 20 lbs. of nectar from basswood in one day;* but usually four or five pounds is considered a

the latter of the Ohio Experiment Station, conducted a series of experiments which closely approximate figures of Prof. Coons, so we are sure they are correct.

WEAK COLONIES, TO STRENGTHEN. See UNITING, sub-head ALEXANDER PLAN; also NUCLEUS.

WHITEWOOD (*Liriodendron Tulipifera*). This is often called the tulip-tree, we suppose from its tulip-shaped flowers.

After writing the foregoing, we concluded we did not know very much about the whitewood, especially the blossoms. So we traveled off into the woods, where we found a tree; but there were only buds to be seen, not blossoms. It must be too early in the season; but hark! whence come those sounds of humming-birds and humming bees? Whence, too, that rare and exquisite perfume? We

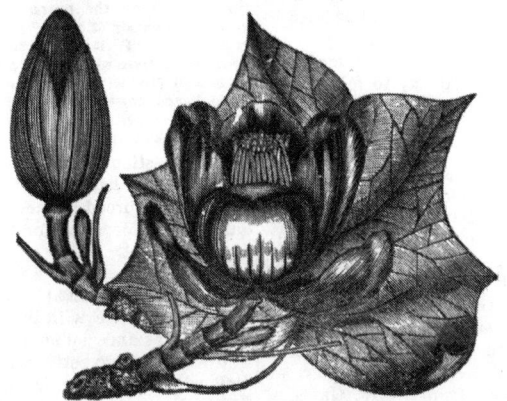

LEAF, BUD, AND BLOSSOM OF THE WHITEWOOD, OR TULIP-TREE.

remarkably big day's work. If we figure that there were, say, in the first instance (20 lbs. per day), 8 lbs. of bees, there would be 38,400 bees. If 20,000 of these were field-bees (estimating 10,000 necessary to carry a single pound of basswood nectar), those bees must have made forty trips. On the same basis of calculation, a colony of equal strength that brought in 5 lbs. would make one-fourth as many trips, or an even ten. This would leave for each trip one hour for ten hours; or, in the case of 20 lbs. a day, twenty minutes.

Both Profs. Gillette and Lazenby, the former of the Colorado Experiment Station and

looked higher, and, away in the misty top of the tree discerned, by the light of the setting sun, multitudes of bees flitting about. Oh that we were just up there! We looked at the rough trunk of the tree, and meditated that we were boys no longer, but forty years of age, or would be in a few months more. We might get up to that first limb: after a good deal of kicking and puffing, we did. The next was a harder pull yet; but soon the limbs were thicker, and finally we began to crawl upward with about as much ease as our year-and-a-half-old baby goes upstairs whenever she can elude maternal vigilance. Up, up, we went, until, on looking down, we really began to wonder what that blue-eyed baby and her mamma would do should our clumsy boots slip, or a dead limb break un-

* We had one colony that brought in over 43 lbs. in three days; and Doolittle 66 lbs. in the same time from basswood.

expectedly. Now we were at the very summit of the tree, and, oh what a wonderful beauty we saw in those tulip-shaped blossoms that peeped from the glossy-green foliage all about us! No wonder there was humming. Bumble-bees, gaudy-colored wasps, yellow Italians, and last, but not least, beautifully plumaged humming-birds, were all rejoicing in a feast of sweets. Every now and then one of the latter paused before our very face, and, as he swung pendulously in mid air, winked his bright little eyes, as much as to say, "Why, what on earth can *you* be doing away up here in our domain?"

We picked off the great orange-colored, mottled blossoms, and looked for the honey. We presume it was the wrong time of day to expect much; but inside, those large petals seemed to be distilling a kind of dark dew that the birds and insects were licking off. It tasted to us more like molasses than honey. In the cut our engraver has tried to show you what we saw in the tree-top.

As the sun had gone down, we commenced in a rather undignified way to follow suit, and, after resting a little, limped home. Although stiff and sore, we carried an armful of whitewood blossoms to surprise the good folks who, probably, had never dreamed of the beauties to be seen only in the tree-tops

Our friends in the South have a great deal to say about what they call "poplar honey;" and, if we are correct, the poplar is the same tree which we call whitewood. It blossoms with them in April and May. We know what time it blossoms here, for we thought about its being the 27th of May, when sliding down out of that tree. Shortly after, we received some bees from G. W. Gates, of Bartlett, Tenn. The combs were filled, even bulged out with a dark honey, such as we have described, and the bees had built fins of snow-white comb on the cover of their shipping-box. From this we infer the honey must be yielded in great abundance in those localities. We have seen it stated that the large flowers sometimes yield a spoonful of honey each. As the tree is often used for ornament, we make the following extract from *Fuller's Forest-Tree Culturist:*

LIRIODENDRON TULIPIFERA *(Tulip-tree, Whitewood).*

Leaves smooth, on slender petioles, partially three-lobed, the middle one appearing as though cut off; flowers about two inches broad, bell-shaped, greenish yellow, marked with orange; seeds winged, in a large cone-shape cluster which falls apart in autumn. The figure shows a single seed as it appears when separated from the mass. It blooms in May and June, and the seeds ripen in late summer or early autumn, and should be sown as soon as

ripe, in good, moderately dry soil. They may remain in the seed-bed two years if desirable, but should receive a slight protection the first winter; tree of large size, sometimes 130 feet high, with a very straight stem; wood light color, greenish white, soft and light, not hard enough to receive a polish. It is much used in cabinet work, and for making panels for carriages, and for any inside work where toughness or a hard surface is not required. There is perhaps no native wood that will shrink more in seasoning than whitewood, for it not only shrinks sidewise but endwise as well; yet when once thoroughly seasoned it remains fixed, and does not warp or twist like many of the hard and tough kinds of wood. There is also much difference in the character of the wood coming from different sections of the country, and mechanics who are conversant with the various kinds and localities will readily tell whether specimens came from the West or East. The latter is of a light greenish color, grain not so smooth and soft, and sometimes rather tough. The wood is but little used, except for the purposes mentioned above, and consequently it is only large trees that are of much value. It is one of the most beautiful ornamental trees we possess, growing in a conical form, and producing an abundance of beautiful tulip-shaped flowers in spring. The roots are soft and sponge-like, and it requires great care in removing to insure success.

The question is often asked, "Is whitewood good for bee-hives?" It may do for sections and brood-frames, but it is very unsatisfactory for hives, for the reasons given in this extract.

WILLOW (*Salix.*) We have had little or no experience with this shrub. It does yield honey and pollen in some localities, and we can do no better than to copy an article with engravings, from the pen of G. M. Doolittle, as given in *Gleanings in Bee Culture*, p. 486, Vol. XVII.:

Among the pollen-bearers we have several kinds of what is known here as "pussy willow" (*Salix*) which put out their blossoms quite irregularly. Some are a month earlier than others, and some of the buds on the same bush are ten days later than others. The kinds which seem to attract the bees most are the black willow, upon which the kilmarnock is budded, and those which produce a long cone-like flower similar to the black willow. The accompanying cut gives a fair representation of the latter, a week or so after it is through blossoming and has partially gone to seed. From these two kinds the bees obtain large quantities of pollen, but, so far as I can ascertain, no honey. As this pollen comes the first of any which we have which amounts to any thing, I esteem it of great value to the bees. Skunk-cabbage gives pollen a little earlier, but we do not have enough of it to amount to much, compared with what these willows give. The flowers are of a rich orange color, having a center out of which spring hundreds of little thread-like filaments, upon which the pollen is supported. It is very interesting to see the bees work on these flowers, as you can see their motions plainly, for the tree or bush does not grow so high but that some of the lower limbs are about on a level with the eye. Here is a peculiarity of the willows, for all those in this section which give pollen grow in bush form, while all of those which yield honey grow to be quite large trees, often reaching six feet in circumference.

PUSSY WILLOW.

The pussy willow naturally grows on low swampy ground; but with a little culture to start, it will grow readily on dry ground. It grows readily from cuttings put in the ground in early spring, as do all of the willow tribe. The above are often set down as "honey-plants;" but, according to Quinby and my own observation, they produce no honey. As they grow plentifully about here, I have made close observation regarding them. To be sure, the bee is continually poking its proboscis into the blossoms, the same as it does when seeking for honey; but after killing many bees and dissecting them, I have been unable to find the least bit of honey in their sacs. This, when bees are at work on any of the honey-bearing flowers, never fails to reveal any honey they are getting.

HONEY-PRODUCERS.

Of these we have three kinds—the golden willow, the white willow, and the weeping willow, and they are of value as honey-producers in the order named. The weeping willow blossoms about three days earlier than the others, which would make it of more value to the bees, even did it not yield honey quite so profusely, if there were enough trees to keep the bees busy; but there are very few trees of this kind about here to render it of any account. None of the three willows mentioned here give any pollen that I ever could discover, for none of the bees at work on these trees ever have any of it in their pollen-baskets. If there is any species of willow which yields both honey and pollen, I am not acquainted with it. The flowers are similar to those which grow on the birch and poplar, being of a long tag-like shape, as large as a slate pencil and from one to two inches long. Those on the golden willow are the longest, and yield honey abundantly.

The engraving presented herewith so nearly represents the golden willow that any one should know it in connection with its yellow bark, which distinguishes it from the other kinds of honey-yielding willow, as all of the rest, so far as I know, have a

light-green bark. When these willows are in bloom, and the weather warm, the bees rush out of their hives at early dawn, and work on it all day long as eagerly as they do on clover or basswood. The blossoms often secrete honey so profusely that it can be seen glistening in the morning by holding the blossom between you and the sun, while the trees resound with that dull busy hum from morning till night, so often heard when bees are getting honey. As this is the very first honey of the season, I consider it of the greatest value to the bees, for brood is now crowded forward with great "vim," giving us the bees which work on white clover, while the honey often helps very greatly in piecing out the depleted stores of the hive. These willows blossom a little in advance of the hard maple, yet hold out equally long; and from the fact that, when I kill a bee at work on these willows I always find honey in its sac, while when I do the same to a bee at work on the maple I never find any, I have been led to think that perhaps those reporting honey from maples might be mistaken, and that the honey really came from the willows. Again, maple blossoms only every other year with us, while the willows never fail; and I have noticed for years that I get fully as much honey in the years when the maples do not bloom as when they do. From the few trees along a small creek near here, my bees frequently make a gain of from six to ten pounds of honey while the willows are in bloom, and one season they made

GOLDEN WILLOW.

gain of 15 pounds. This present spring some of my best colonies gained 8 pounds, while on apple-bloom they did not get more than a living from apple-orchards white with bloom all about. The honey from the willow is quite similar to that from the apple-bloom, and has a nice aromatic flavor. As the willows give the first pollen, and also the first honey each season, it will be seen what a great help they are to all who have them in profusion near their bees. The only drawback is the weather often being unfavorable, for I do not think that more than one year in three gives good weather all through the time willows are in blossom. So far as I know, honey and pollen are always present in the respective kinds when in bloom; but the trouble is, that it is too cold, rainy, cloudy, or windy for the bees to get to the trees so much of the time, at this season of the year, that honey or pollen from this source is not at all certain.

Borodino, N. Y. G. M. DOOLITTLE.

WILLOW-HERB. Often called fire-weed, sometimes Indian pink, and rose bay. The scientific name is *Epilobium angustifolium*. Its growth is confined to the lumbering regions of Northern Wisconsin, Minnesota, Michigan, Canada, Washington State, and Maine, upon areas that have been burned over, hence the name "fireweed." After forest fires it seems to spring up spontaneously, monopolizing the soil to itself. Sometimes it grows in localities never so devastated.

at least so we thought after eating some at one of the Michigan conventions which we attended at Grand Rapids. Mr. Hutchinson styles it the whitest and sweetest honey he ever tasted, and says the flavor, while not very pronounced, is suggestive of spice. The quality of the honey, its unfailing supply from year to year, following right after clover and basswood, and blooming from then on till frost, make it one of the most valuable honey-plants known. Unfortunately its growth is confined almost exclu-

WILLOW-HERB AND ITS HOME (FROM THE BEE-KEEPERS' REVIEW).

It is a handsome plant, usually only a single stalk growing from two to six feet high. The flowers are dark pink, arranged in clusters around the stalk. As the season advances, the first bloom goes to seed; and as the stalk extends upward, more blossoms appear, so the plant keeps in bloom from July till frost. Thus appear on each stalk buds, blossoms, and seed-pods at the same time.

Willow-herb, or fireweed, yields quantities of white honey. Some of it is so light-colored as to be actually as clear and limpid as water, having flavor simply superb—

sively to the regions where forest fires occur. But bee-keepers situated in its vicinity are enabled to secure immense crops of fine white honey. Another remarkable feature of the plant is, it yields every year—at least so continuously that a failure has scarcely been known, even by the oldest inhabitants in the vicinity where it grows.

Mr. Hutchinson estimates there are thousands of acres in Northern Michigan where this plant grows, without bees to gather its delicious nectar. But this condition certainly can not long exist; for where one can produce anywhere from 100 to 125 pounds of comb honey per colony, unoccupied fields will soon be covered by bee-keepers, after the manner of the rush of the gold-seekers to the Klondike.

For the fine illustration on previous page we are indebted to the editor of the *Bee-keepers' Review*. The picture was taken when the willow-herb was out in all its glory. In the background appear the straight black shafts of dead pine-trees that stand out alone as the only survivals of their class from the fires. While we can not but de-

LATION. Some very important information is given under ENTRANCES, and it would be advisable to re-read that article before one takes up the matter further here. For management of bees in the spring, see SPRING MANAGEMENT. For a consideration of the different sizes and shapes of frames for wintering, see HIVES. For the discussion of double-walled or chaff hives, see HIVES.

TWO METHODS OF WINTERING BEES.

There are two methods in vogue. One is called the indoor and the other the outdoor

A. E. MANUM'S HOME APIARY IN WINTER.

plore the loss of the pines that furnish the only timber fit to make hives, we rejoice that they have been succeeded by so valuable a honey-plant.

All attempts to grow willow-herb out of its native habitats have been failures.

WINTERING. Whoever has gone over faithfully the preceding pages is now nearly ready to sum up the matter of wintering. Under the head of ABSCONDING SWARMS, in the opening of the book, and under the subject of UNITING, he has been cautioned against dividing, and trying to winter weak colonies. See *Absconding in Early Spring*, under the head mentioned. In regard to keeping bees warm through the winter with ARTIFICIAL HEAT, see that head. Concerning the effects of different kinds of food or stores on the welfare of bees during winter, see DYSENTERY, FEEDING AND FEEDERS, CANDY FOR BEES. On the subject of fixing the size of the entrances, see ENTRANCES TO HIVES, VENTI-

plan. Which one the reader shall use depends entirely on locality. Where the winters are extremely cold, with *continuous* freezing weather prevailing through December, January, February, and March, without any warm days intervening, the indoor or cellar plan of wintering bees is the one usually followed. In other places, say fifty or one hundred miles south of the great lakes, or where there is an occasional warm day, say one or two a month when bees may fly, the outdoor method of wintering in double-walled hives, or in single-walled hives with winter cases, is the plan generally in vogue. Throughout the Southern States the plain single-walled hives are warm enough without extra protection.

Indoor wintering in the colder localities does not require double-walled hives or winter cases; but when bees are set out in the spring, some protection should be provided.

Although cellar wintering requires less expensive hives, it involves more skill—especially so if the cellar or winter repository does not afford all the favorable conditions. Just what these are will be referred to later. While the outdoor method, on the other hand, demands double-walled hives, winter cases, or something to protect the hives on their summer stands, it does not require that degree of skill made necessary when the bees are confined in the cellar. Therefore, the majority of beginners, especially where the climate is not severe, are by all means advised to winter outdoors.

With either the indoor or outdoor plan it is fair to state that, after a very severe winter in which the mercury plays below the

Indeed, some have wintered their bees winter after winter with a loss not exceeding five per cent, if we throw out of calculation the one year in ten which proves abnormally severe.

OUTDOOR WINTERING.

This is the simpler and easier plan for most beginners to follow, and the principles involved help to lay the foundation for the more difficult problem of indoor or cellar wintering. The prime requisite for both methods of wintering is a large force of young bees reared during the latter part of summer or early fall. A colony made up of old wornout bees with very few young, no matter how strong, will be almost sure to succumb before spring, or reach such a weakened condition as to become practically worthless. As a general rule, in the Northern States brood-rearing ceases right after the honey-flow.

Fig. 2.—We prefer deep a telescoping cover to set over the packing-trays for our outdoor-wintered colonies.

zero-point for weeks at a time, and when spring is very late, with a warm spell followed by a very severe cold one, losses are likely to be heavy, even among the most experienced bee-keepers. But these losses can to a very great extent be minimized, even in bad years, provided one makes a study of his locality, regarding this general subject of wintering. It will, therefore, be the object of this article to set forth as nearly as possible some of the difficulties to be encountered, in order that the reader may intelligently undertake the problem. It is well to state, though, that the very severe winters referred to do not occur more than once in 10 or 20 years, when for some reason the whole year seems to be thrown entirely out of balance; but at all other times, if one follows carefully the directions here given his losses will not exceed ten per cent, and he may keep them down as low as two per cent.

Fig. 3.—Our top packing consists of a tray filled with planer-shavings.

This is perfectly normal where there is no late summer or fall pasturage like buckwheat; but during the latter part of August and the early part of September, brood-rearing should begin again: and unless there are natural sources of nectar the bees will require feeding with thin syrup given in small quantities daily to stimulate. See FEEDING. This stimulative feeding should be continued long enough to get a lot of brood in the hive so there will be a strong force of young bees to go into winter quarters In many localities colonies will be able to gather enough nectar daily to supply themselves with young bees without any special feeding. So far the scheme of raising a large force of young bees is an important requisite for either method of wintering, but especially important where bees are wintered outdoors subjected to extremes of temperature requiring a large consumption of stores in order to keep up necessary heat.

It is unwise to attempt to winter bees outdoors in single-walled hives north of 40 degrees north latitude. While the colonies may come through after a fashion, the shock of the exposure will be so great that they probably will not be good for much to gather honey. It is, therefore, important that

Fig. 4.—The super-cover is made of three-eighths lumber, tin-bound at the ends. This should be sealed down by the bees to insure good wintering at Medina, and covered with the tray shown in Fig. 3.

the hives be protected from high winds, and that the walls surrounding the hive be double and warm. Special double - walled hives are manufactured, having the space between filled with chaff, planer-shavings, leaves, or other suitable material. (See HIVES for detail of construction.) The cover or roof should also be double so that the heat of the cluster will not too readily radiate away, thus causing a great consumption of stores in order to keep up the necessary animal heat; for it should be remembered that, the warmer and better protected the cluster, the less honey they require to eat. It is desirable to have the bees, so far as possible, enter a quiet state of sleep, or semi-hibernation, that practically amounts to a condition of suspended animation. But an extremely cold spell will make it necessary for this cluster to unfold and consume its stores in

order to keep up the temperature. When, therefore, a colony is so poorly protected that it has to overeat in order to keep warm, their intestines become distended, and dysentery or purging is almost sure to follow. This occurring in mid-winter or early spring means the death of the colony, as there is no cure for it but warm weather.

A hive having double walls well packed, with warm cushions on top, and a good cover, makes about as good a winter home as it is possible to construct. A tray containing chaff, planing-mill shavings, or forest leaves resting under the telescope cover keeps the top warm. A large cushion may be used instead but is not so good.

Because double - walled hives are somewhat expensive, many bee-keepers start with single-thickness hives, intending to winter, perhaps, indoors. How shall they be prepared and yet

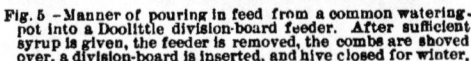

Fig. 5 –Manner of pouring in feed from a common watering-pot into a Doolittle division-board feeder. After sufficient syrup is given, the feeder is removed, the combs are shoved over, a division-board is inserted, and hive closed for winter.

give as good results, practically, as can be obtained from the more expensive double-thickness hives? Very good outside winter cases are obtainable from supply-manufacturers, large enough to telescope down over the hive. The cover of the single-walled hive, if it projects over, as most of them do, should be removed, and what is known as a thin super-cover—that is, a thin board of the same width and length as the hive, substituted. Several folds of newspaper, old carpeting, or any other suitable material, should be laid crosswise and lengthwise over the top of the hive. Enough of them should be put on so that, when the

EXAMINING A COLONY IN A DOUBLE-WALLED CHAFF HIVE; THE CHAFF-TRAY CONTAIN-
ING PACKING-MATERIAL IS SHOWN AT THE LEFT.

W. T. DAVISON'S METHOD OF PACKING BEES IN STRAW FOR OUTDOOR WINTERING.

winter case is put on, it will telescope over, crowding the folds of newspaper or other packing material neatly around the inner

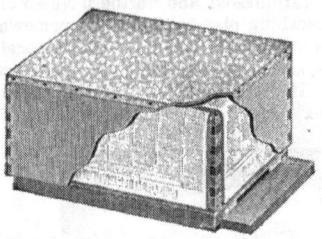

hive. The illustration herewith given will give some idea of the scheme here proposed.

TELESCOPE CAP.

Another plan, somewhat cheaper and possibly just as good, embodying the same principle, may be employed. Instead of having a winter case made of wood, the protection is made up of a large square of medium-weight manilla or roofing paper, laid on top of folds of newspaper as before directed, and then neatly folded down on the sides and ends as one would do up a package, and tied with a string as shown in the accompanying illustration. It should be stated, however, that this paper should be large enough so that, when folded down, it will reach to the

PAPER WINTER CASE.

bottom-board and not part of the way down as shown. It will also be important not to make the mistake of making the folds come down over the end of the hive in such a way that they will catch and hold water. In the two accompanying illustrations the method of wrapping and tying is shown. If one uses manilla paper it would, perhaps, be well to cover it with a coat of grease, or, better

still, linseed oil. In the spring one can examine his bees by loosening the bowknot of the string, lifting off the paper cover, and finally the packing under it. After examination, the paper can be readjusted as before, with the packing material underneath.

In cold localities this packing should not be less than two inches thick. If one can not secure enough newspapers perhaps he can contrive some scheme for using old carpeting or grain-sacks, especially such as are unfit for any other purpose. He can usually obtain quite a quantity of these by going to the farmer or miller; and he may (and probably will) receive free all he can take away.

A WINTER CASE MADE OF SECOND-HAND WRAPPING-PAPER AS USED AT MEDINA.

In selecting a roofing-paper for the purpose, avoid the heavy grades, as they are expensive, and do not fold readily; and, when folded, they will break on removing the string. A greased manilla paper, about like flour-sacking, gives very good results; any paper which will stand weather, and yet fold up flat again in summer after the cold winter weather and spring are over, will answer.

Some use, in place of the string to fasten the paper down, strips of wood tacked on; but a string is just as good, much cheaper, and quicker to apply; and, what is more, it does not in the least disturb the colony to tie it on the hive.

Another method of protecting the single-walled hives is to get some old drygoods-boxes. Pile straw on top of the hives, then push the large box back over the hive. But as these boxes are of such varieties of shapes and sizes they are not usually very satisfactory; and, besides, they do not shed rain unless covered with roofing-paper.

Another scheme is to put the hives in a row under a shed, leaving the point of least exposure in front. Straw is then packed in between the hives and in the rear, after which it is covered with boards to shed water.

sealed cover brings the bees through in better shape. In the colder climates, such as Northern Michigan, Canada, Northern Wisconsin, Minnesota, and Northern New York, the absorbing plan seems to have somewhat the preference, although we find advocates of the sealed-cover principle in these localities. If there is danger of the entrance becoming closed by deep snows or ice for

TOWNSEND'S METHOD OF PROTECTING HIVES AFTER SETTING THEM OUT IN THE SPRING.

But working hives under a shed is very inconvenient in summer, and therefore one is strongly urged to adopt the winter-case plan if he can not afford double-walled chaff hives.

SEALED COVERS OR ABSORBING CUSHIONS OVER THE CLUSTER OF BEES.

There has been considerable discussion in the bee-journals over the question of whether there should be loose porous absorb-

TWO-STORY DOUBLE-WALLED OR CHAFF HIVE.

ing cushions or other material placed above the cluster of bees so that the moisture from a cluster can pass up into the packing, or whether, on the other hand, the top of the hive should be sealed tight, and packing placed on top. In the milder climates it seems to be pretty well proven that the

weeks at a time, upward ventilation through porous packing would probably be safer, for bees must have air.

When the top of the hive is closed tight, the moisture from the bees collects on the under side of the cover, drips down, and passes out at the entrance. The absorbing cushions, on the other hand, in our climate

MODERN ONE-STORY DOUBLE-WALLED HIVE.

often become damp and soggy before spring. When in that condition they will sometimes freeze; and, so far from being a protection, they are a positive detriment. But where the climate is cold and dry, the temperature going down to 10 or 20 below zero, the absorbing cushions will be less damp than in a milder climate subject to more or less dampness on account of moist or rainy weather. When absorbing cushions are used, there must be a space of at least one inch over the top of the packing. In addition, there should be ventilating-holes so that the moisture can escape. But these holes should be so situated as to prevent rain or snow from blowing in.

When sealed covers are used, it takes less packing than when the absorbing plan is employed; but the entrances must be kept clear. If one has not decided which scheme to adopt, we suggest that he try the two side by side. We have tried sheets of glass the exact size of the tops of the hives. These are imbedded in putty, making a tight sealing between the glass and the hive. The packing material is then placed on top. We have wintered most successfully anywhere from one to a dozen colonies, during successive winters, under these sealed glass covers —not because there was any merit in the glass, but because we could better observe conditions. We could never see that this moisture that collects in drops at the corners ever did any harm. We would advise the average bee-keeper to use sealed covers until he determines by comparative tests that the absorbing plan and upward ventilation is better.

BEST KINDS OF PACKING MATERIAL.

Wheat or oat chaff, preferably the former, has been recommended as being the best material to use; but since the advent of new methods of separating the chaff from the wheat by means of a suction-fan, it is not now easy to obtain the chaff. We now recommend dry forest-leaves, plenty of them, or planer-shavings. Cut straw does very well. In milder climates, two thicknesses of old carpeting or burlap sacking will do. In colder climates we could use not less than six inches of packing. If the absorbing scheme is used, eight inches will be better.

SIZE OF ENTRANCES.

Under the head of ENTRANCES, to which the reader is referred, it is shown that the entrance should be reduced down so as not to be larger than ⅜x8 inches; and in the case of some of the smaller colonies it would be better to have the openings ⅜x3 or 4 inches. In all cases of outdoor wintering it is important to keep these entrances cˈe r, and it may, therefore, be necessary to rake out the dead bees now and then which may accumu-

late; for should the entrance become clogged the death of the colony must follow.

WINTER STORES—QUANTITY AND QUALITY.

We have now considered the inclosure, or the hives themselves, for holding a colony for outdoor wintering. Something should be said about the quantity and quality of the stores. It is fair to say that bees outdoors consume nearly twice as much as those indoors; but it is argued, on the other hand, that while the former consume this larger proportion of food they keep stronger numerically and will be in better condition at harvest time than those wintered indoors on half the amount. The opinion of the bee-keeping world is somewhat divided on this whole question; but certain it is that he who winters outdoors should provide twice the amount of stores, or at least see that his colonies, after the main brood-rearing has ceased, have from 20 to 25 lbs. of sealed stores. The beginner will need to weigh up his combs for the first colony or two, to be able to estimate approximately the stores of other colonies.

As a general thing an eight-frame colony should be crowded on six combs, and a ten on an eight. The division-board must be shoved up close to the frames, and empty space, if any, filled with leaves or other packing material. It is desirable that bees have stores given to them at least a month before they go into their winter sleep, so they may have a winter nest around which will be sealed stores within easy reach. As to quality, there is noth ng better than granulated-sugar syrup, although any good first-class table honey, if well ripened, will give as good results. Many bee-keepers pursue the policy of extracting all the honey and feeding sugar syrup. At the present price of sugar and honey one can afford to do this; and, moreover, the very act of feeding will stimulate rearing young bees. This in itself is worth all it costs.

Although a colony has sufficient stores by the middle or latter part of August it may run considerably short by the first of November, especially if a fall flow induces brood-rearing. In any case it is well to go over the colonies just prior to the final preparation for winter, and make sure they do not run short.

WINTERING BEES IN TENEMENT HIVES.

Some prominent bee-keepers, among whom may be named the late E. and N. E. France, of Wisconsin; W. L. Coggshall, of New York, and H. G. Quirin, of Bellevue, Ohio,

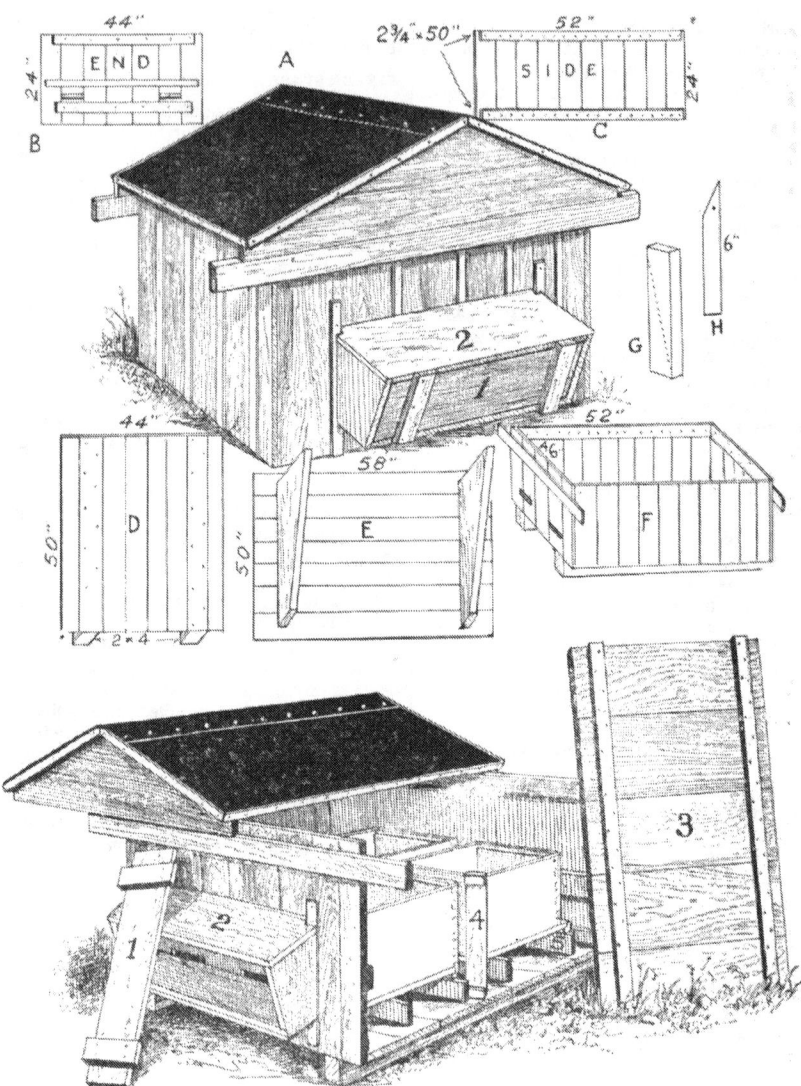

BARTLETT'S WINTER CASE FOR HOLDING FOUR TEN-FRAME COLONIES;
LOWER ILLUSTRATION SHOWING INTERIOR.

winter their bees in double-walled tenement hives. As the name indicates, it consists of two or more hives all under one roof. Of course, one double-walled hive large enough for four or five colonies can be made cheaper than four or five single hives, and this is one factor in their favor. Another is, that two or more colonies together conserve heat. But the objection to these big hives is that they are large, unwieldy, and not suitable for out-apiary work on account of difficulty in transportation. The big covers are heavy and awkward to lift or slide off. It is for this reason that so few bee-keepers, comparatively, use tenement hives.

WINTERING IN CELLARS OR SPECIAL REPOSITORIES.

In discussing methods for wintering bees outdoors, we have already given some principles that apply to cellar wintering. In the first place, we may say that bees do not require more than 10 or 15 lbs. of stores per colony, although it is an advantage to have more, because it is difficult to feed bees in the spring. With a strong force of young bees and good stores we are well equipped to winter bees in the cellar, provided we have reasonable control of temperature and means for ventilation. Before we go into the general subject of cellar wintering it is perhaps, important to specify two or three

IMPORTANT REQUISITES FOR A GOOD BEE-CELLAR.

First is the *control of temperature.* The ideal temperature is about 45 degrees F. It may go up to 50 or it may go down to 40; where possible the extremes should not exceed these figures. A greater variation early in the winter does less harm than later. As the winter approaches spring it becomes increasingly important that the temperature be held as nearly as possible at 45. If it goes too high the windows should be opened at night—never in day time—to let in air, and closed just before daylight. If it becomes too cold, so the temperature goes down below 40, or near freezing, artificial heat must be used. To that end a small stove connected with a chimney may be used to advantage. Build just enough fire to raise the temperature to 45 or a little more. As a general thing it will not be necessary to have a stove; for enough bees in the cellar will keep up the temperature by their own body heat. If a repository during the winter can not be kept cool enough by opening the windows at night, and closing them in the morning, it goes to show very plainly that the bee-keeper had better adopt outdoor wintering, as his climate is not cold enough to keep a cool cellar. A cellar that has a tendency to be too warm most of the time is a very poor place in which to winter bees. But one where the temperature can be kept uniformly at 45, not varying more than two or three degrees through the day, will not require much ventilation. Such a cellar must be mainly underground, and should have double doors to shut out frost, as well as double windows, if any.

It is important that the cellar be kept dark at all times; and by *dark* we mean absolutely so, without any light penetrating anywhere.

It is important, also, that the cellar be reasonably dry, although bees have wintered fairly well in damp cellars. If it is damp, the bottom muddy, and the temperature down much below 45, the effect on bees would not be satisfactory.

VENTILATION.

Authorities are not all agreed as to whether a bee-cellar should be ventilated or not. The question of air change depends almost entirely on the temperature of the cellar and its control. If the mercury can be kept uniformly at 45 throughout the entire winter with not more than two or three degrees variation it may be said that very little ventilation of the cellar will be needed; but if it has a tendency to go to 50 or more, then down, and especially if the bees begin to roar, showing uneasiness, then it is *very* important to let in large quantities of fresh air by opening the cellar-windows at night, or through sub-earth ventilators, as used by some. But if windows are opened they must be closed before daylight in order to shut out light. Some have found it better to let fresh air into an outer cellar and from there into the inner cellar where the bees are. It has been argued that air directly from outdoors has a tendency to stir up the bees; yet we have not found it so. Our experience is that, when bees are uneasy by being too warm, it is also because the air is foul. The obvious remedy is to let in cool air from the outside to reduce the temperature, and at the same time supply fresh oxygen.

Cellars should be large in proportion to the number of bees in them. A room 12 by 12, and 7 feet deep, will winter 50 colonies much better than it will 100. Ten colonies will come through in better condition than 50. The reason of this is simply a question of pure air. In some cases one may have access to a larger cellar that opens up into other compartments. If these compartments are not used, leave the doors open so that the air of the entire cellar can be available for the bees. A bee-cellar only 10 by 10, 7 feet deep, should not be used to winter more than 100 colonies, and will give better results with 50. A larger number may, of course, be crowded in, and will winter properly if enough ventilation can be given both day and night, keeping the temperature down to about 45.

SUB-EARTH VENTILATORS.

The sub-ventilator should be from four to six inches in diameter, made of tile, about 100 feet long, and from four to six feet below the surface of the ground. The outer end is brought to the surface of the ground, and the inner opens near the bottom of the cellar. Cold air entering the ventilator is warmed in passing under ground; and until it enters the cellar, not only supplying the latter with pure air, but at the same time raising its temperature several degrees.

SPECIAL REPOSITORIES OR A CELLAR UNDER THE HOUSE.

The ordinary cellar under a dwellinghouse often affords excellent conditions for wintering bees. Where a furnace is used to warm the house it should be shut off from the bee part by means of a brick wall having a door. Should the bee cellar get too cold the temperature can be raised by opening the door leading into the furnace-room. When it gets too warm, one can open an outside window; or, perhaps, better still, swing wide the cellar-door leading into the furnace, and thence, when tempered, into the bee-room. Hives properly shaded to shut out the direct rays of light will permit the doors left open day and night. If the temperature in the bee part can thus be maintained approximately at 45, the conditions for wintering will be ideal; for a perfect bee-cellar is one where the temperature can be held at about 45, and fresh air admitted every hour of the day. But if opening the cellar-door reduces the temperature that is otherwise uniformly at 45, or causes it to rise, it would be better to keep the bee-cellar closed—not because the ventilation does harm, but because the change of temperature does. House cellars are very often too small, perhaps lack room to put bees and vegetables. And right here let us say it is a bad practice to put bees and garden truck together in the same room. They should be kept separate.

Objection has been raised that the noise overhead in the house cellar disturbs bees ; but no absolute proof has been adduced to show this. We have had some excellent results in wintering in a bee-cellar under a machine-shop where rumbling machinery every now and then was accompanied by the bumping of heavy castings. We have never been able to discover that this noise interfered with good wintering in that cellar.

But where a house cellar is damp, too small, too cold, too warm, or too something else, it may be well to construct a special repository for the bees. This should be located in a side-hill if possible. A little later on we give illustrations of cellars used by some extensive bee-keepers; also other schemes of ventilation.

ARRANGEMENT OF HIVES IN A BEE-CELLAR.

They may be piled up one on top of another in such a way that any one can be removed without disturbing more than the one or two above it. The reason for this will be apparent later. Strong colonies should be put in first, and placed on a 2x4 scantling. On top of these may then be placed the weaker ones. This has no special advantage except the convenience of having the heavy ones at the bottom and the light ones on top. The entrances of the hives should be left about the same as they were during the late fall—⅜ deep by 8 inches wide. Some consider it essential to remove the bottoms of the hives entirely. Others consider it good practice to have a deep space under the frames by raising the hive off the bottom in front and supporting it there by a couple of blocks. But some disastrous results in wintering seem to show *us*, at least, that too much bottom ventilation is bad unless the cellar is kept at a temperature of about *60 and thoroughly ventilated.* The bee is essentially a warm-blooded animal; and if large openings be used under the bottoms of the hives the cluster will come down to shut out the cold from the interior of the hive. We have uniformly secured the best results with a reasonably small entrance, or one about the size used during the fall or late spring. The larger the colony, of course the larger the entrance that will be required. In the case of a strong populous colony we would have the entrance ⅜ deep by the full width of the hive. The colonies of medium strength should have the entrance reduced accordingly.

INSPECTING THE BEES DURING MID-WINTER; AND DEAD BEES ON THE CELLAR BOTTOM.

Experience has proven that, when the temperature is maintained at 45 degrees, very little attention need be paid to the bees, especially in the fore part of the winter. But during the last month or two of confinement the bees require watching more carefully; for if they get to roaring many of them will be lost. It then becomes necessary to make frequent examination to determine the temperature and the quality of the air. It will also be found, perhaps, that a good many dead bees will be found on the cellar bottom. This is not necessarily cause for alarm; because in normally good wintering the old bees will generally come out of the hive and die. Their bodies, however, should not be allowed to stench the living bees but should be swept up often and removed. A disposition to roar should be met by more ventilation, and at the same time the temperature should be reduced. If all the colonies in the cellar should become uneasy during mid-winter it is evident that something must be done at once or the whole lot of bees will be lost. They ought not to become uneasy until late in the spring. If they can not be quieted by infusions of fresh air it may be best to give the uneasy colonies a flight on the first warm day by setting them outdoors and letting them stay there for 24 hours or until they can clean themselves. Dysentery or diarrhea in the bee-cellar is generally the result of too much cold air or too high a temperature, either of which will induce too large a consumption of stores; and where bees are not able to void their feces, the intestines become distended, resulting in purging. A colony so affected should be removed as soon as a warm day comes.

WHEN TO PUT BEES IN THE CELLAR, AND WHEN TO TAKE THEM OUT.

This is a question that depends entirely on locality. Most bees go into the cellar in the Northern States anywhere from the last of November until the first of January; but usually it is advisable to have all bees in before Christmas. As to when the bees should be taken out of the cellar, authorities differ. Some set them out in March, and then put on winter cases. See SPRING MANAGEMENT. Others believe it is better policy to keep bees in late or until the last cold weather is past, and then set them out. We would advise taking the golden mean, waiting until the time natural pollen comes, or, in our locality, soft maples bloom. But when bees are uneasy in the cellar it is advised to set them out earlier than otherwise.

TIME OF DAY TO TAKE BEES OUT.

The usual plan for taking bees from a cellar in the spring is to wait until fairly settled warm weather has come, and then on some warm bright day all the colonies are removed at once. The great trouble with this method is that the bees are likely to become badly mixed, owing to their eager flight without carefully marking the location. This results in a bad state of affairs, and should be avoided.

Another method followed to some extent is to put some of the colonies out during an evening when all appearances indicate that it will be warm and bright the next day. A third of them, perhaps, are taken out, and these fly quite well the next day. The next evening another third is removed. and the last third the night following. The great trouble with this plan is that the bees removed first get to flying well and then start to rob colonies taken out later, thus making a fearful uproar.

Mr. E. W. Alexander, in *Gleanings in Bee Culture*, page 286, Vol. XXXIV., gave a plan open to none of these objections. In his own words it is as follows:

"First get every thing all ready for a big job, and watch the weather closely, especially after a few nice days, for it is quite changeable at this time of the year. Then when the wind gets around in the east, and it commences to become overcast with heavy clouds, and has every appearance of bad weather for the morrow, we commence about sundown and carry out all our bees—yes, even if it takes not only all night but into the next day'; and if it commences to rain before we are done, all the better, for we don't want any to try to fly until they have been out two or three days if we can help it. By this time they will have become nice and quiet; and when a fair day arrives they will commence to fly, only a few at a time, and get their location marked, so there will be no mixing up or robbing, because they all have their first fly together. Then when the day is over we find by examining our hives that nearly every one has apparently retained all its bees."

SHALL WE PUT THE COLONIES BACK ON THE OLD STANDS IN SPRING?

There is this advantage in putting the colonies back: Mr. H. R. Boardman letters each row in his apiary, and numbers every hive, each body and bottom-board bearing the number and the letter of its respective position. In the spring, in carrying bees out he is able to deposit his hive right where it was the preceding fall. "C6," we will say, is to go directly to the C row, and on arrival it is replaced on bottom No. 6. Mr. Boardman does not attach very much importance to bees being put back upon their old stands; though if he can, just as conveniently, he prefers doing so, because some old bees will go back to where they were the previous fall.

CARRIERS FOR HIVES.

A wheeled vehicle is not as good for moving bees in and out of a cellar as some sort of carrier. There are several good ones and we here show a few.

For hives without projections a pair of U-shaped wires bent to form a sort of bail answers nicely. The bottom hooks catch on to the bottom of the hive as shown.

Dr. Miller uses a rope as seen in the next cut. Of course, it can be used only when the hives are cleated at the ends.

Where hives are carried any distance, and help is scarce, the yoke would be better. One man can carry two heavy hives quite easily; descend cellar-steps, and go through doors. The

MILLER'S ROPE CARRIER.

only objection is the rigging, and loading and unloading.

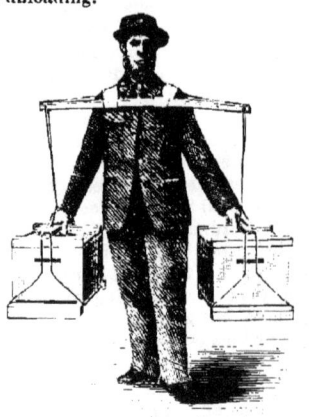

M'FARLAND'S NECKYOKE FOR CARRYING.

The particular form of hive-carrier preferred by many is the one described by Mr.

G. C. Greiner and several others in *Gleanings in Bee Culture.* This is presented in the following illustrations.

Two men can easily carry as many as five hives in this way. Where the cellar is locat-

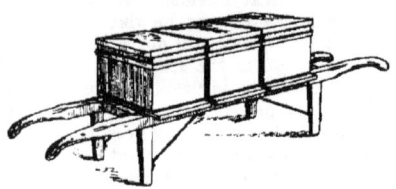

GREINER'S HIVE-CARRIER.

ed some little distance from the apiary we believe this to be the most convenient method yet devised.

Instead of constructing a regular hive-carrier as shown, it is possible to get along quite well by the use of two poles. See illustrations, next page. These should be about two inches square and six or eight feet long. They are placed on the ground in a parallel position, and as many hives placed on them as can be carried; perhaps three hives would be all that could be managed easily with the poles. It is much more satisfactory, however, to have the poles nailed together with a framework, making a regular hive-carrier.

HOW AND WHAT TO FEED BEES DURING MID-WINTER.

It is advisable to avoid feeding any syrup during mid-winter, because it has a tendency to stir up the bees, causing them to consume too largely of their stores; and, as they can not take a cleansing flight, dysentery is likely to follow. Moreover, the feeding of a single colony in a cellar is apt to stir up, by its roar, the other colonies near it.

When an outdoor colony is running short it should be given a comb of sealed stores. To avoid disturbing the winter nest this should be given directly on top of the brood-frames laid upon a couple of sticks. On top of the comb should be placed two other strips and then the packing-material. A comb may be given in the same way in the cellar, but it would be more practicable to take out an empty frame and put the one containing the stores in its place.

If one does not have any combs of honey he may give rock candy, or any kind of bee-candy (Good candy), by putting the same in a wooden tray on top of the brood-frames. In putting the packing-material back, care

CARRYING HIVES ON TWO POLES.

should be taken not to cover the tray so that the bees fail to get at the food.

Some have advised putting the candy right on top of the frames without the dish. But there is some danger that it may be dissolved by moisture from the cluster, and run down between the combs, destroying a good many bees if not the whole colony. So the candy should always be put in some sort of receptacle where, if it melts, it can not do any damage.

Where good hard candy can not be obtained, lumps of loaf sugar may be used; but these should first be moistened with a little water. Great care should be taken not to overdo the wetting-down, as the slightest amount of moisture will be sufficient to make the sugar available to the bees.

BEE - CELLARS VARIOUSLY CONSTRUCTED.

Having stated the general principles of cellar-wintering, we give views and descriptions of some of those used by men who are very successful in wintering.

Mr. N. D. West, of Middleburgh, N. Y., has been very successful in wintering bees in ordinary cellars under dwellinghouses.

CARRYING HIVES FROM THE CELLAR AT THE HOME OF THE HONEY-BEES.

He prefers to have the bee-room separated from the outside door by another room, possibly a vegetable-room, so that the temperature may be controlled more easily.

HOW N. D. WEST ARRANGES HIS HIVES IN THE CELLAR.

keep out the rain and snow, but still allow space for foul or warm air to escape from the bee-room. Any openings that would admit light are closed so as to make the room dark and warm. Mr. West thinks it is advisable to have a spring of running water in one corner, if possible, that the temperature may be kept constant.

In placing his hives in the cellar, Mr. West does not remove the bottom-boards. He makes a platform about four inches above the cellar-floor, and puts one row of hives on this with the back ends resting on a 2 x 5, so that they are four inches higher than the front ends. The next row of hives is placed on top of this row, although set back just a little so that the tiers will not fall over. As will be seen, all the hives will be so placed with the entrances at least four inches lower than the back ends of the hives, so that any dead bees may be easily cleaned out. See illustration.

The door between the two rooms may be left open most of the time, although it can be closed when necessary. An outside ventilator is used through an opening in one of the windows. A wooden box is made 8 inches square and about 2 ft. long. This extends through the window, and the outer end is built up so that the whole ventilator assumes the form of an elbow. The outer opening, which may be 3 ft. from the ground, is then covered in such a way as to

Harry Lathrop, of Bridgeport, Wisconsin, uses a stone bee-cellar built in a side hill. There are two rooms in the cellar, or, more properly speaking, a main room for the bees and a smaller one used as a vestibule. He

HATCH BEE-CELLAR—DIMENSIONS OF INLET, 6x8 INCHES; OUTLET, 8x10 INCHES.

thinks that, in some cases, it is advisable to have a stove in the vestibule. If there is a small opening at the top of the vestibule leading into the bee-room, and another opening at the bottom, artificial heat will cause a circulation. The air can be kept fresh by opening the outside door at intervals. An oil-stove should not be used, ordinarily, for the resulting bad air will be worse for bees than the cold.

With a properly constructed bee-cellar, there should be no need of artificial heat; but, nevertheless, it is best to have the cellar so arranged that a stove can be used if necessary.

The illustration given on the previous page shows Mr. C. A. Hatch's plan for a bee-cellar. It will be seen that the bee-room is almost entirely under the ground. The space between the ceiling and the roof is filled with leaves.

Mr. Hatch thinks it is advisable to have a cellar near the apiary, and built in a side hill if possible. If the entrance is on the level it is very easy to wheel colonies in and out. He thinks that a cellar 12 x 16 feet, inside measure, would be ample for 100 colonies in ten-frame hives, or for 120 colonies in eight-frame hives.

An important point connected with the Hatch bee-cellar is the double entrance, or vestibule. In this way the temperature can be regulated very easily. A temperature of 45 degrees Fahrenheit is considered ideal, but it is probable that a rise or drop of five degrees does no great harm unless continued more than 24 hours. Mr. Hatch agrees with Mr. France in thinking that the three essentials for safe wintering are good feed, proper temperature, and young bees.

HOLTERMANN'S BEE-CELLAR.

One of the largest bee-cellars, as well as one of the best designed, is owned by Mr.

Hull's bee-cellar, built in a side-hill; capacity 200 colonies.

Rear view of Hull's bee-cellar.

Front view of Hull's bee-cellar. Ten inches of sawdust cover the ceiling of the bee-room.

R. F. Holtermann, of Brantford, Ont., Canada, an extensive bee-keeper of that prov-

HOLTERMANN'S CONCRETE BEE-CELLAR AND WORK-SHOP.

INTERIOR VIEW LOOKING DOWN THE AISLES OF THE HOLTERMANN BEE-CELLAR.

ince. The cellar is made wholly of concrete, and, what is of particular interest to bee-keepers, has a scheme of ventilation that is almost ideal. It is not only theoretically perfect, but practically gives results in wintering that can scarcely be surpassed.

The authors have seen this cellar, and, notwithstanding there were about 500 powerful colonies in it at the time, there was perfect quiet and apparently perfect wintering. The temperature was about 43, and the air was pure and sweet. Scarcely any dead bees were found on the cellar bottom.

The bottom illustration, previous page, shows how his big twelve-frame colonies are piled up, having the ordinary entrance and a honey-board on top.

The sub-earth ventilator, in the diagram opposite, extends under ground several hundred feet away from the building where it comes to the surface. At the other end it passes under the floor of the cellar, then up into a small room in which is placed a stove. From this compartment or room the air is distributed all around the cellar by means of a large square wooden pipe suspended from the ceiling. Foul air is taken out at the bottom of the cellar by means of flues reaching down from the roof of the building to within a foot of the cellar floor. The upper story of the building is filled with hives and supers, being, in fact, the place where general shopwork connected with the yard is done.

Right here we can not do better than to give Mr. Holtermann's description and diagrams.

DESCRIPTION OF THE CELLAR.

The bee-house is of concrete—even to the chimney. This has a cowl on top, which veers its back to the wind to assist in getting a draft. On each side of the chimney is a box ventilator projecting through the peak of the roof. This is 12 in. square, with a slide to regulate the amount of air passing through. These shafts enter the cellar at the ceiling above, and are for warm weather. The building is 50 ft. long by 25 wide. The cellar walls are below the level of the ground, in order to get a more uniform temperature from the earth, and less liability for moisture to condense on its walls.

The cellar-ceiling, to secure uniformity of temperature and prevent condensation, has, as seen in the perpendicular-elevation plan, Fig. 2, G, a tongue-and-groove floor; C, E, felt paper; D, air-space; C, tongue-and-groove floor; F, floor of the cellar, is concrete. The only openings from the outside into the cellar are seen in Fig. 1. From B to A are two glazed waterlime-jointed tiling, coming above ground just outside of the bee-house at B B, the wall going down 8 ft. into the ground; then passing under the cellar-wall and floor, entering the cellar at points A, A. Then there is a stairway, C, which is covered by two doors at the level of the ground, and again clos-

ed from the cellar by two doors. Through these doors the bees are brought in and out.

D is a 12-inch glazed pipe with waterlime joints 8 ft. under ground. This enters the cellar in the compartment E, a coal-stove standing over this opening. In this compartment, if the air is not sufficiently tempered by its passage under the ground it can be warmed before it passes into the cellar.

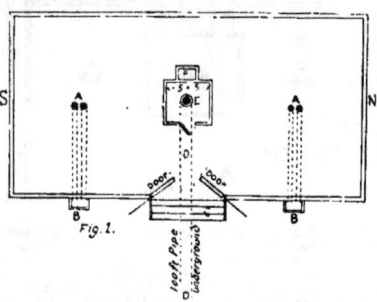

Ground plan of cellar. Inner compartment E has solid concrete walls extending to ceiling. Opening E communicates with a sub-earth ventilator, D. When in-rushing air is too cold a fire is built in the stove, tempering the air then it passes upward to the ceiling, and into the square-box wooden flues shown at D D D D, in Fig. 3, where it is distributed to every point in the cellar.

In Fig. 3 the system of distributing fresh air is shown. The illustration is not quite correct as to the central compartment, however. B is supposed to be the same central compartment as E in Fig. 1, and the distance between it and the west wall should be greater. At the top of this compartment, on the west side, are pipes, D, D, D, which carry the fresh air to the north and south end of the cellar, B E respectively being the north and south ends. From there through many one-inch openings (see arrows also, in B, Fig. 2, and the method of turning the cor-

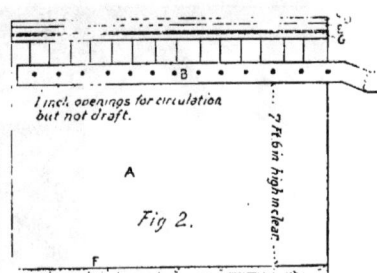

Perpendicular elevation of bee-cellar, showing the square-box ventilating-flue with its one-inch holes as shown in diagram 3.

ner of the wall), the fresh air is evenly distributed through the cellar and carried off in a more or less foul condition through openings in the bottom of chimney F, in Fig. 1, and at ventilators, F F, in Fig. 3, said ventilators showing through the roof on either side of the chimney shown in the exterior halftone view of the cellar.

I have a curtain this winter on the north, south, and west walls, and find it assists in equalizing the temperature. This winter I have had more or less air passing through all the air-passages, yet have kept up a sufficiently high temperature half the time without fire.

Two years ago I darkened all the windows in the bee-house above, and partially opened a trap-door which leads by means of a stairway alongside of the

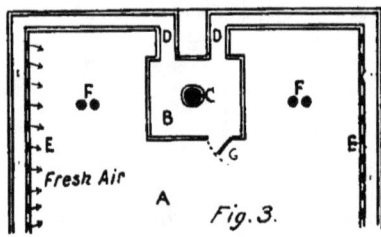

Fresh Air *Fig. 3.*

Horizontal plan showing scheme of ventilation. Room B has solid concrete walls to prevent danger from fire from the stove at C. Under the stove is the sub-earth-ventilator opening that supplies fresh air, which, if too cold, is warmed and then forced through the distributing-flues D D D D, which are perforated by one-inch holes. The flues D D are closed at the ends, and all air must pass out at the holes indicated by the arrows. F F are ventilators carrying foul air and moisture by means of flues extending through the roof.

center compartment to the cellar floor. This, however, gave too rapid variations in temperature and was abandoned. During the last strong gale, with the wind reaching a velocity of over 60 miles an hour, within 24 hours a change from 59 to 12° was experienced; while there was a variation of only 2½° in the cellar without any alteration of the ventilating dampers.

WINTERING BEES IN CLAMPS.

In parts of the country where the soil is sandy and porous, bees are often wintered in trenches dug in the ground. These are about 18 inches deep, large enough to hold two rows of ten hives each. The hives are set upon 2 x 4's to keep them off the ground. Three of these are used, one at each side and one in the middle, with the flat or wide side down. The bottoms are removed from the hives, and the covers raised half an inch or so to provide upward ventilation. About 18 inches of straw is thrown over the hives, and then the dirt shoveled on. The engravings shown on next page illustrate the plan as practiced by E. D. Townsend, of Remus, Michigan. The first engraving shows the dirt partly shoveled away and some of the hives removed. The next illustration shows all of the hives removed in the spring from the pits or clamps and set on their summer stands. It would seem as though there ought to be some provision made for ventilation; but when it is remembered that the soil is sandy and very porous, it is seen that this is not necessary. This plan can not be made use of in a location where the soil is composed largely of clay. Mr. Townsend thinks that it is well to have surface drains along each side of the pits to carry off any water that may come that way.

WHAT TO DO WHEN BEES SPRING-DWINDLE OUTDOORS.

In the spring, especially when cold and backward, many weaker colonies begin to dwindle, and so rapidly that some will have only about a dozen bees or so with their

DAVIDSON'S CONCRETE BEE-CELLAR.

WINTERING COLONIES IN CLAMPS OR TRENCHES DUG IN THE GROUND.
From Bee-keeper's Review.

COLONIES JUST REMOVED FROM THE TRENCHES IN THE SPRING.
From Bee-keeper's Review.

queen. It would seem to be goo l policy to unite all these weak colonies into one good strong one; but experience shows that but very little good comes from so doing—mainly because most of the bees from the several forces go back to their old stands and perish. Better than a cure for spring dwindling is prevention, by having a large force of young bees early in the fall; then just about the time they are taken out of the cellar, when indoor wintering is practiced, weak colonies may be united on the "Alexander plan" by putting them on top of strong ones. See UNITING. If practiced early enough it will anticipate and prevent spring dwindling.

One who has outyards can unite several nuclei into one strong colony, then move that whole aggregation to another yard, where, of course, the united forces will remain in the new location.

WHAT TO DO WITH COMBS FROM HIVES WHERE THE BEES HAVE DIED.

Put them safely out of the way of bees, either in tight hives or in a bee-proof room ; and if you have not bees enough to cover them by the middle of June, or at such a time as you shall find moth-worms at work among them, be sure that all the combs are spread at least two inches apart, as recommended under BEE-MOTH. Now, whatever other precautions you take, you *must* look after these empty combs occasionally. They are very valuable, and should not be allowed to be destroyed. A very good way is to keep them in regular hives, piled one over the other. This keeps them perfectly protected, and yet you can quickly look them all over as often as once a week at least, until they are used.

WINTERING IN THE SOUTHERN STATES.

The directions so far given apply particularly to localities that are subject to zero weather at times, that have more or less of snow, and, during the greater portion of the year, a large amount of frost in the ground, extending down perhaps two feet.

Where bees can fly almost every day in the year, and for ten months are able to gather a little honey or pollen, outdoor wintering in single-walled hives is recommended. Double walled hives would do no harm, and might, during the coldest of the weather, save a little brood; but it is doubtful whether the added expense for the extra walls and packing will compensate for the possible slight loss of brood and bees during a few cold days. While we recommend sin-gle hives for the southern portions of our country, and for some parts of the West, we always urge that the same be located in an inclosure of trees, a tight high board fence, a hedge, or any thing in the way of buildings that will break the prevailing winds. To establish windbreaks is one of the most important requisites in either the northern or southern portions of the country.

While no great skill is needed to winter bees in such localities as are found in Florida, South Carolina, Texas, Louisiana, Georgia, Alabama, and Southern California, yet one must be careful to see that his bees do not run short of stores, as it seems to be a generally acknowledged fact that bees wintered in the South consume much more stores, according to the size of the colony, than in the North. Those in cold climates are compelled to contract into a very small ball for the purpose of concentrating the animal heat; and while in that condition they are in a semi-dormant state, and consume a comparatively small quantity of food. On the other hand, bees in the South, especially in the warmest portions, can have access to all parts of the hive, rear more or less brood, and, as a consequence, when natural flora does not secrete nectar they are liable to run short of stores, and starve. To the Southlander let us urge that the greatest danger is starvation, and the next greatest is more or less of robbing during a dearth of honey. Indeed, all things considered, we believe Southern bees require more watching than those of the North.

In localities like Virginia, Tennessee, and other States lying in about the same latitude, it might be advisable to use double-walled hives; yet we know that the majority of bee-keepers in that latitude winter their bees successfully in single-walled hives; but we believe it is the general practice to place on top of the hive a super containing chaff, leaves, planer-shavings, or some good warm packing-material; moreover, when the colony is not very strong it is advisable to place a chaff division-board on each side of the cluster. In all cases there should not be given a larger cubic capacity than the bees can comfortably fill, spread out as they usually are on a day when the temperature is not below 70 F.

In Colorado it is customary to winter in single-walled hives. A shallow cap or tray containing a few inches of packing is placed on top of the hive. Very often, for further protection, a sort of shed or roof, with its back to the prevailing winds, is built over a row of hives. The Colorado bee-keepers are troubled with sandstorms and fierce piercing winds; while the temperature may go down below zero, it is not likely to remain so for more than a few hours, when one extreme will change to a temperature of 60 or 70 F., and the bees flying. For such conditions double-walled hives and an excess of packing-material have been found to be not at all necessary.

DO BEES HIBERNATE?

In the foregoing pages, under the general subject of WINTERING we have spoken of the quiescent state or sleep into which bees enter when the wintering conditions are been lowered; and this state is somewhat analogous to the torpor experienced by some animals in a state of true hibernation, during which no food is taken, and respiration is considerably reduced. Dr. Marshall Hall has stated that "respiration is inversely as the degree of irritability of the muscular fiber." If the respiration is reduced without this irritability being increased, death results from asphyxia. Hibernation is usually induced by cold; and the animal under its influence attains nearly the temperature of the surrounding atmosphere, yet can not resist *any* amount of cold, although its capacity for doing so varies according to the animal. Some animals bury themselves

VIEW ON SOUVENIR POSTAL CARD SENT OUT BY F. J. MILLER, OF LONDON, ONT., CAN.

ideal. In this period of semi hibernation the bees seem merely to exist. With no activity the consumption of stores is very light. As the reader may wish to pursue this subject a little further we have thought best to take it up to help solve some of the wintering problems, and, perhaps, lead to some good results from an economic point of view.

Hibernation was exploited about 20 years ago, when it was generally decided, and rightly, too, that bees do not hibernate in the ordinary sense of the term (see *American Bee Journal* for 1885). But they do enter a quiescent state when the temperature has in holes, like snakes and frogs; others, like the bear, crawl under a pile of leaves and brush where they are still further covered with snow. Thus buried they will go all winter without food or water; but there is a waste of tissue. Fish may be encased in ice and still live, it is said. A lively frog may be dropped into a pail of water four or five inches deep, and exposed to a freezing temperature. Indeed, there may be a thin coating of ice formed over the animal. The next morning, that frog, though stiff and cold, can be warmed up into activity, but to freeze solidly will kill the creature.

Flies, as is well known, will secrete themselves in window-frames and other hiding-places, subject to cold atmosphere, for weeks at a time, and yet revive on exposure to warmth. As is well known, also, ants have been repeatedly dug out of logs, frozen solid —in fact, fairly enveloped in frost; yet on exposure to warmth they will come to. Some hibernators can endure a freezing temperature, while others, like the bear, woodchuck, and the like, can not. Other very interesting incidents may be taken from natural history; but the purpose of this article is to consider whether bees go into a quiescent state that *approaches* hibernation, in which there is low respiration and a small consumption of stores.

Two or three years ago we put a number of cages of bees with some queens (laying the cages down on cakes of ice) in a refrigerator. The bees were chilled to absolute stiffness. Every day we would take out a cage, and each time the bees would revive, including the queen. This thing was continued for several days, and yet the bees would "come to" each time.

The strange part of it was, that the queens went on laying normally when put back in the hives, instead of laying drone eggs as we expected. Just what the temperature to which these bees were subjected was we can not say — probably something below 40 and something above 35, for the doors of the refrigerator were frequently opened, and the ice was constantly melting.

During one winter, when a very cold snap came on—the temperature going down to zero—we put out some cages of bees, exposing them to the cold wind, which was then blowing a pretty good gale, when the temperature was 5 above zero. We had expected that the bees possibly might be able to survive the shock for a number of hours, and yet revive; but 20 minutes of zero freezing was sufficient to kill them outright. If we had taken the bees and gradually acclimatized them to the cold, first subjecting them to 40, then to 35, and gradually down to the zero point, they would possibly have withstood the shock.

When the weather warmed up a little we took several cages of bees and buried them in the snow, leaving with them a thermometer so that we might know the absolute temperature. We went out and got a cage of bees about every two or three hours, and we found that we could revive them without difficulty; but at the end of 24 hours the bees, when they "came to," seemed somewhat the worse for the experience. The temperature in the snow played around the 32 mark. But the experiments conducted during the summer would seem to show that bees might stand a temperature of 38 for a number of days.

We know it to be a fact that the bees on the outside of the ball or cluster, in an out-door-wintered colony, will often be chilled stiff while those inside have almost a blood temperature. It has occurred to us that, during very severe weather, the outside bees may be gradually replaced by those within the cluster; for we know the bees are in constant movement. Experiments show that a starved bee will not stand as much cold as one that is well filled. Bee-keepers who have had any experience in wintering outdoors know how repeatedly thay have taken clusters of bees that seemed to be frozen stiff, yet when warmed up before a good fire would revive and appear as lively as ever.

In view of the experiments we have thus far conducted, it would appear that bees might be able to stand a temperature of 40, or slightly below that, for a number of days: but if a warm spell does not come within a week, or less, those bees in their chilled condition may starve to death. But if it warms up, the cluster will unfold and the bees take food, and so be ready for another "freeze." The authors have repeatedly seen clusters of bees, after a zero spell, lasting a couple of weeks, that were stone dead; but the honey had been eaten from all around them within a radius of an inch or more. If a zero spell of weather continues more than a week or ten days, we always find some of the weaker colonies frozen to death in the spring.

There are some interesting phenomena in connection with chilled bees—their quiescent sleep, their low respiration, their light consumption of stores—that simulates a condition of semi-hibernation. The bee in a chilled condition can go only a few days without food, while a bear, a true hibernator, may go all winter. When the temperature of a bee-cellar goes up to 50 or 60 the bees are active. Their respiration is normal. They must have ventilation, or die in large numbers. If we can maintain a temperature down to 45, with slight variation, there is a state of sleep where the respiration is ver low, food consumption slight, and consequently fresh air is not needed, or not more than what will percolate through the walls of the repository.

There is a practical side to this matter; for if we can induce semi-hibernation or torpor we cut down the consumption of stores.

BEES FLYING OUT ON CHILLY OR COLD DAYS AND APPARENTLY DYING ON THE GROUND.

In this connection there are a few other interesting facts that are worth recording here. In early winter or early spring, bees will very often fly out on a bright day, whether it is very warm or not. They alight on the ground or some object, become chilled, and apparently die. Cases are on record where bees have flown out, alighted on the ground, become stiff and cold, and were apparently dead. There was one instance in particular of this kind where thousands of bees had flown out and lay on the ground apparently never to return. A cold rain set in and then it began to freeze, followed by some snow. This freezing weather lasted for a couple of days. This was followed by warm sunshine, when, wonderful to relate, those dead (?) bees came to life, took wing, and flew back to their hives. Other authentic reports, showing something similar to this have been sent in. It seems almost unbelievable, but the facts are, that bees can fly out, alight in the snow, chill through, and seem to be dead. If the snow is not too deep it melts away so that the bodies of the bees can become warmed up, when they will often revive; they always revive, if it is warm enough, and they have not been chilled too long.

Bee keepers have written in at many different times, fearing that their bees had flown out in late fall, and, becoming chilled on the ground, were utterly lost; but, when a warm day comes on a little later, these bees, if it has not been too cold, will return to their hives.

Old Dame Nature seems to have made some wonderful provisions to preserve bee-life. We are therefore constrained to believe that bees can stand, under some conditions, chilling cold for some days without killing them.

WOMEN AS BEE-KEEPERS. See BEE-KEEPING FOR WOMEN.

WIRING FRAMES. See COMB FOUNDATION.

X Y Z.

XYLOCOPA. This is the scientific name of the genus to which the carpenter bees belong. Of course they do not gather honey, but we frequently receive large bees from readers which they suppose are some giant form of our own honey-bees. The largest and finest-looking bees in the world belong to the genus *Xylocopa*. There are possibly 10,000 species of bees in the world, of which only eight are regarded as *Apis*. The latter, though small and humble-looking, occupies the top of the class on account of its higher development.

YELLOW SWEET CLOVER. See CLOVER, sub-head SWEET CLOVER.

ZINC, Perforated. See DRONES and EXTRACTED HONEY.

Appendix

[The following article came too late to be inserted in its regular
place in the body of the work.]

The Anatomy of the Bee

BY R. E. SNODGRASS
of the Bureau of Entomology, Washington, D. C.

The three parts of the body of the bee are well separated by constrictions. The head carries the eyes, antennæ, and mouth parts; the thorax, the wings and legs; and the abdomen, the wax-gland and sting.

The *head* is flattened and triangular, being widest crosswise through the upper corners, which are capped by the large compound eyes. It carries the *antennæ*, or feelers, on the middle of the face (Fig. 2, A, *Ant*); the large *compound eyes* (*E*) laterally; three small simple eyes or *ocelli* (*O*), at the top of the face, and the *mouth parts* (*Md*, *Mx*, and *Lb*) ventrally. Each antenna consists of a long basal joint and of a series of small ones hanging downward from the end of the first. The antennæ are very sensitive to touch, and contain the organs of smell. At the lower edge of the face is a loose flap (Fig. 2, A, *Lm*) forming an upper lip called the *labrum*. On its under surface is a small soft lobe called the *epipharynx* on which are located the organs of taste. At the sides of the labrum are the two heavy jaws, or *mandibles* (*Md*), which work sidewise. They are spoon-shaped at their ends in the worker, but sharp-pointed and toothed in the queen and drone. Those of the queen are largest, those of the drone smallest. Behind the labrum and the mandibles is a bunch of long appendages, usually folded back beneath the head, which together constitute the *proboscis* (Fig. 2, A, *Prb*). These organs correspond with the second pair of jaws, or *maxillæ*, and the lower lip, or *labium*, of other insects. In Fig. 2 they are cut off a short distance from their bases, but are shown detached from the head and flattened out in Fig. 3, D. The middle series of pieces (*Smt-Lbl*) constitutes the labium, the two lateral series (*Cd-Mx*) the maxillæ. The labium consists of a basal *submentum* (*Smt*), and a *mentum* (*Mt*), which supports distally the slender, flexible, tongue-like *glossa* (*Gls*), the two delicate *paraglossæ* (*Pgl*), and the two lateral, jointed labial palpi (*Lb Plp*). Each maxilla is composed of a basal stalk, the *cardo* (*Cd*); a main plate, the *stipes* (*St*), and a wide terminal blade (*Mx*) called the *galea*. At the base of the galea is a rudimentary *maxillary palpus* (*MxPlp*), representing a part which in most insects consists of several slender joints.

As before stated, the parts of the maxillæ and the labium together constitute the proboscis, which, as shown in Fig. 2, B, is suspended from a deep cavity (*PrbFs*) on the lower part of the back of the head having a membranous floor. The basal stalks (*Cd*) of the maxillæ are hinged to knobs on the sides of this cavity, while the labium is attached to the maxillary stalks by means of a flexible band called the *lorum* (Fig. 3, D, *Lr*).

When the bee wishes to suck up any liquid, especially a thick liquid like honey or syrup, provided in considerable quantity, the terminal lobes of the labium and maxillæ are pressed close together so as to make a tube between them. The labium is then moved back and forth between the maxillæ with a pump-like motion produced by muscles within the head. This brings the liquid up to the mouth, which is situated above the base of the proboscis, between the mandibles and beneath the labrum. The food is probably then taken into the mouth by a sucking action of the pharynx produced by its muscles.

A more delicate apparatus is probably necessary, however, for sucking up minute drops of nectar from the bottom of a flower. Such a structure is provided within the glossa. This organ (Fig. 3, D, *Gls*), ordinarily called the "tongue," is terminated by a delicate, sensitive, spoon-like lobe known as the labella (Fig. 3, A, B, and D, *Lbl*), and has a groove (*k*) running along its entire length on the ventral side. Within the glossa this groove expands into a double-barreled tube (Fig. 3, E, *Lum*). A flexible chitinous rod (*r*) lies along the dorsal wall of this channel, which is itself provided with a still finer groove (*l*) along its ventral surface. Thus the very smallest quantity of nectar may find a channel suited to its bulk through which it may run up to the base of the glossa by capillary attraction. But since the glossal channels are ventral the nectar must be transferred to the dorsal side of the labium by means of the paraglossæ, the two soft lobes (Fig. 3, D and F, *Pgl*) whose bases are on the upper side of the mentum, but whose distal ends underlap the base of the glossa, and thus afford conduits for the nectar around the latter to the upper side of the labium. The glossa is highly extensible and retractile by means of muscles attached to the base of its rod, and its movements when a bee is feeding are very conspicuous, and interesting to watch.

The *thorax* of any insect carries the wings and the legs. The two wings of the bee on each side are united to each other by a series of minute hooks so that they work together, and the four wings are thus practically converted into two. Each wing is hinged at its base to the back, and pivoted from below upon a small knob of the side wall of the thorax. The up-and-down motion of the wings is produced, not by muscles attached to their bases, but by two sets of enormous muscles, one vertical and the other horizontal, attached to the walls of the thorax, whose contractions elevate and depress the back plates of the thorax. Since the fulcrum of each wing is outside of its attachment to the back, the depression of the latter elevates the wings, and an elevation of the back lowers the wing. But the bee flies by a propeller-like action, or figure-8 motion of the wings. This is produced by two other sets of much smaller muscles acting directly upon the wing bases, one before and the other behind the fulcrum of each. The combined result of all these muscles is that the down stroke of the wing is accompanied by a forward movement and a deflexion of the anterior edge, while the up stroke reverses this.

The legs of the bee are too familiar to need any extensive description here. Their special characters, such as the antennæ-cleaners on the first and the pollen-baskets and brushes on the last, are illustrated in Fig. 4. The tarsi are each provided with a pair of terminal *claws* (E, *Cla*), by means of which the bee clings to rough objects, while between the claws is a sticky pad. the *empodium* (*Emp*), which is brought into play when the bee alights on or walks over any smooth surface like glass.

The hind part of the thorax of bees, wasps, and their allies is composed of a segment which, in other insects, is a part of the abdomen. It is known as the *propodeum*. The middle division of the body of a bee, wasp, or ant, therefore, is not exactly the equivalent of the thorax of a grasshopper, fly, or butterfly.

The *abdomen* of the bee has no appendages corresponding with those of the head or thorax; but it bears two important organs, viz., the wax-glands and the sting. The *wax-glands* are simply specially developed cells of the skin on the ventral surfaces of the last four visible abdominal segments of the worker. There are only six segments visible in the apparent abdomen; but remembering that the propodeum of the thorax is really the first, the wax-glands occur, therefore, on segments four to seven inclusive (Fig. 1, IV-VII). The wax secreted by the glands is discharged through minute pores in the ventral plate of each segment, and accumulates in the form of a little scale in the pocket above the underlapping ventral plate of the segment next in front.

The *sting* is such a complicated organ that it is very difficult to describe it clearly in a few words. Fundamentally it consists of three slender, closely appressed pieces forming the sharp piercing organ that projects from the tip of the abdomen (Fig. 1, *Stn*), and of two soft finger-like lobes, sometimes also visible, all of which arise from three pairs of plates belonging to the eighth and ninth segments of the abdomen, but which are concealed within the seventh segment.

Fig. 5 shows, somewhat diagrammatically, all the parts of the left side. The acute stinging shaft swells basally into a large bulb (*ShB*) which is connected by a basal arm on each side with two lateral plates (*Ob* and *Tri*). The finger-like lobes, called the *palpi of the sting* (*StnPlp*) are carried also by the lower of these two plates (*Ob*) while the upper (*Tri*) carries the third and largest plate (*Qd*) which partially overlaps the lower (*Ob*).

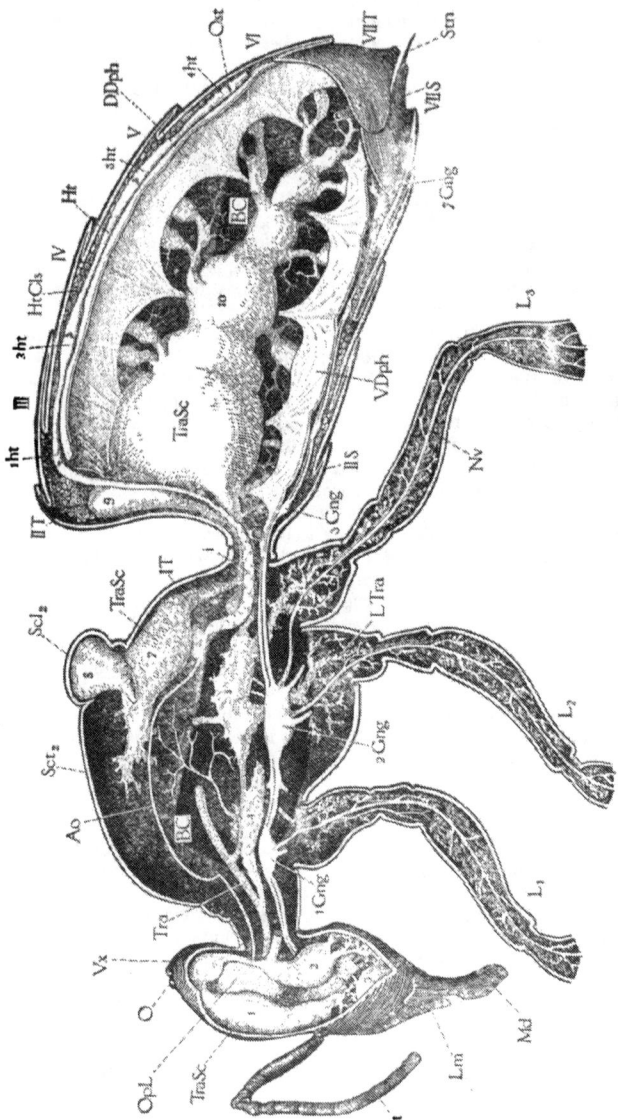

From Bulletin No. 18, "The Anatomy of the Honey-bee," by Snodgrass, Bureau of Entomology, Department of Agriculture, Washington, D. C.

FIG. 1.—Longitudinal, median, vertical section of worker, exposing body cavity (BC) in right side, with alimentary canal (Fig. 6) removed, but showing tracheal system (Tra, LTra, and Tra Sc 1-10), heart (Ht), and aorta (Ao); dorsal diaphragm (DDph), ventral diaphragm (VDph), and nervous system (OpL,1Gng-7Gng). Ao, aorta; Ant, antenna; BC, body cavity; DDph, dorsal diaphragm; Gng, ganglion; 1Gng, 2Gng, first and second thoracic ganglia; 3Gng-7Gng, abdominal ganglia; Ht, heart; 1ht-4ht, chambers of heart; L, convolutions of aorta; L, leg; L1, L2, L3, prothoracic, mesothoracic, and metathoracic legs; Lm, labrum; LTra, lateral trachea; Md, Mandible; N, nerve of leg; O, ocelli; OpL, optic lobe of brain; Ost, ostium (aperture of heart); S, sternum; 1S VII S, sternum, second to seventh sternum; annual sterna; Scl, scutellum of mesothorax; Scl2, scutum of mesothorax; Stn, sting; Tra, trachea; Tra Sc (1-10), tracheal air-sacs; T, tergum; IT, propodeum, or first abdominal tergum; VIII T, seventh abdominal tergum; VDph, ventral tergum; Vx, vertex.

A close examination of the sting proper shows that both the bulb and the tapering shaft are formed of three pieces. One is dorsal (*ShB* and *ShS*) while the other two (*Lct*) are ventral (of course only one of the latter shows in side view). Furthermore, the basal arm on each side is formed of two pieces, one of which (*ShA*) is continuous with the dorsal piece of the sting, while the other (*Lct*) is continuous with the ventral rod of the same side. Since these ventral rods are partially enclosed within a hollow on the under side of the dorsal piece, the latter is called the *sheath of the sting*. It consists of the terminal *shaft* of the sheath (*ShS*), the *bulb* (*ShB*), and of a *basal arm* (*ShA*) on each side. The ventral pieces (*Lct*)

tubular, alkaline gland (*BGl*). By movements of the triangular plates (Fig. 5, *Tri*) the lancets slide back and forth against the sheath while the poison exudes in tiny drops from an opening between them near the tips. The poison-sac has no muscles in its walls, and, hence, can not force the poison through the sting. The poison, in fact, is driven out of the latter by a force-pump inside of the bulb. This consists of two pouch-like lobes situated on the upper edges of the lancets, having their cavities open posteriorly. When the lancets move forward the walls of these pouches collapse; but when the motion is reversed they flare apart and drive the poison contained in the bulb back through the shaft and out at the end.

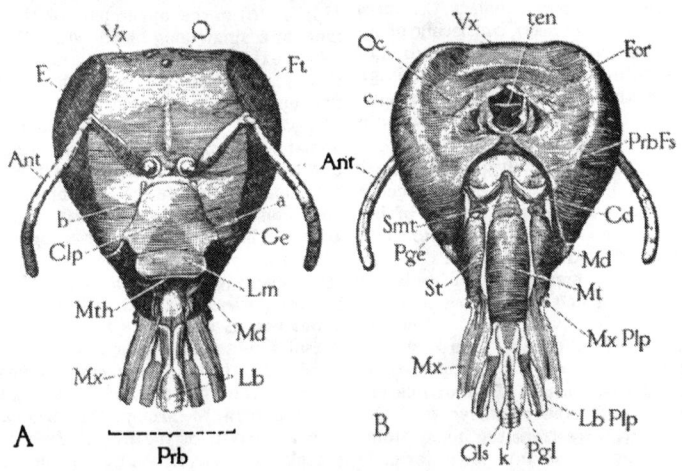

From Bulletin No. 18, "The Anatomy of the Honey bee," by Snodgrass, Bureau of Ent., Dept. of Ag., Washington, D. C.

FIG. 2.—Head of worker with parts of proboscis cut off a short distance from their bases. A, anterior; B, posterior; *a*, clypeal suture; *Ant*, antenna; *b*, pit in clypeal suture marking anterior end of internal bar of head; *c*, pit on occipital surface of head, marking posterior end of internal bar; *Cd*, cardo; *Clp*, Clypeus; *E*, compound eye; *For*, foramen magnum; *Ft*, front; *Ge*, gena; *Gls*, glossa, or "tongue;" *k*, ventral groove of glossa; *Lb*, labium; *LbPlp*, labial palpus; *Lm*, labrum; *Md*, mandible; *Mt*, mentum; *Mth*, mouth; *Mx*, terminal blade of maxilla; *MxPlp*, maxillary palpus; *O*, ocelli; *Oc*, occiput; *Pge*, postgena; *Pgl*, paraglossa; *Prb*, base of proboscis; *PrbFs*, fossa of proboscis; *Smt*, submentum; *St*, stipes; *ten*, small bar of tentorium arching over foramen magnum; *Vx*, vertex.

are slender sharp-pointed rods having barbed extremities, and are known as the *lancets*. The shaft of the sheath is grooved along the entire length of its ventral surface, the groove enlarging into a spacious cavity in the bulb. The lancets lie close together against the ventral edges of the sheath, but slide freely upon minute tracks on the latter. The three parts, therefore, inclose between them a cavity which is tubular in the shaft, but enlarged into a wide chamber in the bulb. The great poison-sac (Fig. 8, *Psn Sc*) of the acid-glands of the sting opens into the base of the bulb along with the smaller,

The *poison* is an acid liquid formed by the glands (Fig. 8, *AGl*, *AGl*, and *Bgl*). Two of these (*AGl* and *AGl*) are simply small enlargements at the ends of two long coiled tubes (*AGlD*), which latter unite into a short single tube that opens into the anterior end of the great poison-sac (*PsnSc*). The secretion of these glands is acid. The third gland (*BGl*) is a short, somewhat twisted tube opening into the bulb of the sting along with the poison-sac. Its secretion is alkaline. Carlet has shown that it is only the mixture of these two secretions that has the full strength in stinging properties.

The *alimentary canal* (Fig. 6) consists of a tube extending through the entire body, and coiled somewhat in the abdomen. The first part above the mouth in the head is widened to form the *pharynx* (*Phy*). Then follows the long slender *œsophagus* (*Œ*), running clear through the thorax and into the front of the abdomen, where it enlarges into a thin-walled bag, called, in general, the *crop*, but which is known as the *honey-stomach* (*HS*) in the bee. Back of the honey-stomach is a short narrow *proventiculus* (*Pvent*), which is followed by the large U-shaped stomach, or *ventriculus* (*Vent*). Then comes the slender *small* intestine (*SInt*) with the circle of *Malpighian tubules* (*Mal*) arising from its anterior end. Finally, forming the terminal part of the alimentary canal, is the *large* intestine, or *rectum* (*Rect*), consisting of an enormous sack, varying in size according to its contents, but often occupying a large part of the abdominal cavity. Six opaque longitudinal bands on its anterior end are known as the *rectal glands* (*RGl*).

The honey-stomach is of special interest in the worker because the nectar gathered from the flowers is held in it, instead of being swallowed on down into the stomach, and is regurgitated into the cells of the comb, or given up first to another bee in the hive. The upper end of the proventiculus sticks up into the lower end of the honey-stomach as a small cone with an X-shaped opening in its summit. This opening is called the *stomach-mouth*. Its four lips are very active, and take whatever food the ventriculus requires from the honey-stomach, for it must all go into the latter first, while at the same time it affords the bees a means of retaining nectar or honey in the honey-stomach.

The natural food of bees consists of pollen, nectar, and honey. The first contains the nitrogen of their diet, and the other two the hydrogen, carbon, and oxygen. Observations made by the writer indicate that the pollen is not digested until it gets into the intestine, for masses of fresh-looking grains nearly always occur in the rear part of the ventriculus, which is otherwise filled with a brownish slime. On the other hand, the nectar and honey is very probably digested in the ventriculus, and in large part absorbed from it.

The *salivary glands*, located in the back part of the head (Fig. 6, *2Gl*) and in the front part of the thorax (*3Gl*) open upon the upper part of the labium (Fig. 3, F, *SalDO*). The saliva can thus affect the liquid food before the latter enters the mouth, or it can be allowed to run down the proboscis upon hard sugar in order to dissolve it, for the latter is eaten with the proboscis, not with the mandibles.

The large glands (Fig. 6, *1Gl*) situated in the front part of the head are supposed, by some students of the bee, to form the white pasty brood food and the royal jelly. Others think that these substances come from the stomach. More investigation of the subject must be made, however, before the question can be decided; but the contents of the stomachs of workers have no resemblance to the brood food.

The *circulatory* system is very simple, consisting of a delicate, tubular, pulsating *heart* (Fig. 1, *Ht*) in the upper part of the abdomen, of a single long blood-vessel, the *aorta* (*Ao*), extending forward from the heart through the thorax into the head, and of two pulsating membranes, the *diaphragms* (*DDph* and *VDph*), stretched across the dorsal and ventral walls of the abdomen, but leaving wide openings along their sides between the points of attachment. The heart consists of four consecutive chambers, *1ht-4ht*, which are merely swellings of the tube, each having a vertical slit or *ostium* (*Ost*) opening into each side. The *blood* is the colorless liquid that fills the spaces about the viscera of the body cavity. The dorsal diaphragm and the heart pulsate forward. The blood in the cavity above the former enters the ostia of the heart, and is pumped forward through the aorta and out into the cavity of the head. From here it percolates back through the thorax and enters the space beneath the ventral diaphragm (*VDph*) of the abdomen. This membrane pulsates backward, and the blood is driven posteriorly and upward, through the lateral openings, around the abdominal viscera, and again into the dorsal or pericardial cavity of the abdomen, where it begins its circulation anew. In insects the principal function of the blood is to distribute the food which dissolves into it from the alimentary canal.

The *respiratory system* is very highly developed in the bee, consisting (Fig. 1) of large air-sacs (*TraSc*, *1-10*) in the head, thorax, and abdomen, and of tubes called tracheæ given off from them (*Tra*, *LTra*). Fig. 1 shows principally the parts in only the right side of the body. In the abdomen a large sac (*10*) lies on each side connected with the exterior by short tubes opening on the sides of the first seven segments. Three other pairs of such openings occur in the thorax; but the last of these, being in the propodeum, really belongs to the abdomen. Thus there are in all ten pairs of breathing apertures, and they are called the *spiracles*. None occur on the head. The tracheal tubes given off from the air-sacs branch minutely to all parts of the body and penetrate into most of the tissues. Hence oxygen is carried directly to the cells that use it, and the blood of insects is thus relieved of the work of distributing it—one of its principal functions in vertebrate animals. The respiratory movements are produced by muscles of the abdomen.

The life processes of the cells of the body result in the formation of products excreted by the cells into the surrounding blood. These products are poisonous to the system unless immediately changed into simpler

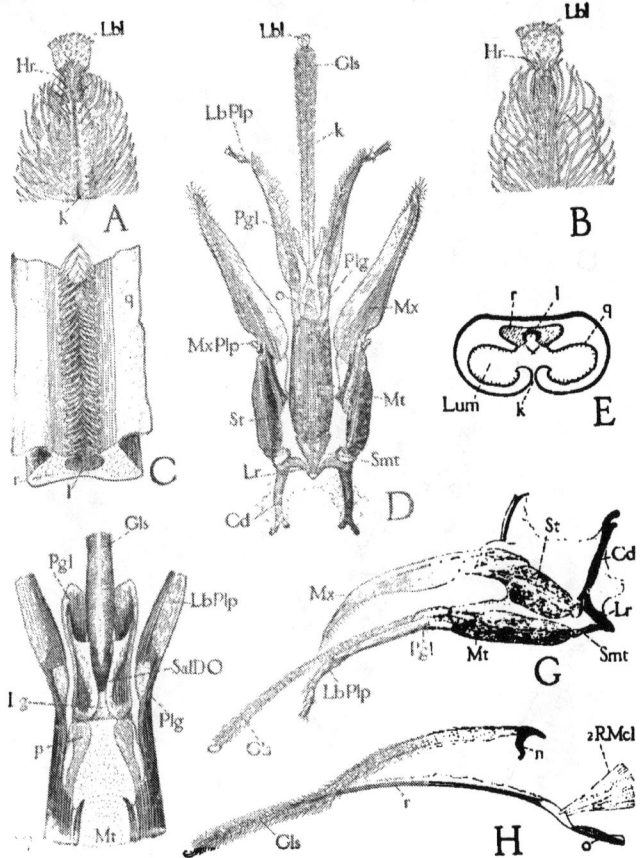

From Bulletin No. 18, " The Anatomy of the Honey-bee," by Snodgrass, Bureau of Ent., Dept. of Ag., Washington, D. C.

FIG. 3.—Details of mouth parts of worker. *A*, tip of glossa, ventral; *B*, tip of glossa, dorsal: *C*, piece of glossal rod (*r*) showing ventral groove (*l*) with parts of walls (*q*) of glossal channel attached; *D*, parts of proboscis (maxillæ and labium) flattened out in ventral view; *E*, cross-section of glossa, showing its channel (*Lum*) open below along the groove (*k*), the internal rod (*r*) in roof of channel, and its groove (*l*): *F*, distal end of mentum (*Mt*), dorsal, showing opening of salivary duct (*SalDO*) on base of ligula; *G*, lateral view of left half of proboscis; *H*, glossa (*Gls*) with its rod (*r*) partly torn away, showing retractor muscles (*2RMcl*) attached to its base; *Cd*, cardo; *Hr*, long stiff hairs near tip of glossa; *k*, ventral groove of glossa; *l*, ventral groove of glossal rod; *Lbl*, labella; *LbPlp*, labial palpus; *Lg*, ligula; *Lr*, lorum; *Lum*, channel in glossa; *Mt*, mentum; *Mx*, terminal blade of maxilla; *MxPlp*, maxillary palpus; *n*, basal process of glossal rod; *o*, ventral plate of ligula, carrying base of glossal rod; *p*, dorsal plates of mentum; *Pgl*, paraglossa; *Plg*, palpiger; *q*, inner wall of glossal channel; *r*, rod of glossa; *2RMcl*, retractor muscle of glossal rod; *SalDO*, opening of salivary duct; *Smt*, submentum; *St*, stipes.

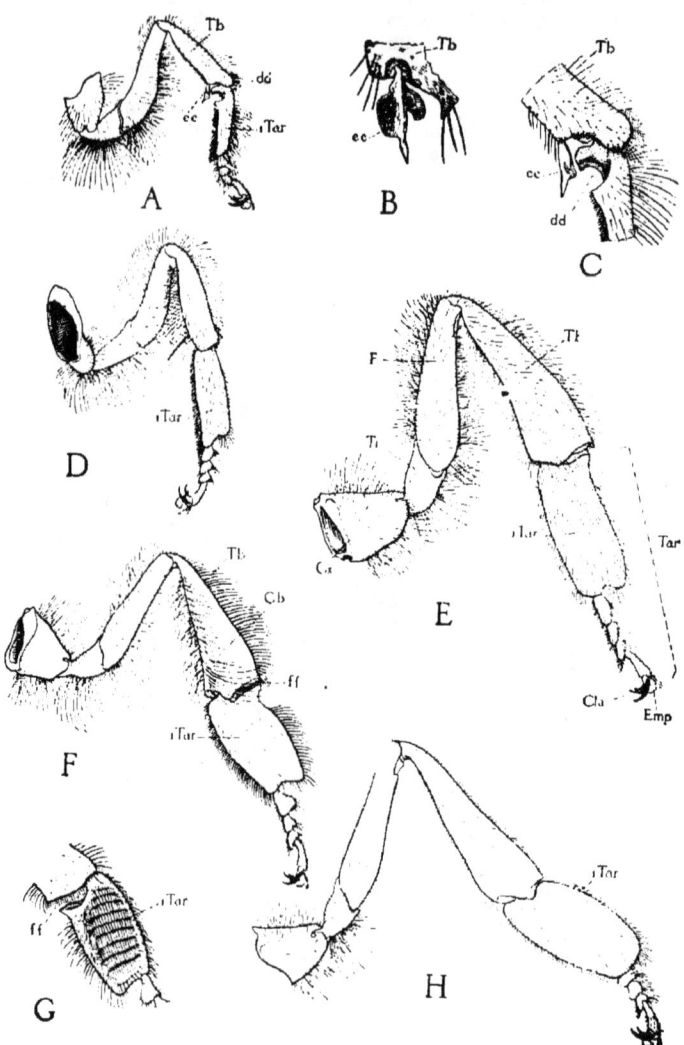

From Bulletin No. 18, "The Anatomy of the Honey-bee," by Snodgrass, Bureau of Ent., Dept. of Ag., Washington, D. C.

FIG. 4.—Details of legs. *A*, front leg of worker, showing position of antenna-cleaner (*dd* and *ee*); *B*, end of tibia of front leg showing spine (*ee*) of antenna-cleaner; *C*, antenna-cleaner, more enlarged; *D*, middle leg of worker; *E*, hind leg of queen; *F*, hind leg of worker, showing pollen-basket; (*Cb*) on outer surface of tibia; *G*, inner view of basal joint of hind tarsus of worker, showing the brush of pollen-gathering hairs; *H*, hind leg of drone; *Cb*, corbiculum, or pollen-basket; *Cla*, claws; *Cx*, coxa; *dd*, notch of antenna-cleaner on basal joint of first tarsus; *ee*, spine of antenna-cleaner on distal end of tibia; *Emp*, empodium, sticky pad between the claws for walking on smooth surfaces); *F*, femur; *ff*, "wax-shears;" *Tar*, tarsus; *1Tar*, first joint of tarsus; *Tb*, tibia

substances. This change is effected partly by the inhaled oxygen combining with the waste products, resulting in the formation of compounds of nitrogen which dissolve in the blood, and of carbonic-acid gas which diffuses into the tracheal tubes and is exhaled. The nitrogen compounds are supposed to be removed by the *Malpighian tubules* (Fig. 6, *Mal*), which are regarded as the kidneys of insects.

The *nervous system* consists of a series of small masses of nerve tissue called *ganglia*, lying along the median ventral line of the body cavity (Fig. 1, *1Gng-7Gng*), the two of the thorax being much larger than those of the abdomen. Each two are connected by a pair of cords called *commissures*. Nerves are given off from these ganglia to the various organs and parts of the body, and to the legs and wings. In the head there are two gan-

spermatozoa are stored during the adult stage of the drone's life. The two vesicles open into the bases of two enormous *mucous glands* (*AcGl*) which come together in a narrow muscular tube, the *ejaculatory duct* (*EjD*). This opens into the anterior end of the *penis* (*Pen*). The last is a complicated organ, shown at E, Fig. 7. It is ordinarily contained within the cavity of the abdomen; but during copulation it is entirely everted, and its basal pouches (*zz*) lock into corresponding pouches of the oviduct of the queen.

The eggs are formed by the *ovaries* of the female (Fig. 8, *Ov*), each of which consists of a thick mass of tubules called the *ovarioles* (*ov*), within which the eggs grow from simple cells at their upper ends into the mature eggs found at their lower ends. The ovarioles of each ovary open into an *oviduct* (*OrD*), which two unite into a wide median

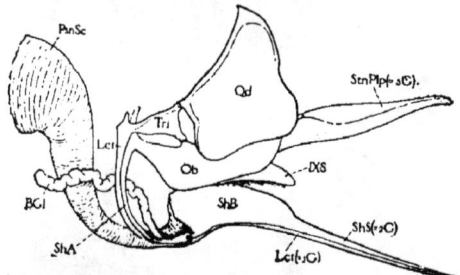

From Bulletin No. 16, "The Anatomy of the Honey-bee," by Snodgrass, Bureau of Ent., Dept. of Ag., Washington, D. C.

FIG. 5.— Left side of sting and its accessory plates, with alkaline gland (*BGl*) and base of poison-sac (*PenSc*) attached. *BGl*, alkaline-poison gland; *Lct*, lancet; *Ob*, oblong plate; *PenSc*, base of poison-sac, holding secretion from acid-gland (see Fig. 8); *Qd*, quadrate plate; *IXS*, median part of ninth abdominal sternum; *ShA*, arm of sheath; *Shb*, bulb of sheath; *ShS*, shaft of sheath; *StnPlp*, palpus of sting; *Tri*, triangular plate.

glionic masses. One is called the *brain* (*OpL*), and is situated above the œsophagus, where it gives off nerves to the eyes, the antennæ, the front, and the labrum. The other called the *subœsophageal ganglion*, lies in the lower part of the head, and innervates the mouth parts, while it is connected by commissures with both the brain and the first thoracic ganglion.

The *reproductive system* consists of those organs that produce the spermatozoa in the male and the eggs in the female and their accessory parts.

The spermatozoa are formed in the *testes* of the male (Fig. 7, A, *Tes*), a pair of small bodies in the front part of the abdomen, said to be developed at their highest in the pupal stage. Each is connected by a coiled tube, the *vas defferens* (*VDef*), with a long sac, the *seminal vesicle* (*Ves*) in which the

tube called the *vagina* (*Vag*) that swells posteriorly into a large pouch known as the *bursa copulatrix* (*BCpx*), opening to the exterior in the eighth segment beneath the base of the sting.

During copulation the drone ejects the spermatozoa into the upper end of the vagina of the queen. The spermatozoa consist of minute vibratory threads (Fig. 7, C), which, probably, by their own motion, make their way up through a small tube opening into the dorsal wall of the vagina, and so reach a globular sac (Fig. 7, *Spm*) called the *spermatheca*. Here they are held during the rest of the lifetime of the queen, to be extruded in small bundles, of about a hundred each, according to Breslaw, upon the eggs passing out of the vagina. Thus are the female eggs *fertilized*, the drone eggs developing without the addition of the male element.

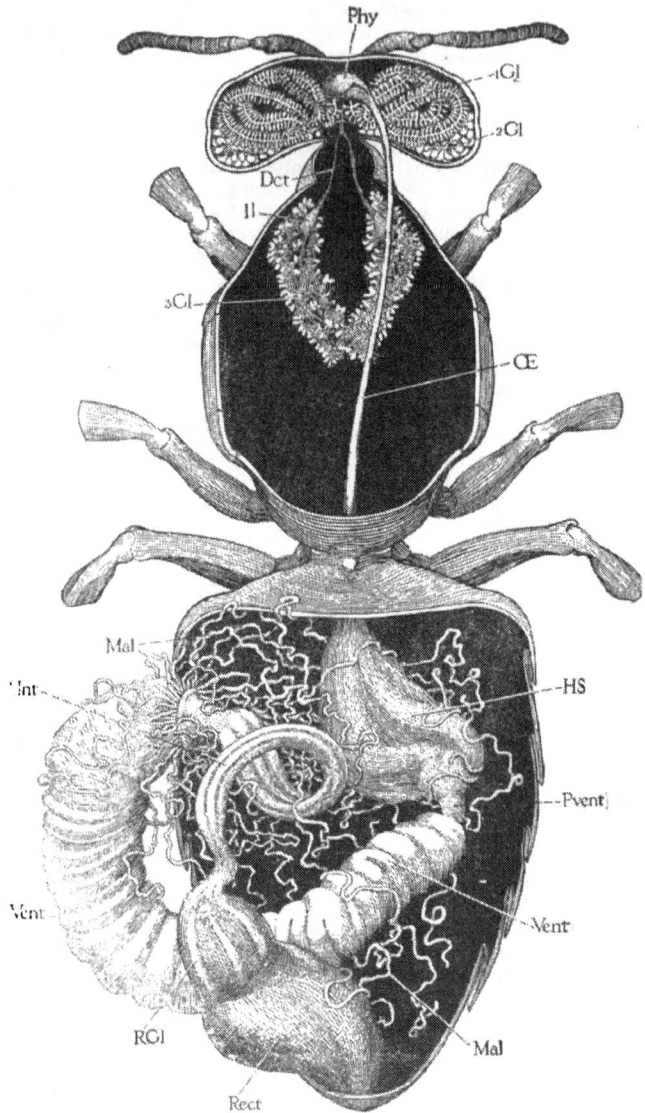

FIG. 6.—Alimentary canal and salivary glands of worker, dorsal. *Dct*, salivary duct; *1Gl*, pharyngeal glands of head (supracerebral glands); *2Gl*, salivary glands of head (postcerebral glands); *3Gl*, salivary glands of the thorax; *HS*, honey-stomach; *ll*, reservoir of thoracic salivary gland; *Mal*, Malpighian tubules; *Œ*, œsophagus; *Phy*, pharynx; *Pvent*, proventriculus; *Rect*, rectum; *Rgl*, rectal glands; *SInt*, small intestine; *Vent*, ventriculus.

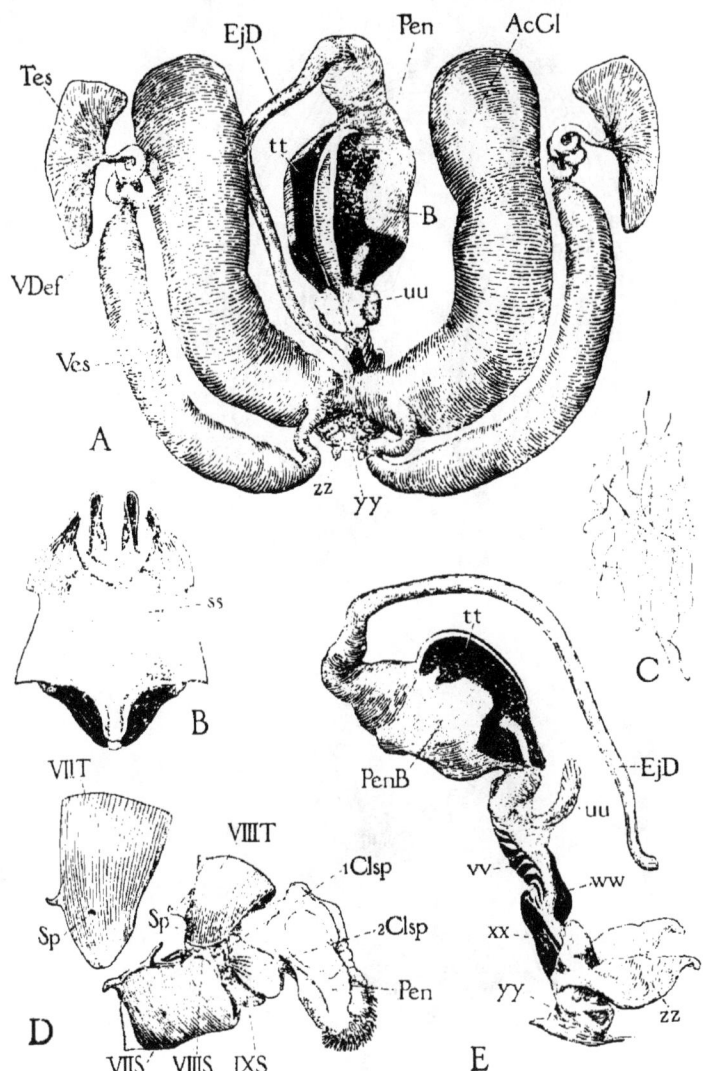

FIG. 7.—A, reproductive organs of drone, dorsal; B, inner view of dorsal wall of bulb of penis; C, group of spermatozoa; D, terminal segments of drone, lateral, showing penis (Pen) partly protruded; E, lateral view of penis and ejaculatory duct (EjD); AcGl, accessory mucous gland; B, bulb of penis; 1Clsp, 2Clsp, clasping organs of ninth abdominal sternum; Pen, penis; PenB, bulb of penis; VIIS-IXS, seventh to ninth abdominal sterna; ss, gelatinous mass of inner wall of bulb of penis; VIIT-VIIIT, seventh and eighth abdominal terga; tt, dorsal plates of bulb of penis; Tes, testis; uu, fimbriated lobe at base of bulb of penis; vv, ladder-like plates of penis; VDef, vas deferens; Ves, seminal vesicle; ww, xx, dorsal and ventral plates in wall of penis; yy, terminal chamber of penis through which the rest is everted; zz, copulatory pouches of penis.

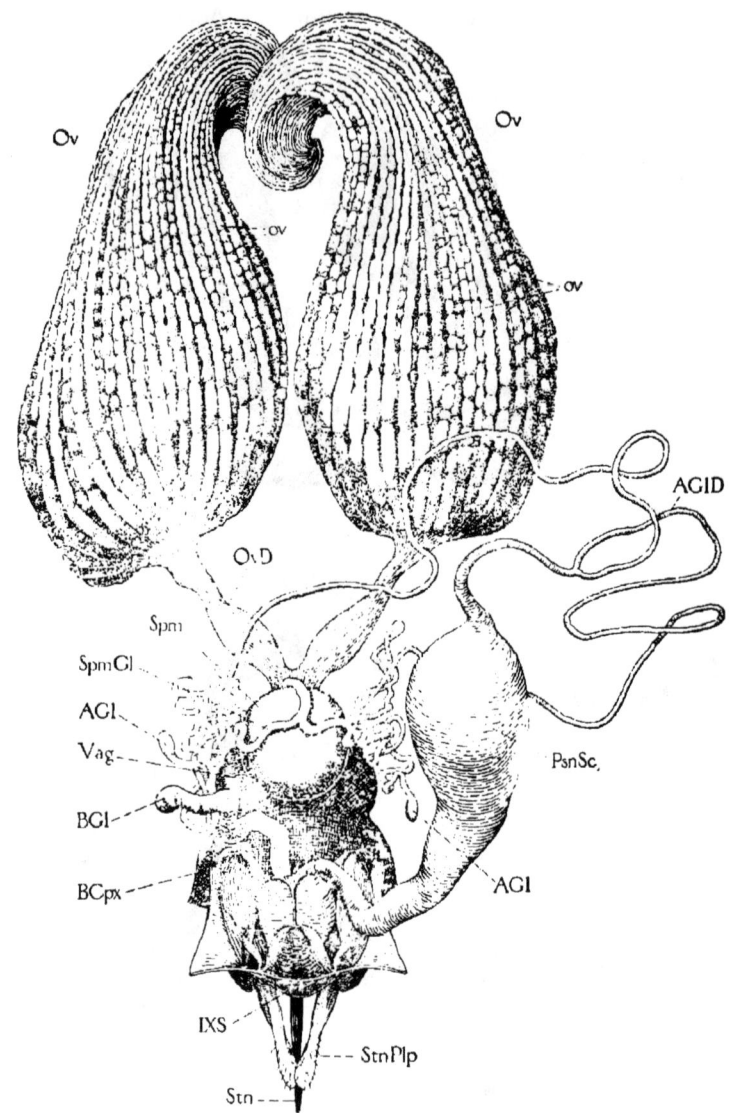

FIG. 8 —Reproductive organs of queen, dorsal, together with sting, its muscles, glands, and poison-sac. *AGl*, acid-glands of sting; *AGlD*, duct of acid-glands; *BCpx*, bursa copulatrix; *BGl*, alkaline gland of sting; *Ov*, ovaries; *ov*, ovarioles; *OvD*, oviduct; *PsnSc*, poison-sac; *IXS*, median part of ninth abdominal sternum; *Spm*, sac of spermatheca; *SpmGl*, spermathecal gland; *Stn*, sting; *StnPlp*, palpus of sting; *Vag*, vagina.

Absconding Swarm.—A swarm which leaves for parts unknown.

Adair Frame.—13⅝ inches long, 11¼ inches deep.

After Swarms.—Swarms which come after the first swarm.

Albino Bee.—A very light-colored variety of the Italian bee.

Alighting-board.—The projection before the entrance to a hive.

American Frame.—12 inches long, 12 inches deep.

Antenna.—Horns of the bee; are the organs of touch, and perhaps other senses.

Anthers.—Tiny double bags containing pollen in the male parts of flowers.

Apiarian.—Relating to bees.

Apiarist.—A bee-keeper.

Apiary.—A collection of bee-hives, colonies, appliances, usually on a spot of ground.

Apiculture.—Bee-keeping.

Apidæ.—The insect family to which bees belong.

Apis.—The genus to which honey-bees belong.

Aphis.—Plant-louse which secrets honey-dew.

Artificial Fecundation.—The impregnation of virgin queens in confinement (never accomplished).

Artificial Fertilization.—Fecundation of virgin queens in confined spaces (not correct term).

Artificial Pasturage.—Plants purposely cultivated for their bee-nectar.

Artificial Pollen.—Rye meal or pea flour fed as a substitute for the pollen of flowers.

Artificial Swarm.—A swarm made by dividing a colony of bees.

Association Frame.—The standard frame of the British Isles. 8½x14 inches.

Bacillus alvei.—Cause of European foul brood. (Cheshire.)

Bacillus Guntheri.—Origin of sour brood. (Burri.)

Bacillus Larvæ.—Cause of American foul brood. (White.)

Balling a Queen.—A mob of bees lightly clustering around a queen in an effort to kill her.

Bar-frame.—The English name for Lang. frames.

Bee-bread.—The pollen of flowers gathered by the bees and deposited in the comb.

Bee-brush.—A brush used in removing bees from off their combs.

Bee Culture.—The care of bees.

Bee-dress.—A suit or dress to wear while working with bees and preventing stings.

Bee-escape.—A trap (or small gin) to allow bees to pass out of a super, but preventing their return.

Bee-gloves.—Generally made of cloth or leather, to protect the hands from stings.

Bee-gum.—A hollow log used for holding a swarm of bees.

Bee-hive.—A box or other contrivance for holding a colony of bees.

Bee-house.—A shelter for bee-hives.

Bee-line.—The shortest distance between two points.

Bee Metamorphosis.—The bee passes through three stages before becoming a perfect insect—first the egg, then the larva, and next the

nymph. The following will serve to show how this is accomplished:

	Queen, days.	Worker, days.	Drone, days.
Incubation of the egg...	3	3	3
Time of feeding the larva	5	5	6
Larva spinning Cocoons.	1	2	3
Resting period.........	2	3	4
Passing from larva to nymph	1	1	1
Time in the nymph state	3	7	7
Total period of growth	15	21	24
Hatching takes place on.	4	4	4
Cell sealed	9	9	9
Bee leaves its cell......	16	22	25
Bee flies	21	38	38

Bee-moth.—A small moth which deposits its eggs in combs.

Bee Paralysis.—A disease which affects adult bees, cause unknown.

Bee Plants.—Flowering plants which produce nectar for bees.

Bee-pest.—Foul brood.

Bee Space.—From ¼ to ⅜ of an inch.

Bee-tent.—Used in covering a hive of bees while it is being operated upon.

Beeswax.—A sort of fat made by the bees and secreted in folds or pockets under the abdomen in the form of scales, which are subsequently kneaded into comb.

Bee-tree.—A hollow tree occupied by a colony of wild bees.

Bee-veil.—A net veil for protecting the head from the attacks of bees.

Black Bee.—A variety of the honey bee from Germany which is nearly black or dark brown and found wild in many parts of the U. S. Huber, Dzierzon and others speak of "black" bees in a hive as separate from the workers and drones.

Bottom Board.—The floor of a bee-hive.

Box Hive.—A plain box used for housing a colony of bees.

Box Honey.—Honey stored in small boxes or sections.

Brace Combs.—Small pieces of comb made as connecting links between two combs.

Brimstoning.—The operation of killing a colony of bees with sulphur fumes.

Brood.—Young bees not yet emerged from their cells.

Brood-comb.—Combs reserved for breeding purposes.

Brood-nest.—The part of hive reserved for breeding only.

Brood-rearing.—Raising bees from the egg.

Brushed Swarm.—An artificial swarm of bees made by brushing a portion of the bees of a full colony into a spare hive. This prevents natural swarming.

Bumble Bees.—Of the genus Bombus. There are many species.

Burr Combs.—Bits of combs which form ladders between the brood chamber and supers.

Bouton or Button.—The spoon of the bees' tongue.

Candied Honey.—Crystallized honey, or honey that has solidified by the action of cold.

Capped Brood.—Young bees in their cells with a covering of wax to protect them.

17

Cappings.—The covering of the cells.

Carniolan Bees.—A variety of the common black bee from Carniola, Austria, said to be larger and gentler than the ordinary bee.

Carton.—A pasteboard box for holding a pound of comb honey.

Cell.—The hexagonal apartment in a comb.

Cell Cups.—Artificial cells for rearing queens.

Chaff Hive.—A hive having double walls filled between with chaff.

Chorion.—Shell of the bee egg.

Chyle Food or Chyme.—A food elaborated in the stomach of mature bees for the purpose of feeding their young. This food varies in strength, the richest being fed to growing queens. The chyle food when given is absorbed not only by the mouth, but also by means of glands in the skin, and for this purpose the larvae actually float in food. It resembles milk.

Chyme.—See Chyle Food.

Chrysalis.—This is applied to the state of the bee in its transformation from a larval condition into an imago or perfect bee. It is synonymous with pupa and nymph.

Claustral Hive.—Having a covered-in entrance with ventilator for winter.

Claws.—A bee has two claws on its feet.

Cloister Hive.—A hive provided with a cloistered entrance, which excludes the light in winter weather to prevent the bees from flying.

Closed-end Frames.—Frames for comb in which the end bars touch all the way down.

Clustering.—This refers to the peculiar manner bees cling together by means of hooklets on their wings.

Clypeus.—The nose of the bee.

Colony.—A swarm of bees, comprising a mass of workers, one queen and some drones (in summer).

Comb.—An arrangement of hexagonal cells made of wax to hold young bees or honey; for workers 5 cells to the inch, and for drones 4 cells.

Comb Basket.—A light box of wood or tin for carrying combs completely covered.

Comb Foundation.—Thin sheets of beeswax stamped to imitate comb, forming a base on which the bees will construct a complete comb.

Comb-Foundation Machine.—A machine for stamping the foregoing.

Comb-guide.—Strips of wood used as a guide in the construction of combs.

Comb Honey.—The product of the bee in a natural state.

Cushion.—A bag filled with some porous loose material for covering the brood nest of a hive.

Cyprian Bee.—The native bee of the island of Cyprus.

Danzenbaker Frame.—17 inches long, 7½ inches deep.

Decoy Hive.—A hive placed with the object of attracting passing swarms.

Dequeen.—Depriving a colony of bees of its queen, to unqueen.

Dividing.—Separating a colony in a manner to produce two or more colonies.

Division Board.—A board of the same length and height as the side of a hive used to contract the size of the chamber.

Drone.—Male bee.

Drone Brood.—The brood of drones, bred in larger cells than worker bees.

Drone Egg.—The egg from which a drone hatches—an unimpregnated egg.

Drumming.—A mode of inducing bees to leave one hive for another by thumping on the sides of the hive in which they have resided. The two hives should touch.

Dysentery.—A bee-keeper's name for catarrh of the intestines in bees caused by bad conditions.

Dzierzon System.—A system of beekeeping founded on 13 propositions written by Baron Berlepsch after a study of the beekeeping methods of the late Father Dzierzon, a renowned German beekeeper.

Edulcoration.—The process by which bees condense, sweeten, transform and acidify the nectar collected by them.

Egyptian Bee.—Apis fasciata. A smaller and more beautiful bee than the Italian, but exceedingly cross.

Embryo.—In the natural history of bees this has reference to the unfertilized eggs in the ovaries of the queen.

Entrance.—An opening in a hive to allow the bees to pass.

Entrance Blocks.—Three-cornered pieces of wood for regulating the size of the entrance.

Extracted Honey.—Honey obtained from combs by means of a centrifugal extractor.

Extractor.—A machine for throwing honey out of combs by centrifugal force.

Fdn.—An abbreviation for the words *comb foundation.*

Feces.—Excreta of bees.

Feeders.—Appliances for feeding bees artificially.

Femur.—Thigh of the honey bee.

Fence.—A slotted separator resembling an ordinary wooden fence. It is used as a guide to enable the bees to build combs that are straight.

Fertile.—Not barren, but productive.

Fixed Frames.—Comb frames which are not loose in the hive, closed-end frames.

Formic Acid.—An acid added to honey by the bees to help preserve it. The same acid is found in the sting and head.

Foul Brood.—A malignant contagious disease of bees affecting the brood.

Foundation.—See Comb Foundation.

Frame.—Four slats of wood to hold a comb invented by the late Rev. L. L. Langstroth of Oxford, Ohio. This frame requires a space ¼ of an inch on all sides to be effective. Can be moved in any direction.

Fumigate.—Generally means to apply sulphur fumes to bees.

Galleria cerella.—Scientific name of the beeswax-moth.

Ganglia.—Nerves of the bee.

Glucose.—A kind of sugar 3-5 as sweet as cane sugar made by the action of dilute acids on starch. Generally speaking it is detrimental to health on account of the presence in it of sulphites acquired in the process of manufacture. Nearly always used as an adulterant. It appears in two forms, one of which is known as corn syrup and the other as crystallized grape sugar.

Go-backs.—Unfinished combs in sections which have to be returned to the hive to be finished.

Grafting.—Applied by beekeepers to the process of removing ordinary larvae from their cells into a queen cell cup with the purpose in view of having them reared into queens.

Green honey.—Unripe honey.

Hatching Brood.—Young bees just gnawing their way out of the cells.

Heddon Frame.—5⅜ inches deep by 18 1-16 in length.

Hermaphrodite Bees.—Bees which belong to no sex—imperfect bees.

Hive.—A home for bees furnished by man.

Holy Land Bees.—A variety of bees from Palestine. Somewhat resemble Italian bees, but are more irritable.

Honey.—The nectar of flowers edulcorated by the bees.

Honey Evaporator.—A machine for removing water from honey when deemed too thin.

Honey Sac.—A special stomach for holding nectar; it is also used to prepare the honey and partially to convert it.

Honey Bee.—Apis mellifica.

Honey-Board.—A board of slats or perforated metal placed between the brood-chamber and the honey-chamber to break the continuity of the two.

Honey Box.—A box for comb honey, closed on all sides, and provided with holes to allow the bees access. Almost obsolete.

Honey-comb.—A wall of double cells of wax, in most cases about an inch in thickness. Empty comb is ⅞ inch thick, and capped nearly an inch. There are 56 cells in one square inch, 28 on each side for worker comb. Drone comb has 32 cells to the inch, 16 on a side. One cell is opposite to three others (in part).

Honey-dew.—A sweet liquid similar to the nectar of flowers deposited on the leaves and branches of plants. It is of two kinds. One is the production of plant lice and the other exudes from around the axils of leaves and flowers.

Honey Extractor.—A machine for throwing the honey from combs by centrifugal force.

Honey Gate.—An iron faucet used for drawing of thick liquids from barrels or other receptacles.

Honey-house.—A small building for the purpose of honey extraction, storage, etc.

Honey Knife.—A double-edged steel knife with a bent handle for shaving off the capping of combs.

House Apiary.—A double-walled building used for the protection of bee hives from the extremes of heat and cold.

Hybrids.—Usually used by beekeepers to designate a cross between the common black bee and the Italian.

Hymettus.—A mountain district of Greece famous for its wild thyme honey celebrated in classic poetry and history.

Imago.—The fully developed bee or other insect.

Introducing.—The manner in which a strange queen may be introduced to a colony of bees in the stead of a former one to which they were much attached. It is usually performed by hanging the queen in a cage in the midst of the strange bees several days until she acquires the odor of the hive.

Introducing Cage.—A small box of wire and wood. See INTRODUCING, in the body of the work

Inversion.—A process of turning a hive upside down to compel the bees to attach their combs to the bottom bar, also to remove honey from brood frames into the supers.

Italian Bee.—Originally from the Italian part of Switzerland, but now bred in this country in a manner to produce a new variety superior to the original.

Italianizing.—Converting an apiary from a race of bees to the Italian variety exclusively. Done by changing the queens.

Jumbo Frame.—17⅝ inches long, 11¼ inches in depth.

Lamp Nursery.—A kind of hot water incubator for bees where queens or cells are placed till wanted.

Langstroth Frame.—17⅝ inches long by 9⅛ inches depth.

Langstroth Hive.—Any hive having frames hanging by shoulders with a bee space all round them is an L. hive.

L. Frame.—A frame of the size first introduced by Langstroth.

L. Hive.—A hive provided with frames of the Langstroth dimensions.

Larva (plural *larvæ* or *larvas*). A bee in the worm state, unsealed brood.

Laying Worker.—A worker bee which has acquired the power of laying eggs; as these have not been impregnated by a drone the eggs laid produce none but drones.

Ligurian Bee.—Italian bee, named for the district in which the best Italian bees are found.

Lining Bees.—Watching the direction of their flight.

Loose Frames.—Loose hanging Langstroth frames which are spaced by the eye.

Mal-de-May.—A peculiar disease of bees occurring mostly in May. As yet it is confined to Europe.

Mandibles.—The jaws of the bee working like a pair of pliers, but sidewise, not up and down, as with ourselves.

May-pest.—Same as Mal-de-May.

Melipona Bees.—A genus of stingless bees inhabiting South and Central America, comprising at least 50 species, some domesticated.

Mel Extractor.—Former name of the honey extractor.

Metal Corner.—Corners for frames on which is the support for the same, used because the bees do not propolize them.

Movable Frame.—A loose comb frame which can be removed completely from the hive for the purpose of examination or use. A Langstroth frame.

Mummy Brood.—An European bee disease.

Natural Swarm.—A swarm of bees issuing spontaneously from the mother hive.

Nectaries.—The parts of a flower wherein is secreted the nectar.

Neuter.—A name sometimes applied to worker bees.

Non-swarming Hive.—A hive so constructed as to control the desire to swarm.

Nucleus.—A small hive of bees used for various purposes, plural *nuclei*.

Nurse Bees.—Young bees less than 14 days old.

Observatory Hive.—A hive largely of glass to allow of the bees being observed at work.

Ocelli.—The three single eyes of the bee.

Overstocking.—A condition reached when there are too many bees for a given locality.

Paraffine.—A white translucent substance somewhat resembling beeswax, derived from mineral oil and sold very largely in the form of candles. It is used by beekeepers to render honey barrels tight.

Parasite.—There are several parasites of bees, the principal being Braula cœca.

Parent Stock.—The mother of a swarm.

Parthenogenesis.—The law that only the female eggs require fecundation or fertilization by the semen of the drone, stored in the spermatheca of the queen. A virgin queen produces drones only.

Perforated Zinc.—Zinc sheet metal having oblong holes 1-6 of an inch in width to allow worker bees alone to pass, and excluding queens and drones.

Pickle Brood.—A mild contagious disease of bees affecting the brood.

Piping.—A quakking noise made by young queens —a note of defiance.

Pistil.—The female organs of a flower collectively.

Plain Sections.—Comb honey sections with no insets or scalloped edges.

Pollen.—The fecundating element in flowers gathered by the bees in the form of a sticky flour kneaded into pellets deposited on their legs.

Pollen Basket.—A cavity on the hind legs of the bee wherein is deposited the pollen gathered from flowers.

Proboscis.—The trunk of a bee in which is the tongue or pump.

Propolis.—A kind of glue or resin collected by the bees and chiefly used to close up cracks and small spaces.

Pupa.—The stage of the bee before becoming a perfect insect, a chrysalis.

Quakking.—Noise made by young queens in answer to each other.

Queen.—A fully developed female bee capable of being the sole mother of a swarm of bees. The mother bee.

Queen Cage.—A small box of wire and wood in which queens are held prisoners.

Queen-cells.—Large cells in which queens are raised.

Queening.—The act of introducing a queen into a queenless colony of bees.

Queenless.—Having no queen.

Queen-rearing.—Raising queens.

Queen Register.—A written history of a queen tacked on a hive.

Queen's Voice.—A sound made by a queen. See Piping.

Quinby Frame.—A plain frame without shoulders and having closed ends. 18½ inches long by 11¼ in depth ; old style 19¼ by 11 deep.

Quinby Hive.—A hive invented by Mr. Quinby based on the hive of Huber's leaf hive of the latter part of the 18th century.

Quilt.—A cover for brood frames made in the form of a thin cushion.

Rabbet.—Usually has reference to a narrow piece of tin folded in a peculiar manner to form a rest for the shoulders of the hanging frames.

Rendering Wax.—The process of melting combs and refining wax from its impurities, usually done by means of hot water or steam accompanied by pressure on the mass of material.

Repository.—An above-ground house resembling a cellar for protecting hives from cold winter weather. Usually erected on a hillside.

Reversing.—Turning over or inverting a hive with bees to accomplish certain results.

*Ripe Honey—*Honey in which the process of edulcoration by the bees has been completed. See Edulcoration.

Robbing.—Pilfering from other hives when flowers are scarce.

Royal Cell.—Queen cell.

Royal Jelly.—A rich food secreted in the chyle stomach of bees and fed only to young queens in the larval condition.

Scent Organ.—Thought to be the antennæ of the bee.

Scaled Brood.—Capped brood, the young bee is not exactly sealed because the capping is porous.

Section Box.—A sectionally constructed box for containing a small honey comb.

Section Holder.—A device for holding sections while in process of being filled on the hive.

Separator.—A thin board or piece of tin placed between combs to insure their being very accurately made by the bees, particularly section comb honey.

Sheet.—A piece of enameled cloth for placing over the brood chamber conserving the heat.

Shook Swarm.—An artificial swarm made by shaking bees from a very populous colony into a fresh hive. By this means natural swarming is closely imitated.

Skep.—Generally used in the country to indicate the old fashioned hives without frames. In England it is synonymous with the word hive.

Skeppist.—An old-fashioned bee-keeper.

Slumgum.—The refuse from a wax extractor.

Smoker.—A machine for making smoke and puffing it to control bees.

Solar Wax Extractor.—A glass covered box melting beeswax by the heat of the sun.

Sour Brood.—Similar to foul-brood ; almost identical.

Spent Queen.—A mother bee whose ovaries are almost or wholly exhausted.

Spermatozoon.—One of the germs contained in the semen of drones.

Spiracles.—Air tubes through which the bee breathes.

Spirochœte apis.—Microbe found in foul brood by Maasen.

Spreading Brood.—The work of transposing combs filled with brood and empty ones that the queen will be provided with empty cells to lay in.

Stamens.—Male organ of flowers producing pollen.

Stigmas.—Female organs of flowers.

Supersede.—A plan the bees have of disposing of a decaying queen and substituting a young one.

Swarm.—A natural division of a hive of bees into two for the purpose of increase. The old queen goes with the first swarm.

Swarm Catcher.—A basket on the end of a pole designed to catch swarms hanging up in trees.

Swarming Season.—The period of the year when swarms usually issue in numbers.

Syrians.—Same as Holy Land bees, light colored, productive and cross.

Tarsus.—The foot of a bee.

Tested Queen.—A queen whose progeny show she has mated with a drone of her own race.

Thorax.—The waist of a bee.

Tiering Up.—Adding supers on the top of a hive.

Transferring.—Ordinarily applied to the process of changing bees and combs from common boxes to movable frame hives.

Transformations.—See Metamorphosis.

Transposition Process.—Transposing a larva from one cell to another with a spoon.

Travel Stain.—A term applied to comb honey with a discolored appearance and supposed to be caused by the dirty feet of the bees, which it is not.

Trigona Bees.—A genus of stingless bees in South America and Asia. Some species bite furiously.

Unqueening.—Removing the queen of a colony of bees.

Unripe Honey.—Honey not sufficiently evaporated and formic acid added by the bees.

Unsealed Larvæ.—Young bees in the worm form not yet covered over with a wax capping.

Virgin Queen.—An unfecundated queen which can lay only drone-producing eggs.

Wax.—A secretion produced from certain glands or pockets on the under side of the abdomen of the bee, a species of fat produced by the consumption of honey or any kind of sugar. It is estimated bees consume from 6 to 20 lbs. of honey in the production of one pound of wax, depending on circumstances. Wax is produced by bees quite spontaneously when the weather is warm and food abundant. In cool weather it requires much more food to produce the wax.

Wax Extractor.—An appliance for rendering wax by the action of heat and also pressure.

Wax Pocket.—The receptacles on the under side of the abdomen wherein the bees secret their wax.

Weaning.—Larvæ intended for workers are weaned ; if not, they become queens.

Wild Bees.—Escaped or feral bees living in hollow trees or in small caves.

Windbreaks.—Either specially constructed fences or barriers composed of growing trees to reduce the force of the wind.

Wintering.—The care of the bees during winter.

Worker Bee.—An undeveloped female bee, dwarfed by withholding stimulating food during the larval condition.

Worker Egg.—A female egg, will produce either queen or worker.

*Zinc.—*See Perforated Zinc.

Picture Gallery of
Apiaries and Bee-exhibits

During the years since our journal, *Gleanings in Bee Culture*, was started, a large number of fine and beautiful engravings of apiaries and of bee and honey exhibits have been presented to our subscribers. These engravings were executed at considerable cost; and as they are instructive, and suggestive of many ideas in regard to apiaries and exhibits, we have thought best to put the better part of them in permanent form right after the body of this work. Instead of going to a large expense in visiting different apiaries, one can see how different bee-keepers arrange their hives, and how their apiaries look. Each engraving in order will be found to contain some hint or distinctive feature which it is hoped will be found valuable. As our space is limited, we give a brief description of each engraving by number. The last of the series show photographic views of The A. I. Root Company's manufacturing and publishing plant.   PUBLISHERS.

No. 1.—A. E. Manum's Side-hill Apiary.

No. 2.—Hauling Honey to the Barn from the Apiary of Thorne & Ercanbreck, Lovelocks, Nevada,

No. 3.—Apiary of W. J. McCarroll, Tropico, Cal.

No. 4.—Making Straw Skeps in England.—*British Bee Journal.*

No. 5.—Apiary of John Bodenschatz, Lemont, Illinois; largely Supported by Sweet Clover Sown in Waste Places by the Owner.

No. 6.—View in a Mexican Apiary.

No. 7.—Solar Wax-extractor, having Artificial Bottom-heat Attachment, Belonging
to Philip Large, Longmont, Colorado.

No. 8.—A Corner of Alexander's Apiary, Showing Nuclei Used in Queen-rearing.

No. 9.—General View of Alexander's Apiary of 750 Colonies; Taken from Northwest.

No. 10 —Honey-house and Bee-cellar of E. W. Alexander, Delanson, N. Y.

No. 11.—Interior of E. W. Alexander's Honey-house, at Delanson. N. Y.

No. 12.—A Swarm of Schoolma'ms and Schoolmasters after Taking Their First Lesson in Bee-keeping at The A. I. Root Company's Home Apiary, Medina, Ohio.

No. 13.—A Fine Honey exhibit at the Wisconsin State Fair, by William E. Prisk.

No. 11.—Apiary of Wessing Brothers, near Nicolaus, California.

No. 15.—Bee-farm of The A. I. Root Company, at Salem, New Jersey.

No. 16.—One of the Out-apiaries of The A. I. Root Company, at Salem, New Jersey, for Breeding Bees.

No. 17.—Apiary of Charles G. Macklin, Morrison, Illinois; Winner of Second Prize in Photo Contest.

No. 18.—W. S. Hart's Apiary, Hawks Park, Florida.

No 12.—Exhibit of The A. I. Root Company, at Omaha, Nebraska.

No. 20.—The 500-colony Apiary of J. F. McIntyre, near Ventura, Cal., looking East.

No. 21.—Mel Bonum Apiary, Goodna, Queensland, Australia. Said to be Largest Queen-rear.ng Establishment in Southern Hemisphere.

No. 22.—Apiary of W. T. Richardson, Simi, California.

No. 24.—Cuban Apiary of J. H. Martin, better known as "Rambler."

No. 24.—L. L. Langstroth in his Eighty-second Year.

No. 25.—Crowder's Extracting-house on Whee's, Selma, California.

No. 26.—An Apiary in Australia.

No. 27.—Out-apiary of J. F. Aitkin, Reno, Nevada.

No. 28.—A Part of the Apiary belonging to Wm. H. Horstman, of Chicago, Ill., showing the Capitol Hive containing three full Colonies and a Nucleus.

No. 29.—Jas. McNeill's Apiary at Hudson, N. Y. Grass Cut and Hives Arranged in Rows.

No. 30.—Dr. C, C, Miller,

No. 31.—Williams' Corrugated-iron Bee-sheds.

No. 32.---Dr. Miller Watching the Flight of his Bees to and from his
Sweet-clover Field.   Rear end of his Home.

No. 33.—Method in Use in Holland of Finding a Queen in a New Swarm.

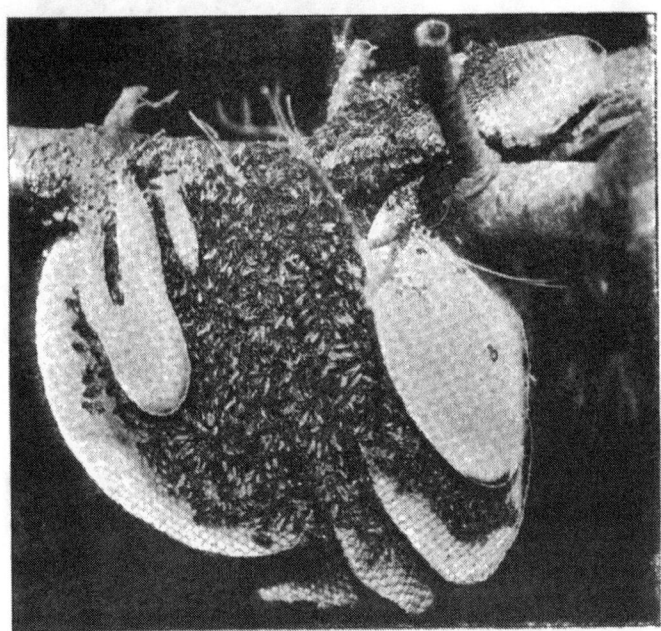

No. 34.—Comb Built in the Open Air Late in the Fall.

No. 85.—Moving Four Wagon-loads of Bees by Traction-engine, in Canada.

No. 36.---Mud Bee-hives in Jez.eel, Palestine.
Photo by I. W. Metcalfe, Oberlin, Ohio.

No. 37.---Stewart's Buick which He Uses for Out-apiary Work.

No. 38.—One of W. Z. Hutchinson's Apiaries in Northern Michigan.

No. 39.—W. C. Sorter's House-apiary.

No. 40.---Interior of Sorter's House-apiary.

No. 41.— *Virgil Sires Portable Gasoline engine Extracting-outfit.*

No. 42 ---A Small Apiary Close to a Car-barn in Harrisburg, Pa.

No. 43.—An Outdoor Colony Found on Sugarloaf Mountain, near
Boulder, Colorado.

No. 44. --The Method of Shaking Bees into a Swarm-box Preparatory to Shipment.

No. 45.---Disinfection of Hives and Supers by Use of Fire.

No. 46.—First-prize Exhibit of Honey at the Canadian National Exhibition.

No. 35.—F. W. Redfield's House Made of Honey for Exhibition Purposes.

No. 36.—The A. I. Root Company's Exhibit at the Jamestown Exposition.

No. 49.—F. Greiner's Apiary, Naples, N. Y., in Mid-winter.

No. 50.—A Swarm of Bees Entering a Hive from the Sack in which They were Captured.

No. 51.—George H. Rex & Son's Permanent Bee-shed.

THE engravings that follow next in order show the hive-manufacturing and publishing plant of The A. I. Root Company, located at Medina, Ohio. As we have hundreds of visitors who come every year to look over this peculiar establishment, the output from which is devoted almost exclusively to the interests of the bee, we thought that many of the readers of this work, living a thousand miles or more away, might like to pay us a visit. We are glad to give them this opportunity so far as it is possible by the aid of the camera.

THE A. I. ROOT COMPANY. By E. R. Root.

Views of a Part of The A. I. Root Company's Lumber-yards.

The A. I. Root Company's Manufacturing Plant. View from the Southeast. Lower Cut shows Court between some of the Buildings.

Birdseye View of a Part of Our Home Apiary in 1906, Showing the Hexagonal Design and the Wall of Evergreens, as Planned by A. I. Root 30 Years Ago.

The A. I. Root Company's Lumber-sheds where an Aggregate of $75,000 Worth of Lumber is Stored at One Time.

Part of The A. I. Root Company's Lumber-yards.

View of Covered Lumber-yard Containing the Material for Bee-keepers' Supplies, as seen from the Top of the Smoke-stack.

Partial View of The A. I. Root Company's Manufacturing Plant, looking from the south.

The A. I. Root Company's Fire-proof Warehouse, 148x48, three stories, with loading-platform and steel bridge connecting old Warehouse on the south.

Two of The A. I. Root Company's Warehouses, with a floor-space of 37,000 square feet.

The East and West Railroad Connections and the Warehouse Facilities of The A. I. Root
Company.

Upper View Shows The A. I. Root Company's Office and Publishing House.   Lower View Shows the Interior of the Printing Department.

Interior View of The A. I. Root Company's New Office.

"Gleanings in Bee Culture" Ready for the Postoffice.

NOTE.—The view shows only about one-third of the list ready to mail.—ED.

Description of Foregoing Engravings.

No. 1.—This picture shows A. E. Manum's side-hill apiary. This spot was selected because the ground is descending, thus affording good drainage, and Mr. Manum thinks the bees can locate their hives better in such a place, especially the young queens when they go out to mate and as every hive can be seen from the honey-house, the attendant can be watching for swarms while working inside. It must not be supposed that this hill is very steep, as the picture would lead one to think, as the descent is very slight neither are the hives arranged on the amphitheater plan, but are set in straight rows. Mr. Manum has three apiaries on level ground, and he finds the water from melting snow often makes it too damp for the bees ; hence his preference for a slope.

No. 2.—This view is thoroughly characteristic of Nevada, showing the bonanza system on which bees are kept in the Sage-brush State. The honey usually obtained is not only conspicuous by its quantity, but its quality as well. Owing to the fact that the honey is mostly collected from alfalfa clover, and the extreme dryness of the climate, the honey of Nevada is never surpassed in color, flavor, or density combined. It is not unusual to see piled up underneath the cottonwood-trees ten or twenty tons of honey awaiting an opportunity to ship it to the eastern markets, where it is highly appreciated. Owing to the extreme dryness of the climate it is wholly impracticable to use wooden packages, and tin takes its place altogether, as is shown by the illustration. Those who look on Nevada as a desert will probably be astonished to know it is an excellent honey-producing State.

No. 3.—This beautiful picture was shown the author of this book (E. R. Root) while he was in Los Angeles. The location is six miles north of Los Angeles, and is an ideal place for wintering. The foot of the mountain, in the background, is such as may be seen there on all unreclaimed land. Between the mountain and hives may be seen a growing crop of alfalfa. The trees at the left are probably orange. Each hive is the center of six others standing around it, and they are far enough apart so one can walk around each hive. The extracting-room is a cloth tent. An iron pipe leads from the extracting-room to the storage-tank. The highest yield Mr. McCarroll has had per colony is 200 lbs. of extracted honey.

No. 4.—This shows how straw skeps are made in England. These are still made in England to a limited extent, and some of the advanced bee-keepers use them for taking down swarms, in temporarily housing swarms, and for various other uses in the apiary. Being light and cool these skeps are handier than a box.

No. 5.—The peculiar feature of this apiary is that the honey is almost wholly obtained from sweet clover which was distributed in waste places by the owner several years previous to the taking of this view. It will be noted the supers are in place and

the crop here represented when gathered weighed 12,000 lbs., nearly all of it from sweet clover. The apiary is situated in the heart of the town of 3500 inhabitants. The building in the background is the honey house. It is evident the owner of this apiary is a keen and successful bee-keeper, and as a matter of fact the honey sold from it enabled its owner to start a drugstore. He admits not being able to keep away from the bees, and the ship-shape appearance of every thing would indicate that to be the case.

No. 6.—This is a thoroughly characteristic view of a Mexican apiary. Just such apiaries exist all over Mexico. The young man, a true son of the soil, is about to hive a swarm in a long basket-work hive which he holds in his hand. He also has a cloth to put over the hive to shade and protect it until evening time when it will be placed among the others. The honey is taken by putting the hives over the fumes of burning sulphur and killing the bees.

No. 7.—During a trip to Colorado in 1900 Mr. Root made a visit to Mr. Philip Large, of Longmont, and was there attracted by the sight of a large solar wax-extractor, elevated as shown in the cut so as to allow of extra heat being applied underneath. At the back end there is a cupboard door communicating with an air-tight compartment. In this is a large lamp placed under the slanting part of the extractor. Mr. Large was greatly pleased with the working of the extractor. For information regarding the practical working of solar extractors, see that subject, page 368.

Nos. 8 and 9.—Views in the famous apiary of 750 colonies, all in one apiary, owned and managed by E. W. Alexander, of New York. It is hardly possible to show in one picture 750 hives but the view marked 10 gives us an idea of the extent of this apiary.

No. 10.—A view of the honey-house and bee-cellar of Mr. E. W. Alexander, at Delanson, New York, who described it in *Gleanings in Bee Culture* for January 15, 1907, as follows: "First, I will describe the building, which is 24 feet wide and 56 long. The longest way is north and south. The cellar occupies 24x40 feet of the ground floor at the north end; then the tank-room occupies 16x24 feet of the south end, and its floor is on the same level with the cellar floor. This room has four doors in it—one wide door opening into the south end of the cellar; also one wide outside door in the south end of the building where we roll out the barrels of honey into the wagon when we ship. Then we have a door on each side of this room, which comes very handy to carry bees in and out of the cellar from the lower part of the bee-yard by putting screens on these two doors; and by leaving them open we get a fine current of air through the tank-room, which has much to do with ripening and thickening the honey. The cellar also has an outside door at the northeast corner, where the greater number of colonies are carried in and out. The shop part is on the upper floor, which is level with the floor of the extracting-room, and is 16x24 feet.

No. 11.—Showing the interior of the honey-house which forms part of the 2-story portion of the house shown in Fig. 10. This extracting-room or store-room is 24x40 feet; and directly over the cel'ar, in the floor of it, we have four trap-doors about 10 feet apart, in size 2x2½ feet, directly over the bees. These we can easily open to any size of hole from a little crack to the whole space, 2x2½ feet, which allows all impure air to pass off into the room above. We can also put a quilt in the place of the large door at the south end of the cellar, which gives fine ventilation into the tank-room and up the stairway into the shop, and up a garret. We have two pipe-holes in the chimney, one of which is always open, and makes a strong current of all foul air out of the building. This steady and gradual ventilation of the cellar into these two large rooms, one at the end and the other directly over the cellar, keeps the air as fresh and healthy where the bees are as it is out-doors.

No. 12.—Represented in this picture are school-teachers from all parts of the United States in the act of holding comb-frames covered with adhering bees. These teachers were part of the summer school (1905) of Wooster University, Wooster, Ohio, where they had been taking instruction in "Nature Study," under the instruction of Dr. E. F. Bigelow, S'amford, Conn., editor of the Nature Department of St. Nicholas Magazine. Dr. Bigelow occupies a sitting posture in the middle foreground with his left foot resting under his right knee. The illustration affords a very striking proof of the gentle nature of the red-clover strain of Italian bees. The picture was taken after their first lesson in bee-keeping.

No. 13.—The honey exhibit made by William E. Prisk, of Mineral Point, Wisconsin, at the State Fair. It might be termed a model exhibit; and any person wishing to make an exhibit at some local fair can obtain ideas from it that will prove useful. Fairs are an excellent means of advertising honey in a very satisfactory manner, as the honey sold quite frequently pays all expenses, and, in addition, customers are gained who will be steady buyers for years after.

No. 14.—This is a view of the Wessing Brothers' apiary, near Nicolaus, Cal., taken by E. R. Root in 1901. The great elevation of the hives is on account of high water there at certain seasons.

No. 15.—The view here shown is that of The A. I. Root Company's apiary, or, rather, bee-breeding farm at Salem, N. J., where great numbers of bees are bred for sale to their regular customers. The region has a mild climate with many nectar bearing flowers in the immediate vicinity. In addition, the bees are steadily fed by means of the Alexander feeder, so as to stimulate brood-rearing to the greatest possible extent. No combs are used except those made on full sheets of foundation properly wired for transportation. The company has found it better to do this than to buy bees from the ordinary farmer bee-keepers, whose combs often contain large patches of drone-comb, and besides are irregular and unwired. On this bee-farm sugar is converted into bees in a wholesale manner.

No. 16.—A view of the bee-breeding apiary of The A. I. Root Co., at Salem, New Jersey. The purpose of the high board fence is to screen off the wind, as the country is flat and the winds are high at certain seasons of the year. The bees that are reared are distributed over the eastern and southwestern States.

No. 17.—This apiary is owned by an amateur, Mr. Chas. G. Macklin, of Morrison, Illinois. The hives are not all shown, for he has over 100 colonies equally well placed as the ones shown in this view. Mr. Macklin is a good specimen of the modern amateur bee-keeper, for he not only keeps a large number of bees but makes them pay a profit.

No. 18.—This picture shows a glimpse of one of the most important apiaries in F'orida—that of W. S. Hart. At the left is a section of bee-sheds covered by scuppernong grapevines. This kind of grape grows enormously, and is going over the palmetto-trees, shutting off the view beyond. This picture was taken July 17, 1890. The principal object in taking it was to show a cabbage palmetto in full bloom, but the buds were not perfected. You will notice Mr. Hart holding a sprig of the bloom over his head. This will give an idea of its size and form. Mr. Hart's reports from this apiary are among the largest and most astonishing the world has ever seen. In 1894 he received from one hive 554¼ lbs., and averaged 355 lbs. from 116 colonies.

No. 19.—This view represents the apicultural exhibit of the authors of this book at the Omaha exposition. It included a general list of all the apiarian implements in general use, and the story is better told by the camera than by the pen. The educational benefits arising from these exhibits is great. After the above view was taken, a still larger exhibit was made by the same company at the great Pan-American exposition in Buffalo, in 1901.

No. 20.—This shows a general view of J. F. McIntyre's apiary, located about three miles from Ventura, Cal., on the Big Sespe River. Those who have the older editions of this work will remember a wood engraving of this apiary, then owned by the father-in-law of Mr. McIntyre, R. Wilkin, a name known the world over among bee-keepers. Mr. McIntyre keeps track of his colonies entirely by the use of a record-book. The hives are all painted white, and look like a miniature city. The surrounding mountains form a very picturesque feature in the scene. At the right in No. 10 is the honey-house. At the left of the honey-house are three large tanks, not shown, holding four tons each. A full description of this, probably the most important apiary in California, will be found in Gleanings in Bee Culture, Oct. 1, 1891.

No. 21.—We have here a very fine view of one of the largest, if not the largest, queen-rearing apiaries in the southern hemisphere. It is operated by Mr. H. L. Jones, of Goodna, Queensland, Aus. This apiary contains about 300 colonies; and while it presents a remarkably neat and orderly appearance, its owner says it was not "got up for the occasion," as a photographer came along unexpectedly. It is very seldom that one sees an apiary in such trim neatness in its usual working order. On the other hand it is not uncommon to see hives in the average yard more or less tipped sidewise, a little out of square with the points of the compass, weather-beaten, unpainted, besides quite an array of old brood-frames, sticks, old covers, old bottom-boards, and other things too numerous to mention. I do not mean to say that bee-keepers of this country are disorderly; but in the rush of the season, when every thing is "hurrah boys!" and "any thing and every thing to 'get there quickly." we are liable to find things not quite' dress-parade style for a snap-shot photo.

No. 22.—The leading honey-producer of Southern California is W. T. Richardson, of Simi. One of his apiaries is represented in the picture, a grotesque appearance being imparted to it by the stones on the hives, to keep the covers from blowing off. The view is one of many taken by Rambler while making the rounds of the bee-yards of California. Mr. Richardson runs about 1200 colonies, in four apiaries, all situated in the Simi Valley. A full account of his history is given in *Gleanings* for 1898, page 720, where a portrait is given of this famous bee-man.

No. 23.—This view was taken by the lamented Rambler a short time before his death, he himself appearing on the left. It was probably owing to his deep devotion to his apicultural interests here that his life was shortened. The ground is very low and even swampy, and the atmosphere there at times very insalubrious; but as these drawbacks were partly compensated for by the great yield of nectar, Mr. Martin located there, dying a few months later.

No. 24.—A full-size view of father Langstroth while taking a walk in one of the parks of Dayton, O. Mr. L. was 82 years of age when this view was taken.

No. 25.—This scheme of an extracting-house on wheels is the best we have yet seen presented. In a series of outyards it makes it possible to use only one extractor and outfit, and to carry away the honey as soon as extracted, where it will not be liable to be stolen. While going to the several yards the men inside the wagon can slick up and get things ready for the next yard. The tank holds about 100 gallons, and in 1899 Mr. Crowder and his brother put 43 cases of honey through it in two days, which is remarkably fast work.

No. 26.—This represents an out-apiary of 95 colonies near the river Murray, Mildura, Australia. We have no particulars concerning it, but would draw attention to the general beauty of the place, where, apparently, thousands of men might assemble. Modern apiculture is making great progress in that wonderful island-continent.

No. 27.—The reader will naturally ask, when he sees this picture, "Why those big stones, one on each hive?" Probably they have some heavy winds near Keno, rendering their use necessary. Mr. Aitkin uses quilts or cloths on top of the frames; and as these are propolized down while the covers are not, he finds it necessary to weight the latter down It is probable the trees on the left are more for the purpose of keeping off stock than to break the force of the wind. The regularity of the rows of hives is very noticeable. The desirableness of this is discussed in the body of this work, under head of "Apiary."

No. 28.—This is a scene in the apiary of W. H. Horstmann, of Chicago, Illinois. The main part of the apiary is not shown, as he has quite a fair-sized apiary on a city lot. This view shows his Capitol hive made by him in his spare moments. It is quite useful since it contains three full colonies of bees and in addition a nucleus. Mr Horstmann is a mail-carrier attached to the Chicago postoffice, but yet he finds time to attend to his bees. His example is worthy of emulation by many others who desire some avocation to occupy spare time.

No. 29.—This is a partial view of the apiary of James McNeill, situated in the village of Hudson, New York. Mr. McNeill has kept bees for many years with conspicuous success. When this view was taken he had about 450 colonies all kept in the same spic-and-span condition shown in the engraving. His average crop he places at 75 lbs. per colony, spring count, and this is mainly secured from white clover, with some sweet clover and basswood. Naturally such honey brings the highest market prices; besides, the apiary is not far away from a very fine market—Albany, New York. For various reasons this may be considered a model apiary.

No. 30.—Some years ago—yes, nearly twenty—I said to Dr. Miller, "You have a peculiar talent for making bright comments in convention, throwing in a few sentences and then sitting down. The comments always enlighten the proceedings. Now, can you not edit a department in *Gleanings* made up of short items of running comment, something after the style of your convention work?"

Turning to me he said, his wonted smile vanishing for the moment into a serious expression, "Ernest, I doubt my ability to carry out your ideas, but I have confidence in your opinion. I will try it. If you do not like the stuff, throw it into the waste-basket."

There, now you have the origin of Stray Straws. We had a department running, as we do now, called "Heads of Grain," and I suggested "Kernels of Wheat'" as an appropriate heading; but Dr. Miller very modestly preferred Stray Straws, as he was not sure that he would be able to glean very much *wheat*. As to the general character of the Straws, and whether they are worth binding along with the other gleanings from many fields, I don't need to say. Our readers have long since settled that by the eager way they grab at the Straw-stack in Marengo.

Dr. C. C. Miller is probably one of the best-known apicultural writers in the world. He reads both the American and European exchanges, and his articles and comments on both sides of the Atlantic have brought him into prominence throughout all beedom.

His writings are further enhanced by a ripe experience of many years, for he is now in his seventy-eighth year, having been for forty years a bee-keeper, and a good one, especially in the production of comb honey; and, if I mistake not, his crops are sold before they are off the hive. This speaks volumes, not only for his method of management but for his careful honest grading, which is all done by the members of his family. The buyers know in advance just exactly what Dr. Miller's honey is going to be, and they are usually willing to pay above the market because they know beyond any question that there will be no after-quibble over the grading, quantity, or quality. There is no reason why many others can not sell their crop in the same way.—*E. R. Root, in Gleanings in Bee Culture for Aug. 1, 1908.*

No. 31.—The front, roof, and back of the sheds are made of corrugated iron fastened to cedar posts set in the ground two feet.

No. 32.—This picture shows Dr. C. C. Miller watching the flight of bees as they fly to and from his field of sweet clover. The lower half is a view of his home from the rear.

No. 33.—This view was taken in Holland, and represents a bee-keeper hunting for the queen. The photograph was furnished us by Mr. Henri Meyer, of Arnhem, Holland. He regrets the backward condition of the people there in regard to bees while science in general is so thoroughly understood there. He says the bee-men kill their bees in the fall, and thus secure a small quantity of inferior honey.

No. 34.—Here is another fine view of comb built in the open air late in the fall. The swarm alighted on a limb of a pine-tree and built comb, even though the weather was getting cold. One piece of comb broke off before the picture was taken, so it was laid on top The combs were built thirty feet from the ground, and were secured by Mr. A. D. Stoneman, of Quasqueton, Iowa.

No. 35.—This illustration represents the moving of four wagonloads of bees by a traction-engine in Canada. The load consisted of 110 twelve-frame hives with one or two supers on each, the racks being filled with straw. The trip of forty miles was made without accident under the management of R. F. Holtermann.

No. 36.—This represents one class of hives peculiar to the Holy Land, this one having been photographed at Jezreel, Palestine. While primitive, there is something about the ingenuity displayed in the construction of such hives that commands our admiration, and they still remind us that "the land which the Lord giveth thee" still flows with honey if not milk.

No. 37.—By means of this automobile he can carry sixty 28-section supers at the rate of twelve to twenty miles an hour. The picture shows a load of that kind.

No. 38.—This is a view of an apiary belonging to W. Z. Hutchinson, editor of the Bee-keepers' Review, and the photograph itself was taken by him. Mr. H. has probably done more to illustrate the bee world with his own camera than any other man—a work in which he delights and excels. The apiary itself is located in the wilds of Northern Michigan, where wild red raspberries cover the ground for miles, yielding generously one of the finest honeys known.

No. 39.—This cut shows the house-apiary of W. C. Sorter, Wickliffe, O. It represents the south side, the north fronting on Lake Erie. It is 60 feet long, and is very satisfactory to the owner. The cloths are designed, being of different colors, to guide the bees to the right place.

No. 40.—This shows the interior of Mr. Sorter's apiary. The colonies are arranged along the south wall on the left. See outer views

No. 41.—This view represents the gasoline-engine extracting-outfit of Virgil S. rea, located on the Yakima Indian reservation, Washington With this outfit he extracted in 1908 twenty tons of honey. At the time of writing he was inclined to think a permanent extracting-house would be cheaper than to draw this one around.

No. 42.—This is a view of a small apiary close to a car-barn in Harrisburg, Pa. The hives have a tar paper covering, and the supers are filled with chaff. They are owned by Mr. A. F. Rexroth.

No. 43.—This singular freak of nature is an outdoor colony of bees found on Sugarloaf Mountain, near Boulder, Col These combs were built on the bough of a tree, and would accommodate a large colony.

No. 44.—This, as will be noticed, embraces three separate views taken at the home apiary of the authors of this book. They illustrate the method of shaking bees into a swarm-box preparatory to putting them in pound cages without brood for shipment.

No. 45.—These four views illustrate the wholesale disinfection of foul-broody hives at the apiary of Louis H. Scholl, New Braunfels, Texas. Fig. 2 shows the pile of hive bodies and supers. Kerosene is poured down the stack of empty bodies, Fig. 3. A lighted bunch of straw, Fig. 4, is thrown in, which sets the whole mass on fire. A spadeful of earth below, Fig. 5, at the draft, and a cover on top, finishes the job.

No 46.—This exhibit received the first prize at the Canadian National Exhibition. It occupied a space 12 by 20 feet, and contained 2000 pounds of honey.

No. 47.—A view of Mr. F. W. Redfield's house made of honey for exhibition purposes. The walls are entirely of cans filled with honey; boards are used to support the cans on the roof. It was shown in Ogden, Utah, in 1909.

No. 48.—This illustrates the bee and honey exhibit of The A. I. Root Company at the Jamestown Exposition, Jamestown, Va., in 1907.

No. 49.—This is one of the best views of an apiary in mid-winter we have ever secured. It belongs to Mr. F. Greiner, of Naples, N. Y., one of the foremost bee-men of the country, and an interesting writer as well. Probably it would be difficult to secure a better covering for the hives in winter than that remarkable non-conductor of heat, "the beautiful snow."

No. 50.—This picture represents a large swarm that clustered in the extreme top of a large elm, and was sent us by Mr. Frank C Pellett, of Atlantic, Ia. The bees may be seen leaving the sack and entering the hive. Mr. Pellett says this was the most difficult feat in his experience in tree-climbing.

No. 51.—This represents George H. Rex & Son's permanent bee-shed, located at Stettlersville, Pa. With this kind of shed there is no need of wintering bees in a cellar, as the hives are kept here all the year.

Index

Printed in the USA
CPSIA information can be obtained
at www.ICGtesting.com
LVHW012000130823
755107LV00005B/302

9 781015 393097